D1760456

Studies in Logic and Computation

Series editor

D. M. GABBAY

Studies in Logic and Computation

What is a
Logical System?

Edited by

D. M. GABBAY

*Department of Computing, Imperial College of Science, Technology
and Medicine, London*

CLARENDON PRESS • OXFORD
1994

Oxford University Press, Walton Street, Oxford OX2 6DP

Oxford New York
Athens Auckland Bangkok Bombay
Calcutta CapeTown DaresSalaam Delhi
Florence HongKong Istanbul Karachi
KualaLumpur Madras Madrid Melbourne
MexicoCity Nairobi Paris Singapore
Taipei Tokyo Toronto
and associated companies in
Berlin Ibadan

Oxford is a trade mark of Oxford University Press

Published in the United States by
Oxford University Press Inc., New York

A catalogue record for this book is available from the British Library

Library of Congress Cataloging in Publication Data
(Data available)

ISBN 0 19 853859 6

Typeset by the author

Printed in Great Britain by
Bookcraft (Bath) Ltd
Midsomer Norton, Avon

Preface

In recent years we have witnessed a very strong and fruitful interaction between traditional logic on the one hand and computer science and Artificial intelligence on the other. As a result, there was urgent need for logic to evolve. New systems were developed to cater for the needs of applications. Old concepts were changed and modified and new concepts came into prominence. The community became divided. Many expressed themselves strongly, both for and against, the new ideas. Papers were rejected or accepted on ideological grounds, as well as technical substance.

In this atmosphere, it seemed necessary to clarify the basic concepts underlying logic and computation, especially the very notion of a logical system. This volume is trying to put forward the current opinions of leading researchers on this basic notion. The views among members of the community are varied and in many cases, very strongly held. There is at one extreme the pluralistic view, expressed to me once in a meeting by a distinguished colleague who said something like 'we use logics like we use computer languages'. At the other end of the spectrum there is the view of those who believe there is only one true logic, and all the rest is nonsense. Of course there exist several proposals for this true logic with their respective bands of followers.

It is clear that such an atmosphere is not conducive for cooperation and joint research, and the community is indeed somewhat fragmented.

We hope that this volume will have an impact, both on the pure researcher and on the applied consumer of logic.

I would like to thank Mrs Jane Spurr, for her dedication and expertise in the organisation and production of this book.

D. M. Gabbay
London, May 1994

Contents

Contributors

P. Aczel
Department of Computer Science
The University, Manchester M13 9PL, UK.

H. Andreka
Mathematical Institute of the Hungarian Academy of Sciences
Budapest, PO Box 127, H 1364, Hungary.

A. Avron
Department of Computer Science
Tel Aviv University, Tel Aviv, Israel.

J. Barwise
Department of Philosophy and Mathematics
Sycamore Hall 120, Indiana University, Bloomington IN 47405, USA.

G. Crocco
Languages et Systemes Informatiques
Université Paul Sabatier, 118 route de Narbonne, F-31062 Toulouse Cedex, France.

K. Došen
Languages et Systemes Informatiques
Université Paul Sabatier, 118 route de Narbonne, F-31062 Toulouse Cedex, France.

L. Fariñas del Cerro
Languages et Systemes Informatiques
Université Paul Sabatier, 118 route de Narbonne, F-31062 Toulouse Cedex, France.

S. Feferman
Mathematics Department
Stanford University, Stanford CA 94035, USA.

D. M. Gabbay
Department of Computing
Imperial College of Science, Technology and Medicine, 180 Queen's Gate, London
SW7 2BZ, UK.

I. Hacking
Institute for the History and Philosophy of Science and Technology
Victoria College, 73 Queen's Park Crescent East, University of Toronto, Toronto,
Ontario M5S 1K7, Canada

E. Hammer
Departments of Philosophy and Mathematics
Sycamore Hall 120, Indiana University, Bloomington IN 47405, USA.

R. A. Kowalski
Department of Computing
Imperial College of Science, Technology and Medicine, 180 Queen's Gate, London
SW7 2BZ, UK.

J. Lambek
Department of Maths and Statistics
Burnside, Hall, McGill University, 205 Sherbrooke Street West QC H3A 2K6,
Canada.

N. Martí-Oliet
SRI International, Menlo Park CA 94025, USA, and Center for the Study of
Language and Information, Stanford University, Stanford CA 94305, USA.

S. Matthews
Max-Planck Institut für Informatik, Im Stadtwald, W-6600 Saarbrücken, Germany.

J. Meseguer
SRI International, Menlo Park CA 94025, USA, and Center for the Study of
Language and Information, Stanford University, Stanford CA 94305, USA.

I. Németi
Mathematical Institute of the Hungarian Academy of Sciences, Budapest,
PO Box 127, H 1364, Hungary.

N. Tennant
Department of Philosophy, 230 North Oval Mall, The Ohio State University,
Columbus OH 43210, USA.

J. van Benthem
University van Amsterdam, Plantage Muidergracht 24, 1018 TV Amsterdam, The
Netherlands.

1

What is Logic?*

Ian Hacking

What follows is a general theory about classical logic. It is not to be expected that logic can be or should be characterized to everyone's satisfaction, for the subject is too ancient, its workers too active, and its scope too vast for that. Instead this chapter falls within one lively and enduring tradition, the one called 'logicist'. It is an organization and development of some of the thoughts of Leibniz, Bolzano, Frege, Russell, and Wittgenstein. The main technical device is due to Gentzen. The chief philosophical idea that has not already been widely used by many writers is taken from the *Tractatus*. The general thrust of the inquiry goes back to Frege and to Leibniz, but although I shall allude to origins I shall not trace them in any detailed way.

A theory is prompted by problems, and it is well to begin by stating some long-standing questions that this one tries to answer. My focus will be the demarcation of logic: what distinguishes logic from the extralogical? The question has been important because it is closely connected with something deeper. What has been achieved by the program, now in disarray, of trying to show that parts of mathematics are analytic? There is a third question that I hope to take up in later work: Which, if any, of the nonstandard logics can in some strict sense be regarded as alternatives to classical logic? Only two at present have sufficiently serious and far-reaching motivations to have anything in their favour. It is an important question, why intuitionist and quantum logic are at least candidates for being called 'logic'. But I shall not address that question now, and shall instead consider only the nature of classical logic. We should start by recalling the fate of Frege's project of reducing arithmetic to logic. That is

*A first version of this chapter was duplicated for a seminar in Cambridge University, November, 1970, and a second version for seminars at the London School of Economics, February, 1971. 1 owe many debts of gratitude to people who have helped me with this project since then. I particularly wish to thank T. J. Smiley for his patient encouragement and advice. Previously published in *The Journal of Philosophy*, Volume LXXVI, No. 6, June 1979.

what gave bite to my question, What is logic ?

1   The analytic program

Frege tried to prove that arithmetic is analytic. 'The problem', he wrote
at the beginning of his *Grundlagen*, 'becomes, in fact, that of finding the
proof of the proposition, and of following it up right back to the primitive
truths. If in carrying out this process we come only on general logical laws
and definitions, then the truth is an analytic one'.[1] General logical laws
and definitions are the crux. The idea is older than Frege, and the very
word 'analytic' recalls Leibniz's doctrine that all necessary truths can be
traced back to logical identities by finite analysis. Frege first cast this idea
into a form precise enough for it to be established or refuted. Hence I speak
of the *analytic* program of showing, for example, that arithmetic can be
obtained from logic and definitions.

The analytic program is not primarily epistemological. It is not trying
to make mathematics certain, nor to provide foundations for a shaky edifice,
although some latter-day logicists had that in mind. Nor, as I understand
the tradition stemming from Leibniz, is the chief interest in 'what there
is'. There are ontological spinoffs to be sure, like the proposed answer
to the question, What is a number? But remarks on certainty and on the
existence of objects are by the way. The chief point is to explain the nature
of at least some kinds of necessary truth.

Logicists have not agreed on whether the analytic program would work
for all necessities. Leibniz argued that the necessary truths are just those
which can be proved from identities by pure logic in a finite number of
steps. Frege, in contrast, maintained that, although Euclidean geometry is
necessarily true, it is synthetic, and founded on what Kant called intuition.
Whatever we may think about such infighting, it seems that the analytic
program as a whole has run into sand. Russell's paradox shook Frege's
confidence that we know the basic laws of logic. Diverging set theories made
it seem that propositions about sets lack the universality and apodictic
certainty claimed for logic. *Principia Mathematica* was a poor tool for
research in higher mathematics. Then Gödel showed that no such system
is able even to analyze computable arithmetic completely.

Despite such discoveries, a philosopher might draw in his horns and
admit that even though not all mathematics is analytic, analyticity remains
a valuable concept. Drilling at mathematics with Frege's tools, we hit
impermeable matter, but that, one might feel, is no reflection on the tools.
If mathematics cannot be fully embedded in logic, that is an important

---

[1] *Die Grundlagen der Arithmetik* (Breslau: W. Koebner, 1884); J. Austin, trans.,
The Foundations of Arithmetic (New York: Harper, 1960), p. 4.

discovery showing that analyticity was indeed a good investigative idea. We cannot, however, rest there. Even in 1936 Quine was launching his critique. Thirty years later, most philosophers had concluded that Frege's drill would hardly make it through a bar of soap. His general laws of logic and definitions: where are they now? A whole system of philosophy has arisen around Quine's demolition of definition, synonymy, analyticity, and meaning. His comments on logic were briefer but as effective, and lead to the chief question posed by this chapter.

2 The demarcation of logic

A logical truth, said Quine, is a truth in which only logical constants occur essentially. But, as Tarski had earlier implied, there is no delineation of the logical constants.[2] We can at best list them. It is as if we could characterize the concept *planet of the sun* only by reciting Mars, Venus, Earth, etc., and could not tell by any general principle whether the heavenly body Epsilon is a planet or not. We have a laundry list of logical constants, but no characterization of what a logical constant is—except the circular one, that logical constants are those which occur essentially in analytic truths.

The question, What is a logical constant? would be unimportant were it not for the analytic program. There is no point in trying to separate logic from other science, except for that profound speculation about the nature and origin of necessary truth. But, because of that speculation, a fruitful definition of 'logical constant' is called for. This chapter to some extent revives the analytic program by providing such a demarcation. Doubtless it is not the only definition that is both rigorous in application and rich in consequences, but it is curiously appropriate to the logistic tradition. It does not go as far as Frege had hoped, but it does include the ramified theory of types. This is just what the authors of *Principia* expected; for in their opinion the ramified theory is logic, but the simplified theory obtained by adding the axiom of reducibility is not logic.

The theory also seems able to resolve a difference between Leibniz and Kant. Leibniz held that all necessary truth is analytic, whereas Kant thought that even $5 + 7 = 12$ is synthetic. Kant is wrong in particular, but right in general. On my theory, truths about individual integers, such as $5 + 7 = 12$, are analytic, but arithmetic as a whole is synthetic. The concept *number* is not explicable by logical constants alone. Hence, even sentences of the form, 'For every natural number x, then ...', are not in general analytic, for the numerical quantifier is not a logical one. The

[2]On the concept of logical consequence, trans. J. H. Woodger from the Polish and German (1936) in *Logic, Semantics, Metamathematics* (Oxford: Clarendon Press, 1956), pp 409–420, esp. p. 420.

concept *number* must be given by what Kant called intuition, or at least by some extralogical practice. This is despite the fact that any particular natural number can be characterized analytically. I must add at once that this rather trivial resolution of an issue between Leibniz and Kant is only an historical oddity. For anyone interested in arithmetic it is, of course, a mere scratching of the surface.

3   Wittgenstein's 'by-product' theory of logic

The interrogative, 'What is logic?' can be used to express two questions. I have just asked how to identify logic, but, having identified something, one can still ask about its essential nature. Had Frege been right, we should have reduced arithmetic to logic and shown that its truth conditions lie in logic itself. But what then is the nature of logical truth? Frege said that laws of logic are laws of thought, not in the sense that they are laws about what men do in fact take for true but because they are 'the most general laws, which prescribe universally the way in which one ought to think if one is to think at all'.[3] He prefers to call them laws of truth, 'boundary stones set in an eternal foundation, which our thought can overflow, but never displace'. So it seems not to make sense to ask what makes them true, for they help constitute the nature of true thought itself.

In the *Tractatus* we find what seems to be an entirely different idea. Wittgenstein tried to explain how some classes of logical truth are a 'by-product' of facts about the use of logical constants. Imagine a language of independent elementary sentences whose meanings are understood. In order to form complex sentences, let logical constants be implanted in this language, and let certain rules determine the truth condition of such complexes as functions of their components. Then some compound sentences take the value true regardless of their components. This fact is a by-product of rules for the introduction of the logical constants. '[W]ithout bothering about sense or meaning, we construct the logical proposition out of others using only *rules that deal with signs*'.[4] The fact that these logical truths are a by-product of rules for signs is taken to explain the necessary, apodictic, and *a priori* character of some of the truths that we call logically necessary.

Recall the positivist slogan that 'mathematical truths are true by virtue of the meanings of the words that express them'. This came to be used in what one can only call a lighthearted way by some writers who seemed not

---

[3] *Grundgesetze der Arithmetik, Begriffsschriftlich abgeleitet*, Bd. I (Jena: H. Pohle, 1893), partially trans. M. Furth, *The Basic Laws of Arithmetic* (Berkeley: Univ. of California Press, 1967), p.12.

[4] *Tractatus Logic-Philosophicus*, D. F. Pears and B. F. McGuinness, trans. (New York: The Humanities Press), 6.126. For an alternative translation see the text for fn 28.

to reflect on the complexities of mathematical reasoning. But when first propounded the slogan had real force, thanks to Frege's analytic program taken together with Wittgenstein's by-product theory. First, the meanings of mathematical expressions are to be analyzed into purely logical terminology. Secondly, the meanings of the logical constants are conveyed by their introduction rules, and these rules have as a by-product the class of logical truths. The meanings of the mathematical terms are given in terms of logic. The meanings of logical constants are conveyed by the introduction rules. Hence, if *both* Frege *and* Wittgenstein had been right, then meanings, in some imprecise sense of that word, would have been responsible for a good deal of mathematical truth. I know of no other plausible motivation for the crisp positivist slogans about 'true by virtue of the meanings' or even 'true by convention'.

Wittgenstein tried to extend his theory of tautology in a natural way to first-order language, anticipating the theory of countable conjunction and disjunction. He had another meaning-oriented—or at least name-oriented—theory for arithmetical identities. Aside from the account of tautology, no one except Ramsey took much of this seriously. However, my demarcation of logic turns out to confirm Wittgenstein's hunch about the logical constants, using Gentzen's devices to take in the first-order quantifiers and even identity. Although Wittgenstein often alluded to the importance of rules and notational conventions of a 'deep' sort, he was never able to say which ones are specifically logical. We are now able to specify a precise class of rules that fits his descriptions, yet includes the whole 'logical' part of *Principia Mathematica*.

I must emphasize at once that the resulting *Tractatus*-like theory is not incompatible with the Fregean doctrine that logic constitutes the laws of truth. Nor is it incompatible with Wittgenstein's later reflections on following a rule, stated in *Remarks on the Foundations of Mathematics*. It is a matter of some delicacy to get straight the relations among these different insights. I attempt it in the concluding section of this chapter, but first we require the demarcation of logic.

4 Deducibility not logical truth

What distinguishes logic from the other branches of knowledge? Quine starts his elementary textbook by implying that logic is a science of truths.[5] That is where I part company. If we must have a one-word answer, logic is the science of deduction. The point is made by Michael Dummett, who accuses Frege himself. Frege's approach was 'retrograde', he says, in that it

---

[5] *Methods of Logic* (New York: Holt, 1950), p. xi.

formalized 'logical systems on the quite misleading analogy of an axiomatized theory'. 'The representation of logic as concerned with a characteristic of sentences, truth, rather than of transitions from sentences to sentences, had highly deleterious effects both in logic and in philosophy'.[6] He implies that we owe the first corrective to Gerhard Gentzen.

I am less sure than Dummett that this is a corrective to Frege, although it is certainly a corrective to the early twentieth-century tradition in mathematical logic. When Frege speaks of logical axioms he commonly does so with some hint of qualification, and when we go back to *Begriffsschrift* we find passages such as the following:

> We have already introduced in the first chapter several principles of [pure] thought in order to transform them into rules for the application of our symbols. The rules and laws to which they correspond cannot be expressed in our 'conceptual notation' because they form its basis.[7]

Tractatus 5.132 says that 'Laws of inference which—as in Frege and Russell—are to justify the conclusions, are senseless and would be superfluous.' This may be a legitimate objection to the primitive propositions *1.1 and *1.11 of *Principia Mathematica*. But if one had the view that anything not expressible in concept-writing is *sinnlos* and can at best be elucidated, one would find less of a difference between *Begriffsschrift* and *Tractatus* than Wittgenstein asserts.

Disregarding this historical issue, I agree entirely with Dummett that the right way to answer the question, What is logic? is to consider transitions between sentences. It is now natural to present rules for such transitions in a metalanguage. To avoid Wittgenstein's strictures, we must insist that such rules are not justifications of transitions. They are descriptions, or, perhaps, codifications of what one knows when one knows how to make certain transitions that we call logical. In one respect this talk of metalanguage is like doing the grammar of English in English. There is evidently a distinction between two uses of the word 'justify'. On the one hand, should an author challenge an editor who has corrected a grammatical solecism, the editor may reply by citing a rule to justify the emendation. It is not to be inferred that in general the rules of grammar 'justify' standard usage. They merely codify it, and are often couched in the very forms that they describe. Yet this is only an analogy; for although English grammar will alter in time and varies a little in different communities, it is an open question whether there is any real alternative to classical logic.

---

[6] *Frege. Philosophy of Language* (London: Duckworth, 1973), p. 432–433.

[7] *Begriffsschrift, eine der arichmetischen nachgebildete Formelsprache des reinen Denkens* (Halle: L. Nebert, 1879), T. W. Bynum, trans., *Conceptual Notation* (Oxford: Clarendon Press, 1972), p. 136.

Deducibility comes first, I have said, and not logical truth. Today we distinguish sharply between syntactic and semantic aspects of transitions between sentences. The opening parts of my discussion will proceed by considerations about deducibility which are intended to be almost neutral between a syntactic and a semantic treatment of the idea. This is not a quirk of the exposition but a feature of the theory, which is quite in the spirit of the older logicists.

The details of my delineation of logic are so indebted to Gentzen as to make that aspect of this chapter only a footnote to his work, although what I do is to turn him upside down. He took a given axiomatized entity, first-order logic, and characterized it by rules of inference.[8] I proceed in the opposite way, using rules of a certain kind to define an entity, namely 'logic.' I give reasons for saying that anything defined by a rule of inference like Gentzen's is a logical constant. Of course, the exact boundary depends entirely on what shall count as 'like' Gentzen's rules. I shall present and defend some general propositions about deducibility and the definition of constants, all of which are in fact true of Gentzen's work, and which, in my opinion, capture its essence. I do not claim this is the only delineation; only that it is remarkably instructive.

5 The sequent calculus

Gentzen invented two kinds of logical calculi, called 'natural deduction' and 'sequent calculus'. He thought that the former gets at the heart of logical reasoning, and used the sequent calculus only as a convenient tool for proving his chief results. Dag Prawitz was able to obtain many of these results directly for the systems of natural deduction.[9] Per Martin-Löf and other workers have found them the best vehicle for investigations of higher mathematics.[10] W. W. Tait has suggested to me that the sequent calculus is right for classical logic, whereas natural deduction best fits a constructive approach. Despite all this, my exposition will without discussion employ only the sequent calculus.

In the present work the sequent calculus is regarded as a metatheory about an object language. We suppose that an object language is given, and that the class of formulas of this language is determinate. Finite (possibly

---

[8] Untersuchungen uber das logische Schliessen, *Mathematisches Zeitschrift*, XXXIX (1935):176–210, 405–431; M. E. Szabo, trans, Investigations into logical deduction, in *The Collected Papers of Gerhard Gentzen* (Amsterdam: North Holland, 1969), pp. 68–131.

[9] *Natural Deduction* (Stockholm: Almqvist and Wiksell, 1965).

[10] See e.g. papers by Girard, Jervell, Kreisel, Martin-Lof, Prawitz, and Tait in J. E. Fenstad, ed., *Proceedings of the Second Scandinavian Logic Symposium* (Amsterdam: North Holland 1971).

empty) sets of formulas are represented by Greek capitals such as Γ and Θ. Individual formulas are represented by Roman capitals, A and B. For brevity we write, for example, 'A, B' to stand for the set whose members are the formulas A and B, and 'Γ, A, B' for the set whose members are A, B and the members of Γ. In the metalanguage we make statements about deducibility relations in the object language, such as 'A is deducible from Γ'. The turnstile abbreviates the converse of this relation: $\Gamma \vdash A$. It is to be emphasized that the turnstile ($\vdash$) is a symbol of the metalanguage, and not a constant of the object language.

There is of course an intended connection between deducibility and logical consequence, so that at least $\Gamma \vdash A$ only if A is a consequence of Γ. But I shall proceed in as syntactic a way as possible, stating certain constraints that will hold on any relation that can be accounted a deducibility relation. Some readers will feel this puts the cart before the horse: we know that my constraints are appropriate to deducibility only because of our understanding of logical consequence. In my opinion, such questions of priority are a red herring. It is not necessary to define deducibility to discover that we have some constraints on this notion. Even the very simple constraints that I cull out are sufficient for a good deal of work, and, wherever they come from, it is a virtue that they can be stated in terms of '$\vdash$' alone.

The notion of deducibility is, however, extended in one slightly loaded way. Gentzen noticed that it is convenient to make statements of the form $\Gamma \vdash \Theta$, where Θ may have several members.[11] On the intended reading, this will be valid only if *some* member of Θ is assigned the value true whenever *each* member of Γ is assigned the value true. It is well known that in Gentzen's calculi, with his rules, intuitionist logic results from insisting that Θ have at most one member. I shall not discuss this seemingly magical fact here.

6 Three facts about classical deducibility

When is a relation between formulas a deducibility relation? Without aiming at necessary conditions, three sufficient conditions will be readily assented to.

1. *Reflexivity: $A \vdash A$.* Leibniz believed that every logical truth is derived from identity statements by definitions. He did not work this out, because he did not have the distinction between object and metalanguage. But, with the distinction, the sequent calculus curiously confirms his hunch. The top statements in any derivation of a theorem are always instances of reflexivity. Reflexivity might be called *the*

---

[11] A general theory is provided in D. J. Shoesmith and T. J. Smiley, *Multiple conclusion Logic* (New York: Cambridge, 1978).

deducibility of identicals. Moreover, as we shall see in Sections 10 and 16, the substantive steps in the derivation may always be regarded as the application of definitions. So Leibniz's claim about the nature of logical truth is vindicated by the sequent calculus.

2. *Dilution:* If $\Gamma \vdash \Theta$, then $\Gamma, A \vdash \Theta$ and $\Gamma \vdash A, \Theta$. Adding a possibly irrelevant premise or consequent does not affect the deducibility relation. This is clear for a classical notion of deducibility and consequence. In a nonclassical language, such as might be suggested by quantum mechanics, the joint assertion of arbitrary sentences might not make sense; so this rule is asserted here only for the classical case. We may call this the *stability of classical deducibility* under the addition of arbitrary sentences. Note that it provides an essential contrast between deductive and inductive reasoning; for the introduction of a new premise may spoil an inductive inference.

3. *Transitivity:* If $A \vdash B$ and $B \vdash C$, then $A \vdash C$. In the context of our other facts about deducibility, this is naturally generalized to the form: If $\Gamma \vdash A, \Theta$ and $\Gamma, A \vdash \Theta$, then $\Gamma \vdash \Theta$. Gentzen called this *cut*, and it will occupy us a good deal.

These three facts about deducibility do not depend on the presence of any logical constants. The elementary sentences of the *Tractatus* were all independent, so there were no relations of deducibility between different sentences. A less ideal primitive language, even if it had no recognized logical constants, might have some relations of deducibility: 'Rachel is a sister ⊢ Rachel is a sibling'. An unanalyzed language of elementary arithmetic is rich in statements of deducibility. And even if all sentences were independent, identical sentences would be interdeducible. So the class of statements of deducibility about a 'prelogical' language will never be entirely vacuous.

7   Building rules

A sequent calculus is a device for deriving statements of deducibility and is thus a metalinguistic instrument. The top statements are all instances of $A \vdash A$, the deducibility of identicals. All nodes in the tree are to be instances of the application of rules of derivation. These rules are of two sorts. Gentzen called one lot *structural.* Since his formulation used sequences rather than finite sets of formulas, these included rules for permutation and for contraction of identical formulas, which we may ignore. The other structural rules are precisely those which correspond to my basic facts about deducibility, namely dilution and transitivity. Thus he had rules for dilution on the left and right of the turnstile, and a rule for cut:

$$\frac{\Gamma \vdash \Theta}{\Gamma, A \vdash \Theta} \qquad \frac{\Gamma \vdash \Theta}{\Gamma \vdash A, \Theta} \qquad \frac{\Gamma \vdash A, \Theta \quad \Gamma, A \vdash \Theta}{\Gamma \vdash \Theta}$$

These rules are to be understood as instructions: having derived the statements of the form shown above the line, one may derive the statement of the corresponding form below the line. Γ and Θ are called *side formulas* and may be empty. For brevity I shall include the deducibility of identicals as a structural rule. It allows one to start a derivation with a statement of the form $A \vdash A$. *The structural rules embody basic facts about deducibility and obtain even in a language with no logical constants at all.*

Gentzen called his other class of rules *operational*. Each of these characterizes a particular logical constant. In the case of conjunction we have, for example:

$$\frac{\Gamma, A \vdash \Theta}{\Gamma, A\&B \vdash \Theta} \qquad \frac{\Gamma, B \vdash \Theta}{\Gamma, A\&B \vdash \Theta} \qquad \frac{\Gamma \vdash A, \Theta \quad \Gamma \vdash B, \Theta}{\Gamma \vdash A\&B, \Theta}$$

The formulas that occur in the top line but not in the bottom line are *components*. The new formula in the bottom line is the *principal formula*. We shall consider only rules with a single principal formula. Statements of deducibility occurring in the top line of a rule of derivation will be called the *premises* of that rule. Gentzen considered only rules with one or two premises, but we allow more and can even generalize to rules with countably many premises.

I shall not repeat Gentzen's calculi here. All his operational rules build up complex formulas from less complex ones. In the case of the sentential connectives, the components are literally subformulas of the principal formula. This is not the case, for example, with the rules for the universal quantifier:

$$\frac{\Gamma, Fa \vdash \Theta}{\Gamma, \forall x Fx \vdash \Theta} \qquad \frac{\Gamma \vdash Fa.\Theta}{\Gamma \vdash \forall x Fx, \Theta}$$

where a does not occur free in the bottom line. Even so, the principal formula is built up out of a part of the component. A generalization of this property is called the *subformula property*, and is defined elsewhere. It has the effect that principal formulas are, according to a certain complexity ordering, more complex than their components, and that they are built up out of parts of their components. *Gentzen's operational rules are all building rules*: according to a natural ordering in terms of complexity, they always pass from less complex to more complex formulas.

8   Cut-elimination

Only the cut rule can have a conclusion that is less complex than its premises. Hence, when cut is not used, a derivation is quite literally constructive, building up more complex formulas from their components. The theorem known as Gentzen's *Hauptsatz* shows that derivations in first-order logic can always have this property, for any statement derived using the cut rule can be obtained without it. If there are derivations of both $\Gamma \vdash A, \Theta$ and $\Gamma, A \vdash \Theta$, then a finite induction on the length and complexity of the derivations shows that they may be rearranged and combined so as to derive $\Gamma \vdash \Theta$ without cut. Haskell Curry called this the *elimination theorem*, for it shows how to eliminate A. Other writers call this result 'cut-elimination' because it shows that the cut rule itself is eliminable. I shall speak of *eliminating rules* in the latter sense, and not in Curry's.

Cut-elimination is useful in proof theory. For an elementary example, we see at once why first-order logic is consistent. If it is inconsistent, there must be some formula A for which both $\vdash A$ and $A \vdash$ are derivable (the latter being interderivable with $\vdash \sim A$). Then, by cut, plain $\vdash$ is derivable. Hence $\vdash$ must be derivable without cut. That is impossible, for none of the other rules decreases complexity.

Gentzen's proof of the consistency of arithmetic uses this sort of consideration, but requires a transfinite induction up to ϵ_0. In systems of natural deduction, cut-elimination corresponds to the result that every proof can be put into a normal form in which one first analyzes certain formulas, and then synthesizes new formulas out of bits and pieces that have been obtained. During the 1960s cut-elimination and normal-form theorems yielded many valuable results in proof-theoretic investigations. The ordinal of the transfinite induction required indicates the degree of constructivity of the proofs. Here, however, we shall be concerned only with finitistic proofs of cut-elimination.

9   Elimination theorems and definition

Gentzen's proof-theoretic work is rich in philosophical asides. For example, he had the idea that his operational rules actually define the logical constants that they introduce. This needs qualification, but first notice where it leads. We commonly require that definitions should be noncreative. Roughly speaking, if the expression w does not occur in a language fragment and is added to that fragment by means of a definition, we require that this does not change what can be said in the fragment without the use of w and its definition. No more should be asserted in the fragment after defining w than could be asserted before. Nothing less should be assertible either. One is usually afraid of creating truths by definition, but one also ought not to destroy any. Wanting to guard against both possibilities, I shall simply say that definitions must be *conservative*.

Now suppose that operational rules are to be regarded as defining logical constants. Then they must be conservative. *Proving cut-elimination is one ingredient in showing that the operational rules are conservative definitions.*

How does this come about? Gentzen's rules are peculiar definitions. We start with an object language, possibly, but not necessarily, lacking logical constants, and for which various statements of deducibility may be made in the metalanguage. Then some operational rules are added, together with syntactic rules for the logical constants thus introduced. Now what should these definitions conserve? Among other things, they should not affect the facts about deducibility that obtain for the original language fragment.

We can put this another way. We add rules for disjunction, the universal quantifier, and so forth, all couched in terms of a deducibility relation denoted by '⊢'. We should ensure that adding these rules does not muck up the basic facts about the deducibility relation noted in Section 6. If those facts no longer obtained, then our rules would have been destructive, and we would have no reason to think that '⊢' still denotes a relation of deducibility. I take this to be the chief moral of Arthur Prior's logical connective 'tonk'.[12] Prior stated inferential rules that introduced a new connective, but these rules led to absurdity. He intended this as a criticism of the very idea of introducing or defining logical connectives by rules of inference. I draw a more familiar moral. All definitions, including Gentzen-like ones, should be conservative. One may state a sequent calculus for Prior's tonk from which one can derive $A \vdash A\text{-tonk-}B$ and $A\text{-tonk-}B \vdash B$; yet there is no way to get $A \vdash B$. So cut-elimination does not hold. If we were to postulate Prior's rules, '⊢' would no longer be transitive. That is, it would no longer be a deducibility relation. Cut-elimination assures that the operational rules, regarded as definitions of the logical constants, still leave ' ⊢' denoting a deducibility relation.

I listed two other facts about deducibility: the deducibility of identicals, and dilution. These also must be conserved. For purposes of proof theory they are either trivial or irrelevant, but if one is to develop Gentzen's suggestion that operational rules provide definitions, then we must check them out. Gentzen himself stated the deducibility of identicals as '$A \vdash A$ for arbitrary formulas'. But a second elimination theorem is that any derivation starting from $A \vdash A$, where 'A' is complex, may be replaced by a derivation starting from the deducibility of identicals for elementary formulas. For example, if we start with $B \vee C \vdash B \vee C$, we could instead start with $B \vdash B$ and $C \vdash C$ and use the operational rules for disjunction.

---

[12]The Runabout Inference-Ticket, *Analysis*, XXI, I (October 1960): pp.38–39.

The requirement is, then, that the deducibility of identicals for arbitrary formulas should be eliminable. It is in fact eliminable for first-order logic.

That is a trivial fact but not a vacuous one. Consider the compound quantifier '$(\forall\exists xy)$', short for '$\forall x\exists y$'. This can be introduced by the rules:

$$\frac{\Gamma, Fab \vdash \Theta}{\Gamma, (\forall\exists xy)Fxy \vdash \Theta} \qquad \frac{\Gamma \vdash Fab, \Theta}{\Gamma \vdash (\forall\exists xy)Fxy, \Theta}$$

In the rule on the left, b does not occur free on the bottom line; for the rule on the right, a does not occur free on the bottom line. Although, assuming the deducibility of identicals, cut-elimination can be proved for this rule, there is no way to derive $(\forall\exists xy)Fxy \vdash (\forall\exists xy)Fxy$ itself. So this is a rule that does not conserve the deducibility of identicals. Likewise, although it is a trivial constraint that dilution should be conserved, the elimination of dilution for complex formulas is not vacuous. Consider these rules for S4:

$$\frac{\Gamma, A \vdash \Theta}{\Gamma, \Box A \vdash \Theta} \qquad \frac{\Box\Gamma \vdash A}{\Box\Gamma \vdash \Box A}$$

In the second rule the side formulas must all start with a box, as indicated. One cannot eliminate the dilution rule for arbitrary formulas even though, when the rule is added, cut-elimination is provable. In general one cannot eliminate the dilution rule (for arbitrary formulas) from systems of modal logic. Since our concern is with object-level logic rather than metalogic, dilution-elimination is a convenient way of excluding metalogic and modal logic from our immediate considerations. I shall presently qualify the suggestion that Gentzen's operational rules can be regarded as definitions. I claim here only that if we are to pursue that idea, we shall require that the definitions be conservative. Cut-elimination, dilution-elimination, and identicals-elimination (all for complex formulas) are necessary conditions for this. Thus we use elimination theorems for purposes quite different from those of the student of proof theory.

I can here forestall an objection raised by Christopher Peacocke against an earlier and more obscure draft of this chapter.[13] Crudely put, it amounts to 'What's so great about cut-elimination ?' More precisely, if we want to define logical constants, why not just give the operational rules, plus the cut rule and any other structural rules we want? The immediate answer is that then the operational rules are certainly not, in themselves, the definitions of the logical constants. But what is wrong with just adding the operational rules and the structural rules stated for arbitrary formulas built up out of the logical constants? Nothing, except that one is not then defining logical

---

[13]What is a logical constant? *The Journal of Philosophy*, LXXIII, 9 (May 1976): 221–240.

constants in connection with some previous language fragment. Rather one is creating, as a totality, a new system of logistic. Moreover, to foreshadow one use I shall make of these ideas, this system could not have added to it rules for yet another logical constant, without then changing the structural rules once again, asserting that they are to hold for yet more complex formulas. When we add only conservative operational rules, however, we never add any structural postulates. They hold for elementary 'prelogical' formulas, and are proved to hold for arbitrary complex formulas. For a rough analogy to textbook cases of creative definition, take a system of first-order logic with identity and an operation 'o' for which there is only an associative axiom: $x \circ (y \circ z) = (x \circ y \circ z)$. Try defining '$e$' by the formula $x \circ e = x$. This is not conservative, for we can now prove $(\exists y)(\forall x)(x \circ y = x)$. To caricature Peacocke's question, why not add this last sentence along with the sentence defining 'e'? There is nothing wrong with that. But it leads to a new theory of 'o' which is substantively different from the old one. One has not defined 'e' for the original system with simply associative 'o'.

I hasten to add that Peacocke's chief objection was that purely syntactic rules could not possibly be expected to be what is fundamental in characterizing logical constants. Logic is concerned with the preservation of truth, and hence with logical consequence and a semantics, so a syntactic approach ought not be basic. My doctrine is, however, that the peculiarity of the logical constants resides precisely in this: that, given a certain pure notion of truth and consequence, all the desirable semantic properties of the constants are determined, as in Section 16, by their syntactic properties. Peacocke is more favourably disposed to the subformula property (which he seems to imply is associated with cut-elimination), but I can give no defense of it as a requirement that the definitions should be conservative.

10   Defining logical constants

If operational rules could be regarded as definitions, then they would have to be conservative. But can they be so regarded? Several quite different kinds of objection arise. First, it is clear that these rules could not define the constants for a being that lacked all logical concepts. One must understand something like conjunction to apply the conjunction rule, and one must have some surrogate for some sort of quantifier to apply the rule for universal quantification. This kind of consideration particularly influences workers trying to find predicative or other constructive foundations for branches of mathematics. They look for definitions that genuinely reduce seemingly nonconstructive concepts or reasonings to ideas that are better understood. I shall not argue that the operational rules serve any such purpose. On the contrary, the operational rules at most *character-ize* the logical constants in a certain way for a person who already has some logical ideas. In fact of course there is a legitimate sense of 'defini-tion' in which a definition characterizes what one already understands. To avoid confusion, however, I shall often speak of the operational rules not as defining but only as characterizing the logical constants. This in no way weakens the demand that the rules be conservative. If they are not, the operational rules themselves fail to characterize the logical constants. A quite different objection arises from the fact that Gentzen wrote only at the dawn of semantic theory. Today we expect that anything worth call-ing a definition should imply a semantics. Since the operational rules are syntactic, they must, it will be urged, fall short of definitions. This objec-tion is partially met by the 'do-it-yourself semantics' of Section 16 below. Let there be assumed a notion of classical truth and falsity for elemen-tary sentences lacking logical constants, and let the deducibility relation be complete for classical logical consequence among the class of such sen-tences. Then one is in a certain sense able to read off the semantics of the logical constants from the operational rules. Given the underlying notions of truth and logical consequence, the syntactic rules determine a seman-tics. The operational rules do not themselves determine this semantics. It is not as if one could somehow fix what truth and logical consequence are, just by stating the operational rules. This bears on a useful observa-tion of Hilary Putnam's. He recalls Gödel's mapping of classical sentential logic into intuitionist logic, in which, for example, classical conjunction is identified with intuitionist conjunction but classical disjunction is identi-fied with intuitionist $\neg(\neg p \& \neg q)$. Then he writes, in italics: *'Contrary to what a number of philosophers—including recently Hacking—have asserted,* [the operational rules] *do not fix the "meanings" of the logical connectives. Someone could accept all of those rules (and all classical tautologies, as well) and still be using the logical connectives in the nonclassical sense just described'.*[14] Putnam makes this observation in the course of urging that if the logical connectives are given a 'quasi-intuitionist' interpretation one can then go on to define 'true', as he puts it, *'exactly à la Tarski. Only* "truth" becomes provability ...)' . On this point my theory does not seem to diverge much from Putnam's ideas. He is avoiding the following ma-neuver: someone says 'I'll first fix the meaning of the logical constants by giving rules of inference; then I'll define "true" à la Tarski, so any indeter-minacy in truth itself will be entirely avoided.' I claim, on the contrary, that the operational rules 'fix the meanings of the logical connectives' in the sense of giving a semantics, only if classical notions of truth and logical consequence are already assumed. So any avoidance of Putnam's indeter-

---

[14] *Meaning and the Moral Sciences* (Boston: Routledge and Kegan Paul, 1978), p. 27.

ectively

minacy would be circular. The minimum classical assumptions on truth and consequence are stated in Section 15 below.

11   Categorical grammar

This discussion of definition may suggest that I want to characterize conjunction or universal quantification or some other specific constant—as if logicians did not already know what they mean! Quite the contrary. I am concerned with a general *form* of definition. Now Gentzen studied a given class of first-order constants. He proceeded in the standard way, first stating the elements of his object language, then giving rules for well-formedness, and finally giving rules of inference. That is good practice for a preassigned set of logical constants, but we shall be concerned with *any* constant that can be introduced in a certain way. Hence we should think of the inferential rules introducing a constant as accompanied by syntactical rules for the grammar of the constant.

These grammatical rules should be effective. The symbol w is to be added to some well-understood language L. Suppose that not only is there an effective test for determining which strings of symbols from L are well-formed, but also that there is an effective procedure for uniquely parsing well-formed formulas of L. Then there should be grammatical rules for w, ensuring that $L + w$ has the same properties. It is well known that Russell introduced the definite description operator so as to make its scope ambiguous; our definitions should avoid that defect.

It would be nice to state the general form for introducing a constant into any language of sufficient complexity. That would require a knowledge of the general form of language itself, and there is no such thing. But we can achieve a remarkably high degree of generality by using the categorical grammar invented by Kasimirz Ajdukiewicz.[15] He intended it as the grammar for the theory of types, but it has recently been generalized and enriched by Richard Montague.[16] We need have no views on how suitable it is for the analysis of English: categorical grammar is plainly adequate for any of the more formal languages used in logic.

This grammar assigns a category to each expression of the language. The notation for the categories indicates how new expressions are to be formed from old and also indicates the category of the resulting expression.

---

[15] Die syntaktische Konnexität, *Studia Philosophica*, I (1935): 1–27; H. Weber, trans., Syntactic connection, in S. McCall, ed., *Polish Logic 1920-1939* , (Oxford: Clarendon Press, 1967), pp. 207–231.

[16] The proper treatment of quantification in ordinary English, in R. H. Thomason, ed., *Formal Philosophy: Selected Papers of Richard Montague* (New Haven, Conn.: Yale, 1974) and other papers in the same volume.

If the primitive categories are s (for formula) and t (for term), then a singulary predicate is of category $(t)/s$, because when applied to a term it yields a sentence. Binary predicates are $(t,t)/s$. Binary sentential connectives are of category $(s,s)/s$, adjectives are $(t)/t$, and so forth. The existential and universal quantifiers of first-order logic are of category $((t)/s)/s$. Such a notation rapidly takes in some of the more complex structures even of ordinary speech. It allows, by indexing, for different kinds of nouns, of adjectives that apply to them, and so forth. By systems of indexing it is well adapted to the theory of types, which was the point for which Ajdukiewicz designed it. I shall not elaborate the cumbersome details of this syntax, relying on the fortunate fact that there is now a reservoir of categorical grammar on which to draw. In practice we consider only language fragments of the sort familiar to logicians, the functional calculi. But I emphasize that this is an altogether general theory. We can investigate the possibility of conservative Gentzen-like-rules as far as others can develop precise and unambiguous categorical grammars. Although I shall not proceed to the discussion of adverbs, for example the road to a logic of adverbs, such as it is, lies open before us. Similarly for the logic of those second-order quantifiers, such as 'every man', retrieved by Montague from scholastic logic.

Suppose, then, that we have a language fragment and wish to introduce a constant by means of a (Gentzen-like rule. It is not enough, in general, to write down some inference schemes. Take the simplest case, a fragment L with no logical constants whatsoever, and whose expressions are all of category s. Let us add a binary connective '*' to this language. The steps are as follows. The grammar of L must be augmented by a category $(s,s)/s$, together with rules for sentence formation with this category. Then it is stated that '*' is of this category. Then operational rules are stated. Using our intuitive (but grammatically formalizable) scheme for representing the rules, we have, say:

$$\frac{\Gamma \vdash A, \Theta \quad \Gamma \vdash B, \Theta}{\Gamma, A * B \vdash \Theta} \qquad \frac{\Gamma, A, B \vdash \Theta}{\Gamma \vdash A * B, \Theta}$$

That completes the characterization of '*'. Next one must check that it is conservative. Yes, the deducibility of identicals, dilution, and cut are all eliminable for formulas with '*'.

Perhaps no one has written down this 'definition' before. What does '*' mean ? That is the best way to put the demand that Gentzen-style definitions ought to provide a semantics. In fact the do-it-yourself semantics of Section 16 does automatically provide a semantics for the above constant. One sees at once that $A * B$ is true in a model if and only if at least one of A or B is false in that model. This '*' is Sheffer's stroke.

The requirement that operational rules be conservative can make un-expected demands. Let us start with a language L of terms and monadic predicates. Its nonempty categories are at least s, t and $(t)/s$. To bring in a universal quantifier we must add the category $((t)/s)/s$. It is stated that the universal quantifier is of this category, and one gives the usual Gentzen rules. But proof of cut-elimination is not yet possible. In the course of restructuring the derivations of $\Gamma, (\forall x)Fx \vdash \Theta$ and $\Gamma \vdash (\forall x)Fx, \Theta$, one will in general require at least one item of category t that does not occur in Γ, Θ. Since there is no upper bound on the number of terms that can occur in Γ, Θ, we shall require a stock of items of category t that cannot be exhausted. In more familiar terms, to add the universal quantifier to a language of monadic predicates, one must also add a countable class of variables. For some purposes it is doubtless true that the variables of first-order logic can be regarded as prepositions and place-holders that could in principle be dispensed with, say by a system of arrows indicating what places fall in the scope of which quantifier. The above remarks are yet another way of making the point that this is not the whole story about variables in logic.

Henceforth it will be assumed that rules for introducing a logical con-stant have two parts. There is the syntactic part determining the rules of well-formedness for the constant. This may include adding stocks of parameters of various categories, required to prove cut-elimination. Then there is the inferential part, giving the rules of derivability of statements in which the constant occurs.

12   What is a logical constant?

Gentzen's rules are built around a deducibility relation. Deduction has seemed, to some, to be the essence of logic. Hence philosophers have long suggested that systems of natural deduction or the sequent calculus pre-cisely capture 'the province of logic'. The phrase is that of William Kneale. Similar ideas were propounded by Karl Popper, independently of Gentzen. Paul Lorenzen's operational logic is a related syntactic development of logic which is also supposed to lead to the semantics of logical constants.[17] One basic idea of all these workers may be that *a logical constant is a constant*

---

[17]W. C. Kneale, The Province of Logic, in H. D. Lewis, ed., *Contemporary British Philosophy, Third Series* (London: Allen and Unwin, 1956). Karl Popper, New foun-dations for logic, *Mind*, LVI, 223 (July 1947): 193–235, and other papers referred to in note 1 to C. Lejewski, *Popper's Theory of Formal Inference*, in P. A. Schilpp, ed., *The Philosophy of Karl Popper*, (La Salle, Ill.: Open Court, 1976), p. 669. Wolfgang Stegmuller, Remarks on the completeness of logical systems relative to the validity-concepts of P. Lorenzen and K. Lorenz, *Notre Dame Journal of Formal Logic*, V, 2 (April 1964): 81–112.

that can be introduced, characterized, or defined in a certain way.

What way? My answer is about the same as Kneale's: a logical constant is a constant that can be introduced by operational rules like those of Gentzen. The question becomes, 'like' in what respects? Different answers will mark off different conceptions of logic. My answer is that the operational rules introducing a constant should (i) have the subformula property, and (ii) be conservative with respect to the basic facts of deducibility. The second clause means (finitistic) provability of the elimination theorems. Why should rules for 'pure logic' have the subformula property and be conservative? There are several kinds of answers. They correspond to criteria of adequacy like the following. (A) The demarcation should give the 'right' logicist class of logical constants and theorems. That is, it should include the traditional (and consistent) core of what logicists said was logic and should exclude what they denied to be logic. (B) Since the demarcation is couched in terms of how logical constants are characterized, it should provide the semantics for the constants called 'logical.' (C) It should explicate why logic is important to the analytic program. Although (A) and (B) are important, (C) is essential. A demarcation of logic that leaves the analytic program unintelligible is of little philosophical interest (unless the point is to show that the analytic program *is* unintelligible).

I shall briefly explain how my demarcation satisfies (A)–(C), then develop these themes more fully. As regards (A), the most coherent conclusion to logicist investigations is *Principia Mathematica*. Its authors held that all of the ramified theory of types (including identity relations for various ramified types) is logic. But they regretfully concluded that the simplified theory of types is not logic. That is exactly our result. Conservative rules having the subformula property can be used to introduce the ramified quantifiers and identity, but they do not go as far as full second-order logic.[18] So criterion (A) is satisfied. In Section 13 I shall discuss whether this is really desirable: is it now known that Russell excluded something truly logical or included something that is not? I don't think so.

As for criterion (B), I have already mentioned that 'do-it-yourself semantics' is generated from Gentzen's operational rules for first- order logic. Indeed, what makes it work is precisely the subformula property and the elimination theorems. Section 15 gives some indication of how criterion (B) is satisfied.

Criterion (C) is fundamental. To delineate logic without explicating the intuitions underlying the analytic program is to forget the point of the whole exercise. Without the idea of analyticity, who cares exactly what logic *is*? Quine, in contending that logic coincides with first-order logic,

---

[18]For the ramified theory of types and second-order logic, see Prawitz, *op. cit.* note 10, pp. 62–73. For identity, see my On the reality of existence and identity, *Canadian Journal of Philosophy*, Vlll, 4 December 1978): 613–632.

is as usual entirely germane. He thinks that the intuitions underlying the analytic program are fundamentally mistaken. Hence his answer to the question, 'What is logic?' does indeed satisfy criterion (C), albeit vacuously. He thinks there are few ultimately coherent intuitions to explicate. In the concluding sections of the chapter I argue that the present demarcation of logic, in terms of a form of definition, does elucidate some of these intuitions in a more positive way.

13   First- and second-order

Russell said that the ramified theory of types is logic. The axiom of reducibility, the simplified theory of types, and even full second-order logic are not, then, logic. By my criterion (A), I took it as a virtue of my demarcation that it agrees with the logicist answer. But it would be no virtue if the logicists were just wrong. I now wish to examine a few putative counterexamples to show that the logicist thesis is at least not manifestly absurd.

To stop halfway between first- and second-order logic is to leave oneself in the middle of an uncomfortable slanging match. On the one hand is the position favoured by Quine. He once denied that we can stake out a separate preserve for logic. Now he says that if logic is a special kind of entity, it can only be first-order logic.[19] That is not much of a shift of position. Part of the original argument was that nothing distinguishes the peculiarly logical. Now we relax: there is after all one firm distinction, namely, the distinction between first-order logic and everything else. This is buttressed by ontological considerations. Quine does not want to quantify over predicates, and so excludes second-order quantification. Then there are powerful formal results: for example, first-order logic is the strongest complete compact theory with a Löwenheim–Skolem theorem.[20] It is well known that Richard Montague, in contrast, urged that second-order logic is the very tool for mathematical inquiries and that it is also the foundation of the categorical grammar of English. George Boolos has recently vigorously

---

[19]Existence and quantification, in *Ontological Relativity and Other Essays* (New York: Columbia, 1969), esp. pp. 111–113; *Philosophy of Logic* (Englewood Cliffs, NJ.: Prentice Hall, 1970), chs 5, 6.

[20]Per Lindström, On Extensions of Elementary logic, *Theoria*, xxxv, 1 (1969): 1–11. I refer of course to a countable Löwenheim–Skolem theorem, and not to generalizations such as are found in Jon Barwise, Matt Kaufmann, and Michael Makkai, Stationary Logic, *Annals of Mathematical Logic*, XIII (1978): 171–224. Note that stationary logic also falls between first- and second-order logic. There are numerous other investigations showing either that first-order logic has all of certain desirable properties, or else is the strongest logic with certain desirable properties e.g. J. Zucker, The adequacy problem for classical logic, *Journal of Philosophical Logic*, viii (1979).

defended second-order reasoning.[21] He stands up to the ontological threats and he asks, for example, why on earth compactness, whatever its virtues, should be definitive of logic itself. My theory of logic goes between these two extremes. It appears to have some of the advantages that each party claims for its own side, while lacking some of the faults that each party finds in the other. Logic, on my account, includes the ramified theory of types, but goes no further toward a higher-order logic. This may seem an inauspicious claim, for the ramified theory is now generally held to have been a mistake. But that is because of the historical accident that the authors of *Principia* tried to find a foundation for all mathematics. They thought that logic stopped at the ramified theory, which is too weak for much set theory. Hence they added an extralogical postulate, the axiom of reducibility. As Ramsey noticed, this makes ramification redundant; since then, no one has been much interested in the ramified theory. But if we accept the fact that logic is not going to provide a foundation for mathematics and if we do not add an extralogical axiom of reducibility, then the ramified structure is untouched, and has, I believe, certain merits. Consider, for example, the fact that second-order logic has no chance of a completeness theorem unless one ventures into intensional entities and possible worlds. I sympathize with the extensionalist objection to these devices, and am glad that the completeness proof for ramified theory is entirely extensional. One does not need to posit any class of entities larger than the class of inscriptions demanded by the theory itself, although the intensionalist may, if he so wishes, suppose that one is quantifying over certain well-circumscribed classes of properties.[22] Ramified theory is not adequate even for the analysis of recursive arithmetic, and the second-order theorist will object to this fact. In my opinion, this is, on the contrary, something that we have learned: arithmetic is not logic. There are many ways to do arithmetic, and not all demand second-order theorizing, but there is one new and prospering discipline that has thus far been conducted only in a second-order way. This is Montague's grammar. Montague was of course a champion of second-order theory in mathematical investigations as well as in the sphere of grammar. Let us keep these separate. Although second-order theory provides a powerful grammar for all sorts of fragments of English, we should not jump at once to conclusions. We should consider whether we need the full force of second-order logic to effect Montague's analysis of bits of ordinary language that we well understand. I tentatively propose that there is nothing in the more accessible parts of the analysis which cannot also be provided by a ramified theory.

---

[21] On second-order logic, *The Journal of Philosophy*, LXXII, 16 (Sept. 18, 1975): 509–526.

[22] There is an unpublished extensional semantics for ramified theory, due to David Kaplan.

A Löwenheim–Skolem theorem holds for anything which, on my delineation, is logic. It follows from Per Lindström's result that logic is not compact. Defending second-order theory, Boolos asks why logic should be compact? Compactness is a handy property, but there is no argument that it is of the essence of logic. On my account, however, classical logic has a property that we might call *proof-compactness*. I allow countably many premises. The question then arises whether we could obtain additional theorems by allowing proofs with more than finitely many steps, using an ω-rule. The answer is that no new theorems arise in this way. This property of proof-compactness has a venerable tradition behind it. It was Leibniz's original demarcation of the logically necessary: that which can be proved in finitely many steps. The second-order logician has one telling objection against his first-order antagonist. Leon Henkin[23] proved that there is no first-order treatment of branching quantifiers such as

$$rl(x)(\exists y)$$
$$(Pxy \& Qzw \& Ryw) \qquad (1)$$
$$(z)(\exists w)$$

Branching quantifiers do not seem to involve any idea that is fundamentally different from ordinary quantification; so why, it is asked, should we exclude them from the province of logic? We understand them, it is said, in just the way that we understand ordinary universal quantification. The second-order logician does have a rendering of branching quantifiers, namely:

$$(\exists f)(\exists g)(x)(z)(P(x, fx) \& Q(z, gz) \& R(fx, gz)) \qquad (2)$$

The question of branching quantifiers also leads to another rival theory on the nature of logic, the game-theoretic semantics being developed by Jaakko Hintikka and his students.[24] Hintikka claims it as a virtue of his theory that it provides an analysis of real sentences of English. To use an example due to Janet Beehner,

Some melody of every big band from the forties is copied in some hit song of every rock'n roll star. (3)

Students of English grammar are by no means agreed on whether such sentences do bear the branching quantifier reading.[25] Such current issues

---

[23] Some remarks on infinitely long formulas, in *Infinitistic Methods: Proceedings of a Symposium on Foundations of Mathematics* (New York: Pergamon, 1961).

[24] *Logic, Language Games and Information* (Oxford: Clarendon Press, 1973), ch III; Quantifiers vs. quantification theory, *Linguistic Inquiry*, V (1974): 153–177.

[25] For some relevant considerations on these tentative matters I am indebted to Laure Carlsen and Alice ter Meulen, Informational independence in intensional contexts, in E. Saarinen *et al.* eds, *Essays in Honour of Jakko Hinitkka* (Boston: Reidel, 1979), pp. 61–72; and to an unpublished paper by Jon Barwise.

will take a number of years to settle down, and here I wish only to warn against too speedy a slide: 'If you look at these sentences, you see they involve no idea basically different from the sort of thing we do in first-order logic; we can indeed explain everything in terms of individuals. So you must count branching quantifiers as much a part of "logic" as first-order logic'. Then comes: 'the natural abstraction of the idea of branching quantifiers produces a theory formally as strong as full second-order logic'. I would interject that there is nothing that we understand in (3) that cannot be understood by (2) where f and g are restricted to very low-grade ramified functions. I don't know whether (3) has to have a branching reading in English syntax. But, if it does, then it can be represented in a way that stops short of full second-order logic. To express matters in a modest way, the ramified theory once again shows itself to be a buffer between first- and second-order logic.

14   Other logics

A demarcation can be bad in two distinct ways. It can be too strait, denying the existence of borderline cases, or it can be too vague, muttering that there will always be a messy border. A good criterion is one which is sharp but which can also be relaxed in various ways. For example, a good criterion of 'grammatical sentence' is one that provides a natural measure of degrees of being grammatical. Likewise, we should allow that a core definition of 'logic' can forge out in various directions. Here are some examples of how my demarcation does this.

I say that a Gentzen-like rule should have the subformula property. Now a number of workers have prepared Gentzen versions of Hilbert's ϵ-calculus, where cut-elimination does not hold. Linda Wessells has recently offered a cut-free sequent calculus for Hilbert's ϵ, but her rules do not, strictly speaking, have a subformula property.[26] (It may be possible to find a more encompassing but not merely *ad hoc* property that they do have.) On present evidence we should say not that Hilbert's ϵ is not logical but that it fails to fall under the logicist conception of logic in an entirely specific and well-defined way. A much better understood extension of the logicist conception of logic concerns the power of proofs of cut-elimination. I have considered only finitistically provable cut-elimination. Transfinite induction up to limit ordinals provides more and more generous classifications of logic. Many readers will say that is how we ought to go, for the restriction

---

[26]Cut-elimination in a Gentzen-style ϵ-calculus without identity, *Zeitschrift für Mathermatische Logik und Grundlagen der Mathematik*, XXIII (1977): 527–538. For a debate on whether Hilbert's 'ϵ' is a logical constant, see Thomas Bjurlöf, A note on logical constants, *Analysis*, XXXVIII (1978): 119–121, and Christopher Peacocke, A reply to Bjurlöf's objection, *idib*, 122–124.

to finitistic proofs is provincial or old-fashioned. There are many things to say on that score. One logicist defense might recall Leibniz's idea that a proof of a necessary proposition must have a finite number of steps. Now take a theory like arithmetic for which one proves an elimination theorem using transfinite induction. That does not imply that cut-free proofs in the object-level theory itself have to be infinite in length; for any particular use of the cut rule can be dealt with in a finite number of steps. So Gentzen's object-level theory of arithmetic is not to be faulted on that Leibnizian score. But there is also a logicist conception that logic is the very canon of consistency. If, for Leibnizian reasons, proofs in logic are things that stop, then only when logic is construed in terms of finitistically provable elimination theorems do we have a theory whose consistency can be established by logic itself.

Modal logics provide yet another direction in which to extend logic. Obviously, the principles underlying this extension must be quite different from those which lead on to arithmetic. Our demarcation displays this very nicely. It is not provability of cut-elimination that excludes modal logic, but dilution-elimination, as was shown in Section 9. The serious modal logics such as $T, S4$ and $S5$ have cut-free sequent-calculus formalizations, but the rules place restrictions on side formulas. Gentzen's rules for sentential connections are all 'local' in that they concern only the components from which the principal formula is built up, and place no restrictions on the side formulas. Gentzen's own first order rules, though not strictly local, are equivalent to local ones. That is why dilution-elimination goes through for first-order logic but not for modal logics. What does this formal difference amount to? The meaning is clearer when one thinks of natural-deduction formulations. To place a restriction on side formulas is to insist that whether a step in a proof is valid depends on the history of the proof and on the forms of the sentences that occur higher up in the proof. Modal logic is in this sense metalogical, and our criterion picks out object-level classical logic. This is not to deny that modal logic is in some general sense logic, but rather to specify precisely a formal respect in which it differs from first-order and ramified logic. Thus the subformula property, finitistic cut-elimination, and dilution-elimination may all be relaxed to provide different kinds of extension of my core logicist demarcation of logic. That is as it should be. The difference between first-order and modal logic shows up in a more familiar way at the semantic level. Models for modal logic use domains of possible worlds. The seriously motivated nonclassical logics, such as are inspired by intuitionist mathematics or quantum physics, also have different semantics. I believe that the difference between such nonclassical logics and classical logics lies in the deducibility relation itself and in the corresponding semantic relation of logical consequence. The nonclassical logics assume a different underlying semantic framework. I shall develop this idea in the next two sections.

15   Semantic frameworks

Suppose that Gentzen-like operational rules are to be added to a language fragment. If the initial bit of language is something one can understand, then it ought to be possible to understand this fragment augmented by the constants introduced by the rules. If not, the rules are not definitions.

We must, then, provide a semantics for the new logical constants, presupposing a semantics for the original language fragment. That assumes some substantive and precise analysis of the fragment. The assumption has two parts: first, a general assumption about the form that the semantics should take, and, second, a specific account of thc language fragment to hand.

By the form of the semantics I mean an initial abstraction about the nature of truth and logical consequence. What I have to say in detail about this abstraction does not depend on any philosophy, but it is well to offer one philosophical setting, which the reader need not accept. I do not believe that English is by its nature classical or intuitionistic or whatever. Classical and intuitionistic truth are both abstractions made by logicians. We all know that logicians attend to numerous different objects that might be served by uttering 'if ... then. ...' sentences. The abstractions that result include the material conditional, several kinds of strict implication, and a panoply of stronger connectives of which relevant implication is the current favourite. In a more ambitious way classical and some serious nonclassical logics abstract from the very point of making statements. Classical logic is one of several interesting abstractions. If the point of uttering sentences (perhaps only with some selected topics of conversation) is to say what can be established, or to say what makes sense in microphysics, then one is drawn to nonclassical abstractions.

These remarks about abstraction are intended chiefly as a flag, posting quicksand. It might well be the case that there are decisive arguments in favour of classical, intuitionist, or quantum logic (to mention only views that are widely attributed to Kripke, Dummett, and Putnam in turn). I here contend only that none of these is the logic of English. When I speak of a semantic framework for a language fragment, I mean an abstraction from the point of uttering declarative sentences. It is art, not nature, that determines the semantics of natural languages.

A semantic framework is to be the general form of the semantics of a language. It may well be that I include too little in the framework, and then smuggle in more assumptions as part of the semantics of specific languages. Perhaps I focus too much on what has been the subject of recent discussion. But I shall make two assumptions only, one about truth, and the other about logical consequence. The strongest version of the assumption about truth is that every sentence of the language fragment should be assigned the value true or false but not both. The second assumption is that a set of sentences Θ is a logical consequence of the set of sentences Γ if no matter what values are assigned to the members of Γ, Θ, some member of Θ is true when every member of Γ is true. We make only these two assumptions. The language fragment might have a rich field of logical consequence, or it might be a 'prelogical' language of independent elementary sentences like that envisaged by the *Tractatus*, in which there are no nontrivial consequences.

There is an important connection between the structural rules and this classical semantic framework. Let us say that a set of rules of deducibility is *complete* with respect to a language with a classical semantic framework when Γ ⊢ Θ is derivable if and only if Θ is a logical consequence of Γ. *Then the structural rules are complete with respect to a prelogical classical language.* Or to put it differently, Θ is a logical consequence of Γ in any classical language whatsoever, if and only if Γ ⊢ Θ is derivable by the structural rules alone. I began in Section 6 writing out general constraints on anything that could count as a relation of deducibility. These constraints had already been recognized by Gentzen as the structural rules of his sequent calculus. They also pick out the minimum facts of logical consequence that obtain from a classical point of view. Thus the structural rules formalize the 'pure' theory of classical logical consequence. It is my contention, not developed here, that a nonclassical logic has a right to be called logic (and not merely another logical algebra) only if there is a different semantic framework, with respect to which some nonclassical structural rules are complete.

16   Do-it-yourself semantics

The rules for logical constants always take the following form. Since the requirement of dilution-elimination means that all rules are local in the sense of placing no restrictions on side formulas, side formulas may be disregarded. Omitting side formulas, the form of the rules is:

$$\frac{\{\Pi_i \vdash \Sigma_i\}}{A \vdash} \qquad \frac{\{\Pi_j \vdash \Sigma_j\}}{\vdash A}$$

The formulas in Π and Σ are components of A. A set of statements $\{\Pi_j \vdash \Sigma_j\}$ from which one may derive ⊢ A is called a *right protopremise*; $\{\Pi_i \vdash \Sigma_i\}$ above is a *left protopremise*. Consider a Gentzen-like rule which is to add a constant to a language fragment. A semantics and a class of models for the language is assumed. A model assigns every sentence of this language the values T or F. We are concerned with how to assign values to complex sentences in terms of a model for the original language. Thanks to the subformula property an inductive definition may be used.

A takes the value T in a model iff there is a right protopremise for A, $\{\Pi_i \vdash \Sigma_i\}$, such that for each j some member of Σ_j takes T or some member of Π_j takes F.

Thanks to the elimination theorems, it is possible to establish a matching assertion,

A takes the value F iff there is a left protopremise for A, $\{\Pi_i \vdash \Sigma_i\}$ such that for each i some member of Σ_i takes T or some member of Π_i, takes F.

There is nothing more to be said about sentential logic. More complicated languages have more structured models. In Section 11 it was pointed out that provability of cut-elimination for first-order logic might require the addition of countably many items of category t, that is, an infinite stock of variables. This applies only to languages which already have some terms and predicates and for which we assume models with a nonempty domain of individuals. For each model M of the original language, we now need all models obtained by assigning the new variables to individuals in the domain of M. This indicates a general technique for ramified logic, and is possible because variables of a given category are added only to a language that already has items of that category and, hence, whose models already have a nonempty class of objects for items of that category.

This semantics is not directly applicable to Gentzen's quantifier rules. His rule for the universal quantifier is stated on the left below. Instead we use the equivalent ω-rule on the right, which is local in the sense of Section 14, that is, places no restrictions on the side formulas. (That such a rule is equivalent is implied already by Gentzen's Lemma 3.10 'redesignating of free object variables'.)

$$\frac{\Gamma \vdash Fa, \Theta}{\Gamma \vdash \forall x Fx, \Theta} \text{ where } a \text{ does not occur in the bottom line}$$

$$\frac{\{\Gamma \vdash Ft_i, \Theta\}_i}{\Gamma \vdash \forall x Fx, \Theta} \text{ where } t_i \text{ runs over all terms}$$

Such devices may be immediately generalized to ramified logic. Charles Parsons points out that such ω-rules precisely parallel the *Tractatus* account of the first-order quantifiers.

The completeness theorem states that, under the above semantics, $\Gamma \vdash \Theta$ is derivable if and only if Θ is a logical consequence of Γ. I have stated some details of the proof elsewhere.[27] This do-it-yourself semantics is of course a fraud. It purports to be a mechanical way of providing the semantics of the logical constants. But in fact it needs a thoroughly hand-crafted semantics for the original language fragment in order for the whole thing to work. In the case of the quantifiers with the ω-rule above, one would have to understand something like arithmetic, or at least counting, to deploy the semantics. This is not a problem for the present chapter, for I have tried only to find a demarcation of the logical constants. The claim is that the constants are those which can be introduced into a language in a certain way. They can be introduced by rules of a certain form. The rules are syntactic in character. Yet they are such that if strong semantic assumptions of a general kind are made, then the specific semantics of the individual logical constants is thereby determined. The rule for '*' in Section 11 will illustrate this. What are the truth conditions for '$A * B$'? The rules stated above show that $A * B$ takes the value T if and only if at least one of A or B is F. So the do-it-yourself semantics is not vacuous; for one could well have failed to understand what the '*' meant, and then found it out by these semantics.

17   Prelogical language

The *Tractatus* imagines a language of elementary sentences that lack logical constants, which has in addition sentential connectives for forming compound sentences. The truth tables exhibit the character of these connectives and show how the truth conditions for complex sentences may be explained in terms of simpler sentences. One could carry this myth one step further, and consider the fragment of the language consisting just of elementary sentences. Then one could imagine the logical connectives being added to that language, and their use being conveyed by syntactic rules and the truth tables. The point of this extra myth would not be to show how the connectives are in fact learned, but rather to display something about the logical connectives—'they are words of this peculiar sort, that one can imagine them being planted in the language in this way'.

There is no part of the *Tractatus* of which Wittgenstein became more scornful than the myth of elementary sentences. But having been taught some of the lessons of later philosophy, one can still usefully deploy the myth. It is an instructive myth because it is the purest form of the idea of

---

[27]Do-it-yourself semantics for classical sequent calculi, including ramified type theory, in R. Butts and J. Hintikka, eds., *Logic, Foundations of Mathematics and Computability Theory* (Boston: Reidel, 1977), pp. 371–390.

a purely descriptive part of language. This myth, and the task of distinguishing nondescriptive logical constants, is foreshadowed by the schoolmen. The signs of quantity, 'some', 'all', and 'no', were central examples of syncategorematical terms. But what, it was asked, distinguishes them from descriptive terms? It was natural to contrast *velus* (meaning 'veil') and *vel* (meaning something like inclusive disjunction) but there was never an agreed basis to the distinction. In general one tried to say as much, or more, about what it is to be descriptive as about what it is to be syncategorematical. Much the same holds for similar dichotomies in judgments, say between the empirical and the *a priori*, or in faculties, say between sensibility and the understanding. It is a virtue of my demarcation that it enables one to characterize the logical constants without being forced to say what is on the other side of the dichotomy. One does not have to say what pure descriptive constants are. A logical constant is a constant that can be added to any language of a certain sort.

Yet the myth of the prelogical or entirely descriptive language still has some force. It enables us to ask, What are the minimum conditions on a language, in order that logical constants should be added by means of operational rules? If the rules are to be regarded as something like definitions, then we suppose the formulas of a prelogical language are themselves intelligible. Such understanding might be achieved by providing a theory of truth for the language, or a formal semantics, or: the language is simply understood. A number of philosophers have recently been reinforcing the point that the stating of meanings comes to an end, and languages are in the end just understood. A fact about the terminology of the *Tractatus* has been widely overlooked. Wittgenstein speaks of *truth conditions* for compound sentences. He shows how truth conditions of compounds are determined by their components. But he does not speak of truth conditions for elementary sentences. He does speak of their truth possibilities, but not of their truth conditions.[28] This thought could be combined with a recent doctrine of Putnam's. He urges that the theory of understanding a language is not to be couched in terms of truth conditions and correspondence, although those ideas are important for explaining the success of discourse. Without taking a stand on such matters, one could urge that understanding the prelogical language is indeed not to be explained in terms of truth conditions. Complex sentences, obtained by adding logical constants, however, may have their truth conditions explained in terms of more elementary sentences.

It may well be asked whether a prelogical language could be understood

---

[28]For *Wahrheitsbedingungen*, see, 4.431, 4.442, 4.45, 4.46, 4.461, 4.463; for *Wahrheitsmöglichkeiten*, see 4.3, 4.31, 4.4, 4.41, 4.42, 4.43, 4.431, 4.44, 4.442 4.45, 4.46, 5.101. Note that in 4.063 (b) the word sometimes translated as 'conditions' is *Umständen*.

by a being that had no logical concepts. I doubt that there are any compelling arguments one way or the other, and the question is idle because prelogical language is a myth. Beneath any 'elementary' sentence—be it 'this is black', said pointing at this letter 'r'—there *is* a swarming underworld of logically germane sentences that bear on the sentence in more than a merely empirical or inductive way. The best metaphor may be that of an hourglass, of endless constructions which converge on a collection of what are at one level simple sentences, but which, when they pass through the narrow point of the hourglass, open up again in endless complexity. The elementary sentences of the *Tractatus* are merely the elements that occur at a narrowing in an hourglass, and are not ultimate. Logic, depth grammar, structuralism, and the like should postulate points of convergence or condensation, not atoms.

18   Logical truth

My criterion (C) insists that a demarcation of logical constants should connect with the analytic program. The immediate Fregean aim had been to reduce arithmetic to logic, proving thereby that arithmetic is not synthetic. The results are negative. Recursive arithmetic cannot be reduced to logic, strictly construed. If, however, one were to extend the definition of logic to allow for transfinite proofs of cut-elimination, then arithmetic does get included as 'logic'. In Section 14 I have expressed some reservations about this strategy.

   The strict demarcation of logic provides some vindication for both Leibniz and Kant. In the ramified hierarchy cumbersome definitions enable one to prove that $5 + 7 = 12$. So, on my explication, Kant's immediate claim about arithmetic is wrong. *That* sum is not synthetic. But although Leibniz may win this battle he loses the war, for the concept *natural number* cannot itself be categorically characterized in pure logic. We can say only that the natural numbers are those which come in the sequence $1, 2, 3, \ldots$. We do have an intuition of this sequence. Perhaps, as Kant supposed, it is connected to the intuition of succession in time.

   Arithmetic was a special project for the analytic program. More generally, it aimed at understanding the nature of logical truth. A. J. Ayer could say, in the great days of enthusiasm, that 'there is nothing mysterious about the apodictic certainty of logic and mathematics. Our knowledge that no observation can ever confute the proposition "$7 + 5 = 12$" depends simply on the fact that the symbolic expression "$7 + 5$" is synonymous with "12", just as our knowledge that every oculist is an eye doctor depends on the fact that the symbol "eye-doctor" is synonymous with "oculist". And the same explanation holds good for every other *a priori* truth.'[29] No one would dare say this sort of thing any more, but there is a lingering belief in the maxim, 'Necessary truths are true in virtue of the meanings of the words used to express them'.

The by-product theory of logical truth, which in Section 3 I attributed to the *Tractatus*, gives some credibility to that idea. Intended originally for the truth-functional connectives, it is readily extended to any constant introduced by Gentzen-like rules satisfying my criteria. 'Without troubling ourselves about a sense and a reference, we form the logical theorems out of others by rules that deal with signs alone.' That fits the operational rules rather well. Rules for a notation are provided, in consequence of which certain complex sentences come out as theorems. As the *Tractatus* continues, 'All theorems of logic are of equal status; there are not some that are essentially primitive and others deduced from these'. 'Logic can always be conceived so that every theorem is its own proof.'[30] In the sequent calculus every theorem has, indeed, its own analysis, and no theorems are primitive. Moreover this analysis answers rather exactly to Leibniz's idea of the finitely long analysis of necessary propositions.

This way of thinking makes the existence of theorems in logic look like a by-product of the rules that convey the use of logical constants. It guards against the supposition that theorems represent constraints on how the world must be. The only constraints arise from the system for forming complex sentences. Some complexes that are built up using logical constants describe complex possibilities, but theorems and contradictions are only limiting cases that arise from the rules for the notation itself. As Leibniz well understood, the concept *logically necessary proposition* is to be explained in terms of proof, and not in terms of truth in all possible worlds (as if necessity represented some constraint on what worlds can be created).

It is not to be inferred that logical truths are in any instructive sense true by convention. Imagine that notational conventions in the form of operational rules were added to a 'prelogical' language. Even in that mythical case convention would not completely account for logical truth. There would remain the question prompted by Lewis Carroll's Achilles and the Tortoise,[31] and elaborated by Quine long ago.[32] By what conventions, it would be asked, do we apply the rules as we do when we derive theorems in the calculus? Even when we deliberately adopt a convention (say with

---

[29] *Language, Truth and Logic*, 2nd edn (London: Gollancz, 1946), p. 85.

[30] *Tractatus* 6.126, 6.127, 6.1265 for this discussion one must translate *Satz* as 'theorem'.

[31] What the tortoise said to Achilles, *Mind*, IV (1895): 278–280.

[32] Truth by convention, 1936, in W. V. Quine, *The Ways of Paradox* (New York: Random House, 1966), pp 70–99.

the rule that turned out to introduce Sheffer's stroke in Section 11) that convention is not the *complete* account of the logical theorems that result.

To reject truth by convention is not to reject truth by virtue of meaning. The operational rules display certain features of logical constants. These constants do have a 'meaning', aspects of which are displayed by these rules. The rules do not produce or create or justify logical truths, but set out what it is about their meaning that is connected with logical truth. Note that a particular objection to 'truth by virtue of meaning' is irrelevant here. It is rightly observed that 'It is raining or it is not raining' cannot be true in virtue of the meaning of the words, because the proposition expressed would be true even if we used quite different words. Yet this tautology is still a product of meanings, not (except adventitiously) of the English signs 'or' and 'not', but of the abstract 'meaning' that is conveyed by the operational rules that we happen to label as disjunction and negation. Whatever be the signs we associate with those rules, there will be a corresponding tautology.

These considerations are all of a negative sort: logical *truth* has no source outside language and whatever makes language possible. There still remain the familiar questions as to what it is to grasp the meaning. Undoubtedly we understand some constants before formulating any rules, and, even if we did not, there would be questions about following the rules. It may be, however, that certain positive conclusions are to be drawn from the theory of operational rules. For it is not as if they justify talk of logical truth. All we get from applying the rules are some sentences with the deducibility sign in front. To construe these as truths we require a semantics.

I have contended that the semantic framework has nothing to do with particular logical constants. Given a semantic framework for a language, one may use operational rules to characterize logical constants; the do-it-yourself semantics shows how the semantics for the language works out for the constants that are thus introduced. This leads one to recall some remarks of Frege quoted earlier.[33] Analytic truths are those whose proofs may be traced back to 'general logical laws'. But these general laws were not to be primitive propositions written down in the object language. What are these 'most general laws, which prescribe universally the way in which one ought to think if one is to think at all'? I believe that in the end they are not about particular logical ideas, such as the quantifier or the conditional. They must be what Frege calls 'laws of truth'. A law of truth would concern the nature of the semantic framework itself.

The analytic program has come full circle. In an attempt to understand

---

[33] References for Frege's remarks are given in notes 1, 3, and 7. Frege himself appears to have abandoned the analytic program late in life; see his Neuer Versuch der Grundlegung er Arithmetik, in H Hermes *et al.* eds *Nachgelassene Schriften* (Hamburg: Felix Meiner, 1969), p. 298.

the idea of analyticity, one considered the logical truths. A logical truth is a truth in which only logical constants occur essentially. So one searched for a demarcation of the logical constants. Having used the theory of deducibility to find it, we then see that although the existence of particular theorems of logic may be explained in terms of rules that define individual constants, the notion of logical truth depends on the notion of truth for a language. If a nonstandard logic is possible, in a way that is not parasitic upon classical logic, then a nonclassical notion of truth and consequence is possible. But if a nonstandard logic must ultimately be explained using classical logic, then indeed we would have found something that 'our thought can overflow, but never displace'.

2

Logic Without Model Theory

Robert Kowalski

1 Introduction

Arguably, model theory serves two main functions: (1) to explain the relationship between language and experience, and (2) to specify the notion of logical consequence. In this chapter I shall propose the notion of 'knowledge assimilation', the assimilation of new information into a knowledge base, as an alternative understanding of the way in which a knowledge base formulated in logic relates to externally generated input sentences that describe experience. I shall argue that the notion of logical consequence can also be understood within a knowledge assimilation framework, in terms of sentences that must hold no matter what stream of input sentences might arise in the future.

Classical model theory can be understood as dealing with static relationships among individuals. It leads naturally therefore to possible world semantics and modal logic, in which models are understood as related to one another by accessibility relations. I shall argue in favour of a non-model-theoretic alternative to possible world semantics, an alternative which employs a syntactically rich vocabulary of terms representing time, events, situations and theories.

Similarly to the way in which possible worlds can be viewed as arising from classical models, situations which cut across time and space in situation semantics can be viewed as arising from possible worlds. I shall argue for representing situations syntactically as theories and amalgamating object language and metalanguage as an alternative to situation semantics.

Logic is an important object of study in such diverse disciplines as mathematics, philosophy, psychology, linguistics, computing, artificial intelligence and law. It is used informally in every other intellectual discipline: in the natural sciences, social sciences and humanities. Despite the all-pervasive nature of logic, however, there is little agreement among

experts and lay people alike about whether or not humans are truly logical; and, if they are, about what that logic might be like. Even worse,
there seems to be little communication between experts in logic working in
different fields.

In this chapter I will outline a computational approach to logic that has
proved useful for building non-trivial applications in computing, artificial
intelligence and law. I will argue that such a logic can also be used to
understand human reasoning in both computational and logical terms. For
ease of reference, I will call this computational logic 'CL'.

The computational logic, CL, is not entirely well-defined. It is an evolving system of logic, which has its basis in the clausal and logic programming
(LP) forms of logic, but which is undergoing continual refinement and rein-
terpretation. In this chapter I will not be concerned with the theoretical
foundations of CL, but rather with the practical characteristics which make
it useful for building complex applications and for modelling human reasoning. These characteristics include the use of a rich vocabulary of terms
and the combining of object language and meta-language, to represent and
reason about time, events, states of affairs, and theories.

Johnson-Laird and Byrne [16], in their book on human deduction, dismiss clausal logic and by implication LP, as psychologically implausible and
propose instead a model-theoretic account of human reasoning. They argue
that their 'mental model' theory explains human performance on reasoning
tasks better than proof-theoretic approaches that assume humans reason
by applying rules of inference.

The mental model view of human reasoning is similar to the model-
theoretic approach to databases, in which a database is regarded as a
model-theoretic structure and a closed query is evaluated by determining its truth value in the database. The model-theoretic approach is also
common in modal logic, where possible world semantic structures are often
used directly as temporal databases or 'knowledge bases'. It is, perhaps,
taken to its greatest lengths in situation semantics [2], where all information
is directly associated with situations, viewed as extra-linguistic semantic
structures.

Situation semantics, motivated largely by problems in linguistics, and
mental models, developed in the field of psychology, share a common assumption that human logical thinking is based upon the processing of certain kinds of semantic structures. In this chapter I will present and defend
the contrary view that both computer and human reasoning are better
viewed proof-theoretically as reasoning with sentences formulated in an
internal, 'mental' language.

I will begin in Section 2 by considering the two main goals of model
theory: (1) to explain the relation between language and experience, and
(2) to specify the notion of logical consequence. In Section 3, I will present

an alternative, more pragmatic approach to the first goal—one based upon the proof-theoretic assimilation of observational sentences into a knowledge base of sentences formulated in a language such as CL. Whereas in model theory 'truth' is a relationship between language and reality, in the alternative approach 'truth' is a relationship between sentences of the knowledge base and observational sentences.

The language considered in Section 3 is the mental language of an agent that is forced to make sense of a continuous stream of experience formulated in terms of observational sentences. In Section 4, I consider the case where the observations which need to be assimilated are utterances of natural language sentences, and I argue that the *meaning* of such sentences is best understood syntactically as the result of translating them into other sentences of the agent's mental language.

In Section 5, I consider the second goal of model theory, to specify the notion of logical consequence, and I outline an alternative specification based upon the hypothetical consideration of all possible, complete input streams of observational sentences. The alternative specification differs from the orthodox model-theoretic specification by making no assumptions about the existence of individuals, functions and relations apart from those 'projected' by the vocabulary of the language. Although the alternative specification is entirely syntactic, it can also be understood 'pseudo-model-theoretically' in terms of Herbrand interpretations.

In Sections 6 and 7, I consider possible world semantics and situation semantics respectively. In both cases I propose syntactically-based alternatives. In the case of temporal possible world semantics in particular, I propose the use of a rich vocabulary of terms representing time and events directly in the language. In the case of situation semantics, in Sections 8 and 9, I propose the use of metalanguage, in which terms represent situations regarded syntactically as theories. In Section 10, I conclude.

2   What is model theory?

Arguably, model theory has two main functions. First, it aims to clarify the relationship between language and experience, by considering the concept of truth as a relationship that holds between a sentence and a semantic structure. The semantic structure, called an *interpretation* associates individuals with constant symbols of the language, functions with function symbols, and predicates or relations with predicate symbols. An atomic, variable-free sentence is said to be *true* in the interpretation (and the interpretation is said to be a *model* of the sentence) if and only if the individuals associated with the terms appearing in the sentence stand in the relation associated with the predicate symbol of the sentence. As an explanation of

the relationship between language and experience, model-theoretic semantic structures incorporate an assumption that experience is caused by an
independently existing reality, and they serve as mathematical idealisations
of that reality.

The other main purpose of model theory is to specify the relationship of
logical consequence between a set of sentences T and a sentence P as holding
if and only if P is true in every interpretation in which all the sentences of
T are true. The model-theoretic definition of logical consequence formalises
the intuitive understanding that P holds whenever T holds, no matter what
meaning is associated with the symbols in T and P.

I shall argue that model theory fails in its first goal, of giving a good
explanation of the relationship between language and experience; and it
is only partially successful in its second goal, of specifying the notion of
logical consequence. In both cases, the assumption of model theory that
there exists a reality composed of individuals, functions, and relations,
separate from the syntax of language, is both unnecessary and unhelpful.

3   A more pragmatic view of the relationship between language and experience

Computer systems that interact with the world and that use logic to reason in the context of those interactions suggest a very different and more
pragmatic view of the relationship between language and experience. In
this view, the symbolic representations which are constructed and manipulated by the computer can be thought of as sentences of a '*knowledge base*'
formulated in an internal '*mental language*'.

Here the notion of mental language needs to be understood liberally,
analogously to the way in which computer languages are understood in
Computing. Computer programs written in a high-level language can be
compiled into lower-level languages and even into hardware, in such a way
that their high-level origins can be practically unrecognisable. None the
less, to understand and reason about the behaviour and 'semantics' of
such programs it is generally useful to view them as though they were still
written in the high-level language and as though they were executed on a
high-level 'virtual machine' appropriate to the high-level language. Even
programs implemented directly at lower-levels are often better understood
by 'decompiling' them and imagining them to have been written in a high-
level language.

The fundamental thesis of logic programming is that appropriate forms
of logic can serve as a high-level programming language. It follows that
such forms of logic can also be used to understand and reason about computations which actually take place at a lower software, hardware or even

biological level.

Logic programs can also function as deductive databases or knowledge bases. But databases, like programs, can usefully be understood at several different levels. The *external level* is what the user sees—perhaps a natural language, graphical, menu-driven or forms interface. The *physical level* is what the computer 'sees'—typically a collection of obscure data structures and complicated algorithms that exploit the physical properties of the computer to achieve efficiency. The *conceptual level* is what the designers and implementers of the database system see when they want to understand and reason about the intended behaviour of the database. It is at this conceptual level that the database can be understood as a logical theory—some collection of sentences in logical form.

It is also at the conceptual level that an intelligent computing agent can be understood as representing beliefs about its interactions with the world in the form of a theory or 'knowledge base' of sentences formulated in a 'mental', logical language.

Such theories or knowledge bases are really 'theory presentations' from which logical consequences are derived, both in order to solve problems and in order to assimilate new 'information'. Logically equivalent theories, which entail the same logical consequences, can have very different pragmatic characteristics, in the same way that different, but equivalent, programs can have very different computational properties.

In the general case, the knowledge base of an agent consists both of observational *sentences*, which record inputs and which correspond directly to experience, and of theoretical *sentences*, which do not have direct counterparts in experience. Observational sentences are *ground* (i.e. variable-free) atomic sentences, which identify individuals, classify them, and record both their attributes and their relationships with other individuals. With the aid of theoretical sentences, other ground atomic sentences can be derived from input observational sentences; and these derived sentences can be compared with previous and future observational sentences. A ground atomic sentence might be regarded as 'true' if it corresponds exactly with some such past or future input observation.

For example, the knowledge base might record an input observation that

there is smoke coming from the kitchen.

Appropriate 'mental constants' would be used as symbolic representations of 'the smoke' and 'the kitchen'. These might be constants already occurring in the knowledge base, in the case of individuals about which there already exists some previous 'knowledge', or they might be new constants for new individuals. The record might use a predicate symbol to represent the relationship 'coming from'. The time of the observation might be recorded explicitly by some form of mental time-stamping (in the manner of CL) or implicitly by a modal operator. The entire record of the observation might then take the form

> isa (smoke$_1$, smoke)
> isa (kitchen$_1$, kitchen)

and either

> coming-from (smoke$_1$, kitchen$_1$, time$_1$), or
> coming-from (smoke$_1$, kitchen$_1$)

where in the first case the third argument place of 'coming-from' indicates that 'time$_1$' is the time of the happening, whereas in the second case there is an implicit modality indicating that the event took place at the present time.

Theoretical sentences in the knowledge base (in one form or other) might represent such beliefs as

> whenever and wherever there is smoke, there was an earlier event of ignition which happened and which caused the smoke

and

> whenever and wherever an event of ignition happens, there is a state of fire soon afterwards.

With the aid of such theoretical sentences it would be possible to derive the conclusion that there is, or soon will be, fire in the kitchen. This conclusion can be compared with other observational sentences coming from other observations made at the same or other times. Once observations have been recorded in the mental language of the knowledge base, these comparisons between derived and input sentences are purely syntactic (relative to the mental language). A record of observing fire in the kitchen would confirm (the 'truth' of) the derived conclusion. A record of observing a smoke machine would probably refute it.

That part of the knowledge base, which includes observational sentences and those theoretic sentences which can be used to derive conclusions that can be compared with observational sentences, is often referred to as a *world model*. This use of the term is potentially confusing because the notion is completely syntactic and quite different from the notion of model in model theory.

World models are tested by comparing the conclusions that can be derived from them with other sentences that record inputs, which are observational sentences extracted from experience. In the idealised case, where observational sentences are assumed to be faultless, they serve as the standard against which the world model can be tested. Thus, a ground atomic sentence derivable from the 'model' can be regarded as '*true*' if it is identical to an input observational sentence. Moreover, such an input need not be added to the 'model' because it is already derivable and therefore redundant. The negation of a ground atomic sentence derivable from the 'model' can be regarded as '*false*' if it is the negation of an input observational sentence. In such a case assimilation of the input would involve (perhaps non-deterministically) removing or modifying some sentence in the knowledge base that leads to the derivation of the false conclusion, and adding the 'true' input to the knowledge base.

In the idealised and unrealistic case where the observational sentences constitute a complete and correct description of all experience, then the '*truth*' or '*falsity*' of all sentences in the world model can be determined. Thus, for example, given such a complete and faultless set of observation sentences O a sentence of the form

$$\forall X p(X)$$

would be '*true*' *relative to* O, if every ground instance

$$p(t)$$

is '*true*' relative to O, where t is any ground term occurring in O, and it would be '*false*' otherwise.

Moreover, a negative sentence

$$\neg P$$

is '*true*', relative to O, if and only if P is not in O. Thus it is the assumption that the observations are complete that warrants concluding $\neg P$ if P cannot be validated by the observations. This is similar to the assumption of completeness used to justify negation as failure in logic programming [5].

Obviously, the notion of an idealised, faultless and complete set of observational sentences has much in common with the notion of model in model theory. In model theory, there is a real world, consisting of real individuals, functions and relations. In the more pragmatic theory, however, there is only an inescapable, constantly flowing input stream of observational sentences, which the agent is forced to assimilate. To inquire into the source of this input stream and to speculate about the nature of the source is both unnecessary and unhelpful. For all the agent can ever hope to determine, the source might just as well be some form of *virtual reality*.

Hallucinations can be explained as a lack of coherence among the input sentences themselves, rather than as any lack of correspondence between input sentences and reality. Identifying an appropriate record of experience to be rejected or otherwise modified, as such an hallucination, can be a non-deterministic process, like any other process of restoring consistency to an inconsistent set of sentences.

In model theory, truth is a static correspondence between sentences and a given state of the world. In the computationally inspired, pragmatic theory, however, what matters is not so much 'truth' and correspondence between language and experience, but the appropriate *assimilation* of an inescapable, constantly flowing input stream of observational sentences into an ever changing knowledge base. Correspondence between an input sentence and a sentence that can be derived from the knowledge base is only a limiting case. In other cases some weaker form of coherence may be all that can be obtained. In the most extreme form of incoherence, which arises in the case of inconsistency, assimilation of an input might require a non-deterministic revision of the knowledge base.

A related process of *belief revision* was considered by Gärdenfors [12] and by Alchourrón, Gärdenfors and Makinson [1], who formulated a number of postulates about the relationship between a given state of a knowledge base, an input, and the resulting successor state of the knowledge base. These postulates embody a number of idealised assumptions, about the knowledge base containing all its logical consequences and about there being a unique successor state, which are not computationally feasible. Perhaps, more importantly though, the belief revision theory shares with the knowledge assimilation theory presented here the property that model-theoretic considerations are unnecessary. Moreover, Gärdenfors [12] shows how belief revision can give an alternative account of the semantics of logic, somewhat in the spirit of the account presented later in Section 5 of this chapter.

The process of *knowledge assimilation*, proposed in [18], was intended as a computationally feasible account of how input sentences might be assimilated into a given set of sentences constituting a 'theory'. The proposal was intended to include such diverse applications as updating a database, understanding a natural language discourse, enlarging and testing a scientific theory, and assimilating observations into the knowledge base of an intelligent, computing agent. A related, computationally-oriented theory of human cognition in general and of human communication in particular has been developed by Sperber and Wilson [33].

In knowledge assimilation, the relationship between a given state T of a theory, an input sentence P, and a successor state T' of the theory is determined by resource-constrained deduction. There are four cases:

1. P is a logical consequence of T.

2. Part of T is logically implied by P together with the other part of T,

that is, $T = T_1 \cup T_2$ and T_2 is a logical consequence of $T_1 \cup \{P\}$.

3. P is inconsistent with T.

4. None of the relationships (1)–(3) hold.

Input sentences, P, occur as items in a constantly flowing input stream. Normally there is little time available to process one input before the next appears. Although it is sometimes possible to interrupt the processing of the first input, process the second and return to the first, most inputs need to be assimilated 'on-line' in the relatively small gap between that input and the next. Thus detecting any of the logical relationships (1)–(3) outlined above is generally subject to severe limitations on the processing time available.

To make the best use of the limited computational resources, proof procedures for detecting logical consequences need to be as efficient as possible. For this reason they need to avoid generating obvious redundancies and irrelevancies. One way to reduce the generation of redundancies is to avoid explicitly putting them there in the first place. This is the purpose of cases (1) and (4).

One way to reduce the generation of irrelevancies is to focus on the input. This can be done by reasoning forward from P in cases (2) and (3), so that every conclusion generated depends non-trivially on P; and, similarly, to reason backwards from P in cases (1) and (2). Another way is to avoid unnecessary and computationally unmotivated use of the thinning rule, which derives

$$A \lor B \text{ from } A.$$

Such strategies for improving the efficiency of deduction in classical logic have been developed in the field of automated reasoning. Many of these strategies are based upon some restricted use of the resolution rule of inference [29]. These strategies implement classical logic, but derive only *relevant* conclusions, without using relevance logic. Related restrictions on the deductive processing of information have been proposed by Sperber and Wilson [33].

The successor state T' , which results from processing an input sentence P in a given state T of a theory, depends upon what logical relationships can be determined between T and P within the limited computational resources available.

In case (1) the input is determined to be redundant, and the theory does not need to change, that is, $T' = T$. However, although the input does not contain any new logical (or 'semantic') information, it does have pragmatic value. It identifies some subtheory T^* of T used to derive P.

This subtheory can be most easily determined by reasoning backward from the input P. To the extent that all the sentences in T^* are *relevant* to the derivation of P, the input P lends support to the sentences in T^*. The increased support given to T^* could be recorded in the form of metalogical *labels* [10] which somehow measure the *degree of confirmation* or *utility* of the sentences in T^*.

The term 'degree of confirmation' comes from philosophy of science, where it indicates the extent to which an hypothesis conforms to observational evidence. Here, I use the term more in the sense of Gärdenfors' [12] *epistemic entrenchment* and Sperber and Wilson's [33] *strength* of an assumption, to indicate the extent to which a sentence has proved useful for the deductive processing of other sentences in the past or the extent to which is expected to prove useful in the future.

In case (2), the input provides useful information, which renders part, T_2 of T redundant. Therefore the input can replace T_2 in the successor state of the theory, that is, $T' = T_1 \cup \{P\}$. Assuming that T itself is the result of a previous sequence of knowledge assimilation steps, and therefore that it contains no 'obvious' redundancies or inconsistencies, the generation of T_2 can be performed by reasoning forward from P, thereby restricting the conclusions contained in T_2 to ones in which the contribution of P is *relevant*. Moreover, if degree-of-confirmation labels are associated with sentences in the theory, then the labels associated with sentences in the set T^*, used to derive conclusions in T_2, can be revised to record a higher degree of confirmation.

In case (3), the test for inconsistency can be performed by reasoning forward from P, on the assumption that the search for inconsistency can be restricted to proofs in which the contribution of P is relevant [30]. The derivation of an inconsistency identifies a subset T^* of $T \cup \{P\}$, containing P, which needs to be revised in order to avoid the inconsistency. In general, this can be done in many different ways, and therefore the choice of successor state T' will be non-deterministic, that is, different choices of T' will have the desired effect of avoiding the inconsistency. In some domains, such as database updates, it is common simply to ignore the input, and so $T' = T$. In other domains, where the input can be regarded as recording 'true' observations, some other way of restoring consistency needs to be found. In these and other cases, degree-of-confirmation labels can help to identify candidate sentences to be removed or otherwise modified. In any case, it may not be possible to identify a unique successor state T', in which case the agent may need to explore alternative successor states, whether in sequence or in parallel. Notice, moreover, that exploring alternative, mutually incompatible successor states in parallel might give an external observer the misleading impression that the agent is irrationally committed to holding simultaneously incompatible beliefs.

In case (4), where none of the other logical relationships can be determined in the time (and space) available, it may be necessary to add the input to the theory, obtaining $T' = T \cup \{P\}$. In many domains, however, it is more appropriate (and more coherent) to determine an *abductive explanation* Δ such that $T \cup \Delta$ implies P and to let $T' = T \cup \Delta$. Other constraints that are normally imposed upon Δ include that (a) $T \cup \Delta$ be *consistent*, (b) Δ be *minimal*, that is, no strict subset Δ' of Δ is such that $T \cup \Delta'$ implies P, and (c) Δ be *basic*, i.e. not derivable (by deduction or abduction) from $T \cup \Delta'$, where $\Delta' \neq \Delta$. As in case (3), the choice of T' will often be non-deterministic. Again, degree-of-confirmation labels can help to compare different derivations and to choose a Δ such that the relevant subset T^* of T used with Δ to derive P has a greater (or at least no worse) degree of confirmation than other relevant subsets used with other abductive explanations. As in case (1), the generation of the *relevant* set T^* needed to derive P can be performed by reasoning backward from the input P.

Adding an abductive explanation in place of the input to obtain a successor state of the knowledge base violates the Alchourrón–Gärdenfors–Makinson rationality postulates, but accords well with the Sperber–Wilson Relevance Theory. A survey of the extension of logic programming to incorporate abduction is given by Kakas, Kowalski and Toni [17].

For the sake of efficiency, cases (1) and (4) can be combined, using resolution to reason backward from the goal P, reducing it either to the empty set of subgoals (case 1) or to a set of abducible subgoals (case 4). Cases (2) and (3) can also be combined, using resolution to reason forward from the assertion P, either to derive conclusions already in T (case 2) or to derive an obvious inconsistency (case 3). Furthermore, the test (case 4) that an abductive explanation Δ is consistent with T, can be subsumed by treating Δ as a new set of inputs to be assimilated.

Compared with knowledge assimilation, model theory can be regarded as dealing with the special and limiting case where the input sentences constitute a correct and complete description of the world, and are given entirely in advance. Cases (1)–(4) of knowledge assimilation are roughly analogous to the recursive definition of truth in model theory. The big difference, however, is that model theory assumes the existence of semantic structures containing individuals, properties and relationships, separate from the syntactic structures of the language. Knowledge assimilation, on the other hand, assumes only that there is a constant stream of input sentences that need to be assimilated.

In the normal case, the input sentence to be assimilated is an observational sentence—for example, some record of a natural language utterance. Such observational sentences typically have the form of ground atomic sentences. However, an agent might also generate its own hypothetical inputs, as in the case of abduction, induction, or theory formation more generally. The four cases of knowledge assimilation apply also to such hypothetical input sentences, in which case (2) assumes a special importance, because it indicates the *explanatory power* of the hypothesis. The greater the number (and degree-of-confirmation) of sentences T_2 derivable from the hypothesis, the greater the explanatory power and utility of the hypothesis.

In summary, knowledge assimilation provides a syntactic and pragmatic alternative to model theory as an account of the relationship between language and experience. It assumes that experience takes the form of an inescapable stream of input sentences, which needs to be assimilated into a constantly changing knowledge base. The knowledge base serves to organise and provide efficient access to useful information. Not only do its consequences need to correspond as much as possible with experience, but ideally they need to provide coherent explanations as well.

In the next two sections, I will discuss natural language processing and logical consequence in knowledge assimilation terms. In the following sections I will discuss syntactic alternatives to possible world semantics and situation semantics.

4   Natural language processing

Natural language understanding can also be understood in knowledge assimilation terms—but with two complicating factors: The first concerns the relationship between language and thought. Presumably, there is or there ought to be some close relationship between the structure of a natural language utterance and the structure of some sentence in the mental language of the communicator. In the simplest case, the utterance conveys the communicator's thought as directly and as simply as possible. In other cases, the utterance may be ambiguous or misleading. In yet others, it might attempt to articulate a new thought, as part of the communicator's process of assimilating a new hypothesis into its own knowledge base. In many cases, the correspondence between a natural language utterance and its intended meaning might be very imperfect indeed.

The second complication concerns the difference in the meaning of an utterance as understood by the communicator compared with its meaning as understood by the recipient. For the recipient, this means that the utterance needs to be understood in terms of both the recipient's own point of view as well as the recipient's understanding of the communicator's point of view.

Consider, for example, the process of attempting to understand and assimilate the consecutive sentences in a text such as the one constituting this chapter. Arguably, the reader has a two-fold task. The first is to understand the text in its own terms, assessing the extent to which the presumed meanings of individual sentences cohere with the previously determined meanings of the sentences which preceded them. The second is to understand the significance of the text for the reader's own beliefs, assessing the extent to which the meanings conveyed can be coherently assimilated into the reader's own knowledge base. In the simplest case, understanding a straightforward account of some historical event, for example, the two tasks might collapse into one if the recipient has sufficient faith in the communicator. In a more complicated case, however, the recipient might not only decide to reject the information, but also to conclude that the communicator is using the communication for some ulterior motive. An example, where the recipient would have benefited from reasoning in such a way, is the crow in Aesop' s fable of the fox and crow.

Notice that throughout the preceding discussion I have implicitly assumed that the '*meaning*' (and by implication the '*semantics*') of natural language sentences is be obtained by translating such natural language sentences into other sentences of a mental language. This is a kind of '*correspondence theory*' of meaning—not a correspondence between natural language utterances and actual states of affairs, but rather a correspondence between natural language utterances and mental language sentences.

In the standard account of natural language understanding, the observational sentences that are input to a recipient record only the syntactic form of the utterance. The recipient needs to process this syntactic form to generate a representation of its 'semantics'.

Consider, for example, the natural language sentence

'All humans are mortal.'

A typical natural language processing program would first generate an internal representation of its syntax, for example a list such as

['All', 'humans', 'are', 'mortal', '.']

and then a representation of its meaning, for example,

$$\forall X(h(X) \rightarrow m(X))$$

The program might usefully record the source and context of the input by means of appropriate metalevel sentences such as

said $(c_o,$ john, ['All', 'humans', 'are', 'mortal', '.'])
said-that $(c_o,$ john, '$\forall X(h(X) \rightarrow m(X))$')

where the second sentence would be derived from the first. Here the first argument, c_o, is some representation of the context—possibly a time indicator, an event identifier, or even a situation in the spirit of situation

semantics. By reference to this argument, the agent trying to assimilate
the input can gain access to previous inputs in the same discourse.

Having obtained a metalevel representation of the presumed meaning
of the input, the agent would then attempt to assimilate this metalevel
sentence into its knowledge base, perhaps deriving such object level conclusions as

$$\forall X(h(X) \rightarrow m(X)) \qquad \text{or}$$

$$\text{logician (john)} \vee \text{psychologist (john)}.$$

In the first case, the conclusion might be derived by means of a metalevel
sentence[1]

$$\text{believes } (X,Y) \leftarrow \text{said-that } (X,Y) \wedge \text{trustworthy } (X)$$

together with a scheme[2] that combines an object level conclusion with a
metalevel condition

$$Y \leftarrow \text{believes } (X, \text{'}Y\text{'}) \wedge \text{wise } (X)$$

and with object level sentences that express that John is both trustworthy
and wise.

In the second case, the conclusion might be derived from other, quite
different assumptions in the knowledge base, for example

$$\text{logician } (X) \vee \text{psychologist } (X) \leftarrow \text{said-that } (X,Y) \wedge \text{logic-example } (Y)$$

In both cases what is assimilated is not an object level sentence expressing that all humans are mortal, but rather a metalevel sentence expressing
that John said that all humans are mortal.

In general it is important to distinguish between information coming
from direct experience and information coming from communication. Although both kinds of information are appropriately expressed by means of
observational sentences, information which comes from direct experience is
most naturally expressed in object level form, for example

$$h \text{ (john)}.$$

a record of an observation that john is human, whereas information which
is communicated is most naturally expressed in metalevel form, for example

---

[1] Upper case symbols are used here and elsewhere in this chapter for variables. Any
variable occurring in a sentence is assumed to be universally quantified, even when
the quantifiers are not written explicitly. Note also that I use '$p \rightarrow q$' and '$q \leftarrow p$'
interchangeably.

[2] A simpler representation of this scheme as a combined object-level, metalevel sentence without quotation will be given in Section 8.

said (c_o, john, ['All', 'humans', 'are', 'mortal', '.'])

Of course, such metalevel observational sentences are also, in a sense, object level sentences which record direct experiences of the communication itself.

The example shows how difficult it is to test whether or not a computing agent processes information logically, and, if it does, what kind of logic the agent employs. A psychologist, for example, who poses logic puzzles in natural language, cannot simply assume that the agent receiving the communication assimilates the information communicated directly in object level form as though it were the result of its own direct experience. To determine whether or not the agent reasons logically, the interrogator would need to know the contents of the agent's knowledge base and understand how the agent assimilates the communication (not the information communicated!) into that knowledge base.

5 The specification of logical consequence

I believe that the considerations presented in the previous two sections call into question the usefulness of model theory in providing a useful account of the relationship between language and experience. Model theory helps to explain neither the relationship between mental language and the world nor the relationship between natural language and its meaning.

But perhaps the more significant achievement of model theory is its providing a specification of logical consequence, which is arguably more compelling than simply providing a proof procedure. In this respect, model theory (non-constructively) specifies the notion of logical consequence in much the same way that a program specification specifies a program. In contrast, proof theory provides a non-deterministic, but constructive definition of logical consequence, which is analogous to a non-deterministic program.

Model theory formalises the intuitive specification of logical consequence, which can be put informally in the form

a set of sentences T logically implies a sentence P
if and only if
for every interpretation I of the language L
in which T and P are formulated,
P holds in I if all sentences in T hold in I.

Model theory formalises the notion of interpretation in this informal specification in terms of set theoretic or algebraic structures, which have a different nature from the linguistic structures of the language L. I have

already argued that, for the purpose of understanding the relationship between language and experience, such extra-linguistic semantic structures
are neither necessary nor useful. I have argued instead that the notion
of assimilating a dynamically changing input stream of observational sentences can give a better account both of the relationship between mental
language sentences and experience and of the relationship between natural
language sentences and their meanings. I shall now argue that a similar,
purely syntactic notion, in which interpretations are understood as idealised, complete and faultless input streams of observational sentences, can
be used to formalise the specification of logical consequence. This notion
is, in fact, similar to the notion of Herbrand interpretation in model theory.

The syntactic specification of logical consequence is especially transparent in the case of sentences formulated in clausal form, which is the
basis for both resolution and LP. Clausal form is normally considered as
an implementation of classical first-order logic (FOL). However, although
clausal form has some disadvantages compared with FOL, it can also be
considered as a knowledge representation formalism in its own right [18].
Its main advantage is its simplicity and the fact that trivial syntactic differences between sentences are avoided by the use of a canonical form. For
example, a conjunction of sentences, $A \wedge B$, is represented as a set $\{A, B\}$;
double negation, $\neg\neg A$, is automatically eliminated; and negation is only
applied to atomic formulae. Existential quantifiers are avoided by introducing 'skolem' constants and function symbols, which make existential
commitments more explicit than existential quantifiers. For example, the
sentence

$$\forall X \exists Y \text{ father } (Y, X)$$

becomes a clause

$$\forall X \text{ father } (\text{dad}(X), X),$$

where the function symbol 'dad' is distinct from any other function symbol
used elsewhere.

In general, a *clause* can be written either as a universally quantified
disjunction of literals or as a universally quantified implication of the form

$$\forall X_1, \ldots, X_k (A_1 \wedge \ldots \wedge A_n \rightarrow B_1 \vee \ldots \vee B_m)$$

where the A_i and B_j are atoms and $X_1, \ldots, X_l$ are all the variables occurring in the A_i and B_j. In LP, the number of conclusions m is always less
than or equal to one. If m is zero, then the clause is equivalent to a denial

$$\forall X_1, \ldots, X_k \neg [A_1 \wedge \ldots \wedge A_n].$$

Because all variables are universally quantified it is usual to omit explicit
universal quantifiers.

The semantics of clausal form is normally defined in terms of Herbrand interpretations, which are sets of ground atoms. I shall show that this semantics can also be understood in knowledge assimilation terms. Given a set of clauses S, a *Herbrand interpretation* of S is any set of ground atoms constructed from the vocabulary of predicate symbols, function symbols, and constant symbols occurring in S. Thus Herbrand interpretations can be understood purely syntactically as a complete and faultless set of possible observational sentences, where every ground term of the language is regarded as the name of a 'conceivably' observable individual and every predicate symbol as the name of an observable predicate or relation.

To show that a set of clauses T *logically implies* a sentence P, the denial, $\neg P$, of P is converted into a set of clauses P^* and it is shown that $T \cup P^*$ is *inconsistent*. This is done by showing that every Herbrand interpretation of $T \cup P^*$ falsifies some clause in $T \cup P^*$. A Herbrand interpretation I *falsifies* a clause if it falsifies some ground instance

$$A_1 \wedge \ldots \wedge A_n \rightarrow B_1 \vee \ldots \vee B_m$$

of the clause. Such a variable-free clause is *falsified* by I if all of $A_1, \ldots, A_n$ belong to I, but none of $B_1, \ldots, B_m$ belong to I.

It is possible to execute the semantics of clausal form directly, to determine whether a set, S, of clauses is inconsistent, using the method of semantic trees [21], originally developed to prove the completeness of resolution. The semantic tree procedure can be viewed as an idealised process of assimilating all possible input streams of complete observations and showing that each such stream falsifies some clause in the set of clauses S. There is a one-to-one correspondence between such input streams and Herbrand interpretations of S.

The process of assimilating all possible input streams of complete observations can be formulated as a process of growing a binary-branching tree of partial input streams, and terminating the growth of a branch when the observations recorded on that branch already falsify some clause in S. If S is inconsistent, the process will terminate after only a finite number of steps.

To be more precise, given S, first some procedure for enumerating all ground atoms

$$A_1, \ldots, A_n, \ldots$$

constructible from the vocabulary of S is defined. This determines a one-to-one correspondence between Herbrand interpretations I of S and sequences

$$l_1, \ldots, l_n, \ldots$$

where each l_i is either A_i, if A_i belongs to I, or $\neg A_i$, if A_i does not belong to I. The collection of all such sequences can be presented in the form of a binary tree:

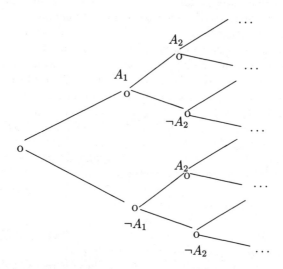

When a new node l_n of the tree is generated, the new information l_n is assimilated into the theory consisting of S together with the earlier part of the branch $l_1, \ldots, l_{n-1}$. If $S \cup \{l_1, \ldots, l_n\}$ is inconsistent (i.e. the information on the branch so far already falsifies some clause in S), then the branch is terminated, and all possible input streams extending this branch are eliminated from further consideration.

The semantic tree procedure has all the hallmarks of a program specification. Although it is executable, it is inefficient, especially if the enumeration of atoms determining the growth of branches is not dependent on the structure of the clauses in S. Its efficiency can be greatly improved both by choosing an enumeration which is sensitive to the structure of the set of clauses and by appropriately choosing different enumerations on different branches.

Arguably, the semantic tree procedure is also a good semantics, because it considers all possible (syntactically characterised) meanings of the vocabulary occurring in a given set of clauses. It is not, however, model-theoretic, because it makes no assumptions about the existence of possible individuals, functions, and relations independently from the syntax of the language.

The semantic tree procedure can also be viewed as a form of reasoning by means of hypothetical cases, somewhat similar in spirit to the way in which a lawyer might argue in favour of a general principle by appealing to imaginary cases. Such reasoning by means of cases is an important characteristic of legal reasoning and of practical reasoning in general. It may be tempting to understand such hypothetical, case-based reasoning in model-theoretic terms. The semantic tree procedure and the example of legal reasoning show that it can also be understood more simply in purely linguistic terms.

Curiously, the semantic tree procedure also has a purely proof-theoretic interpretation. Extending a branch by creating two new successor nodes can be interpreted as the application of a rule

$$\frac{\{A\} \cup S \vdash \bot \quad \{\neg A\} \cup S \vdash \bot}{S \vdash \bot}$$

Recognising that a partially constructed branch already falsifies some clause can be interpreted as the application of a complex, premise-free rule

$$\overline{\{A_1, \ldots, A_n, \neg B_1, \ldots, \neg B_m, C\} \cup S \vdash \bot}$$

where $A_1 \wedge \ldots \wedge A_n \rightarrow B_1 \vee \ldots \vee B_m$ is a ground instance of C.

Clearly, there is a one-to-one correspondence between a semantic tree demonstration that a set of clauses S is inconsistent and a proof of $S \vdash \bot$ using these deduction rules. Moreover, this correspondence between semantic tree demonstrations and deduction rule proofs is obviously very like the correspondence between the semantic and proof-theoretic interpretations of the semantic tableau procedure.

The examples of the semantic tree and semantic tableau procedures are not unique. Many other proof procedures are ambiguous and can be interpreted both semantically and proof-theoretically. For example, the model-elimination procedure [23], as its name implies, was originally understood in purely model-theoretic terms. Today this interpretation has largely been forgotten. On the other hand, the clausal theorem-prover SATCHMO [24] and its parallel variant MGTP [9] are still commonly regarded as model-theoretic procedures, even though, in my opinion, it is more useful to understand them purely proof-theoretically.

In the light of such examples, as Wilfred Hodges has observed [14], it is easy to understand how Johnson-Laird might argue that human beings reason in model-theoretic rather than in proof-theoretic terms.

6 From model theory to possible worlds

The model-theoretic approach to logic leads naturally both to the notion of possible worlds and to the enrichment of FOL by means of modal operators. The more pragmatically-oriented, CL approach, on the other hand, leads to the use of a rich vocabulary of terms representing such entities as time, events, situations, and theories without leaving FOL and without introducing new logical operators.

Given the seemingly static view of the world inherent in the semantic structures of classical model theory, it is natural to view time as transforming one static state of the world into another. Thus the possible world semantics of modal logic replaces the simple model-theoretic interpretations of FOL by complexes of interpretations (possible worlds) connected by accessibility relations. In the simplest and most commonly occurring case, the concepts of time, events, states, and state transitions are present in the possible worlds semantic structures, but are absent from the language itself. In their place, the modal language contains modal operators, which are used to form sentences whose truth values are determined by reference to the accessibility relation between possible worlds. Thus, for example

> a sentence **future** P is true in a possible world I
> in a possible worlds structure W
> if and only if P is true in some possible world I'
> accessible from I in W.

The notion that a modal theory T logically implies a conclusion P is defined, analogously to the case for FOL, as holding if and only if

> for every world structure W and every
> possible world I in W, if T is true in I in W
> then P is true in I in W.

Modal logic and its possible world semantics seem to be adequate for reasoning about change in an unchanging environment. This is the case, for example, when reasoning about general properties of programs. In such a case, possible worlds correspond to possible program execution paths; and sentences true in all possible world structures correspond to program properties, such as correctness and termination, that hold no matter what execution path the program might take. That the modal language does not allow explicit reference to specific states of computation is not a limitation, because properties of specific states are not needed for proving general program properties.

The situation is quite different, however, when modal logic is used to record incoming observations that change over the course of time. For example, an observation that

> mary is at work

might be recorded by a simple sentence of the form

location (mary, work).

But, immediately after the observation has been completed, the further sentence

past location (mary, work)

would need to be added to the knowledge base. Both sentences would need to be retained until mary leaves work, at which time the first sentence would need to be deleted.

Maintaining modal sentences becomes even more complicated when they express expectations about the future. For example, should a sentence such as

future location (mary, home)

be deleted when the observation

location (mary, home)

is first recorded? Or, rather, should the expectation be retained as part of a default strategy which expects facts to persist until they are explicitly terminated? If the latter, then how should such default rules be formulated?

Because of such problems of maintaining modal sentences in a changing environment, many applications of modal logic abandon the notion of logical consequence and use possible world structures directly as temporal databases or knowledge bases instead. Incoming information about the present state is input into a possible world representing the present state. Information about the past or future is appropriately recorded in past or future possible worlds. As time changes, the possible world representing the present state changes accordingly.

Using possible world structures as knowledge bases is a natural extension of using classical models as relational databases. In the relational database case, the database consists only of ground atomic sentences. Sentences more general than ground atoms can occur only as queries or integrity constraints. They are evaluated by determining their truth values in the database regarded as a model-theoretic structure. By assuming that the database is complete (i.e. the 'closed world assumption'), a ground negative literal ¬A is assumed to be true if A does not belong to the database.

By analogy with relational databases, the most obvious way to use possible world structures as databases or knowledge bases is to associate only ground atoms with possible worlds and to restrict more general sentences to queries and integrity constraints. Unfortunately, not only does this greatly restrict the kind of information that can be stored in a knowledge base, but it also involves enormous duplication. Facts, such as location(mary, work)

that hold in several possible worlds must be included in all the worlds in which they hold. Moreover, general statements, such as

whenever mary stays late at work,
she drives the car to work in the morning,

do not fit into such a possible world structure.

Many authors have argued for using deductive theories rather than model-theoretic structures as databases. The most obvious advantage is that the database can then contain sentences more general than just ground atoms. Moreover, a relational database can be considered as a special case in which the deductive theory is a set of ground atoms augmented with a completeness assumption [11].

Similar arguments apply to possible world structures. A possible world structure can be regarded as a special case of a non-modal theory in which the fact that a relationship

$\langle\langle r, a_1 \ldots a_n \rangle\rangle$ holds in a possible world s

is represented by a sentence such as

holds $(\langle\langle r, a_1 \ldots a_n \rangle\rangle, s)$.

Such a non-modal approach to the representation of modal concepts is exemplified by McCarthy's situation calculus, Allen's interval logic, the event calculus of Kowalski and Sergot, and many other formalisms for the representation of temporal information both in database systems and in artificial intelligence. Moreover, Gabbay [36] has developed a general methodology, called 'labelled deductive systems' by means of which possible world structures can be translated directly into classical logic.

7 From possible worlds to situation semantics

Situation semantics can be viewed as arising from possible world semantics in a similar way to that in which possible world semantics can be viewed as arising from model theory. Whereas a possible world, in the context of temporal reasoning, can be viewed as representing an instantaneous time slice of an entire world state, a *situation* is most naturally viewed as representing partial information that cuts across time and space. Typical situations might include, for example,

s_1, the situation consisting of all of Mary's activities at work on 1 April 1993, and s_2, the situation consisting of all the information I have about Mary.

Situations '*support*' items of information, which are semantic entities called *infons*, similar to the way in which relationships between individuals hold in the semantic structures of classical model theory and possible world semantics. In addition to recording 'ordinary' relationships between individuals, infons also record locations, times and polarities. A polarity of 1 indicates that a relationship holds; a polarity of 0 that it doesn't. For example

$$\sigma_1 = \langle\langle\text{location,mary, work, 1 April 1993, 1}\rangle\rangle$$
$$\sigma_2 = \langle\langle\text{location,mary, work, 1 April 1993, 0}\rangle\rangle$$

where the first argument, 'location', is the relation name, the third argument, 'work' or 'home', names the actual location and the fourth argument, '0' or '1', indicates whether or not the relationship actually holds.

Compound infons can be constructed by means of conjunction, disjunction, universal, and existential quantification. The only negation allowed in most treatments of situation semantics is that provided by the polarity '0', which can be associated with basic (non-compound) infons. (This restricted use of negation is similar to the restricted use of negation in the clausal form of logic.) However, there is normally no connective for constructing compound infons by means of implication (as in the standard treatment of clausal form, but not in the treatment presented in Section 5).

To a first approximation [8], (the external form of) the mental state of an agent can be understood as a collection (or knowledge base) of *propositions* of the form

$$s \vDash \sigma$$

expressing that a situation s *supports* an infon σ. (The distinction between the external and internal form of a belief is discussed below in Section 9.) Information that persists over time can be recorded, by means of a proposition such as

$$s_1 \vDash \forall T \in [10:00,\ 10:50]\langle\langle\text{lecturing, mary, work}, T, 1\rangle\rangle$$

for example. Situation semantics can also relate information about one situation to information about another, by means of 'constraints' between situation types. Such constraints serve the function of implication as a logical connective in ordinary FOL. For example, let S_1 and S_2 be the *situation types* (rather like sets)

$S_1 = [\mathbf{s_1} \mid \mathbf{s_1} \vDash \langle\langle\text{location, mary, work, } \mathbf{t}, 1\rangle\rangle \wedge \langle\langle\text{late, } \mathbf{t}\rangle\rangle \wedge \langle\langle\text{day, } \mathbf{t}, \mathbf{d}\rangle\rangle]$

$S_2 = [\mathbf{s_2} \mid \mathbf{s_2} \vDash \exists T(\langle\langle\text{drives, mary, work, } T, 1\rangle\rangle \wedge T < \mathbf{t} \wedge \langle\langle\text{day}, T, \mathbf{d}\rangle\rangle)]$

Then the proposition

$$w \vDash S_1 \Rightarrow S_2$$

expresses, as part of the information supported by the world state, w, that, for every situation in which mary works late, there exists a situation in which she drives to work earlier in the same day.

More generally, a *constraint* of the form

$$S \Rightarrow S'$$

expresses that if s is any situation of type S then there is a corresponding situation s' of type S', possibly extending s.

Constraints can also convey information about a single state. For example, the constraint

$$S_3 \Rightarrow S_4$$

where

$$S_3 = [\mathbf{s} \mid \mathbf{s} \vDash \langle\langle\text{kisses, } \mathbf{a}, \mathbf{b}, \mathbf{l}, \mathbf{t}, 1\rangle\rangle]$$
$$S_4 = [\mathbf{s} \mid \mathbf{s} \vDash \langle\langle\text{touches, } \mathbf{a}, \mathbf{b}, \mathbf{l}, \mathbf{t}, 1\rangle\rangle]$$

can be understood as expressing that if a person $\mathbf{a}$ kisses a person $\mathbf{b}$ at location $\mathbf{l}$ and time $\mathbf{t}$ in situation $\mathbf{s}$ then $\mathbf{a}$ touches $\mathbf{b}$ at location $\mathbf{l}$ and time $\mathbf{t}$ in the same situation $\mathbf{s}$.

A knowledge base consisting of propositions in situation semantics is analogous to a possible worlds structure used directly as a temporal knowledge base. In both cases, logical consequence and proof procedures play no role. In both cases, the alternative is to use an ontologically rich vocabulary of terms representing time, events, and theories, to use theories (sets of sentences) as knowledge bases, and to use proof procedures to deduce logical consequences. In this alternative approach, situations are represented by theories, infons by ordinary sentences, and the 'supports' relation by a metapredicate

$$\text{demo } (T, P)$$

which expresses that the conclusion named P can be demonstrated from the theory named T.

8 Combining object language and metalanguage

Metaprogramming is a powerful, commonly used technique for implementing expert systems, natural language processing systems, theorem-provers, interpreters and compilers in Prolog and in other logic programming languages. Its use has also been proposed for theory construction [4] (including the construction and manipulation of modules viewed as theories), knowledge assimilation [18, 3]) and the representation of knowledge and belief in multi-agent systems [22]. Many of these applications require that object language and metalanguage be combined, similarly to the way in which modal logic combines sentences with and without modal operators.

Following the results of Tarski [34], who showed that inconsistencies can arise when object language and metalanguage are combined in an unrestricted manner, it has been generally held that object language and metalanguage should be separated in an hierarchical fashion, so that self-reference cannot occur. Moreover, Montague [25] and Thomason [35] showed that object language and metalanguage cannot be combined consistently in the more restricted manner of modal logic. However, more recent studies (e.g. [26, 27, 7, 31]) indicate ways in which object language and metalanguage can be combined, provided that appropriate restrictions are imposed.

At least two other objections have been raised against systems that combine object language and metalanguage. One is that the naming conventions necessary to distinguish between object level expressions and their metalevel names are syntactically cumbersome. The other is that using syntactic expressions to represent intensional concepts, such as knowledge and belief, is too fine grained, in the sense that it distinguishes, as different beliefs, logically equivalent sentences that are trivial variants of one another.

One possible approach to the first objection is to abandon naming conventions altogether and to allow syntactic expressions to function as terms which name themselves. This is the approach taken informally in much Prolog programming practice (including the so-called non-ground naming of variables [13]) and more formally in the micro-Prolog programming language [6]. Semantic foundations for using syntactic expressions as their own names were laid by Richards [28] and Gabbay [10] and have been further developed by Jiang [15].

The use of syntactic expressions as their own names allows combined object level metalevel sentences such as

$$\forall X, Y (X \leftarrow \text{believes }(Y, X) \wedge \text{wise }(Y)).$$

In common with other universally quantified sentences, such sentences can be understood as standing for the set of all their ground instances, for example, for such instances as

likes (john, mary) ← believes (john, likes (john, mary)) ∧ wise (john).

The second objection, that the use of syntactic expressions to represent intensional concepts is too fine grained, has been partly addressed by the discussion in Section 5, where it was pointed out that clausal form (and other canonical forms) eliminates trivial syntactic distinctions between otherwise identical sentences. In this respect, the relationship between clausal form and the standard form of FOL might be regarded as similar to the relationship between the 'deep structure' which expresses the 'meaning' of natural language sentences and the 'surface structure' exhibited by the sentences themselves.

None the less, syntactic representations of intensionality (even in canonical form) are much finer grained than modal representations. Thus, for example, the two sentences

believes (john, $\forall X$ (human (X) → mortal (X)) ∧ human (john))
believes (john, $\forall X$ (human (X) → mortal (X)) ∧ human (john)
                  ∧ mortal (john))

are logically equivalent in modal logic, where 'believes' is a modal operator, because the two sentences

$\forall X$ (human (X) → mortal (X)) ∧ human (john)
$\forall X$ (human (X) → mortal (X)) ∧ human (john) ∧ mortal (john)

are logically equivalent. However, they are not equivalent in metalogic, where 'believes' is a metapredicate, unless they become so as a consequence of non-logical axioms such as

believes (T, P) ← believes $(T, P ← Q)$ ∧ believes (T, Q)
believes $(T, P ∧ Q)$ ← believes (T, P) ∧ believes (T, Q)

As Konolige [37] observes, the finer granularity of syntactic representations of belief potentially avoids the omniscience problem of conventional modal representations: that if an agent holds a belief then it holds all logical consequences of that belief. In fact, however, Konolige treats belief as a modal operator, but gives it a syntactic interpretation, in which an agent is regarded as holding a belief if (and only if) the agent can prove that belief from its 'knowledge base'. That the agent **a** can prove **p** is determined by an 'attachment rule', which associates a knowledge base $Kb_\mathbf{a}$ and inference system $\vdash_\mathbf{a}$ with **a** and shows that

$$Kb_\mathbf{a} \vdash_\mathbf{a} p$$

by directly applying the inference rules of $\vdash_\mathbf{a}$ to $Kb_\mathbf{a}$.

In metalogic programming it is natural to interpret the 'believes' predicate as a two argument proof predicate

$$\text{demo}\,(T, P)$$

where the first argument T names a theory (the knowledge base of an agent) and the second argument P names a sentence which is believed by the agent because it can be derived (or 'demonstrated') from T. The 'demo' predicate can be defined by such non-logical axioms as

(d1) $\text{demo}(T, P) \leftarrow \text{demo}(T, P \leftarrow Q) \wedge \text{demo}(T, Q)$

(d2) $\text{demo}(T, P \wedge Q) \leftarrow \text{demo}(T, P) \wedge \text{demo}(T, Q)$

identical (except for the different predicate symbol) to those for 'believes' given before. Alternatively, it can be implemented by means of an attachment (or reflection) rule, similar to that of the modal language of Konolige.

In CL, the theory parameter T of the 'demo' predicate names a set of clauses. A finite set of clauses can be represented either by a list or by a conjunction of the clauses in the set. The two representations are identical for conjunctions

$$C_1 \wedge \ldots \wedge C_{n-1} \wedge C_n$$

written in the canonical form

$$C_1 \wedge (\ldots \wedge (C_{n-1} \wedge (C_n \wedge \text{true}))\ldots)$$

where '$\wedge$' functions as an infix list constructor and 'true' as a list terminator or empty list. That a sentence is provable from a set of sentences because it belongs to the set can be expressed by the non-logical axioms

(d3) $\text{demo}\,(P \wedge Q, P)$

(d4) $\text{demo}\,(P \wedge Q, R) \leftarrow \text{demo}\,(Q, R)$

similar to the axioms defining list membership.

Thus, for example,

$$\text{demo}\,((p \leftarrow q) \wedge (q \wedge true), p)$$

can be proved by using (d3) and (d4) to show

$$\text{demo}\,((p \leftarrow q) \wedge (q \wedge \text{true}), p \leftarrow q)$$
$$\text{demo}\,((p \leftarrow q) \wedge (q \wedge \text{true}), q)$$

and then using (d1).

An alternative and often more useful way of representing theories and other syntactic objects is by means of constants [19]. Membership of a sentence in a set of sentences constituting a theory, represented by a constant, can be expressed by means of appropriate non-logical axioms. Thus, if the constant c names the theory

$$\{c_1, \ldots, c_n, \ldots\}$$

then membership in the set can be defined, for example, by enumeration

$$\text{demo}(c, c_1)$$
$$\vdots$$
$$\text{demo}(c, c_n)$$
$$\vdots$$

The use of constants as names of theories can even be used for infinite sets of sentences. For example, the infinite set of ground, object level clauses of unbounded length

> prime (2) ← true
> prime (3) ← ¬ divides (2,3) ∧ true
> $\vdots$
> prime (N+1) ← ¬ divides (N, N+1)
> ∧(...∧ (¬ divides (2, N+1) ∧ true)...)
> $\vdots$

can be named by a constant, say 'prime', and membership in the infinite set can be defined by the three clauses

demo (prime, prime (N+1) ← X) ← conditions (N,N+1, X)
conditions (1, N, true)
conditions (M+1, N, ¬ divides (M+1, N) ∧ X)← conditions (M, N, X)

Naming theories by constants is especially useful when the 'demo' predicate represents belief. In such cases it is not realistic to name a knowledge base by an explicit conjunction of sentences, either because the knowledge base is too large or because its complete contents are not known.

If an agent has a unique knowledge base (or set of beliefs), then the agent's name can conveniently double as the name of the knowledge base. Thus the metasentences

demo (john, $p \leftarrow q$)
demo (john, q)

can be interpreted as expressing that john both believes $p \leftarrow q$ and also believes q. From these sentences it is possible to derive the conclusion

demo (john, p)

using the clause (d1).

9   Situations as theories

From a purely formal point of view, much of situation semantics can be formalised in metalogic by using theories to represent situations, sentences to represent infons, and the 'demo' predicate to represent the 'supports' relation. There is even a formal correspondence between the definition of the 'demo' predicate and certain properties of the 'supports' relation, including, for example, such properties as

$$s \vDash \sigma_1 \wedge \sigma_2 \text{ iff } s \vDash \sigma_1 \text{ and } s \vDash \sigma_2$$

which is formally like the clause (d2) of the definition of 'demo'.

Unlike the use of constraints between situation types to represent conditional statements in situation semantics, CL uses ordinary implication instead. Thus a conditional statement such as

'If a person kisses a person at a
time and a location, then the first
person touches the second person at the
same time and the same location'

can be formulated as an ordinary object level sentence

kisses $(A, B, T, L) \rightarrow$ touches (A, B, T, L).

It can also be expressed at the metalevel, either in the form

(m1) demo $(S,$ kisses $(A, B, T, L)) \rightarrow$ demo $(S,$ touches $(A, B, T, L))$

or in the form

(m2) demo $(S,$ kisses $(A, B, T, L) \rightarrow$ touches $(A, B, T, L))$.

Whereas the first of these metalevel formulations is analogous to the formulation by means of a constraint in situation semantics, the second is analogous to the prohibited use of implication to construct compound infons. (m1) can be derived from (m2) using (d1).

Constraints between different situation types can also be formalised in CL by means of metalevel implications. For example, the constraint that

for every situation in which
Mary works late there exists a
situation in which she drives to work
early that same day

can be formulated by means of the metalevel statement

$[demo(earlier(S), drive(mary, work, before(T)))$
$\wedge\ before\ (T) < T \wedge day\ (before(T), D)]$
$\leftarrow demo\ (S, location\ (mary, work, T) \wedge late\ (T) \wedge day\ (T, D)).$

Here the 'Skolem' function symbol 'earlier' constructs a name for the situation $earlier(S)$ which exists as a function of the universally quantified variable S, thereby eliminating the need for an existential quantifier. Similarly, the function symbol 'before' avoids the use of an existential quantifier for the time before T which exists as a function of T.

In situation semantics, an infon can occur as part of a meaningful statement only in the context of a situation which supports it. In CL, on the other hand statements can be formulated at either the object level or the metalevel, as is most appropriate. Thus it would be simpler and possibly also more appropriate to formulate the connection between Mary's working late and driving to work by the purely object level statement

$[drive\ (mary, work, before\ (T)) \wedge before\ (T) < T \wedge day\ (before(T), D)]$
$\leftarrow location\ (mary, work, T) \wedge late\ (T) \wedge day\ (T, D).$

The possibility of formalising situation semantics in the metalogical component of CL glosses over an important philosophical difference between the two approaches. Situation semantics views and represents mental states of an agent and their relationship to the world objectively from an external 'theoretician's' point of view. CL, on the other hand, is conceived of as a mental language in which an agent subjectively constructs internal representations of its experience and beliefs and uses those representations to derive logical consequences.

Thus, for example, situation semantics would represent the external content of John's belief that it is raining by the proposition

$$s \vDash \langle\langle raining, t_0, 1 \rangle\rangle$$

as seen externally by the 'theoretician', where s is John's immediate environment at the time t_0 that he holds the belief. Devlin [8, p. 165], in discussing this example, denotes the internal structure of John's belief by

$$\langle Bel, -, raining\sharp, now\sharp, 1 \rangle$$

where $raining\sharp$ is John's notion of raining, $now\sharp$ is John's notion of present time, and the dash in the second argument indicates that the belief is 'situated', that is, does not itself involve a notion of the situation s that figures in the external content of John's belief. This internal structure, which is neither an infon nor a proposition, is not of direct concern to situation theory.

In CL there is no 'theoretician' and no external content of beliefs, only agents and their internal representations of their own beliefs, as well as their internal representations of other agents' beliefs. Thus, John might represent his own belief, that it is raining, in the object level form

$$\text{raining } (t_0)$$

where t_0 records the time of the event, or in the more informative form

$$\text{raining } (l_0, t_0)$$

where l_0 records the location of the event. For John's internal purposes these two parameters, l_0 and t_0, alone are likely to constitute an adequate indication of the situation in which the raining takes place.

Another agent, say Mary, might have her own representation of John's belief, perhaps in the form

$$\text{demo (john, raining } (l_0, t_0)).$$

This representation, while external to John, would be internal to Mary.

Agents may be inclined to associate objective status to their beliefs, regarding them as objectively 'true'. They may be similarly inclined to regard other agents' beliefs as 'true' if they accord with their own beliefs.

Thus, for example, if Mary believes

    human (john)
    mortal $(X) \leftarrow$ human (X)
    $\neg$ (superhuman $(X) \wedge$ human (X))
    demo (john,$\forall X$ (mortal $(X) \leftarrow$ human (X)))
    demo (john, superhuman (john))

then she will believe

$$\neg \text{ superhuman (john)}$$

as a logical consequence of her beliefs. Moreover, she will probably regard John's belief that he is superhuman as false. Of course, John himself might not actually believe that he is superhuman. So, from John's point of view, Mary's belief that John believes that he is superhuman would be false.

10   Conclusion

In this chapter I have outlined an agent-centred, computationally-oriented, and purely syntactic account of the relationship between language and experience. In this account, an agent interacts with its environment through a constant stream of inputs, which it assimilates in the form of observational sentences into an evolving knowledge base of beliefs. Both the knowledge base and the inputs are formulated as sentences in the agent's internal mental language.

The assimilation of inputs is constrained by the computational resources available. Consequently the agent's knowledge base should be structured to make the best use of the limited computational resource. For the sake of efficiency, redundant derivations of the same conclusion should be avoided. For the sake of more effective problem-solving, beliefs which are more useful should be easier to derive than beliefs which are less useful.

The resource-constrained nature of an agent's ability to derive logical consequences from its knowledge base is an essential aspect of its 'pragmatics', because what matters in practice is not whether a consequence follows from the knowledge base in the ideal case, but rather whether it follows in the case at hand. Thus, for example, a logically inconsistent knowledge having many useful consequences might well be more 'logical' than a consistent one which gives access to only few useful consequences, especially if the inconsistency is inaccessible in practice or if it can be prevented from polluting the rest of the knowledge base if and when it is found.

In the knowledge assimilation account of the relationship between language and experience, it is unnecessary and unhelpful to be concerned about the existence and the nature of the 'world' which generates the input stream. In this respect, the knowledge assimilation account diverges from model theory, which posits the existence of an external reality having a 'semantic' structure which is analogous to the syntactic structure of the language of the knowledge base.

I have argued also that the notion of logical consequence can be specified in purely syntactic, knowledge-assimilation terms, without the extra-syntactic structures of model theory. Not only is the syntactic specification executable, but it leads directly to more efficient and more conventionally defined proof procedures.

The model-theoretic view of logic leads naturally to possible world semantics and potentially to situation semantics. The knowledge assimilation view, on the other hand, leads to the employment of a syntactically rich language with a vocabulary of terms representing such objects as time, events, and theories. For this purpose it is necessary to combine object level and metalevel in the same language. Moreover, for the sake of simplicity and naturalness of expression, it is useful to allow syntactic objects to be named both by themselves and by constant symbols or other ground terms. The use of constant symbols as names of theories is especially useful for representing situations and other agents' knowledge bases as theories in the combined object level and metalevel language.

This chapter was written partly in reaction to Johnson-Laird's theories about the model-theoretic nature of human deduction. His work and that of his colleagues have two parts: an experimental part which establishes certain empirical data, and a theoretical part which attempts to explain the empirical results. I regret that I have not had time to investigate the extent to which the computationally-oriented CL approach to deduction and knowledge assimilation might provide an alternative explanation for the same empirical results. None the less, I hope that I have drawn attention to some of the difficulties involved in assessing whether or not an agent understands natural language logically, and that I have raised some doubts about whether seemingly model-theoretic reasoning is truly model-theoretic and not simply proof theory in disguise.

I am aware of other holes I have left in my argument. I have said very little, for example, about how an agent might generate outputs which affect its environment and which have a subsequent affect on its own and other agents' future inputs. Clearly, such an output will normally be generated by some plan formation process in the context of the agent's 'resident goals'. The agent will record the output, predict its expected effect on the environment using its 'world model', and compare its expectations against its later observations. The relationships between inputs and outputs and between goals and actions, within the knowledge assimilation framework outlined in this chapter, undoubtedly requires further investigation.

I have said very little, too, about the characteristics of CL which support such pragmatically important properties as relevance and even paraconsistency. Here I will mention again only that we should look for such properties to emerge as the result of the need for efficiency which arises from resource-constrained deduction. Thus, to make the best use of the limited resources available, both redundancies and irrelevancies have to be avoided as much as possible. In the case of resolution-based proof procedures, irrelevancies are avoided both by focusing on the input and by eliminating the thinning rule, which allows $A \vee B$ to be derived from B. The elimination of thinning does not introduce a new logic, but simply makes classical logic more efficient. Resource limitations also mean that inconsistencies can exist without being detected and without leading to the derivation of arbitrary and irrelevant consequences. Such paraconsistency does not require a new logic, but simply emerges as a property of classical logic when it is used in a practical context.

I began this chapter by referring to the multitude of different disciplines in which logic plays a central role. In this chapter, I have explicitly considered only computing and artificial intelligence to any significant extent, and linguistics and psychology to a much lesser degree. However, two other disciplines, philosophy of science and law, have also contributed implicitly to the approach presented here. The notion of knowledge assimilation, in particular, owes much to the concepts of observational and theoretical sentences, confirmation, falsification, and explanation developed in philosophy of science. On the other hand the idea of a canonical language, CL, based on resolution and logic programming, and combining object language with metalanguage has been greatly supported by investigations of legal reasoning and the formalisation of legislation [32, 20].

I also set out as my ultimate goal, in the introduction of this chapter, to outline an approach to logic that could be used to explain human reasoning in both logical and computational terms. This goal was deliberately ambiguous with respect to explaining competence or performance, where *competence* is concerned with how humans ought to reason, and *performance* with how they actually reason in practice. I chose not to distinguish between these two goals because in the case of designing an artificial agent there is no reason why the two kinds of reasoning should be distinguished. Moreover, in the case of a human agent, it seems to me that the theory is applicable to both goals.

A performance theory of human reasoning would be interesting for scientific reasons. But from a purely practical point of view, a competence theory would be even more important, because it could be used by people to improve their own natural reasoning skills. This, after all, is the original and ultimate goal of logic, viewed as a discipline in its own right. It would be a pleasant irony if computationally-oriented logics, originally developed for use by machines, should also prove convenient for use by human beings.

Acknowledgements

I am grateful to Jon Barwise and Dov Gabbay for helpful discussions and for comments on an earlier draft of this chapter. This work was supported both by the ESPRIT Basic Research project Compulog and by Fujitsu Research Laboratories.

References

[1] Alchourrón, C.E., Gärdenfors, P. and Makinson, D. On the logic of theory change: partial meet functions for contraction and revision. *Journal of Symbolic Logic*, **50**, 510–530, 1985.

[2] Barwise, J. and Perry, J. *Situations and Attitudes*. MIT Press, 1983.

[3] Bowen, K. A. and Kowalski, R. A. Amalgamating language and meta-language in logic programming, in *Logic Programming* K. L. Clark and S.-A. Tärnlund, (eds.), Academic Press, pp. 153–173, 1982.

[4] Brogi, A., Mancarella, P., Pedreschi, D., Turini, F. Composition operators for logic theories, in *Proc. Symposium on Computational Logic*, Springer-Verlag, 1990.

[5] Clark, K. L. Negation by failure, in *Logic and Databases*, H. Gallaire and J. Minker, (eds.), Plenum Press, pp. 293–322, 1978.

[6] Clark, K.L. and McCabe, F.G. *Micro-Prolog: Programming in Logic*. Prentice Hall, 1984.

[7] des Rivires, J. and Levesque, H. J. The consistency of syntactical treatments of knowledge, in *Proceedings of the 1986 Conference on Theoretical Aspects of Reasoning about Knowledge*, J. Halpern, (ed.), pp. 115–130, 1986.

[8] Devlin, K. *Logic and Information*. Cambridge University Press, 1991.

[9] Fujita, M., Hasegawa, R. Miyuki, K. and Fujita, H. Model generation theorem provers on a parallel inference machine, in *Proc. Fifth Generation Computer Systems 1992*, pp. 357–375, 1992.

[10] Gabbay, D. Metalevel features in the object level. In *Intensional Logics for Programming*, L. Fariñas del Cerro and M. Penttonen, (eds.) Oxford University Press, pp. 85–123, 1992.

[11] Gallaire, H., Minker, T. and Nicolas, J.-M. Logic and databases: a deductive approach, *ACM Computing Surveys*, **16**, pp. 153–185, 1984.

[12] Gärdenfors, P. *Knowledge in Flux: Modelling the dynamics of epistemic states*. A Bradford Book, MIT Press, 1988.

[13] Hill, P. M. and Lloyd, J. W. Analysis of metaprograms, in *Metaprogramming in Logic Programming*, H. D. Abramson and M. H. Rogers, (eds.), MIT Press, pp. 23–52, 1989.

[14] Hodges, W. The Logical Content of Theories of Deduction. Queen Mary College, London, 1993.

[15] Jiang, Y. Ambivalent logic as the semantic basis of metalogic programming I, in *Proceedings o fthe Eleventh International Conference on Logic Programming*, P Van Hentenryck, ed., MIT Press, pp. 387–401, 1994.

[16] Johnson-Laird, P.N. and Byrne, R.M.J. *Deduction*. Lawrence Erlbaum Associates Ltd, Hove, East Sussex, 1991.

[17] Kakas, A., Kowalski, R. and Toni, F. Abductive logic programming, *Journal of Logic and Computation*, **2**, 719–770, 1992.

[18] Kowalski, R. *Logic for Problem Solving*, North Holland Elsevier, 1979.

[19] Kowalski, R. A. Problems and promises of computational logic, in *Proceedings Symposium on Computational Logic*, J. Lloyd, ed., Springer-Verlag, pp. 1–36, 1990.

[20] Kowalski, R. A. Legislation as logic programs, in *Logic Programming in Action*, G. Comyn, N. E. Fuchs, M. J. Ratcliff, eds., Springer-Verlag, pp. 203-230, 1992.

[21] Kowalski, R. and Hayes, P. J. Semantic trees in automatic theorem-proving, in *Machine Intelligence 4*, B. Meltzer and D. Michie, (eds.), Edinburgh University Press, pp. 87–101, 1969. Also in *Anthology of Automated Theorem-Proving Papers*, Vol. 2, J. Siekmann and G. Wrightson, eds., Springer-Verlag, pp 217–232, 1983.

[22] Kowalski, R. and Kim, J. S. A metalogic programming approach to multi-agent knowledge and belief, in *Artificial Intelligence and Mathematical Theory of Computation*, V. Lifschitz, (ed.), Academic Press, 1991.

[23] Loveland, D. *Automated Theorem Proving: A Logical Basis*, North Holland, 1978.

[24] Manthey, R. and Bry, F. SATCHMO: A theorem prover implemented in Prolog, in *Proc. Ninth Int. Conf. on Automated Deduction (CADE)*, 1988.

[25] Montague, R. Syntactical treatments of modality, with corollaries on reflection principles and finite axiomatizability, *Acta Philosophic Fennica*, **16**, 153–167, 1963.

[26] Perlis, D. Languages with self-reference I: foundations. *J. of Artificial Intelligence*, **25**, 301–322.

[27] Perlis, D. Language with self-reference II: knowledge, belief and modality, *Artificial Intelligence*, **34**, 179–212.

[28] Richards, B. A Point of reference. *Synthese*, **28**, 431–445, 1974.

[29] Robinson, J. A. A Machine oriented logic based on the resolution principle. *J. ACM*, **12**, 23–41, 1965.

[30] Sadri, F. and Kowalski, R. A. A theorem proving approach to database integrity, in *Foundations of Deductive Databases and Logic Programming*, J. Minker, (ed.), Morgan Kaufmann, pp. 313–362, 1987.

[31] Sato, T. Metaprogramming through a truth predicate. In *Proc. JIC-SLP*, MIT Press, pp 526–540, 1992.

[32] Sergot, M. J., Sadri, F., Kowalski, R. A., Kriwaczek, F., Hammond, P. and Cory, H. T. The British Nationality Act as a logic program, *CACM*, **29**, 370–386, 1986.

[33] Sperber, D. and Wilson, D. *Relevance: Communication and cognition*, Basil Blanckwell Ltd., Oxford, U.K, 1986.

[34] Tarski, A. Der Wahrheitsbegriff in den formalisierten Sprachen, *Studia Philosophia*, **1**, 261–405, 1936. English translation The concept of truth in formalised languages in A. Tarski, (ed.), *Logic, Semantics, and Mathematics*, Oxford, 1956.

[35] Thomason, Richmond H. A note on syntactic treatments of modality, *Synthese*, **44**, 391–395, 1980.

[36] Gabbay, D. Classical versus non-classical logic. In *Handbook of Logic in Artificial Intelligence and Logic Programming*, D. Gabbbay, C. Hogger and J.A. Robinson, (eds.), Oxford University Press, 1993.

[37] Konolige, K. *A Deduction Model of Belief*, Pitman Research Notes in Artificial Intelligence, Pitman, 1986.

3

Diagrams and the Concept of Logical System

Jon Barwise and Eric Hammer*

1 Introduction

This volume is devoted to an interesting and important question: *what is a logical system?* The question is interesting because a good answer could do much to systematize and unify a bewildering logical landscape; it is important because if an answer were widely accepted, it could help guide research in logic in the years to come.

In attempting to answer this question, there are various approaches that could be taken. One would be to look at the things people have called logical systems and try to develop a natural framework which would encompass most or many of these, and then explore the consequences of the framework, seeing what else falls under the framework and what the consequences of the general notion happen to be. This was basically the approach taken, for example, in Barwise [1], one of the early attempts to develop such a framework.

This approach has much to recommend it, but it also has at least two serious drawbacks. It is too dependent on accidents of history, what particular systems of logic people happen to have developed. There is at least the theoretical possibility that biases of precedent and fashion have played a significant role in the way things have gone. If so, the abstraction away from practice has the danger of codifying these historically-contingent biases, making them appear to be necessary features of a logical system. The flip side of this problem is that there may well be some unnatural logical

---

*This chapter represents collaborative work of the authors, but was written largely by the second named author. The first named author acknowledges several years of collaboration with John Etchemendy on topics related to this chapter, see especially [3]. Both authors would like to thank the members of the Visual Inference Laboratory at Indiana University for many interesting and useful discussions on the topic presented here.

systems which contort the framework. But how else could one proceed in an attempt to obtain a principled notion of a logical system?

Another approach, the one we take here, is to look at the existing logical systems that people happened to have developed but to try to see what they were up to in more general terms. Our hope is to find some interesting natural phenomenon lurking behind these systems, a 'natural kind', if you will. If there is such a natural phenomenon, it could be used to guide the formulation of an abstract notion of a logical system.

If a characterization of logical systems could be found using this approach, it would have potentially two significant advantages over the more orthodox approach. First, it would provide a basis from which one could give a principled critique of existing systems claimed to be logical systems. Second, though, it would point out gaps, logical systems which have yet to be developed.

Thus, in this chapter we argue that there is a natural way to understand most logical systems, that this leads to a natural notion of a logical system (though we do not completely spell out the details here), and that there are indeed many logical systems yet to be developed. To be honest, though, the chapter was motivated in the opposite way, from our conviction that there are many logical systems yet to be developed, logical systems that are quite different in some important respects from most of the logical systems being studied. Thus, our reasons for writing this chapter are largely cautionary: to warn against the danger of developing notions of a logical system based solely on previously developed systems, as opposed to those that could and no doubt will be developed.

2   The standard story

Let's begin by rehearsing the story one usually tells by way of motivating the study of some particular formal system of logic.

Motivation comes from trying to capture formally certain sorts of instances of logical consequence. For example, from 'Ahab is neither tired nor wants to go home', one can infer 'It is not the case that Ahab is either tired or wants to go home'. And from 'Sue is tired and wants to go home' follows 'Sue wants to go home'.

Any number of different logical systems can model the validity of such inferences. Propositional logic, one of the simplest logical systems, begins with the observation that these inferences do not depend on the particular meanings of 'Ahab', 'Sue', 'is tired', or 'wants to go home'. Their validity is due solely to the meanings of the words 'and', 'neither...nor',' 'or', and 'not'. It looks at these statements in terms of grammatical units built up from atomic sentence letters using 'and', 'or', and 'not', and interprets these sentence letters by truth values, interpreting more complex sentences in such a way as to respect the intuitive meaning of the connectives. The first inference mentioned above would be represented in the system by replacing 'Ahab is tired' by some letter 'P' and 'Ahab wants to go home' by some other letter 'Q'. The premise would then be represented by 'not-P and not-Q' and the conclusion by 'not-(P and Q)'. The validity of the inference would then be captured in the system by the fact that any assignment of truth values to 'P' and 'Q' making the premise true is also an assignment which makes the conclusion true.

Such a system may also include syntactic rules for deriving one sentence from another which preserves truth value. So a second way the inference might be modelled in the system is by the existence of a proof in the system of the conclusion from the premise using these syntactic rules.

Beyond such familiar targets of logical analysis, that is, those concepts traditionally thought of as 'logical constants', logical systems can account for the validity of inferences involving *any* well-defined concept. For example, from the premises 'There are infinitely many primes' and 'Only one prime is even' it follows that 'There are infinitely many primes that are not even' by virtue of the meanings of 'infinitely many', 'only one', and 'there are'. Just as with inferences depending on the meanings of 'and', 'or', and 'not', there are logical systems which model inferences depending on the meaning of 'infinitely many'. Similarly, there are logics for dealing with inductive definitions, transitive closures of relations, cardinalities like 'uncountably many', and so on.

When we look beyond mathematics we find logical systems which attempt to model inferences involving concepts expressed by words like 'necessarily', 'possibly', 'always', 'knows', and the like. There are also logical systems which break away from strictly logical inference, trying to model notions of plausible inference and default inference.

Further logical systems have attempted to model 'natural reasoning'. Relevance logics, for example, were originally motivated by the desire to model the difference between using relevant and irrelevant information in the course of carrying out some argument. In another direction, distinctions between natural deduction systems and Hilbert-style deduction systems rest on how they model the process of reasoning. New developments, like linear logic, attempt to model reasoning where resource considerations are vital. For example, if we are attempting to develop automatic proof systems, we may want to restrict the ability to use a given premise more than once.

Logical systems always have either a mathematical semantics or a proof theory; sometimes they have both. A model-theoretic semantics for a logical system, when one is given, is a mathematical model explicating what it is that makes one sentence a logical consequence of another sentence. A proof theory, by contrast, gives a precise answer to the question as to how we can go about showing in the system that one sentence is a consequence of others. Based on the observations above, we propose the following informal characterization of logical system:

Thesis A *logical system* is a mathematical model of some pretheoretic notion of consequence and an existing (or possible) inferential practice that honors it.

The thesis is intended to be relatively neutral between logical systems based primarily on semantic considerations and those based primarily on proof-theoretic considerations. The difference is seen as a matter of what aspect of inference one is modeling. Some logical systems model both aspects explicitly while others leave one or the other aspect implicit, as not being something the model is trying to capture.

It is not to be thought that everything that has been called a logical system fits perfectly with this thesis, any more than that everything that has been called gold is gold. But we do claim that most of the systems people have called logical systems do fit the thesis, and that it provides a useful way to understand work on logical systems. It allows us to judge them on their own merit; to relate existing systems; and to develop, investigate, and use new logical systems.

Mathematical models of inference

The thesis can be refined in several ways. For one thing, in this chapter we intend that 'inference' be taken to concern relationships among structured representations in some sort of conventional representation system. A broader notion of inference would include non-conventional inference. For example, it could be said that one infers the sentence 'There's someone at the door' from certain knocking sounds heard at certain places. While it is of interest to develop mathematical models of inference thus broadly construed, we are not inclined to think of them as *logical* systems, so we restrict attention to the narrower class.

An understanding of the thesis obviously presupposes an understanding of the nature of mathematical modeling more generally. Mathematical modeling we take to be the process whereby some natural phenomenon is idealized and represented within the universe of mathematical objects. Consider mathematical models of the weather. Such a model may be a good one or a poor one, depending on how close a fit there is between the model and the actual weather. One of the ways we judge a mathematical model is to see how well its predictions conform to our experience with the phenomenon modeled. A good model has a good fit and can then be used in interesting ways. For example, it might be simulated on a computer to make long-range predictions.

There is much to be said about mathematical modeling, but space restricts us to three points that are most important for our project. The first is that there is a difference between a model and the thing modeled. No one would confuse a mathematical model of the weather with the weather itself. The weather can flood the basement; the model can't.

The second point is that the same phenomenon (in our case the same inference practice) can be modeled in many different ways. Consider, for an example, the different sorts of systems of first-order logic: Hilbert-style systems, natural deduction systems, resolution systems, analytic tableaux systems, Gentzen systems and so on. In a sense these are all mathematical models of the very same inference practice since they are extensionally equivalent. They all agree with one another on what follows from what, on what is inconsistent, and on what is logically true, etc.

While these systems are all models of the same inference practice, say first-order inference in mathematics, they none the less each provide a different perspective on it. Hilbert-style systems, for example, provide a particularly simple and elegant model of what can be shown to follow from what, but they fail to reflect accurately the actual rules of proof employed. Natural deduction systems are much less elegant, yet fairly nicely reflect the structure of the proofs people actually give. Resolution systems again are a perfectly good model of derivability, but similarly fail to reflect the proof structure of actual practice. But resolution systems remain of interest since they are much easier to implement on a computer than natural deduction or Hilbert-style systems. Finally, Gentzen systems are of interest because they are particularly well-suited to metamathematical study of the model itself.

A model of first-order inference must at least capture its most coarse-grained features: it must provide a characterization of logical consequence which is faithful to the informal practice being modeled. For just this purpose a mere non-effective listing would suffice. But one is generally interested in more than just pure extensional adequacy, hence the diversity of systems of first-order logic. Different systems capture various of the more fine-grained features of the inference practice. One may provide an effective procedure for listing all logical truths, another may reflect the structure of the informal proofs given, and so on.

This same point holds for any other phenomenon to be mathematically modeled. Any model of the weather, for example, must satisfy certain minimal conditions, such as providing an accurate description of weather conditions. But just as with modeling inference, there are also more fine-grained features one may also be interested in, such as how current conditions depend on larger weather patterns. For any given phenomenon to be modeled, there simply is no single mathematical model of interest.

The third point about models has to do with the idealizations necessary for mathematical modeling of natural phenomena. The world is typically too complex to model everything that is relevant to some phenomenon. Idealizations must be made to even get the project off the ground; this is just one of the rules of the game.

Part of the evidence for our thesis is that it is fairly easy to see the idealizations being made in typical logical systems. They include such things as the following, though some may be irrelevent in the case of logical systems that ignore either consequence (semantics) or inference (proof theory):

Idealization 2.1 Each representational object of the system has an unambiguous syntactic structure.

In other words, for each such representational object it is determinate what its parts are and how they are arranged.

Idealization 2.2 The well-formed representations are finite and linear in form and so can be modeled by finite sequences of symbols.

This is to say that it is assumed that the well-formed representations resemble the sentences of a written human language, in contrast to something like a picture or a diagram.

Idealization 2.3 The content of a given well-formed object is unambiguous.

While in actual practice context may be needed to disambiguate a given syntactic object, this assumption presupposes that this context has been adequately captured by the system.

Idealization 2.4 The consequence relation between meaningful objects of the system is a function of this syntax alone, whether or not there are effective rules for determining this relation.

This idealization arises from the assumptions that the content of representation is completely determined by its syntactic structure, and that the consequence relation is a function of the contents of the representations.

Idealization 2.5 The grammar and the semantics of the system are finitely specifiable.

Idealization 2.6 Limitations on the complexity or size of the well-formed objects and of proofs are ignored.

There are certainly examples of logical systems that do not make all of these idealizations. This only points out that they are idealizations, ones that may turn out to be a problem. If a model is based on the assumption that some particular aspect of a phenomenon is peripheral, and that aspect is in fact a major aspect, then the model will be flawed. For example, one may be interested in developing a formal system with the property of having a fixed polynomial $P(n)$ such that for every sentence of length n provable in the system, there is a proof of it in the system of length less than $P(n)$, all of the sentences of which are also bounded in length by $P(n)$. For this sort of system, one cannot make Idealization 2.6, since it abstracts away from the very features one is interested in.

Given that these are idealizations, ones which may have to be abandoned, the question arises as to which if any should be built into an analysis of the notion of a logical system. We intend our thesis to be silent on this matter. We think that it should be possible to develop interesting models which abandon any of these idealizations, though maybe not all at once.

As a particular type of example of logical systems not meeting all the idealizations above, in this chapter we examine several *diagrammatic* systems and several *heterogeneous* systems, both types of which violate Idealization 2.2. By a 'heterogeneous' system we mean one that seeks to model inferences carried out between two or more different types of representations. Of particular interest is inference between sentences and diagrammatic or other non-linguistic representations.

As examples of diagrammatic logics we discuss logics of Venn diagrams, Euler diagrams, existential graphs, and geometry diagrams. As examples of heterogeneous logics we discuss Hyperproof, a logic of charts and sentences, and a logic of first-order sentences and Venn diagrams. These are all examples of inferential practices where Idealization 2.2 is clearly and importantly false.

After presenting these example systems we examine some of the properties of diagrammatic and heterogeneous systems. In particular, we address the following sorts of questions. Can anything useful be said about the general features that make a representation system diagrammatic? Are there, as is usually assumed, special difficulties with having a sound diagrammatic logic? What are the potential advantages of using a diagrammatic system to model a given inference practice? What domains are particularly well-suited for diagrammatic/heterogeneous treatment? And, finally, in the light of the various systems examined, what can be said about what a logical system is?

3   Examples of diagrammatic logics

Venn diagrams and Euler circles

The following is a sketch of a formalization of a system of Venn diagrams incorporating ideas found in [15, 11, 14, 7]. The well-formed diagrams of the system are built up from the five basic types of primitive objects: rectangles used to represent the universe, closed curves used to represent subsets of it, shading used to assert emptiness of a set, and Xs connected by lines used to assert non-emptiness. Well-formed diagrams consist of a rectangle

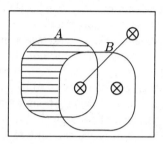

Figure 1: A Venn diagram.

within which are drawn any number of closed curves (labeled by names), with the restriction that they overlap one another in an appropriate way. Any area can be shaded and any area can contain a chain of Xs connected by lines. This is all described more fully in [14, 7].

Figure 1 displays a well-formed diagram. The shading or hatching asserts that the set represented by that region is empty, that nothing is A and not B. The single X asserts non-emptiness of the set represented, that something is B and not A; the chain of two Xs connected by a line asserts that something is either both A and B or else neither.

The semantics for the system is simply a mathematical representation of the intuitive meaning just sketched. Models[1] consist of a set along with an interpretation function mapping the rectangle to the whole set and closed curves to subsets of it, mapping curves sharing the same label to the same subset. Whether a diagram is true in a model depends on which of its areas are shaded and which of them have a chain of Xs connected by lines. A diagram D is a 'logical consequence' of a set Δ of diagrams if and only if every model of each diagram in Δ is a model of D.

Formal proofs can also be carried out by means of rules of inference including the following:

Extending sequences Any chain of Xs can be extended by additional Xs separated by lines. This rule corresponds to the addition of new disjuncts to a sentence.

---

[1]Here 'model' is being used in its standard model-theoretic sense as opposed to its use above in 'mathematical model'. It should always be clear from the context in what way we are using the term.

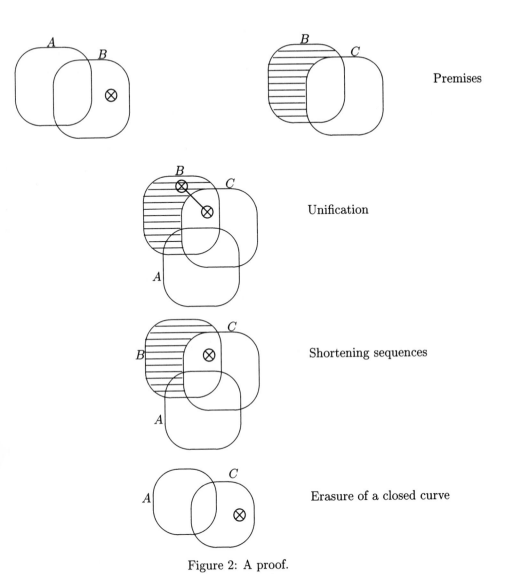

Premises

Unification

Shortening sequences

Erasure of a closed curve

Figure 2: A proof.

82   *J. Barwise and E. Hammer*

Erasure The shading occurring in any region can be erased. Any entire
X-sequence can be erased. A closed curve can be erased provided
that each minimal region having shading that would be unbounded
upon erasure of the curve is first erased. This rule is the counterpart
of conjunction-elimination.

Shortening sequences A link of an X-sequence can be removed and the
two halves reconnected provided that the link falls within the shading.

Unification D_3 follows from D_1 and D_2 by unification if the set of labels
of D_3 is the same as the set of labels occurring in either D_1 or D_2,
and for each shading (X-sequence) occurring in a region of either D_1
or D_2 there is a corresponding region of D_3 also having a shading
(X-sequence), and vice versa. This rule is similar to conjunction-
introduction, allowing one to combine the information of two diagrams.

An example of a proof is given in Figure 2. Shin [14] proved that for finite
sets Δ, a diagram is provable from Δ if and only if it is a logical consequence
of Δ; the result is extended to arbitrary sets Δ in [7].

A variation of the system above utilizes an alternative to shading for
asserting the emptiness of a set, namely containment or disjointness of
curves. The syntax of this system allows curves to be drawn within a
rectangle in any arrangement whatsoever. Shading and X-sequences are
allowed to appear in diagrams as before. A well-formed Euler diagram is
shown in Figure 3.

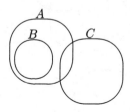

Figure 3: A Euler diagram.

Models are exactly as in the Venn system; truth of a diagram D in a
model is slightly different, though X-sequences and shading are handled as
before. An additional clause states that if A and B are sets that partition
the set of curves of a diagram D (one of them possibly empty) and there
is no area of D falling within each curve in A and outside each curve in B,
then the intersection of the interpretations of all the curves in A is such that
subtracting from it each of the interpretations of the curves in B results in
the empty set. So the diagram in Figure 3 asserts that no B is C, all B
are A, and, subsequently, that nothing is simultaneously A, B, and C, etc.

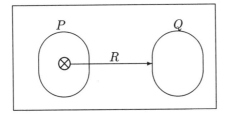

Figure 4: An example of a higraph.

Directed edges can also be added to the syntax as a mechanism for representing binary relations diagrammatically as in [9, 6]. An example is shown in Figure 4; intuitively it asserts that some P bears the relation R to every Q, and, by the arrangement of the closed figures, that no P is Q. Additional rules of inference for such a system allow one to manipulate edges appropriately; for example, if an end of an edge contacts a closed curve within which occurs an X-sequence, then the end can be moved inwards to that X-sequence. This would be similar to a form of universal instantiation.

Peirce's existential graphs

The Alpha part of Peirce's existential graphs is a diagrammatic system equivalent in expressive and deductive power to propositional logic. It was proposed in Peirce [11] and later studied and modified in [16, 12]. The Beta part, discussed in the following section, is equivalent to first-order logic. Further extensions of the system studied by Peirce incorporate higher-order and modal quantification.

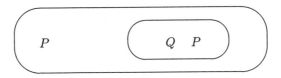

Figure 5: An existential graph.

The grammatical resources of the system are minimal. Graphs are construted from propositional letters $P, Q, \ldots$ and 'cuts' or drawn closed figures. The syntax is simple: any two cuts of a graph must be such that one is contained within the other or else is entirely separated from the other, and any letter must fall either entirely within or entirely outside of each cut.

Juxtaposition of elements of a graph has the same effect as conjunction. A cut acts as the negation of the 'conjunctive' claim within. Figure 5 displays an alpha graph. This graph can be read in many different but logically equivalent ways: it can be read as asserting $\neg(P \wedge \neg(Q \wedge P))$; alternatively, it can be read as a conditional, with what is nested within one cut being the antecedent and what is nested within two cuts the consequent, as $P \to (Q \wedge P)$.

It is fairly obvious what the semantics of the graphs will be. An 'assignment function' assigns truth values to letters. Such an assignment function is then uniquely extendable to an evaluation v assigning truth values to entire graphs according to the following restrictions. A subgraph consisting of the juxtaposition of sentence letters is assigned truth if and only if each sentence letter is. A subgraph consisting of a cut drawn around another subgraph is assigned falsehood if and only if at least one of the enclosed immediate subgraphs is assigned falsehood. Finally, the juxtaposition of several subgraphs is assigned truth if and only if each of the juxtaposed subgraphs is assigned truth. This is explained more explicitly in the references cited.

The rules of inference are very simple. Call a subgraph 'evenly enclosed' if it falls within an even number of cuts or else does not fall within a cut. Otherwise it is 'oddly enclosed'. The following rules are sound and complete with respect to the semantics:

Double cut Two cuts may be drawn around or removed from any subgraph of a graph. This corresponds to double negation.

Erasure Any evenly enclosed subgraph may be erased. This corresponds to strengthening an antecedent.

Insertion Any graph may be drawn on an existing graph provided it is thereby oddly enclosed. This corresponds to weakening a consequent.

Iteration Any subgraph occurring in a graph may be recopied on the graph provided it is enclosed by every cut enclosing the subgraph copied. This is similar to the rule: from $A \to B$ infer $A \to (A \wedge B)$.

Deiteration Any subgraph which could have been drawn by an application of the Iteration rule can be erased. This is analogous to: from $A \to (A \wedge B)$ infer $A \to B$.

The Beta part of Peirce's existential graphs is a diagrammatic logical system equivalent to first-order logic. The propositional letters of the Alpha

part are replaced by predicates of each arity. Each n-ary predicate symbol
has n 'hooks' or argument places that can be quantified over.

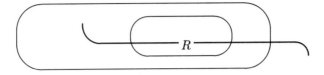

Figure 6: A Beta graph.

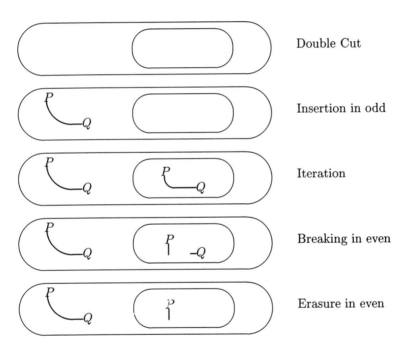

Figure 7: A proof in Beta of $\exists x(P(x) \wedge Q(x)) \rightarrow \exists x P(x)$.

The Beta equivalent of a quantifier is a drawn, heavy 'line of identity'. A
single line of identity can have any number of branches and still be a single
line, provided all these branches are connected. Each line corresponds to a

distinct quantifier.

The syntax is the same as for the Alpha part, except for the follow-ing two conditions. Lines of identity can cross cuts, and each hook of a predicate must be contacted by exactly one line of identity.

Cuts behave just as in the Alpha part. The precedence of one quantifier (line of identity) over another is determined by whether the one has some portion less deeply nested within cuts than the other. First, therefore, those lines having parts enclosed by no cuts are read, then those having parts enclosed by one cut are read, then those whose least enclosed parts are enclosed by two cuts, and so on.

Consider the Beta graph in Figure 6. It has two lines of identity, a one-place predicate P and a two-place predicate R. The right-hand line of identity is the one with a least deeply embedded part, so it takes prece-dence over the other. Inelegantly, translating cuts as negations and lines of identity as existential quantifiers, it would be read as $\exists x \neg (\exists y \neg R(y, x))$. A more sympathetic reading would translate the oddly embedded line of identity universally here: $\exists x \forall y R(y, x)$.

Rules for the Beta part extend those of the Alpha part. A full descrip-tion is rather involved, as can be seen from [16] so some examples will have to suffice: the rule of Double Cut is as before, except that lines of identity are allowed to cross both cuts; the rule of Breaking a Line of Identity al-lows one to erase part of an evenly enclosed line of identity. A proof of the Beta analog of $\exists x (P(x) \wedge Q(x)) \to \exists x P(x)$ is shown in Figure 7. In actual practice one would not recopy the original with each step, but rather erase and add to a single graph. To capture the dynamic process on the printed page, however, it is necessary to recopy a graph each time a rule is applied.

A logic of geometry diagrams

The most notorious fallacies involving the use of diagrams have been in geometry. Nevertheless, by making the syntax and semantic content of the sort of diagrams typically used clear, one can use them in perfectly rigorous proofs. This topic of the formal logic of geometry diagrams in heteroge-neous and diagrammatic proofs is currently being studied by Luengo [10].

Diagrams are taken to be configurations of various syntactic primitives like drawn lines, points, labels, congruence indicators for angles and line segments, and parallel line indicators, all drawn within a rectangle. For example, Figure 8 displays a diagram of such a formal system. Intuitiveiy it asserts that the two lines labeled by '$\int$' refer to parallel lines, and that line AB intersects these lines at point A and point B.

There are some particularly interesting issues concerning such geometry diagrams. One involves the construction rules typically employed in their informal use. Geometry diagrams assert something about a structured

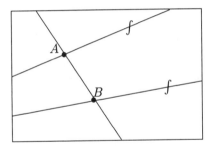

Figure 8: A geometry diagram.

domain satisfying various constraints, perhaps Hilbert's axioms. These constraints ensure the existence of various objects, such as a point between any two points on a given line or a point not on a given line, a line through any two points, and so on. To be faithful to actual practice, the semantics of a diagrammatic system must legitimate such construction rules.

The following is an outline of such a semantics. A model M for a diagram D consists of disjoint sets of 'points' and 'lines' and of a 'lying on' relation between points and lines, a 'between' relation between triples of points, a 'parallel' relation between pairs of lines, and a 'congruence' relation between pairs of pairs of points (congruence of segments) and between pairs of pairs of lines (congruence of angles). These must satisfy, say, Hilbert's axioms. M also assigns a line to each drawn line in D and a point to each drawn point in D, which is true in M provided these interpretations are such that the congruence and parallel assertions made in the diagram by use of the indicators drawn are preserved by the interpretation in the obvious way, and likewise for the diagrammatic assertions of a point being on a particular line.

The notion of logical consequence is then defined in such a way as to allow the application of construction rules to D as well as other rules (such as erasure of a point or a line or an indicator). For example, the fact that it is valid to draw a new point between two points of D falling on some single drawn line follows from the fact that one can extend the interpretation function of M so as to assign a point in the model bearing the appropriate relations to the referents of the two original, drawn points. Logical consequence, then, is defined in terms of being able to extend interpretation functions in appropriate ways.

Such a definition fairly accurately reflects actual usage of diagrams in plane geometry proofs. One typically constructs a diagram step-by-step, perhaps starting with given assumptions, then adding new lines and points to it in accordance with the nature of the space in question. Finally, having manipulated the diagram in useful ways, one is able to read conclusions

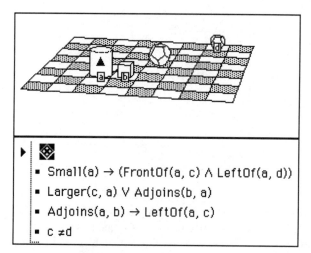

Figure 9: Show *Small*(*a*) independent of the given information.

off the diagram, thereby showing them to be consequences of the original premises. The sort of semantics discussed here validates such inferential practices.

4 Examples of heterogeneous logics

Heterogeneous logical systems are logics having both linguistic and non-linguistic elements, such as diagrams, charts, tables, etc. They are very important with respect to our main thesis since a great deal of inference involving non-linguistic representations combines the non-linguistic with the linguistic. Sentences are commonly inferred from diagrams, tables, and charts; likewise, sentences are commonly applied to existing diagrams, tables, and charts. Accurate models of such inference will need to take this heterogeneity into account. We now describe some examples of heterogeneous logics.

Hyperproof

Historically the first example of a formal, heterogeneous system is Hyperproof, a pedagogical proof system implemented for the Macintosh computer (Barwise and Etchemendy [2, 3]).

The proof system in Hyperproof contains as a proper part a (Fitch-style) natural deduction system for full first-order logic. But it also allows

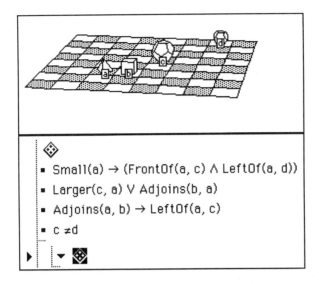

Figure 10: Case where tet is small and 'c' names medium dodec.

diagrams as representations, ones that can be assumed in subproofs or asserted at any stage of a proof. These proofs integrate interpreted first-order sentences with diagrams depicting the target domain, allowing for structurally rich inference back and forth between sentences and diagrams as well as between two diagrams or between two sentences. The system serves as an example of the sort of heterogeneous inference found everywhere in actual reasoning practice.

We illustrate Hyperproof by means of a sample problem. We choose as a sample problem one that illustrates a striking feature of certain heterogeneous systems, namely, their ability to allow us to give formal proofs of consistency and independence claims in addition to the more familiar consequence claims.

Figure 9 displays premises consisting of the diagram and four sentences shown. The diagram says that the domain has four objects, one cube referred to by 'b', one medium dodecahedron, one small dodecahedron referred to by 'd', and one tetrahedron of unknown size (indicated by the barrel icon) referred to by 'a'. The remaining, linguistic premises are self-explanatory, with 'FrontOf' meaning further forward but not necessarily on the same column and 'LeftOf' meaning further left but not necessarily in the same row. The goal of the problem is to show that the sentence $Small(a)$ is independent of the premises; that is, neither it nor its negation follows from the premises. Obviously standard logical systems do not allow for formal proofs of this sort of fact.

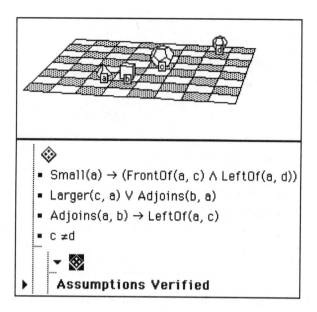

Figure 11: Using **CTA** to verify a case where premises hold.

To solve the problem one breaks into two cases. In the first one, shown in Figure 10, a diagram is temporarily assumed in which the barrel icon has been transformed to a small tetrahedron icon and the medium dodecahedron has been named 'c'. In the second case a diagram is temporarily assumed in which the barrel has been transformed to a medium tetrahedron icon, and in which the medium dodecahedron has been named 'c'. So each of these temporary assumptions constitutes a different way the partial description of the given diagram can be fleshed out. In each of the two cases the rule 'CTA' will be applied, a rule which effectively verifies that the diagram assumed in the subcase depicts a world in which all of the premises are true. For the first case this is shown in Figure 11; the second case is handled in an identical manner. Since the rule 'CTA' checks out in both these cases, and since $Small(a)$ is true in one but false in the other, Hyperproof allows one to conclude that it is independent of the premises, finishing the proof.

In the two cases, one has in effect built two diagrammatic partial representations of worlds in which all the given information comes out true, one in which $Small(a)$ holds and the other in which it doesn't. The first case shows that $Small(a)$ is at least consistent with the given information and the second shows that its negation is as well. This sort of use of diagrams as partial specifications of models allows students to grasp fundamental concepts like joint satisfiability and independence in a particularly clear and visual manner.

Much more complicated reasoning tasks are possible than the one given here. For example, the system allows one to give formal proofs of such things as that the size of some object a is independent of some sentences and/or diagram, but that one can still infer $Cube(a) \vee Tet(a)$ from them. So one can show that the particular size of a is independent but that it can be narrowed down to two possibilities.

Besides the rule 'CTA', another useful rule in Hyperproof is 'Cases Exhaustive' which allows one to break into a number of diagrams that, given some sentences, exhaust the range of possible arrangements of the world. This allows one to carry out reasoning tasks such as showing that, given certain sentences, there must be at least two but not more than four objects in front of a given object. Or it can allow one to show that every model of some set of sentences consists of either three cubes or else three tetrahedrons.

A logic of charts

We next look at a different sort of heterogeneous logic, one that uses charts as first-class representations. Charts exist because they provide a very convenient way of presenting some kinds of information. They are also very useful in certain sorts of reasoning, especially reasoning involving systematic matching of objects: last names with first names, owner with dog, etc. Typical examples of such reasoning tasks are found in the sort of problems given in the analytic section of the Graduate Record Exam or in logic puzzle books, though charts are obviously of use in many other contexts. Since they are also simple, they serve as a good case study of how one can give a rigorous mathematical model of an existing inferential practice that clearly violates Idealization 2.2.

For problems usefully solved with a chart, one typically chooses a particular sort of chart tailored to the peculiarities of the problem at hand. Making a good choice of representational conventions is always important in solving a problem, but it is especially true of charts. This sensitivity of type of chart to the particularities of the task at hand makes a very general logic of charts useless. There are as many logics of charts as there are different sorts of charts that can be useful in solving problems. So the specific system presented here should be taken to be illustrative rather than as exhaustive of the topic. It is merely a system for solving a particular sort of chart problem. For modeling the reasoning involved in other sorts of chart problems, one would likely want a formal system having entirely different well-formed charts.

The sort of problem dealt with here involves a finite domain of say n

elements, each of which can be named in m different ways. The problem is to figure out which names denote the same object. We think of this in terms of the matching names of m different types, where each type has n names of that type, each of which refers to a different object. Since there are n objects, every name of some type refers to the same object as some name from each of the other types. The task, then, is to match each name of each type with those names of each other type that co-refer. For example, one may be given four sorts of names (first names, last names, horse names, and jockey names) and, for each of the four sorts, five names of that sort. The problem may be to determine for five people their first names, their last names, the name of the horse they own, and the name of the jockey of the horse they own.

A chart logic of this sort, then, is relative to a particular selection of sorts and names of that sort:

$$\text{Sort } \alpha_1 \text{ having names } a_1^1, \ldots a_n^1$$
$$\text{Sort } \alpha_2 \text{ having names } a_1^2, \ldots a_n^2$$
$$\ldots$$
$$\text{Sort } \alpha_m \text{ having names } a_1^m, \ldots a_n^m$$

Given such a choice, a well-formed chart is of the following form (letting m be four and n three):

α_1	α_2	α_3	α_4

For convenience, if sort 'α_i' labels a column, it will be referred to as 'column α_i'. For such a chart, any name of sort α_i can be written in a box of column α_i provided that it does not already occur in the chart. These are the only conditions on well-formed charts.

Each sort is treated as a unary predicate symbol, though not every predicate symbol need be a sort. A problem will also involve linguistically-presented assumptions. To model these, we use a standard first-order predicate language with identity. Some of the premises of a problem will typically be non-identities or identities among the names in question, such as $a_3^3 \neq a_3^2$. Other premises may involve other predicates, like $R(a, b) \wedge \neg R(a, c)$ for names a, b, and c and relation R.

A model for such a system consists of an n-membered structure M for the language in question satisfying the condition that for each sort α, the domain of M is the set $\{a^M \mid a \text{ is a name of sort } \alpha\}$, where a^M is the element of M assigned to the name a. Due to this assumption, we will take as linguistic axioms sentences asserting that every object is named by exactly one of the names of each sort.

We need to say what it means for a chart to be true in a model, but this should be obvious. Whether a chart is true in a model is a function solely of whether pairs of names occurring in the chart occur in the same row or not. If they do, they must be assigned the same object. If the two names occur in different rows, they must be assigned different objects. If these conditions hold for all pairs of names occurring in the chart, the chart is true in the model.

To model the inferential practice of reasoning with charts, we need some rules of inference. In addition to the usual first-order axioms and rules (in any form), we need rules for charts. Here are some examples of how we can use charts in reasoning.

$=$-**Extract:** If both a and b occur in the same row of the chart, then it is legitimate to infer the sentence $a = b$. This principle is justified by the truth conditions given above.

$=$-**Apply:** 1. Let a be of sort α and b be of sort β. From $a = b$ and a chart with a in row n, one can write b in column β of row n. This is again justified by the semantic principles noted in the paragraph above.

2. Suppose one has established the sentence $a = b$ where a is of sort α and b is of sort β. Suppose neither a nor b occur in the chart, and that only empty rows of the chart are such that both columns α and β of a row are empty. Then one can write a in column α and b in column β of any such row.

3. Suppose neither a nor b appears in a chart and that there is only one row having both columns α and β empty. Then from the sentence $a = b$, one can write a in column α of that row and b in column β of that row.

$\neq$-**Extract:** If a and b occur in different rows of the chart, then one can infer $a \neq b$.

$\neq$-**Apply:** 1. Let a be of sort α and b be of of sort β, suppose a occurs in row n of a chart but b does not occur, and suppose there is only one row of column β other than n having no name. Then from $a \neq b$, one is entitled to write b in that row.

2. Let a be of sort α and b be of of sort β, suppose α occurs in row n of a chart, and suppose every other row having nothing in column β has no name in any column. Then from $a \neq b$, one is entitled to write b in any such row of column β.

3. Let a be of sort α and b be of of sort β, suppose neither a nor b occurs in a chart, and suppose that every two distinct rows m and n having no names in column α or β, respectively, are empty rows. Then one can choose any such m and n and put a in row m and b in row n.

4. Let a be of sort α and b be of of sort β, suppose neither a nor b occur in a chart, and suppose that m and n are the only two distinct rows having no names in column α or β, respectively. Then one can put a in row m and b in row n.

Column completion: If exactly $n - 1$ of the names of sort α occur in column α of the chart, then one can write the remaining name of that sort in the blank row of the column.

Name insertion: If a is of sort α and each of the rows in which there is no name in column α is completely empty, then one can put a in any such row of column α.

Empty chart: An empty chart can be asserted without justification.

Weakening: Any name can be erased from a chart.

Notice that each of these rules is valid and that each involves charts. Some of them have to do with getting information into charts from sentences. Some have to do with getting information from charts to sentences. Some have to do with inference between charts. Moreover, the rules given, along with the axioms mentioned and some complete set of first-order axioms and rules, form a complete set. In other words, given any set Γ of sentences and possibly a chart, if ϕ is either a chart or a sentence such that every model in which every member of Γ is true is a model in which ϕ is true, then ϕ can be proved from Γ using only the rules above, the axiom described above, and the first-order rules.

A logic of sentences and Venn diagrams

Any of the diagrammatic systems described above can be extended to be heterogeneous by adding appropriate sentences, enriching the syntax of the diagrams if needed, and providing rules of inference allowing inference between the two types of representations. For example, the addition of interpreted first-order sentences built from predicates like $Between(x, y, z)$, $On(x, y)$, etc., to the system of geometry described above, along with appropriate linguistic axioms and heterogeneous rules, would allow one to carry out rigorous heterogeneous proofs very much like those actually given in plane geometry.

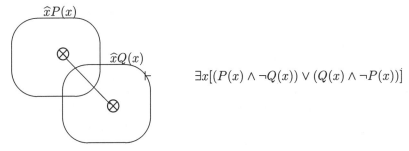

$$\exists x[(P(x) \land \neg Q(x)) \lor (Q(x) \land \neg P(x))]$$

Figure 12: An instance of the rule of Existential-observe.

Similarly, one can combine first-order sentences with a version of the system of Venn diagrams presented above, as in [5]. We will briefly describe such a system.

Sentences are built up from constant symbols and predicate symbols of each arity. Diagrams are just as in the system above, except that each closed curve is tagged by a 'set term' rather than an atomic label as in the system above. These set terms are formed by abstracting over the free variable in an open formula, as with '$\hat{x}P(x)$' and '$\hat{y}(Q(y) \lor \exists z R(y, z))$'. Models for the system are extensions of first-order models. The interpretation of a closed curve in a model is as expected: it is assigned the set of objects satisfying the open formula labeling the curve in the model. Truth in a model for sentences is as usual; truth in a model for diagrams is just as in the Venn system above.

The diagram-to-diagram rules are exactly as above; for sentence-to-sentence rules one can take any complete set of first-order rules and axioms. The occurrence of set terms as labels of closed curves obviously enriches the syntax of the diagrams sufficiently to allow one to formulate explicit and effective diagram-to-sentence and sentence-to-diagram rules. One way to do this is to associate regions of a diagram with set terms in a systematic manner based on those occurring as labels in the diagram. The region enclosed by a curve is associated with the set term labeling it. If a region r is associated with some set term $\hat{x}\phi$, then the region within the rectangle but outside of r is associated with $\hat{x}\neg\phi$. Similarly, overlap of regions is associated with conjunction, the combination of two regions is associated with disjunction, and so on. Given this relation, effective rules of inference can be stated. For example, if a diagram has shading in region r, and the region within the rectangle but outside r is associated with $\hat{x}\phi$, one can infer $\forall x\phi$. Figure 12 displays an instance of a heterogeneous rule in this system. Completeness of the system is proved in [5].

The issue arises with many heterogeneous systems of whether a 'sentence-elimination theorem' is provable (see [6]). In other words, if a diagram is a logical consequence of another diagram (or a set of diagrams) in a heterogeneous system, can it be proved from the other without using heterogeneous and linguistic rules of inference?

This sort of property is an issue of concern for the logic of charts above, for example. If one chart is a logical consequence of another, it would be very inefficient to have to translate the first into sentences, then manipulate these sentences using first-order rules, and finally translate the resulting information back into chart form. A theorem is clearly needed to show that this sort of roundabout process is always unnecessary for chart-to-chart inference, that in such cases a direct proof can always be given.

The sentence-elimination property does not hold for the heterogeneous Venn system because of the potentially complex logical structure allowed in the labels of the diagrams. However, such a theorem does hold with respect to a weaker, 'diagrammatic' notion of logical consequence holding between two diagrams when no analysis of the logical structure of the labels occurring in the diagrams is needed to verify that one is a consequence of the other. This sort of 'canceling out' of the linguistic components in heterogeneous reasoning and representation is of potential computational as well as theoretical interest.

5   Classifications of diagrammatic systems

There are some features that have been invariant among the logics examined here and elsewhere, whether linguistic, diagrammatic, or heterogeneous. Namely, each must have a *grammar*, each must have a class of *structures*, each must have a notion of *logical consequence* holding among well-formed objects defined by means of structures, and each must have some (possibly empty) set of *rules of inference*. These four components can be characterized by the following very provisional conditions. (We certainly don't want to rule out logical systems that cannot be easily subsumed under these specific conditions.)

A *grammar* consists of a classification of external representations into types. First of all, it has finitely many sorts of 'primitive grammatical objects'. Secondly, it has finitely many 'primitive grammatical relations' which can hold among primitive objects. A 'well-formed unit' or 'well-formed representation' of the grammar consists of finitely many primitive objects standing in various primitive relations. These well-formed units classify external representations according to whether they consist of appropriate tokens of the primitive objects standing in the appropriate primitive relations to one another.

Any logical system of the kind we have in mind has implicit in it the idea that well-formed units contain information about some target domain. It is typical to model the target domain by a mathematical *structure*. Each such structure models a possible way things could be, consistent with the information given by the representation. Typically, a structure $M = (U, S_1, \ldots, S_m, I, \ldots)$ consists of some (possibly empty) set U of objects (possibly organized into sorts), a class of relations S_i holding among the objects, and a function I assigning objects of the structure to some or all of the grammatical primitive objects. A structure may have other features and may put various restrictions on its various components. The class of all *structures* that could model the target domain, consistent with some well-formed units, is then used to classify the content of those units.

A relation of *truth in a structure* is a relation between the structures and well-formed units. Whether the relation holds or not between a structure $M = (U, S_1, \ldots, S_m, I, \ldots)$ and a well-formed unit ϕ depends on each of the primitive grammatical relations holding among the grammatical primitives of ϕ. For each such grammatical relation R holding among grammatical primitives $a_1, \ldots, a_n$, a fixed condition among the relations of the structure must be met. In other words, with the fact that R holds among grammatical primitives $a_1, \ldots, a_n$ is associated some condition $\Phi_R(M, a_1, \ldots, a_n)$. If for each such grammatical primitive relation R of ϕ the corresponding condition Φ_R is met by M, ϕ is true in M. Various conditions may be put on the relation of truth in a structure, such as preservation of truth in a structure under isomorphic copies of it for some particular notion of isomorphism.

A relation of *logical consequence* is a relation holding among well-formed units, defined in terms of truth in a structure. Whether a well-formed object ϕ is a logical consequence of some set of well-formed objects Γ is a function of ϕ and the class of all structures M such that every member of Γ is true in M.

A *rule of inference* is a relation holding between sets of well-formed units and well-formed units. Whether this relation holds is a function purely of the grammatical relations holding among the diagrammatic primitives of the various well-formed units in the set.

This description of the components of a logic should be nothing too unusual, though the notion of a grammar is slightly more inclusive than usual. Of greater interest are the further, more fine-grained classifications of systems suggested by the diagrammatic and heterogeneous systems presented above, a matter to which we now turn.

Logical systems have traditionally been classified according to considerations along the following lines: whether every class of structures definable in one system is definable in some other system; whether the class of denumerable structures is definable in a given system; whether elementary equivalence of two structures entails isomorphism; whether a certain type of isomorphism entails elementary equivalence; whether the set of valid sentences is effectively enumerable; and whether the Beth property holds for a system.

The systems considered here, however, suggest some very different potential classifications of logical systems. First of all, they focus attention on the representational level of proof in addition to the level of content of proof. Secondly, they display some very unusual relationships between representations and what a system seeks to represent, suggesting the possibility of a mathematical study of representation and how it represents, beyond the usual mathematics of inference and consequence.

For example, where standard analyses are concerned with various notions of isomorphism between structures of a system, some of the systems under examination here suggest investigation of various notions of isomorphism between structures M of a system and those representations that are true in M. One may very well be interested in defining some notion of isomorphism '$\cong$' having the property: if a representation R is true in M, then $R \cong M$, where $R \cong M$ provides more illumination into the connection between representation and structure than 'R is true in M'. As in the case of Hyperproof, these special relationships between representations and structures may allow for non-standard deductive practices, such as allowing one to prove satisfiability of a sentence or non-consequence. One could think of such a study of representation as a formalization of some of the informal semiotics of iconic representation that has been carried out since Peirce.

Homomorphic systems

In the remainder of the chapter we briefly examine some of these new criteria by which logics, especially diagrammatic and other non-linguistic ones, can be compared. To begin with, we will provide an explicit definition of a 'homomorphic' or 'diagrammatic' system for purposes of comparison rather than as a cut-and-dried, definitive definition:

1. Objects in the domain of a structure, 'target objects' are represented by tokens of diagrammatic primitive objects, 'icon tokens', with different sorts of objects represented by different types of tokens.

2. If π is the interpretation function of a structure, then for those representations true in the structure, π preserves the grammatical structure holding among the icon tokens constituting such representations in the following ways:

   - If icon tokens of a representation stand in some relevant relationship R, that is, they hold of a primitive grammatical relation, then there is a corresponding relationship S holding among the objects of the domain to which they are assigned by π, a 'target relation'.

- The converse holds as well.

- If a grammatical relationship among icon tokens has some structural property (like transitivity, asymmetry, irreflexivity, etc.), then this same property must hold of the objects assigned to the tokens by π.

- The converse holds as well.

- If a token t of some type T (say closed curve) has some special property P (say being shaded), then $\pi(t)$ is an object of some type $\pi(T)$ having some special property $\pi(P)$ on the domain (say, an empty set rather than just a set).

- The converse holds as well.

3. Every representation is true in some structure.

Call a system 'more diagrammatic/ more homomorphic' or 'less diagrammatic/ less homomorphic' in virtue of having more or fewer of these features listed above, and also by virtue of having stronger or weaker versions of them.

We illustrate these definitions with some examples. Let's start with a very extreme case of a diagrammatic logic, a logic for reasoning about the relationships of containment of drawn closed figures within other drawn figures. A structure of this logic consists of a number of drawn figures standing in relations of containment or non-containment with one another. Each drawn figure (as a syntactic object) is interpreted in a structure as some drawn closed figure. Truth of a diagram in a structure depends simply on whether the relationships of containment and non-containment among the drawn figures is (literally) preserved under their interpretation in a structure. So the system has a particularly strong version of Condition 1 and also a particularly strong version of the first clause of Condition 2. One reasons about certain relationships among certain types of objects with these objects and relationships themselves; one reasons with the target objects and target relations.

Let's now look at another, slightly less extremely diagrammatic, system. The primitives consist of names $a, b, c \ldots$ and a bar $-$. Diagrams consist of finitely many names separated by bars, like $a - b - c - b - a - d$. The only grammatical relation is the left-of relation among names. In this system, unlike the system above, names are not interpreted as names but rather as arbitrary objects, so that it has a weaker version of Condition 1. The only relevant relation among objects of the domain is the left-of relation. For truth in a structure, the left-of relation must be preserved under the interpretation function. Again, it has a very strong version of the first clause of Condition 2. For example, $a - b - d$ is a logical consequence of $a - b - c - d$, and any diagram is a logical consequence of $a - b - c - b$, since this last is unsatisfiable.

Both of the logics above have rather extreme diagrammatic features. In each case the single primitive grammatical relation is required to be literally preserved under interpretation functions. The first logic is even more extremely diagrammatic than the second since the primitive syntactic components, closed figures, represent objects of the very same sort: closed figures. An even more extreme case could have them representing themselves.

It is clearly far too much to ask of a logic that it have such extremely homomorphic features as the two logics above to qualify as diagrammatic. In most diagrammatic systems, grammatical relations among grammatical objects are not required to be preserved literally under the interpretation function. For example, consider a logic with the same grammar as the drawn-figure logic above, but with figures now interpreted as sets, and containment among figures now corresponding to the subset relationship among the sets they denote. In this system it is obviously not literally the same relationship required to be preserved from representation to domain for truth in a structure. The grammatical relation is a physical relation between physical objects, the target relation it represents is an abstract one among abstract objects.

Other clearly diagrammatic logics enjoy an even less direct connection between grammatical relations and target relations. With most diagrammatic systems there is no one-to-one correspondence between grammatical relations and relations in the domain as with the previous three systems; in other words, with most diagrammatic logics it is not the case that with each grammatical relation R there is a unique target relation S required to hold of the referents of grammatical objects whenever they hold for R in a diagram and vice versa; it is not generally the case that when a diagram is true in a structure, the structure's interpretation function is a homomorphism from diagram to structure.

This is most obvious with a system like existential graphs, where most of the syntactic objects are not referential and where the syntax is entirely isomorphic to linguistic systems. So in general, the following sort of connection between representation and structure is all that is required for truth in the structure. For each grammatical relation R holding among grammatical primitives, a fixed condition Φ_R must be met involving the representation's grammatical relations and objects, the target objects and relations, the target, and the interpretation function.

Since this alone is obviously insufficient to distinguish diagrammatic from non-diagrammatic systems, there is a need for further criteria for determining the extent to which such systems are diagrammatic. While this matter demands a much more detailed treatment than can be given here, a temporary solution is simply to call one such logic more diagrammatic than another if the correspondence between grammatical relations and relations on the domain required for truth in a structure in the first logic is more natural than for the other. Obviously the 'naturalness' of a diagrammatic system is at least somewhat relative to the capacities of the particular processing system at hand, whether this is a human system or some particular computational system.

To conclude the discussion of the definition above, consider Condition 3, which we illustrate using the system of Venn diagrams described above. The Venn system does not satisfy this condition since the same region can be both shaded and have an X-sequence. Therefore it is less diagrammatic than a system that enjoys all the features the Venn system has, while having the feature that every representation is satisfiable. However, it does have a weaker version of Condition 3 since there is an effective procedure for determining, for any given diagram, whether it is satisfiable. So it is more diagrammatic than a system having the same homomorphic features except that the satisfiability of its diagrams is not effectively decidable.

Even linguistic systems can have homomorphic properties. For example, the temporal ordering of spoken English sentences describing a succession of events can have the effect of being an assertion of the same temporal ordering among the events mentioned. Thus, the three sentences 'Ahab ate his salad. Then he ate his soup. Then he ate his cheese', describe a different succession of events than does 'Ahab ate his salad. Then he ate his cheese. Then he ate his soup', solely by virtue of the three event descriptions occurring in a different order. One can find many other homomorphic features in various languages.

Heterogeneity and language in inference

What is special about highly homomorphic systems is that they can very closely and naturally mirror objects and properties being represented. We saw that in extreme cases the very objects and properties themselves can be used in the representations reasoned with.

Perhaps unfortunately, the expressive generality of a system is often incompatible with its capacity for being diagrammatic. If a system needs to be able to represent the left-of or subset relation it can do so in a highly diagrammatic manner. But if it is to represent *arbitrary* binary relations, say, its potential for being homomorphic drops dramatically. It is hopeless to try to have a separate diagrammatic representation for every binary relation: one for father-of, one for owns, one for front-of, one for taller-than, etc. If a combinatorial explosion of notation is to be avoided, the only homomorphic features that are retainable concern those properties of binary relations common to all of them, such things as having two argument places, having a distinguishable order among the argument places, and being distinguishable from one another. The strongly diagrammatic features characteristic of the systems having only to represent a few particular relations have been necessarily traded for economy of representational resources, elegance, and readability. The problem obviously worsens for a system needing to be able to represent, say, arbitrary n-ary relations, arbitrary second-order properties, and so forth.

Despite this trade-off between degree of homomorphism and expressive range, heterogeneous systems can allow one to balance expressive range with homomorphic representation, to have one's cake and eat it too. Since they are essentially combinations of two or more systems, each subsystem of a heterogeneous system can be specially adapted to a particular aspect of the domain to be represented. Representational labor can thereby be divided.

As a real-life example of this sort of division of representational labor, consider the case of circuit design. Here it is typical to appeal simultaneously to timing diagrams, state charts, circuit diagrams, and language in reasoning about a single piece of hardware. The reason these different sorts of representations are used in the same reasoning process is that each one is specially attuned to a different aspect of the type of hardware in question. The state diagrams are attuned to the issue of control, circuit diagrams to the construction from logic gates, timing diagrams to the value of a wire as it changes through time, and language to high-level description. To attempt to combine these various representational tasks into a single type of representation would result in chaos. It is much more useful to keep them separate and to reason back and forth between them.

What is needed in cases of heterogeneous reasoning is usually not some supersystem able to represent everything in some canonical fashion. Rather, what is needed is a semantic underpinning tying the different types of representations together, as illustrated by the heterogeneous systems presented above. By utilizing different sorts of representational systems simultaneously, one is able to exploit the homomorphic power of various formalisms without restricting one's expressive power in the process by their specificity of application.

It may be that dividing representational labor in some cases tends to result in a corresponding increase in complexity in the heterogeneous rules needed to translate between the different components of such systems in some cases. We leave this matter to further study.

Besides generality, a second limitation on the degree of homomorphism a system can have concerns the fact that some expressive tasks simply leave very little room for it. Disjunction of assertions, for example, is not ripe with representational possibilities. Infix notation in a language is more-or-less as diagrammatic a mechanism as is possible. One might call the expression of disjunction a 'thin' representational task, one which is expressible as well by language as by diagram. Other thin representational tasks include conjunction, negation, universal quantification, and so on.

Diagrammatic systems built around the representation of thin concepts show a marked lack of the representational perspicuity sought in diagrams. Peirce's system of existential graphs, for example, is a diagrammatic system only able to represent thin concepts; hence, its structural isomorphism with certain first-order linguistic systems having the same expressive range (see [16]).

On the other hand, representational tasks like the expression of a linear ordering or the inclusion relation among sets are 'thick' in allowing for a much greater range in degree of homomorphism among different representations of them. They have more elaborate and specific properties than do thin tasks, thus allowing these specific properties to be closely mirrored in a represention. Diagrams are especially useful for thick representational tasks, and perhaps any other sort of job is best left to other kinds of representation.

Scalability

Many have expressed the concern that, nice as diagrammatic and heterogeneous formalisms can be in simple cases, they are simply not scalable to more complex cases. By way of addressing this worry, we would like to make three comments. First of all, the same worry might easily be directed towards various first-order formal systems. It is not at all obvious that a few trivial-looking rules and axioms like modus ponens or universal generalization would be useful at all in a real-life, complex domain like mathematics or computer science. However, the appearance is clearly misleading in this case and perhaps in the case of some diagrammatic and heterogeneous systems as well.

Secondly, heterogeneous systems allow one to do such things as extend standard linguistic systems for such purposes as allowing a more perspicuous expression of common cases or key features (such as in mathematical proofs). So they can increase (or at least not decrease) the power of already quite powerful linguistic systems.

Thirdly, many non-linguistic systems are able to express very large amounts of data in a compact way. Topographical charts are an example of this. Practically an infinite amount of information can be expressed by means of very few lines with one of these. A linguistic expression of the same information would be much more complex. So at least in some cases, scalability is more of a problem for linguistic systems than for diagrammatic ones. Because of these sorts of considerations we do not feel that the problem of scalability is an unavoidable obstacle, though it may be a problem in certain cases.

Valid and invalid reasoning with diagrams

There is also a concern that reasoning involving diagrams is essentially non-rigorous. Indeed, despite the fact that they have been used for thousands of years in mathematics, they are notorious for having led to fallacies, classic examples of which are found in Euclid. We describe two ways in which a diagrammatic logic can encourage invalid reasoning and discuss how a good diagrammatic logic can facilitate valid reasoning.

A diagrammatic system invites error when natural interpretations of grammatical relations are superseded in favor of less natural ones. For example, were '$b - c - a$' in the system above to be reinterpreted as meaning that a is left of c which is left of b, error would be avoided only with difficulty. The obvious and natural interpretation would have been superseded.

Similarly, from a diagram having a point labeled 'A' falling within a drawn triangle in a system of geometrical diagrams, one would be strongly tempted to infer that the point falls within the triangle. But one's semantics need not assign this meaning to the diagram. Depending on the semantics, the point could be any point, inside or outside the triangle. This pitfall would be all the more dangerous if one's semantics were only vaguely specified, as was the case with the diagrams in Euclid's *Elements*. Fallacy is avoidable given carefully specified semantics but easily avoidable given a natural semantics, one in which diagrammatic relations are mapped in a conceptually natural way to target relations. This point has been made in Shimojima [13].

Ideally, one should rely on natural diagrammatic constraints both in the demarcation and interpretation of the well-formed units whenever possible rather than on purely conventional stipulations. If one wants to reason about some transitive relation and chooses a transitive grammatical relation to represent it like the left-of ordering, one has wisely exploited the physical properties of the grammar; one has allowed part of the inferential burden to be carried by one's representations.

6   Conclusion

The thesis underlying this chapter has been that logical systems are meant to serve as mathematical models of informal inference practices and pre-theoretic consequence relations underlying these practices. It was noted that particular systems arise not only from the inference practice being modeled, but also from what idealizations are made about it. We argued that the diversity of logical systems arising from taking both of these variables into consideration is not handled well by means of standard accounts of what constitutes a logical system.

Though any of the idealizations mentioned could be dropped with an increase in coverage, we concentrated on logical systems violating Idealization 2.2, the assumption that the external representations of an inference practice can be adequately modeled by means of a linear sequence of symbols. When one drops this assumption, the resulting systems display many logical properties not readily expressible in terms of linguistic systems. For example, the representations of some of these systems display close relationships to structures themselves, sometimes serving as representations of them, allowing one to deductively establish facts usually obtainable only model-theoretically. Other systems allow one to hard-wire part of one's inferential burden into the representations themselves. Others provide a more accurate model of inference practices involving charts, tables, diagrams, etc. For example, heterogeneous systems appear when Idealization 2.2 is dropped, thus allowing one to model many features of actual reasoning not easily capturable by linguistic or strictly diagrammatic systems. As is often done in actual practice, such systems allow one to divide representational labor among different types of representations and to transfer information from one type to another.

Many of these systems also have interesting logical properties, a topic we were able to treat only cursorily. For example, heterogeneous systems suggest the study of how one representational component of such a system can be isolated either proof-theoretically or model-theoretically from the others. Does a restricted completeness theorem hold within a single component of the heterogeneous system or not? How do the various components compare in terms of expressive range?

A great deal of real-life reasoning and representation is heterogeneous, diagrammatic, graphical, and so on. We hope to have pointed out some of the topics of concern that will arise in a logical treatment of this area and to have made it obvious that there are many other such topics not yet discovered. We hope also to have provided motivation for the development of a potentially very fruitful new field.

References

[1] Jon Barwise. Axioms for abstract model theory. *Annals of Mathematical Logic*, **7**, 221–265, 1974.

[2] Jon Barwise and John Etchemendy. Visual information and valid reasoning. *Visualization in Teaching and Learning Mathematics*, pp 9–24,

W. Zimmerman and S. Cunningham, eds. Washington: Mathematical
Association of America, 1991.

[3] Jon Barwise and John Etchemendy. *Hyperproof.* 254pp. CSLI, Stanford, distributed by Cambridge University Press, 1995.

[4] Jon Barwise. Heterogeneous reasoning. *Conceptual Graphs and Knowledge Representation.* G. Mineau, B. Moulin, and J. Sowa, eds. New York: Springer Verlag, to appear.

[5] Eric Hammer. Reasoning with sentences and diagrams. *The Notre Dame Journal of Formal Logic.* To appear.

[6] Eric Hammer. Representing relations diagrammatically. In *Working Papers on Diagrams and Logic*, pp. 77–119, The Visual Inference Laboratory, Indiana University, 1993.

[7] Eric Hammer and Norman Danner. Towards a model theory of diagrams. In *Working Papers on Diagrams and Logic*, pp. 144–168, The Visual Inference Laboratory, Indiana University, 1993.

[8] David Harel et al. On the formal semantics of statecharts. *Proc. of the Second Annual IEEE Symposium on Logic in Computer Science.* Ithaca, 1987.

[9] David Harel. On visual formalisms. Carnegie Mellon University Computer Science technical report 87-126, 1987.

[10] Isabel Luengo. A diagrammatic system for Euclidean geometry. Unpublished paper, 1993.

[11] Charles S. Peirce. *The Collected Papers of Charles S. Peirce, volume 4.* Charles Hartshorne and Paul Weiss, eds. Cambridge: Harvard University Press, 1933.

[12] Don Roberts. *The Existential Graphs of Charles S. Peirce.* The Hague: Mouton and Co., 1973.

[13] Atsushi Shimojima. The default syntax of diagrams. Unpublished paper, 1992.

[14] Sun-Joo Shin. Valid Reasoning and Visual Representation. Diss. Stanford University, 1991.

[15] John Venn, *Symbolic Logic.* 2nd edn. New York: Burt Franklin, 1971.

[16] J. Jay Zeman. The Graphical Logic of C.S. Peirce. Diss. University of Chicago, 1964.

4

General Dynamic Logic

Johan van Benthem

A 'logical system' is a complex architecture for analysing one or more styles
of reasoning. This paper approaches this notion by example, focussing
on current 'dynamic' conceptions of logic, as being concerned both with
declarative propositions and with cognitive procedures of update, revision,
etc. The semantic model proposed for this purpose is a general dynamic
logic (inspired by dynamic logic in computer science). We show how this
architecture leads to (1) new perspectives on logical constants (essentially,
these become invariants in an infinite hierarchy of process simulations), (2)
notions of inference (which may be classified via sets of structural rules and
corresponding representation theorems) as well as (3) a systematic study of
switching mechanisms between static and dynamic levels, effecting a flow
of information between short-term and long-term reasoning.

1   What is a logical system?

The title of this volume illustrates a significant recent shift in perspective,
moving from the definite to the indefinite article. The term 'logical system'
has become a common noun, rather than a proper name, as a result of the
diversity and flexibility of current logical theorizing. Thus, the essence of
the subject no longer lies in the possession of one particular calculus (say,
Frege's 'predicate logic' or Heyting's 'intuitionistic logic'), but rather in
a certain logical skill or 'modus operandi'. Of course, in some ways, this
makes it harder to circumscribe where 'logicality' resides, and therefore,
some people are still waging rear-guard actions holding on to specific inference rules of 'monotonicity' or 'permutation', or other supposed shibboleths
of 'true logic'.

Some noticeable features of current logical systems are the following. First, there is a growing interest in the fine-structure of intended applications. Logical systems often represent an intuition concerning some particular field of reasoning, which may come with its own most appropriate notions of inference and expressiveness. In particular, there is no reason for blindly copying the old connectives and quantifiers from standard calculi: one should dare to pursue conscious design, asking which key patterns should be brought out by the new formalism. Moreover, it is becoming an acknowledged fact that, instead of one fixed canon from predicate logic, there are often different bona fide styles of inference, appropriate to specific tasks. And finally, current systems often display a heterogeneous architecture, mixing various reasoning styles and data types. All this means that a 'logical system' is no longer a calculus having this or that specific notion of consequence, or specific logical vocabulary, but rather a calculus exemplifying a certain degree of 'logicality', for instance in its level of abstraction and exactness of procedure.

We shall not attempt here to pinpoint these notions more precisely in abstract terms. One might think of 'logical constants' in terms of their 'invariance' for changes in semantic content, as proposed in van Benthem [47]. Likewise, there are presumably various broad constraints on what might count as a genuine 'inference relation'. Instead, in this chapter, we shall develop a general system of 'dynamic logic', which we take to be quite typical of the above trend, in order to demonstrate all the mentioned tendencies at work. (Further details of this enterprise may be found in the monograph by van Benthem [47], Part VI.) Thus, we hope to define a suitably broad notion of 'logical system' by example.

2 Modelling logical dynamics

2.1 A procedural turn

2.1.1 General motivation

Many central cognitive notions have a dual character. For instance, *judgment* stands for both an intellectual action and the content of that action, and likewise *reasoning* denotes both an intellectual process and its products. This interplay between 'static' contents and 'dynamic' actions is also to be observed in our ordinary use of the term 'natural language', which can be either a static mathematical structure of words and rules, or a dynamic social activity with many systematic conventions that are not necessarily encoded in explicit syntax. In the mainstream of contemporary logic and linguistics so far, static aspects have been predominant; witness the emphasis on isolating so-called 'truth conditions' for linguistic discourse.

Here, what may be called Boolean propositional structure is paramount, with various logical operators creating complex forms of description, such as negation, conjunction, or disjunction. In other words, the emphasis lies on 'that' or 'whether' certain statements are true about a situation, not so much on 'how' they come to be seen as true. To some, this 'declarative' bias, as opposed to a 'procedural' one, is even a laudable hall-mark of logical approaches as such. But, in recent years, there has been a growing tendency in logical and linguistic research to move dynamic considerations of cognitive action to the fore, trying to do justice to the undeniable fact that human cognitive competence consists of procedural facility just as much as communion with eternal truths.

What may be discerned behind current proposals in the field is a general model for construing the interplay of content and action, whose mathematical core is derived from existing systems of relational algebra and dynamic logic. We shall develop its further details in what follows. Such a general model allows us to start raising systematic questions of 'dynamic logic' across various fields. In particular, we shall study such issues as the proper choice of fundamental dynamic logical constants, charting the variety of dynamic forms of inference, and the systematic interplay between newer forms of procedural logic and the original standard systems in an optimal logical architecture. Finally, the model also invites reflection in the end on its most appropriate realizations. We shall discuss a number of pertinent questions, such as the ontological status of 'transitions' as a new basic category, or the complexity of more procedural systems of logic.

In all this, our focus is on language and cognition, but not exclusively so: the 'general dynamics' of this chapter applies also to non-linguistic activities, such as digging or playing. This seems the proper strategic depth from which to start logical analysis of these phenomena, before looking at the peculiarities of cognitive action, or within the latter realm again, at specifics of lexically or syntactically encoded cognitive action. In this way, many similarities emerge between logic, linguistics, philosophy and computer science that may become of mutual benefit.

2.1.2 States, transitions, and procedures

The most general model of dynamics is simply this: some system moves through a space of possibilities. Thus, there is to be some set S of relevant *states* (cognitive, physical, etc.) and a family $\{R_a \mid \in A\}$ of binary *transition relations* among them, corresponding to actions that could be performed to change from one state to another. These may be thought of as an 'atomic repertoire'. Procedural aspects of action or cognition then have to do with the way in which such transitions can be combined to obtain certain desired effects (the 'procedural repertoire'). For instance, one can think of an instruction manual for building a model airplane, or a computer program guiding some computation, or a linguistic text as it modifies the information state of its reader. For the moment, we do not constrain these examples any further.

'Logic' now enters as a study of the structure of complex procedures on binary relational models and their general effects. If one wishes, this may be contrasted with the 'standard approach', where logical systems strive for description of *unary* propositional *properties* of states, which can only be tested for truth or falsity. The difference is reflected in the greater number of natural operators for constructing procedures arising in the dynamic perspective, over and above the Boolean algebra of mere sets of states. It is easy, however, to exaggerate here: and our view will be that the standard approach retains its value, too, both intuitively and in the technical sense of being able to *reduce* the dynamic one by 'translation' if the need arises.

Specific dynamic systems will usually specify a more detailed set of states, in order to introduce meaningful *basic actions*. These can have quite diverse forms, such as

real action	put the block on the table
playing games	serve the ball
computation	assign some value to a register
information flow	update the current state.

Relevant 'states' here can be either concrete physical states, or more abstract procedural ones, or mixtures of both (the most frequent case in practice). Not only different types of activity induce different kinds of state. Even one and the same activity may be studied using states with different degrees of detail. For instance, in the above transition models, one can make a standard shift from individual states to *finite sequences* of states, being the 'traces' of some relational process, which allow for more detailed description of computational processes or physical activities. Or, one can also give single states different components, recording different aspects of a process taking place.

2.1.3 A budget of examples

Let us briefly consider a number of dynamic 'genres', seeing how the above features are exemplified in them.

- **Real action** in the world changes actual physical states. Basic actions are defined either by the intrinsic properties of a process, such as 'moving', or by a desired end state: 'to put a block on the table'. In both cases, a logical mechanism is at work generating an action from some descriptive statement: either the 'resultative' ! describing the resulting state, or some 'imperative' linked to a pure description of the desired transition itself. The procedural repertoire of actions includes all Boolean operations: 'walk and whistle' (intersection), 'walk, don't run' (complement), 'take it or leave it' (union), and also various 'ordering operations' such as 'hit and run' (composition), 'put it back' (converse). Finally, real action involves a natural interplay between dynamic instructions and descriptive tests, as shown in 'take the tram if you are late' or 'run until you are safe'. There are also various natural logical relations between physical actions, ranging from 'implication' to one action's 'enabling' another to achieve a certain effect.

- **Playing games** is another form of action with a clear procedural structure. Here, the notion of state can be more complex, involving both physical components and more ephemeral obligations and commitments of participants. Examples range from sports to cognitive games, such as those introduced into logic by Lorenzen [32], Hintikka [24]. Again, basic actions include both physical actions ('serving a ball', 'drawing an object to be inspected') and tests ('the ball is in', 'a player is over-committed'). As for operations on games, the most natural ones seem to be those of *choice* and sequential *composition*. Already in a two-person game, the former leads in fact to two options, depending on whose choice is involved. To see this, identify such games with Parikh [36] as relations between states representing a win for player I if she plays her best strategy. Then starting with a choice for player I amounts to Boolean union, but starting with a choice for player II amounts to Boolean intersection. Moreover, the two roles suggest a natural operation of 'role switching', which amounts to switching of winning and losing states: that is, to Boolean complement in this representation. Of course, subtler representations for games are possible, too: modelling them, for instance, with both possible transitions and sets of distinguished winning states. Then, for example, role switching might affect only the latter coordinate. But this is just an earlier point about all our examples: activities and processes can be modelled at different levels of 'grain size'.

- **Computation.** Perhaps the most important process of state change, as far as logical theory is concerned, is that of *computation*. In the simplest set-up, states are *environments* mapping variables ('identifiers') in a programming language to values in some data structure. These represent snapshots of the registers during computation. Basic actions are then *assignments* $x := t$ and *tests* ε? for so-called 'Boolean conditions' ε. Procedural structure of programs has been investigated since Floyd [12], with operators including 'sequential composition', 'conditional choice', and 'guarded iteration'. The latter is often taken to be characteristic of computation: but see [46] for more general cognitive uses of such operators, for instance, when recording continuing commitment in a dialogue. The semantics of imperative programming contains many cues for a more general logic of dynamics. Again, there is no single notion of state here serving all computational purposes. For instance, Pnueli [37] has a mixture of physical environments and internal recording of 'control'. Incidentally, even the semantics of declarative programming may be viewed in the same spirit, with sets of ground atoms serving as states, that are transformed via deductive 'approximation operators' for logic programs, computing their Herbrand models as fixed points. (Van Benthem [49] shows how the dynamic logic to be proposed below fully applies to Horn clause programming.)

- **Linguistic activities** provide a final source of inspiration. In the field of natural language, dynamic ideas have been around for a long time. For instance, in semantics, incremental growth of discourse representations had already been advocated, amongst others, in Seuren [40], with modern implementations in Heim [21], Kamp [28], Seuren [41]. And in pragmatics, the tendency dates back to at least Stalnaker [43], who proposed 'context change' as a driving force. Here again, there is a great variety of states and prominent operations, depending on the particular speech act or linguistic 'mode', such as evaluating a sentence against a given model, constructing some partial model, querying a certain predicate, etc.

2.2   State transition models

Let us now turn to a more technical modelling of the above dynamic paradigm.

2.2.1   Relational algebra

What are most general operations on actions? Ubiquitous examples are *sequential composition* and *choice*. But others occur frequently too, such as *undoing* an action. A convenient formalism for studying this repertoire is that of *relational algebra*, being the study of logical operations on binary relations initiated by Schröder and Tarski (see Jónsson [26], Németi [35]). Basic operations here are the following:

$-, \cap, \cup$	set-theoretic Booleans	complement, intersection and union
$\circ,\ \check{}$	ordering operations	composition and converse
Δ	one constant entity	the identity relation

More precisely these are, for example, $R \circ S = \{(x,y) \mid \exists z : Rxz \& Szy\}$ and $R\check{} = \{(x,y) \mid Ryx\}$. Intuitively, $\cup$ models 'choice', $\circ$ 'sequencing' and $\check{}$ 'reversal' of binary relations. These operations O form a completely general procedural apparatus, which is 'logical' in the sense of being independent of any specific structure of states. Technically, this may be seen in their so-called *invariance under permutations* of states. For instance, in the binary case, we have that

for every permutation π of the state set S, $\pi[O(R,S)] = O(\pi[R], \pi[S])$.

Thus, not surprisingly, operations from relational algebra return across many concrete systems of dynamics, making more specialized choices for their state space.

Next, what are the inferential properties of these algebraic operators? A well-known list of axioms looks as follows. One starts with all basic axioms of Boolean algebra, and then adds the following equations:

$$R \circ \Delta = R = \Delta \circ R \qquad\qquad R\check{}\check{} = R \qquad\qquad (-R)\check{} = -R\check{}$$
$$(R \cup S)\check{} = R\check{} \cup S\check{} \qquad\qquad (R \circ S)\check{} = S\check{} \circ R\check{}$$
$$(R \circ S) \circ T = R \circ (S \circ T) \qquad R \circ (S \cup T) = (R \circ S) \cup (R \circ T)$$
$$(R \cup S) \circ T = (R \circ T) \cup (S \circ T) \quad (R\check{} \circ -(R \circ S)) \cup -S = -S.$$

(It is known, however, that no finite axiomatization can capture all valid principles of relational algebra over set relations.)

It may not be clear *a priori* why the 'static' mathematical notion of validity chosen here, namely that of universally true algebraic identities, should be suitable in all dynamic settings. Indeed, we shall see below that a dynamic approach generates plausible new varieties of consequence, just as it generates new kinds of logical operator. For instance, genuine dynamic validity of an inference might consist of the following sequential prescription for achieving some desired effect:

first process all premise instructions successively, then see if the resulting transition is successful for the conclusion.

But the latter notion will turn out to be reducible to the above format.

Relational algebra as introduced so far is a subsystem of *first-order predicate logic*. Therefore, algebraic calculations may always be replaced by predicate-logical reasoning using explicit variables for states. (Full relational algebra is known to be an undecidable fragment of first-order logic.) This gives at least a general reduction from dynamic reasoning to standard formalisms, which is useful for technical purposes, such as establishing standard meta-properties or finding initial estimates of complexity. In addition to first-order operations, however, there are also other natural *infinitary* operations on binary relations. These correspond to 'unlimited' structures in action, such as endless repetition. The most prominent technical example is the *transitive closure R^** of a relation R:

$$R^* = \{(x,y) \mid some \; finite \; sequence \; of \; successive \; R \; transitions \; links \; x \; to \; y\}$$

This operation also satisfies various algebraic principles, such as

$$R \cup R^* = R^* \qquad R^{**} = R^* \qquad (R \cup S)^* = (R^* \circ S^*)^*.$$

Digression 2.1 (Relations versus functions over state spaces)
Some current dynamic frameworks employ *functions* rather than relations, as 'transformations' of states. In principle, there is no conflict with our approach so far. In one direction, functions are nothing but *deterministic total* relations, and hence the functional perspective is subsumed in the present one. And conversely, every binary relation R on S induces a function $R^\sharp$ from $\text{pow}(S)$ to $\text{pow}(S)$, by setting

$$R^\sharp(X) = \quad R[X] \quad (= \{y \in S \mid \exists x \in X \, Rxy\}).$$

Moreover, nothing is lost in this larger setting, as these 'lifted' functions can be uniquely retrieved via a well-known mathematical property:

Fact 2.2 A function $F: \text{pow}(S) \to \text{pow}(S)$ is of the form $R^\sharp$ for some binary relation R on S if and only if F is *continuous*, in the sense of commuting with arbitrary unions of its arguments.

The reason is that continuous maps F can be computed 'locally' from their values at singleton arguments only. The existence of such 'liftings' and 'lowerings' between various levels of set-theoretic representation can also be studied more systematically (see van Benthem [45, Ch. 3]). For example, here is a similar reduction of maps on sets of states to 'propositions' in the standard style, being subsets of S:

Fact 2.3 A unary operation F on $\text{pow}(S)$ is both continuous and *introspective* (i.e. $F(X) \subseteq X$ for all $X \subseteq S$) if and only if it represents some unary property P via the rule $F(X) = X \cap P$.

2.2.2 Dynamic logic

Relational algebra is powerful enough to embed standard declarative propositions, namely as special 'test relations'. Nevertheless, there is much to be said for a richer two-level architecture merging propositional dynamics with statics. Thus, let us also allow unary properties $P, Q, \ldots$ of states henceforth. Then the following picture arises, connecting 'propositions as tests' on states with 'propositions as programs' for changing states:

unary properties	$\rightarrow$	**modes**	$\rightarrow$	binary relations
of states	$\leftarrow$	**projections**	$\leftarrow$	between states

propositional	program
operators	operators
(Boolean algebra)	(Relational algebra)

The motivation for this system lies partly in its mathematical elegance, but is mainly conceptual: there remains a clear independent intuition behind classical propositions. And there is also a practical advantage. Procedural effects are 'local', leaving no traces in short-term memory, while classical propositions are closer to eventual stored content that can be recalled afterwards. Thus, operating with two (or more) levels of 'short-term logic' and 'long-term logic' may be just what is needed in cognitive practice.

The above picture brings out several *mechanisms* for switching from one perspective to another, which correspond to plausible moves that we make in practice. For instance, classical propositions provide 'descriptive contents' for different kinds of action:

testing $?P$ $\lambda xy \bullet y = x \wedge Py$
realizing $!P$ $\lambda xy \bullet Py.$

These proposition-driven *modes* of action deserve independent logical investigation. For instance, ordinary argument has clear modes. A transition 'so' from premises to conclusion signals a shift from a processing mode for the premises to a testing mode for the conclusion. Going in the opposite direction, there are also various natural *projections* from transition processes to classical statements recording their behaviour:

domain   dom (R) $\lambda x \bullet \exists y \, Rxy$
diagonal   diag (R) $\lambda x \bullet Rxx$
(where the latter describes the 'fixed points' of the transformation R) .

The above system is inspired by 'dynamic logic' as developed by Pratt and others (see Harel [19]). The core system of propositional dynamic logic has 'formulas' and 'programs' defined by mutual recursion. Basic operators on formulas are the Boolean connectives, while programs are joined by means of the so-called 'regular operations':

; sequential composition   ∪ Boolean choice   ∗ Kleene iteration

There is one 'test mode' ? taking formulas to programs, and one 'projection modality' <> from programs and formulas to formulas: $< \pi > \varphi$ is a 'weakest precondition' true at only those states where π can be performed so as to achieve the truth of φ. This system encompasses standard operators on programs such as

Conditional choice	IF ε THEN π_1 ELSE π_2	$((\varepsilon)?; \pi_1) \cup ((\neg\varepsilon)?; \pi_2)$
Guarded iteration	WHILE ε DO π	$((\varepsilon)?; \pi)^*; (\neg\varepsilon)?$

Moreover, it expresses various useful types of statement about the execution of programs:

Correctness	$\varphi \to [\pi]\psi$	precondition φ implies postcondition ψ after successful execution of program π
Termination	$< \pi > T$	program π terminates
Enabling	$[\pi_1] < \pi_2 > \varphi$	program π_1 'enables' program π_2 to produce effect φ.

The restriction to regular program operations, as compared to full relational algebra, makes the resulting logic *decidable*. Its core is a perspicuous set of principles for computing weakest preconditions plus one 'induction axiom':
Segerberg axioms

$$< \pi_1; \pi_2 > \varphi \leftrightarrow < \pi_1 >< \pi_2 > \varphi \quad < \pi_1 \cup \pi_2 > \varphi \leftrightarrow < \pi_1 > \varphi \vee < \pi_2 > \varphi$$
$$< \varphi? > \psi \leftrightarrow \varphi \wedge \psi \qquad\qquad\quad < \pi^* > \varphi \leftrightarrow \varphi \vee < \pi >< \pi^* > \varphi$$
$$(\varphi \wedge [\pi^*](\varphi \to [\pi]\varphi)) \to [\pi^*]\, \varphi$$

This calculus generalizes various natural systems of reasoning, such as 'regular algebra', 'propositional modal logic' and 'Hoare calculus' for correctness assertions. Like relational algebra, dynamic logic is an open-ended enterprise. For instance, adding the earlier *converse* operation on programs, running them backwards, gives rise to what may be called a two-sided 'tense-logical' variant of the system. Moreover, in the literature, the missing Booleans $\cap$ and - have been brought in after all, be it at the price of loss of decidability (cf. Goranko and Passy [17]).

2.3 Dynamic design

The above perspective is at work in various systems of dynamic interpretation and inference in the recent literature. What it encourages us to do is bring out procedural intuitions behind standard notions, using deliberate variation on their original design.

2.3.1 Tarskian variations

The standard Tarski truth definition explains the notion

$\mathbb{D}, I, b \vDash \varphi$
formula φ is true in structure $\mathbb{D}$
under interpretation I and variable assignment b.

In this scheme, various 'semantic parameters' may be varied dynamically. For instance, evaluation of formulas may be viewed as a process which changes the assignment b, as is particularly clear with the usual clause for the existential quantifier, which involves some kind of 'domain search' for an appropriate value. Heim [21], Barwise [3] and Groenendijk and Stokhof [18] provide different technical implementations of this intuition. But then, one can also change the interpretation function I: for instance, when incorporating the answer to a *question* 'who wants an ice cream?' into one's partial picture of predicate denotations in the model. And even the whole structure $\mathbb{D}$ itself may be changed when learning about new individuals and new facts. (All these possibilities are demonstrated rather nicely in the graphics of the program 'Tarski's World', Barwise and Etchemendy [4].) Here is a basic system of this kind couched in our general framework. The 'dynamic predicate logic' of Groenendijk and Stokhof has assignments for its states, and essentially two kinds of basic action:

$x := -$ random assignment to the variable x
$P?$ test for the atomic assertion P

Its further operations are sequential composition, as well as a test of strong negation:

$$\sim R \;\; = \;\; \{(x, x) \mid \neg \exists y Rxy\}$$
(The latter can be defined in relational algebra as $\Delta \cap -(T \circ R^{\smile})$.)

Thus, dynamic predicate logic is a relational algebra of random assignment with a limited number of algebraic operations on propositions. Note how there is no independent instruction for quantifiers in this set-up. The existential quantifier corresponds directly to random assignment, while the universal quantifier may be viewed as a test defined out of this. What this suggests is that there need not be any sensible 'quantified dynamic logic' (but there are some current attempts at 'dynamizing' the theory of generalized quantifiers in terms of genuine change of domains). Finally, from the point of view of 'free design', it would make sense to give up predicate-logical timidity and study the full relational algebra of random assignment.

As a further example of changing interpretation functions I, one can think of the earlier 'realizing' instructions $Px!$. These drive a 'state', now consisting of a pair (b, I), to a new state (b, I') in which the object $b(x)$ has been added to the denotation $I(P)$: $I'(P) = I(P) \cup \{b(x)\}$. We

shall not go into such systems here: the main principle will be clear. Even
more intricate semantic settings are conceivable. For instance, in Hintikka's
game-theoretical semantics, evaluation involves finite sampling from a given
structure. In that case, states consist of partial assignments plus some finite
subset of the individual domain where these take their values. Thus, an
existential quantifier $\exists x$ will become an instruction for drawing one more
object from the background (or, shifting an item from long-term to short-
term memory). Then further distinctions arise. For instance, a universal
quantifier may now be read as either referring to the sample, or to the total
domain. More generally, there is a plausible distinction now between local
procedures operating on a sample and global procedures operating on a
structure as a whole.

2.3.2 Kripkean variations

Supplying further detail about the state set S does not only show up in
specific basic actions: it may also produce further complex procedural operations. Here is an illustration, this time concerning the dynamics of
'information flow' rather than of 'interpretation'. Suppose that cognitive
states are ordered by some pattern of *inclusion* $\subseteq$ by informational content,
as happens in Kripke models for intuitionistic logic. Then, there arises a
much richer array of operators in dynamic logic, such as

Propositional modes

updating	up (P)	$\lambda xy \bullet x \subseteq y \wedge Py$
minimal updating	μ-up (P)	$\lambda xy \bullet x \subseteq y \wedge Py \wedge \neg \exists z(x \subset z \subset y \wedge Pz)$
downdating	down (P)	$\lambda xy \bullet x \supseteq y \wedge Py$

Propositional operators

| possibility | poss (P) | $\lambda x \bullet \exists y(x \subseteq y \wedge Py)$ |

Relational operators

| upward part | upw (R) | $\lambda xy \bullet Rxy \wedge x \subseteq y.$ |

This brings us to the possibility of creating explicit dynamic versions
of modal logic. These will bring out 'cognitive procedures' behind various
clauses in the semantics of intuitionistic logic, which is intuitively concerned with the *growth* of knowledge for an epistemic agent. (For example,
an intuitionistic negation describes excursions into the epistemic future,
telling us that all of these end in failure.) Here, atomic propositions p can
be interpreted as standing for updates, either general or 'minimal' in the
above sense. Moreover, one can read the modal operator $\Diamond$ *itself* as a name
for the inclusion relation ('random upward jump'). The procedural repertoire will then include further algebraic operations as connectives, such as
sequential composition or testing for domainhood of some relation. Here is
one concrete system of 'dynamic modal logic'.

Propositions denote transition relations in a possible worlds model $M = (W, R, V)$ of 'information states' ordered by some relevant relation R (that is, 'inclusion' $\subseteq$ as above, or perhaps 'cognitive preference'):

$$[\![q?]\!] = \{(w, w) \mid w \varepsilon V(q)\} \quad [\![q!]\!] = \{(w, v) \mid v \varepsilon V(q)\} \quad [\![\Diamond]\!] = R$$
$$[\![\mathrm{up}(q)]\!] = \{(w, v) \mid Rwv \text{ and } v \varepsilon V(q)\}$$
$$[\![\mu - \mathrm{up}(q)]\!] = \{(w, v) \mid Rwv, v \varepsilon V(q) \text{ and no } u \varepsilon V(q)$$
lies strictly in between w and v}
$$[\![\varphi \wedge \psi]\!] = [\![\varphi]\!] \circ [\![\psi]\!] \quad [\![\neg\varphi]\!] = \{(w, w) \mid \text{ for no } v, (w, v) \varepsilon [\![\varphi]\!]\}.$$

This is just one basic system, which may be shown to be decidable by embedding it into its standard counterpart. But one may add further relational operations, too, such as Boolean intersection or complement. And even a full dynamic logic over these transition models is possible, having both static and dynamic formulas, incorporating the initial atomic modes uniformly for the former (van Benthem [48]). The resulting system becomes at least as powerful as the theory of cognitive updating and revision developed in Gärdenfors [16], once we add the downward direction of inclusion throughout, as in models for temporal logic. An idealized intuitionist mathematician will always move forward along the inclusion order; ordinary human beings can be observed plodding on more zigzagging tracks; and hence a logic of cognitive processes needs both directions. This system can be studied via extensions of standard modal techniques (De Rijke [9] has various results on model-theoretic expressiveness, an axiomatic completeness theorem and a proof of undecidability for the richest version).

There is a wide variety of congenial logical models for information flow. Gärdenfors [15] starts from cognitive states and propositions as operations on these, and then explains logical operations via constructs from *Category Theory*, including composition and 'equalizers'. This theory imposes very strong constraints, such as idempotence and symmetry of composition, to force things back into the mould of standard intuitionistic logic. Gärdenfors [16] gives a more concrete version, using deductively closed sets of statements and probability distributions over a formal language. But already Allen [1] proposes temporal data networks that get updated via an algorithm producing the outcome 'true' for a statement in case its processing leaves the initial network state unaffected. Kamp [27] also has partial data bases for its states—which then became generalized in Kamp [28]— whose 'discourse representation structures' serve as cognitive states which are transformed by each successive proposition that gets incorporated. A simpler, 'non-representational' model of information stems from the logical folklore, cf. Heim [21], Veltman [52]. Its states are merely classes of valuations, models or indices, which get narrowed down as further propositions are learnt. This model can accommodate various further epistemic operators. For instance, in conditional logic, implications have been traditionally explained in terms of 'preferences' among models: 'the conclusion must be true in all *most preferred* worlds where the antecedent is true'. Thus, a state becomes a set of worlds with a preference order. Logical operations may now affect not just the descriptive content of a state, but also its preference pattern. This is the main idea in Spohn [42], Veltman [52], Sandewall [39], when explaining the cognitive effect of heuristic default rules.

In addition to cognitive *states*, a logic of information flow must specify *basic actions* and *procedural operations* over these. In 'constructive' systems, basic actions will consist of adding or removing pieces of code, perhaps followed by closure under some deductive algorithm. Little systematic theory of this kind has been developed so far. In the more 'external' account with sets of models, options are a little easier to classify. Basic actions may be the intersection of these models with some fixed set, increasing descriptive content, or changing the preference pattern over them in some uniform manner. As for procedural operations, here is a sample from Veltman [52], which is concerned with the 'deterministic' case where all relevant relations are functions:

$$
\begin{aligned}
[\![q]\!](X) &= X \cap Q \\
[\![\varphi \wedge \psi]\!](X) &= [\![\psi]\!]([\![\varphi]\!](X)) \\
[\![\varphi \vee \psi]\!](X) &= [\![\varphi]\!](X) \cup [\![\psi]\!](X) \\
[\![\neg\varphi]\!](X) &= X - [\![\varphi]\!](X) \\
[\![\Diamond\varphi]\!](X) &= X \quad \text{if } [\![\varphi]\!](X) \neq \varnothing \\
&\quad\ \varnothing \quad \text{otherwise}
\end{aligned}
$$

All these operations move an agent 'forward', to ever smaller sets of possibilities. Backward movement ('epistemic retreat') would be produced by a qualifier like 'unless φ', which adds the whole range $[\![\varphi]\!]$ to the information state again. Without the modality, this is still a purely descriptive system whose propositions φ map states X to their intersection with the standard models for φ (all such functions are still continuous). With a preference relation as outlined above, more complex instructions may be formulated. For instance, incoming propositions may be taken with a 'heuristic' surplus of information, as with the non-continuous atomic update:

$[\![q]\!](X)$ consists of only the *most preferred* states in $X \cap Q$.

Then, order of presentation becomes important, as in the earlier dynamic logic: there will be different dynamic effects for $p \circ q, q \circ p$ or $p \cap q$.

3   Key issues in dynamic logic

In the above procedural framework, a number of general questions arise concerning logical dynamics, of which we discuss three salient ones. These will serve to illustrate the more general notion of 'logicality' required in current theorizing, though still taking their point of departure in standard notions and results.

3.1 Logical constants

3.1.1 Relational algebra revisited

Boolean algebra has clear-cut central truth-functional operations on propositions, by the usual functional completeness theorem. By contrast, relational algebra provides a plethora of possible operations on relations. So, one immediate question is what are most natural operations on dynamic propositions, the 'logical constants' in a dynamic setting. This question probably has no definitive answer, but there is at least a systematic approach. One basic theme in semantics is measurement of the expressive power of a formalism against its invariance for similar models that 'simulate' each other to some extent. Now, one natural notion of simulation for dynamic processes derives from ordinary model theory. To compare two structures of states-cum-transitions, one must trace similar processes on either side across suitably connected states and transitions:

Definition 3.1 A relation C from S_1 to S_2 linking points with points and ordered pairs with ordered pairs is a 2-*simulation* between two models $(S_1, \{R_{1_a} \mid a \in A\}), (S_2, \{R_{2_a} \mid a \in A\})$ if it satisfies the following two conditions:

- *Partial isomorphism*
  matching points and pairs satisfy corresponding relational transitions R_{1_a}, R_{2_a}.

- *Zigzag*
  if xCy and $z \in S_1$, then $\exists u \in S_2 : xzCyu$,   and vice versa.

Then, a formula $\varphi(x, y)$ is *invariant for 2-simulation* if its truth value is unaffected by passing from evaluation in one model to C-corresponding points in the other one. Within first-order logic, this notion can be described purely syntactically:

Proposition 3.2 *A first-order formula $\varphi(x, y)$ is invariant for 2-simulation iff it can be written using the two variables x and y only (free or bound).*

Examples are defining schemata for the following operations from relational algebra:

Booleans	$\lambda xy \bullet \neg Rxy$	$\lambda xy \bullet Rxy \wedge Sxy$
Conversion	$\lambda xy \bullet Ryx$	
Identity	$\lambda xy \bullet x = y$	
Domain	$\lambda xy \bullet \exists x Ryx$	(no fresh variable z is needed!)

By contrast, three variables are involved essentially in

Composition $\lambda xy \bullet \exists z(Rxz \wedge Szy)$

This tells us the following about the algebra of relations. For procedural structure that involves essentially just computation over two 'registers' x, y when traversing states, the following limited set of operations suffices:

Proposition 3.3 (Henkin–Monk–Tarski [22]). *Each first-order formula $\varphi(x, y)$ with two free variables using only x, y has a variable-free notation with the following algebraic operators:*

Booleans	$-, \cap, \cup$	Conversion	$\check{\ }$
Identity	Δ	Domain	*Do*

The complete relational algebra of Section 2.2.1 moves one step up:

Proposition 3.4 (Henkin–Monk–Tarski [22]). $\{-, \cap, \cup, \check{\ }, \Delta, \circ\}$ *provides a complete variable-free notation for all first-order formulas $\varphi(x, y)$ containing only the three variables x, y, z.*

Again there is a model-theoretic characterization of the three-variable formalism, this time using 3-*invariance* under simulation of states, pairs of states, and triples of states. These propositions reflect a more general effective correspondence, between 'finite variable fragments' and complete finite sets of algebraic operators (cf. Gabbay [13]). In general then, the following Hierarchy arises:

level 1	is that of the Boolean operations
levels 2, 3	have been described above
further levels	will contain still more complex relational operators.

Corresponding invariances will provide ever finer views of processes. 2-simulation only preserved the structure of successive transitions, while 3-simulation allows decomposition of transitions into components, while making comparisons on both sides. And this finite-variable hierarchy extends indefinitely (van Benthem [47]):

Theorem 3.5 *The full first-order language over state structures is not exhausted by any of its k-variable fragments, and hence no finite set of algebraic operations is functionally complete for all of relation algebra in this wider sense.*

Our general conclusion is this:

'Logicality' in a dynamic setting is a notion of invariance across situations, or insensitivity to specific content. Moreover, this is not an absolute notion, as it admits of gradations, depending on the strength of simulation.

Remark 3.6 (Fine-structure). The above analysis also reveals the 'fine-structure' of proposed dynamic operations. For instance, 'strong negation' lies within the two-variable fragment:

$$\sim R \quad = \quad \lambda xy \bullet y = x \wedge \neg \exists x Ryx.$$

By contrast, composition is essentially of three-variable complexity—but taking *domains* of compositions involves only two variables:

$$\text{dom}(R \circ S) \quad = \quad \lambda x \bullet \exists y (Rxy \wedge \exists x Syx).$$

In our modal logic, ordinary updates lie within the two-variable fragment:

$$\lambda xy \bullet x \subseteq y \wedge Py \qquad \text{(algebraically } \subseteq \cap Do(P?)).$$

But the more complex minimal updates require three variables essentially:

$$\lambda xy \bullet x \subseteq y \wedge Py \wedge \neg \exists z (x \subset z \wedge z \subset y \wedge Pz).$$

3.1.2 Dynamic logic revisited

From a standard model-theoretic point of view, it is natural to consider both unary formulas $\varphi(x)$ and binary ones $\varphi(x, y)$. This brings us back to the earlier dynamic logic, where the above invariance analysis makes sense just as well. For the basic propositional dynamic logic, one needs so-called *modal zigzags*, that is, 2-simulations whose back-and-forth clauses refer only to taking R_a-successors of C-connected single states. This amounts to tracing a process entirely via successive atomic actions. Again, a characterization exists (van Benthem [44]):

Theorem 3.7 *The first-order formulas $\varphi(x)$ that are invariant for bisimulation are precisely those that are equivalent to translations of modal formulas (in a poly-modal logic with possibility operators for each atomic relation).*

This result can be extended to include complex programs with composition and union. (Statements involving *intersection* or *complement* need no longer be preserved.) Bisimulation invariance is a structural notion, and does not depend on any specific (first-order) formalism. In fact, a modal zigzag exists between two models if and only if these have the same theory in a poly-modal logic with arbitrary infinite conjunctions. (More technical details on this theme may be found in van Benthem [48].)

J. van Benthem

Other natural 'model shifting' constraints, relating evaluation of instructions in one model to that in its extensions, may throw a different light on our procedural repertoire. For instance, which relations $[\![\pi]\!]$ expressed in our language have the following

> *Persistence property*
> 'if M_1 is a submodel of M_2, then $[\![\pi]\!]_{M1}$ is the set-theoretic restriction of $[\![\pi]\!]_{M2}$ to the domain of M_1?'

This time, Boolean operations are completely harmless, but it is, rather, *composition* which may fail to be persistent. A transition might be decomposable into certain steps in the larger model which are not available in the smaller. And a similar observation applies to the earlier negation test $\sim \varphi$. This kind of model theory for dynamic logic still remains to be explored.

3.2 Varieties of inference

What would be a proper notion of *valid consequence* in a dynamic setting? As with 'logical constants' in earlier sections, the matter is no longer so clear-cut as in standard logic: there are many attractive options. Here is one natural imperative recipe:

I. *Achieving an effect*
   Process all premises successively, then see if the resulting transition is successful for the conclusion.

   Inclusion and *composition* are the key notions here: as we are demanding $[\![\varphi_1 \circ \ldots \circ \varphi_n]\!] \subseteq [\![\psi]\!]$. But there are other reasonable options, too, such as (Groenendijk and Stokhof [18]):

II. *Enabling a conclusion*
   Process all premises, then see if a transition can be made for the conclusion.

   Likewise, one could *test* the conclusion in the range of the composed premises (II@), thus mixing dynamic processing with static testing (cf. Veltman [53]). But there are still further options, such as the following more 'declarative' notions from Veltman [52], van Eyck and de Vries [50], respectively:

III. *Inclusion of fixed points*
   See if the conclusion 'holds' at all states where all premises 'hold'

   (where a proposition *holds* at a state if that state is among its fixed points).

IV. *Inclusion of domains*
The domain of the composition of all premises should be included in the domain of the conclusion.

Relational algebra provides a unifying perspective here. All the above notions of consequence may be reduced to the original proposal using standard relational operations (precise details are omitted here):

II. Range $(\varphi_1 \circ \ldots \circ \varphi_n) \subseteq$ Domain (ψ)
(the variant with test would have 'Diagonal(ψ)' on the right)

III. Diagonal$(\varphi_1 \cap \ldots \cap$ Diagonal$\varphi_n) \subseteq \psi$

IV. Domain$(\varphi_1 \circ \ldots \circ \varphi_n) \subseteq$ Domain (ψ)

These various notions of inference have quite different structural logical behaviour, which may be measured using the so-called *structural rules* of standard logic. For instance, the 'classical' style III has all the general properties of standard inference:

$$
\begin{array}{lll}
 & /\ \ C \Rightarrow C & \text{Reflexivity} \\
X \Rightarrow D \quad Y, D, Z \Rightarrow C & /\ \ Y, X, Z \Rightarrow C & \text{Cut rule} \\
X, P_1, P_2, Y \Rightarrow C & /\ \ X, P_2, P_1, Y \Rightarrow C & \text{Permutation} \\
X, P, Y, P, Z \Rightarrow C & /\ \ X, P, Y, Z \Rightarrow C & \text{Contraction} \\
X, P, Y, P, Z \Rightarrow C & /\ \ X, Y, P, Z \Rightarrow C & \text{Contraction} \\
X, Y \Rightarrow C & /\ \ X, P, Y \Rightarrow C & \text{Monotonicity}
\end{array}
$$

By contrast, the dynamic style I satisfies only reflexivity and cut, as is easy to check. Indeed, there are several *representation results* showing that such packages of structural rules determine these styles of inference precisely.

Proposition 3.8 {*monotonicity, contraction, reflexivity, cut*} *completely determine the structural properties of classical inference III.*

Proposition 3.9 {*reflexivity, cut*} *completely determine the structural properties of dynamic inference I.*

By way of illustration, we prove the first result in more detail.

PROOF. Let R be any abstract relation between finite sequences of objects and single objects satisfying the classical structural rules. Now, define

$$
A^* = \{X \mid X \text{ is a finite sequence of objects such that } XRA\}.
$$

Then, we have $X_1, \ldots, X_k RA$ only if $X_1^* \cap \ldots \cap X_k^* \subseteq A^*$, using cut and contraction, while the converse follows by reflexivity and monotonicity. ∎

But new religions need not be defined by listing the old dogmas they accept or reject. Their point may be precisely that these old dogmas are too crude as they stand. Inferential styles may in fact modify standard structural rules, reflecting a more delicate handling of premises. For instance, the above mixed style $II^@$ has none of the above structural properties (counter-examples are easy to produce), but it does satisfy

$$X \Rightarrow C \quad / \quad P, X \Rightarrow C \qquad \text{Left monotonicity}$$
$$X \Rightarrow D \quad Y, X, D, Z \Rightarrow C \quad / \quad Y, X, Z \Rightarrow C \quad \text{Left cut}$$

These principles even characterize this style of inference:

Proposition 3.10 {*left monotonicity, left cut*} *completely determine the structural properties of mixed inference* $II^@$.

PROOF. The following map from syntactic items to binary relations will work here:

$$A^\sharp = \{(X, X) \mid X \Rightarrow A\} \cup \{(X, XA) \mid \text{ all sequences } X\}.$$

■

For completeness' sake, without proof, here are complete sets of structural rules for the remaining two dynamic styles, which again involve suitable representations:

II.	$X \Rightarrow C$ / $P, X \Rightarrow C$		Left monotonicity
IV.	/ $C \Rightarrow C$		Reflexivity
	$X \Rightarrow C$ / $X, P \Rightarrow C$		Right monotonicity
	$X \Rightarrow D$ $Y, D \Rightarrow C$ / $Y, X \Rightarrow C$		Right cut

The general outcome of our analysis is this:

> Styles of inference correspond to different clusters of structural rules, each encoding its own 'processing mechanism' for determining validity.

Remark 3.11 (Power of relational algebra). Structural rules have the form of universal Horn clause assertions about propositions. Relational algebra has the power to formulate its own universal properties, at least in one important special case:

Fact 3.12 *For set relations, universal clauses involving algebraic identities are reducible to single identities.*

This property rests on the following observation. Any universal clause of the form 'universal prefix $\forall R_1 \ldots \forall R_n$, followed by a disjunction of equalities and inequalities between terms in $R_1, \ldots, R_n$' may be reduced as follows. By Boolean Algebra, it suffices to consider equalities of the form

'$A = 1$' . Next, inequalities may be replaced by equalities because of the key equivalence $A \neq 1$ iff $1 \circ -A \circ 1 = 1$. Finally, even one equality suffices for the remaining disjunction of equalities, thanks to chains of equivalences like the following (where '$A^\sharp$' abbreviates '$1 \circ -A \circ 1$') : $A = 1 \vee B = 1$, $\neg(A \neq 1 \wedge B \neq 1)$, $\neg(A^\sharp = 1 \wedge B^\sharp = 1)$, $A^\sharp \cap B^\sharp \neq 1$, $(A^\sharp \cap B^\sharp)^\sharp = 1$. Therefore, a large part of the structural properties of varieties of dynamic inference lies encoded within relational algebra itself. $\square$

Digression 3.13 (Special types of proposition). Besides general rules of inference, there are special inferential classes of dynamic propositions that can be studied. For instance, we have

Tests which do not change states:

$$\forall x \forall y (Rxy \rightarrow y = x) \qquad (\text{i.e. } R \subseteq \Delta).$$

Idempotent relations whose repetition will produce no further effect:

$$\forall x \forall y (Rxy \rightarrow Ryy) \qquad (\text{i.e., Domain}(R) \subseteq \text{Diagonal}(R)).$$

The latter property is plausible for 'updating' as well as 'testing' and 'realizing'.

Further special informational behaviour arises on models with inclusion, such as the 'updating' property of being a subrelation of $\subseteq$. Here, we only point at a general analogy with linguistics. Information may be compared with matter or time, and we have a so-called 'aspectual calculus' (Dowty [11], Krifka [30]) for various kinds of informative behaviour of propositions. In particular, there will be syntactic criteria to this effect. Which syntactic forms in the relational algebra over inclusion are updating? How do standard algebraic operations create, or modify this property? These concerns are a counterpart to standard questions in modal logic concerning syntactic recognition of 'hereditary' propositions.

3.3   Logical architecture

A third noticeable phenomenon in our dynamic logic is the co-existence of different components with possibly different logical constants and styles of inference, whose interaction is largely handled by modes and projections. We shall consider two aspects of 'logical management' that arise naturally in such a multi-level architecture.

3.3.1   Static tracing of dynamic procedures

One obvious concern is 'static tracing' of dynamic processes. For this purpose, a well-known technique from computer science may be used. Behaviour of imperative programs is often explained in terms of 'preconditions' and 'postconditions'. Starting from some set of states described by a predicate P, execution of a program π moves us to a new set of states (the 'image of P under π'), defined by the *strongest postcondition* of P under $\pi : SP(P,\pi)$. Conversely, one may also compute *weakest preconditions* for a resulting predicate under a program ('inverse images'): $WP(\pi, P)$. The two are related by conversion: $SP(P,\pi) = WP(\pi^\smile, P)$. Often, these operators may be computed recursively, in the style of the reduction axioms for $<\pi> \varphi$ in propositional dynamic logic, at least for suitable relational operators.

In particular, for dynamic predicate logic a simple mechanism computes the transient 'classical' informational contents of a dynamic process, via these decompositions:

$$
\begin{aligned}
WP(At, P) &= P \wedge At \\
WP(x := -, P) &= \exists x P \\
WP(\varphi_1 \circ \varphi_2, P) &= WP(\varphi_1, WP(\varphi_2, P)) \\
WP(\sim \varphi, P) &= P \wedge \neg WP(\varphi, T) \qquad \text{('}T\text{' for 'true').}
\end{aligned}
$$

This reduction also works for strongest postconditions, since dynamic predicate logic is closed under conversion $((At)^\smile = At, (x := -)^\smile = x := -, (\varphi \circ \psi)^\smile = \psi^\smile \circ \varphi^\smile, (\sim \varphi)^\smile = \sim \varphi)$. More direct recursion clauses look like this:

$$
\begin{aligned}
SP(P, At) &= P \wedge At \\
SP(P, x := -) &= \exists x P \\
SP(P, \varphi \circ \psi) &= SP(SP(P, \varphi), \psi) \\
SP(P, \sim \varphi) &= P \wedge \neg WP(\varphi, T) \ (!).
\end{aligned}
$$

Here is a sample computation on a sequence of dynamic formulas, with trace points indicated in bold-face subscripts:

$$
{}_0\exists x_1 (Ax_2 \circ Bx_3).\exists x_4 Cx_5.(\sim \exists x Dx)_6
$$

SP	0	T	1	$\exists x T = T$	2	Ax
	3	$Ax \wedge Bx$	4	$\exists x (Ax \wedge Bx)^*$	5	$\exists x (Ax \wedge Bx) \wedge Cx,$
	6	$\exists x (Ax \wedge Bx) \wedge Cx \wedge \neg \exists x Dx$		etcetera.		

At the trace point *, the initial $\exists x$ becomes an ordinary quantifier after all.

Similar calculations apply to other dynamic systems. For example, Veltman's update semantics admits of the following recursion clauses for on-line computation of classical content, in the modal logic S5:

$$
\begin{aligned}
SP(P, q) &= P \wedge q \\
SP(P, \varphi \wedge \psi) &= SP(SP(P, \varphi), \psi) \\
SP(P, \varphi \vee \psi) &= SP(P, \varphi) \vee SP(P, \psi) \\
SP(P, \neg \varphi) &= P \wedge \neg SP(P, \varphi) \\
SP(P, \Diamond \varphi) &= P \wedge \Diamond SP(P, \varphi)
\end{aligned}
$$

3.3.2   Uniformity of design

Despite the diversity of our architecture, there is also a clear mathematical uniformity. Most of the earlier techniques used in analyzing logical constants within Boolean or relational algebra make sense for their connecting categories of operators, too, when viewed in a suitable *type-theoretic* perspective. For instance, modes like 'test' or projections like 'domain' are both invariant for permutations of the underlying states in an obvious extended sense. Moreover, both of them are 'continuous' in that they commute with arbitrary unions of their arguments. All possibilities of this kind can be classified by prior reasoning:

Fact 3.14 *The only permutation-invariant continuous modes are those definable by a schema of the form*

$$\lambda P \bullet \lambda xy \bullet \exists z (Pz \wedge \text{'Boolean condition on } \{=, x, y, z\}\text{'}).$$

For instance, 'Test' reads:

$$\lambda P \bullet \lambda xy \bullet \exists z (Pz \wedge z = x = y).$$

All other possibilities are simple variations.

Fact 3.15 *The only permutation-invariant continuous projections are those definable by a schema of the form*

$$\lambda R \bullet \lambda x \bullet \exists yz (Ryz \wedge \text{'Boolean condition on } \{=, x, y, z\}\text{'})$$

'Fixed points' is one example here: $\lambda R \bullet \lambda x \bullet \exists yz (Ryz \wedge x = y = z)$, and so are 'Domain' ($\lambda R \bullet \lambda x \bullet \exists yz (Ryz \wedge x = y)$) and 'Range'. The other options are again simple variations.

Another management question concerning projections is whether there exists some map from procedures to statements preserving all relevant logical structure. In particular, one might expect that composition of procedures will reduce to conjunction of the corresponding declarative statements. But here, a negative result arises (provable by the techniques of van Benthem [45]):

Fact 3.16 *There is only one logical Boolean homomorphism from procedures to propositions, namely the diagonal fixed point map.*

The proof is based on a recipe for 'deflating' (logical) Boolean homomorphisms of a type $((a, t), (b, t))$ to arbitrary (logical) maps of the type (b, a), and then counting all mathematical possibilities there. But the diagonal map Δ does not match the operation o with $\cap$: $\Delta(\{(1, 2)\}o\{(2, 1)\}) = \{1\} \neq \varnothing = \Delta(\{(1, 2)\}) \cap \Delta(\{(2, 1)\})$. As for modes, we have the following

Fact 3.17 *Among the logical (permutation-invariant) modes, exactly two are Boolean homomorphisms:* $\lambda P \bullet \lambda xy \bullet Py, \lambda P \bullet \lambda xy \bullet Px$ *('left and right expansion') .*

Remark 3.18 (Translating inference). The above is related to the following statement. The two-level system has inference going on both between propositions and between procedures. Say, propositions have standard inference and procedures the earlier dynamic inference. Then, we want to see whether one mechanism can be related systematically to the other. One direction is easy: standard inference may be simulated within the dynamic style using the test mode ?:

$$P_1, \ldots, P_n \vDash_{\text{classs}} C \quad \text{iff} \quad ?(P_1), \ldots, ?(P_n) \vDash_{\text{dyn}} ?(C).$$

In the opposite direction, however, the diagonal fix point operator Δ will not work. By a simple argument, such a reduction would make dynamic reasoning monotonic: quod non.   □

Other modes and projections are not without mathematical structure either. For instance, both test and domain had the important Boolean property of 'continuity'. As with homomorphisms, all continuous logical modes and projections can easily be classified: and they turn out to form a finite set.

Our conclusion is this:

> Dynamic logic admits of a perspicuous architecture in which the same notions of logicality, as well as other general semantic properties, make sense across components of different types. Moreover, the interaction between components may be described by means of systematic computational mechanisms.

4   Elaborating the paradigm

The main claim of this paper is that the above systems of relational algebra and dynamic logic provide a convenient architecture for bringing out essential logical features of action and cognition. Further evidence for this view may be found in [9], which investigates dynamic modal logic in more technical detail, and in Van Eyck and de Vries [50, 51] which apply Hoare-style correctness fragments of dynamic logic to matters of linguistic interpretation and inference. Nevertheless, this picture also needs some *clair-obscur*.

There are obvious refinements of the relational paradigm. Each proposition may also be assigned the 'trace set' of finite sequences of atomic transitions traversed during its successful computations, recording intermediate stages that are lost in an 'extensional' input–output account of dynamics. In fact, 'transition models' $(S, \{R_a \mid a \in A\})$ can be mapped to 'trace models' S^* whose domains consist of all *finite sequences* of states from S. Evaluation of complex propositions in trace models may then follow its own intuitions. In particular, compositions $P \circ Q$ will now refer to *concatenation* of sequences in $[\![P]\!], [\![Q]\!]$, respectively, having matching ends and beginnings. The latter approach takes us closer to the 'language models' studied in [47]: trace models are families of 'transition languages' for processes. Hence, the resulting logic is related to 'occurrence logics' in the linguistic paradigm of categorial grammar. An even finer view of dynamic processes would be provided by introducing various forms of 'process algebra', preserving more information about traces of computations (Milner, [34], Harel, Kozen and Parikh [20], Bergstra and Klop [7]). The latter direction would be quite in line with the emphasis on 'bisimulation' of processes emphasized in Section 3.1 above (cf. Bergstra and van Benthem [8]).

The modelling given so far may eventually prove not radical enough. After all, if logical dynamics is of equal importance to logical statics, then the two ought to be accorded equal ontological status. This means that *transitions* would come to be viewed, not as ordered pairs of states, but rather as independent basic objects in their own right. Thus, the relevant mathematical paradigm would no longer be relational algebra with its intended set-theoretic semantics, but rather some form of 'arrow logic' ([47, 54]), manipulating sets of transition arrows connected by 'composition' and other relations. Transition arrows can be extensionally the same in having equal starting and finishing points, without being intensionally identical. Moreover, not every ordered pair of states needs to be represented by an arrow. This paradigm can still be developed in an analogy with modal logic, which makes it congenial to the systems investigated here.

The latter move might also alleviate a problem of computational complexity. Relational algebra is known to be a more complex theory than Boolean algebra. More generally, many currently proposed dynamic logics tend to be more complex than their static counterparts. (This is in fact a disturbing paradox, given the practical motivation of current 'cognitive dynamics', as being supposedly closer to the reasoning practice of human agents. Somehow, our current theories still get the 'balance of labour' wrong in some essential way, that is still ill-understood.) Indeed, relational algebra is undecidable: such being the price of its greater expressive power. But arrow logics are often decidable, combining sophistication with simplicity (cf. [2, 33] for the current state of the art in this enterprise).

In the end, it remains to be seen how much procedural structure can be captured in our semantic approach. Many important procedural aspects of cognition seem deeply linked to the actual syntactic lay-out of arguments, or the actual course of games. What compositional semantics tends to do is provide only limited access here, by discarding the syntactic structure that produced its denotations. (Admittedly, for some purposes, that is precisely its strength.) This is unnatural, since humans do have short-term recall of syntactic structure: so, why not make use of it? In this respect, recent proof-theoretic approaches, like those of Kracht [29], Ranta [38], Gabbay and Kempson [14] may have their advantages, identifying states with more proof-theoretic 'contexts', allowing for a more flexible dynamics, switching between what was said and how it was said.

Finally, once more, we admit to a free-wheeling attitude toward (natural) 'language' in the design of a logical system. The crucial issue is to understand human action and cognition, whether or not it is fully encoded linguistically. It would be wilful suppression of the evidence to stick with the 'letter' of cognition rather than its 'spirit' (cf. Levelt [31]). And indeed, the procedural perspective is rather unorthodox, in that one is equating lexical expressions, such as 'and', 'if' or 'not', with discourse particles like 'so', or even just punctuation signs, such as commas or dots. (See Jennings [25], Došen [10] for earlier views of logical constants as 'punctuation marks'.) In fact, even typographical devices may be obvious 'mode switchers', witness question or exclamation marks, or semicolons inside a sentence. And from graphics, the border line to acoustics, or even just abstract game conventions 'in the air', becomes quite fluid, in line with the 'heterogeneous design' of various current paradigms (cf. Barwise and Etchemendy [5]). This attitude has already been advocated in Hintikka [23], Barwise and Perry [6]: studying cognition entirely via one dimension amounts to an 'existential projection' which might be more complex than the full picture. Logical analysis is entitled to the use of any rational clue in discourse and argumentation.

Addendum

Proliferation of 'logical systems' is characteristic of current research. This phenomenon has led to some largely unpublished but quite persistent debate in the logical community concerning boundaries and definitions. I will use this opportunity to present some thoughts on this matter.

Does anything go these days, or can one rightfully dismiss at least some new-fangled proposals as 'non-logical' in some proper sense? This debate is partly substantial and partly terminological and, as usual, the latter admixture tends to make discussions only more acrimonious. For instance, mainstream logicians have negative gut reactions to current non-monotonic systems (such as circumscription or preferential entailment), feeling that these have forfeited their logical birth-right. And those who can live with non-monotonicity have been known to object to current non-commutative systems (such as categorial or dynamic logics): even down the slippery slope, people want to draw a line somewhere ... This reaction persists all the way, as the distance from classical systems gets larger. Recently, linear logicians, who have been willing to give up both monotonicity and (to some extent) commutativity, have voiced vehement objections to giving up associativity for logical premisses (as happens in recent logics of syntactic structure). Everybody has a last stand, it seems, but where is it to be fought?

I think that this situation calls for an entirely different analysis from the received one. Let us first formulate what seems to be the general view behind the above reactions. There is a dominant opinion among logicians and philosophers that what makes a system 'logical' is to be located in certain axioms or rules of inference (or even in certain desirable meta-properties, such as cut elimination). Like most received views, this one usually comes without explicit motivation except perhaps the scholarly point that this is what our founding fathers thought. As it happens, though, a well-argued statement of this kind of position may be found in Dana Scott's celebrated paper 'On Engendering an Illusion of Understanding', which has been justly influential for its clarity and elegance. The proposal for a demarcation line given there is the following. The core topic of Logic is the study of 'inference relations', and the latter can be characterized by three structural properties that capture the essentials of transmitting inferential information: Reflexivity, Transitivity (Cut) and Monotonicity. To be sure, other formal relations between propositions may be interesting too, but they are then not 'logical'. This conception of Logic is very attractive, and indeed, it is precisely that proposed in the early nineteenth century in Bernard Bolzano's 'Wissenschaftslehre'. But this historical reference also illustrates a problem. Bolzano thought that inference relations were what Logic is all about, but he certainly did not specify any fixed core of specific structural rules in advance. Instead, he studied a wide variety of styles of inference (including 'domestic', 'statistical', 'strict'), carefully recording their rather divergent structural properties without taking any a priori stand.

Indeed, I would like to suggest that no 'core canon' of structural properties exists that could form a rock bottom for 'logical' system-building. This agnosticism on my part (like its religious counterpart) was prompted by the lack of consensus among believers. But its most important motivation is one of principle. What matters in 'logicality', in my view, is not located in any 'extensional' behaviour of an inference relation; rather, what matters are certain general qualities of a logical system, more elusive than a list of structural rules and much more difficult to capture in simple terms. Here is an attempt. To a first approximation, I would call a system 'logical' if it satisfies two conditions, an empirical one of descriptive relevance and a methodological one of mathematical spirit: the system should bring out some broad mechanism occurring in 'natural reasoning', and it should be designed using 'logical standards' of clarity and precision. The process of bringing out broad mechanisms of reasoning is an ongoing and perhaps open-ended enterprise: recent examples are various forms of 'resource-awareness' (as in linear logic or categorial logic) and 'procedural awareness' (as in dynamic logics). Of course, the great core systems of standard logic embody insights concerning natural reasoning that are of at least the same order of magnitude! Once such a general phenomenon is well-analysed by a logical system, its possible 'non-monotonicity' or 'non-commutativity' will be seen to be a secondary, predictable behaviouristic issue. For instance, even the non-declarative systems of 'dynamic inference' found in this Chapter must be considered logical by these criteria, because they reflect important aspects of actual reasoning (order dependence, procedurality), and can be designed and studied by the same rigorous techniques, and by researchers with the same unmistakeable 'logical mind set', as earlier systems.

In this light, the real question for discussion will now come to shift. Having said what a logical system is, perhaps we should go on to say what a 'good' logical system is. Compare the situation in the sciences, where the main point of interest would not seem to be whether a proposed system is, say, 'physical', but whether it is good physics. This viewpoint also allows us to add some fine-structure to the above general criteria. For instance, two requirements of a good theory may be found in the philosophy of science which relate it to the preceding core of its discipline. One is that a new theory should preferably shed additional light upon its predecessors, perhaps even explaining why they did so well within their own assumptions. The other is that it should enrich the agenda of the field in novel ways. Many current 'logical systems' indeed meet these further criteria. For instance, linear logic, non-monotonic preferential logics or dynamic logics all 'explain' classical logic as a natural idealization from their richer perspective, while raising new theoretical issues of their own.

Thus, the present proposal does not disqualify earlier views: it merely puts them in a broader perspective. This seems the normal course of scientific research, and Logic is no exception. The natural mathematization of many inferential mechanisms will reveal a broad 'landscape' of new options, and providing some 'systematic parametrization' might well be a general methodological requirement for good logical system building! Now, such landscapes will have 'natural ridges', which dominate their environment. For instance, the Tarski–Scott analysis certainly identifies one landmark which cannot be missed by any sensible traveller. (Another instance of this style of analysis is the well-known landscape of invariances for different notions of 'logicality' of operators.) And I am willing to go one step further, again borrowing an analogy from physics. In all recent systems of logic, a Bohr-style 'Correspondence Principle' seems at work. 'In the limit', the new systems all reduce to classical logic (think of intuitionistic logic with 'total information', preferential logic with 'universal indifference', linear logic with 'unbounded resources', or dynamic logic with 'successful testing'). Perhaps a more refined Tarski-Scott Thesis is tenable, namely that under appropriate idealizations any genuine 'logical system' should contain classical logic as a special case.

Finally, this alternative view has some side-benefits. Constructively, it encourages one to move away from arid taxonomies of axioms or structural rules to broad phenomena. Moreover, it provides a much more dynamic view of the 'treasures' of our discipline: not in museum boxes labeled with some particular axiom or rule or even calculus (whether Frege's, Heyting's or Girard's), but rather in broad notions and techniques. Thus, what is essential to Logic is not the structure of its products but the structure of its activities. The latter view seems to have the greater evolutionary survival value, too.

Of course, I cannot hope to have convinced those who prefer short lunchtime debates and clear dogmatic opinions. My account is more philosophical, less clear-cut and to a large extent dependent on 'good sense'. But I do feel that 'logicality' is just that way.

References

[1] J. Allen. Maintaining knowledge about temporal intervals. *Communications of the Association for Computing Machinery*, 26:832–843, 1983.

[2] H. Andréka, A. Kurucz, I. Németi, I. Sain and A. Simon. Exactly which logics touched by the dynamic trend are decidable? In P. Dekker and M. Stokhof, eds., *Proceedings of the 9th Amsteram Colloquium*, pp. 44–66, Institute for Logic, Language and Computation, University of Amsterdam, 1993.

[3] J. Barwise. Noun phrases, generalized quantifiers and anaphora. In P. Gärdenfors, editor, *Generalized Quantifiers. Logical and Linguistic Approaches*, pages 1–29. Reidel, Dordrecht, 1987.

[4] J. Barwise and J. Etchemendy. *Tarski's World*. Academic Software, 1988.

[5] J. Barwise and J. Etchemendy. Reasoning in hyper-proof. Technical report, Center for the Study of Language and Information, Stanford University, 1991.

[6] J. Barwise and J. Perry. *Situations and Attitudes.* Bradford Books / MIT Press, Cambridge (Mass.), 1983.

[7] J. Bergstra and J.-W. Klop. Process algebra for synchronous communication. *Information and Control*, 60:109–137, 1984.

[8] J. van Benthem and J. Bergstra. Logic of Transition Systems. Technical Report CT-93-03, Institute for Logic, Language and Computation, University of Amsterdam, 1993. To appear in *Journal of Logic, Language and Information.*

[9] M. de Rijke. Extending Modal Logic. PhD thesis, Institute for Logic, Language and Computation, University of Amsterdam, 1993.

[10] K. Došen. Logical constants as punctuation marks. *Notre Dame Journal of Formal Logic*, 30:362–381, 1989.

[11] D. Dowty. *Word Meaning and Montague Grammar.* Reidel, Dordrecht, 1979.

[12] R. Floyd. Assigning meanings to programs. In *Proceedings AMS Symposia in Applied Mathematics 19*, American Mathematical Society, Providence, (R.I.), pages 19–31, 1967.

[13] D. M. Gabbay. Functional completeness in tense logic. In U. Mönnich, editor, *Aspects of Philosophical Logic*, pages 91–117. Reidel, Dordrecht, 1981.

[14] D. M. Gabbay and R. Kempson. Natural-language content: A proof-theoretic perspective. Technical report, Department of Computing, Imperial College / Department of Linguistics, School of Oriental and African Studies, London, 1991.

[15] P. Gärdenfors. Propositional logic based on the dynamics of belief. *Journal of Symbolic Logic*, 50:390–394, 1984.

[16] P. Gärdenfors. *Knowledge in Flux. Modelling the Dynamics of Epistemic States.* Bradford Books / MIT Press, Cambridge (Mass.), 1988.

[17] V. Goranko and S. Passy. Using the universal modality: Gains and questions. Technical report, Mathematical Institute, Kliment Ohridski University, Sofia, 1990.

[18] J. Groenendijk and M. Stokhof. Dynamic predicate logic. *Linguistics and Philosophy*, 14:39–100, 1990.

[19] D. Harel. Dynamic logic. In D. Gabbay and F. Guenthner, editors, *Handbook of Philosophical Logic, vol. II*, pages 497–604. Reidel, Dordrecht, 1984.

[20] D. Harel, D. Kozen, and R. Parikh. Process logic: Expressiveness, decidability, completeness. *Journal of Computer and Systems Sciences*, 25:144–170, 1982.

[21] I. Heim. The Semantics of Definite and Indefinite Noun Phrases. PhD thesis, Department of Linguistics, University of Masssachusetts, Amherst, 1982.

[22] L. Henkin, D. Monk and A. Tarski. *Cylindric Algebra, Part II*, North-Holland, Amsterdam, 1985.

[23] J. Hintikka. *Logic, Language Games and Information*. Clarendon Press, Oxford, 1973.

[24] J. Hintikka. Quantifiers versus quantification theory. *Dialectica*, 27:329–358, 1973.

[25] R. Jennings. Logic as punctuation. In W. Leinfellner and F. Wuketits, editors, *The Tasks of Contemporary Philosophy*. Schriftenreihe der Wittgenstein Gesellschaft, Hölder-Pichler-Tempsky Verlag, Wien, 1986.

[26] B. Jónsson. The theory of binary relations. Technical report, Department of Mathematics, VanderBilt University, Nashville (Tenn.), 1984.

[27] H. Kamp. Instants, events and temporal discourse. In R. Bäuerle, U. Egli and A. von Stechow, editors, *Semantics from Different Points of View*, pages 376–417. Springer Verlag, Berlin, 1979.

[28] H. Kamp. A theory of truth and semantic representation. In J. Groenendijk, Th. Janssen and M. Stokhof, editors, *Truth, Interpretation and Information*, pages 1–41. Foris, Dordrecht, 1984.

[29] M. Kracht. How to say "it". Technical report, Mathematisches Institut, Freie Universität, Berlin, 1988.

[30] M. Krifka. Nominal reference, temporal constitution, and quantification in event semantics. In R. Bartsch, J. van Benthem and P. van Emde Boas, editors, *Semantics and Contextual Expression*, pages 75–115. Foris, Dordrecht, 1989.

[31] W. J. Levelt. *Speaking. From Intention to Articulation*. The MIT Press, Cambridge (Mass.), 1989.

[32] P. Lorenzen. *Metamathematik*. Bibliographisches Institut, Mannheim, 1962.

[33] M. Marx, Sz. Mikulas, I. Németi and I. Sain. Investigations in arrow logic. In M. Marx and L. Pólos, eds., *Arrow Logic and Multimodal Logics*, CCSOM, University of Amsterdam, 1994.

[34] R. Milner. *A Calculus of Communicating Systems*. Springer Verlag, Berlin, 1980.

[35] I. Németi. Algebraizations of quantifier logics: an introductory overview. Technical report, Institute of Mathematics, Hungarian Academy of Sciences, Budapest, 1990. (Shortened version in *Studia Logica*, **50**, 485–569, 1991.)

[36] R. Parikh. The logic of games and its applications. Technical report, Department of Computer and Information Sciences, Brooklyn College, SUNY, New York, 1984.

[37] A. Pnueli. The temporal logic of programs. In *Proceedings 18th IEEE Symposium on Foundations of Computer Science*, American Mathematical Society, Providence, RI, pages 46–57, 1977.

[38] A. Ranta. Intuitionistic categorial grammar. Technical report, Institute for Language, Logic and Information, University of Amsterdam, 1990. Appeared in *Linguistics and Philosophy*, **14**, 203–239, 1991.

[39] E. Sandewall. The semantics of non-monotonic entailment defined using partial interpretations. In M. Reinfrank, J. de Kleer, M. Ginzberg, and E. Sandewall, editors, *Non-Monotonic Reasoning*, pages 27–41. Springer Verlag, Lecture Notes in Artificial Intelligence, 1989.

[40] P. Seuren. *Tussen Taal en Denken*. Oosthoek, Scheltema en Holkema, Utrecht, 1975.

[41] P. Seuren. *Discourse Semantics*. Blackwell, Oxford, 1986.

[42] W. Spohn. Ordinal conditional functions: A dynamic theory of epistemic states. In W. L. Harper, R. Stalnaker and G. Pearce, editors, *Causation in Decision, Belief Change and Statistics II*, pages 105–134. Kluwer, Dordrecht, 1988.

[43] R. Stalnaker. Pragmatics. In D. Davidson and G. Harman, editors, *Semantics of Natural Language*, pages 380–397. Reidel, Dordrecht, 1972.

[44] J. van Benthem. *Modal Logic and Classical Logic*. Bibliopolis, Naples, 1985.

[45] J. van Benthem. *Essays in Logical Semantics*. Reidel, Dordrecht, 1986.

[46] J. van Benthem. Modal logic as a theory of information. Technical Report LP-89-05, Institute for Language, Logic and Information, University of Amsterdam, 1989. In J. Copeland, ed., *Proceedings Arthur Prior Memorial Conference*, Christchurch, New Zealand, Oxford University Press, 1994.

[47] J. van Benthem. *Language in Action. Categories, Lambdas and Dynamic Logic*, volume 130 of *Studies in Logic*. North-Holland, Amsterdam, 1991.

[48] J. van Benthem. Logic and the flow of information. Technical Report LP-91-10, Institute for Logic, Language and Computation, University of Amsterdam, 1991. To appear in D. Prawitz, B. Skyrms and D. Westerståhl, eds., *Proceedings 9th International Congress of Logic, Methodology and Philosophy of Science. Uppsala 1991*, North-Holland, Amsterdam, 1993, pages 693–724.

[49] J. van Benthem. Logic as programming. Technical report, Institute for Logic, Language and Computation, University of Amsterdam, 1991. Appeared in *Fundamenta Informaticae*, **17**, 295–317, 1992.

[50] J. van Eyck and F.-J. de Vries. Dynamic interpretation and Hoare deduction. *Journal of Logic, Language and Information*, 1(1):1–44, 1992.

[51] J. van Eyck and F.-J. de Vries. A sound and complete calculus for update logic. Technical report, Centre for Mathematics and Computer Science, Amsterdam, 1992.

[52] F. Veltman. Update semantics. Technical report, Institute for Language, Logic and Information, University of Amsterdam, 1988.

[53] F. Veltman. Defaults in update semantics. Technical report, Institute for Language, Logic and Information, University of Amsterdam, 1990. To appear in *Journal of Philosophical Logic*.

[54] Y. Venema. A crash course in arrow logic. To appear in M. Masuch and L. Polos, editors, *Arrow Logic and Multimodal Logics*, Oxford University Press.

5

What is a Deductive System?

Joachim Lambek

1 Introduction

We discuss various styles of presnting deductive systems, with and without structural rules, paying some attention to equality between deductions.

A deductive system should deal with

(a) formulas, (b) deductions, alias proofs, (c) equality between de-

ductions.

While most, if not all, logicians would agree with (a) and (b), they have often neglected (c), the importance of which is now becoming apparent under the influence of category theory and computer science. Computer scientists may even go further and replace the equality in (c) by a partial order called 'reduction'.

We may distinguish a number of different styles of presenting a logical system, according to the shape of the deductions.

1. Hilbert style: deductions have the form $f : \ \to B$, meaning that f is a proof of B without any hypotheses. We usually just write $f \in B$.

2. Lawvere style: deductions have the form $f : A \to B$, meaning that f is a proof of B from A.

3. Gentzen intuitionistic style: deductions have the form $f : A_1 \cdots A_m \to B$, meaning that f is a proof of B from the hypotheses $A_1 \cdots A_m$, $m \geq 0$.

4. Gentzen classical style: deductions have the form $f : A_1 \cdots A_m \to B_1 \cdots B_n$, meaning that f is a proof of of the alternatives $B_1 \cdots B_n$ from the hypotheses $A_1 \cdots A_m$, $m, n \geq 0$.

5. Schütte style: deductions have the form $f : \quad \to B_1 \cdots B_n$, meaning that f is a proof of the alternatives $B_1 \cdots B_n$ without any hypotheses.

As to deductions of the form $A \to$ (deriving a contradiction from A), $A \to B_1 \cdots B_n$ (deriving a bunch of alternatives from A) and $A_1 \cdots A_m \to$ (deriving a contradiction from a bunch of hypotheses), they follow by arrow reversal from (1), (3) and (5) respectively. It is assumed here that m and n are non-negative integers.

The above descriptions leave out the occasional necessity of declaring variables. Often the arrow in a deduction is decorated with a subscript $X = \{x_1, \cdots, x_k\}$, say $f : A_1 \cdots A_m \underset{X}{\to} B$ in Case 3, where the x_i exhaust all the variables which may occur freely in the A_j and B.

What are formulas? It is usually assumed that formulas are constructed from certain atomic formulas with the help of certain connectives and sometimes quantifiers. The atomic formulas may themselves have structure, for example they may be of the form $a = b$ or $a \in \alpha$, where a, b and α are terms of certain types. We shall not pursue this possibility further in the present exposition. On the other hand, formulas may be variables X, Y, $\cdots$; we shall concentrate on this possibility here. As to compound formulas, we will allow, for example, the nullary connective $\top$, which may also be regarded as an atomic formula, $A \wedge B$ and $A \Rightarrow B$, where $\wedge$ and $\Rightarrow$ are binary connectives and A and B are previously given formulas. We might also allow such expressions as $\forall_x F(x)$, where $\forall_x$ is a quantifier, and $F(x)$ is a previously given formula in which the free variable x has been displayed for purposes of substitution. Here we shall confine attention to expressions $\forall_X F(X)$, where X is a propositional variable, ranging over formulas, already mentioned as an atomic formula above.

Assuming that we are acquainted with the formulas, let us take a closer look at deductions and equations between them. As regards (5), these deductions were introduced by Schütte [28] and championed by Schwichtenberg [29]. They play a basic rôle in Girard's [8] discussion of proofnets. I have yet to make use of them in my own work and will consider them here only reluctantly, though with arrows reversed.

2   Hilbert style proofs

In this section we shall assume given a binary connective $\Rightarrow$ called 'implication'. For the purpose of illustration, we shall present the proof theory of *intuitionistic* implication, even if Hilbert might turn over in his grave at the mention of the restrictive adjective. Given proofs a of A (write $a \in A$) and f of $A \Rightarrow B$, one may obtain a proof $f'a$ (read f *of* a) of B, by an ancient construction called 'modus ponens'. Axioms for intuitionistic implication may now be stated as follows:

$I_A \in A \Rightarrow A,$

$K_{AB} \in A \Rightarrow (B \Rightarrow A),$

$S_{ABC} \in (A \Rightarrow (B \Rightarrow C)) \Rightarrow ((A \Rightarrow B) \Rightarrow (A \Rightarrow C)).$

From these axioms one can form other proofs by modus ponens, for example,

$(*) \quad S_{(B \Rightarrow C)BC} \, {}^\backprime I_{B \Rightarrow C} \in ((B \Rightarrow C) \Rightarrow B) \Rightarrow ((B \to C) \Rightarrow C),$

$(**) \quad (S_{ABA} \, {}^\backprime K_{AB}) {}^\backprime K_{AB} \in A \Rightarrow A.$

The system is intuitionistic, for example, because it allows no proof of the classical tautology $((A \Rightarrow B) \Rightarrow A) \Rightarrow A$.

We shall write $x \in A$ for an assumption that A holds, or rather for a particular occurrence of this assumption in a proof, since A may be assumed more than once in the same proof. The usual *deduction theorem* may now be stated as follows:

Given a proof $\phi(x)$ of B based on the assumption x of A, there exists a proof f of $A \Rightarrow B$.

Now what about equations between proofs? For example, are we to regard $(S_{ABA} {}^\backprime K_{AB}) {}^\backprime K_{AB}$ as equal to or different from I_A? We shall return to this question later.

It is customary to postulate the following equations suggested by Schönfinkel:

1. (i) $I_A {}^\backprime x = x,$

2. (ii) $(K_{AB} {}^\backprime x) {}^\backprime y = x,$

3. (iii) $((S_{ABC} {}^\backprime u) {}^\backprime v) {}^\backprime x = (u {}^\backprime x) {}^\backprime (v {}^\backprime x),$

based on the assumptions $x \in A$, $y \in B$, $u \in A \Rightarrow (B \Rightarrow C)$ and $v \in A \Rightarrow B$. With the help of these equations, one can improve the deduction theorem as follows:

Given a proof $\phi(x)$ of B based on the assumption x of A, there exists a proof f of $A \Rightarrow B$ such that $f {}^\backprime x = \phi(x)$.

The proof of this result should be ascribed to Schönfinkel, but with two reservations. First, he had a functional interpretation in mind, for example, he thought of f not as a proof but as a function from A to B. Perhaps he did not even realize the connection, later pointed out by Curry, between his result and the deduction theorem. Secondly, he omitted all mention of the formulas A, B and C and wrote I, K and S without subscripts. His result whould be better phrased in the language of universal algebra:

Given an algebra with one binary operation ${}^\backprime$ and three nullary operations I, K and S satisfying the identities (i) to (iii), every polynomial $\phi(x)$ can be written in the form $\phi(x) = f {}^\backprime x$, where f is a constant.

The constant f will be unique, provided we postulate:

(iv) if $f'x = g'x$ then $f = g$.

It then follows that $(S_{ABA}'K_{AB})'K_{AB} = I_A$, once one shows that $((S_{ABA}$ $'K_{AB})'K_{AB})'x = I_A'x$ with the help of (**). In fact, Schönfinkel had taken advantage of this result to *define* I as $(S'K)'K$.

The fact that (iv) is an implication and not an equation goes counter to the spirit of universal algebra. In fact, Curry (see e.g. Curry and Feys [7]) succeeded in replacing (iv) by a family of identities. For a more recent derivation of such a set of equations, see Lambek [17].

Making use of the equations replacing (iv), we can improve the deduction theorem once more and obtain the following:

Given a proof $\phi(x)$ of B based on the assumption x of A, there exists a unique proof f of $A \Rightarrow B$ such that $f'x = \phi(x)$.

Under the intended functional interpretation, this may be restated as a theorem about a many-sorted algebra with a type forming operation $\Rightarrow$ satisfying (i) to (iii) and the identities replacing (iv):

Given a polynomial $\phi(x)$ of type B in the indeterminate x of type A, there exists a unique constant f of type $A \Rightarrow B$ such that $f'x = \phi(x)$.

This property has been called 'functional completeness' by Rosenbloom [26]. One usually writes $f = \lambda_{x \in A}\phi(x)$, so that the existence and uniqueness of the constant f are expressed as follows:

$$(\beta') \quad (\lambda_{x \in A}\phi(x))'x = \phi(x),$$
$$(\eta) \quad \lambda_{x \in A}(f'x) = f.$$

Exploiting the universal property of indeterminates, we may replace (β') by the more familiar:

$$(\beta) \quad (\lambda_{x \in A}\phi(x))'a = \phi(a),$$

where a is a constant of type A and $\phi(a)$ is the result of substituting a for x in $\phi(x)$.

In the account of equality given in this section, we have neglected to *declare variables* in order to simplify the exposition. (For a clue how variables ought to be declared, see Section 5 below.)

I do not like the Hilbert approach for several reasons. It won't work for a logical system which lacks the connective $\Rightarrow$. The axioms seem rather artificial, as though they had been pulled out of a hat. The discussion of equality between proofs can become quite complicated, see, for example, Curry and Feys [7], certainly not as transparent as equality of arrows in a cartesian closed category.

3 Lawvere style deductions

Evidently, we require for each formula a deduction:

$$1_A : A \to A$$

and the following *rule of inference*, or recipe for creating new deductions from old:

$$\frac{f : A \to B \qquad g : B \to C}{gf : A \to C}.$$

Had we not been interested in distinguishing different deductions from A to B, we could have omitted the labels f and g, in which case we would just be stating the usual reflexive and transitive laws of the arrow, viewed as a binary relation between formulas. However, we wish to allow the possibility of having different deductions of B from A, but we should at least insist on the following equations:

$$f1_A = f, \ 1_B f = f, \ (hg)f = h(gf),$$

where it is assumed that $h : C \to D$. A deductive system subject to these equations is called a *category*.

Lawvere's [23] basic insight was that one can now introduce the connectives $\top$, $\wedge$ and $\Rightarrow$ and the quantifier $\forall_X$ in a natural way as 'adjoint functors'. Let $\mathcal{C}$ be the category of formulas and deductions, $\mathbf{1}$ the *terminal* category consisting of one object and one arrow and $\mathcal{C} \times \mathcal{C}$ the cartesian product of $\mathcal{C}$ with itself, then

$$\top : \mathbf{1} \to \mathcal{C}, \ \wedge : \mathcal{C} \times \mathcal{C} \to \mathcal{C}, \ A \Rightarrow - : \mathcal{C} \to \mathcal{C}$$

may be defined as right adjoints to the following functors respectively:

$$\circ_{\mathcal{C}} : \mathcal{C} \to \mathbf{1}, \ \Delta_{\mathcal{C}} : \mathcal{C} \to \mathcal{C} \times \mathcal{C}, \ A \wedge - : \mathcal{C} \to \mathcal{C},$$

where $\circ_{\mathcal{C}}$ is the unique functor $\mathcal{C} \to \mathbf{1}$ and $\Delta_{\mathcal{C}}$ the 'diagonal' functor. In the same spirit, one could introduce

$$\forall_X : \mathcal{C}[X] \to \mathcal{C}$$

as the right adjoint of the inclusion functor

$$I_X : \mathcal{C} \to \mathcal{C}[X],$$

provided we can make sense out of $\mathcal{C}[X]$, which should be a deductive system obtained from $\mathcal{C}$ by somehow adjoining an indeterminate formula X.

I am sure that, by now, I have lost those of my readers who are not steeped in the language of category theory. Fortunately, it is possible to translate all this into ordinary prose.

We begin by postulating the following deductions and rules of inference:

$$\circ_A : A \to \top; \qquad \pi_{AB} : A \wedge B \to A, \qquad \varepsilon_{AC} : A \wedge (A \Rightarrow C) \to C,$$
$$\pi'_{AB} : A \wedge B \to B,$$

$$\frac{f:C\to A \qquad g:C\to B}{<f,g>:C\to A\wedge B;} \qquad\qquad \frac{f:A\wedge B\to C}{f^*:B\to A\Rightarrow C.}$$

So far, every logician will recognize a simple presentation of the positive intuitionistic propositional calculus. However, to give a complete translation of Lawvere's categorical formulation, we must also insist on the following equations between deductions:

$$f = \circ_A; \qquad \pi_{AB} < f,g >= f, \qquad \varepsilon_{AC} < \pi_{AB}, f^*\pi'_{AB} >= f,$$
$$\pi'_{AB} < f,g >= g, \qquad (\varepsilon_{AC} < \pi_{AB}, g\pi'_{AB} >)^* = g.$$
$$< \pi_{AB}h, \pi'_{AB}h >= h;$$

It is here assumed that

$$f : A \to \top, \qquad\qquad h : C \to A \wedge B, \qquad\qquad g : B \to A \Rightarrow C,$$

in the respective columns.

The kind of category described by the above equations is called a *cartesian closed category* (CCC) and was introduced by Lawvere in his thesis, although our equational presentation is more recent. We shall leave discussion of the universal quantifier to a later section.

If $\mathcal{C}$ is a CCC, it is possible to make sense out of $\mathcal{C}[x]$, where $x : \top \to A$ is an *indeterminate* arrow, and to consider *polynomial* arrows $\phi(x) : \top \to B$ living in $\mathcal{C}[x]$. To a logician, $x : \top \to A$ is just an occurrence of the assumption A in a proof and $\phi(x) : \top \to B$ is a proof of B from this assumption. The usual deduction theorem tells us that there should exist a proof $g : A \to B$ without any assumption. In fact, it has been shown that there is a unique arrow $g : A \to B$ in $\mathcal{C}$ such that $gx = \phi(x)$ in $\mathcal{C}[x]$. We call this property 'functional completeness' as in Section 2.

To prove functional completeness one must generalize it to allow polynomials of the form $\phi(x) : C \to B$, which form a set closed under composition. For details of the proof see the work of Lambek [17] or Lambek and Scott [22].

As pointed out by Lawvere long ago, there is an obvious one-to-one correspondence between arrow $g : A \to B$ and $f : \top \to (A \Rightarrow B)$, where $f = \ulcorner g \urcorner$ and $g = f^`$ are defined thus:

$$\ulcorner g \urcorner = (g\pi'_{AT})^*, \quad f^` = \varepsilon_{AB} < 1_A, f\circ_A > .$$

Hence there is a unique arrow f in $\mathcal{C}$ such that $f'x = \phi(x)$ in $\mathcal{C}[x]$. Writing $f = \lambda_{x \in A}\phi(x)$, we may also express this statement as follows:

$$\lambda_{x \in A}\phi(x)'a = \phi(a), \ (\lambda_{x \in A}f)'x = x,$$

where $a : \top \to A$ has been substituted for $x : \top \to A$.

The reader will recognize these as the basic equations (β) and (η) of the usual λ-calculus. In view of π_{AB}, π'_{AB} and $< -, - >$, we actually have the lambda calculus with surjective pairing. This establishes, in one direction, the so-called Curry-Howard isomorphism between the proof theory of the positive intuitionistic propositional calculus and the lambda calculus with surjective pairing. For more details in the above argument and for the converse proof, the reader is referred to Lambek and Scott [22].

For the reader familiar with category theory, it should now be evident that CCC is a category, whose morphisms are functors which preserve the cartesian closed structure on the nose. The forgetful functor from CCC to Cat, the category of categories, or to Grph, the category of graphs, will have a left adjoint. Less technically expressed: one can form the CCC freely generated by a category or graph. The problem of finding all arrows $A \to B$ in this freely generated category can be attacked by Gentzen's cut elimination theorem; but this requires a different presentation of the deductive system (see (3) above). The problem of deciding when two arrows $A \to B$ are equal can be attacked by reducing each of them to some kind of normal form. In fact, once it is realized that the arrows $A \to B$ correspond to lambda-terms of type $A \Rightarrow B$, there is a standard procedure for doing this.

There is, however, another answer that can be given to the question of when two deductions are equal. For example, the two projections

$$\pi_{AB} : A \wedge B \to A, \ \pi'_{AB} : A \wedge B \to B,$$

upon identifying B with A, specialize to two arrows

$$\pi_{AA} : A \wedge A \to A, \ \pi'_{AA} : A \wedge A \to A.$$

These must be distinguished, because they give rise to distinct mappings in the cartesian closed category of sets. In Lambek [15], I stated a criterion which, in the present context, would assert: two deductions in a freely generated cartesian closed category are equal if and only if they have the same *generality*. My attempt to make this notion precise and to give a formal proof of the criterion (for a different deductive system) was unfortunately flawed, but I still believe the criterion has some merit and hope to return to it some day. See also Section 6 below.

4 Polymorphism

It is not difficult to incorporate universal quantifiers into the above description, assuming one has made sense out of $C[X]$. One must stipulate the following additional deduction and rule of inference:

$$\pi_A : \forall_X F(X) \to F(A),$$

$$\frac{f(X) : C \to F(X)}{\Lambda_X f(X) : C \to \forall_X F(X)},$$

and the following additional equations:

$$\pi_A \Lambda_X f(X) = f(A), \quad \Lambda_X(\pi_X g) = g,$$

where $g : C \to \forall_X F(X)$. It is assumed here that C is an object of $\mathcal{C}$.

We thus obtain an equational presentation of the so-called *second order positive intuitionistic propositional calculus*. Alternatively, we shall speak of a *cartesian closed category* with formal *products* (CCCP). However, it is not enough to consider a single such category; one must look at $\mathcal{C}, C[X], C[X, Y]$, etc., simultaneously, together with arrows $\forall_X : C[X] \to \mathcal{C}$, $\forall_Y : C[X, Y] \to C[X]$, etc., which are right adjoint to the obvious inclusions $I_X : \mathcal{C} \to C[X]$, $I_Y^X : C[X] \to C[X, Y]$, etc., For a rigorous treatment of this concept, see Seely [30] and Lambek [19].

5 Gentzen's intuitionistic sequent calculus

Among the different styles of presenting logical systems, my favorite is that developed by Gentzen for intuitionistic logic. He called the deductions of the form $f : A_1 \cdots A_m \to B$ *sequents*, so he was probably not aware of the fact that they may also be viewed as *operations* in a multisorted algebraic theory, provided proper attention is paid to equality between sequents. (See Higgins [10] and Birkhoff and Lipson [3] for discussion of multisorted algebraic theories.)

Gentzen stipulated, for each formula A, a sequent

$$1_A : A \to A \qquad \text{(identity)}$$

and the inference rule

$$\frac{f : \Lambda \to A \qquad g : \Gamma A \Delta \to B}{g < f >: \Gamma \Lambda \Delta \to B} \qquad \text{(cut)}.$$

We have used capital Greek letters to denote strings of formulas, for example, $\Lambda = A_1 \cdots A_k$. In addition, he postulated three so-called *structural rules*:

$$\frac{f : \Gamma A B \Delta \to C}{f^i : \Gamma B A \Delta \to C} \qquad \text{(interchange)},$$

$$\frac{f : \Gamma AA\Delta \to C}{f^c : \Gamma A\Delta \to C} \quad \text{(contraction)},$$

$$\frac{f : \Gamma \Delta \to C}{f^w : \Gamma A\Delta \to C} \quad \text{(weakening)}.$$

To get a proper grip on the notion of equality between sequents, we pass from the sequent calculus to its associated language. We now view the formulas as *sorts*, alias *types*, and introduce countably many variables of each sort. We define *terms* of different sorts inductively:

(i) variables are terms of their sorts;

(ii) if $f : A_1 \cdots A_m \to B$ is a sequent and a_i is a term of sort A_i, then $fa_1 \cdots a_m$ is a term of sort B.

Finally, we introduce an equality relation between terms, or rather a whole slew of equality relations $\underset{X}{=}$, X being a finite set of variables. It is understood that $a \underset{X}{=} b$ makes sense only when a and b are terms of the same sort and X contains all the variables occurring (freely) in a and b. Aside from the obligatory reflexive, symmetric and transitive laws, we also require the obvious rule

$$\frac{a \underset{X}{=} b}{a \underset{Y}{=} b},$$

when $X \subseteq Y$, and two substitution rules:

$$\frac{a_i \underset{X}{=} a_i' (i = 1, \cdots, k)}{fa_1 \cdots a_k \underset{X}{=} fa_1' \cdots a_k'}, \qquad \frac{a(z) \underset{X \cup \{z\}}{=} b(z)}{a(c) \underset{X \cup Y}{=} b(c)}.$$

In the second of these, we have displayed the variable z of sort C in $a(z)$ to show that $a(c)$ is the result of replacing z by c, where c is a term of sort C and Y contains all the variables occurring (freely) in c.

Once this tiresome machinery has been set up, we can state appropriate equations accompanying each of Gentzen's rules; but we shall skip the subscripts on the equality symbol:

$$1_A x \;=\; x, \qquad x \text{ being a variable of sort } A;$$

$$g < f > \bar{u}\,\bar{x}\,\bar{v} \;=\; g\bar{u}f\overline{x}\bar{v}, \qquad \text{where } \bar{x} = x_1 \cdots x_k \text{ and } x_i \text{ is a variable}$$
$$\text{of type } A_i, \; \Lambda = A_1 \cdots A_k, \text{ and}$$
$$\text{similarly for } \bar{u} \text{ and } \bar{v};$$

$$f^i \overline{u} y x \overline{v} \;=\; f \overline{u} x y \overline{v};$$
$$f^c \overline{u} x \overline{v} \;=\; f \overline{u} x x \overline{v};$$
$$f^w \overline{u} x \overline{v} \;=\; f \overline{u} v.$$

The algebraically inclined reader can now think of the variables as *indeterminates*, of the sequents as *operations* and of the terms as *polynomials*. We call two operations $f, g : A_1 \cdots A_m \to B$ *equal* if the corresponding polynomials are provably equal in the associated language, that is, if we can prove

$$f x_1 \cdots x_m = g x_1 \cdots x_n.$$

Functional completeness here takes the following form: given any term $b = \varphi(x_1, \cdots, x_m)$ of type B, with variables occurring in b displayed, there is a unique operation $f : A_1 \cdots A_m \to B$ such that

$$f x_1 \cdots x_m = \varphi(x_1, \cdots, x_m).$$

Thus every polynomial is generated by a unique operation.

The logically inclined reader will think of the variables x_i as instances of the assumptions A_i in the proof b of B. Functional completeness is then a strengthened form of a kind of deduction theorem, which here asserts that every Prawitz style natural deduction is generated by a uniquely determined Gentzen style sequent.

The logical connectives may of course be introduced into a Gentzen style framework as into a Lawvere style one, although lacking the motivation of adjoint functors. Without getting too technical, they may be described with the help of one-to-one correspondences between sequents

$$\Gamma \Delta \to C \quad \text{and} \quad \Gamma \top \Delta \to C,$$
$$\Gamma A B \Delta \to C \quad \text{and} \quad \Gamma (A \wedge B) \Delta \to C,$$
$$\Gamma A \to B \quad \text{and} \quad \Gamma \to A \Rightarrow B,$$
$$\Gamma \to F(X) \quad \text{and} \quad \Gamma \to \forall_X F(X), \text{ where } X \text{ is not free in } \Gamma.$$

However, in view of the structural rules, there are other ways of introducing these connectives. Thus $A \wedge B$ is usually described by a one-to-one correspondence between pairs of sequents

$$(\Gamma \to A, \Gamma \to B) \quad \text{and} \quad \Gamma \to A \wedge B$$

and $\top$ is usually described by stipulating a unique sequent $\Lambda \to \top$.

6   Logic without structural rules

One advantage of the Gentzen style presentation is that it allows one to ask: what happens if some or all of the structural rules are dropped? Such *substructural* logics have received much attention lately. For example, in *relevance logic* one drops weakening, in Girard's *linear logic* one drops weakening and contraction, and in the author's *syntactic calculus* one drops all three structural rules. In comparison with Girard's work, this might also be called *intuitionistic bilinear logic.* It should be mentioned in this context that Bourbaki [4] had the same idea as Gentzen when he defined the tensor product by a one-to-one correspondence between bilinear maps $AB \to C$ and linear maps $A \otimes B \to C$.

The analogue of an algebraic theory without structural rules has been called a *multicategory* see Lambek [16]. In retrospect, it might have been called a *contextfree grammar*, although the *derivations*, alias sequents, here have a direction opposite to that customary in generative grammars, provided equality between derivations is paid proper attention to, as in the work of Hotz [11] and Benson [2].

Into a contextfree grammar one may introduce the connectives $\top$, $\wedge$, $\Rightarrow$, and $\Leftarrow$ as in Section 5, although the last two will fail to be converses of one another in the absence of the interchange rule. However, we shall replace these symbols by I, $\otimes$, $\backslash$ and $/$ respectively. In addition to and distinct from these, one may also consider the usual lattice operations $\top$, $\wedge$, $\perp$ and $\vee$, hence the change of notation. For some reason, Girard calls these connectives 'additive'.

All these connectives may be introduced with the help of rules of inference which already incorporate all the required cut rules. To keep this exposition within bounds, we shall ignore the lattice operations here and also quantifiers. Here are the remaining introduction rules:

$$i: \quad \to I \ , \qquad \frac{f : \Gamma\Delta \to C}{f^{\#} : \Gamma I \Delta \to C}$$

$$\frac{f_0 : \Gamma \to A \quad f_1 : \Delta \to B}{\{f_0, f_1\} : \Gamma\Delta \to A \otimes B} \ , \qquad \frac{f : \Gamma AB\Delta \to C}{f^{\S} : \Gamma(A \otimes B)\Delta \to C}$$

$$\frac{f : \Gamma A \to B}{f^{*} : \Gamma \to B/A} \ , \qquad \frac{f : \Lambda \to A \quad g : \Gamma B \Delta \to C}{g[f] : \Gamma(B/A)\Lambda\Delta \to C} \ ,$$

$$\frac{f : A\Delta \to B}{f^{\dagger} : \Delta \to A\backslash B} \ , \qquad \frac{f : \Lambda \to A \quad g : \Gamma B \Delta \to C}{g\{f\} : \Gamma\Lambda(A\backslash B)\Delta \to C} \ .$$

A cut elimination theorem for this system was proved in Lambek [13]. Equality of sequents may be treated as in Section 5 (for details see Lambek [20]).

We can now look at the problem of determining all sequents $f : \Gamma \to A$ in the syntactic calculus freely generated by a contextfree grammar, even if this is only the trivial grammar with no arrows except identity arrows.

The cut elimination theorem will tell us that every sequent constructed with the help of the cut rule is equal to one constructed without the cut rule, assuming that all required cuts have already been incorporated into the introduction rules as above. As each of these rules introduces a connective on the right or on the left, we can work from the bottom up, starting with $\Gamma \to A$, eliminating one connective at a time, and see whether we end up with an axiom, that is, the above sequent i or an arrow of the given contextfree grammar. It may be worth pointing out that also all instances of the reflexive law $1_A : A \to A$ can be eliminated, unless A belongs to the original contextfree grammar. For example, $1_I = i^{\#}$.

It was for this syntactic calculus, though without the connective I, that the notion of generality was originally developed. As an example, consider two cutfree derivations of $S/((S/N)\backslash S) \to S/((S/N)\backslash S)$, one of which generalizes to a derivation of $S/((S'/N)\backslash S'') \to S/((S'/N)\backslash S'')$ and the other to a derivation of $S'/((S/N)\backslash S') \to S''/((S/N)\backslash S'')$. The former is easily seen to be the identity arrow, whereas the latter clearly is not. Thus, we have constructed two arrows of different generality in the syntactic calculus (alias residuated multicategory or biclosed monoidal category) freely generated from a discrete contextfree grammar consisting of 'axioms' $A \to A$, where $A = N, S, S', S'', \ldots$. We may rightly infer that the two arrows of different generality are distinct.

Unfortunately things go wrong when we replace S by I in the above argument. (It should be noted that then $I \to I$ is no longer an axiom, but is derived from the axiom $\to I$.) The two derivations of $I/((I/N)\backslash I) \to I/((I/N)\backslash I)$ then appear to have the same generality, even though they must be counted as distinct arrows, as is seen from the example of a vector space N over a field I, where one usually writes N^* for I/N and $N\backslash I$ and finds two distinct linear transformations $N^{***} \to N^{***}$.

Things turn out differently in another example. There are two distinct derivations of $((S/N)\otimes N)/N \to ((S/N)\otimes N)/N$ of different generality, but this time there appears to be only one arrow $((S/I)\otimes I)/I \to ((S/I)\otimes I)/I$.

7 Classical Gentzen style deductions

When dealing with classical logic, we can exploit the properties of negation to move formulas from one side of the arrow to the other. Thus we may discuss sequents of the form $f : \Gamma \to \Delta$, as Gentzen did for classical logic, or even restrict attention to sequents of the form $f :\quad \to \Delta$, as Girard did for classical linear logic. I do not wish to discuss the former system in any detail here; but the reader will get the flavour of what is possible by looking at the following version of *classical bilinear logic*, which goes back to Grishin [9] and Abrusci [1] and is called BL2 in Lambek [18], and compare it with the intuitionistic bilinear logic of Section 6. In view of the symmetry afforded by arrow reversal, one may also introduce connectives O and $\oplus$ dual to I and $\otimes$ and connectives $\doteq$ and $\dot{\frown}$ dual to $/$ and $\backslash$, although we shall not do so here. Here are the new introduction rules, again with all required cut rules already incorporated:

$$i: \quad \to I \;, \qquad\qquad \frac{f: \Gamma\Delta \to \theta}{f^{\#} : \Gamma I\Delta \to \theta} \;,$$

$$\frac{f_0 : \Gamma \to \Phi A \quad f_1 : \Delta \to B\Psi}{\{f_0, f_1\} : \Gamma\Delta \to \Phi(A\otimes B)\Psi} \;, \qquad \frac{f: \Gamma AB\Delta \to \theta}{f^{\S} : \Gamma(A\otimes B)\Delta \to \theta} \;,$$

$$\frac{f: \Gamma A \to \Phi B}{f^{*} : \Gamma \to \Phi(B/A)} \;, \qquad \frac{f: \Lambda \to A\Psi \quad g : \Gamma B\Delta \to \theta}{g[f] : \Gamma(B/A)\Lambda\Delta \to \theta\Psi} \text{ with } \Delta \text{ or } \Psi \text{ empty,}$$

$$\frac{f: A\Delta \to B\Psi}{f^{\dagger} : \Delta \to (A\backslash B)\Psi} \;, \qquad \frac{f: \Lambda \to \Phi A \quad g : \Gamma B\Delta \to \theta}{g\{f\} : \Gamma\Lambda(A\backslash B)\Delta \to \Phi\theta} \text{ with } \Gamma \text{ or } \Phi \text{ empty.}$$

A proof of the cut elimination theorem for this system was attempted in Lambek [18]. However, some subcases had been overlooked and the result is not valid, as shown by Abrusci [1], though it still holds for the weaker systems called BL1 and BL1(a) in [18].

A somewhat simpler presentation of classical bilinear logic can be given in terms of the connectives I, $\otimes$, O, $\perp$ and $^{\top}$, where $A^{\perp} = A\backslash O$ and $A^{\top} = O/A$. The new symbols obey the following introduction rules:

$$0 \to \qquad\qquad \frac{\Lambda \to \Phi\Psi}{\Lambda \to \Phi O\Psi}$$

$$\frac{\Delta \to B\Psi}{B^{\top}\Delta \to \Psi} \;, \qquad \frac{\Gamma A \to \Phi}{\Gamma \to \Phi A^{\top}} \;,$$

$$\frac{\Gamma \to \Phi B}{\Gamma B^{\perp} \to \Phi} \;, \qquad \frac{A\Delta \to \Psi}{\Delta \to A^{\perp}\Psi} \;.$$

One may then define $B/A = B \oplus A^{\top}$ and $A\backslash B = A^{\perp} \oplus B$.

In Section 5 we looked at Gentzen's intuitionistic sequents as operations in a multisorted algebraic theory and this viewpoint can be extended to Section 6, provided we talk about *multilinear* operations. It can even be extended to Section 7, provided we shift attention from algebras to *bialgebras*. The associated language should then admit not only variables but also *covariables*.

8   Dual Schütte style deductions

As has already been mentioned, classical bilinear logic may also be presented by Schütte style deductions $f : \; \to \Delta$. Personally, I prefer the dual presentation by means of deductions $f : \Gamma \to \;$, because we may then think of f as a *multilinear operation* $f : \Gamma \to O$. (In the presence of Gentzen's three structural rules, one would be tempted to think of O as the type of *truth-values* and of deductions $A_1 \cdots A_n \to O$ as an m-sorted *relation*.) We might even introduce variables to form terms (multilinear polynomials) $f x_1 \cdots x_n$ of type O in the associated language, although we shall desist from doing so here.

Of course, the reader is free to reverse all the arrows (and to interchange $\otimes$ and I with $\oplus$ and O respectively), but then she would have to think of the less familiar co-operations and covariables. In the presence of Gentzen's three structural rules, one could say that a co-operation $I \to \Delta$ establishes a bunch of alternatives, while an operation $\Gamma \to O$ shows the inconsistency of a set of assumptions.

In this section, we shall deal with a form of bilinear propositional logic that makes use of the connectives $\otimes, I, \oplus, O, {}^{\perp}$ and ${}^{\top}$. The first four of these are to satisfy the following *introduction rules*:

$$\frac{f : \Gamma\Delta \to}{f^{\#} : \Gamma I \Delta \to} \; ; \qquad \frac{f : \Gamma A B \Delta \to}{f^{\S} : \Gamma A \otimes B \Delta \to} \; ;$$

$$o : O \to \; ; \qquad \frac{f : \Gamma A \Gamma' \to \qquad g : \Delta' B \Delta \to}{[f, g] : \Delta' \Gamma A \oplus B \Delta \Gamma' \to} \; \text{provided } \Gamma' \text{ or } \Delta' \text{ is empty .}$$

The connectives ${}^{\perp}$ and ${}^{\top}$ are subject to the following rules, which should be counted as *structural* rather than introduction rules: the *axiom scheme*

$$\varepsilon_C : C C^* \to \; ,$$

and the *cut rule*

$$\frac{f : \Phi C^* \Phi' \to \qquad g : \Psi' C \Psi \to}{g \&_C f : \Psi' \Phi \Psi \Phi' \to} \; ,$$

provided Φ' or Ψ' is empty. Here C^* may always stand for $C^{\perp}$; but, if $C = A \otimes B$, I, $A \oplus B$, O or $A^{\top}$, it may also stand for $B^* \oplus A^*$, O, $B^* \otimes A^*$, I or A respectively. The star should be thought of as a symbol in the metalanguage.

The cut rule contains as special cases the following *helical rules*:

$$\frac{g : C\Psi \to}{g^+ : \Psi C^{**} \to} \; , \qquad \frac{f : \Phi D^{**} \to}{f^- : D\Phi \to} \; ,$$

where $g^+ = g\&\varepsilon_{C^*}$ and $f^- = \varepsilon_D\&f$. The first of these rules allows the following argument:

$$\frac{\dfrac{g : ABC \to}{g^+ : BCA^{**} \to}}{g^{++} : CA^{**}B^{**} \to} \quad ,$$

etc. In case the two negations coincide, that is, $A^{\perp} = A^{\top}$, we may put $A^{**} = A$ and the helical rules become 'cyclic' in the sense of Yetter [34].

If we assume that all formulas are freely generated from a discrete set of basic formulas by means of the six connectives, we can prove a *cut elimination* theorem:

Every deduction $f : \Gamma \to$ may be replaced by a cutfree deduction $f^o : \Gamma \to$.

Moreover, by adopting an appropriate notion of equality of deductions, one can ensure that $f = f^o$. It also turns out that the axioms $\varepsilon_C : CC^* \to$ need only be stated when C^* is $C^{\perp}$ or $C = D^{\top}$ and $C^* = D$, as otherwise ε_C may be defined, for example, $\varepsilon_{A\oplus B} = [\varepsilon_A, \varepsilon_B]^\S$. An alternative approach is to define $C^{\perp}$ and $C^{\top}$ for *compound* formulas by De Morgan rules; then ε_C is only needed for basic formulas C. These results will be proved in a forthcoming article [21]. See also Abrusci [1], who does so for a Schütte style presentation.

9 Bimodules revisited

The remainder of this article will be devoted to a possible generalization of the intuitionistic style sequent calculus without structural rules, also known as a multicategory or contextfree grammar.

Let Σ be the set of formulas, alias sorts; then a sequent, also known as deduction, operation or derivation, has a source and a target: whereas the target is an element of Σ, the source is a string of elements of Σ, that is, an element of Σ^*, (the underlying set of) the free monoid generated by Σ. The algebraic example which had originally motivated the present author to study multicategories was the theory of bimodules $_RA_S$, A being an abelian group with rings R and S operating on the left and right respectively such that $(ra)s = r(as)$ for all $r \in R, a \in A$ and $s \in S$.

Thus $A \otimes B$ was inspired by the tensor product of $_RA_S$ and $_SB_T$ with respect to S, C/B by the bimodule of T-homomorphisms $_SB_T \to _RC_T$ and $A\backslash C$ by the bimodule of R-homomorphisms $_RA_S \to _RC_T$. As pointed out in Lambek [14], the resulting bimodules have the form $_R(A\otimes B)_T$, $_R(C/B)_S$ and $_S(A\backslash C)_T$ respectively. But, already in the linguistic application [13], some of this information was thrown away, as though the rings R, S and

T were necessarily the same. In retrospect, it appears that this may have been a mistake.

If we think of the elements of Σ as bimodules, then Σ should be viewed not as a set but as an oriented *graph*: its nodes are the rings R, S, $T, \cdots$ and its edges are the bimodules $_RA_S$, etc. Thus Σ^* is not (the underlying set of) the free monoid but (the underlying graph of) the free category generated by Σ.

From quite different considerations, the linguist Brame [5, 6] has proposed a grammar whose derivations have the form $f : \Gamma \to B$, where Γ and B are edges of Σ^* and Σ respectively, of course between the same nodes. The way I interpret his idea may be illustrated by the following motivating example.

Let 1, A, N, S be given nodes and consider the following edges:

$$_1\mathrm{the}_A \ , \ _A\mathrm{man}_N \ , \ _N\mathrm{works}_S \ ;$$

$$_1\mathrm{ART}_A \ , \ _A\mathrm{NOUN}_N \ , \ _N\mathrm{VP}_S \ , \ _1\mathrm{NP}_N \ , \ _1\mathrm{SENTENCE}_S \ .$$

The following derivations are postulated in a usual contextfree grammar, though without the present subscripts and with arrows reversed:

$$_1\mathrm{the}_A \to_1 \mathrm{ART}_A \ , \ _A\mathrm{man}_N \to {}_A\mathrm{NOUN}_N \ , \ _N\mathrm{works}_S \to_N \mathrm{VP}_S \ ,$$

$$_1\mathrm{ART}_A \ _A\mathrm{NOUN}_N \to {}_1\mathrm{NP}_N \ , \ _1\mathrm{NP}_N \ _N\mathrm{VP}_S \to {}_1\mathrm{SENTENCE}_S \ .$$

From these 'axioms' one easily proves:

$$(*) \qquad {}_1\mathrm{the}_A \ _A\mathrm{man}_N \ _N\mathrm{works}_S \to {}_1\mathrm{SENTENCE}_S \ .$$

Without the subscripts, this would be the usual way of analysing the sentence '*the man works*' in a contextfree grammar. The reader will notice, however, that the subscripts (nodes) do half the work. In fact, Brame suggests that they could do all the work: we don't really need the edges ART, NOUN, VP and NP. We may admit the derivation $(*)$ for no other reason than that the nodes match.

Recently Todd Trimble [33] has come up with a very original idea which exploits a bimodule technique for obtaining and comparing deductions in linear logic, or even logic without structural rules. Although a single ring (or node of Σ) suffices for his purpose, he shows that bimodules provide a nice conceptual explanation of Girard's [8] 'longtrip' criterion for correctness of proofnets. He also suggested that the original ring theoretical bimodules be generalized to the bimodules of Lawvere [24], who replaced the category of Abelian groups by any symmetric closed category V. Quite independently, I had been investigating the special case when V is the category $\cdot \to \cdot$, where bimodules become downward closed subsets of $X^{op} \times Y$, X and Y being posets, and Kimmo Rosenthal [27] has looked at Lawvere bimodules as modelling classical bilinear logic.

10   Acknowledgements

I wish to thank Kosta Došen, Jean-Pierre Marquis and Todd Trimble for their careful reading of the preliminary version and their helpful comments. Support from the Social Sciences and Humanities Research Council of Canada is acknowledged.

References

[1] V. M. Abrusci. Phase semantics and sequent calculus for classical linear propositional logic. *J. Symbolic Logic*, **56**, 1403–1451, 1991.

[2] D. B. Benson. The basic algebraic structures in categories of derivations. *Information and Control*, **28**, 1–29, 1975.

[3] G. Birkhoff and J. D. Lipson. Heterogeneous algebras. *J. Combinatorial Theory*, **8**, 115–133, 1970.

[4] N. Bourbaki. *Algèbre multilinéaire*. Hermann, Paris, 1948.

[5] M. Brame. Recursive categorical syntax and morphology I. *Linguistic Analysis*, **14**, 265–287, 1984.

[6] M. Brame. Recursive categorical syntax and morphology II. *Linguistic Analysis*, **15**, 137–176, 1985.

[7] H. B. Curry and R. Feys. *Combinatory Logic*. North Holland, Amsterdam, 1958.

[8] J.-Y. Girard. Linear logic. *J. Theoretical Computer Science*, **50**, 1–102, 1987.

[9] V. N. Grishin. On a generalization of the Ajdukiewicz-Lambek system. In *Studies in non-classical logics and formal systems*, pages 315–343. Nauka, Moscow, 1983.

[10] P. J. Higgins. Algebras with a scheme of operators. *Math. Nachrichten*, **27**, 15–132, 1963.

[11] G. Hotz. Eindentigkeit und mehrdeutigkeit formaler sprachen. *Elektronische Informationsverarbeitung und Kybernetik*, **2**, 235–247, 1966.

[12] S. C. Kleene. *Introduction to Metamathematics*, Van Nostrand, New York 1952.

[13] J. Lambek. The mathematics of sentence structure. *Amer. Math. Monthly*, **65**, 54–159, 1958.

[14] J. Lambek. *Lectures on Rings and Modules*. Ginn, Waltham, 1976: Chelsea, New York, 1986, 1966.

[15] J. Lambek. Deductive systems and categories I. *Math. Systems Theory*, **2**, 278–318, 1968.

[16] J. Lambek. Deductive systems and categories II. In *LNM86*, pages 76–122. Springer-Verlag, 1969.

[17] J. Lambek. From λ-calculus to cartesian closed categories. In J. P. Seldin and J. R. Hindley, editors, *To H. B. Curry*. Academic Press, 1980.

[18] J. Lambek. From categorial grammar to bilinear logic. In K. Došen and P. Schroeder-Heister, editors, *Substructural Logics*, pages 207–237. Oxford University Press, 1993.

[19] J. Lambek. Least fixpoints of endofunctors of cartesian closed categories. *Mathematical Structures in Computer Science*, **3**, 229–257, 1993.

[20] J. Lambek. Logic without structural rules. In K. Došen and P. Schroeder-Heister, editors, *Substructural Logics*, pages 179–206. Oxford University Press, 1993.

[21] J. Lambek. Cut elimination for classical bilinear logic. *Fundamenta Informaticae*, To appear.

[22] J. Lambek and P. J. Scott. *Introduction to higher order categorical logic*. Cambridge University Press, Cambridge, 1986.

[23] F. W. Lawvere. Adjointness in foundations. *Dialectica*, **23**, 281–296, 1969.

[24] F. W. Lawvere. Metric spaces, generalized logic and closed categories. *Rend. del Sem. Mat. e Fis. di Milano*, **43**, 135–166, 1973.

[25] D. Prawitz. *Natural Deduction*, Almquist and Wiskell, Stockholm 1965.

[26] P. C. Rosenbloom. *The elements of mathematical logic*. Dover, New York, 1950.

[27] K. I. Rosenthal. *-autonomous categories of bimodules. Technical report, Union College, Schenectady, 1993.

[28] K. Schütte. Schlussweisen-kalküle der predikatenlogik. *Math. Annalen*, **22**, 47–65, 1950.

[29] H. Schwichtenberg. Proof theory: some applications of cut-elimination. In J. Barwise, editor, *Handbook of mathematical logic*, pages 867–895. North Holland, Amsterdam, 1977.

[30] R. A. G. Seely. Categorical semantics for higher order polymorphic lambda calculus. *J. Symbolic Logic*, **52**, 969–989, 1987.

[31] M. E. Szabo (ed). *The Collected Papers of Gerhard Gentzen*, Studies in Logic and the Foundations of Mathematics, North Holland, Amsterdam, 1969.

[32] M. E. Szabo. *Algebra of Proofs*, North Holland, Amsterdam, 1978.

[33] T. H. Trimble. The bimodule interpretation of linear logic, Rutgers University Thesis, 1993.

[34] D. N. Yetter. Quantales and (non-commutative) linear logic. *J. Symbolic Logic*, **55**, 41–64, 1990.

6

The Transmission of Truth and the
Transitivity of Deduction*

Neil Tennant

Frege assigned to logic the task of 'discovering the laws of truth'[1] Logical proofs preserve truth from their premisses to their conclusions. Logic is also said to be a matter of form, not content. I intend in this essay to stay with considerations of just truth and logical form, in order to address the question of the transitivity of deduction.

I shall investigate in very general terms the principles that we might be concerned to lay down for a system of logic whose deducibility (and consequence) relation is not unrestrictedly transitive. The choice of principles we eventually make might not only rule some systems out and some systems in; it might also serve to constrain exactly how a system of rules of inference is to be set up in order to generate the field of its deducibility relation.

We shall draw throughout only on notions of great generality: that of *being true* (according to whatever semantics is chosen); that of *uniform substitution*, an effective operation by which syntactic objects of a logical kind (formulae, proofs) are produced from other syntactic objects of the same kind; and other notions that can be defined in terms of these, such as *perfect validity, soundness* and *perfect proof*. These notions have application across all logical systems.

A word of warning in advance: I shall be defining a very special sense of soundness, whose importance will emerge in the course of my discussion. Standardly, one says an argument is sound just in case it is truth-preserving (under all interpretations of non-logical expressions) *and* its premisses (hence also its conclusion) are true (under interpretation in the 'ac-

---

*Given as an invited paper to the Eastern Division Meeting of the American Philosophical Association, Washington, December 1992. I am grateful to Stewart Shapiro for several helpful comments.
[1]'Thoughts', at p. 1 in Gottlob Frege, *Logical Investigations*, edited by P. T. Geach, Blackwell, Oxford, 1977.

tual world'). This is not, however, the sense in which I shall be using the term 'sound'. Details will emerge below.

Another word of warning in advance: when speaking of proofs I shall be confining myself to systems of natural deduction, even when the notions in play might find application in other systems of proof as well.

Before defining the notion of a sound argument, let us speak informally of *good* arguments.

A good argument transmits truth from its premisses to its conclusion. But its premisses may be false, while yet the argument still be good. So a good argument is one that *would* transmit truth from its premisses to its conclusion, whenever the premisses turned out to be true. But one cannot transmit what one could not acquire. So one is tempted to say of a good argument: it must be possible for its premisses to turn out true.

Prima facie, then, we have a problem if we regard as good an argument whose premisses cannot all be true.

Unless, of course, the argument establishes just that: namely, that the premisses form an inconsistent set. Such an argument is called a *reductio ad absurdum* (its conclusion is absurdity). It has every right to be regarded as good (or, anticipating: as sound). So we must be more cautious in stating our preceding conclusion: *prima facie* we have a problem if we regard as good an argument *for a conclusion other than absurdity* whose premisses cannot all be true. The principle of proof by *reductio ad absurdum* must remain intact.

A problem for the logical analyst is emerging here. Two desiderata sit uneasily together:

1. you cannot transmit what you do not have

2. sometimes you can show you cannot have it

Satisfiability of premisses and validity of *reductio* pull in opposite directions— or so it would seem.

Logic, as noted above, is a matter of form, not content. Form can be gross or fine. Grossly, one is obviously justified in holding that $A\&B$ logically implies B. This justification survives upon substitution for finer discriminations: $A\&\sim A$ logically implies $\sim A$ even though $A\&\sim A$ cannot be true. So *some* arguments with conclusions other than absurdity proceed soundly from inconsistent premisses. But one may still be able to ensure that the way they do so can be represented at a grosser level in such a way that the inconsistency of the premisses is masked and the reasoning can be seen to make no illicit use of it.

It would be very different, however, with the unsound argument

$$A, \sim A \therefore B.$$

With this argument, there is no way of ascending to a grosser level to mask the inconsistency of the premises while still maintaining soundness of the resulting grosser argument.

Dually, one would not wish to obtain logical truths from falsifiable premises. This would rule out the argument $A \therefore A \lor \sim A$; until one observed that this argument is a substitution instance of $A \therefore A \lor B$, whose conclusion is *not* logically true. At the grosser level the logical truth of the conclusion might be masked, and the reasoning be seen to make no illicit use of it. It would be very different, however, with the unsound argument $B \therefore A \lor \sim A$. With this argument, there is no way of ascending to a grosser level to mask the logical truth of the conclusion while still maintaining soundness of the resulting grosser argument.

Perfectly sound reasoning would make no use of unnecessary assumptions. Consider the argument $(A \lor B) \supset C, A \therefore B \supset C$. It has the following two proofs:

$$
\begin{array}{cc}
\dfrac{A}{A \lor B} \quad (A \lor B) \supset C & \dfrac{\overline{}\ (1)}{B} \\[2mm]
\dfrac{C}{B \supset C} & \dfrac{A \lor B \quad (A \lor B) \supset C}{\dfrac{C}{B \supset C}\ (1)}
\end{array}
$$

The first proof may be regarded as somehow defective in that it uses both premises when (as one can see from the second proof) the second premiss will do. But this defect is only apparent. For the first proof is a substitution instance of the proof

$$
\dfrac{\dfrac{A}{A \lor B} \quad (A \lor B) \supset C}{\dfrac{C}{D \supset C}}
$$

This proof establishes the argument $(A \lor B) \supset C, A \therefore D \supset C$; and this argument *does* need both its premises. For both the proper sub-argument $(A \lor B) \supset C \therefore D \supset C$ and the proper sub-argument $A \therefore D \supset C$ admit of counterexamples (that is, interpretations making their premises true and their conclusions false). Such a proof I shall call a *perfect* proof.

Let a *non-trivial* substitution on a proof be one that is not induced by a one-one mapping of atomic sentences to atomic sentences. A *perfect proof* in a system S is then defined as one that is not a non-trivial substitution instance of any proof in system S. The idea is that a perfect proof captures the 'bare bones' of a piece of reasoning, ignoring (that is, not representing) any occurrence of a logical operator that is not actually exploited in the reasoning involved. Imagine doing the following with any proof. Highlight the dominant occurrence of the logical operator on which the formal correctness of the application of any rule of inference turns. Let that highlighting be inherited at the appropriate occurrences of that formula as a subformula either above or below; ... and so on. The idea is that in a perfect proof every operator occurrence in every formula occurrence would end up being highlighted. So in a perfect proof there are no otiose operator occurrences. A perfect proof works, moreover, with the *shallowest possible* level of logical analysis of the premises and conclusion that will enable one to make the moves that make up the proof. In particular, it minimizes repetitions of occurrences of propositional variables.

The notion of perfect proof, therefore, is a very general one, and can be applied across widely different systems (systems of natural deduction for, say, minimal, intuitionistic or classical logic). It is therefore apt for the formulation of independently motivated constraints on one's choice of such a logical system, or of principled re-formulation of it. I have in mind here constraints that might incline one, say, to the choice of some 'relevantized' version of one of these systems.

It was emerging that soundness is more than standard validity. I want to explicate the notion of soundness adumbrated here; and consider what might happen to deducibility when we require deductions to be sound, that is, to establish only sound sequents (or arguments).

One subsidiary notion that is in play already is that of an argument *needing all its premises* in order to secure its conclusion. Another subsidiary notion is that of an argument (whose conclusion is not absurdity) *needing its premises to form a satisfiable set*. These notions apply most naturally to what one might call 'stand-alone' arguments. There is no requirement that they should apply to any of the *sub-arguments* of a stand-alone argument. That, indeed, is the implicit problematic of this chapter: to fashion a notion of soundness that is compositional across argument structure.

Think for a moment in terms of classical sequents $X : Y$, where X and Y are sets of sentences. Dropping one or more premises in X yields a *proper subsequent* of $X : Y$. To say that the argument $X : Y$ *needs all its premises* is to say that any proper subsequent of this kind admits of counterexample. Likewise, dropping any members of Y yields a proper subsequent of $X : Y$. In the special case where Y is a singleton $\{A\}$, dropping its sole member A produces the proper subsequent $X : \varnothing$, which states that X is unsatisfiable. To say that the argument $X : A$ *needs its conclusion* is to say that the proper subsequent $X : \varnothing$ admits of counterexample. We now define the main notions involved:

$X : Y$ *admits of counterexample* iff some interpretation makes all of X true and makes all of Y false[2]

$X : Y$ is *valid* iff $X : Y$ admits of no counterexample

$X : Y$ is *perfectly valid* iff $X : Y$ is valid and every *proper* subsequent of $X : Y$ is *invalid*, that is, admits of counterexample

$X : Y$ is *sound* iff $X : Y$ is a substitution instance of a *perfectly* valid sequent

These definitions capture the spirit of what has come to be known as the Geach–Smiley–von Wright condition, but which Smiley himself attributes to W. E. Johnson.[3]

Thus $A\&\sim A : A$ and $A\&\sim A :\sim A$ are sound; while $A\&\sim A : B$ is not. This looks promising.

Also, $A : A \vee B$ is sound, and $A \vee B, \sim A : B$ is sound; while $A, \sim A : B$ is not. While each of these results in itself is promising, their combination may appear unsettling. For what it tells us is that sound arguments (or their proofs) *do not always accumulate*. Another way of putting this is to say that soundness (and deducibility) *is not unrestrictedly transitive*. Or, more succinctly: *Cut fails. That is, the structural rule of Cut is not admissible for sound arguments*:

$$\frac{X : A \quad Y, A : B}{X, Y : B} \text{ Cut}$$

One aim of this essay is to justify the reaction 'So what?!' Such failure of Cut is to be *welcomed*. When Cut fails, it *ought* to fail. Failure of Cut is *logically enlightening*. It represents *epistemic gain*. I share Smiley's diagnosis[4] of the paradox of irrelevance as resulting

> from ascribing to an intuitive concept of entailment (which requires a connexion of meanings between premises and conclusion that is quite lacking in the 'paradoxical' [$A\&\sim A$ entails B]) the property of unrestricted transitivity ...

but demur from his further claim that this property is

> ... admittedly essential to any entailment-relation that is to be put to sustained use as a logical instrument.

---

[2] Or, in case there are alternatives to truth besides falsity: '...makes all of Y not true'.

[3] T. J. Smiley, 'Entailment and deducibility', *Proceedings of the Aristotelian Society 1959*, pp. 233–253; at p. 239.

[4] T. J. Smiley, *loc. cit.*, p. 233.

Smiley writes[5] of

> (t)he need for an unrestrictedly transitive entailment-relation
> for serious logical work

and claims that

> the need itself is undeniable: the whole point of logic as an
> instrument, and the way in which it brings us new knowledge,
> lies in the contrast between the transitivity of 'entails' and the
> non-transitivity of 'obviously entails', *and all this is lost if tran-*
> *sitivity cannot be relied on.* Of course if there is an effective way
> of predicting when transitivity will hold then most of the ob-
> jection vanishes; there is such a way where the . . . system . . . is
> decidable (so that inferences can be checked directly); but I do
> not see how the thing might be done in, say, predicate logic
> . . . [my emphasis].

Smiley's worry emphasized in this last quotation is, I submit, mistaken.
What is needed of logic as an instrument of knowledge is only that chains
of obvious entailments should yield entailments on *satisfiable sets of pre-*
misses; and that all unsatisfiable sets should provably be so (that is, should
be *inconsistent*). This will suffice for mathematics (on the assumption that
it is not inconsistent) and for the hypothetico-deductive method in science.
And *this* kind of guarantee can be forthcoming regardless of the decidability or otherwise of the logic in question. We simply do not need Cut in
order for our logic to be a useful (indeed, completely adequate) instrument
of knowledge.

By Cut I mean the principle above claiming the *unrestricted* transitivity of sound argumentation. With soundness defined above as a semantic
notion, it is apparent that we would need (pending a metatheorem to the
effect that the sound arguments were exactly those that admitted of proof)
to consider the correlative principle of Cut for deducibility. That principle
would read

$$\frac{\text{There is a proof of } X : A \quad \text{There is a proof of } Y, A : B}{\text{There is a proof of } X, Y : B}$$

This principle of Cut for deducibility would follow from, but not in general imply, the following principle of Cut for proofs, which provides for
accumulation of proofs in a system of proof:

---

[5] *loc. cit.*, p. 242.

Cut for Proofs by Proof Accumulation

Given any proof Π of A from X, and any proof Σ of B from Y, A the result of grafting (copies of) Π onto appropriate assumption occurrences of A in Σ is itself a proof of B from X, Y:

$$
\begin{array}{c}
X \\
\Pi \\
Y, \, (A) \\
\Sigma \\
B
\end{array}
$$

This indeed is more or less the way in which Gentzen incorporated Cut as a structural rule of his sequent systems. The point of his *Hauptsatz* was then to show that applications of Cut could be eliminated from proofs, and their results still be secured by means of the remaining rules of the system.

It may turn out for some systems that the straightforward operation of accumulation may not be enough to secure the sought proof of $X, Y : B$. That is, one would not in general find a proof of the overall result $X, Y : B$ by chaining the proofs Π and Σ together in any straightforward sense. This would happen if, for example, proofs were defined so as to be in normal form. The result Φ of straightforward accumulation might not itself be in normal form, hence not, on this definition, a proof. But one might be able to *normalize* such an object Φ so as to obtain a proof Θ, in normal form, that establishes the overall result $X, Y : B$. So what we are envisaging in general here is the possibility that there may be some more complicated (but still effective) operation f that can be performed on the given proofs Π and Σ so as to furnish a proof Θ of that overall result. Θ need not in any way be a straightforward composite (*qua* labelled tree) of the two proofs Π and Σ, or even of multiple copies thereof. Yet Θ would be obtained effectively from Π and Σ. We may summarize this line of thought as follows.

Principle of Cut for Proofs by Proof Conversion

There is an effective operation f that will turn any proof Π of A from X and any proof Σ of B from Y, A into a proof Θ of $X, Y : B$:

$$
\begin{array}{ccc}
X \\
\Pi \\
A \quad f \quad X \cup Y \\
\quad \rightarrow \quad \Theta \\
Y, A \qquad B \\
\Sigma \\
B
\end{array}
$$

Note that the crucial thing about both Principles of Cut for Proofs (that by Accumulation and that by Conversion) is that they provide for proofs *of the overall result* $X, Y : B$. This is precisely what unrestricted transitivity of deduction consists in. If a system's deducibility relation does not obey dilution (thinning) it is possible for that deducibility relation not to be *unrestrictedly* transitive. Such, indeed, is the case with the systems of truth table logic, intuitionistic relevant logic and classical relevant logic.[6]

The principle that I shall recommend we should choose instead of Cut (for proofs) will be called Paste. Paste will be formulated below, in an *ordinary* form and in a *perfect* form. The way that Paste differs from Cut is that Paste provides in general only for a proof of *some subsequent* of the erstwhile overall result $X, Y : B$. That is, the proof Θ obtained by Paste may have for its set of undischarged assumptions some *proper subset* of X, Y; and it may have absurdity ($\bot$) for its conclusion.

Cut, indeed, should never have been laid down as a feature of the deducibility relation of any decent logical system. It would be an interesting topic, but not one for this chapter, to enquire into the reasons why Cut ever became a respectable part of orthodox logic. There may have been an interesting historical interplay between closure operations in algebra and nascent notions of logical consequence in the early twentieth century. Topologically, the closure of the closure of a set is just its closure: $[[X]] = [X]$. To say, by way of analogy, that the deductive closure of the deductive closure of a set of sentences is just its closure is just to say that deducibility is unrestrictedly transitive, that is, that Cut holds.

Another notion that we shall have occasion to bring into play is that of a (uniform) substitution instance. The substitution instance itself is the finer object; that of which it is a substitution instance is the grosser object. Generally I shall write $\Phi \Leftarrow \mathbf{\Phi}$ to indicate that the finer object Φ is a substitution instance of the grosser object $\mathbf{\Phi}$. These objects may be sentences or sequents or proofs.

Let us return to the point that Cut fails for a more stringent notion of soundness than is involved in the usual semantical treatments of logical consequence, be they intuitionistic or classical. I shall work towards a careful statement of exactly how and where Cut might fail (both for soundness and for the associated notion(s) of deducibility) and exactly how and where it might hold. I shall argue that the new Paste principle of *epistemically gainful but restricted transitivity* should be adopted for deducibility. This principle, which I shall state for single-conclusion arguments, is as follows:

---

[6]For sources, see footnotes that follow.

Paste for Proofs by Conversion

If $X : A$ is sound and $Y, A : B$ is sound then *some subsequent* of $X, Y : B$ is sound. Indeed, there is an effective operation f that will turn any proof Π of A from X and any proof Σ of B from Y, A into a proof Θ of some subsequent of $X, Y : B$:

$$
\begin{array}{c}
X \\
\Pi \\
A \quad f \quad Z \qquad\quad Z \\
\qquad \rightarrow \quad \theta \quad \text{or} \quad \Theta \quad \text{where } Z \subseteq (X \cup Y) \\
Y, A \qquad\quad \perp \qquad\quad B \\
\Sigma \\
B
\end{array}
$$

Here A is called the *paste formula*. We require only that the operation f be effective, not feasible. Thus when I speak below of epistemic gain, I should, strictly, speak of *potential* epistemic gain. Note that the principle states that one can (in principle, but not necessarily feasibly) paste proofs together and thereby obtain proof of a result *at least as good as, and often better than*, the result that the old rule of Cut would have furnished. This we have seen with the attempted proof-by-accumulation of the Lewis paradox. Taking Π as the proof

$$
\frac{A}{A \vee B}
$$

and taking Σ as the proof

$$
\frac{A \vee B \quad \dfrac{\sim A \quad \overline{A}^{\,(1)}}{\perp} \quad \overline{B}^{\,(1)}}{B}{}^{(1)}
$$

all we get by pasting them in the system of intuitionistic relevant logic, and then converting,[7] is the proof

$$
\frac{\sim A \quad A}{\perp}
$$

---

[7]which process would involve *normalization* and *extraction*. Extraction is the process of getting rid of applications of the absurdity rule. An extraction theorem is in effect a dilution-elimination theorem.

We do *not* get any proof of B from $\sim A, A$.

So far so good with blocking the Lewis paradox itself. But what assurance do we have that the transforms that we *do* obtain via f applied to proofs Π and Σ never *themselves* involve anything rum from the relevantist's point of view? How can we be sure that $f(\Pi, \Sigma)$ does not itself trade illicitly on some hidden inconsistency among its undischarged assumptions in order to establish its conclusion, or trade illicitly on the logical truth of its conclusion while yet making it look as though it follows from those assumptions?

The guarantee that there is nothing rum on the part of the transform would have to take the form of this strengthened Paste principle:

Principle of Paste for Proofs by Conversion and with Perfection

There is an effective operation f that will turn any proof Π of A from X and any proof Σ of B from Y, A into a proof Θ of some subsequent of $X, Y : B$; and Θ is, moreover, a substutition instance of a proof $\boldsymbol{\Theta}$ that establishes a perfectly valid sequent:

$$
\begin{array}{c}
X \\
\Pi \\
A \\
\end{array}
\quad f \quad
\begin{array}{c}
Z \\
\Theta \\
\bot \\
\end{array}
\quad \text{or} \quad
\begin{array}{c}
Z \\
\Theta \\
B \\
\end{array}
\quad \text{where } Z \subseteq (X \cup Y) \text{ and } \Theta \Leftarrow \boldsymbol{\Theta}
$$
$$
\begin{array}{c}
Y, A \\
\Sigma \\
B \\
\end{array} \rightarrow
$$

The new second part in this statement of the principle goes exactly as far as we need. It assures us that whatever stronger result $Z : B$ we may thus obtain (where B is not $\bot$), we may rest assured that it in turn *will not have been obtained by any sort of irrelevance within the proof* Θ *that establishes it*. Its proof Θ will exploit only such logical structure as will fail to reveal the inconsistency of its set Z of premises, or the logical truth of its conclusion B; and will, moreover, need each of its premises to obtain that conclusion. This is guaranteed by the existence of the perfect proof $\boldsymbol{\Theta}$ of which Θ is a substitution instance. The inferential moves made in Θ are, so to speak, acceptable via their schematization as the corresponding steps in $\boldsymbol{\Theta}$; so since $\boldsymbol{\Theta}$ by definition contains nothing rum (how could it?—it establishes a perfectly valid sequent), nor, then, will Θ. So the result of pasting and transforming by means of the mapping f will give a *bona fide* sound result— even if it does happen to be a proper subsequent of $X, Y : B$. And if it is a proper subsequent of $X, Y : B$ then we can at least claim *epistemic gain*.

Logic will have been an adequate instrument of knowledge—indeed, *more* than adequate in the usual way. For the conversion of Π and Σ will have produced a stronger logical result than $X, Y : B$. We might learn that not all of X,Y is needed in order to obtain the conclusion B—perhaps even that B is itself a logical truth; or we might learn that (some subset of) X, Y is inconsistent.

The motivation for the Principle of Paste for Proofs by Conversion (PPPC) comes, somewhat surprisingly, from a very familiar and apparently orthodox source: the truth tables. The system of *truth table logic*[8] provides a natural setting for our main idea. It is very easy to establish that PPPC holds for this system. Part of the reason why this is so easy is that accumulation and conversion of proofs in truth table logic can only ever take place when the bottom conclusion (that is, the conclusion of Σ) is absurdity ($\perp$). This is because the paste formula A has to stand as the major premiss for an application of an elimination rule within the proof Σ; and all elimination rules in truth table logic have absurdity as their overall conclusion.

It would be useful, however, to generalize our means of reasoning so that applications of elimination rules can lead to conclusions other than absurdity. By modifying the rules of inference of the system of truth table logic in a principled and controlled way we can achieve this end. We obtain thereby the system of *intuitionistic relevant logic*.[9] I have proved elsewhere[10] that PPPC holds for intuitionistic relevant logic. But the newly modified rules considerably complicate attempts to prove analogously that the Principle of Paste for Proofs by Conversion **and with Perfection** also holds for this system. I simply conjecture this at present.

PPPC holds also for *classical relevant logic*.[11] And if the Principle of Paste for Proofs by Conversion **and with Perfection** holds for intuitionistic relevant logic, then it holds also for classical relevant logic.

---

[8] N. Tennant, 'Truth table logic, with a survey of embeddability results', *Notre Dame Journal of Formal Logic*, **30**, 1989, p 459–484.

[9] N. Tennant, *Autologic*, Edinburgh University Press, 1992, pp. 6–11, p. 39. See also N. Tennant, 'Delicate proof theory', in J. Copeland (ed.), *Logic and Reality: Essays in Pure and Applied Logic, In Memory of Arthur Prior*, Oxford University Press, forthcoming.

[10] N. Tennant, 'Intuitionistic Mathematics Does Not Need *Ex Falso Quodlibet*', forthcoming in *Topoi*.

[11] N. Tennant, 'Perfect validity, entailment and paraconsistency', *Studia Logica*, XLIII, 1984, pp 179–198.

Suppose we have materials for a paste:

$$X$$
$$\Pi$$
$$A$$

$$Y, \; (A)$$
$$\Sigma$$
$$B$$

and suppose moreover that there *is* a proof of B from (some subset Z of) $X \cup Y$. It is possible, however, that the mapping f in our statement of PPPC (with or without Perfection) might go to work on the proofs Π and Σ in such a way as to miss this fact. $f(\Pi, \Sigma)$ might turn out to be a proof of $\perp$ from some other subset W of $X \cup Y$. Thus as a special case, there might be as supposed a proof of B from $X \cup Y$ itself (that is, $Z = X \cup Y$) while yet $f(\Pi, \Sigma)$ turn out to be a proof of $\perp$ from some subset W of $X \cup Y$; perhaps even from $X \cup Y$ itself. Or, Z could be $X \cup Y$, and $f(\Pi, \Sigma)$ turn out to be a proof of B from some *proper* subset W of $X \cup Y$. That B follows from Z would here go unremarked by the operation of f.

The worry, then, is that there might be some kind of *transitive lacuna* even within an epistemically gainful system. We could have $X : A$ sound, $Y, A : B$ sound and $X, Y : B$ sound. We could even have the assurance that every proof in general is a substitution instance of a perfect proof, and that perfect proofs establish only perfectly valid sequents. Thus in having a proof Π of $X : A$, we learn that $X : A$ is sound; in having a proof Σ of $Y, A : B$ we learn that $Y, A : B$ is sound; but we might be unable to operate on Π and Σ with f so as to obtain a proof that would enable us to learn that $X, Y : B$ is sound. We might miss some gross fact about deducibility when the materials (the proof Π and Σ) constituting some of the patchwork facts are in hand. Our Paste principle has the overall form

$$\begin{array}{cc} X & Y, A \\ \exists f \; \forall \Pi & \forall \; \Sigma \qquad \exists Z \subseteq (X \cup Y) \quad f(\Pi, \Sigma) \text{ is a proof of } B \text{ or of } \perp \text{ from } Z \\ A & B \end{array}$$

and

$$\exists \Theta (\Theta \text{ is perfect and } f(\Pi, \Sigma) \Leftarrow \Theta)$$

and the worry is now that there *could well be* some proof Ξ of B from $X \cup Y$ itself but that $f(\Pi, \Sigma)$ might not establish the same sequent (namely, $X, Y : B$) as Ξ!

This is a worry that one may simply have to live with. The point still stands that $f(\Pi, \Sigma)$, if it establishes a result other than $X, Y : B$, represents epistemic gain. For that result will have the form $Z : B$, for some *proper* subset Z of $X \cup Y$, or the form $Z : \perp$ (that is, $Z : \varnothing$), for some subset Z of $X \cup Y$.

One can see how the transitive *lacuna* arises.[12] We supposed above that we had a result to the effect that every proof is a substitution instance of a perfect proof. Thus the proof Π of $X : A$ could be a substitution instance of some perfect proof $\mathbf{\Pi}$ of $\mathbf{X} : \mathbf{A_1}$, and the proof Σ of $Y, A : B$ could be a substitution instance of some perfect proof $\mathbf{\Sigma}$ of $\mathbf{Y, A_2} : \mathbf{B}$; but $\mathbf{A_1}$ and $\mathbf{A_2}$ could be so different that a straightforward cut or paste would not be possible. $\mathbf{A_1}$ and $\mathbf{A_2}$ could be distinct formulae. One could try to find a unifier A^* (that is, a common substitution instance of $\mathbf{A_1}$ and $\mathbf{A_2}$) for these two formulae, which would induce a substitution instance Π_1 of Π and a substitution instance Σ_2 of Σ, and *then* use A^* as the paste formula in order to operate with f (on Π_1 and Σ_2, hence, in some sense, on Π and Σ via $\mathbf{A_1}$ and $\mathbf{A_2}$); but would there be any guarantee that we would thereby avoid unwanted epistemic gain, as it were? Would there be any guarantee that we could obtain an f-transform $\Theta(= f(\Pi_1, \Sigma_2))$ whose perfected version Θ established a (perfectly valid) sequent of which $X, Y : B$ was a substitution instance?

Note that epistemic gain can occur even when both Π and Σ are perfect. Thus

$$\frac{A}{A \vee B}$$

is perfect, as is the IR proof

$$\frac{\cfrac{\overline{\sim A} \quad \overset{-}{A}\,{}^{(1)}}{A \vee B \quad \perp}}{B}{}^{(1)} \quad \cfrac{\overline{B}\,{}^{(1)}}{}{}^{(1)}$$

but there is no perfect IR proof establishing a sequent of which $A, \sim A : B$ would be a substitution instance. The result of pasting is converted instead to the simple proof

$$\frac{\sim A \quad A}{\perp}$$

But suppose that Π is a perfect proof of A from X and that Σ is a perfect proof of B from Y, A and, moreover, that $X, Y : B$ is *sound*. Should we then require of our mapping f that it produce from Π and Σ some proof Θ of the result $X, Y : B$? *Can* we so require? If we can, should we also require that Θ itself be perfect? This latter requirement *could* be imposed

---

[12] cf. Smiley, *loc. cit.*, p. 242.

(so there would be no loss in requiring that it *should*) if we had a general method for turning proofs Θ into the perfect proofs Θ of which they were substitution instances. That general method could then be tacked on as the last part of the mapping f itself, in our statement of the Paste principle.

The ideas that are emerging here call at this point for summary. I shall state some candidate principles that it would be good to have. But first, three preliminaries:

1. two formulae A_1, A_2 are said to *unify* via the substitution σ if and only if $\sigma A_1 = \sigma A_2$

2. **X** : **A** is a *suprasequent* of $X : A$ if and only if $X : A$ is a substitution instance of **X** : **A**

3. **Π** is a *supraproof* of Π if and only if Π is a substitution instance of **Π**

Perfectibility
There is an operation π such that for every proof Π, $\pi(\Pi)$ is a perfect supraproof of Π

Perfect soundness[13]
Every perfect proof establishes a perfectly valid sequent.

Soundness
Every proof establishes a sound sequent.

Completeness
Every sound sequent has a proof.

Perfect Pasting of Perfect Proofs
There is an effective operation f such that:
for every perfect proof Π of $X : A_1$ and for every perfect proof Σ of $Y, A_2 : B$
if A_1 and A_2 unify via σ
    and there is a proof of $\sigma X, \sigma Y : \sigma B$
then $f(\Pi, \Sigma)$ is a perfect proof of a suprasequent of $\sigma X, \sigma Y : \sigma B$.

Note that there is no perfect completeness theorem to the effect that every perfectly valid sequent has a perfect proof. As a counterexample, consider the perfectly valid sequent $A, A \supset (B\&C) : B\&C$.

Perfectibility with the weaker Principle of Paste for Proofs by Conversion implies the stronger Principle of Paste for Proofs by Conversion and with Perfection. The weaker principle has already been established for the

---

[13]Note that this soundness requirement embodies a requirement of relevance. It rules out standard classical and intutionistic logic, since they contain the perfect proof of Lewis's first paradox that is constructed by one step of negation elimination followed by one step of *ex falso quodlibet*.

full system of first-order intuitionistic relevant logic.[14] Thus Perfectibility is an important goal as a metatheorem.

Even if we attain that goal, however, we will not necessarily thereby have Perfect Pasting of Perfect Proofs. With Perfectibility, however, it will be enough, for Perfect Pasting of Perfect Proofs, to prove the slightly weaker result.

Perfectible Pasting of Perfect Proofs

There is an effective operation f such that:
for every perfect proof Π of $X : A_1$ and for every perfect proof Σ of $Y, A_2 : B$
if A_1 and A_2 unify via σ
    and there is a proof of $\sigma X, \sigma Y : \sigma B$
then $f(\Pi, \Sigma)$ is a(n ordinary) proof of a suprasequent of $\sigma X, \sigma Y : \sigma B$.

Both Principles of Pasting of Perfect Proofs involve the hypothesis that $\sigma X, \sigma Y : \sigma B$ is *sound*. They might therefore be called principles of Pasting of Perfect Proofs for a Sound Result. Of course, we already have the

Principle of Pasting of Perfect Proofs for a Perfect Result

There is an effective operation f such that:
for every perfect proof Π of $X : A_1$ and for every perfect proof Σ of $Y, A_2 : B$
if A_1 and A_2 unify via σ
    and there is a perfect proof of $\sigma X, \sigma Y : \sigma B$
then $f(\Pi, \Sigma)$ is a perfect proof of a suprasequent of $\sigma X, \sigma Y : \sigma B$.

The stronger hypothesis here to the effect that there is a perfect proof of $\sigma X, \sigma Y : \sigma B$ rules out the prospect of epistemic gain by proof of a proper subsequent. For, since perfect proofs establish only perfectly sequents, $\sigma X, \sigma Y : \sigma B$ will be perfectly valid. Thus one will be forced, via the operation f of PPPC, to find a proof of $\sigma X, \sigma Y : \sigma B$ itself. By perfectibility, we can then turn this proof into a perfect proof of a suprasequent of $\sigma X, \sigma Y : \sigma B$.

But why should we go so far as to require that we have Perfect Pasting for Sound Results, if these results are not themselves perfect? Why should the way of getting *to* A embodied in the proof Π and the way of getting *from* A embodied in the proof Σ always guarantee a way to the overall (sound but not perfect) result $X, Y : B$? Choice of lemmata A after all serve only a strategic purpose. They can reduce dramatically the computational effort involved in finding the proofs Π and Σ as opposed to finding an outright and

---

[14]'Intuitionistic Mathematics Does Not Need *Ex Falso Quodlibet*', op. cit.

direct proof Θ of the overall result. But the logical *quid pro quo* exacted for this saving of investigative effort is that when we come to paste the proofs Π and Σ and convert the result, we have to be prepared to make do with whatever (epistemically gainful) result the process delivers.

In serious scientific work, when logic is being used as an instrument to discover the *truth*, this is all that matters. Better a subsequent of $X, Y : B$ than $X, Y : B$ itself! Since X and Y will both be subsets of our set of axioms, or of our set of scientific hypotheses and observational statements, we will always be interested in (i) their mutual consistency, and (ii) how little of their combined forces are needed, should they be consistent, to deliver the consequence B.

It is only a very special and narrow concern (even in the presence of perfectibility) that is catered for by the demand that we should design our logical system in such a way as to guarantee the truth of the Principle of Pasting of Perfect Proofs for a Sound Result. The sound result will still be *discoverable* by *some* means or other anyway, since it admits of (direct) proof. Why insist that someone who has chosen a judicious lemma A and has found a proof Π of $X : A$ and a proof Σ of $Y, A : B$, should, simply by virtue of the soundness (but not perfect validity) of $X, Y : B$ itself, be able to bring out *that* fact of soundness by putting together those particular proofs Π and Σ and operating on them in some effective way?

Lemmata are but points of logical access; each furnishes a pair of perspectives on the overall problem. Through a lemma, one sees, Janus-like, two aspects of truth-transmission, looking up and looking down. Looking up at the premises X from the lemma A, one sees A as having been derived by virtue of a particular delineation of logical structure. Looking down to the conclusion B from the lemma A and other premises Y, one sees B as following from Y, A by virtue of a possibly different delineation of logical structure. The lemma A conforms to both delineations by being the unification of its counterparts in the upper proof and the lower proof. If the overall argument $X, Y : B$ is indeed sound, and one wants to see *this*, and *not* rest content with any epistemically gainful proof of some proper subsequent of $X, Y : B$, then one must work to do so directly, from X, Y to B without breaking the job down into a passage *to* some lemma A and a passage *from* it.

The job of logic is to transmit truth as *economically* as possible. There is economy in the 'proper subsetting of sequents' that yields epistemic gain. There is economy in proof-search when premises have to be relevant to their conclusions.[15] And there is computational economy in seeking proofs

---

[15]Or *should* be. This is why I object to the Anderson–Belnap system R of propositional logic—it is undecidable. By contrast, my method of relevantising a logical system does not increase the complexity of its decision problem. See my book *Autologic*, Edinburgh University Press, 1992, for a full discussion of all aspects of this consideration.

of and from judiciously chosen lemmata. If that makes deduction fail to be unrestrictedly transitive, then so be it.

7

What is a Logical System?

D. M. Gabbay

1 Introduction

There is an increasing demand from computer science, linguistics and philosophy for a variety of logical systems. This is prompted by the extensive applications of logic in theoretical computer science, artificial intelligence and logic programming. In these fields there is a growing need for a diversity of semantically meaningful and algorithmically presented logical systems which can serve various applications. Therefore renewed research activity is being devoted to analysing and tinkering with old and new logics.

This activity has produced a shift in the notion of a logical system. Traditionally a logic was perceived as a 'consequence relation' between *sets* of formulas. Problems arising in application areas have emphasized the need for consequence relations between structures of formulas (such as multisets, sequences or even richer structures). The general notion of a *structured consequence relation* was put forward in [9]. This finer-tuned approach to the notion of a logical system introduces new problems which call for an improved general framework in which many of the new logics arising from computer science applications can be presented and investigated.

This chapter is a systematic study of the notion of what is a logical system. It will incrementally motivate a notion of logical system through the needs of various applications and applied logical activity. The chapter proposes an increasingly more detailed image of a logical system. The initial position is that of a logical system as a consequence relation on sets of formulas. Thus any set theoretical binary relation of the form $\Delta \mathrel{\vdash\!\!\!\sim} \Gamma$ satisfying certain conditions (reflexivity, monotonicity and cut) is a logical system. Such a relation has to be mathematically presented. This can be done either semantically, or set theoretically or it can be algorithmically generated. There are several options for the latter. Generate first the $\{A \mid \varnothing \mathrel{\vdash\!\!\!\sim} A\}$ as a Hilbert system and then generate $\{(\Delta, \Gamma) \mid \Delta \mathrel{\vdash\!\!\!\sim} \Gamma\}$

or generate the pairs (Δ, Γ) directly (via Gentzen rules) or use any other means (other proof theories)?

The concepts of a *logical system, semantics* and *proof theory* are not sharp enough even in the traditional literature. There are no clear definitions of what is a proof theoretic formulation of a logic (as opposed to e.g. a decision procedure algorithm) and what is e.g. a Gentzen formulation. Let us try here to propose a working definition, only for the purpose of making the reader a bit more comfortable and not necessarily for the purpose of giving a definitive formulation of these concepts.

- We start with the notion of a well formed formula of the language **L** of the logic.

- A consequence relation is a binary relation on finite sets of formulas, Δ, Γ written as $\Delta \mathrel{\vert\!\sim} \Gamma$, satisfying certain conditions, namely reflexivity, monotonicity and cut.

- Such a relation can be defined in many ways. For example, one can list all pairs (Δ, Γ) such that $\Delta \mathrel{\vert\!\sim} \Gamma$ should hold. Another way is to give Δ, Γ to some computer program and wait for an answer (which should always come).

- A semantics is an interpretation of the language **L** into some family of set theoretical structures, together with an interpretation of the consequence relation $\mathrel{\vert\!\sim}$ in terms of the interpretation. What I have just said is not clear in itself because I have not explained what 'structures' are and what an interpretation is. Indeed, there is no clear definition of what a semantics is. In my book [6], following Scott I defined a *model* as a function **s** giving each wff of the language a value in $\{0,1\}$. A semantics $\mathcal{S}$ is a set of models, and $\Delta \mathrel{\vert\!\sim_{\mathcal{S}}} \Gamma$ is defined as the condition:

$$(\forall \mathbf{s} \in \mathcal{S})[\forall X \in \Delta(\mathbf{s}(X) = 1) \rightarrow \exists Y \in \Gamma(\mathbf{s}(Y) = 1)]$$

- There can be algorithmic systems for generating $\mathrel{\vert\!\sim}$. Such systems are not to be considered 'proof theoretical systems' for $\mathrel{\vert\!\sim}$. They could be decision procedures or just optimal theorem proving machines.

- the notion of a proof system is not well defined in the literature. There are some recognized methodologies such as 'Gentzen formulations', 'tableaux', 'Hilbert style' but these are not sharply defined. For our purpose, let us agree that a *proof system* is any algorithmic system for generating $\mathrel{\vert\!\sim}$ using rules of the form:

$$\frac{\Delta_1 \mathrel{\vert\!\sim} \Gamma_1; \ldots; \Delta_n \mathrel{\vert\!\sim} \Gamma_n}{\Delta \mathrel{\vert\!\sim} \Gamma}$$

and 'axioms' of the form:

$$\frac{\varnothing}{\Delta \hspace{1pt}\vdash\hspace{-3pt}\sim \Gamma}$$

The axioms are the initial list of $(\Delta, \Gamma) \in \hspace{-3pt}\sim$ and the other rules generate more. So a proof system is a particular way of generating $\vdash\hspace{-3pt}\sim$. Note that there need not be structural requirement on the rule (that each involves a main connective and some subformulas, etc.).

A Hilbert formulation is a proof system where all the Δs involved are $\varnothing$. A Gentzen formulation would be a proof system where the rules are very nicely structured (try to define something reasonable yourself; again, there is no clear definition!). A Gentzen system can be viewed as a higher level Hilbert system for the 'connective' '$\vdash\hspace{-3pt}\sim$'.

A tableaux formulation is a syntactical countermodel construction relative to some semantics. We have $\Delta\vdash\hspace{-3pt}\sim\Gamma$ if the countermodel construction is 'closed' i.e. must always fail. It is also possible to present tableaux formulations for logics which have no semantics if the consequence $\vdash\hspace{-3pt}\sim$ and the connectives satisfy some conditions.

The central role which proof theoretical methodologies play in generating logics compels us to put forward the view that a logical system is a pair $(\vdash\hspace{-3pt}\sim, \mathbf{S}_{\vdash\hspace{-3pt}\sim})$, where $\mathbf{S}_{\vdash\hspace{-3pt}\sim}$ is a proof theory for $\vdash\hspace{-3pt}\sim$. In other words, we are saying that it is not enough to know $\vdash\hspace{-3pt}\sim$ to 'understand' the logic, but we must also know how it is presented (i.e. $\mathbf{S}_{\vdash\hspace{-3pt}\sim}$).

The next shift in our concept of a logic is when we observed from application areas whose knowledge representation involves data and assumptions the need to add structure to the assumptions and the fact that the reasoning involved relies on and uses the structure. This view also includes non-monotonic systems. This led us to develop the noton of *Labelled Deductive Systems* and adopt the view that this is the framework for presenting logics. Whether we accept these new systems as logics or not, classical logic must be able to represent them.

The real departure from traditional logics (as opposed to just giving them more structure) comes with the notion of aggregating arguments. Real human reasoning does aggregate arguments (circumstantial evidence in favour of A as opposed to evidence for $\neg A$) and what is known as quantitative (fuzzy) reasoning systems make heavy use of that. Fortunately *LDS* can handle that easily. The section concludes with the view that a proper practical reasoning system has 'mechanisms' for updates, inputs, abduction, actions, etc., as well as databases (theories, assumptions), and that a proper logic is an integrated *LDS* system together with a specific choice of such mechanisms.[1]

2   Logical systems as consequence relations

Traditionally, to present a logic **L**, we need to present first the set of well formed formulas of that logic. This is the *language* of the logic. We define the sets of atomic formulas, connectives, quantifiers and the set of arbitrary formulas. Secondly we define mathematically the notion of consequence, namely, for a given set of formulas Δ and a given formula Q, we define the consequence relation $\Delta \vdash_L Q$, reading 'Q follows from Δ in the logic **L**'.

The consequence relation is required to satisfy the following intuitive properties: (Δ, Δ' abbreviates $\Delta \cup \Delta'$).

Reflexivity

$$\Delta \vdash Q \text{ if } Q \in \Delta$$

Monotonicity

$$\Delta \vdash Q \text{ implies } \Delta, \Delta' \vdash Q$$

Transitivity (cut)[2]:

$$\Delta \vdash A; \ \Delta, A \vdash Q \text{ imply } \Delta \vdash Q$$

---

[1]My personal view is that this is a logic i.e. Logic = *LDS* system + several *mechanisms*. In AI circles this might be called *an agent*. Unfortunately, the traditional logic community are still very conservative in the sense that they have not even accepted non-monotonic reasoning systems as logics yet. They believe that all this excitement is transient, temporarily generated by computer science and that it will fizzle out sooner or later. They believe that we will soon be back to the old research problems, such as how many non-isomorphic models does a theory have in some inaccessible cardinal or what is the ordinal of yet another subsystem of analysis. I think this is fine for mathematical logic but not for the logic of human reasoning. There is no conflict here between the new and the old, just further evolution of the subject.

[2]There are several versions of the **cut rule** in the literature, they are all equivalent for the cases of classical and intuitionistic logic but are not equivalent in the context of this section. The version in the main text we call **transitivity (lemma generation)**. Another version is:

$$\frac{\Gamma \vdash A; \quad \Delta, A \vdash B}{\Delta, \Gamma \vdash B}.$$

This version implies **monotonicity**, when added to **reflexivity**.
Another version we call **internal cut**:

$$\frac{\Delta, A \vdash \Gamma; \quad \Delta \vdash A, \Gamma}{\Delta \vdash \Gamma}.$$

The consequence relation may be defined in various ways. Either through an algorithmic system $\mathbf{S}_{\vdash}$, or implicitly by postulates on the properties of $\vdash$.

Thus a logic is obtained by specifying $\mathbf{L}$ and $\vdash$. Two algorithmic systems $\mathbf{S}_1$ and $\mathbf{S}_2$ which give rise to the same $\vdash$ are considered the same logic.

If you think of Δ as a database and Q as a query, then reflexivity means that the answer is yes to any Q which is officially listed in the database. Monotonicity reflects the accumulation of data, and transitivity is nothing but lemma generation, namely if $\Delta \vdash A$, then A can be used as a lemma to obtain B from Δ.

The above properties seemed minimal and most natural for a logical system to have, given that the main applications of logic were in mathematics and philosophy.

The above notion was essentially put forward by [18] and is referenced to as Tarski consequence. [17], following [3], generalised the notion to allow Q to be a set of formulas Γ. The basic relation is then of the form $\Delta \vdash \Gamma$, satisfying:

Reflexivity

$$\Delta \vdash \Gamma \text{ if } \Delta \cap \Gamma \neq \varnothing$$

Monotonicity

$$\frac{\Delta \vdash \Gamma}{\Delta, \Delta' \vdash \Gamma}$$

Transitivity (cut)

$$\frac{\Delta, A \vdash \Gamma; \Delta' \vdash A, \Gamma'}{\Delta', \Delta \vdash \Gamma, \Gamma'}$$

Scott has shown that for any Tarski consequence relation there exist two Scott consequence relations (a maximal one and a minimal one) that agree with it (see my book [7]).

A more restricted version of cut is **unitary cut**:

$$\frac{\Delta \vdash A; A \vdash Q}{\Delta \vdash Q}$$

The above notions are monotonic. However, the increasing use of logic in artificial intelligence has given rise to logical systems which are not monotonic. The axiom of monotonicity is not satisfied in these systems. There are many such systems, satisfying a variety of conditions, presented in a variety of ways. Furthermore, some are proof theoretical and some are model theoretical. All these different presentations give rise to some notion of consequence $\Delta \mathrel{\vdash\mkern-9mu\sim} Q$, but they only seem to all agree on some form of restricted reflexivity $(A \mathrel{\vdash\mkern-9mu\sim} A)$. The essential difference between these logics (commonly called *non-monotonic logics*) and the more traditional logics (now referred to as *monotonic logics*) is the fact that $\Delta \mathrel{\vdash\mkern-9mu\sim} A$ holds in the monotonic case because of some $\Delta_A \subseteq \Delta$, while in the non-monotonic case the entire set Δ is used to derive A. Thus if Δ is increased to Δ', there is no change in the monotonic case, while there may be a change in the non-monotonic case.

The above describes the situation current in the early 1980s. We have had a multitude of systems generally accepted as 'logics' without a unifying underlying theory and many had semantics without proof theory. Many had proof theory without semantics, though almost all of them were based on some sound intuitions of one form or another. Clearly there was the need for a general unifying framework. An early attempt at classifying non-monotonic systems was [4]. It was put forward that basic axioms for a consequence relation should be *reflexivity, transitivity (cut)* and *restricted monotonicity*, namely:

Restricted monotonicity

$$\frac{\Delta \mathrel{\vdash\mkern-9mu\sim} A; \Delta \mathrel{\vdash\mkern-9mu\sim} B}{\Delta, A \mathrel{\vdash\mkern-9mu\sim} B}$$

A variety of systems seem to satisfy this axiom. Further results were obtained [14, 16, 15, 19, 20] and the area was called 'axiomatic theory of the consequence relation' by Wójcicki.[3]

Although some classification was obtained and semantical results were proved, the approach does not seem to be strong enough. Many systems do not satisfy restricted monotonicity. Other systems such as relevance logic, do not satisfy even reflexivity. Others have richness of their own which is lost in a simple presentation as an axiomatic consequence relation. Obviously a different approach is needed, one which would be more sensitive to the variety of features of the systems in the field. Fortunately, developments in a neighbouring area, that of automated deduction, seem to give us a clue.

---

[3]In general, the exact formulations of transitivity and reflexivity can force some form of monotonicity.

3 Logical systems as algorithmic proof systems

The relative importance of automated deduction is on the increase, in view of its wide applicability. New automated deduction methods have been developed for non-classical logics, and resolution has been generalized and modified to be applicable to these logics. In general, because of the value of these logics in theoretical computer science and artificial intelligence, a greater awareness of the computational aspects of logical systems is developing and more attention being devoted to proof theoretical presentations. It became apparent to us that a key feature in the proof theoretic study of these logics is that a slight natural variation in an automated or proof theoretic system of one logic (say L_1), can yield another logic (say L_2).

Although L_1 and L_2 may be conceptually far apart (in their philosophical motivation, and mathematical definitions) when it comes to automated techniques and proof theoretical presentation, they turn out to be brother and sister. This kind of relationship is not isolated and seems to be widespread. Furthermore, non-monotonic systems seem to be obtainable from monotonic ones through variations on some of their monotonic proof theoretical formulation.

This seems to give us some handle on classifying non-monotonic systems.

This phenomenon has prompted us to put forward the view that a logical system L is not just the traditional consequence relation $\vdash$ (monotonic or non monotonic) but a pair $(\vdash, S_\vdash)$, where $\vdash$ is a mathematically defined consequence relation (i.e. the set of pairs (Δ, Γ) such that $\Delta \vdash \Gamma$) satisfying whatever minimal conditions on a consequence one happens to agree to, and $S_\vdash$ is an algorithmic system for generating all those pairs [5]. Thus according to this definition classical propositional logic $\vdash$ perceived as a set of tautologies together with a Gentzen system $S_\vdash$ is not the same as classical logic together with the two valued truth table decision procedure $T_\vdash$ for it. In our conceptual framework,$(\vdash, S_\vdash)$ is *not the same logic* as $(\vdash, T_\vdash)$.

To illustrate and motivate our way of thinking, observe that it is very easy to move from $T_\vdash$ for classical logic to a truth table system $T_\vdash^n$ for Łukasiewicz n-valued logic. It is not so easy to move to an algorithmic system for intuitionistic logic. In comparison, for a Gentzen system presentation, exactly the opposite is true. Intuitionistic and classical logics are neighbours, while Łukasiewicz logics seem completely different. In fact for a Hilbert style or Gentzen style formulation, one can show proof theoretic similarities between Łukasiewicz's infinite valued logic and Girard's Linear Logic, which in turn is proof theoretically similar to intuitionistic logic.

This issue has a bearing on the notion of 'what is classical logic'. Given an algorithmic proof system $\mathbf{S}_{\vdash_c}$ for classical logic $\vdash_c$, then $(\vdash_c, \mathbf{S}_{\vdash_c})$ is certainly classical logic. Now suppose we change $\mathbf{S}_{\vdash_c}$ a bit by adding heuristics to obtain $\mathbf{S}'$. The heuristics and modifications are needed to support an application area. Can we still say that we are essentially in 'classical logic? I suppose we can because $\mathbf{S}'$ is just a slight modification of $\mathbf{S}_{\vdash_c}$. However, slight modifications of an algorithmic system may yield another well-known logic. In fact $\mathbf{S}'$ may be linear logic. So is linear logic essentially classical logic, slightly modified, or vice versa?

We give an example from goal directed implicational logic. Consider a language with implication only. It is easy to see that all wffs A have the form $A_1 \rightarrow (A_2 \rightarrow \ldots \rightarrow (A_n \rightarrow q)\ldots)$, q atomic, where A_i has the same form as A. We now describe a computation with database a multiset Δ of wffs of the above form and the goal a wff of the above form. We use the metapredicate $\Delta \vdash A$ to mean the computation succeeds i.e. A follows from Δ. Here are the rules:

1. $\Delta, q \vdash q$, q atomic and Δ empty. (Note that we are not writing $A \vdash A$ for arbitrary A. We are not writing a Gentzen system.)

2. $\Delta \vdash A_1 \rightarrow (A_2 \rightarrow \ldots \rightarrow (A_n \rightarrow q)\ldots)$ if $\Delta \cup \{A_1, \ldots, A_n\} \vdash q$. Remember we are dealing with multisets.

3. $\Delta' = \Delta \cup \{A_1 \rightarrow (A_2 \rightarrow \ldots (A_n \rightarrow q)\ldots)\} \vdash q$ if $\Delta = \Delta_1 \cup \Delta_2 \cup \ldots \cup \Delta_n$, $\Delta_i, i = 1, \ldots, n$ are pairwise disjoint and $\Delta_i \vdash A_i$.

The above computation characterizes linear implication. If we relinquish the side condition in (3) and let $\Delta_i = \Delta'$ and the side condition (1) that Δ is empty, we get intuitionistic implication.

The difference in logics is serious. In terms of proof methodologies, the difference is minor. More examples in [5].

4 Logical systems as algorithmic structured consequence relations

Further observation of field examples shows that in many cases the database is not just a set of formulas but a structured set of formulas. The most common is a list or multiset.[4] Such structures appear already in linear and concatenation logics and in many non-monotonic systems such as priority and inheritance systems. In many algorithmically presented systems much use is made (either explicitly or implicitly) of this additional structure.

---

[4]Classical logic cannot make these distinctions using conjunction only. It needs further annotation or use of predicates.

A very common example is a Horn clause program. The list of clauses

$$(a_1) \quad q$$
$$(a_2) \quad q \to q$$

does not behave in the same way as the list

$$(b_1) \quad q \to q$$
$$(b_2) \quad q$$

The query $?q$ succeeds from one and loops from the other.

It is necessary to formulate axioms and notions of consequence relations for structures. This is studied in detail in [9]. Here are the main features:

- Databases (assumptions) are structured. They are not just sets of formulas but have a more general structure such as multisets, lists, partially ordered sets, etc. To present a database formally, we need to describe the structures. Let $\mathcal{M}$ be a class of structures (e.g. all finite trees). Then a database Δ has the form $\Delta = (M, \mathbf{f})$, where $M \in \mathcal{M}$ and $\mathbf{f} : M \mapsto$ wffs, such that for each $t \in M, \mathbf{f}(t)$ is a formula. We assume the one point structure $\{t\}$ is always in $\mathcal{M}$. We also assume we know how to take any single point $t \in M$ out of M and obtain $(M', \mathbf{f}'), \mathbf{f}' = \mathbf{f} \restriction M$. This we need for some versions of the cut rule and the deduction theorem.

- A structured-consequence relation $\mathrel{|\!\sim}$ is a relation $\Delta \mathrel{|\!\sim} A$ between structured databases Δ and formulas A. (We will not deal with structured consequence relations between two structured databases $\Delta \mathrel{|\!\sim} \Gamma$ here. See [9].)

- $\mathrel{|\!\sim}$ must satisfy the minimal conditions, namely

Identity

$$\{A\} \mathrel{|\!\sim} A$$

Surgical cut

$$\frac{\Delta \mathrel{|\!\sim} A; \Gamma[A] \mathrel{|\!\sim} B}{\Gamma[\Delta] \mathrel{|\!\sim} B}$$

where $\Gamma[A]$ means that A resides somewhere in the structure Γ and $\Gamma[\Delta]$ means that Δ replaces A in the structure. These concepts have to be defined precisely. If $\Delta = (M_1, \mathbf{f}_1)$ and $\Gamma = (M_2, \mathbf{f}_2)$ then $\Gamma[A]$ displays the fact that for some $t \in M_2$, $\mathbf{f}_2(t) = A$. We allow for the case that $M_2 = \mathbf{f}_2 = \varnothing$ (i.e. taking A out) We need a notion of substitution, which is a three place function $\mathbf{Sub}(\Gamma, \Delta, t)$, meaning that for $t \in M_2$ we substitute M_1 in place of t. This gives us a structure $(M_3, \mathbf{f}_3)$ according to the definition of $\mathbf{Sub}$. $(M_3, \mathbf{f}_3)$ is displayed as $\Gamma[\Delta]$, and $\Gamma[\varnothing]$ displays the case of taking A out.

Many non-monotonic systems satisfy a more restricted version of surgical cut:

$$\frac{\Gamma[\varnothing/A] \hspace{0.1cm}\vdash\hspace{-0.3cm}\sim\hspace{0.1cm} A; \Gamma[A] \hspace{0.1cm}\vdash\hspace{-0.3cm}\sim\hspace{0.1cm} B}{\Gamma[\Gamma[\varnothing/A]] \hspace{0.1cm}\vdash\hspace{-0.3cm}\sim\hspace{0.1cm} B}$$

Another variant would be

Deletional cut

$$\frac{\Gamma[\varnothing/A] \hspace{0.1cm}\vdash\hspace{-0.3cm}\sim\hspace{0.1cm} A; \Gamma[A] \hspace{0.1cm}\vdash\hspace{-0.3cm}\sim\hspace{0.1cm} B}{\Gamma[\varnothing/A] \hspace{0.1cm}\vdash\hspace{-0.3cm}\sim\hspace{0.1cm} B}$$

- A logical system is a pair $(\hspace{0.1cm}\vdash\hspace{-0.3cm}\sim\hspace{0.1cm}, \mathbf{S}_{\vdash\hspace{-0.25cm}\sim})$, where $\hspace{0.1cm}\vdash\hspace{-0.3cm}\sim\hspace{0.1cm}$ is a structured-consequence and $\mathbf{S}_{\vdash\hspace{-0.25cm}\sim}$ is an algorithmic system for it.

Of course we continue to maintain our view that different algorithmic systems for the same structured consequence relation define different logics. Still although we now have a fairly general concept of a logic, we do not have a general framework. Monotonic and non-monotonic systems still seem conceptually different. There are many diverse examples among temporal logics, modal logics, defeasible logics and more. Obviously, there is a need for a more unifying framework. The question is, can we adopt a concept of a logic where the passage from one logic to another is natural, and along predefined acceptable modes of variation? Can we put forward a framework where the computational aspects of a logic also play a role? Is it possible to find a common home for a variety of seemingly different techniques introduced for different purposes in seemingly different intellectual logical traditions?

5 Logical systems as labelled deductive systems

To find an answer, let us ask ourselves what makes one logic different from another? How is a new logic presented and described and compared to another? The answer is obvious. These considerations are performed in the metalevel. Most logics are based on modus ponens anyway. The quantifier rules are formally the same anyway and the differences between them are metalevel considerations on the proof theory or semantics. If we can find a mode of presentation of logical systems where metalevel features can reside side by side with object level features then we can hope for a general framework. We must be careful here. In the logical community the notions of object level vs metalevel are not so clear. Most people think of *naming* and *proof predicates* in this connection. This is not what we mean by metalevel here. We need a more refined understanding of the concept. There is a similar need in computer science.

We found that the best framework to put forward is that of a *Labelled Deductive System, LDS,* see [10]. Our notion of what is a logic is that of a pair $(\mathord{\vdash}, \mathbf{S}_{\vdash})$ where $\mathord{\vdash}$ is a structured (possibly non-monotonic) consequence relation on a language $\mathbf{L}$ and $\mathbf{S}_{\vdash}$ is an *LDS*, and where $\mathord{\vdash}$ is essentially required to satisfy no more than *Identity* (i.e. $\{A\} \mathrel{\vdash} A$) and a version of *Cut*. This is a refinement of our concept of a logical system presented in [5]. We now not only say that a logical system is a pair $(\mathord{\vdash}, \mathbf{S}_{\vdash})$, but we are adding that $\mathbf{S}_{\vdash}$ itself has a special presentation, that of an *LDS*.

As a first approximation, we can say that an *LDS* system is a triple $(\mathbf{L}, \mathcal{A}, \mathbf{M})$, where $\mathbf{L}$ is a logical language (connectives and wffs) and $\mathcal{A}$ is an algebra (with some operations) of labels and $\mathbf{M}$ is a discipline of labelling formulas of the logic (from the algebra of labels $\mathcal{A}$), together with deduction rules and with agreed ways of propagating the labels via the application of the deduction rules. The way the rules are used is more or less uniform to all systems.

To present an *LDS* system we need first to define its set of formulas and its set of labels.

For example, we can take the language of classical logic as the formulas (with variables, constants and quantifiers) and take some set of function symbols on the same variables and constants as generating the labels. More precisely, we allow ordinary formulas of predicate logic with quantifiers to be our *LDS* formulas. Thus $\exists x A(x, y)$ is a formula with free variable y and bound variable x. To generate the labels, we start with a new set of function symbols $t_1(y), t_2(x, y), \ldots$ of various arities which can be applied to the *same* variables which appear in the formulas. Thus the labels and formulas can share variables, or even some constants and function symbols. In other words in some applications it might be useful to allow some labels to appear inside formulas A. We can form declarative units of the form $t_1(y) : \exists x A(x, y)$. When y is assigned a value $y = a$, so is the label and we get $t_1(a) : \exists x A(x, a)$. The labels should be viewed as more information about the formulas, which is not coded inside the formula, (hence dependence of the labels on variables x makes sense as the extra information may be different for different x). A formal definition of an algebraic *LDS* system will be given later, meanwhile, let us give an informal definition of an *LDS* system and some examples which help us understand what and why we would want labels.[5]

Definition 5.1 (Prototype *LDS* system). Let $\mathcal{A}$ be a first order language of the form $\mathcal{A} = (A, R_1, \ldots, R_k, f_1, \ldots, f_m)$ where A is the set of terms of the algebra (individual variables and constants) and R_i are predicate symbols (on A, possibly binary but not necessarily so) and $f_1, \ldots, f_m$ are function symbols (on A) of various arities. We think of the elements of A as atomic labels and of the functions as generating more labels and of the predicates as giving additional structure to the labels. A typical example would be (A, R, f_1, f_2) where R is binary and f_1, f_2 are unary.

A *diagram* of labels is a set M containing elements generated from A by the function symbols together with formulas of the form $\pm R(t_1, \ldots, t_k)$, where $t_i \in M$ and R is a predicate symbol of the algebra.

Let **L** be a predicate language with connectives $\sharp_1, \ldots, \sharp_n$, of various arities, with quantifiers and with the *same* set of atomic terms A as the algebra.

We define the notions of a declarative unit, a database and a label as follows:

1. An atomic label is any $t \in A$. A label is any term generated from the atomic labels by the symbols $f_1, \ldots, f_m$.

---

[5]The idea of annotating formulas for various purposes is not new. A. R. Anderson and N. Belnap in their book on Entailment, label formulas and propagate lables during proofs to keep track of relevance of assumptions. Term annotations (Curry–Howard formula as type approach) are also known where the propagation rules are functional application. The Lambek Calculus and the categorial approach is also related to labelling. The extra arguments sometimes present in the Demo predicate of metalogic programming are also a form of labelling. What is new is that we are proposing that we use an arbitrary algebra for the labels and consider the labelling as part of the logic. We are creating a discipline of *LDS* and claiming that we have a unifying framework for logics and that almost any logic can be given an *LDS* formulation. We can give $\vdash\!\!\!\sim$ an *LDS* formulation provided $\vdash\!\!\!\sim$ is reflexive and transitive and each connective is either $\vdash\!\!\!\sim$ monotonic or antimonotonic in each of its arguments. See [8]. We are claiming that the notion of a logic is an *LDS*. This is not the same as the occasional use of labelling with some specific purpose in mind. We are translating and investigating systematically all the traditional logical concepts into the context of *LDS* and generalising them.

I am reminded of the story of the Yuppy who hired an interior decorator to redesign his sitting room. After much study, the decorator recommended that the Yuppy needed a feeling of space and so the best thing to do is to arrange the furniture against the wall, so that there will be a lot of space in the middle. The cleaning lady, when she first saw the new design was very pleased. She thought it was an excellent idea. 'Yes', said the Yuppy, 'and I paid £1000 for it'. 'That was stupid', exclaimed the cleaning lady, 'I could have told you for free! I arrange the furniture this way every time I clean the floor!'.

Of course she is right, but she used the idea of the new arrangement only as a side effect!

2. A formula is any formula of **L**.

3. A declarative unit is a pair $t : A$, where t is a label and A is a formula.

4. A database is either a declarative unit or has the form $(a, M, \mathbf{f})$, where M is a finite diagram of labels, $a \in M$ is the distinguished label, and $\mathbf{f}$ is a function associating with each label t in M either a database or a finite set of formulas. (Note that this is a recursive clause. We get simple databases if we allow $\mathbf{f}$ to associate with each label t only single or finite sets of formulas. Simple databases are adequate for a large number of applications.)

Definition 5.1 is simplified. To understand it intuitively, think of the atomic labels as atomic places and times (top of the hill, 1 Jan. 1992, etc.) and the function symbols as generating more labels, namely more times and more places (*behind*(x), *day after*(t), etc.). We form declarative units by taking labels and attaching formulas to them. Complex structures $(a, M, \mathbf{f})$ of these units are databases. This definition can be made more complex. Here the labels are terms generated by function symbols from atomic labels. We can complicate matters by using databases themselves as labels. This will give us recursively more complex, richer labels. We will not go into that now. The first simplification is therefore that we are not using databases as labels. The second simplification is that we assume constant domains. All times and places have the same elements (population) in them. If this were not the case we would need a function U_t giving the elements residing in t, and a database would have the form $(A, M, \mathbf{f}, U_t)$.

Example 5.2 Consider a language with the predicate $VS900(x, t)$. This is a two sorted predicate, denoting Virgin airline flight London–Tokyo, where t is the flight date and x is a name of an individual. For example $VS900$ (Dov, 15.11.91) may be put in the database, denoting that Dov is booked on this flight scheduled to embark on 15.11.91.

If the airline practices overbooking and cancellation procedures (whatever that means), it might wish to annotate the entries by further useful information such as

- Time of booking;

- Individual/group travel booking;

- Type of ticket

- ± VIP.

This information may be of a different nature to that coded in the main predicate and it is therefore more convenient to keep it as an annotation, or label. It may also be the case that the manipulation of the extra information is of a different nature to that of the predicate.

In general, there may be many uses for the label t in the declarative unit $t : A$. Here is a partial list:

- Fuzzy reliability value:
  (a number $x, 0 \leq x \leq 1$.) Used mainly in expert systems.

- Origin of A:
  t indicates where the input A came from. Very useful in complex databases.

- Priority of A:
  t can be a date of entry of updates and a later date (label) means a higher priority.

- Time when A holds:
  (temporal logic)

- Possible world where A holds:
  (modal logic)

- t indicates the proof of A:
  (which assumptions were used in deriving A and the history of the proof). This is a useful labelling for Truth Maintenance Systems.

- t can be the situation and A the infon (of situation semantics).

Example 5.3 Let us look at one particular example, connected with modal logic. Assume the algebra $\mathcal{A}$ has the form $(A, <)$, with a set of atomic labels A, no function symbols and a binary relation $<$. According to the previous definition, a diagram of labels would contain a (finite) set $M \subseteq A$, together with a set of pairs of the form $\{t < s\}$, $t, s, \in M$. A database has the form $(a, M, \mathbf{f})$, where M is a finite diagram and $\mathbf{f}$ is a function, say giving a formula $A_t = \mathbf{f}(t)$, for each $t \in M$.

The perceptive reader may feel resistence to the idea of the label at this stage. First be assured that you are not asked to give up your favourite logic or proof theory, nor is there any hint of a claim that your activity is now obsolete. In mathematics a good concept can rarely be seen or studied from one point of view only and it is a sign of strength to have several views connecting different concepts. So the traditional logical views are as valid as ever and add strength to the new point of view. In fact, manifestations of our *LDS* approach already exist in the literature in various forms, they were locally regarded as convenient tools and there was not the realization that there is a general framework to be studied and developed. None of us is working in a vacuum and we build on each other's work. Further, the existence of a general framework in which any particular case can be represented does not necessarily mean that the best way to treat that particular case is within the general framework. Thus if some modal logics can be formulated in *LDS*, this does not mean that in practice we should replace existing ways of treating the logics by their *LDS* formulation. The latter may not be the most efficient for those particular logics. It is sufficient to show how the *LDS* principles specialize and manifest themselves in the given known practical formulation of the logic.

The reader may further have doubts about the use of labels from the computational point of view. What do we mean by a unifying framework? Surely a Turing machine can simulate any logic. Is that a unifying framework? The use of labels is powerful, as we know from computer science. Are we using labels to play the role of a Turing machine? The answer to the question is twofold. First that we are not operating at the metalevel, but at the object level (see point 4 below). Second, there are severe restrictions on the way we use *LDS*. Here is a preview:

1. The only rules of inference allowed are the traditional ones, modus ponens and some form of deduction theorem for implication, for example.

2. Allowable modes of label propagation are fixed for all logics. They can be adjusted in agreed ways to obtain variations but in general the format is the same. For example, it has the following form for implications:

   Let $LDS_{\twoheadrightarrow}$ be a particular *LDS* system with labels $\mathcal{A}$, and with $\twoheadrightarrow$ a special implication characteristic to this particular *LDS* system. Then there exists a fixed set of labels Γ, which can characterize $\twoheadrightarrow$ as follows. For any theory Δ (of labelled wffs) we have: Δ proves $(A \twoheadrightarrow B)$ with label t iff $\forall x \in \Gamma$ [B can be proved from Δ and $x : A$ with label $t + x$], where Γ is a set of labels characterizing the implication in that particular logic. For example Γ may be restricted to atomic labels only, or to labels related to t, or some other restrictions. The freedom that different logics have is in the choice of Γ and the (possibly not only equational) properties of '$+$'. For example we can restrict the use of modus ponens by a wise propagation of labels.

3. The quantifier rules are the same for all logics.

4. Metalevel features are implemented via the labelling mechanism, which is object language.

The reader who prefers to remain within the traditional point of view of:

assumptions (data) proving a conclusion

can view the labelled formulas as another form of data.

There are many occasions when it is most intuitive to present an item of data in the form $t : A$, where t is a label and A is a formula. The common underlying reason for the use of the label t is that t represents information which is needed to modify A or to supplement (the information in) A which is not of the same type or nature as (the information represented by) A itself. A is a logical formula representing information declaratively, and the additional information of t can certainly be added declaratively to A to form A', however, we may find it convenient to put forward the additional information through the label t as part of a pair $t : A$.

Take for example a source of information which is not reliable. A natural way of representing an item of information from that source is $t : A$, where A is a declarative presentation of the information itself and t is a number representing its reliability. Such expert systems exist (e.g. Mycin) with rules which manipulate both t and A as one unit, propagating the reliability values t through applications of modus ponens. We may also use a label naming the source of information and this would give us a qualitative idea of its reliability.

Another area where it is natural to use labels is in reasoning from data and rules. If we want to keep track, for reasons of maintaining consistency and/or integrity constraints, of where and how a formula was deduced, we use a label t. In this case, the label in $t : A$ can be the part of the data which was used to get A. Formally in this case t is a formula, the conjunction of the data used. We thus get pairs of the form $\Delta_i : A_i$, where A_i are formulas and Δ_i are the parts of the database from which A_i was derived.

A third example where it is natural to use labels is time stamping of data. Where data is constantly revised and updated, it is important to time stamp the data items. Thus the data items would look like $t_i : A_i$, where t_i are time stamps. A_i itself may be a temporal formula. Thus there are two times involved, the logical time s_i in $A_i(s_i)$ and the time stamping t_i of A_i. For reasons of clarity, we may wish to regard t_i as a label rather than incorporate it into the logic (by writing, for example, $A^*(t_i, s_i)$).

To summarize then, we replace the traditional notion of consequence between formulas of the form $A_1, \ldots, A_n \vdash B$ by the notion of consequence between labelled formulas

$$t_1 : A_1, t_2 : A_2, \ldots t_n : A_n \vdash s : B$$

Depending on the logical system involved, the intuitive meaning of the labels varies. In querying databases, we may be interested in labelling the assumptions so that when we get an answer to a query, we can record, via the label of the answer, from which part of the database the answer was obtained. Another area where labelling is used is temporal logic. We can time stamp assumptions as to when they are true and query, given those assumptions, whether a certain conclusion will be true at a certain time. Thus the consequence notion for labelled deduction is essentially the same as that of any logic: given assumptions does a conclusion follow?

Whereas in the traditional logical system the consequence is defined using proof rules on the formulas, in the *LDS* methodology the consequence is defined by using rules on both formulas and their labels. Formally we have formal rules for manipulating labels and this allows for more scope in decomposing the various features of the consequence relation. The meta-features can be reflected in the algebra or logic of the labels and the object features can be reflected in the rules of the formulas. Recall, however, that there are severe restrictions on how we use *LDS* rules, as we discussed earlier.

The notion of a database or of a 'set of assumptions' also has to be changed. A database is a hierarchical configuration of labelled formulas. The configuration depends on the labelling discipline. For example, it can be a linearly ordered set $\{a_1 : A_1, \ldots, a_n : A_n\}, a_1 < a_2 < \ldots < a_n$. The proof discipline for the logic will specify how the assumptions are to be used. See for example the logic programming case study.

We summarize our current position on what is a logical system. A logical system is a pair $(\vdash, LDS_{\vdash})$, where $\vdash$ is a consequence relation between labelled databases Δ and declarative units $t : A$ and $LDS_{\vdash}$ is an algorithmic system for $\vdash$.

We need one more component to the notion of a logical system. In previous subsections, a logical system was presented as $(\vdash, S_{\vdash})$, where $\vdash$ is a structured consequence relation satisfying *Identity* and *Surgical Cut* and $S_{\vdash}$ is an algorithmic proof system for computing $\vdash$. We are now saying that we need to refine this notion and deal with *Labelled Deductive Systems*, where $\vdash$ is a consequence relation between labelled databases Δ and declarative units $t : A$ and that $S_{\vdash}$ is replaced by some specific *LDS* discipline (algorithm) for computing the above. We need to be able to retrieve the old notion i.e. $(\vdash_1, S_{\vdash_1})$ from the new notion $(\vdash_2, LDS_{\vdash_2})$. In other words, we must add into *LDS* the capability of proving and reasoning without labels. To achieve this we can first reason with labels and then strip the labels and give a conclusion without labels. The additional algorithm which we can use to strip the labels is called *flattening*. Thus a labelled theory Δ may prove $t_i : A$ and $s_i : \neg A$, with many different labels t_i and s_i, depending on various labelling considerations and proof paths. The *flattening* algorithm will allow us to decide whether we flatten the pair of sets $(\{t_i\}, \{s_i\})$ to $+$ or $-$ i.e. whether we say $\Delta\!\!\sim\!\! A$ or $\Delta\!\!\sim\!\!\neg A$.

For example, if the labels represent moments of time or priorities, we may say the value is $+$ if max $\{t_i\} \geq \max\{s_j\}$. Or we may *interlace* the flattening with the deduction itself.

Thus, given a structured theory Δ (without labels) and a candidate A, we can have the following procedure, using *LDS*, for deciding whether $\Delta\!\!\sim\!\!?A$.

- Label the elements of Δ with completely different atomic labels, representing the existing structure in Δ.

- Use the *LDS* machinery to deduce all possibilities $\Delta\!\!\sim\!\! t_i : A$ and $\Delta\!\!\sim\!\! s_i : \neg A$.

- Flatten and get A (or interlace with flattening and get A).

Example 5.4 Here is an example of interlacing. The database has

$$t_1 : A$$
$$t_2 : \neg A$$
$$t_3 : \neg A \to B$$
$$t_4 : A \to \neg B.$$

Assume priority is $t_1 < t_2 < t_3 < t_4$, and assume a flattening process which gives higher priority rules superiority over low priority rules and similarly for facts but gives lexicographic superiority for rules over facts. Thus $t_4 t_1$ is stronger than $t_3 t_2$. If we deduce and then flatten, we get

$$t_4 t_1 : \neg B$$
$$t_3 t_2 : B$$

The flattening process would take $\neg B$.

If we pursue an interlace argument, we first flatten the premises and take $\neg A$ and then perform the modus ponens and get B.

6 Aggregated systems

So far all our logical systems have either proved or not proved a conclusion A. There was no possibility of aggregating arguments in favour of A as against arguments in favour of negation of A. The lack of aggregation is a basic characteristic which currently separates the symbolic, qualitative school of reasoning from the numerical, quantitative one.

There are many systems around (many are recognized as probabilistic systems, expert systems, fuzzy systems) which attach numerical values to assumptions and rules, use various functions and numerical procedures to manipulate these values and formulas and reach conclusions.

In many cases we get systems which give answers which seem to make sense, which can be very successfully and profitably applied but which cannot be recognized or understood by traditional logic. The main feature common to all of these numerical systems (which is independent of how they calculate and propagate their values) is that their 'proofs' aggregate. They can add the numbers involved and thus aggregate arguments. The spirit is: *Five good rumours are better than one proof.*

To further illustrate, consider the following example:

Example 6.1 The assumptions are:

$$t_1 : A \to C$$
$$t_2 : B \to C$$
$$t_3 : A$$
$$t_4 : B$$
$$t_5 : D \to \neg C$$
$$t_6 : D$$

Here we can conclude C in two different ways and conclude $\neg C$ in one way.

Non-monotonic systems like defeasible logic will not allow us to draw any conclusion unless one rule defeats all others. If we had a numerical evaluation of the data, say t_i are numbers in $[0\ 1]$, then we could aggregate our confidence in the conclusion. Thus we get:

$$(t_1 \cdot t_3 + t_2 \cdot t_4) : C$$
$$t_5 \cdot t_6 : \neg C$$

the two numbers can be compared and a conclusion reached.

If we operate in the context of *LDS*, we can use the labels to aggregate arguments. Any conclusion is proved with a label indicating its proof path. These can be formally (algebraically) added (aggregated) and an additional process (called *flattening*) can compare them.

In consequence relation terms, the property of aggregation destroys the cut rule. The reason is as follows:

Assume $\Delta, A \mathrel|\!\!\sim B$. This now means that the aggregated proofs in favour of B are stronger than the aggregated proofs in favour of $\neg B$. Similarly $\Gamma \mathrel|\!\!\sim A$ would mean the balance from Γ is in favour of A.

If we perform the cut we get

$$\Delta, \Gamma \mathrel|\!\!\sim ? B$$

Δ and Γ may interact, forming new additional proofs of $\neg B$, which outweigh the proofs for B.

Cut is a very basic rule in traditional logical systems and can be found in one form or another in each one of them. Thus it is clear that aggregation of arguments is a serious departure from traditional formal logic. Yet, it cannot be denied. In practical reasoning we do aggregate arguments and so logic, if it is to be successfully applied and be able to mirror human reasoning, must be able to cope with aggregation. Classical logic, if it is to be a universal language, must also be able to deal naturally with aggregation.

One form of cut is still valid. The unitary cut:

$$\frac{\Delta \mathrel{\vdash\!\!\!\sim} A; A \mathrel{\vdash\!\!\!\sim} B}{\Delta \mathrel{\vdash\!\!\!\sim} B}$$

This holds because there is nothing for Δ to interact with.

We thus require from our reasoning system that it satisfy only *Identity* $(A \mathrel{\vdash\!\!\!\sim} A)$ and *Unitary Cut*.

To show how real and possibly destructive aggregation can be, consider the example of Prince Karlos and Princess Laura.

Example 6.2 The prince and princess are separated. Both made it clear to the press that no third parties were involved and the separation was purely due to a personality clash. However, the editor Mr Angel of the *Daily Tabloid*, thought otherwise. First he observed that after her separation the princess moved to a house very near the Imperial Institute of Logic, Language and Computation. This in itself did not mean much, because both the Institute and the residence were in the centre of town. However, Mr Angel further found out that in the past two years, whenever the princess went on a European holiday, there was an Esprit project meeting in the same hotel, and surprisingly all projects involved a certain professor from the Institute. Again, this could be a coincidence, because it is a well known fact that Esprit project consortia find it most inspiring to be in the most expensive holiday resorts in Europe and it is equally well known that certain dynamic professors participate in many such projects.

However the plot thickens when the princess, as part of her general social activity, seems to actively support the new logics for computation. This could also be a coincidence because after all, this subject is going to transform the nature of our society. The various little arguments do seem to be aggregating, though not conclusively enough to risk an article in such a responsible paper as the *Daily Tabloid*. The situation changed when it became known that the princess actively supports Labelled Deductive Systems and the Universality of classical logic. Under this aggregation of arguments an obvious conclusion could be drawn!

7   Practical reasoning systems

Our discussion so far has generalized the notion of a *deductive system*; namely, given a database Δ and a formula Q, we ask the basic question, does Δ prove Q? The various concepts we have studied had to do with what form do Δ and Q take and what kinds of consequence relations $\hspace{-1pt}\vdash\hspace{-3pt}\sim$ and algorithmic systems $\mathbf{S}_{\hspace{-1pt}\vdash\hspace{-3pt}\sim}$ are involved.

In practical reasoning systems, the *deductive* question is but one of many which interest us. Other operations such as *updating, abduction, action, explanation* are also involved. If we rethink of Q as an *input*, we can partially list the kind of operations which may be involved. These operations are performed using algorithms which accompany the deductive component. We refer to them as *mechanisms*.

- The input Q is a query from Δ. We are interested in whether $\Delta \hspace{1pt}\vdash\hspace{-3pt}\sim Q$ and possibly ask what proofs are available.

- The input Q is an update. We want to insert Q into Δ to obtain Δ'. We may possibly have to deal with inconsistency and restructuring of Δ.[6]

- The input Q is an abductive stimulus (goal). We are interested in Δ' such that $\Delta + \Delta' \hspace{1pt}\vdash\hspace{-3pt}\sim Q$. Where $+$ is a symbol (to be precisely defined) which 'adds' or 'joins' Δ and Δ' to 'combine' their declarative information.

  The $+$ operation may or may not be the same as update. The abductive question is to find (possibly the minimal) Δ' which helps prove the input.[7]

- The input Q may be a stimulus for action on the database outputting a new database or outputting an explanation or any other output of interest.

The new possibilities of a formula Q interacting with a database Δ (via action or abduction or other mechanisms) allow for a new way of answering queries from Δ. To see this, consider the query $\Delta?Q$. In the declarative aspect, we want an answer, namely we are asking whether $\Delta\hspace{-1pt}\vdash\hspace{-3pt}\sim Q$. This can be checked via $\mathbf{S}_{\hspace{-1pt}\vdash\hspace{-3pt}\sim}$, or semantically. Q does not act or change Δ in any way. In the interactive case, we trigger an action. Q acts on Δ to produce a new Δ'. Q is read imperatively. We can write $\Delta!Q$ to stress this fact.

---

[6]Such a view has been presented in Chapter 13 of Bob Kowalski's book [13]. The systematic study of updates and theory change was initiated in [1].

[7]For a given system $(\hspace{-1pt}\vdash\hspace{-3pt}\sim, \mathbf{S}_{\hspace{-1pt}\vdash\hspace{-3pt}\sim})$, the abductive mechanism is usually dependent on $\mathbf{S}_{\hspace{-1pt}\vdash\hspace{-3pt}\sim}$, the particular algorithmic proof system involved. Different applications might require different abductive procedures.

The result of the interaction is Δ'. Thus $\Delta!Q = \Delta'$. Thus given a Δ and a Q, we have two options. We can ask whether $\Delta \mathrel{\vdash\!\!\!\sim} Q$ holds (written $\Delta?Q$, with $\mathrel{\vdash\!\!\!\sim}$ implicit) or we can let Q act on Δ, written $\Delta!Q$, where ! denotes the action. When an action ! is given, it is possible to derive a new consequence relation $\mathrel{\vdash\!\!\!\sim}$ dependent on the action ! (really we should write $\mathrel{\vdash\!\!\!\sim}_!$). The new $\mathrel{\vdash\!\!\!\sim}$ is defined by $\Delta \mathrel{\vdash\!\!\!\sim} Q$ iff $\Delta!Q = \Delta$. This view was put forward particularly by F. Veldman and pursued by J. van Benthem.

Let us introduce clearly our current view on the question of what is a logical system:

Definition 7.1 (Current tentative view of a logical system). A logical system has the form $(\mathrel{\vdash\!\!\!\sim}, \mathbf{S}_{\vdash\!\!\!\sim}, \mathbf{S}_{\text{abduce}}, \mathbf{S}_{\text{update}}, \ldots)$ where $\mathrel{\vdash\!\!\!\sim}$ is a labelled consequence relation, $\mathbf{S}_{\vdash\!\!\!\sim}$ is a *Labelled Deductive System* with *Flattening* procedures and $\mathbf{S}_{\text{abduce}}, \mathbf{S}_{\text{update}}$, etc. are *mechanisms* which are dependent on (make use of) $\mathbf{S}_{\vdash\!\!\!\sim}$.

It would be instructive to construct a logical system in the sense of the above definition. We now present one incrementally.

Example 7.2 Our starting point is minimal propositional implicational logic with a constant for falsity. The language contains atomic propositions $\{p, q, r, \ldots\}$ and the implication connective $\{\rightarrow\}$ together with the falsity constant $\{\perp\}$. As a Hilbert system, minimal logic satisfies the following schemas:

- $A \rightarrow (B \rightarrow A)$

- $(A \rightarrow (B \rightarrow C)) \rightarrow ((A \rightarrow B) \rightarrow (A \rightarrow C))$

and the rule of modus ponens

- $\dfrac{A; A \rightarrow B}{B}$.

The following theorems can be proved

- $\vdash A \rightarrow A$

- $\vdash (A \rightarrow (B \rightarrow C)) \rightarrow (B \rightarrow (A \rightarrow C))$.

A consequence relation $\mathrel{\vdash\!\!\!\sim}_m$ can be defined by:

- $A_1, \ldots, A_n \mathrel{\vdash\!\!\!\sim}_m B$ iff (def) $\vdash A_1 \rightarrow (A_2 \rightarrow \ldots \rightarrow (A_n \rightarrow B) \ldots)$

Note that in minimal logic $\perp$ does not imply anything in particular, just itself. If we add the axiom schema $\perp \rightarrow A$, we get intuitionistic logic based on the connectives $\{\rightarrow, \perp\}$.

The following additional Hilbert axioms yield full minimal logic with $\wedge$ and $\vee$.

- $A \rightarrow (B \rightarrow A \wedge B)$

- $A \wedge B \rightarrow A$

- $A \wedge B \rightarrow B$

- $(A \rightarrow C) \rightarrow ((B \rightarrow C) \rightarrow (A \vee B \rightarrow C))$

- $A \rightarrow A \vee B$

- $B \rightarrow A \vee B$

We have now defined $\mathrel|\joinrel\sim_m$, the consequence relation of our logic. We proceed to define $\mathbf{S}_m$ (actually $\mathbf{S}_{\mathrel|\joinrel\sim_m}$), an algorithmic proof system for $\mathrel|\joinrel\sim_m$. There are many options to choose from, such as Gentzen systems, Tableaux, Term Translation into Classical logic, etc. We choose a goal directed formulation.

Definition 7.3

1. First note that any formula B of the language (without $\vee$ and $\wedge$) has the form $B = (B_1 \rightarrow (B_2 \rightarrow \ldots \rightarrow (B_n \rightarrow q)\ldots))$, where q is atomic and B_i has the same form as B. q is called the *head* of B and $\{B_i\}$ is the *body*. If we allow $\wedge$ in the language, then every formula is equivalent to a set of wffs of the above form. This holds because of the following equivalences in minimal logic:

$$A \wedge B \rightarrow C \text{ and } A \rightarrow (B \rightarrow C)$$
$$A \rightarrow (B \wedge C) \text{ and } (A \rightarrow B) \wedge (A \rightarrow C)$$

2. A *theory* Δ is a list of wffs of the logic.

3. We define the following metapredicates:

   - $\Delta ? A = 1$, reading 'the goal A succeeds from the theory Δ'.
   - $\Delta ? A = 0$ reading 'the goal A finitely fails from Δ'.

   The definition is as follows:

   (a) $\Delta ? q = 1$, for q atomic if q is listed in Δ.

   (b) $\Delta ? q = 0$, for q atomic if q is not the head of any element in Δ.

   (c) $\Delta ? A_1 \rightarrow (\ldots (A_n \rightarrow q)\ldots) = 1$ (resp. 0) if $\Delta * (A_1, \ldots, A_n)?q = 1$ (resp. 0) where $*$ is concatenation.

   (d) $\Delta ? q = 1$ if for some $B = (B_1 \rightarrow \ldots \rightarrow (B_n \rightarrow q)\ldots)$ in Δ we have that $\Delta ? B_i = 1$, for $i = 1, \ldots, n$.

   (e) $\Delta ? q = 0$ if for each B in Δ of the form $B_1 \rightarrow (B_2 \ldots (B_n \rightarrow q)\ldots)$ there exists an $1 \leq i \leq n$ such that $\Delta ? B_i = 0$.

Theorem 7.4 $A_1, \ldots, A_n \mathrel{\vdash_m} B$ *iff* $(A_1, \ldots, A_n)?B = 1$.

PROOF. See [5].   ∎

To obtain a proper algorithm for $\mathbf{S}_{\vdash_m}$, we need to specify exactly how we compute $\Delta?Q$. It is convenient for the purpose of ease of control to let the goal be a list of formulas Γ, as in some PROLOG interpreters. Thus clause 7.3(3d) will now read:

$\Delta?q * \Gamma = 1$ if for some $B = (B_1 \to (\ldots \to (B_n \to q)\ldots))$ in Δ we have
$$\Delta?(B_1, \ldots, B_n) * \Gamma = 1.$$

We can agree to search the list Δ top down and agree where to continue the search when starting a new goal in the list of goals. The policy of some PROLOG interpreters is always to start the search at the top of the database list Δ. This would yield a precise algorithm but may cause loops. For example $(q \to q)?q$ will loop. With a loop checker, however, we get decidability in P-space.

We now proceed with the incremental definition of our logic. We need next the notion of a database. This will contain integrity constraints and some clauses as data. The data are divided into two parts, permanent data and added hypothetical data. (e.g. to show $A \to B$, we hypothetically assume A and try to show B). The next definition does the job.

Definition 7.5

1. A formula of the form $B_1 \to (\ldots \to (B_n \to \bot)\ldots)$ where $\bot$ does not appear in $B_i, i = 1, \ldots, n$, is called *an integrity constraint*.

2. A formula in the pure $\to$ fragment (i.e. without $\bot$) is called *a clause*.

3. A *simple database* is a concatenation of three (possibly empty) lists of formulas of the form $\Delta = \Delta_I * \Delta_P * \Delta_A$, where Δ_I is a list of integrity constraints, Δ_P is a list of clauses, called the *protected* clauses (the significance of Δ_P will emerge later when we update), and Δ_A is another list of clauses called the *additional* clauses.

4. A database Δ is *inconsistent* if $\Delta?\bot = 1$. Note that Δ is also a *theory*, so $\Delta?\bot$ can be computed.

Definition 7.6

1. Let $\Delta = \Delta_I * \Delta_P * \Delta_A$ be a consistent database with $\Delta_A = (C_1, \ldots, C_m)$ and let Q be a clause. We define the *update* of Δ by Q, denoted by $\Delta!Q$, to be the following database Δ':

   • $\Delta' = \Delta$ if $\Delta_I * \Delta_P * (Q)$ is not consistent.

- Otherwise, let Δ' be $\Delta_I * \Delta_P * (C_i, C_{i+1}, \ldots, C_m, Q)$ where i is the least number ≥ 1 such that the above theory is consistent.

An update $\Delta!Q$ insists, if possible, on putting Q into Δ and maintains consistency by taking out from Δ those assumptions that are unprotected (i.e. in Δ_A) and old (i.e. earlier in the list Δ_A). If Q is inconsistent with $\Delta_I * \Delta_P$, then and only then do we reject the input.

In Definition 7.3, the algorithm $\mathbf{S}_{\vdash_m}$ for computing $\Delta?A \to B$ is based on the deduction theorem and the query $\Delta?A \to B$ is reduced to $\Delta *$ $(A)?B$. In minimal logic, where Δ is a theory, $\Delta * (A)$ is always consistent, because we do not mind deriving $\bot$, and there is no notion of inconsistency. When we move to the notion of databases, integrity constraints and clauses, databases can be inconsistent and the old reduction of $\Delta?A \to B$ to $\Delta *$ $(A)?B$ may need to face the fact that $\Delta * (A)$ is inconsistent. However, we do have in this case the notion of the update $\Delta!A$, and we could reduce the query $\Delta?A \to B$ to that of $\Delta!A?B$. This new reduction actually defines a new conditional implication $A \Rightarrow B$, meaning B would be true if A were true i.e. update Δ by A and then (query) check B. The next definition gives the details. We are going to keep using the '$\to$' symbol for both kinds of implication and the context will decide what meaning we give to '$\to$'. See [11].

Definition 7.7 (Computation for conditional $\to$). We define a new computation $\Delta?!Q = 1$ and $\Delta?!Q = 0$ for clauses Q as follows:

(a) $\Delta?!q = 1$ if q is in Δ, for atomic q.

(b) $\Delta?!q = 0$ for q atomic, if q is not the head of any clause in Δ.

(c) $\Delta?!B_1 \to (B_2 \to \ldots \to (B_n \to q) \ldots) = 1$ (resp. 0) iff $(((\Delta!B_1)!B_2)$ $\ldots !B_n)?!q = 1$ (resp. 0).

(d) $\Delta?!q = 1$ if for some $B_1 \to (\ldots (B_n \to q) \ldots)$ in Δ we have $\Delta?!B_i = 1$, for $i = 1, \ldots, n$.

(e) $\Delta?!q = 0$ if for each $B_1 \to (\ldots \to (B_n \to q) \ldots)$ in Δ there exists an i such that $\Delta?!B_i = 0$.

(f) $\Delta?!\bot$ is not defined. We only compute $\Delta?\bot$.

We now have an update mechanism and a new consequence relation. Let us define some more mechanisms. First we deal with normal defaults of the form $\frac{A:B}{B}$, reading: if A is in Δ and it is consistent to add B then we do add B. Note that the default notion we are proposing here is straightforward and tailored for our case and is not a general theory of default. We are building a 'new logic' and we want to put some default aspects to it.

Definition 7.8

1. A normal default δ is a pair $\delta = (A, B)$ where A and B are clauses.

2. A default database is a concatenation of several lists of clauses and constraints containing at least the following

$$\Delta = \Delta_I * \Delta_P * \Delta_A * \Delta_D$$

   where Δ_D is a list added because of default.

3. We now define the default update $\Delta!\delta$ as follows

$$\Delta!\delta = \Delta_I * \Delta_P * \Delta_A * \Delta_D * (B)$$

   provided this theory is consistent and $\Delta?A = 1$.

So far we have built a logical system with a consequence relation, an algorithmic procedure for it and some mechanisms such as updates and default. We will add one more mechanism and then rest our case. This time we add *abduction*.

From the purely logical point of view, abduction is a syntactical action on a theory Δ and a goal Q, consistent with Δ, in a logic $(\vdash, \mathbf{S}_{\vdash})$, yielding some additional data Δ_B, consistent with Δ (denoted by $\Delta_B = Abduce\,(\Delta, Q)$), such that $\Delta, \Delta_B \vdash Q$. That is, we 'answer' the question of 'what do we need to consistently add to Δ to make it prove Q'?

Let us define $Abduce(\Delta, Q)$ for the logic $(\vdash_m, \mathbf{S}_{\vdash_m})$. The definition will be by induction on the computation steps of Q from Δ, as in Definition 7.3.

Definition 7.9 Let Δ be a theory and Q be a goal in the minimal logic $\vdash_m$ of example 7.2 (for the language with $\rightarrow$, $\perp$ and possibly $\wedge$), using the algorithm $\mathbf{S}_{\vdash_m}$ of definition 7.3(3) which is complete by Theorem 7.4.

We define a formula $Abduce(\Delta, Q)$ in the full language of minimal logic, with $\wedge$ and $\vee$ such that:

- $\Delta * Abduce\,(\Delta, Q) \vdash_m Q$

1. $Abduce(\Delta, Q) = \top$ if $\Delta?Q = 1$.

2. $Abduce(\Delta, q) = q$, for q atomic such that q is not the head of any clause in Δ.

3. $Abduce(\Delta, A_1 \rightarrow (A_2 \rightarrow \ldots (A_n \rightarrow q) \ldots)) = A_1 \rightarrow \ldots (A_n \rightarrow Abduce\,(\Delta * (A_1, \ldots, A_n), q) \ldots)$

4. Let q be atomic and let $B^j = (B_1^j \to \ldots \to (B_{n_j}^j \to q) \ldots)$, $j = 1, \ldots, m$ be all clauses in Δ with head q. Then $Abduce(\Delta, q) = \bigvee_{j=1}^m \bigwedge_{i=1}^{n_j} Abduce\,(\Delta, B_i^j)$.

5. In case we have conjunctions;
$Abduce(\Delta, A \wedge B) = Abduce\,(\Delta, A) \wedge Abduce\,(\Delta, B)$.

Note that clause 4 of the above definition of *Abduce* may be simplified to be that any one of the disjuncts (say of the first B^j in the list Δ) is always chosen. However, when we take the disjunction we get a logically weaker abduced formula. Also note that clause 5 may give rise to inconsistency; $Abduce(\Delta, A)$ and $Abduce(\Delta, B)$ may be consistent but not necessarily their conjunction.

If we adopt the policy of taking disjunctions in clause 4, we increase the chances of finding a consistent abduced formula. In the $\to$ fragment, of course, we do not want disjunctions.

Examples 7.10

1. Let Δ be $\{a\}$ and let the goal be q. The abduced formula is $Abduce((a), q) = q$. Note that if we were to take $\gamma = (a \to q)$ then certainly

$$\Delta, \gamma \hspace{-0.3em}\not\vdash_m q$$

so the abduced formula is not the logically weakest which can be added to Δ to prove the goal (since $\gamma \hspace{-0.3em}\not\vdash_m q$ but $q \hspace{-0.3em}\vdash_m \gamma$). However, in the presence of Δ it is the weakest.

2. Let Δ be

    (a) $a \to (b \to q)$

    (b) a

    (c) $(c \to d) \to q$

    and let the goal be q.

    The abduced theory is $b \vee (c \to d)$

Lemma 7.11 $\Delta, Abduce(\Delta, Q) \vdash_m Q$.

PROOF. The proof is by induction on the definition of the abduced formula.

1. If the abduced formula is $\top$ then this means $\Delta \vdash_m Q$.

2. Assume that $Q = q$ is atomic and that it is not the head of any clause. Then the abduced formula is q and clearly $\Delta, q \vdash_m q$.

3. Assume Q has the form

$$Q = (A_1 \rightarrow \ldots \rightarrow (A_n \rightarrow q)\ldots).$$

Then the abduced formula is

$$A_1 \rightarrow \ldots \rightarrow (A_n \rightarrow \ Abduce \ (\Delta * (A_1, \ldots, A_n), q), \ldots).$$

We need to show

$$\Delta, A_1 \rightarrow (\ldots \rightarrow (A_n \rightarrow \ Abduce \ (\Delta * A_1, \ldots, A_n), q)\ldots)\!\sim_m Q.$$

By the induction hypothesis

$$\Delta, A_1, \ldots, A_n, \ Abduce \ (\Delta * (A_1, \ldots, A_n), q)\!\sim_m q,$$

hence

$$\Delta, A_1, \ldots, A_n, A_1 \rightarrow \ldots (A_n \rightarrow \ Abduce \ (\Delta*(A_1, \ldots, A_n), q)\ldots)\!\sim_m q,$$

hence

$$\Delta, A_1 \rightarrow (\ldots A_n \rightarrow \ Abduce \ (\Delta * (A_1, \ldots, A_n), q)\ldots)\!\sim_m Q.$$

4. Assume $Q = q$ is atomic and let $B^j = (B_1^j \rightarrow \ldots \rightarrow (B_{n_j}^j \rightarrow q)\ldots), j = 1, \ldots, m$, be all the clauses in Δ with head q.

Then we need to show

$$\Delta, \ Abduce \ (\Delta, q)\!\sim_m q$$

where

$$Abduce \ (\Delta, q) = \bigvee_{j=1}^{m} \bigwedge_{i=1}^{n_j} Abduce \ (\Delta, B_i^j).$$

By the induction hypothesis for j fixed, we have

$$\Delta, \ Abduce \ (\Delta, B_i^j)\!\sim_m B_i^j$$

for $i = 1, \ldots, n_j$.

Hence for each j, since B^j is in Δ, we have:

$$\Delta, \bigwedge_{i=1}^{n_j} Abduce(\Delta, B_i^j)\!\sim_m q.$$

Hence

$$\Delta, \bigvee_{j=1}^{m} \bigwedge_{i=1}^{n_j} Abduce(\Delta, B_i^j)\!\sim_m q.$$

This completes the induction step and the lemma is proved.   ∎

Remark 7.12 The above defined abduction mechanism gives rise to abduced formulas which may be disjunctions, but not necessarily. If we are dealing with the → fragment only, we will not be able to add the abduced formula into Δ. We notice however, that conjunctions are no problem because in the → fragment, every formula with conjunctions is equivalent to a conjunction of pure → formulas. This conjunction can be added to Δ as an additional list. We have already observed that disjunctions arise from the fact that an atom q may have several clauses in the database with head q (item 4 of the inductive definition). Since all clauses are ordered, we can choose as part of our abduction policy to use only an agreed one of them (say the top of the list). This will give us no disjunctions. Call such a modified abduction algorithm by $Abdtop(\Delta, Q)$.

Example 7.13 Consider the database Δ with one integrity constraint in it and one data item in it.

1. $a \wedge s \wedge e \rightarrow \perp$

2. a

We are using conjunction but it can be eliminated. We can write item 1 as

$$a \rightarrow (s \rightarrow (e \rightarrow \perp)).$$

Consider the following two goals.

- $Q_1 = a \wedge e$

- $Q_2 = a \wedge e \rightarrow \perp$

Note that for conjunctions the obvious rule to use (at the risk of integrity constraints being violated) is:

- $Abduce(\Delta, A \wedge B) = Abduce\ (\Delta, A) \wedge\ Abduce(\Delta, B)$

Therefore for our example:

$$Abduce(\Delta, Q_1) = Abduce(\Delta, a) \wedge\ Abduce(\Delta, e) = Abduce(\Delta, e)$$

Clearly $Abduce(\Delta, e) = e$, as the only way to prove e from Δ is to abduce e itself (note we do not have $\perp \hspace{-0.3em}\sim_m e$).

We now try to abduce the second goal, Q_2:

$$Abduce(\Delta, Q_2) = (a \wedge e \rightarrow Abduce(\Delta * (a) * (e), \perp) = a \wedge e \rightarrow s$$

Since

$$Abduce(\Delta * (a) * (e), \perp) = Abduce(\Delta * (a) * (e), a \wedge s \wedge e) = s$$

Remark 7.14 There is a sense in which $Abduce(\Delta, q)$ is the logically minimal addition to Δ which can prove Q, namely:

If $\Delta, X \vdash_m Q$, then $\Delta', X \vdash_m Abduce(\Delta, Q)$, where Δ' is some completion of Δ. It is not clear to me at this stage exactly what Δ' should be. Consider the following:

$$\Delta = \{a \to b\}, Q = b. \; Abduce(\Delta, Q) = a.$$

Clearly, $\Delta, b \vdash Q$ but $\Delta, b \not\vdash a$. However, Clark's completion $\Delta' = \{a \leftrightarrow b\}$ does the job; $\Delta', b \vdash a$.

There is work for Horn clauses in this direction in [2], but our language here contains embedded implications.

Example 7.15 (An example of a logical system). We can now define an example of a 'logical' system in our sense as follows:

- The language has $\to$ only.

- The notion of a theory and of a consequence relation is that of minimal logic $\vdash_m$.

- The algorithmic system is $S_{\vdash_m}$ of definition 7.3. Theorem 7.4 shows the algorithm is complete and sound.

- The abduction mechanism is $Abdtop$ of Remark 7.12. The result is appended at the end of the Δ_B list.

- A database is comprised of several lists of clauses and integrity constraints of the form

$$\Delta = \Delta_I * \Delta_P * \Delta_B * \Delta_A * \Delta_D$$

  where Δ_I is the integrity constraint, Δ_P is the permanent data, Δ_B is the abduced data, Δ_A is the additional data and Δ_D is the default data.

- The update mechanism is as in Definitions 7.6 and 7.7, where for the purpose of performing an update the list Δ_B is considered 'protected' data while $\Delta_A * \Delta_D$ is considered 'additional data'. This gives defaults higher priority than hypotheticals.

- Input of hypotheticals is appended to the end of the Δ_A list.

- The default mechanism is as in Definition 7.8 and the result of default is appended at the end of the Δ_D list

Note that some of our decisions in defining the logic of Example 7.5 are not the most reasonable. They need to be refined. We can be more careful how we update and more careful where to input the results of abduction by looking at what part of the database was used in the abduction. For example if we abduce q because of default rules, it makes more sense to put the result in the default database than in the abduced database.

However, for the purpose of illustrating what we mean by a logical system with mechanisms, the above is sufficient.

In the most general case, databases are *LDS* databases and not just lists. In this case the mechanisms and algorithms will be more complex.

8 Semantics

We cannot address the problem of what is a logical system without saying something about our view of semantics. The traditional view, for classical, intuitionistic, or modal logic is to have some notion of a class of models and of an evaluation procedure of a formula in a model. Thus we may have a set $\mathcal{K}$ of models and a notion of validity in $\mathbf{m} \in \mathcal{K}$ of a formula A of the logic. We use the notation $\mathbf{m} \vDash A$. Given no details on the internal structure of $\mathbf{m}$ and on how $\mathbf{m} \vDash A$ is evaluated, all we can say about the model is that $\mathbf{m}$ is a $\{0,1\}$ function on wffs. Completeness of $\mathcal{K}$ for $\vdash\!\!\!\sim$ means that the following holds:

- $A\vdash\!\!\!\sim B$ iff for all $\mathbf{m} \in \mathcal{K}$ (if $\mathbf{m} \vDash A$ then $\mathbf{m} \vDash B$).

We would like to present a different view of semantics.

We would like to remain totally within the world of logical systems (in our sense, i.e. *LDS* with mechanisms) and to the extent that semantics is needed, we bring it into the syntax. This can obviously and transparently be done in modal logic where the labels denote possible worlds and the proof rules closely reflect semantical evaluation rules. This in fact can also be done in general. So what then is the basic notion involved in a purely syntactical set up? What replaces the notions of a 'model', 'evaluation', and completeness? We give the following definition.

Definition 8.1 (Syntactical semantics). Let $\vdash\!\!\!\sim$ be a consequence relation and let $\mathcal{K}$ be a class of consequence relations, not necessarily of the same language. For each $\vdash\!\!\!\sim^* \in \mathcal{K}$, let $\mathbf{k}_{\vdash\!\!\!\sim^*}$ be an interpretation of $\vdash\!\!\!\sim$ into $\vdash\!\!\!\sim^*$. This involves mapping of the language of $\vdash\!\!\!\sim$ into the language of $\vdash\!\!\!\sim^*$ and the following homomorphic commitment:

- $A\vdash\!\!\!\sim B$ implies $A^*\vdash\!\!\!\sim^* B^*$ (where A^* is $\mathbf{k}_{\vdash\!\!\!\sim^*}(A)$ and resp. B^*).

We say $\vdash\!\!\!\sim$ is complete for $(\mathcal{K}, \mathbf{k})$, iff we have

- $A \hspace{-0.1em}\mid\hspace{-0.6em}\sim\hspace{-0.1em} B$ iff for all $\mid\hspace{-0.6em}\sim^* \in \mathcal{K}, A^* \mid\hspace{-0.6em}\sim^* B^*$.

Example 8.2 The following can be considered as semantical interpretations in our sense:

1. The Solovay–Boolos interpretation of modal logic **G** (with Löbs axiom) in Arithmetic, with $\square$ meaning 'provable'.

2. The interpretation of intuitionistic propositional logic into various sequences of intermediate logic whose intersection is intuitionistic logic (e.g. the Jaskowski sequence).

3. The interpretation of modal logic into classical logic.

Remark 8.3 We gave a definition of interpretation for consequence relations $\mid\hspace{-0.6em}\sim$. Of course, there are always trivial interpretations which 'technially' qualify as semantics. This is not intended. Further note that in the general case, we have a general *LDS* proof system with algorithmic proof systems $\mathbf{S}_{\mid\hspace{-0.4em}\sim}$ and various mechanisms. These should also be interpreted. Each algorithmic move in $\mathbf{S}_{\mid\hspace{-0.4em}\sim}$ should be interpreted as a move package in $\mathbf{S}_{\mid\hspace{-0.4em}\sim^*}$, and similarly for mechanisms.

It is possible to justify and motivate our syntactical notion of semantics from the more traditional one. Let us take as our starting point the notion of Scott-semantics described in [6].

Definition 8.4 Let **L** be a propositional language, for example the modal language with $\square$ or intuitionistic language with $\rightarrow$.

1. A model for the language is a function s assigning a value in $\{0, 1\}$ to each wff of the language.

2. A *semantics* S is a class of models.

3. Let Δ be a set of wffs and A a wff. We say $\Delta \vDash_S A$ iff for all $\mathbf{s} \in S$ if $\mathbf{s}(B) = 1$ for all $B \in \Delta$ then $\mathbf{s}(A) = 1$.

The above definition relies on the intuition that no matter what our basic concepts of a 'model' or interpretation is, sooner or later we have to sa whether a formula A 'holds' in it or does not 'hold' in it. Thus the technical 'essence' of a model is a $\{0, 1\}$ function $\mathbf{s}$ (we ignore the possibility of no value).

It can be shown that this notion of semantics can characterise any monotonic (syntactical) consequence relation i.e. any relation $\mid\hspace{-0.6em}\sim$ between sets Δ (including $\Delta = \varnothing$) of wffs and wffs A satisfying *reflexivity, monotonicity* and *cut*. Thus for any $\mid\hspace{-0.6em}\sim$ there exists an S such that $\mid\hspace{-0.6em}\sim$ equals $\vDash_S$.

The semantics S can be given further structure, depending on the connectives of $\mathbf{L}$. The simplest is through the binary relation $\leq$, defined as follows:

- $\mathbf{t} \leq \mathbf{s}$ iff (definition) for all wffs $A, \mathbf{t}(A) \leq \mathbf{s}(A)$.

Other relations can be defined on S. For example, if the original language is modal logic we can define:

- $\mathbf{t}R\mathbf{s}$ iff for all $\Box A$ of $\mathbf{L}$ if $\mathbf{t}(\Box A) = 1$ then $\mathbf{s}(A) = 1$.

One can then postulate connections between values such as:

- $\mathbf{t}(\Box A) = 1$ iff $\forall \mathbf{s}[\mathbf{t}R\mathbf{s} \Rightarrow \mathbf{s}(A) = 1]$

or for a langauge with $\rightarrow$:

- $\mathbf{t}(A \rightarrow B) = 1$ iff $\forall \mathbf{s}(\mathbf{t} \leq \mathbf{s}$ and $\mathbf{s}(A) = 1$ imply $\mathbf{s}(B) = 1)$.

In some logics and their semantics the above may hold. For example, the respective conditions above hold for the modal logic $\mathbf{K}$ and for intuitionistic logic. For other logics, further refinements are needed.

The nature of what is happening here can be best explained through a translation into classical logic. The language $\mathbf{L}$ can be considered as a Herbrand universe of terms (i.e. the free algebra based on the atomic propositions and the connectives acting as function symbols), and the models considered as another sort of terms, (i.e. the names of the models can be terms). The 'predicate' $\mathbf{t}(A) = 1$ can be considered as a two sorted predicate $\mathbf{Hold}(\mathbf{t}, A)$. Thus the reductions above become

- $\mathbf{Hold}(\mathbf{t}, \Box A)$ iff $\forall \mathbf{s}(\mathbf{t}R\mathbf{s} \Rightarrow \mathbf{Hold}(\mathbf{s}, A))$,
  where $\mathbf{t}R\mathbf{s}$ is $\forall B(\mathbf{Hold}(\mathbf{t}, \Box B) \Rightarrow \mathbf{Hold}(\mathbf{s}, B))$.

This condition reduces to

- $\forall \mathbf{s}[\forall X(\mathbf{Hold}(\mathbf{t}, \Box X) \Rightarrow \mathbf{Hold}(\mathbf{s}, X)) \Rightarrow \mathbf{Hold}(\mathbf{s}, A)] \Rightarrow \mathbf{Hold}(\mathbf{t}, \Box A)$

This is an internal reduction on $\mathbf{Hold}$.

In general, we want to define $\mathbf{Hold}(\mathbf{t}, \sharp(A_1, \ldots, A_n))$ in terms of some relations $R_i(x_1, \ldots, x_{n_i})$ on sort $\mathbf{t}$ (first coordinate of $\mathbf{Hold}$), and the predicates $\mathbf{Hold}(x, A_j)$ for subformulas of $\sharp(A_1, \ldots, A_n)$. $R_i(\mathbf{t}_1, \ldots, \mathbf{t}_{n_i})$ in turn, are expected to be defined using $\mathbf{Hold}(\mathbf{t}_i, X_j)$ for some formulas X_j.

Thus in predicate logic we have formulas φ_i and $\Psi_\sharp$ such that:

- $\mathbf{Hold}(\mathbf{t}, \sharp(A_i, \ldots, A_n))$ iff $\Psi_\sharp(\mathbf{t}, R_i \mathbf{Hold}(x_i, A_j))$

- $R_i(\mathbf{t}_1, \ldots, \mathbf{t}_{n_i})$ iff (definition) $\varphi_i(\mathbf{t}_1, \ldots, \mathbf{t}_{n_i} \mathbf{Hold}(\mathbf{t}_j, X_k))$.

Together they imply a possible closure condition on the semantics

- **Hold**$(\mathbf{t}, \natural(A_1, \ldots, A_n))$ iff $\Psi_\natural(t, \varphi_i(\ldots, \mathbf{Hold}(\mathbf{t}_j, X_k), \mathbf{Hold}(x_i, A_k))$

which may or may not hold.

Remark 8.5 (Representation of algebras). The above considerations can be viewed as a special case of a general set-representation problem for algebras. Let $\mathcal{A}$ be an algebra with some function symbols f_i satisfying some axioms. Take for example the language of lattices $\mathcal{A} = (A, \sqcap, \sqcup)$. We ask the following question: Can $\mathcal{A}$ be represented as an algebra of sets? In other words, is there a set S and a mapping $h(a) \subseteq S$, for $a \in A$ and a monadic first-order langauge $\mathbf{L}_1$ on S involving possibly some relation symbols $R_1, \ldots, R_k$ on S such that for all $s \in S$ and function symbol f of the algebra we have the following inductive reduction, for all $x_1, \ldots, x_n \in A$

$$s \in h(f(x_1, \ldots, x_n) \text{ iff } \vDash \Psi_f(s, h(x_1), \ldots, h(x_n))$$

where Ψ_f is a non-modadic wff of $\mathbf{L}_1$ involving $R_1, \ldots, R_k$ and the subsets $h(x_j)$.

If the relations $R(t_1, \ldots, t_m)$ on S can be defined using h by some formula φ_R of the algebra (involving the classical connectives and equality and the monadic predicates on the algebra $T_i(x)$ meaning $t_i \in h(x)$), then

$$\vDash R(t_1, \ldots, t_m) \text{ iff } \mathcal{A} \vDash \varphi_R(T_1, \ldots, T_m, R).$$

Remark 8.6 (Dependent semantics). The above considerations are not the most general and do not reflect all that might happen. The considerations explain nicely semantics like that of modal $\mathbf{K}$ but we need refinements.

Consider the logic $\mathbf{K}_1$ obtained by collecting all theorems of modal logic $\mathbf{K}$ together with the schema $\Box A \rightarrow A$ and the rule of modus ponens. Necessitation is dropped, so although $K_1 \vdash \Box A \rightarrow A$, we can still have $\mathbf{K}_1 \nvdash \Box(\Box A \rightarrow A)$. This logic is complete for the class of all Kripke structures of the form $\mathbf{m} = (S^{\mathbf{m}}, R^{\mathbf{m}}, a^{\mathbf{m}}, h^{\mathbf{m}})$, where $a^{\mathbf{m}} R a^{\mathbf{m}}$ holds. Completeness means

1. $\mathbf{K}_1 \vdash A$ iff for every $\mathbf{m}$ as above $a^{\mathbf{m}} \vDash A$

Let $\mathbf{a_m}$ be the function satisfying

2. $\mathbf{a_m}(A) = 1$ iff $a_{\mathbf{m}} \vDash A$

and let

3. $\mathcal{S}_0 = \{\mathbf{a_m} \mid \mathbf{m} \text{ as above}\}$.

Then we have here a semantics $\mathcal{S}_0 \subseteq \mathcal{S}$ (of the langauge $\mathbf{L}$ of modal logic) where $\mathbf{a_m}(\Box A)$ cannot be recuced to values of $\mathbf{s}(A)$ for $\mathbf{s} \in \mathcal{S}_0$, but can be reduced to values $s(A)$, for $s \in S$. This is so because when we evaluate $a^{\mathbf{m}} \vDash A$, we evaluate at points $b \in S^{\mathbf{m}}$ such that $a^{\mathbf{m}} R^{\mathbf{m}} b$ and the Kripke structure $(S^{\mathbf{m}}, R^{\mathbf{m}}, b, h^{\mathbf{m}})$ is a **K** structure, but not necessarily a $\mathbf{K_1}$ structure, as bRb need not hold. Let $\mathbf{b^m}$ be the function defined by

4. $\mathbf{b^m}(A) = 1$ iff $b \vDash A$ in **m**. We get

5. $\mathbf{a_m}(\Box A) = 1$ iff for all $s \in \{\mathbf{b^m} \mid a^{\mathbf{m}} Rb\}$, we have $s(A) = 1$.

   Let $\varphi(\mathbf{a}, \mathbf{b})$ mean as follows:

6. $\varphi(\mathbf{a}, \mathbf{b})$ iff (definition) for some $\mathbf{m}, \mathbf{a} = \mathbf{a_m}$ and $b = \mathbf{b^m}$ and $a^{\mathbf{m}} Rb$.

   Then we have that $\mathbf{K_1}$ is characterised by a designated subset S_0 of S and the truth definition:

7. $s(\Box A) = 1$ iff for all $s' \varphi(s, s')$ and sRs' imply $s'(A) = 1$.

8. $A \vDash B$ iff for all $s \in S_0, s(A) = 1$ implies $s(B) = 1$.

We are now ready to say what it means to give technical semantics t a consequence relation $\mathrel{\vdash\mkern-9mu\sim}$.

Definition 8.7 (What is semantics for $\mathrel{\vdash\mkern-9mu\sim}$). Let $\mathrel{\vdash\mkern-9mu\sim}$ be a consequence relation (reflexive and transitive) in a language with connectives. Then a semantics for $\mathrel{\vdash\mkern-9mu\sim}$ is any set theoretic representation (in the sense of Remark 8.6 of the free term algebra based on $\mathrel{\vdash\mkern-9mu\sim}$.

The previous definition does not take account of Remark 8.6. If we want a better concept of what is semantics, we need to talk about *fibred semantics* and *label dependent connectives*. These topics are addressed in [10].

9 Conclusion

We have, incrementally, gone through several notions of 'what is a logical system' and have ended up with Definition 7.1 and Example 7.15 to illustrate it. This new concept of a logic is very far from the traditional concept. In artificial intelligence circles, what we call a 'logic' is perceived as an 'agent' or 'intelligent agent'. This is no accident. Whereas traditional logical systems (classical logic, intuitionistic logic, linear logic) model mathematical reasoning and mathematical proof, our new concept of logic attempts to model, and stay tuned to, human practical reasoning. What we tried to do is to observe what features and mechanisms are at play in human practical reasoning, and proceed to formalize them. The systems emerging from this formalization we accept as the new 'logics'. It is therefore no surprise that in AI circles such systems are perceived as intelligent agents. However, compared with AI, our motives are different. We are looking for general logical principles of human reasoning and not necessarily seeking to build practical applied systems.

There is one more point to make before we can close this chapter. The above 'logics' manipulate formulas, algebraic terms and in general syntactical symbols. We have maintained already in 1988 [12] that deduction is a form of *stylized movement*, which can be carried out *directly* on natural objects from an application area. Thus 'logic' can be done not only on syntactical formulas, but on any set of structured objects, naturally residing in some application area.

To reason about gardening, for example, we can either represent the area in some language and manipulate the syntax in some logic, or we can directly manipulate and move the plants themselves and 'show' the conclusion. The style of movement is the 'logic'. This concept of *logic as movement* is clearly apparent in automated reasoning. Different kinds of 'shuffling' licensed by a theorem prover can lead to different 'logics', because then different sets of theorems become provable. Our insight was that similar movements can be applied directly on the objects of the application areas, and therefore reasoning can be achieved directly in the application area without formalization. This philosophy has been carried out on Discourse Representation Structures in [12].

Our approach is compatible with the more mixed approach in the contribution by Barwise and Hammer in this volume.

Acknowledgements

The author is currently sponsered by a SERC Senior Fellowship, GR/H01014. The research reported here was supported by SERC project *Syntactical Foundations for Non-monotonic Reasoning*, GR/G46671. I am grateful to R. A. Kowalski for valuable comments on the chapter.

References

[1] C. E. Alchourrón, P. Gärdenfors, and D. Makinson. On the logic of theory change: partial meet contraction and revision functions. *The Journal of Symbolic Logic*, **50**, 510–530, 1985.

[2] L. Console, D. T. Dupre, and P. Torasso. On the relationship between deduction and abduction. *Journal of Logic and Computation*, **1**, 661–690, 1991.

[3] D. Gabbay. Semantic proof of the Craig interpolation theorem for intuitionistic logic. In *Logic Colloquium '69*, pp. 391–410, North-Holland, 1969.

[4] D. Gabbay. Theoretical foundations for nonmonotonic reasoning in expert systems. In K. Apt, editor, *Logics and Models of Concurrent Systems*, pp. 439–459, Springer-Verlag, Berlin, 1985.

[5] D. Gabbay. Theory of algorithmic proof. In *Handbook of Logic in Theoretical Computer Science, Volume 1*, eds S. Abramsky, D. Gabbay and T. Maibaum, pages 307–408. Oxford University Press, 1992.

[6] D. M. Gabbay. *Semantical Investigations in Modal and Temporal Logics*. D. Reidel, 1976.

[7] D. M. Gabbay. *Investigations in Heyting intuitionistic logic*. D. Reidel, 1986.

[8] D. M. Gabbay. Classical vs nonclassical logic. In D. M. Gabbay, C. J. Hogger, and J. A. Robinson, editors, *Handbook of Logic in AI and Logic Programming, Volume 1*, pp. 349–489, Oxford University Press, 1993.

[9] D. M. Gabbay. General theory of structured consequence relations. In *Substructural Logics*, Kosta Došen and P. Schröder-Heister, eds, pp. 109–151, Studies in Logic and Computation, Oxford University Press, 1993.

[10] D. M. Gabbay. *Labelled Deductive Systems, Vol. 1*. Oxford University Press, 1994. First draft 1989. Preprint, Department of Computing, Imperial College London SW7 2BZ. 1st intermediate draft February 1991, 165p. Published as CIS Bericht-90-22, Centrum für Informationssysteme und Sprachverarbeitung, Universität München, Germany. 3rd Intermediate draft 470pp, published by the Max Planck Institut, Saarbrücken Technical Report series, MPI-I-94-223, May 1994.

[11] D. M. Gabbay, A. Martelli, L. Giordano and N. Olivetti. Conditional logic programming. Technical report, University of Turin, 1993. To appear in *Proceedings of ICLP '94*, MIT Press.

[12] D. M. Gabbay and U. Reyle. Direct deductive computation on discourse representation structures. Technical report, University of Stuttgart, 1988. To appear in *Linguistics and Philosophy*.

[13] R. A. Kowalski. *Logic for Problem Solving*. North Holland, 1979.

[14] S. Kraus, D. Lehmann, and M. Magidor. Nonmonotonic reasoning, preferential models and cumulative logics. *Artificial Intelligence*, **44**, 167–207, 1990. A preliminary version, with authors Kraus and Lehmann only, was presented under the title 'Nonmonotonic logics: models and proofs' to *JELIA: European Workshop on Logical Methods in Artificial Intelligence*, Roscoff France, June 1988. Another preliminary version, with all three authors, appeared under the title 'Preferential models and cumulative logics', Technical Report TR 88-15, Department of Computer Science, Hebrew University of Jerusalem, November 1988.

[15] D. Lehmann and M. Magidor. What does a conditional knowledge base entail? *Artificial Intelligence*, **55**, 1–60, 1992. This paper gathers together and extends the material of Technical Report 88-16 by Lehmann and Magidor, Department of Computer Science, Hebrew University of Jerusalem, November 1988.

[16] D. Makinson. General theory of cumulative inference. In M. Reinfrank et al., editors, *Non-Monotonic Reasoning*, volume 346 of *Lecture Notes on Artificial Intelligence*, pages 1–18. Springer-Verlag, Berlin, 1989.

[17] D. Scott. Completeness and axiomatizability in many valued logics. In *Proceedings of the Tarski Symposium*, pages 411–436, Providence, Rhode Island, 1974. American Mathematical Society.

[18] A. Tarski. On the concept of logical consequence. In *Logic, Semantics, Metamathematics*. Oxford University Press, 1936.

[19] R. Wójcicki. *Theory of Logical Calculi*. Reidel, Dordrecht, 1988.

[20] R. Wójcicki. An axiomatic treatment of non monotonic arguments. *Studia Logica*, to appear.

8

What is a Logical System?*

Arnon Avron

Introduction

What is a logical system? Well, one possible answer is that this is what all mathematical logicians had thought they knew until they were seriously asked to give a precise answer.... Personally, I was forced to start thinking about this question when I participated, back in 1986, in the construction of the Edinburgh LF ([18], [2]) - the first computerized system aiming to provide a 'logical framework' for implementing a variety of logical systems. The results of my first investigations on this question were published in [5]. They were further elaborated and extended in [7]. Below I shall heavily draw on these two papers, which still contain most of what I have to say about the issue. Neither of them provides a complete answer, though, and I don't believe that anybody has one yet. Still, a lot of progress has been made by now. I believe, first of all, that we understand now what should be the three main ingredients of any logical system. Moreover, we completely understand at least one of them (and I believe that it is safe to say that we understand two), and we have a substantial (though partial) understanding of the other(s).

The three main components of any logical system are:

1. A formal language

2. A consequence relation

3. Applicability through a notion of schematic substitution.

*Most of the research in this chapter was done while the author was visiting the Computer Science Department of Edinburgh University and was supported by grants from the British Academy of Science and the UK Science and Research Council (Visiting Fellowship number GR/G 5547

In the rest of this chapter, I shall do my best to analyse these three components. Then I shall add some remarks about semantics and the way logical systems are *used*.

1   Formal languages

It is a common wisdom that logic has to do with arguments which we accept because of their *form*. When constructing a logical system we need, first of all, a tool for making the relevant forms explicit. The only such tool which I know is a *formal language*.

What exactly is a formal language? This can easily be turned into another 'big' question, if so one wishes—but I do not. The meaning of this term seems to me clear enough for our needs here: a formal language is specified, first, by some (finite) set of symbols [1] called the 'alphabet'. Next there are several syntactic categories. Each such category is a set of finite strings of (or lists of, or trees labelled by—it does not really matter) symbols from the alphabet. Finally, there should be a given set of grammatical rules that have no exceptions and completely determine (at least in principle) the various categories.[2]

Are there any special requirements for a formal language *of a logical system*? Well, there exists at least one, quite trivial: that one of the categories should be called 'the category of well-formed formulas' (wff). Another might be that all the categories should be recursive, or at least r.e. sets. Personally, I would like to impose this requirement, but if someone maintains that certain 'model-theoretic logics' [10] are indeed logics, then I am not going to insist on this point, and I shall be satisfied with some kind of relative recursiveness.

What is really crucial about a formal language of a logical system is that it should have an appropriate *notion of substitution*. This, however, is the third component which was mentioned above, and it is discussed in Section 3.

---

[1] As long as the alphabet is at most denumerable (as I believe it should be) we can assume that it is finite.

[2] One might like to add also the condition that any symbol or term should belong to exactly one category. This certainly makes things easier from the point of view of implementing formal systems. It forbids, however, polymorphic use of symbols which are intended to correspond to words like 'and' or 'or'. The condition might, therefore, be too restrictive.

2 The notion of a consequence relation

2.1 Axiomatic systems

Traditionally a 'formal system' is understood to include the following components:

1. A formal language L as above.

2. An effective set of wffs called 'axioms'.

3. An effective set of rules (called 'inference rules') for deriving theorems from the axioms.

The set of 'theorems' is usually taken to be the minimal set of wffs which includes all the axioms and is closed under the rules of inference.

Systems of this sort have many names in the literature. Here we shall call them *axiomatic systems*. Undoubtedly they constitute the most basic kind of formal systems. One can argue that in fact all other, more complicated deduction formalisms reduce to systems of this sort. This is true, though, for *every* recursively defined system. Take for example the wffs in the propositional calculus. One can regard them as the 'theorems' of an axiomatic system in which the 'wffs' are strings of symbols, the 'axioms' are the propositional variables and the 'inference rules' are the usual formation rules.[3] The concept of theoremhood in systems of the above sort is not sufficient, therefore, to characterize the notion of a *Logic*. It is too broad a concept. On the other hand the notion of theoremhood of wffs is, at the same time, also too narrow to characterize what a logical system concerning these wffs is all about.

Let us make our last point clearer with two very simple examples from the domain of three-valued logics.[4] Consider Kleene's three-valued logic. It has 3 'truth-values': 1, 0 and -1, of which 1 is taken as the only designated one. The operations corresponding to the usual connectives are: $\neg a = -a$, $a \vee b = \max(a, b)$, $a \wedge b = \min(a, b)$. Suppose that L is the language of propositional calculus where the wffs are defined as usual. It

---

[3] In some recent systems of typed constructive mathematics (see e.g. [20]) this resemblance is taken rather seriously and both 'proposition' and 'theorem' are taken as (different) 'judgments' so that there is no significant difference between possible proofs of these 'judgments'!

[4] A many-valued logic is a logic which is specified by providing (i) a set A of 'truth-values' (like $\{\mathbf{t}, \mathbf{f}\}$ in classical logic), (ii) a set of operations which are defined on A (and correspond to the primitive connectives of the language of the logic. In classical logic these operations are defined by the usual truth-tables), (iii) A subset Tr of A of the 'designated' truth-values (in classical two-valued logic this is just $\{\mathbf{t}\}$). A sentence is logically valid in such a logic iff it gets a designated value under every possible assignment in A which respects the operations.

is immediate then that *no* wff is a theorem of this logic (i.e. there is no wff that is given a designated value under all assignments). The notion of theoremhood seems to be vacuous for this logic. One might ask therefore in what sense it is a 'logic'.

On the other hand, consider the case in which we take both 1 and 0 to be designated. It is easy then to see that a wff is a theorem of the new logic iff it is a classical tautology. From the point of view of theoremhood there is no difference between this logic and the classical, two-valued one. But are they really the same? Obviously not, a major difference is, for example, that the 'new' three-valued logic is *paraconsistent*: It is possible for inconsistent theory to be non-trivial in this logic. (It is possible e.g. for P and $\neg P$ to be both 'true' while Q is 'false'.)

2.2   Consequence relations

Both examples above show that sets of 'logical truths' are not enough for characterizing logics. The second example indicates that what is really important is what wffs follow from what theories. Indeed, in modern treatments of logic another concept, that of a *consequence relation*(C.R.)[5] is taken as fundamental. Unfortunately, the notion of a C.R. has in the literature several (similar, but not identical) meanings. We shall define first the one which we are going to use here (which is rather general) and then discuss some possible reasonable variations.

Definition 2.1 A *consequence relation*(C.R.) on a set Σ of formulas is a binary relation $\vdash$ between (finite) multisets of formulas s.t.:

(I) Reflexivity: $A \vdash A$ for every formula A.

(II) Transitivity, or 'Cut': if $\Gamma_1 \vdash \Delta_1$, A and $A, \Gamma_2 \vdash \Delta_2$, then Γ_1, $\Gamma_2 \vdash \Delta_1$, Δ_2.

In the last definition we use the notion of a 'multiset'. By this we mean 'sets' in which the number of times each element occurs is significant, but not the order of the elements. Thus, for example, $[A, A, B] = [A, B, A] \neq [A, B]$ (In this example we use $[\cdot]$ to denote a multiset. We shall also use ',' for denoting the operation of multiset-union (so $[A, A, B], [A, B] = [A, A, B, A, B]$), and omit the '$[\,]$' whenever there is no danger of confusion.) Now, the notion of multiple-conclusioned C.R. was introduced in [22] and [23]. It was a generalization of Tarski's notion of a consequence relation, which was single-conclusioned (see below). Our notions of consequence relations are, however, not identical to the original ones of Tarski and Scott. First, they both considered *sets* (rather than multisets) of formulas.

---

[5]See, e.g., [22, 17, 15, 25, 26, 14, 13, 5, 11]

Second, they imposed a third demand on C.R.'s: that of monotonicity (see below). Today it does not seem perhaps to be necessary to explain the importance of investigating non-monotonic logics, but why multisets?

To explain this, we should return to the original and still the most basic (though certainly not the only) tool for defining consequence relations: axiomatic systems. Given such a system S we usually define the associated consequence relation $\vdash_S$ as follows. $A_1, \ldots, A_n \vdash_S B$ iff there exists a *proof* in S of B from $A_1, \ldots, A_n$. Now proofs in axiomatic systems should most naturally be taken in the form of labelled *trees*. The reflexivity condition means then just that the trivial tree:

$$A.$$

is a proof of A from A, while the transitivity condition means that given two proof trees:

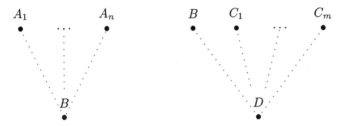

we can combine them into the proof tree:

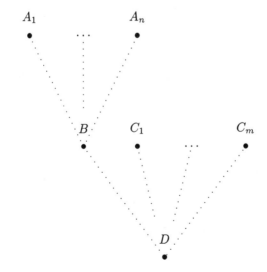

Obviously, in the resulting tree, formulas at the leaves might be repeated more than once. Hence what we *see* is a proof from a *multiset* of formulas. Now insisting on having a proof from a set of formulas means that we should take proofs as directed acyclic graphs. This is less natural. Moreover, combining two proofs into one then becomes much more complicated and less intuitively justified (note also that as long as we understand proofs as defining a relation between the formulas at the root and the formulas at the leaves, the induced relations need not be monotonic).

We conclude that the notion of a proof from hypothesis in an axiomatic system naturally induces a relation of the following type.

Definition 2.2 (1) A *Tarskian* consequence relation on L is a binary relation between finite multisets of L and *formulas* of L such that:

(I) $[A] \vdash A$ for every A.

(II) If $\Gamma \vdash A$ and $\Delta, [A] \vdash B$ then $\Gamma, \Delta \vdash B$.

Because of the primary role that axiomatic systems have for understanding logics, we believe that this definition is the right abstraction for single-conclusioned consequence relations.[6]

A natural objection at this point might be that we have given no ground for using *multiple-conclusioned* C.R.'s. On the contrary: our considerations lead only to single-conclusioned ones. The answer is that a scientific theory should not only make good abstractions, but also good generalizations. Logic obviously carries a great deal of symmetry. This symmetry cannot be fully exploited in the framework of the asymmetrical, single-conclusioned C.R.'s. It seems, therefore, that moving from single-conclusioned C.R.'s to multiple-conclusioned is the right generalization. Moreover, the role of the basic connectives and the relations between them can best be understood in the framework of multiple-conclusioned C.R.'s (see [5, 6]). In particular, the presence of a *real* negation practically turns every single-conclusioned C.R. into a multiple-conclusioned one.

Returning to the subject of multisets and of the best definition of the notion of a consequence relation, it should be noted that by now there are many logics (e.g. linear logic, relevant logic and certain many-valued logics) that can be understood only in the framework of our notion, and not in the original one of Scott. Still, in many cases it is more intuitive to think of C.R.'s in terms of *sets* of formulas (as Tarski and Scott did). It is not difficult, in fact, to introduce a corresponding precise notion of C.R.'s. All we have to do is to replace conditions (I) and (II) of 2.1 by the following two conditions:

---

[6] We give here an absolute priority to the proof-theoretical point of view, since we believe that logic is, above all, concerned with proofs, definitions, arguments, etc.!

I′ $\{A\} \vdash \{A\}$ for all A.

II′ If $\Gamma_1 \vdash \Delta_1 \cup \{A\}$ and $\{A\} \cup \Gamma_2 \vdash \Delta_2$ then $\Gamma_1 \cup \Gamma_2 \vdash \Delta_1 \cup \Delta_2$ ($\Gamma_1, \Gamma_2, \Delta_1, \Delta_2$ are here *sets of formulas*) [7].

It is more useful, however, to be able to apply one unified theory instead of two: one for multisets, another for sets. The following definition and the proposition that follows it will enable us to treat sets-C.R.'s as a special case of multisets-C.R.'s.

Notation

Set (Γ), where Γ is a multiset, is the set which has exactly the same elements as Γ.

Definition 2.3 A *regular* C.R. is a C.R. $\vdash$ which satisfies the following condition: if $\mathrm{set}(\Gamma) = \mathrm{set}(\Gamma')$ and $\mathrm{set}(\Delta) = \mathrm{set}(\Delta')$ then $\Gamma \vdash \Delta$ iff $\Gamma' \vdash \Delta'$.

Proposition 2.4 *Suppose $\vdash$ is a relation between finite sets of formulas. Define a corresponding relation between multisets as follows: $\Gamma \vdash^* \Delta$ iff $\mathrm{set}(\Gamma) \vdash \mathrm{set}(\Delta)$. Then $\vdash^*$ is a C.R. iff $\vdash$ satisfies (I') and (II') above (in which case $\vdash^*$ is regular). Conversely: suppose $\vdash$ is a relation between multisets of formulas and $\vdash'$ – its restriction to sets. Then $\vdash'$ satisfies (I') and (II') iff $\vdash$ is regular. Moreover if $\vdash$ is a relation between sets which satisfies (I') and (II') then $(\vdash^*)' = \vdash$ while if $\vdash$ is a regular C.R. then $(\vdash')^* = \vdash$.*

The last proposition means that C.R.'s between sets and regular C.R.'s are essentially the same thing. In most propositions and definitions below we may adopt whatever point of view we like (provided we understand the expression Γ, Δ as $\Gamma \cup \Delta$ in the relations-between-sets interpretation).

As we have already noted above, Tarski and Scott not only defined a C.R. to be a relation involving sets of formulas (rather than multisets) but they also imposed a third demand: that of monotonicity.

Definition 2.5 (1) A C.R. $\vdash$ is called *monotonic* if $\Gamma, \Gamma' \vdash \Delta, \Delta'$ wherever $\Gamma \vdash \Delta$.

(2) A C.R. $\vdash$ is called *ordinary* iff it is both regular and monotonic.

---

[7]In condition (II′), A may or may not be an element of Γ_2 or Δ_1. It might be thought that restricting condition (II′) to the case: $A \notin \Delta_1 \cup \Gamma_2$ is plausible here (the relevance system $R_{\rightarrow}$ is strongly related to such an understanding), but this would lead to counterintuitive results. Suppose e.g. that we consider minimal C.R.'s which contain all substitution instances of certain schemes, including, for example, $A, B, \vdash A \wedge B$. If we assume only the weak form of (II′) then we have that $A \vdash A \wedge A$ and $A \wedge A, B \vdash (A \wedge A) \wedge B$ and so $A, B \vdash (A \wedge A) \wedge B$ whenever A and B are different atomic variables. Substituting $A \wedge A$ for B is not possible, though: $A, A \wedge A \nvdash (A \wedge A) \wedge (A \wedge A)$. (Note that this difficulty does not arise if we assume monotonicity – as Scott and Tarski did.)

Note

Regularity and monotonicity are, of course, independent properties, and so one can consider monotonic C.R.'s which are not regular (like that of the logic BCK of [21] or the C.R. induced by the Łukasiewicz implication (see [6])).

Monotonicity, again, is a very natural restriction. It fails, however, for any system for non-monotonic reasoning, as well as for some C.R.'s based on linear logic and relevance logics.

2.3 Some examples

2.3.1 First-order logic

Let $A_1, \ldots, A_n$ and $B_1, \ldots, B_m$ be formulas of some first-order language L (i.e. they may contain free variables).

Truth: $A_1, \ldots, A_n \vdash_t B_1, \ldots, B_m$ iff every assignment in a first-order structure for L which makes all the A_is true does the same to one of the B_is.

Validity: $A_1, \ldots, A_n \vdash_v B_1, \ldots, B_m$ iff in every first-order structure (for L) in which all the A_is are *valid* at least one of the B_is is valid too (by 'valid' in a structure we mean: true relative to all assignments).

The above are examples of two important C.R.'s which are frequently associated with first-order logic. It is important to note that they are *not* identical—not even in the case $m = 1$. $\forall x p(x)$ follows, for example, from $p(x)$ according to the second, but not according to the first. On the other hand, the classical deduction theorem holds for the first, but not for the second. The two consequence relations *are* identical, though, from the point of view of *theoremhood*: $\vdash_v A$ iff $\vdash_t A$. Moreover: if all formulas of Γ are closed then $\Gamma \vdash_t A$ iff $\Gamma \vdash_v A$. In [8] we show that resolution is based on $\vdash_v$ while the tableaux method is based on $\vdash_t$.

The single-conclusioned fragments of both C.R.'s defined above can be extended to multiple-conclusioned C.R.'s in more than one interesting way, but we shall not go into the details.

2.3.2 Propositional modal logic

Truth: $A_1, \ldots, A_n \vdash_t B$ iff given a frame and a valuation in that frame, B *is true* in *every world* (of the frame) in which all the A_is are true.

Validity: $A_1, \ldots, A_n \vdash_v B$ iff given a frame, every valuation which makes all the A_is valid (in that frame) does the same to B (by 'valid' we mean: true in all the worlds).

The above are two important *single-conclusioned* C.R.'s. The situation concerning them is similar to that in the previous case: $A \vdash_v \Box A$ but $A \not\vdash_t \Box A$, the deduction theorem obtains for $\vdash_t$ but not for $\vdash_v$. Again the two C.R.'s are identical as far as *theorems* are concerned.[8]

2.3.3 Three-valued logics

Assume again a propositional language with the connectives $\neg$, $\lor$, $\land$. Let corresponding operations on the truth values $\{-1, 0, 1\}$ be defined as in Section 2.1. We now define five different (multiset-) C.R.'s based on the resulting structure. In these definitions v denotes an assignment of truth values to formulas which respects the operations, $\Gamma = A_1, \ldots, A_m$ and $\Delta = B_1, \ldots, B_n$.

Kl: $\Gamma \vdash_{Kl} \Delta$ iff for all v, $v(B_i) = 1$ for some i or $v(A_j) \in \{-1, 0\}$ for some j.

Pac: $\Gamma \vdash_{Pac} \Delta$ iff for all v, either $v(B_i) \in \{1, 0\}$ for some i or $v(A_j) = -1$ for some j.

Lt: $\Gamma \vdash_{Lt} \Delta$ iff for all v, either $v(B_i) = 1$ for some i or $v(A_j) = -1$ for some j, or $v(B_i) = v(A_j) = 0$ for some i, j.

Sob: $\Gamma \vdash_{Sob} \Delta$ iff for all v, either $v(B_i) = 1$ for some i or $v(A_j) = -1$ for some j or $v(A_i) = v(B_j) = 0$ for *all* i, j.

Luk: $\Gamma \vdash_{Luk} \Delta$ iff for all v, either $v(B_i) = 1$ for some i or $v(A_j) = -1$ for some j or at least *two* formulas in Γ, Δ get 0 (under v).

Notes

1. The first three of these C.R.'s are ordinary. The last two are not (see below).

2. $\vdash_{Kl}$ corresponds to taking 1 as the only designated value, and so it is the obvious C.R. defined by the three-valued logic of Kleene (given above as an example of a logic with no logical theorems). It was originally introduced by Kleene for the study of recursive functions, and today it is extensively used, for example, in the VDM project (see [9] or [19]). The standard interpretation of 0 in it is 'undefined'.

3. $\vdash_{Pac}$ corresponds to taking both 1 and 0 as designated. As noted above, it has the same set of theorems as classical propositional calculus, but it is *paraconsistent* ($P, \neg P \not\vdash_{Pac} Q$). Moreover: it is a

---

[8]The distinction between the two C.R.'s was crucial for the efficient implementation of both in the Edinburgh LF. See [2] for further details.

maximal paraconsistent ordinary C.R. in its language. As such it might prove to be important for future use of inconsistent knowledge bases.

4. $A_1, \ldots, A_m \vdash_{Lt} B_1, \ldots, B_n$ iff for every v, $v(A_1 \wedge A_2 \wedge \ldots \wedge A_m) \leq v(B_1 \vee B_2 \vee \ldots \vee B_n)$. This C.R. also has no theorems. In fact, if $\Gamma \vdash_{Lt} \Delta$ then both Γ and Δ are non-empty.

5. $A_1, \ldots, A_n \vdash_{Sob} B$ iff $A_1 \rightarrow (A_2 \rightarrow \ldots \rightarrow (A_n \rightarrow B) \ldots)$ is valid where $\rightarrow$ is defined as in Sobociński three-valued logic.[9] Moreover, $A_1, \ldots, A_m \vdash_{Sob} B_1, \ldots, B_n$ iff $\vdash_{RM_3} A_1 \rightarrow (A_2 \rightarrow \ldots (A_m \rightarrow (B_1 + \ldots + B_n)) \ldots)$, where $A + B \overset{\text{def}}{=} \neg A \rightarrow B$ and RM_3 is the strongest in the family of logics created by the Relevantists school.[10] *This C.R. is not monotonic*: weakening fails for it on both sides. It is maximally paraconsistent as well.

6. $A_1, \ldots, A_n \vdash_{Luk} B$ iff $A_1 \rightarrow (A_2 \rightarrow \ldots \rightarrow (A_n \rightarrow B) \ldots)$ is valid in Łukasiewicz three-valued logic (using negation, it is easy to give a corresponding interpretation for *every* sequent). Its main property is that *contraction fails for it* (on both sides). It is therefore completely necessary to understand it as a *multiset* C.R..

7. The classical C.R. (our first example) can also be characterized in the present framework by: $\Gamma \vdash \Delta$ iff for every v either $v(A_i) = -1$ or $v(B_j) = 1$ or at least one formula in $\Gamma \cup \Delta$ gets 0 (the proof of this claim uses known proof-theoretical reductions).

For more information about these logics, see [6].

2.4   Classification of basic connectives

Our general framework allows us to give a completely abstract definition, *independent of any semantical interpretation*, of standard connectives. These characterizations explain why these connectives are so important in almost every logical system (and so their study is necessarily a significant part of the science of logics).[11]

---

[9]This logic was introduced in [24]. It has 0 and 1 as designated and $a \rightarrow b$ is defined in it as $\max(b, -a)$ in case $a \leq b$, $\min(b, -a)$ otherwise.

[10]It is obtained from Sobociński's logic by adding to it the connectives $\wedge$, $\vee$ as defined above. See [1] or [12] for more details.

[11]It should perhaps be emphasized that I am not trying here to capture the meaning of 'or', say, as is used in English or mathematical English (I do not believe, by the way, that it has just one meaning there!). On the contrary, I am doing my best below to characterize connectives in a way which is completely independent of their possible meanings in certain interpretations. The phenomenon I had in mind is precisely that certain connectives are included in almost any logical system, despite the fact that their

2.4.1 Internal connectives

Given C.R., an internal connective relative to it is one that makes it possible to transform a given sequent to an equivalent one that has a special required form. By 'equivalent' here we mean that one sequent obtains iff the other does (but in most important cases it can be interpreted in a much stronger sense).

In what follows assume $\vdash$ to be a fixed C.R.. All notions defined are taken to be relative to $\vdash$.

Internal disjunction

We call a binary connective $+$ an internal disjunction if for all Γ, Δ, A, B:

$$\Gamma \vdash \Delta, A, B \text{ iff } \Gamma \vdash \Delta, A + B.$$

Internal conjunction

We call a binary connective $\circ$ an internal conjunction if for all Γ, Δ, A, B:

$$\Gamma, A, B \vdash \Delta \text{ iff } \Gamma, A \circ B \vdash \Delta.$$

Internal negation

We call a unary connective $\neg$ a right internal negation if for all Γ, Δ, A:

$$\Gamma, A \vdash \Delta \text{ iff } \Gamma \vdash \Delta, \neg A.$$

We call a unary connective $\neg$ a left internal negation if for all Γ, Δ, A:

$$\Gamma \vdash \Delta, A \text{ iff } \Gamma, \neg A \vdash \Delta.$$

Since it can be shown that $\neg$ is a right internal negation iff it is a left one, we use the term *internal negation* to mean either. It is important to note that such a negation is *necessarily* involutive (i.e. $A \vdash \neg\neg A$ and $\neg\neg A \vdash A$).

Internal implications

We call a binary connective $\rightarrow$ an internal implication if for all Γ, A, B:

$$\Gamma, A \vdash B \text{ iff } \Gamma \vdash A \rightarrow B.$$

We call $\rightarrow$ a *strong* internal implication if for all Γ, Δ, A, B:

$$\Gamma, A \vdash \Delta, B \text{ iff } \Gamma \vdash \Delta, A \rightarrow B.$$

The importance of the internal connectives should be obvious. Thus internal disjunction allows us to assume that there is exactly one conclusion in any argument, while internal conjunction allows us to assume that there

---

intended meaning can be very different (if there is any intended meaning. Girard had no clear interpretation of his 'par' in [16]. Still, its *ROLE* is very clear!).

is exactly one premise. Negation allows both possibilities (although not simultaneously). Its main role is to introduce symmetry and to blur the distinction between single-conclusioned and multiple-conclusioned C.R.'s. Finally, internal implication reflects the consequence relation within the language and frequently makes it possible to concentrate on *theoremhood* rather than on consequence.

2.4.2 The combining connectives

Among the rules that can be associated with the internal connectives there are rules that take *two* sequents and return a single one. In all of these rules, however, the resulting combination is not reversible: the premises cannot always be recovered from the conclusion. Indeed, one cannot expect to be able to combine *any* two sequents into one which contains exactly the same information as is included in the original two. It *is* possible, though, in one important case: when the two sequents to be combined are identical in all formulas except (perhaps) one. The two sequents can then be combined through their exceptional formulas by using a new type of connective which we call *combining* connectives. Two particularly useful ones are the following:

Combining conjunction
We call a connective $\wedge$ a combining conjunction iff for all Γ, Δ, A, B

$$\Gamma \vdash \Delta, A \wedge B \text{ iff } \Gamma \vdash \Delta, A \text{ and } \Gamma \vdash \Delta, B.$$

Combining disjunction
We call a connective $\vee$ a combining disjunction iff for all Γ, Δ, A, B

$$A \vee B, \Gamma \vdash \Delta \text{ iff } A, \Gamma \vdash \Delta, A \text{ and } B, \Gamma \vdash \Delta.$$

Note:
The combining connectives are called 'additives' in linear logic (see [16]) and 'extensional' in relevance logic. The internal ones correspond, respectively, to the 'multiplicatives' and to the 'intensional' connectives.

Several well-known logics can be defined using the above connectives:

'Multiplicative' linear logic
This is the logic which corresponds to the *minimal* (multiset) C.R. which includes all the internal connectives. The system is neither regular nor monotonic.

Propositional linear logic
(Without the the 'exponentials' and the propositional constants.) This corresponds to the minimal consequence relation which contains all the connectives introduced above. Again, it is neither regular nor monotonic.

It is important to note that its internal connectives behave quite differently from its combining ones!

$R_{\underset{\rightarrow}{\sim}}$ the intensional fragment of the relevance logic R^{12}

This corresponds to the minimal C.R. which contains all the internal connectives and is *closed under contraction*. It is still neither regular nor monotonic.

R without distribution:

This corresponds to the minimal C.R. which contains all the connectives which were described above and is closed under contraction.

$RMI_{\underset{\rightarrow}{\sim}}{}^{13}$

This corresponds to the minimal *regular* C.R. which contains all the internal conectives.

Classical propositional logic

This of course corresponds to the minimal ordinary C.R. which has all the above connectives. Needless to say, there is no difference in it between the combining connectives and the corresponding internal ones.

Note

The meaning of the term 'minimal' which is used in these characterizations is not as obvious as it seems. A thorough investigation of various notions of minimality is given in [7].

For more information and discussion of the issues discussed in this section see [5, 6] and [7].

2.5 Representations of C.R.'s

The notion of a C.R., as defined in the first section and exemplified in the second, is an *abstract* one. We have seen above several ways, semantical as well as syntactical, of defining or characterizing C.R.'s. However, in order to use a certain abstract C.R. in practice one needs a *concrete* way of *representing* it. This is usually done by using a formal system. There are two basic demands that such representations of a C.R. ⊢ should meet. These are:

Faithfulness

If the representation can be used to show that $\Gamma \vdash \Delta$ then this is actually the case.

Effectiveness

If someone uses the representation to show that $\Gamma \vdash \Delta$ then his success in

---

[12] see [1] or [12]
[13] see [3, 4].

doing so can be checked mechanically. If we accept Church's thesis then this means that the set of sequents that can be shown to hold by a given formal representation is an r.e. set.

A third property that we would like an adequate representation of ⊢ to have, but that can in principle be achieved (by Church's thesis) only if the represented C.R. is r.e., is:

Completeness
Whenever $\Gamma\vdash\Delta$ the representation can be used to show this.

A study of the use of axiomatic systems, Gentzen-type systems, natural deductions and other methods (like high-order sequents and treating several C.R.'s simultaneously) can be found in [5] and [7].

3   Applicability and substitution

3.1   The basic idea

One of the main features of a logical system LS that is worthy of this name is that it is meant to be *applied*. This means that given some application language L', there might be cases in which we shall claim that a formula B' of L' logically follows by LS from other formulas $A_1', \ldots, A_n'$ of L'. The justification of such a claim will be due, of course, to the logical form(s) that $A_1', \ldots, A_n', B'$ have, when they are analysed in terms of the vocabulary of LS. These logical forms are represented by formulas of the language of LS (call it L), of which $A_1', \ldots, A_n', B'$ are taken to be (substitution) instances. In other words: B' follows by L from $A_1', \ldots, A_n'$ iff there are formulas $A_1, \ldots, A_n, B$ of L such that $A_1, \ldots, A_n\vdash_{LS}B$ and of which $A_1', \ldots, A_n', B'$ are, in some sense, simultaneous (substitution) instances.

It follows that a main factor of any logical system LS is a *notion of substitution* which allows us to see formulas of other languages as instances of formulas of L. Another, related, factor is the vocabulary of L. It consists of the logical concepts which LS is designed to capture and which are reflected in the *constants* of its language. In classical (and many other) propositional logics, for example, these are the standard connectives, which correspond to certain meanings of words like 'not' 'or' 'and', etc. In the predicate calculus we also have the constants for the standard quantifiers, and in modal logic we have, in addition connectives like □ corresponding to 'It is necessary that...'. It may also have, however, other interpretations like:'It is known that...', 'It is provable that...', and many more. The chosen interpretation depends on the application language. It is not completely free, though. The consequence relation of LS imposes certain constraints on the possible interpretations, despite the fact that the formulas of L provide only forms. In principle these constraints might even practically determine just one possible interpretation. This is the case, I believe, with classical propositional logic.

Since a formula φ of *LS* provides a form for formulas of some other language(s) L' and these forms are connected with certain logical concepts, it is obvious that one can substitute in the appropriate places of φ formulas of L' which themselves are connected with these very concepts. A formula of L' might not have, therefore, a single logical form (from the point of view of the constants of L). Moreover, it is obvious that there are forms which are instances (or refinements) of other forms. It follows that the notion of substitution of L should, first of all, apply to itself. In fact, every formula of L should have an infinite set of substitution instances within L (i.e., an infinite set of possible refinements of the forms it represents).[14]

3.2 The logical substitution—instance relation

Now it is reasonable to argue that it does not make much sense to try to characterize a logical system *LS* abstractly in terms of its relations to some unknown possible application languages. I believe, however, that the essence of the potential of substituting into formulas of the language of *LS* should be reflected already in the substitution–instance relation between this language and itself. Below I shall try to give a characterization of such relations, but I admit in advance that what is given below is not necessarily the final word on this issue.

Definition 3.1 Let L be a formal language as in Section 1 and let $\vdash$ be a consequence relation on the formulas of L. An abstract substitution-instance (si) relation on L (relative to $\vdash$) is a relation between finite sequences of formulas of L having the same length. The relation should satisfy the following conditions:

1. $(A_1, \ldots, A_n) si (A_1, \ldots, A_n)$.

2. If $(A_1, \ldots, A_n) si (B_1, \ldots, B_n)$ and $(B_1, \ldots, B_n) si (C_1, \ldots, C_n)$ then $(A_1, \ldots, A_n) si (C_1, \ldots, C_n)$.

3. If $(A_1, \ldots, A_n) si (B_1, \ldots, B_n)$ and $B_i = B_j$ then $A_i = A_j$.

4. If $(A_1, \ldots, A_n) si (B_1, \ldots, B_n)$ and π is a permutation of $\{1, \ldots, n\}$, then
   $(A_{\pi(1)}, \ldots, A_{\pi(n)}) si (B_{\pi(1)}, \ldots, B_{\pi(n)})$.

5. If $(A_1, \ldots, A_n) si (B_1, \ldots, B_n)$ and $k < n$ then $(A_1, \ldots, A_k) si (B_1, \ldots, B_k)$.

---

[14]One might object that there might be degenerate forms with no internal instances at all, like the propositional constants $\top$ and $\bot$. We shall later return to this issue.

6. If $A'_1, \ldots, A'_n, A_1, \ldots, A_n$ and B are in L and $(A'_1, \ldots, A'_n)si(A_1, \ldots, A_n)$ then there exists a formula B' in L so that $(A'_1, \ldots, A'_n, B')si(A_1, \ldots, A_n, B)$.

7. If $(A'_1, \ldots, A'_n, B'_1, \ldots, B'_m)si(A_1, \ldots, A_n, B_1, \ldots, B_m)$ and $A_1, \ldots, A_n \vdash B_1, \ldots, B_m$ then $A'_1, \ldots, A'_n \vdash B'_1, \ldots, B'_m$.

8. There exists a formula A which has an infinite number of different substitution instances.

The eight properties above are obvious necessary properties of a substitution–instance relation. From a logical system, however, we intuitively expect more. To try to determine exactly what, let us turn to see better what is meant by the 'vocabulary of L'. For this let us introduce the following two types of symbols of the alphabet of L (given si as above):

- A symbol s is a constant of L if whenever $(B_1, \ldots, B_n)si(A_1, \ldots, A_n)$ the number of occurrences of s in A_i is less than or equal to the number of occurrences of s in B_i $(i = 1, \ldots, n)$.

- A symbol s is a (logical) variable iff every sequence $(A_1, \ldots, A_n)$ in which s occurs has an infinite number of substitution instances.

Given this terminology, we can formulate two conditions that I believe are characteristic of every logical system:

1. Any symbol in the alphabet is either a constant or a variable.

2. Any well-formed formula contains at least one variable (and so has an infinite number of instances).

Notes

1) The definitions of 'a constant' and 'a variable' are only first approximations. With regard to constants, for example, we really want something stronger: that substitution somehow preserves the structure of a formula. We have in mind, for example, conditions like the following: Let $*$ be a k-ary connective of L. Then for every $A_1, \ldots, A_n, C_1, \ldots, C_k, A'_1, \ldots, A'_n, B'$ in L we have that $(A'_1, \ldots, A'_n, B')si(A_1, \ldots, A_n, *(C_1, \ldots, C_k))$ iff there exist $C'_1, \ldots, C'_k$ such that

$$B' = *(C'_1, \ldots, C'_k) \text{ and } (A'_1, \ldots, A'_n, C'_1, \ldots, C'_k)si(A_1, \ldots, A_n, C_1, \ldots, C_k).$$

This works fine for a special kind of constant: connectives. When it comes to other types, quantifiers, for example, formulating a similar condition is not so easy. Formulating the idea in general terms seems even more difficult. It might be possible, though, if (i) we allow the enriching of the original language L with extra-syntactic categories, especially abstractions, and (ii) use the mechanism of the λ-calculus for identifying syntactic objects. This idea is the core of the Edinburgh LF ([18, 2]) theory of logical systems. Thus the quantifier '$\forall$' is regarded there as connected not directly to formulas but to abstractions (of type '$i \to o$'). Using this method the compositionality condition can be formulated much more generally. On the other hand this method involves the extension of the si relation to arbitrary sequences of grammatically 'meaningful' strings (not necessarily of the same type) where the 'grammatical' criterion refers to the extended grammar. I am not sure yet if and how this can always be done. The LF theory is not completely satisfactory yet, and it is not certain that it is always applicable (a general operation of transitive closure, for example, seems to provide a counterexample). Still its existence and success indicate that a fully adequate theory might be found.

(2) It should be clarified what I have in mind when I talk about 'a (logical) variable' and 'a (logical) constant' of a logical system. This can best be done by an example. Take classical first-order logic. In the literature it is actually difficult to find what single formal system, if any, one refers to when speaking about this logic. It seems that it is a name for a *class* of formal systems, each characterized by its chosen signature. According to my analysis what deserves the name 'classical first-order logic' is only the *pure* system, which has infinitely many constants, and for every n a denumerable set of predicates and a denumerable set of function symbols of arity n.[15] In this pure system every predicate symbol P_i^n, for example, functions as a *variable* for which one can substitute any compatible formula (more precisely, perhaps, any abstraction of the appropriate type, but this formulation relies on the more concrete view of substitution which I have mentioned above). Thus $P_1^1(f_1^2(x)) \to P_5^2(C_3, x)$ is a substitution instance of $P_1^2(x)$ and $\forall x(P_1^1(f_2^1(x)) \to P_5^2((C_3, x))$ is a substitution instance of $\forall x P_1^2(x)$. Similarly, any closed term may be substituted for any 'constant' symbol C_i of the language.[16] In contrast the standard first-order system of Peano arithmetic is an example of an *application* system. Its constants: $+, \cdot$, etc., are not variables and in its usual presentation a closed formula

---

[15]Variants which defer w.r.t. the actual symbols used should be identified somehow, and so a more abstract (categorical?) approach to languages should perhaps be taken, but I consider such problems to be of secondary significance. Similarly I also ignore differences w.r.t. to the actual choice of the constant symbols, for example, '$\wedge$' versus '&'. Like everywhere else in mathematics, everything is defined at the end only up to isomorphism.

[16]Note again that in this description the substitution relation goes beyond the abstract one defined above, which was only between finite sequences of formulas. I emphasize again that I don't yet have a satisfactory theory which will fill the gap on the one hand, and is general enough on the other.

has no instances, and so it has no logical (or schematical) variables.[17]

(3) A very important distinction that should be made is between the logical (or schematical) variables which we discuss above and internal variables that the language might have. The difference may be explained as follows: substitution for the schematical variables is, in principle, external to the language, and it always preserves the consequence relation. Internal variables, on the other hand, are variables for which there is a binding mechanism in the language (and so substitution is done within the language). It should not be related, however, to the consequence relation. In first-order logic we have, for example, a binding mechanism for the syntactic category of (internal) variables $v_0, v_1, \ldots$, and there is an internal notion of substitution for them. Whether or not it is a compatible with the logical notion of substitution which is associated with the language and the C.R. depends on the way we define this notion on the consequence relation. Thus $p(x) \vdash_v \forall x p(x)$ (See 2.3.1 for definition of $\vdash_v$.) Hence $(p(C_1), \forall x p(x))$ does not stand in the corresponding *si* relation with $(p(x), \forall x p(x))$, although internally $p(C_1)$ is a substitution instance of $p(x)$. Externally, the only thing that can be substituted (with care) for a variable in $\vdash_v$ is another variable.

External, logical substitution and internal substitution can, of course, be compatible (i.e. internal substitution can form a part of the logical notion of substitution which is associated with the language and the C.R.). In first-order logic, for example, this is the situation with respect to $\vdash_t$. The *LF* paradigm of logical systems is based, in fact, on assuming such a compatibility in general. Indeed, in the *LF*, one should try as much as possible to identify 'variables' of the language with variables of the *LF* (*without* having a special category of object-language variables). Experience with the *LF* shows that this cannot always be done!

(4) I believe that *every* formula of a pure logical system should contain a logical (schematical) variable. On the other hand, it is common to use propositional constants like ⊤ and ⊥ in the formulations of many logical systems. I always believed this to be an artificial procedure. Thus one usually interprets '⊥' in arithmetic as '0 = 1', although '1 = 2' can be chosen just as well. Still, even propositional constants can almost always be taken as schematic variables. Thus one can usually substitute for ⊤ any theorem of the system that is built from it using the system's connectives, or even every theorem of the system. Similar classes can be found for ⊥. The upshot is that (in my view, at least) the propositional constants are not really constants (i.e. they are never used for representing *forms* of sentences) but

---

[17]Unless one takes two α-variants of a formula as substitution instance of each other. This only means, however, that our definitions should be refined and clarified. For example, we should be talking about *proper* instances, where A is a proper instance of B if $AsiB$ but the inverse is not true. I apologize again that in this chapter I try to convey the main ideas of a research which is far from being complete.

a special kind of variable. This should, indeed, be clear from the fact that the test whether a given sentence in a possible application language can be used as an interpretation of such a 'constant' always depends on the *truth value* of the sentence, not on its *form*.

3.3   The applied substitution-instance relation

As was emphasized above, the *si* relation on a logical language L is not an end in itself, but only a mean for the goal of applying a logic to other languages, usually semantically oriented ones. Again the application is done through a substitution relation between sequences of formulas of L and the application language L'. How this relation is defined is usually a difficult question. When it comes to something near natural languages (to say nothing about natural languages themselves) it is usually not defined at all. One only decides in particular cases what sequence in L can a given sequence of formulas of L' usefully be viewed as an instance of. Even this might be a difficult question and I know no set of rules that can be applied when L' is, say, English. What is obvious is that formulas of L usually do not represent concrete forms of formulas of L', but some abstract form. Thus we usually understand the negation symbol '$\neg$' as corresponding to 'not', but, unlike in $\neg A$, the word 'not' is almost never put in (English) before the sentence we want to negate.

What we can again do is to give a list of properties that any such *si*-relation should have. The basic list is similar to (1)–(8) from the beginning of 3.2, with the exclusion of (1) and with the obvious needed modifications. Thus in (6) $A'_1, \ldots, A'_n, B'$ are in L' , while (7) is more a *definition* of the consequence relation induced by the given logic than a property of *si*. Property (2) is particularly important. In the present context, $A_1, \ldots, A_n, B_1, \ldots, B_n$ are usually in L while $C_1, \ldots, C_n$ in L'. The first *si* is the reflexive *si*-relation in LS while the second – that between L and L'. The resulting condition entails that the interpretations of the logical constants should somehow be uniform.

It is possible also that L' above is the language of another logical system LS'. If so, then (7) is not a definition anymore, but a true condition, while in (2) it is possible also that $A_1, \ldots, A_n$ are in L, $B_1, \ldots, B_n, C_1, \ldots, C_n$ are in L' and the first *si* is the relation between L and L' while the second is between L' and itself. If (2)–(8) obtain ((2) in its two possible readings) then we say that the logic LS is *contained* in the logic LS'. Thus classical propositional logic is contained in this sense in classical first-order logic.

Obviously, if a logic LS is contained in another logic LS' then every application of LS' to some language L' induces an application of LS to L' by composing the two *si* relations to obtain a *si* -relation between L and L'. In this case (2) gets a third reading, where the three occurrences of *si* correspond each to a different substitution–instance relation.

4   Some words about semantics

My discussion so far has deliberately ignored any reference to semantical issue. The reason is that unlike other authors (see, for example, [13]), for me semantics is *not* a part of the logical system. Still, I cannot ignore this aspect here completely because it is extremely important for a lot of issues related to logical systems. So without going into exact definitions of semantical concepts, let me just list the roles of semantics:

(1) **Motivation:** The constants of a logical system almost always have some preliminary intuitive meaning which motivates the construction of the system.[18]

(2) **A tool for defining consequence relations:** Semantical notions are frequently used for this task, especially if they are connected to the intuitions that stand behind the construction of the logic. All the examples we gave above were defined, in fact, using semantical concepts (one should remember, however, that logical systems can be, and frequently were, defined using pure proof-theoretical means. Modal systems were originally introduced in that way while Kripke structures, for example, were introduced much later).

(3) **The applications of a logic:** The semantics of the application language usually dictates in what ways the logic is going to be used. In other words, it is the main factor in the construction of the *si* relation. Usually this is done according to some correspondence between the semantics of L' (the application language) and the intuitive semantics behind L (the language of the logic).

(4) **A technical instrument for investigating logics:** Semantical issues can be used for answering technical problems concerning logics, like decidability, interpolation properties and so on. Sometimes the semantical notions used have little to do with the semantical intuition behind the construction of the logics. Examples are the well known topological semantics of the modal logic S4 or Heyting algebras in the study of intuitionistic logic.

References

[1] Anderson A.R. and Belnap N.D. *Entailment* vol. 1, Princeton University Press, Princeton, N.J., 1975.

---

[18]One should note again, though, that a system can get in applications interpretations which are very different from the original ones. Modal logic is a case in point.

[2] Avron A., Honsell F., Mason I. and Pollack R. Using typed lambda calculus to implement formal systems on a machine, To appear in the *Journal of Automated reasoning*, **9**, 309–354, 1992.

[3] Avron A. Relevance and paraconsistency - a new approach, *Journal of Symbolic Logic*, **55**, 707–732, 1990.

[4] Avron A. Relevance and paraconsistency - a new approach Part II: the formal systems, *Notre Dame Journal of Formal Logic*, **31**, 169–202, 1990.

[5] Avron A. Simple consequence relations, *Journal of Information and Computation*, **92**, 105–139, 1991.

[6] Avron A. Natural 3-valued logics—characterization and proof theory, *Journal of Symbolic Logic*, **56**, 276–294, 1991.

[7] Avron A. Axiomatic systems, deduction and implication, *Journal of Logic and Computation*, **2**, 51–99, 1992.

[8] Avron A. Gentzen-type systems, resolution and tableaux, *Journal of Automated Deduction*, **10**, 265–281, 1993.

[9] Barringer H., Cheng J.H., and Jones C.B., A logic C undefiness in program proofs, *Acta Informatica*, **21**, 251–269, 1984.

[10] Barwise J. and Feferman S. *Model-Theoretic Logics*, Pespectives in Mathematical Logic, Springer-Verlag, New York, 1985.

[11] Cleave J. P., *A Study of Logics*, Oxford Logic Guide Clarendon Press, Oxford, 1991.

[12] Dunn J.M. Relevant logic and entailment, in: *Handbook of Philosophical Logic*, Vol III, ed. by D. Gabbay and F. Guenthner, Reidel: Dordrecht, Holland; Boston: USA, 1984.

[13] Epstein R. L. *The Semantic Foundations of Logic, Propositional Logics*, Kluwer Academic Publishers, 1990.

[14] Fagin R., Halpern J.Y, and Vardi Y. What is an inference rule?, *Journal of Symbolic Logic*, **57**, 1017-1-45, 1992.

[15] Gabbay D. *Semantical investigations in Heyting's intuitionistic logic* , Reidel: Dordrecht, Holland; Boston: USA, 1981.

[16] Girard J.Y., Linear logic, *Theoretical Computer Science*, **50**, 1–101, 1987.

[17] Hacking I. What is logic, The *Journal of Philosophy*, **76**, 285–318, 1979.

[18] Harper R., Honsell F., and Plotkin G. A framework for defining logics, *Journal of the Association for Computing Machinery*, **40**, 143–184, 1993.

[19] Jones C.B., *Systematic Software Development Using VDM* Prentice-Hall International, UK, 1986.

[20] Martin-löf P. *Intuitionistic Type Theory*, Bibliopolis, Napoli, 1984.

[21] Ono H. and Komori, Y., Logics without the contraction rule, The *Journal of Symbolic Logic*, **50**, 169–201, 1985.

[22] Scott D. Rules and derived rules, in: Stenlund S. *Logical Theory and Semantical Analysis*, pp. 147–161, Reidel: Dordrecht, 1974.

[23] Scott D. Completeness and axiomatizability in many-valued logic, in: *Proceeding of the Tarski Symposium*, Proceeding of Symposia in Pure Mathematics, vol. XXV, American Mathematical Society, Rhode Island, (1974), pp. 411–435.

[24] Sobociński B. Axiomatization of partial system three-valued calculus of propositions, The *Journal of Computing Systems*, **11**, 23–55, 1952.

[25] Urquhart A. Many-valued logic, in: *Handbook of Philosophical Logic*, Vol III, ed. by D. Gabbay and F. Guenthner, Reidel: Dordrecht, Holland; Boston: USA, 1984.

[26] Wojcicki R., *Theory of Logical Calculi*, Synthese Library, vol. 199, Kluwer Academic Publishers (1988).

9

Structure, Consequence Relation and Logic

G. Crocco and L. Fariñas del Cerro

1 Introduction

Traditionally logic is defined using set theoretical concepts since historically, the main application of formal logic was mathematical concepts. Systems alternative to classical logic were proposed very early on. However, the new application of logic to computer science requires us to express concepts very different from those handled by the standard set operations.

The characteristics of these new logics has very often been represented by modifications or extensions of the language, such as removing some classical theorems or adding modal operators that express necessity or temporal proposition qualities. But these suggestions do not lead to a unified framework.

A possible unifying approach which represents a general framework to compare and analyse different logics, can be found in Gentzen sequent systems. As is well known in the domain of automated reasoning, G. Gentzen has introduced a very general apparatus, based on the notion of sequent, to represent and mechanise the notion of logic [17]. Its principal advantage is the capability to define the properties of the deduction relation '⊢' independently of the structures it manipulates (the structures on the left and right of the deduction symbol). These structures may be sets but they may also be lists, binary trees, multi-sets, sets of multi-sets and so on. Objects with more structure than sets can be used to define substructural logics such as Lambek's logic, relevant logic, linear logic, etc. The general qualities of information that we want to treat can therefore be expressed first of all by defining the data structure, and then by identifying the possible operations on it. These operations correspond directly to logical connectives. In this chapter we will try to generalise Gentzen apparatus in order to analyse, as a case study, a family of systems which have recently become very relevant in the field of computer science: conditional logics. We will define a non-standard sequent system for one of these logics which can be adapted for certain others. The logic we treat has been proved [7] to be syntactically equivalent to a cumulative non-monotonic inference relation [13]. The Gentzen-style analysis of conditional logics will lead us to make some general suggestions about the way in which they relate to substructural logics. We believe that similar conclusions can be drawn about non-monotonic inference systems. The general point we want to stress, is that applications of logics to computer science require, firstly, logics defined by means of structures of information more expressive than those that are given classically, and secondly to have a mechanism to control the composition of these structures i.e. composition of different deductive contexts.

The next section is devoted to a presentation of the Gentzen systems for classical and substructural logics, in order to prepare a comparison with the Gentzen system for conditional logics to be presented in Section 4.

2 Traditional and substructural logics

Let us consider a language L. Let M be the set of all finite lists of L-formulae. A classical deducibility relation or a *classical Gentzen system* is a binary relation '$\vdash$' on M. Every element $X \vdash Y$ of $\vdash$, is called a *sequent*. X is the *antecedent* and Y the *succedent* of the sequent. In order to define a Gentzen system, a set of *initial sequents* and a list of *rules* must be given. All pairs belonging to the relation can be generated by using them. The notion of *derivation* is the tool used to generate the pairs.

A sequent $X \vdash Y$ is *derivable* if there is a tree, such that the root is $X \vdash Y$, all the leaves are initial sequents, and every father node is produced from the child node(s) using one of the rules of the system.

The rules can be divided into two types: *structural rules* and *logical rules*.

The *structural rules* are rules which allow us to consider the antecedent and the succedent of sequents as purely syntactical objects. These rules give a particular meaning to the comma that separates the elements in the antecedent and the succedent. We recognise two kinds of structural rule. Firstly, *data rules* which define the fundamental structure of the objects to be treated. Several data structures may exist, to represent, for example, independent objects, actions or resources. In classical logic the structural rules

contraction:

$$\frac{X, A, A, Z \vdash Y}{X, A, Z \vdash Y} \qquad \frac{X \vdash Y, B, B, Z}{X \vdash Y, B, Z}$$

expansion:

$$\frac{X, A, Z \vdash Y}{X, A, A, Z \vdash Y} \qquad \frac{X \vdash Y, B, Z}{X \vdash Y, B, B, Z}$$

and exchange:

$$\frac{X, A, B, Z \vdash Y}{X, B, A, Z \vdash Y} \qquad \frac{X \vdash Y, C, D, Z}{X \vdash Y, D, C, Z}$$

transform the antecedent and succedent, originally defined as lists of symbols, into sets. Therefore, if we define, from the outset, antecedents and succedents as sets, contraction, expansion and exchange become superfluous. Note that the components of a set are independent by definition, and the notion of a context or of a number of occurrences of an object are not definable in a set structure.

Reasoning rules, the second kind of structural rules, define the properties of the deducibility relation. The typical examples of reasoning rule is: cut:

$$\frac{X \vdash Y, A \qquad A, Z \vdash U}{X, Z \vdash Y, U}$$

cut rule defines the deducibility relation as transitive. This rule has two principal features: identity and proof composition. Identity is the property expressed statically by initial sequents: $A \vdash A$. Cut rule is the dynamic counterpart of the identity axiom: the presence of the cut rule in a system allows two identical occurrences of a formula in a proof (one in the antecedent of a sequent and the other in the succedent of a sequent) to be identified and removed. At the same time, the identification of these occurrences means that proofs can be composed i.e. formulae can be substituted by their proofs.

The introduction rules for connectives or *logical rules* represent the different operations which can be applied to the sequents *in the object language*. Logical rules represent classical set operations such as union, intersection and complement, if the elements in M are sets. Logical rules can be represented by double line rules (see [24], also [2, 10]). For example the rule of conjunction transforms the comma in the antecedent into a connective:

$$\frac{X, A, B \vdash Y}{X, A \land B \vdash Y}$$

This rule can be read either in the top-down or in the bottom-up direction. The conjunction can then be introduced directly in the succedent of a sequent using identity and two applications of cut as follows:

$$
\cfrac{X_2 \vdash B, Y_2 \qquad \cfrac{X_1 \vdash A, Y_1 \qquad \cfrac{A \wedge B \vdash A \wedge B}{A, B \vdash A \wedge B}}{X_1, B \vdash A \wedge B, Y_1}}{X_1, X_2 \vdash A \wedge B, Y_1, Y_2}
$$

The above derivation can be rewritten as the following derived rule:

$$
\frac{X_1 \vdash A, Y_1 \qquad X_2 \vdash B, Y_2}{X_1, X_2 \vdash A \wedge B, Y_1, Y_2}
$$

Note that we can use another double line rule to introduce conjunction :

$$
\frac{X \vdash A, Y \qquad X \vdash B, Y}{X \vdash Y, A \wedge B}
$$

Conjunction is represented here as the operation which combines two sequents differing only in the two formulae A and B.

If this rule is considered in the bottom-up direction the derived rule:

$$
\frac{X, A \vdash Y}{X, A \wedge B \vdash Y}
$$

is obtained in exactly the same way as the former derived rule.

It is well-known that these two double line rules are derivable one from the other by applying the weakening and contraction rules. Structural rules are therefore fundamental for the identification of connectives: the operations represented by the former double line rules can be identified in some structural contexts.

In the presence of *cut rule and identity*, logical rules can be seen as rules for the manipulation of sequents in the object language. The presence of cut rule ensures that the characterization of the connectives is stable under composition of proofs. So, double line rules characterize logical constants, as expressing the same operation in the antecedent and in the succedent of a sequent.

Systems weaker than traditional Gentzen systems can be considered by rejecting some structural rules. Such logics are called substructural logics, such as:

- the non-exponential fragment of linear logic [18], which lacks weakening and contraction,

- variants of relevant logics [1], which lack weakening,

- BCK logics [22], which lack contraction,

- Lambek calculus which lacks contraction, weakening and permutation [19].

In a general way a *substructural logic* can be defined by fixing the following three entities :

1. The language (L)

2. A structure M of formulae for the antecedent, and a structure M' for the succedent.

3. The relation $\vdash$ on $M \times M'$.

We consider that the deductive relation '$\vdash$' possesses at least the properties of identity and some form of composition of structures (expressed by the cut rule). The necessity of cut for the composition of proofs and for the definition of connective rules seems to us to justify that choice.

A set of initial sequents and a set of rules are used to define the third point. In the original Gentzen presentation, where the comma is associative, the antecedent and the succedent of each sequent are structured as lists of formulae which represent the order in which things are written. In traditional logics (within which contraction, expansion and exchange are basic structural rules) lists are transformed into sets. However, there is no reason to use lists as basic structures for sequents.

The two main features of substructural logics are as follows: firstly, a logic is a tool used to represent and reason about the 'qualities' of objects, for example their lasting power (using the idea that objects are resources), their influence (by considering that objects are actions), etc. The character of a quality is formalised by a structure, that is the left and right of $\vdash$, for example, multisets for resources or lists for actions. The second feature concerns the language which expresses operations on the structure. The set of logical connectives associated with each logic depends on the structure of the antecedent and the succedent. The characterization of a connective is invariant for all possible structures, provided that it has been adapted (via the cut rule) to the particular structure considered.

So, as classical Gentzen systems are based on sets, classical connectives obviously represent set operations. The two different double line rules for conjunction presented in Section 2 are not equivalent in all cases. Where, for example, multisets are used and weakening and contraction are forbidden, they represent two different operations: the union of multisets in which copies are identified:

$$\frac{X \vdash A, Y \qquad X \vdash B, Y}{X \vdash A \wedge B, Y}$$

and the union of multisets in which copies are not identified :

$$\frac{X \vdash A, Y \qquad X \vdash B, Y}{X, X \vdash A \bullet B, Y, Y}$$

These two types of conjunction (fusion and extensional conjunction) as well as the two corresponding disjunctions arise naturally in this structure and exist in relevant, BCK and linear logics. Connectives such as those described above are adaptations of classical connectives, in specific contexts, but others, totally new, could be added according to the following proviso: the choice of a connective set in a substructural logic must preserve the structure defined by data rules, and the properties of the deducibility relation defined by reasoning rules. This is especially important if we consider that some connectives bring with them a structural power, or more generally, that some properties that can be attributed to connectives at the same time transform the structure. We will consider a consequence of this case in Section 4, but a clear example is given by the axiom of distribution of additive conjunction on additive disjunction in relevant logics such as R [1]. If this property is required, the structure of the antecedent must be split into two different contexts, an intensional one and an extensional one (see [1, Vol 1, Ch 5, §28]).

Let us conclude this section with a simple remark on the cut rule. Since proofs can be composed using the cut rule, definition must be according to structure. Consider, for example, concatenation logic defined by Gabbay in [16] which is a fragment of the associative Lambek calculus. The structure is a list of formulae in the antecedent and a single formula in the succedent. The only structural rule is a cut for the lists (called by Gabbay 'surgical cut'):

$$\frac{[A_1, \ldots, A_i, B, A_{i+1}, \ldots, A_n] \vdash C \qquad [B_1, \ldots, B_n] \vdash B}{[A_1, \ldots, A_i, B_1, \ldots, B_n, A_{i+1}, \ldots, A_n] \vdash C}$$

In the sequent representing the conclusion of the rule the list structure is preserved. B in the consequent of the left premises of the rule is identified with B in the antecedent of the right premises. Respecting the ordering of the list, the first antecedent structure, represented by the list of formulae $[B_1, \ldots, B_n]$, is composed with the second antecedent structure $[A_1, \ldots, A_i, B, A_{i+1}, \ldots, A_n]$.

3 Implicit contexts and composition of proofs

In the previous section, the cut rule, together with identity, was said to be a minimal property of deduction relations for formal systems that have to be considered as logics. Two principal reasons supported that claim: the role of the cut rule in the composition of proofs (i.e. in composition of structures of formulae in sequents) and the importance of the cut rule in the definition of connective rules considered as operations on structures. The composition of proofs seems to be an unavoidable property for deduction in any theory where the formalization task has been completely performed. In such theories all the information relative to the objects treated by the theory appears explicitly, according to the aim of the formalization and to the relevant features of the 'world' that are being formalised.

Nevertheless most of the problems that computer science pretends to resolve necessitate the use of implicit information, as, for example, in the domain of planning, taxonomic inheritance or revision of databases. Different grounds can be evoked for using theories with implicit information. On one hand they are more advisable for pragmatical reasons of economy of representation. On the other hand they are needed in every dynamic representation of knowledge. What is regarded as an object in a formal theory depends on what we are formalising and the reasons for doing it; a dynamic account of these choices, has, as a result, an incomplete theory where some of the properties of the objects should be considered implicit in the formalisation.

The use of implicit knowledge induces the adoption of controlled composition of proofs. Let us take a simple example.

Suppose that we affirm $A, H_1 \vdash B$ and $B, H_2 \vdash C$, where A and H_1 are are structures of information (respectively B and H_2) from which a transitive deduction relation allows us to conclude B (respectively C). Suppose further that H_1 and H_2 are implicit, and that we cannot express their contents in the theory we have defined. Nevertheless, we claim that the two deductive relations hold for these implicit structures of information. If we apply unrestricted composition of proofs to $A, H_1 \vdash B$ and $B, H_2 \vdash C$ then we obtain $A, H_1, H_2 \vdash C$ without considering whether H_1 and H_2 are *compatible* (that is not only logically consistent but in a more general way meaningful). So in order to preserve consistency and deductive meaning with implicit contexts, composition of proofs should be restricted.

Two main mechanisms can be brought into play to prevent unrestricted composition of proofs.

The first is basically *extra-logical* and allows us to discriminate, in the class of all proofs, some subset having features appropriate to the problem that is being formalised. Consider for example planning problems : we can avoid giving an explicit notion of action but characterise a special class of proofs interpretable as sequences of actions [5].

Different strategies can be applied to obtain such appropriate subclasses: explicit ordering in the application of rules or labelling of formulae in such a way that only some arrangements of labels are acceptable. In both cases only some proof generated by the system is meaningful for the original problem: composition of proof is not directly prevented, but is obtained indirectly by the external characterisation of what a 'good' proof is.

The second mechanism tries to control composition of proofs by *logical* tools. One such tool directly defines in the system some restriction of transitivity of the deduction relation. We will consider in the following section, as a case study, some of the counterfactual conditional logics, a family of modal logics that has recently received a great attention in various areas of computer science such as non-monotonic inference relations, belief revision and update (see [12, 4, 14]).

Substructural logics are a family of logics based on the notion of structure. We believe that important questions arising from this concern whether conditionals may be analysed in terms of some structural operations and what those structural operations could represent. Fuhrmann [15] is one of the pioneers of this area. An initial approach to these questions involves the adaptation of the standard Gentzen system described earlier to define rules for conditional operators.

There is a twofold aim in searching for a structural interpretation of conditional logics: a better understanding of the deductive power of these logics, and a concrete analysis of what controlling composition of proofs by logical tools means.

4   A case study: conditional logics

4.1   Conditionals, structures and sequent of second degree

A conditional is a binary 'modal' operator, noted by '$\Rightarrow$', that is, roughly speaking a non-transitive modal implication, by opposition to the well known strict implication which is transitive. Conditionals can be used to formalise counterfactual propositions of natural language such as:

'If the match had been struck it would have lit.'

they can be used also to formalise generic sentences such as:

'Usually, if a match is struck, it lights.'

What is common to these two propositions is the fact that they can be interpreted as a short and implicit way to affirm a more complex proposition such as:

'According to certain conditions of humidity, pressure and oxygen availability..., a well-made match will light if it is struck.'

This is the metalinguistic interpretation of counterfactual conditionals given in the 1940s by Chisholm and Goodman, and it leads us to consider the conditional connective $\Rightarrow$ as a representation, in the object language, of a deduction symbol containing an implicit hypothesis. Let us improve the syntactical comparison between strict implication and the counterfactual conditional. Strict implication represents, in the object language, a metalinguistic relation affirming that there exists a deduction from A to B according to which, it has been considered as a tool to formalise the notion of derived rule in a system, as suggested by [24]. The counterfactual conditional $(A \Rightarrow B)$, expresses in the object language a deductive relation $A, H \vdash B$, affirming the existence of a deduction from A and further non-specified hypothesis H, having B as conclusion. Thus the counterfactual conditional formalises the notion of a derived rule but only in relation with a partially specified antecedent, that is, according to a deductive context that cannot be combined with other contexts as it is partially implicit.

This means that a sequent system for the counterfactual conditional must be based on a structure that avoids unrestricted composition of proofs.

Our basic idea is to use sequents of second degree,[1] that is, sequents possessing two kinds of deductive relations, a principal one (symbolised by '$\vdash_P$') and, auxiliary one (symbolised by '$\vdash_a$'). Principal sequents can have collections of formulae (as in the classical case), or, exclusively, collections of auxiliary sequents in the antecedent and in the succedent such as in:

$$\{A_1 \vdash_a B_1\}, \ldots, \{A_n \vdash_a B_m\} \vdash_P \{C_1 \vdash_a D_1\}, \ldots, \{C_n \vdash_a D_n\}.$$

The intuitive idea is that restrictions on the composition of proofs are represented at the second auxiliary level. So, there are structural and logical operations on the principal level, and structural and logical operations on the auxiliary level.

The system contains rules for passing from the principal classical level to the second auxiliary level as for example:

$$\frac{B_1, \ldots, B_k \vdash_P C}{\{A \vdash_a B_1\}, \ldots, \{A \vdash_a B_k\} \vdash_P \{A \vdash_a C\}}$$

and rules to transform expressions like $\{F \vdash_a K\}$ in expression of the object language as $F \Rightarrow K$.

A deduction in our system beginning in the principal sequents with formulae, using rules of classical logic, comes into the auxiliary level in a particular deductive context represented by the antecedent of the auxiliary sequent. Rules on the auxiliary sequents allow us to calculate further information in this restricted context.

---

[1] Our Gentzen system is inspired by the second degree Gentzen systems for modal logics $S4$ and $S5$, defined by K. Došen [9].

From the structural point of view, our principal deduction relation is defined on sets (eventually reduced to singletons) of auxiliary structures that are *sets of pairs of deductive contexts with implicit hypotheses*. The auxiliary deduction relation (as the conditional connective '⇒') is not transitive. The main interest in studying the properties of '$\vdash_a$', is to test what kinds of structural and logical operations are acceptable for a non-transitive deduction relation formalising deductions with implicit hypotheses via a modal connective in the object language.

The answer to this question is a natural consequence of what the cut rule expresses, apart from transitivity of the deduction relation. Remember we noticed in Section 2 that the cut rule is a dynamic form of identification of two occurrences of formulae within different contexts. If $A \vdash B$ and $B \vdash C$ then using the cut rule the occurrence of B, in the consequent of $A \vdash B$, is identified with the occurrence of B in the antecedent of $B \vdash C$, in order to be substituted by the formula from which it is derivable and to conclude $A \vdash C$. So, if transitivity is rejected, the cut rule can be replaced by more restricted rules, which, avoiding composition of proofs, allow *identification* of formulae in deductions. These rules, in the framework of conditional logics, express criteria for substituting conditional antecedents by conditional antecedents, without passing through transitivity. We can recognise three kinds of identification criteria. Let us consider these criteria from the axiomatic point of view.

1. The first and weakest criteria is based on classical equivalence. It is expressed by the rule known as RCEA in the conditional literature:

$$\frac{A \leftrightarrow B}{A \Rightarrow C \leftrightarrow B \Rightarrow C}$$

   Let us interpret the rule from the metalinguistic point of view: if C is deductible from A (and further implicit hypotheses) then A can be identified with every formula classically equivalent to it. So classically equivalent formulae are 'compatible' (in the sense of preserving consistency and meaning) with the same implicit deductive context.

2. The second criterion is based on the positive counterfactual relations between formulae, as in:

$$((A \Rightarrow B) \wedge (B \Rightarrow A)) \rightarrow ((A \Rightarrow C) \leftrightarrow (B \Rightarrow C))$$

   which means that counterfactually equivalent formulae can be identified. Not only equivalence but also inclusion of antecedents can be considered as formalised by axioms like:

$$((A \Rightarrow C) \wedge (A \Rightarrow B)) \rightarrow (A \wedge B \Rightarrow C)$$
$$((A \Rightarrow C) \wedge (B \Rightarrow C)) \rightarrow (A \vee B \Rightarrow C)$$

The antecedent A, which represents a partial specification of the premises that allows C to be deduced, can be identified by $A \wedge B$ and $A \vee B$, if, respectively, $A \Rightarrow B$ and $B \Rightarrow C$. Under these provisos, A and respectively $A \wedge B$ and $A \vee B$ are compatible with the same implicit deductive contexts.

3. The third and last criteria is based on the counterfactual consistency between formulae: negative counterfactual implications are taken into account to establish the identity of contexts, as in:

$$\neg(A \Rightarrow \neg B) \wedge \neg(B \Rightarrow \neg A) \to ((A \Rightarrow C) \leftrightarrow (B \Rightarrow C))$$

where if A and B are mutually counterfactually consistent, then they can be identified. Symmetrically to the second criteria, we have form of inclusion such as that expressed by the axioms:

$$((A \Rightarrow C) \wedge \neg(A \Rightarrow \neg B)) \to (A \wedge B \Rightarrow C)$$
$$((A \vee B \Rightarrow C) \wedge \neg(B \Rightarrow C)) \to (A \Rightarrow C).$$

So conditional logics can be divided in three groups, according to the identification criteria they have. All the logics included in the logic CK (see [6]) belong to the first group, the only identification criteria being classical equivalence. The logics CO and WC (see [21]), belong to the second one. They consider what is deductible in the system to establish what is compatible with a given implicit deductive context. The third group are about counterfactual consistency. The Lewis logic VW [20] and the Stalnaker logic CEM [25] belong to that group.

According to these three criteria of antecedent identification, we have nice correspondences between syntactical axioms, structures of the sequents systems we defined and, partially, with semantical properties, as will be presented in the next section.

4.2 Sequent systems for conditional logics

In this section a non-standard Gentzen system for the conditional logic $\text{CO}\S^2$ is presented.

Let us briefly reiterate an axiomatic presentation of the logics. The logic $\text{CO}\S$ is the smallest conditional logic containing all the axioms and inference rules of classical logic together with the following rule and axioms:

$$\text{(RCK)} \quad \frac{B_1 \wedge \ldots \wedge B_n \to B}{(A \Rightarrow B_1 \wedge \ldots \wedge A \Rightarrow B_n) \to (A \Rightarrow B)} \quad n \geq 0$$

---

[2]The system $\text{CO}\S$ is obtained by the system CO presented by Nute [21], but removing the axiom $(A \Rightarrow B) \to (A \to B)$ and the axiom $(\neg B \Rightarrow B) \to (A \Rightarrow B)$.

(ID) $A \Rightarrow A$

(CSO) $((A \Rightarrow B) \wedge (B \Rightarrow A)) \rightarrow ((A \Rightarrow C) \leftrightarrow (B \Rightarrow C))$

The system is based on identification criteria belonging to the second group of the last section. Classically and counterfactually equivalent formulae are compatible with the same implicit deductive contexts, as is expressed by the axiom CSO and by the rule RCEA, which is provable in the system. In the sequent system presented below, identification criteria are coded by augmentation and reduction rule, which are some kinds of restricted cut and restricted weakening. In the sequel we will give some idea of how this system is extended to the other two logics WC§, and VW§.

The logic WC§ is obtained by the axiomatic system for CO§ plus the axiom:

(CA) $((A \Rightarrow C) \wedge (B \Rightarrow C)) \rightarrow (A \vee B \Rightarrow C)$.

The logic VW§ is obtained from WC§ by adding the axiom:

(VC) $((A \Rightarrow C) \wedge \neg(A \Rightarrow \neg B)) \rightarrow (A \wedge B \Rightarrow C)$.

The flat fragment of these three conditional logics was proved to be equivalent, respectively, to the cumulative, preferential and rational non-monotonic system.

In [8] a cut free variant of all these sequent systems was presented. It is basically obtained by adding introduction logical rules in the succedent of auxiliary sequents. Let us now present the system for CO§.

Let D (for deduction) be a sequent system of higher level for the conditional logic CO§:

Vocabulary of $\mathcal{D}$.

1. The vocabulary of CO§

2. $\{,\}$, the comma, $\vdash_P, \vdash_a$, (where the subscript) 'P' and 'a' stand respectively for principal and auxiliary).

Formulae of $\mathcal{D}$

1. $\Gamma \vdash_P \Delta$ is a formula of $\mathcal{D}$ called a principal sequent iff Γ is a set of formulae of the conditional language, or a set of auxiliary sequents and Δ is a set of formulae of CO§ or auxiliary sequents.

2. $X \vdash_a Y$ is a formula of $\mathcal{D}$ called a secondary sequent iff X and Y are sets of formulae of the language.

As a convention we will use upper-case latin letters (A, B, C) to represent variables that range over formulae of $\mathcal{D}$; and we will use upper-case greek letters Γ, Δ and Λ to represent antecedent or succedent sets of a principal sequent.

We use the letters X, Z, Y to represent the antecedent and succedent sets of a secondary sequent. Let us say that in the sequent:

$$\Gamma, \{X \vdash_a Y\} \vdash_P \{X' \vdash_a Y'\}, \Lambda$$

the set Γ and $\{X \vdash_a Y\}$ are the members of the antecedent set of the principal sequent, and $\{X' \vdash_a Y'\}, \Lambda$ are the members of the succedent set of the principal sequent.

With the aim of simplicity, rules will sometimes be presented using only the secondary sequents, for example:

$$\frac{X \vdash_a Y}{X' \vdash_a Y'} \ .$$

The rules of the sequent system for CO§ are as follows:

1. For *principal sequents* not containing secondary sequents, classical structural rules will be used, with the addition of the following:

   - Prefixing

     $$\frac{B_1, \ldots, B_k \vdash_P C}{\{X \vdash_a B_1\}, \ldots, \{X \vdash_a B_k\} \vdash_P \{X \vdash_a C\}}$$

     where $k \geq 0$.

2. For principal sequents, containing auxiliary sequents, add the following rule:

   - Weakening

     $$\frac{\Gamma \vdash_P \Lambda}{\Gamma, \{X \vdash_a B\} \vdash_P \Lambda}$$

   - Cut

     $$\frac{\Gamma \vdash_P \{X \vdash_a B\} \quad \{X \vdash_a B\}, \Delta \vdash_P \Lambda}{\Gamma, \Delta \vdash_P \Lambda}$$

   - General augmentation:

     $$\frac{\{X_1 \vdash_a B_1\}, \ldots, \{X_k \vdash_a B_k\} \vdash_P \{Y \vdash_a C\}}{\{X_1, A \vdash_a B_1\}, \ldots, \{X_k, A \vdash_a B_k\} \vdash_P \{Y, A \vdash_a C\}}$$

- Local augmentation and reduction

$$\frac{\{X \vdash_a B\}}{\{X, Y \vdash_a B\}} \text{ iff } \{X \vdash_a z\} \in \Gamma \text{ for every } z \in Y$$

where Γ is the antecedent of the principle sequent in which the premises of the rule occur. (Double line rules are interpreted as in Section 2.)

- Descending

$$\frac{\{X_1 \vdash_a B_1\}, \ldots, \{X_{n-1} \vdash_a B_{-1}\} \vdash_P \{X_n \vdash_a B_n\}}{A_1 \Rightarrow B_1, \ldots, A_i \Rightarrow B_i \vdash_P A_n \Rightarrow B_n}$$

where

- $i \le n - 1$ and for every j, $i < j \le n - 1$, such that $\{Aj \vdash_a Bj\}$ is in the premise of the rule, holds $Aj \vdash_P Bj$.

- for every i, $1 \le i \le n$, the conjunction of the element of Xi are equivalent to Ai.

Remarks

The prefixing rule allows a principal sequent to pass to the auxiliary level. Reduction and augmentation rules allow the antecedent of auxiliary sequents (that is, partially specified deductive contexts) to be augmented and reduced in order to prove theorems in the system. The structure for conditionals consists of pairs of deductive contexts. Operations on them are intended to calculate which contexts are compatible with which others, according to the three criteria of Section 4.1. Reduction and augmentation rules for the antecedents of auxiliary sequents are, in the absence of transitivity, the logical tools to identify deductive contexts. In the system CO§ the augmentation and reduction rules are structural ones. They are restricted forms of weakening and cut, whose provisos refer to the structure of the principal antecedent. The descending rule[3] transforms auxiliary sequents in conditional formulae of the object language. Take for example

---

[3]The descending rule contains two special provisos which have only a technical meaning. The first eliminates from the antecedent of the principle sequent conditional formulae which are instances of the identity axiom or are derivable from it. The second one represents a way to allow equivalent classical formulae in the antecedent of the conditional to be identified. Other technical devices could be used but this is not our point here.

the following deduction in the system for the logic CO§:

$$\frac{\dfrac{\dfrac{\dfrac{C \vdash_P C}{B, C \vdash_P C}}{\{A \vdash_a B\}, \{A \vdash_a C\} \vdash_P \{A \vdash_a C\}}}{\{A \vdash_a B\}, \{A, B \vdash_a C\} \vdash_P \{A \vdash_a C\}}}{A \Rightarrow B, A \wedge B \Rightarrow C \vdash_P A \Rightarrow C}$$

The first and second lines of the deduction are as in classical logic (identity and weakening). With the prefixing rule we fix a context, that is, A (third line). The augmentation rule is applied in the fourth line: in the auxiliary consequent of the principal sequent, the antecedent A can be augmented as $\{A \vdash_a B\}$ belongs to the principal antecedent.

Two principles of variation can be recognised on the sequent systems for conditional logics so defined. First, the presence or the absence of reduction and augmentation rules. These rules are typical of logics of the second and third group. Logics of the first group have only prefixing, weakening and descending rules. So, the logics of the first group can differ in the way the context is fixed or in the provisos concerning the descending rule.

Second, the presence or the absence of a weakening rule for the auxiliary sequent in the principal sequent. For CO§, and for the other logics of its group we have the following weakening rule:

$$\frac{\Gamma \vdash_P \Lambda}{\Gamma, \{X \vdash_a B\} \vdash_P \Lambda}$$

But there is no corresponding weakening rule for the principal consequent as:

$$\frac{\Gamma \vdash_P \Lambda}{\Gamma \vdash_P \Lambda, \{A \vdash_a B\}}$$

So, for the logic CO§, if Δ is a set of formulae of the language then '$\vdash_P$' is a classical deductibility relation. If Δ is an auxiliary sequent, '$\vdash_P$' is an intuitionistic deductibility relation. This uni-conclusion property of the principal relation in the auxiliary level is peculiar to the logics belonging to the first and second group presented in the previous section. In fact only logics having identification criteria based on the counterfactual consistency (the third group) need multi-conclusion sequents. The sequent system for the logic VW§,[4] [8] allows weakening rules in the consequent in the principal sequent as expressed by the previous rule.

---

[4]This is the Lewis logic VW, minus the axiom $(A \Rightarrow B) \to (A \to B)$ and $(A \wedge B) \to (A \Rightarrow B)$. It contains the axiom $((A \Rightarrow C) \wedge \neg(A \Rightarrow \neg B)) \to (A \wedge B \Rightarrow C)$.

We said that in CO§ augmentation and reduction rules are restricted forms of weakening and cut, that is, structural rules on the auxiliary antecedents. For other logics of the second group, augmentation and reduction rules are also logical. Consider the logic WC§. To formalise it we also need augmentation and reduction in terms of the disjunction connective. These rules can also be seen as logical rules with a structural import[5] e.g.

- local ∨-augmentation in the principal succedent

$$\frac{\Gamma \vdash_P \{A \vdash_a C\}}{\Gamma \vdash_P \{A \vee B \vdash_a C\}} \text{ iff } \{B \vdash_a C\} \in \Gamma$$

So logics of the second group (as CO§ and WC§) differ in the type of augmentation and reduction rules, as they could be structural or logical. Nevertheless, for all the logics of the second group, the provisos on the augmentation and reduction rules concern only the structure of the principal antecedent.

In contrast, for the logics of the third group, the provisos, concerning the applications of the augmentation and the reduction rules, take into account not only the auxiliary sequents in the antecedent of the principal one, but also the auxiliary sequents in the consequent of the principal one. For example the rules of local ∨-augmentation in the principal antecedent become for the logic VW§:

$$\frac{\Gamma \vdash_P \{A \vdash_a C\}, \Delta}{\Gamma \vdash_P \{A \vee B \vdash_a C\}, \Delta} \text{ iff } \{B \vdash_a C\} \in \Gamma, \text{ or } \{B \vdash_a C\} \in \Delta.$$

These correspondences are summarised by the Table 1.

There exist partial correspondences between this syntactical characterisation and the semantics available for the logics. For the first group we have only semantics with selection functions (see [6]). For the logics belonging to the second group we can define a semantics with an ordering relation, defining an ordering on the formulas such as: $A < B =_{\text{def}} (B \Rightarrow A) \wedge \neg(A \Rightarrow B)$ (see [12]). For the third criteria we have sphere semantics such as Lewis semantics where the ordering on formulas is $A \leq B =_{\text{def}} \neg(A \vee B \Rightarrow \neg B)$.

5   Further remarks on systems without any admissible cut rule

The logic considered in the previous section can be considered syntactically as a simply typographical variant of the so-called preferential non-

---

[5]This is similar to the situation in normal modal logics. Some of the systems (namely S4 and S5) are characterizable by structural operations in higher-order Gentzen systems; others are obtained by adding logical rules which have a structural consequence.

Table 1:

Criteria	Sequents
classical equivalence: $$\frac{A \leftrightarrow B}{A \Rightarrow C \leftrightarrow B \Rightarrow C}$$	uni-conclusion sequents
conditional implication such as: $((A \Rightarrow B) \wedge (B \Rightarrow A)) \rightarrow$ $((A \Rightarrow C) \leftrightarrow (B \Rightarrow C))$	uni-conclusion sequents reduction-augmentation rules with provisos on the principle antecedent structure
conditional consistency such as: $\neg(A \rightarrow \neg B) \wedge \neg(B \Rightarrow \neg A) \rightarrow$ $((A \Rightarrow C) \leftrightarrow (B \Rightarrow C))$	multi-conclusion sequents reduction-augmentation rules with provisos on the principle antecedent and consequent structures

monotonic inference system. If in the sequent:

$$\{A \vdash_a B\}, \{A \vdash_a C\} \vdash_P \{A \wedge B \vdash_a C\}$$

the symbol $\vdash_P$ is replaced by the horizontal line of the deduction rule, and the symbol $\vdash_a$ by the non-monotonic deduction symbol $\vdash\!\sim$, then the following preferential rule is obtained:

$$\frac{A \vdash\!\sim B \quad A \vdash\!\sim C}{A \wedge B \vdash\!\sim C}$$

where $A \vdash\!\sim B$ can be read 'B is a plausible consequence of A'.

It is well-known that neither transitivity nor the cut rule are admissible in non-monotonic systems. In fact, as we argued for the corresponding rule for conditionals:

$$\{X \vdash_a A\}, \{X, A \vdash_a C\} \vdash_P \{X \vdash_a C\}$$

the so-called cut rule for the preferential system:

$$\frac{X, B \vdash\!\sim C \quad X \vdash\!\sim B}{X \vdash\!\sim C}$$

does not allow proof composition.

So in a general way the non-monotonic inference systems are modal systems, as their non-monotonic consequence relation is constructed from the classical one. However they do not represent the metalinguistic relation $\vdash$ in the object language by the modal connective $\Rightarrow$. In both systems composition of proofs is logically controlled by restriction of transitivity (respectively on $\vdash$ and $\Rightarrow$).

There also exist systems which introduce logical restrictions on transitivity. The principal problem with the absence of the cut rule is that definition of connectives cannot be controlled i.e. it cannot be ensured that the structure and the properties of the deduction relation will not be modified by the connectives introduced. Consequently a connective cannot be characterised by a double line rule as in Section 2. The real problem is the way in which trivial cases should be distinguished from non-trivial ones. Let us illustrate two examples which represent trivial cases. If we consider the famous 'tonk ' operator, invented by Prior [23], trivialisation of the deduction relation could be avoided if the cut rule was not an admissible rule. In fact, it is the cut rule (together with the introduction rule for 'tonk') that trivializes the consequence relation:

$$\frac{\dfrac{A \vdash A}{A \vdash A \text{ tonk } B} \quad \dfrac{B \vdash B}{A \text{ tonk } B \vdash B}}{A \vdash B}$$

So, we could even argue that the problem with tonk concerns only the transitivity of proofs by which means contexts can be composed indefinitely without paying attention to modifications of contexts. Our opinion is that a tonk operator would continue to be a silly one in every context.

A more subtle consequence, which can be observed defining connectives in a system without the cut rule, comes from the intuitionistic relevant logic of Neil Tennant [26], who defines a relevant logic where the difference between multiplicative and additive connectives are neglected. In a deduction relation context without weakening, he defines a single disjunction connective as a multiplicative one (noted in the relevant literature by $+$) in the antecedent:

$$\frac{X_1, A \vdash Y_1 \quad X_2, B \vdash Y_2}{X_1, X_2, A + B \vdash Y_1, Y_2}$$

and an additive one in the succedent:

$$\frac{X \vdash A}{X \vdash A \vee B}$$

in order to conserve disjunctive syllogism ($\neg A, A \vee B \vdash B$).

However, his fundamental problem is to give an inferential relevance to the antecedent and the succedent, to avoid, in particular, inferences such as $A \wedge \neg A \vdash B$.

Since the definition of disjunction in the succedent, and application of cut would give:

$$\frac{\neg A \vdash \neg A \vee B \quad \neg A \vee B, A \vdash B}{\neg A, A \vdash B}$$

Tennant banishes the cut rule from the system.

There is an inherent problem with this strategy; composition occurs by definition of the multiplicative disjunction. Therefore, even if $A \wedge \neg A \vdash B$ is not a theorem for all B, it is a theorem in the particular form: $A \wedge \neg A \vdash (A \vee B) \rightarrow (A \wedge B)$, which does not seem justifiable from the point of view of inferential relevance. The direct elimination of the cut rule to avoid the reintroduction of weakening is not sufficient to prevent all forms of weakening, which are derived from the weakening power inherent in the definition of a multiplicative disjunction.

Such kinds of problems do not appear when the restriction on transitivity is performed on the modal level as in conditional logics and non-monotonic inferences.

6 Conclusion

We have not answered the main question of this book directly, but we hope we have indicated some clues, based on the notion of structure.

First, a logic can be seen as a system for reasoning about particular data structures with a deduction relation and logical operations in the object language. The choice of the structure depends on the particular qualities of the objects under discussion. The logical connectives are the tools which allow us to represent the different operations which can be applied to sequents. This analysis applies nicely to substructural logics, as we can separate clearly structural operations from logical ones, which are the same for all logics of the family.

Second, we believe that structures are able to support reasoning with implicit information, that become the main source of inspiration for logic in the last decade. They provide a reasonable 'canon' of inference patterns to handle exceptions.

As a case study, we have shown how the notion of structure is useful from a deductive point of view. In fact, conditional logics can be interpreted as formalisations of the notion of a deductive context with implicit information. A context cannot be combined in any way with other deductive contexts unless the rules of the system allow us to recognise them as identical or compatible. This is the 'raison d'être' of the augmentation and reduction rules in the antecedents of auxiliary sequents. They represent a way in which antecedents can be modified, with the aim of recognition of identity of context. There is no notion of relevance in this method of treating antecedents, only a strategy for preserving implicit deductive contexts from any alteration coming from inadmissible combination with other contexts. The analysis of conditional in terms of structures makes it clear how the notion of compatible contexts can vary. Conditional logics are based on more or less relaxed criteria of what is to be considered compatible with given implicit contexts.

References

[1] A. R. Anderson and N. D. Belnap Jr, *Entailment, Vol 1*, Princeton University Press, 1975.

[2] A. Avron, Simple consequence relations, *Information and Computation*, **92**, 105–139, 1991.

[3] N. D. Belnap, Jr, Tonk, plonk and plink, *Analysis*, **22**, 130–134, 1962.

[4] J. Bell, Pragmatic logic, in *Conference in Knowledge Representation*, pp. 50–61, H. J. Allen, R. Fikes and E. Sandewall, eds, Morgan Kaufmann, 1991

[5] W. Bibel, L. Fariñas del Cerro, B. Fronhofer and A. Herzig, Plan generation by linear proofs: on semantics. In *Proceedings of the 13th German Workshop on AI*, D. Metzing, ed., Springer-Verlag, 1989.

[6] B. Chellas, Basic conditional logic, *Journal of Philosophical Logic*, **1**, 133–153, 1975.

[7] G. Crocco and Ph. Lamarre, *On the connection between conditional logics and non monotonic inference systems*, Proceedings of KR '92, pp. 565–572, B. Nebel, C. Rich and W. Swartout, eds, Morgan Kaufmann, 1992.

[8] G. Crocco, Fondements logiques du raisonement contextuel, PhD Thesis, University Paul Sabatier, Toulouse, 1993.

[9] K. Došen, Sequent systems for modal logics, *The Journal of Symbolic Logic*, **50**, 149–168, 1985.

[10] K. Došen, Sequent systems and groupoid models I. *Studia Logica* **XLVII**, 353–385, 1988.

[11] M. Dunn. Relevant logics and entailment. In *Handbook of Philosophical Logic, Vol. III: Alternatives to Classical Logics*, D. Gabbay ad F. Guenthner, eds, pp. 117–229, Reidel, Dordrecht, 1986.

[12] H. Katsuno and K. Satoh, A unified view of Consequence relation, Belief revision and Conditional logics. In *IJCAI,91*, pp. 406–412, Morgan Kaufmann, 1991.

[13] S. Kraus, D. Lehmann and M. Magidor, Nonmonotonic reasoning, preferential models and cumulative logics, *Artificial Intelligence*, **44**, 1990.

[14] L. Fariñas del Cerro, J. Lang and A Herzig, From ordering-based nonmonotonic reasoning to conditional lgoics. *Journal of Artificial Intelligence*, **66**, 375–393, 1994.

[15] A. Furhmann, Nonmonotonic Inference as Substructural Draft March 92, Department of Philosophy, University of Konstanz.

[16] D. Gabbay, A general theory of structured consequence relations, *Third European Summer School in Language, Logic and Information, Saarbrucken*, 1991.

[17] G. Gentzen, Recherches sur la deduction logique (translation of Untersuchungen über das logische schliessen 1934) R. Feys and J. Ladriere P.U.F., Paris, 1955.

[18] J.Y. Girard, Linear logic, *Theoretical Computer Science*, **50**, 1–102, 1987.

[19] J. Lambek, The mathematics of sentence structure. *The American Mathematics Monthly*, **68**, 154–178, 1958.

[20] D. Lewis, *Counterfactual*, Basil Blackwell, Oxford, 1986.

[21] D. Nute, *Topics in conditional logics*, D. Reidel, Dordrecht, 1980.

[22] H. Ono and Y. Komori, Logics without the contraction rule, *J. Symbolic Logic*, **50**, 263–286, 1985.

[23] A. N. Prior, The runabout Inference-ticket, *Analysis*, **21**, 1960.

[24] D. Scott, On engendering an illusion of understanding, *Journal of Philosophy*, **68**, 787–807, 1971

[25] R. Stalnaker. A theory of conditionals. In *Studies in Logical Theory*, R. Rescher, ed., Blackwell, 1968.

[26] N. Tennant, *Anti-realism and Logic*, Clarendon Press, London, 1987.

10

Schematic Consequence *

Peter Aczel

Introduction

Nowadays we are well aware that there are many different logics. There are computer systems which are meant to be used to implement many logics. But there is no generally accepted account of what a logic is. Perhaps this is as it should be. We need imprecision in our vocabulary to mirror the flexible imprecision of our thinking. There are a number of related phrases that seem to have a similar imprecision e.g. formal system, language, axiom system, theory, deductive system, logical system, etc.... These are sometimes given technical meanings, often without adequate consideration of the informal notions.

When a logic has been implemented in a computer system the logic has been represented in the logical framework that the computer system uses. The logical framework will involve a particular approach to syntax, which may differ from the approach to syntax taken when the logic was first presented. This means that in order to represent the logic, as first presented, in the framework a certain amount of coding may be needed and the question will arise whether the logic as first presented is indeed the logic that has been represented in the framework. To make this question precise it is necessary to have a notion of a logic that abstracts away from particular approaches to syntactic presentation.

So we want to have a formal abstract definition of the notion 'a logic'. It is probable that there is no single notion to be captured but rather several related notions hiding under the single phrase. Nevertheless it would seem to be very worth while to try to analyse the situation and come up

---

*An earlier version of this chapter was called *The Notion of a Logic* and was based on a talk given at the workshop on 'Deductive Systems' at Oberwolfach in May 1991. My attention was drawn to the adjoint situations in the topic by a question after my talk. This work was partially supported by the Esprit Basic Research Action 'Logical Frameworks' and an SERC research Fellowship.

with some technical definitions that can be used to capture the various facets of the notion(s) of a logic. Of course there has been previous work on this topic. An important ingredient in all recent work is the notion of a consequence relation. This is essentially due to Tarski, who developed a fairly general theory of consequence operators and deductive systems in the 1920s. Dana Scott has more recently focused on the notion of a consequence relation. Another important development was Barwise's abstract model theory ([2]), which gave a model theoretic approach to a general class of logics, those based on classical first order semantic structures. A further stage of abstraction gives rise to Goguen and Burstall's notion of an institution ([3]). This level of abstraction seems to be needed to capture the variety of logics that seem to be of relevence in computer science and linguistics. The notion of an institution only focuses on the semantic aspect of logical consequence. Meseguer, in [6], has given a definition of a logic which uses an institution to capture the semantic aspect but also uses an entailment system to capture the operational aspect. An entailment system is roughly a system of consequence relations indexed by signatures. In Meseguer's notion of a logic the consequence relations of the entailment system are required to be sound with respect to the semantic consequence relations of the institution. The notion of an entailment system has also been used in [4], where they called it a logical system or logic.

At this point we should also mention the Edinburgh Logical Framework ([5]) and other systems playing similar roles in connection with computer systems for implementing logics. These logical frameworks provide an environment in which the operational, non-semantic aspects of a logic can be specified, provided that a syntax for the logic is acceptable to the framework or can be made acceptable without essentially changing the logic. One approach to the notion of a logic might be to choose a logical framework and require that the operational part of a logic must have a representation in the logical framework.

What are the key issues in connection with the notion(s) of a logic? We list some of them.

1. Logic is concerned with what follows from what i.e. with logical consequence.

2. Logic is generally applicable i.e. a logic should have a range of possible applications so that if A follows logically from B in a logic then in every application (or interpretation or context) where A is true B is true.

3. Logic is schematic e.g. the rule of modus ponens, that B follows logically from A and $A \to B$, is not expressed in the language of any particular application of the logic, but in a language of schematic

expressions involving parameters which can be instantiated in any application language.

In the next section below we give some definitions relevent to the first issue. We focus on finitary traditional consequence. More general notions are of interest. See, for example, [1]. But the more restricted and familiar notion of a consequence relation will be good enough for our present purposes. We also introduce several other notions which are relevent in connection with the formation of consequence relations either operationally from an axiomatic system or semantically from a semantic system. Both methods of formation can be seen to use the notion of a truth system. We also define a hybrid notion incorporating a semantic system with an axiomatic system that is sound.

We address the second issue above by indexing the above notions in Section 3. Finally we address the third and less familiar issue in Section 4. There is a good deal more to be said on these topics and we hope to produce an expanded version of this chapter. In Section 2 we make a slight detour from the main topic to consider the connections with Scott's notion of an information system and domains.

1 Finitary traditional consequence

We describe five categories relevent to an abstract theory of finitary traditional consequence and study the relationships between them.

Axiomatic systems

An *axiomatic system* (A, Φ) consists of a set A and a set $\Phi \subseteq (finA) \times A$, where $finA$ is the set of finite subsets of A. Axiomatic systems form a category AS. A map $\pi : (A, \Phi) \to (A', \Phi')$ of AS is a function $\pi : A \to A'$ such that

$$(\Gamma, \theta) \in \Phi \ \Rightarrow \ (\pi\Gamma, \pi\theta) \in \Phi,$$

where $\pi\Gamma = \{\pi\gamma \mid \gamma \in \Gamma\}$ if $\Gamma \in finA$.

We think of an axiomatic system as specifying a notion of proof whose inference steps have the form

$$\frac{\gamma_1 \cdots \gamma_n}{\theta},$$

where $(\{\gamma_1, \ldots, \gamma_n\}, \theta) \in \Phi$. Here of course $\gamma_1, \ldots, \gamma_n$ are the premises of the inference step and θ is the conclusion.

Consequence relations

A *consequence relation* $(A, \vdash)$ is an axiomatic system satisfying the following:

$$
\begin{aligned}
\textbf{reflexivity} \quad &: \quad \{\theta\} \vdash \theta \\
\textbf{monotonicity} \quad &: \quad \Gamma \vdash \theta \;\Rightarrow\; \Gamma \cup \{\varphi\} \vdash \theta \\
\textbf{transitivity} \quad &: \quad \Gamma \vdash \varphi \text{ and } \Gamma \cup \{\varphi\} \vdash \theta \;\Rightarrow\; \Gamma \vdash \theta.
\end{aligned}
$$

Consequence relations form a full subcategory CR of AS.

Proposition 1.1 The inclusion functor $CR \hookrightarrow AS$ has a left adjoint $AS \to CR$ which associates with each axiomatic system (A, Φ) the consequence relation $(A, \vdash_\Phi)$ *generated* by (A, Φ) i.e. $\vdash_\Phi$ is the least relation including Φ such that $(A, \vdash_\Phi)$ is a consequence relation, or alternatively,

$$
\Gamma \vdash_\Phi \theta \iff \theta \text{ is in the smallest } \Phi\text{-closed set including } \Gamma,
$$

where $X \subseteq A$ is Φ-*closed* if whenever $(\Gamma, \theta) \in \Phi$

$$
\Gamma \subseteq X \;\Rightarrow\; \theta \in X.
$$

Truth systems

A *truth system* (A, M) consists of a set A and a set $M \subseteq pow A$, where $pow A$ is the set of all subsets of A. Truth systems form a category TS, where a map $\pi : (A, M) \to (A', M')$ of TS is a function $\pi : A \to A'$ such that

$$
X \in M' \;\Rightarrow\; \pi^{-1} X \in M.
$$

With each axiomatic system (A, Φ) we may associate the truth system $(A, cl(\Phi))$ where $cl(\Phi)$ is the set of Φ-closed subsets of A.

Proposition 1.2 $(A, \Phi) \mapsto (A, cl(\Phi))$ can be made into a functor $AS \to TS$ which factorises $AS \to CR \to TS$. Moreover $CR \to TS$ has a right adjoint $TS \to CR$ which associates with each truth system (A, M) the consequence relation $(A, \models_M)$ where

$$
\Gamma \models_M \theta \iff (\forall X \in M)[\, \Gamma \subseteq X \;\Rightarrow\; \theta \in X \,].
$$

Closure systems

A *closure system* is a truth system (A, M) such that

1. $\bigcap \mathcal{X} \in M$ for all $\mathcal{X} \subseteq M$ (where we take $\bigcap \mathcal{X} = A$ when $\mathcal{X} = \emptyset$),

2. $\bigcup \mathcal{X} \in M$ for all directed $\mathcal{X} \subseteq M$.

Let CS be the full subcategory of TS whose objects are the closure systems.

Proposition 1.3 The adjoint functors $CR \to TS$ and $TS \to CR$ have factorisations $CR \to CS \hookrightarrow TS$ and $TS \to CS \to CR$ which are also adjoints. Moreover the functors $CR \to CS$ and $CS \to CR$ are inverses of each other, so that $CR \cong CS$.

Semantical systems

A *semantical system* $(A, Mod, \models)$ consists of a set A, a class Mod and a class relation $\models$ that is a subclass of $Mod \times A$. Semantical systems form a category SS, where a map $(\pi_1, \pi_2) : (A, Mod, \models) \to (A', Mod', \models')$ of SS consists of a function $\pi_1 : A \to A'$ and a function $\pi_2 : Mod' \to Mod$ such that for $m' \in Mod', \theta \in A$

$$(\pi_2 m') \models \theta \iff m' \models' (\pi_1 \theta).$$

Each truth system (A, M) determines a semantical system $(A, M, \ni_M)$ where $m \ni_M \theta \iff \theta \in m \in M$. This gives a functor $TS \to SS$.

Proposition 1.4 The functor $TS \to SS$ has a right adjoint $SS \to TS$ which associates with each semantical system $(A, Mod, \models)$ the truth system

$$(A, \{th(m) \mid m \in Mod\}),$$

where, for each $m \in Mod$,

$$th(m) = \{\theta \in A \mid m \models \theta\}.$$

Note that the composition $SS \to TS \to CR$ gives a functor $SS \to CR$ that sends each semantical system $(A, Mod, \models)$ to the consequence relation $(A, \models)$ where

$$\Gamma \models \theta \iff (\forall m \in Mod)[\, (\forall \gamma \in \Gamma)(m \models \gamma) \Rightarrow m \models \theta \,].$$

Axiomatic system with semantics

We now describe a hybrid notion. An *axiomatic system with semantics* $(A, \Phi, Mod, \models)$ consists of an axiomatic system (A, Φ) and a semantical system $(A, Mod, \models)$ such that

$$soundness: \quad \Gamma \vdash_\Phi \theta \Rightarrow \Gamma \models \theta.$$

The axiomatic system with semantics is *complete* if the converse holds i.e.

$$\Gamma \models \theta \;\Rightarrow\; \Gamma \vdash_\Phi \theta.$$

Axiomatic systems with semantics form a category ASS in the obvious way.

Summary

We have defined the four categories AS, CR, TS, SS with functors

$$AS \to CR \cong CS \hookrightarrow TS \to SS$$

which have right adjoints

$$AS \hookleftarrow CR \cong CS \leftarrow TS \leftarrow SS.$$

There is also the hybrid category ASS with the obvious forgetful functors $ASS \to AS$ and $ASS \to SS$. All these categories and functors are 'over the category of sets'; i.e. for each of these categories $\mathbf{C}$ there is a forgetful functor $\mathbf{C} \to Sets$ and for each of the above functors $\mathbf{C} \to \mathbf{C}'$ the diagram

$$\mathbf{C} \;\longrightarrow\; \mathbf{C}'$$
$$\searrow \quad \swarrow$$
$$Sets$$

commutes.

Lindenbaum algebras

A more abstract algebraic treatment of traditional consequence will work with (meet) semilattices and the Lindenbaum algebra construction. Consider the following natural way to make a (meet) semilattice $(A, \leq)$ into a consequence relation $(A, \vdash_\leq)$, where

$$C \vdash_\leq a \;\Leftrightarrow\; \bigwedge C \leq a.$$

This gives rise to a functor from the category SL of semilattices to the category CR. We can characterise the Lindenbaum algebra construction as a left adjoint $CR \to SL$ to this functor, that maps $(A, \vdash)$ to $(Q, \leq)$ where Q is a quotient of $finA$ with respect to the equivalence relation $\equiv$ given by

$$C_1 \equiv C_2 \;\Leftrightarrow\; \text{for all } a \in A \;\; C_1 \vdash a \text{ iff } C_2 \vdash a$$

and $\leq$ is the partial ordering on Q given by

$$[C_1] \leq [C_2] \;\Leftrightarrow\; C_1 \vdash a \text{ for all } a \in C_2.$$

2 Consequence relations and Scott's information systems

This section is really a detour from the main topic. As in the previous section the categories and functors that we will consider are all 'over the category of sets'.

There is an interesting relationship between the notion of a consequence relation and Scott's notion of an information system (see [7]). This gives rise to a relationship between closure systems and Scott domains. Essentially a Scott Information System can be viewed as a consequence relation $(A, \vdash)$ and a *consistency notion* Con for it i.e. $Con \subseteq finA$ such that for all $C \in finA, a \in A$

1. $C \cup \{a\} \in Con \Rightarrow C \in Con$,

2. $C \not\vdash a \Rightarrow C \in Con$,

3. $C \vdash a$ and $C \in Con \Rightarrow C \cup \{a\} \in Con$.

Given such a consistency notion we can call a $\vdash$-closed set $X \subseteq A$ *consistent* if $finX \subseteq Con$. Then the set $Cl(A, \vdash, Con) = \{X \in cl(\vdash) \mid X$ is consistent$\}$ if 'elements' of the information system form a Scott domain, when partially ordered by the subset relation. It is a standard fact that every Scott domain is isomorphic to one of these.

We call a truth system (A, M) a *weak closure system* if it satisfies the two conditions of a closure system, except that, in condition 1, $\bigcap \mathcal{X} \in M$ need only hold for non-empty $\mathcal{X} \subseteq M$. So a closure system is simply a weak closure system (A, M) such that $A \in M$. We may form the category wCS which is the full subcategory of CS consisting of weak closure systems. Also let CRC be the category whose objects are triples $(A, \vdash, Con)$ where $(A, \vdash)$ is a consequence relation and Con is a consistency notion for it. The maps $\pi : (A, \vdash, Con) \to (A', \vdash', Con')$ in this category are the maps $\pi : (A, \vdash) \to (A', \vdash')$ in CR such that for all $X \in finA$

$$\pi X \in Con' \Rightarrow X \in Con.$$

Then we get an isomorphism

$$CRC \cong wCS$$

given by mapping $(A \vdash, Con)$ in CRC to $(A, Cl(A, \vdash, Con))$ in wCS. The inverse of this isomorphism maps (A, M) in wCS to $(A, \vdash_M, Con_M)$ in CRC, where the map $(A, M) \mapsto (A, \vdash_M)$ is given by the functor $wCS \hookrightarrow TS \to CR$ and

$$Con_M = \{C \in finA \mid C \subseteq X \text{ for some } X \in M\}.$$

Given a consequence relation $(A \vdash)$, there are two extreme ways to form a consistency notion Con for it. The maximum consistency notion is given by $Con = finA$. The minimum consistency notion is given by

$$Con = Con(A, \vdash) = \{X \in finA \mid X \nvdash a \text{ for some } a \in A\}.$$

Of course in some cases the two consistency notions may coincide so that the consequence relation has a unique consistency notion. But in familiar cases we expect the two notions to be distinct (e.g. in a logic with negation we might expect that $\{b, \neg b\} \vdash a$ for all a so that if $X = \{b, \neg b\}$ then X is in $finA$, but not in $Con(A, \vdash)$). Can there be other consistency notions for a given consequence relation? I was initially surprised to observe that:

Proposition 2.1 For any consequence relation the two extreme consistency notions are the only possible ones.

To see why this is so let Con be a consistency notion for the consequence relation $(A, \vdash)$ which is different from $Con(A, \vdash)$. It follows that there is some $C \in Con$ such that $C \vdash a$ for all $a \in A$. We want to show that any $X \in finA$ is in Con. So let $X = \{a_1, \ldots, a_n\} \in finA$. As $C \vdash a$ we get that $C \cup \{a_1\} \in Con$. As $C \vdash a_2$ we get $C \cup \{a_1\} \vdash a_2$ so that $C \cup \{a_1, a_2\} \in Con$. Continuing in this way we eventually get that $C \cup X \in Con$. As $X \subseteq C \cup X$ it follows that $X \in Con$.

The two ways to construct consistency notions give rise to functors in a natural way, though for the second way a little care is needed. In the first case we have the functor $CR \to CRC$ that maps $(A, \vdash)$ to $(A, \vdash, finA)$.

Proposition 2.2 The above functor $CR \to CRC$ is left adjoint to the forgetful functor $CRC \to CR$ that maps $(A, \vdash, Con)$ to $(A, \vdash)$.

For the other consistency notion construction we need to restrict to surjective functions. Let CR' be the subcategory of CR having the same objects as CR but having as maps only those maps of CR that are surjective as functions. Similarly we may define categories CRC', CS', etc.... The above functor $CR \to CRC$ can be restricted to give a functor $CR' \to CRC'$ which is still a left adjoint to the forgetful functor on CRC'. But we also have another functor $CR' \to CRC'$ that maps $(A, \vdash)$ to $(A, \vdash, Con(A, \vdash))$. It is not possible to extend this to CR.

Proposition 2.3 The latter functor $CR' \to CRC'$ is right adjoint to the forgetful functor $CRC' \to CR'$.

So we get a sequence of three functors between CR' and CRC' where the first functor in each successive pair is left adjoint to the second:

$$
\begin{array}{llll}
CR' & \to & CRC' & (A, \vdash) & \mapsto & (A, \vdash, finA) \\
CRC' & \to & CR' & (A, \vdash, Con) & \mapsto & (A, \vdash) \\
CR' & \to & CRC' & (A, \vdash, Con(A, \vdash)) & \mapsto & (A, \vdash).
\end{array}
$$

The isomorphisms

$$CR \cong CS \text{ and } CRC \cong wCS$$

induce isomorphisms

$$CR' \cong CS' \text{ and } CRC' \cong wCS'$$

and hence give rise to a corresponding sequence of functors between CS' and wCS':

$$
\begin{array}{lll}
CS' & \hookrightarrow wCS' & (A, M) \mapsto (A, M) \\
wCS' & \rightarrow CS' & (A, M) \mapsto (A, M \cup \{A\}) \\
CS' & \rightarrow wCS' & (A, M) \mapsto (A, \overline{M}).
\end{array}
$$

where $\overline{M}$ is $M - \{A\}$ if this is a weak closure system and is M otherwise.

There is a close connection between the collections of weak closure systems and Scott domains. But it is too strong to assert that the category *Scott* of Scott domains and continuous maps is equivalent to the category wCS. We do get an equivalence if we restrict to categories of isomorphisms. To get a better result we can consider the contravariant functor $wCS \rightarrow Scott^{op}$ which, on objects, maps (A, M) to $(A, \subseteq_M)$, where $\subseteq_M$ is the subset relation on M, and, on maps, assigns to each $\pi : (A, M) \rightarrow (A', M')$ of wCS the inverse image continuous function $\pi^{-1} : (M, \subseteq_M) \rightarrow (M', \subseteq_{M'})$. This functor is an equivalence if *Scott* is modified so that only certain continuous functions are allowed as maps.

3 Indexed consequence

One aspect of a logic is that there is a notion of signature, so that associated with each signature is a set of sentences that can be formed with the signature. So we postulate a category SIG over the category of sets, the functor $SIG \rightarrow Sets$ being the functor associating with each signature Σ of SIG the set $sent(\Sigma)$ of sentences of Σ.

As an example first order logic could use the category SIG whose objects consist of sets of individual constant symbols and n-place function and predicate symbols for $n > 0$. The signature maps of SIG are functions from symbols to symbols that map individual constants to individual constants, n-place function symbols to n-place function symbols and n-place predicate symbols to n-place predicate symbols. Now $sent(\Sigma)$ can be the set of first order sentences formed in the standard way using the symbols of Σ, logical symbols and individual variables.

Given SIG and $SIG \rightarrow Set$ we get *SIG-indexed notions* as functors from SIG over the category *Set*. For example a *SIG-indexed consequence relation* is a functor $SIG \to CR$ over Set. This is Meseguer's notion of an entailment system and also the Harper, Sanella and Tarlecki notion of a logical system.

A version of the notion of an institution is a category SIG over Set together with a SIG-indexed semantical system $SIG \to SS$ over Set.

Let CRS be the full subcategory of ASS consisting of $(A, \vdash, Mod, \models)$ in ASS where $(A, \vdash)$ is in CR. Now Meseguer's notion of a logic is a category SIG over Set together with a *SIG-indexed consequence relation with semantics $SIG \to CRS$ over Set*.

4   Schematic consequence

We wish to capture the schematic aspects of logic. A logic is axiomatised by giving schematic axioms and rules of inference which can be instantiated to get inference steps. Instantiations may themselves be schematic so that we are interested in the notion of a derived rule of inference obtained by composing instances of the axioms and rules. (Note: We need only focus on rules, as an axiom is simply a rule with no premises.)

Substitution

We want a syntax free way of talking about instantiation. We are led to focus on substitution. We will assume that the substitutions on a set A are functions $s : A \to A$ that form a submonoid of $(A^A, id_A, \circ)$. Here A^A is the set of all functions $A \to A$, $id_A : A \to A$ is the identity function of A and if $s, s' : A \to A$ then $s \circ s' : A \to A$ is their composition. If Sub is such a submonoid then we call (A, Sub) a *concrete monoid*. The instances of $a \in A$ are the elements of A of the form sa for $s \in Sub$.

Concrete monoids form a category CM where a map $(\pi_1, \pi_2) :$ $(A, Sub) \to (A', Sub')$ consists of a function $\pi_1 : A \to A'$ and a monoid homomorphism $\pi_2 : Sub \to Sub'$ such that for all $a \in A, s \in Sub$

$$\pi_1(sa) = (\pi_2 s)(\pi_1 a).$$

We can now give schematic versions of axiomatic systems, consequence relations, etc.

Schematic axiomatic systems

A *schematic axiomatic system* (A, Sub, Φ) consists of a concrete monoid (A, Sub) and an axiomatic system (A, Φ). In an obvious way we get a category SAS of schematic axiomatic systems.

Schematic consequence relations

A *schematic consequence relation* $(A, Sub, \vdash)$ is a schematic axiomatic system such that $(A, \vdash)$ is a consequence relation and for all $s \in Sub$

$$s : (A, \vdash) \to (A, \vdash) \text{ in } CR;$$

i.e.

$$\Gamma \vdash \theta \implies s\Gamma \vdash s\theta.$$

We can now let SCR be the full subcategory of SAS consisting of schematic consequence relations.

Proposition 4.1 The inclusion functor $SCR \hookrightarrow SAS$ has a left adjoint $SAS \to SCR$ which associates with each schematic axiomatic system (A, Sub, Φ) the schematic consequence relation $(A, Sub, \vdash_\Phi)$ *generated* by (A, Sub, Φ) i.e. the least relation including Φ such that $(A, Sub, \vdash_\Phi)$ is a schematic consequence relation, or alternatively,

$$\Gamma \vdash_\Phi \theta \iff \theta \text{ is in the smallest } Sub\Phi\text{-closed set including } \Gamma \text{ where}$$
$$Sub\Phi = \{(s\Gamma, s\theta) \mid s \in Sub \text{ and } (\Gamma, \theta) \in \Phi\}.$$

If $\Gamma \vdash_\Phi \theta$ then (Γ, θ) is a *derived rule of* Φ (relative to (A, Sub)).

Schematic truth systems

A *schematic truth system* (A, Sub, M) consists of a concrete monoid (A, Sub) and a truth system (A, M) such that $s : (A, M) \to (A, M)$ in TS for all $s \in Sub$ i.e.

$$X \in M \implies s^{-1}X \in M$$

for all $s \in Sub$.

STS is the category of schematic truth systems, with the obvious notion of map. With each schematic axiomatic system (A, Sub, Φ) we may associate the schematic truth system $(A, Sub, cl(Sub\Phi))$.

Proposition 4.2 $(A, Sub, \Phi) \mapsto (A, Sub, cl(Sub\Phi))$ can be made into a functor $SAS \to STS$ which factorises $SAS \to SCR \to STS$. Moreover $SCR \to STS$ has a right adjoint $STS \to SCR$ which associates with each schematic truth system (A, Sub, M) the consequence relation $(A, Sub, \models_M)$ where $\models_M$ is obtained from M as in $TS \to CR$.

References

[1] A. Avron, Axiomatic Systems, Deduction and Implication, Tech. Report 203/91, Institute of Computer Sciences, Tel-Aviv University.

[2] J. Barwise, Axioms for abstract model theory, *Annals of Mathematical Logic*, **7**, 221–165, 1974.

[3] J. Goguen and R. Burstall, Institutions: Abstract Model Theory for Specification and Programming, Edinburgh LFCS Report 90-106.

[4] Harper, Sannella and Tarlecki, Structure and Representation in LF, in *Proceedings of the Fourth Annual Symposium on Logic in Computer Science*, IEEE, Computer Science Press, 1989.

[5] Harper, Honsell and Plotkin, A framework for defining logics In *J. Assoc. Comp. Mach.*, **40**, 143–184, 1993.

[6] J. Meseguer, **General logics**, *Proc. Logic Colloquium '87*, edited by H.D. Ebbinghaus et al., North Holland, 1989.

[7] D. Scott, Domains for Denotational Semantics, in the *Proceedings of ICALP, Springer Lecture Notes in Computer Science 140*, 1982.

11

Logical Constants as Punctuation Marks*

Kosta Došen

1 Introduction

This chapter presents a proof-theoretical approach to the question 'What is a logical constant?' The approach starts with the assumption that logic is the science of formal deductions, and that basic formal deductions are structural deductions, i.e. deductions independent of any constant of the language to which the premises and conclusions belong. Logical constants, on which the remaining formal deductions are dependent, may be said to serve as 'punctuation marks' for some structural features of deductions. This punctuation function, exhibited in equivalences which amount to analyses of logical constants, is taken as a criterion for being a logical constant. The chapter presents an account of philosophical analysis which covers the proposed analyses of logical constants. Some related assumptions concerning logic are also considered. In particular, since a logical system is completely determined by its structural deductions, alternative logical systems arise by changing structural deductions while having constants with the same punctuation function. Some other approaches to the question 'What is a logical constant?', grammatical, model-theoretical, and proof-theoretical, are briefly considered.

*This chapter is based on the philosophical part of my doctoral thesis [9], and on lectures delivered in 1984 at the University of Constance, in 1985 at the Mathematical Institute in Belgrade and in 1987 at the University of Notre Dame. I would like to acknowledge my debt to Michael Dummett, who supervised my work on [9]. I am also indebted to Peter Schroeder-Heister, who invited me to Constance, and who encouraged me in a number of discussions to try to explicate the ideas propounded here. Michael Detlefsen has been very kind to invite me to Notre Dame, and to show an interest in my work. I would like to thank him and Michael Kremer for reading and discussing my text. I am grateful to the *Notre Dame Journal of Formal Logic* for the permission to reprint this article from Volume **30** (1989, pp. 362–381), where it first appeared in a very slightly different version.

It is clear that an answer to the question 'What is a logical constant?' would provide us with the means to answer the question 'Where are the limits of logic?' Since the latter question is obviously very close to the question 'What is the subject matter of logic?' one could legitimately assume that our question 'What is a logical constant?' is among the central questions of the philosophy of logic.

Apart from its intrinsic philosophical interest, the problem of the demarcation of logic is obviously of crucial importance to the logicist program in the foundations of mathematics. However, no definite criterion for this demarcation seems to have come out of the work of the logicists, with which modern logic started. On the other hand, one of the main reasons why logicism was abandoned was that at some point it was felt that the limits of logic must have been transgressed in the logicist reconstruction of mathematics. The problem of the demarcation of logic is also in the background of the discussion concerning the status of second-order logic, which started with Quine's attack upon second-order logic (see [6]).

In spite of all that, it doesn't seem that logicians, even those who are philosophically inclined, are trying very hard to answer the question 'What is a logical constant?' A much more characteristic attitude in modern logic is that of a certain scepticism as to whether the distinction between logical and nonlogical expressions can be clearly drawn. Most logicians, like so many followers of Protagoras, are content with just listing what they take as logical constants. A clear exponent of this scepticism, and probably one of those who made it the accepted position, is Tarski in his famous paper on the notion of logical consequence [40]. It is interesting that Bolzano anticipated Tarski not only in his definition of the semantical notion of logical consequence, but also in the belief that it is doubtful that a criterion can be found for drawing the distinction between logical and nonlogical expressions (see [5, Section 148] and [23, p. 366]).

Occasionally, however, attempts do arise to find this criterion. Without trying to ascertain their merits, let us just mention some of these attempts.

In [36] Quine proposed to distinguish logical constants from other expressions (his terms are, respectively, 'particles' and 'lexicon') by saying that the grammatical categories of the latter are 'infinite and indefinite' (see pp. 28–30, 59). In [43] Wang examined some proposals, including a grammatical one, linked with Quine's, but in general he was in a rather sceptical mood (see pp. 143–165). It is interesting that in a lecture from 1966 [42] Tarski seems to have abandoned his scepticism up to a point, and to have found a criterion for the demarcation of logic by elaborating ideas suggested by Klein's *Erlanger Programm*, and some model-theoretical results of Lindenbaum and Tarski [25]. Chief among these results is that '... every relation between objects (individuals, classes, relations, etc.) which can be expressed by purely logical means is invariant with respect to every one-one mapping of the *world* (i.e. the class of all individuals) onto itself ...' ([41, p. 385]; Tarski's lecture of 1966 is criticized in [28]). The proposal for the demarcation of logical constants found in [14, pp. 21-22], which is in principle grammatical (essentially, it takes as logical constants functors from sentences and predicates to sentences and singular terms), also has a footnote dealing with identity, in which a view very similar to Tarski's conception of 1966 is propounded. Finally, Lindström in [26] and [27] suggested a rather technical model-theoretical criterion for the demarcation of logic, by showing that the Löwenheim–Skolem theorem together with the compactness theorem for denumerable sets of sentences cannot be extended to first-order logics with generalized quantifiers that properly extend ordinary first-order logic.

The purpose of this chapter is to give a summary of the philosophical part of [9], which represents yet another attempt to answer the question 'What is a logical constant?' This attempt is neither grammatical nor model-theoretical, but proof-theoretical. In principle, it is not impossible that such a proof-theoretical approach be at least extensionally equivalent with another approach, grammatical or model-theoretical, in the sense that the same constants will be selected as logical in both approaches. However, we shall not investigate the possible connections between these various approaches here. After presenting our approach in the next four sections of this chapter, in the last section we shall briefly consider some similar proof-theoretical programs for the demarcation of logic.

2 Thesis [I]

Our proof-theoretical attempt to answer the question 'What is a logical constant?' starts with the following assumption about logic:

[**A**] Logic is the science of formal deductions.

This conception of logic, despite its aura of antiquity, is neither the only possible nor the dominant conception of logic. There is a strong tradition in modern logic, which starts with Frege, and pervades not only model theory, but also Hilbert-style proof theory, that assumes that logic is the science of a certain kind of truths, rather than deductions. A clear assessment of the role that this conception, and the alternative conception expressed by [A], have played in modern logic can be found in [14, pp. 432–435]; (cf. also [21]).

It is also rather unclear how the logic mentioned in [A] could cover the vast number of mathematical subjects studied in model theory, recursion theory, set theory, or category theory, which all go today under the label of logic. So, 'logic' in [A] should probably be taken as referring only to a certain traditional core of logic. In modern logic, the conception of [A] is clearly present only in Gentzen-style proof theory: the comparatively narrow, but doubtless important, tradition that starts with Gentzen's seminal thesis [18].

Sometimes [A] is expressed by saying that logic is the science of *valid* formal deductions. This use of 'valid' is slightly misleading, since separating valid formal deductions from invalid ones obviously involves considering both.

Assumption [A] does not leave any room for an informal logic. If someone insists (often without much reason) upon using the word 'logic' for the description of the function of all sorts of words (in principle, philosophically interesting), then we must emphasize that the 'logic' of [A] should be understood as 'formal logic' (a subject which does not have many things in common with, for example, 'the logic of colour words').

However, this leaves us with the task of specifying what *the formal deductions* we appeal to in [A] are. To accomplish this task, we first assume the following:

[**B**] Basic formal deductions are structural deductions.

The term 'structural' in [B] should be understood in the sense this word has in Gentzen's sequent-systems in [18]. Structural deductions are deductions that can be described independently of the constants of the *object language*, i.e. the language from which our premises and conclusions come. In other words, in describing structural deductions, everything in the object language is schematic.

With the apparatus of Gentzen's sequent-systems a description of structural deductions is obtained as follows. Let $A, B, C, \ldots$ be schemata for formulae of an object language, and let $\Gamma, \Delta, \ldots$ be schemata for collections of formulae of this language; these collections can be either sets, multisets (i.e. collections with possibly more than one occurrence of each element, in which order is unimportant), or sequences. (A very general approach is to consider Γ as a term made up of formulae of the object language with the help of a binary comma, which need not even be associative; cf. [3] and [12].) Then we can interpret a *single-conclusion* sequent $\Gamma \vdash A$ as saying that there is a deduction from the premises in Γ to the conclusion A. If Γ is empty, $\Gamma \vdash A$ amounts to the assertion that A is a theorem. A *multiple-conclusion* sequent $\Gamma \vdash \Delta$, where Δ has more than one member, can be understood as referring to a deduction where in each line we have a collection of formulae, rather than a single formula. In classical logic, these collections can be sets, in which formulae are tied by an implicit disjunction (cf. [7]). Another possibility is to understand multiple-conclusion deductions in the style of Shoesmith and Smiley [39]. Multiple-conclusion sequents can also be related to a natural generalization of Tarski's semantical notion of consequence (cf. [38, pp. 413–418]).

That the appropriate form of deductions in classical logic is given by multiple-conclusion deductions does not seem to be generally acknowledged. Though, on the technical side, these deductions have some clear advantages, as was demonstrated by Gentzen in [18], intuitively they may well look like an invention of logicians, not to be found in ordinary usage. But perhaps we shall find them in ordinary usage, too, if we assume that there they occur in an *enthymematic* form. Usually, a deduction is enthymematic if some true premises are omitted; but we could just as well say that a deduction is enthymematic if some false alternative conclusions are omitted. For example, the single-conclusion deduction of A from $\neg\neg A$ may be matched by the enthymematic multiple-conclusion deduction obtained from:

$$\frac{\overline{\quad\top\quad}}{\underset{\perp}{A \qquad \neg A \qquad \neg\neg A}}$$

by omitting the true premise $\top$ and the false alternative conclusion $\perp$; the formulae A and $\neg A$ are derived as alternative conclusions from $\top$.

Structural deductions can now be described by restricting the sequent language to *structural sequents*, i.e. schematic sequents in which no constant of the object language occurs. Valid structural deductions will be codified by retaining in a sequent-system only axiom-schemata like $A \vdash A$, and structural rules like permutation, contraction, thinning, and cut. Another structural rule (not mentioned by Gentzen) that may be added to these is the rule of *substitution for variables*:

$$\frac{\Gamma \vdash \Delta}{S_a^x \Gamma \vdash \Delta \mid}\,,$$

where the lower formula stands for the sequent obtained from $\Gamma \vdash \Delta$ by substituting uniformly a for the free occurrences of x; the schematic letter a stands for an expression of the same grammatical category as x, which, as usual, contains neither a free variable that will become bound after the substitution, nor a variable-binding operator that will bind a free variable of $\Gamma \vdash \Delta$.

It seems clear that deductions described independently of any constant of the object language may legitimately be called *formal*. These are the *basic formal deductions*, by which all other formal deductions are determined according to the following assumption:

[C] Any constant of the object language on whose presence the description of a nonstructural formal deduction depends can be ultimately analysed in structural terms.

In the next section we shall explain in more detail what we mean by 'ultimately analysed in structural terms'. For the time being, we shall explain [C] only with the help of a metaphor.

Assumption [C] enables us to get a uniform picture of logical form. Logical form is primarily exhibited by structural deductions, and when logical constants are introduced, they serve, so to speak, as *punctuation marks* of the object language for some structural features of deductions. Which structural punctuation function pertains to the customary logical constants of first-order logic (implication →, conjunction ∧, disjunction ∨, the constant true proposition ⊤, the constant absurd proposition ⊥, the universal quantifiers $\forall x$, the existential quantifiers $\exists x$, and equality =), and to the necessity operator of the modal systems S4 and S5, was mentioned in [10]. Here we shall consider as our main examples the punctuation function of implication and of the universal and existential quantifiers; the rest will be mentioned only briefly.

The connective of implication in $A \to B$ says that A and B are connected in this formula of the object language like a premise and a conclusion in a deduction. This means that for implication we have assumed a *deduction theorem* and *modus ponens*. In a sequent framework, this corresponds to the assumption of the following *double-line rule*:

$$(\to) \quad \frac{\Gamma, A \vdash \Delta, B}{\Gamma \vdash \Delta, A \to B},$$

where the double line means that we have two rules, one going downward and the other upward, and Γ, A stands for the collection obtained by taking the union of Γ and $\{A\}$, or by concatenating A to Γ, or something analogous. The downward rule clearly corresponds to the deduction theorem, whereas the upward rule is equivalent to $A \to B, A \vdash B$, in the presence of the axiom-schema $C \vdash C$ and cut. Axiomatizations with double-line rules like $(\to)$ were propounded by Kneale in [22] and [23], and by Scott in [38] and some other of his papers from the same period. However, the notion is implicit in Gentzen's [18], as a number of authors, starting with Ketonen in the 1940s, have realized.

The double-line rule $(\to)$ can serve to characterize various sorts of implications: classical, intuitionistic, and relevant. What in these characterizations distinguishes various implications is not $(\to)$, which is always the same, but assumptions concerning structural deductions. For example, intuitionistic implication can be obtained from classical implication by abolishing *thinning on the right*:

$$\frac{\Gamma \vdash \Delta}{\Gamma \vdash \Delta, A},$$

which has the same effect as permitting only single-conclusion sequents (this is analogous to the way Gentzen obtains his intuitionistic sequent-system from his classical sequent-system in [18]). Relevant implication, i.e. the implication of the relevant system R of Anderson and Belnap, is obtained by further abolishing *thinning on the left*:

$$\frac{\Gamma \vdash \Delta}{\Gamma, A \vdash \Delta} \cdot$$

The situation is analogous for the other logical constants of first-order logic, and for the necessity operators, mentioned above: they can all be characterized in alternative logical systems by fixing double-line rules for them, and changing only structural assumptions. (Various alternative logical systems, obtained in this way, are investigated in [10, 11, 12].[1])

What we want to stress here is that in the upper sequent of ($\rightarrow$) everything from the object language is purely schematic, so that this sequent is structural. According to ($\rightarrow$), implication is a kind of substitute in the object language for the turnstile $\vdash$, i.e. for the deducibility relation. Implication can reduce a sequent like $A \vdash B$, which says that B can be deduced from A, to a theorem of the object language $A \rightarrow B$: with ($\rightarrow$), we have that $A \vdash B$ and $\vdash A \rightarrow B$ are interdeducible. The logical form of $A \rightarrow B$ mirrors a structural feature of deductions, viz. the relation between a premise A and a conclusion B, independently of any constants A and B may have.

The universal and existential quantifiers can be characterized by the following double-line rules:

$$(\forall) \quad \frac{\Gamma \vdash \Delta, A}{\Gamma \vdash \Delta, \forall x A} ,$$

$$(\exists) \quad \frac{\Gamma, A \vdash \Delta}{\Gamma, \exists x A \vdash \Delta} ,$$

with the following proviso: *the variable x does not occur free in either Γ or Δ*. As with implication, by varying structural rules the same double-line rules ($\forall$) and ($\exists$) can serve for various alternative logical systems, provided we have assumed the structural rule of substitution for variables (see [10]). And as with ($\rightarrow$), the upper sequents of ($\forall$) and ($\exists$) are structural. Since the rule of substitution for variables permits us to read the x that may occur free in A as 'any', according to ($\forall$) and ($\exists$), the two quantifiers express something about the place of 'any' in deductions. If 'any' is in a conclusion, and nowhere else, it becomes 'every', and if it is in a premise,

---

[1] (added in 1992) Among the substructural logics, i.e. logics with restricted structural rules, of [12] we find in particular linear logic and the Lambek calculus.

and nowhere else, it becomes 'some'. So the logical form of $\forall x A$ and $\exists x A$ mirrors a structural feature of deductions, viz. the presence of a variable in a conclusion A, or in a premise A, a variable which doesn't occur free anywhere else in the deduction.

For the remaining constants of first-order logic, mentioned above, we have the following double-line rules:

$$(\wedge) \quad \frac{\Gamma \vdash \Delta, A \quad\quad \Gamma \vdash \Delta, B}{\Gamma \vdash \Delta, A \wedge B} \quad,$$

$$(\vee) \quad \frac{\Gamma, A \vdash \Delta \quad\quad \Gamma, B \vdash \Delta}{\Gamma, A \vee B \vdash \Delta} \quad,$$

$$(\top) \quad \frac{\vdash \Delta}{\top \vdash \Delta} \quad, \quad\quad (\bot) \quad \frac{\Gamma \vdash}{\Gamma \vdash \bot} \quad,$$

$$(=) \quad \frac{S_a^x \Gamma \vdash \Delta \mid}{\Gamma, x = a \vdash \Delta} \quad.$$

The double-line rules $(\wedge)$ and $(\vee)$ should be interpreted as if the pairs of upper sequents were tied by a conjunction; so, for example, the upward direction of $(\wedge)$ gives two rules, one with the conclusion $\Gamma \vdash \Delta, A$ and the other with the conclusion $\Gamma \vdash \Delta, B$. According to $(\wedge)$ and $(\vee)$, conjunction and disjunction serve to economize: they reduce to one deduction two deductions that differ only at one place in the conclusions or in the premises. The constant $\top$ is a substitute for the empty collection of premises ($\vdash \Delta$ can be understood as referring to a demonstration of one of the conclusions in Δ), and $\bot$ is a substitute for the empty collection of conclusions ($\Gamma \vdash$ can be understood as referring to a refutation of one of the premises in Γ). Equality serves to indicate substitution possibilities in a deduction: what holds for a also holds for whatever is assumed to be equal to a.

The double-line rule for the necessity operator $\square$ of S4 and S5 is based on sequents of higher levels, i.e. sequents that have collections of sequents on the left and right of the turnstile (see [10]; cf. [11]). Without entering into details, let us only mention that $\square A$ can be understood as indicating that A is assumed as a theorem.

The connective of equivalence $\leftrightarrow$ can either be explicitly defined by $A \leftrightarrow B =_{df} (A \to B) \wedge (B \to A)$, or we can give the following double-line rule for it:

$$(\leftrightarrow) \quad \frac{\Gamma, A \vdash \Delta, B \quad\quad \Gamma, B \vdash \Delta, A}{\Gamma \vdash \Delta, A \leftrightarrow B} \quad.$$

The assumptions [A], [B] and [C] naturally yield the following thesis concerning constants of our object language:

[**I**] A constant is logical if, and only if, it can be ultimately analysed in structural terms.

In the next section we shall try to explain what we mean by the expression 'ultimately analysed in structural terms', which occurs in assumption [C] and in thesis [I].

3 Analysis

Let us first settle what 'ultimately' means in 'ultimately analysed'. An expression is *ultimately* analysed if, and only if, it is either analysed or it can be explicitly defined in terms of analysed expressions. Next, we must say what we mean by 'analysed'. This is a more difficult matter. It presupposes a general account of philosophical analysis, which we proceed to sketch.

In the philosophical tradition that continues to be called 'analytical', but which has gone through many significant changes in this century, it seems that the most precise account of analysis that can be found, and to which many accepted opinions can still be traced, is in the writings of G. E. Moore. On the other hand, this account, which ultimately treats analysis as a kind of explicit definition, cannot be supported by many examples of significant philosophical analyses that conform to its standards. Our account of analysis will differ from Moore's by drawing a distinction between analysis and explicit definition. (In that, and in some other respects, it follows [24], which contains a detailed critique of Moore's account of analysis and of those accepted opinions that can be traced to his account.)

Let us suppose that we have an expression α of a language L and that we want to analyse α. Then we must specify a language M, to which α does not belong, in which we shall formulate the analytic equivalent of α, i.e. the analysans. Below we shall consider more closely the relation between L and M; for the time being it is enough to say that M, as a vehicle of our analysis, must be a language we understand. Our first condition concerning analysis specifies the *form* an analysis should take; it says that

1. An analysis consists of establishing that a sentence **A** in M plus α, in which α occurs only once, is equivalent to a sentence **B** in M.

The second condition concerning analysis specifies that an analysis must be *sound and complete*: it says that

2. From the equivalence of (1), and from the understanding of M and L minus α, we can infer every sentence of L analytically true in L and no sentence of L not analytically true in L.

K. Došen

That a sentence is analytically true in L means that its truth may be recognized by appealing only to the understanding of the language L. Our third condition concerning analysis says that an analysis must characterize *uniquely* the expression analysed, in the following sense:

3. The expressions α_1 and α_2 can receive the same analysis if, and only if, α_1 and α_2 have the same meaning.

An equivalence can satisfy our three conditions for analysis without amounting to an explicit definition. There are at least two additional conditions that an explicit definition is normally assumed to satisfy, which need not be satisfied by an analysis.

The first of these additional conditions, which we may call *Pascal's condition*, says that

The definitional equivalence should enable us to find for every sentence of M plus α a sentence of M with the same meaning.

If M is equal to L minus α, this amounts to the requirement that in every sentence of L we must be able to eliminate a defined expression by its definiens, without changing the meaning. (Such a requirement is implied by Pascal in [29, pp. 244, 279–282], cf. [4, pp. 504–505]. A similar implication might be found in Aristotle's *Topica*, Z.4, 142 b.) Pascal's condition implies that for **A** in (1) there will be a **B** with the same meaning.

The second condition for explicit definitions we shall call the *conservativeness condition*; it says that

Every sentence of L minus α analytically true in L is analytically true in L minus α.

This implies that from the definitional equivalence, and from the understanding of M and L minus α, we should not be able to infer a sentence of L minus α, analytically true in L, but not analytically true in L minus α.

Strengthening our weaker notion of analysis to explicit definability of some sort, which should presumably satisfy Pascal's condition and conservativeness, threatens to exclude most philosophically interesting analyses, and may reduce us to the recording of more or less lexicographical facts, like the fact that 'a is a brother' is equivalent to 'a is a male sibling'.

To illustrate this, consider first Ramsey's analysis of the predicate 'is true', given by the equivalence:

'A' is true if, and only if, A.

Here, L is a fragment of English, α is 'is true', and M is our fragment of English without α, extended by the schema A for sentences of L (our fragment of English presumably contains quotation marks, or a similar device, transforming expressions of the grammatical category of sentences into expressions of the grammatical category of nouns; A is of the grammatical category of sentences). It is plausible to hold that Ramsey's analysis satisfies (1)–(3), and even conservativeness (provided we have restricted our fragment of English so that Liar-type paradoxes cannot be derived). However, it will not satisfy Pascal's condition, since we are unable to eliminate 'is true' from a sentence like 'Everything Socrates said is true' (at least not without introducing in M further logical paraphernalia, such as propositional variables and propositional quantifiers binding these variables). It can plausibly be argued that the point of having 'is true' in ordinary English is to enable us to say things that cannot be said without this predicate (cf. [19]).

Consider now Russell's analysis of the definite description 'the king of France', given by the equivalence:

The king of France is P if, and only if, there is a single individual
that is a king of France and that individual is P.

Here, L is again a fragment of English, α is 'the king of France' and M is our fragment of English without α (but with the predicate 'is a king of France'), extended by the predicate schema P. Granted that Russell's analysis satisfies (1)–(3), and even Pascal's condition, it is clear that it does not satisfy conservativeness, since on Russell's analysis the analytical truth 'The king of France is equal to the king of France' yields 'There is a king of France', which cannot be analytically true in L minus α.

Let us call an expression α *inconsistent*, relative to a language K without α, if in K not every sentence is analytically true, but in K plus α every sentence is analytically true. Some expressions, like the predicate 'is a round square', which it would be natural to call inconsistent, are not inconsistent in our sense. An example of an inconsistent expression in our sense is Peano's μ (see [30] and [2]), the analysis of which is given by the equivalence:

$$\frac{a}{b}\,\mu\,\frac{c}{d} = e \text{ if, and only if, } \frac{a+c}{b+d} = e,$$

where $a, b, c, d,$ and e are schematic letters for rational numbers. The operation μ is inconsistent, relative to the language K of the arithmetic of rationals: introducing μ into this arithmetic would give rise to inconsistencies, and since an inconsistency implies everything, every sentence will be made analytically true in K plus μ.

Can an inconsistent expression be analysed? As we have just seen above with μ, the answer is yes, provided we have assumed we have such an expression in L. No doubt, inconsistent expressions are to be avoided, and languages containing them should not be constructed for actual use. But constructing a language is something we do before trying to analyse the expressions of this language, and if we have been so unreasonable, or unfortunate, as to construct a language with inconsistent expressions, the fact that these too can be analysed is not a defect in analysis. There is no reason to require that the conditions for analysis should single out inconsistent expressions as unanalysable, so that analysis should be impracticable with unreasonably constructed languages. On the contrary, analysis can sometimes help us in investigating an unreasonably constructed language, and in locating the source of the trouble.

Since we can analyse inconsistent expressions, *a fortiori* we can analyse an expression that does not satisfy the conservativeness condition. A language L with such an expression α, even if it does not give rise to inconsistencies, is also unreasonable in some sense. Such is, indeed, our L that contains the expression 'the king of France'. The possibility of ascertaining in L supposedly analytical truths like 'There is a king of France' (obtained from 'The king of France is a king of France') makes L unreasonable. Russell's analysis can help us in locating the source of the trouble.

The situation is different with definitions. In this case there will be no pre-existing language L in which α has a meaning, but the definitional equivalence will add α to L minus α, and give meaning to α. And if we want L to be reasonable, our definition must define only α, and not also something in L minus α. Hence, the conservativeness condition should be satisfied, even if Pascal's condition is not. If the definition is to be counted as explicit, it should also satisfy Pascal's condition. Of course, analysis will satisfy conservativeness whenever we deal with a 'reasonably constructed' language L. (For a related discussion of conservativeness in the theory of meaning see [14, pp. 453–455, 396–397].)

Some other remarks should be made concerning condition (1). In it we require that α occurs in **A** *only once*. We think that this requirement is justified, since otherwise it could not be said that we are analysing α, rather than a series of occurrences of α. However, a more relaxed view of analysis may perhaps be envisaged, in which this restriction is lifted. In another respect, condition (1) could be strengthened, viz., we could require that the same schematic letters should occur in **A** and **B**, or something more elaborate of this kind. (There is no absolute necessity that schematic letters occur in **A** and **B**, but in general they will, as our examples show, too.) This requirement would presumably make the analytic equivalence resemble a kind of relevant mutual implication, since 'variable sharing' conditions are typical for relevant implication.

Though an analysis doesn't give the meaning of an expression, as an explicit definition would, it follows from conditions (2) and (3) that an analysis is very closely tied to the meaning of the expression analysed, and that the analytic equivalence should presumably be a kind of relevant equivalence. But this presumed relevant equivalence need not yield an equivalence as strong as identity of meaning, or propositional identity: otherwise we would be in danger of excluding practically all philosophically interesting analyses. However, it is unclear how the relevance involved can be explained formally, and simple sharing of schematic letters need not capture it. Consider, for example, Church's thesis:

> An arithmetical function f is computable if, and only if, f is Turing computable.

It may well be held that this equivalence gives an analysis of the predicate 'is computable', L being mathematical English and M the language of the theory of Turing machines. Some relevance condition is presumably satisfied by this equivalence, but the relevance involved is not exhausted by the sharing of the schematic letter f.

In general, when the relevant analytic equivalence does not amount to propositional identity, this has to do with a difference in grammatical form between **A** and **B**. Analogously, we have that A and $A \wedge A$ are, no doubt, relevantly equivalent, but they do not stand for the same proposition. In our examples of analyses, save in Church's thesis, there is a difference in grammatical form between **A** and **B**. (It seems plausible to say that Church's Thesis satisfies not only (1)–(3), but also Pascal's condition and conservativeness; hence, this thesis might be taken not only as an analysis but as an explicit definition as well. And, indeed, this is how it is sometimes understood.)

It seems that (1)–(3) cannot represent all the necessary conditions for a philosophically significant notion of analysis. In particular, they say nothing about the *clarificatory value* of an analysis. It is not enough merely to assume that the language M is a language we understand. It is usually, and rightly, further assumed that M is of a different order than L, in that it is more *basic*, in the sense that it makes fewer assumptions, and that the understanding of L is somehow dependent on a previous understanding of M, and not the other way round. If we are allowed to use the term 'basic' without further explanation, a fourth condition for analysis can be stated as follows:

4. The language M should be more basic than the language L.

Do the examples of analysis we have mentioned up until now satisfy this condition? In these examples, M differed from L in lacking a certain problematic expression we wanted to analyse, but, on the other hand, we supposed that M contained schematic letters, and it may seem that the presence of such technical devices as schematic letters makes this language less basic. However, in our understanding of 'basic', M should be taken as more basic, because schematic letters serve only to make explicit certain very elementary grammatical regularities, which are indeed presupposed by the understanding of ordinary English. The possibility of generating an unlimited number of sentences like 'The king of France is bald', 'The king of France is brave', etc., as soon as we have figured out that 'the king of France' functions as something in the grammatical category of nouns, amounts to an implicit understanding of the schematic letter P for predicates. The fact that in M these implicit features are made explicit does not mean that M is less basic. In the same sense, we could say that a book of English grammar is more basic than a novel in English. It may seem less basic to a native speaker of English, but not so to a foreigner: the book of grammar makes fewer assumptions—the understanding of the novel is in a certain sense dependent on a previous understanding of the grammar, and not the other way round.

So we suppose that condition (4) is satisfied in all of our examples of analysis, including Church's thesis, where M, the language of the theory of Turing machines, is more basic in a mathematical sense.

Finally, note that nothing in what we have said excludes the possibility that two literally different equivalences both represent an analysis of the same expression α.

Even if we cannot pretend that (1)–(4) are *all* the necessary conditions that a certain notion of analysis should satisfy, it can still be argued that they are a plausible approximation, and that they could be strengthened to yield a sufficient condition by developing something which they already contain implicitly.

What we have tried to do here is to give necessary conditions only for a certain notion of analysis, and not for all possible notions. Many philosophically interesting analyses are not given exactly in the form of a single equivalence. Indeed, they need not be given in the form of equivalences at all, but, presumably, analysis in the form of equivalence has a certain primacy among all possible notions of analysis.

Let us see now, in the light of this account of analysis, how we can analyse logical constants in structural terms. We shall concentrate only on the analysis of implication given by the double-line rule ($\rightarrow$). Here implication is directly analysed, whereas in [10] other constants are only *ultimately* analysed i.e. explicitly defined in terms of analysed constants: for example, negation $\neg$ is defined in terms of implication $\rightarrow$ and the absurd $\perp$ by $\neg A =_{df} A \rightarrow \perp$, while $\rightarrow$ and $\perp$ are directly analysed.

In the analysis of implication given by ($\rightarrow$) the language L is the language of propositional, or first-order, logic, and M is the deductive metalanguage in which we speak about structural deductions; more precisely, M is the language of structural sequents. The sentence **A** is the lower sequent of ($\rightarrow$), and **B** is the upper sequent of ($\rightarrow$). Since the double line stands for an equivalence, our analysis has the form prescribed in condition (1). In [10] it was shown that (→) serves to characterize implication, soundly, completely, and uniquely, in classical, intuitionistic, and relevant logical systems; i.e. conditions (2) and (3) are satisfied. Finally, we suppose that our structural analysis of implication satisfies condition (4), since we suppose that the language M of structural sequents is more basic than the language L of propositional, or first-order, logic. This last supposition can be justified by referring to our assumptions [A] and [B]. If formal deductions are the subject matter of logic, and basic formal deductions are structural deductions, the language M is indeed more basic than a language L in which formal deductions are not explicit any more, and where we get only nonstructural truths based on logical constants. (Some further remarks on M and L will be made in the next section.)

On the other hand, the structural analysis of implication given by (→) need not satisfy Pascal's condition, since in a single-conclusion sequent-system we may be unable to eliminate implication from the sequent $A \to B \vdash C$. Conservativeness can also fail in some cases: for example, if we add (→) to a sequent-system with thinning on the right only, we can derive thinning on the left, and this may make L nonconservative with respect to L minus →. However, in the analysis of classical, intuitionistic, and relevant implication, conservativeness will be satisfied.

4 Assumptions [D] and [E]

We shall now consider two further assumptions concerning logic, relevant to the discussion of Section 2. The first assumption is the following:

[**D**] Logic is independent of subject matter.

Although this is an assumption found quite often in the philosophy of logic, it is far from being clear. A possible paraphrase of at least part of the import of [D] is that only logical constants are essential for a logical system—everything else can be schematic. In this sense, [D] seems uncontroversial, almost a truism. But sometimes [D] is meant to express more: it is meant to imply that, independently of what we are dealing with, we should rely on the same logical laws. It is very questionable to what extent this stronger version of [D] can be sustained.

Of course, [D] cannot mean that logic is independent of the subject matter of logic, and if we are right in assuming by [A] that formal deductions are the subject matter of logic, we can claim that the same logical laws are always in force only if a single type of formal deduction is recognized as valid. Since by [C] all formal deductions are determined by structural deductions, the question arises whether only one type of structural deduction is valid. Without trying to answer this question with precision, we surmise that the type of valid structural deduction may depend on the object language, and on the subject matter of that language.

For example, consider an object language where sentences can be asserted if, and only if, they are *provable*. Presumably, the corresponding valid structural deductions should be codified by a single-conclusion sequent-system. And if sentences of our object language can be asserted if, and only if, they are *true*, the corresponding valid structural deductions should be codified by a multiple-conclusion sequent-system. Whereas the connection between *proof* and single-conclusion sequents seems to be rather clear, the connection between *truth* and multiple-conclusion sequents involves an element of discovery (a discovery which should be ascribed to Gentzen). In some other cases, for example, the language of quantum phenomena, where a sentence can be asserted if, and only if, it is *verifiable with existing instruments*, it is not clear that any corresponding form of valid structural deductions can, or indeed should, be discovered.

Sometimes [D] is invoked to justify the introduction of quantificational logical systems *free* of existential assumptions, i.e. whose theorems are valid in the empty domain, too. Now, we have seen in Section 2 that first-order quantificational logic can be understood as the logic of 'any', or, semantically, as the logic of arbitrary individuals. The assumption that there are some individuals can then be understood as proceeding directly from the subject matter of this logic. Presumably, quantificational logic cannot be independent of its own subject matter. The producing of a free logic, though it need not involve an actual contradiction, may well seem unreasonable: on the one hand, we want a logic whose subject matter consists of arbitrary individuals, but on the other hand, we want this logic to be applicable even when its subject matter is missing. (To make an analogy, it is like giving library rules meant to be applied even in libraries without books: the question whether an empty domain is a domain is like the question whether a library without books is a library.) Since logic cannot be independent of the subject matter of logic, [D] understood in such a way that it justifies the introduction of free logics does not seem warranted.

The second additional assumption concerning logic that we shall consider is the following:

[E] The level of discourse of logic is higher than the level of discourse in which we treat of a particular subject matter relying on logical principles.

Part of what [E] can mean is contained in the uncontroversial part of [D], which says that in a logical system everything except logical constants is schematic, i.e. made of metavariables. But another ingredient of [E] may be that a logical system is formulated properly in a *higher* language, a deductive metalanguage, like the language of sequents, whereas we treat of a particular subject matter in a *lower* language, an object language from which we draw our premises and conclusions.

Understood in this latter sense, assumption [E] probably expresses the lesson taught by Achilles and the Tortoise in [8]. The Tortoise (its head low on the ground) is unable to see anything above the lower language. The picture of language in Quine's 'Two Dogmas' [35] and the general conception that logic is the science of logical truths of the object language (cf. [14, p. 596] and [15, p. 353]) are misleading because they disregard [E]. (However, [E] seems to be assumed by Quine in his critique of conventionalism in [34].)

Assumption [E] is in perfect harmony with [A], [B], [C], and thesis [I]. Logical constants are expressions of the lower language that have their *raison d'être* in some features of the higher language. When we treat of a particular subject matter, some structural features of the higher language are only implicit in the activity of making deductions. Logical constants serve to make explicit these features in the lower language: they help us to reduce structural truths of the higher language to truths of the lower language. In other words, they reduce truths of the language M of structural deductions to truths of the language L of propositional, or first-order, logic. This is why we can say metaphorically that logical constants are punctuation marks for some structural features of deductions. This metaphor underlies thesis [I].

The analogy between logical constants and punctuation marks should be taken with a certain reservation. Ordinary punctuation marks usually directly exhibit certain features of the activity of speech in all contexts in which they may occur, whereas logical constants directly exhibit certain structural features of the activity of deducing only when they occur in a particular way in a deduction, viz., as the main constant of a conclusion or of a premise. Some logical constants are analysed by double-line rules in which they occur on the right-hand side of the turnstile, and others by double-line rules in which they occur on the left-hand side of the turnstile; for some other constants, like $\forall, \exists, \top, \bot$, and $=$, there may be additional conditions concerning the respective double-line rules. When a constant occurs in the lower language, or in a context of the higher language, where it cannot be eliminated by using the respective double-line rule, we may still say that it mirrors the corresponding punctuation function, but only in a derived sense. Generalizing condition (2) for analysis, we may assume that whatever holds for this constant, in any context of the lower or higher language, should be derivable from the corresponding double-line rule. The fact that logical constants cannot always be eliminated, i.e. the fact that they need not satisfy Pascal's condition, indicates that there might be a real gain in introducing them not only in the lower language but also in the higher language: they may enable us to say things that cannot be said without them.

To conclude our discussion of thesis [I], let us examine how effective the criterion it provides is. It can be inferred from [10] and [11] that the customary logical constants of first-order logic with identity, and the modal constants of classical and intuitionistic S4 and S5, are all logical. (It is also not difficult to give an analysis in structural terms of some other constants, like the Hilbert ε-operator.) In general, thesis [I] can effectively be applied to show that a constant *is* logical: if it is ultimately analysed in structural terms we can claim that it is logical. On the other hand, this thesis does not seem to be effective in showing that a constant is *not* logical, for it is not clear on what grounds we could claim that an ultimate analysis in structural terms is impossible. So the effective use of thesis [I] in settling disputed cases may be limited, if we don't state more precisely what form a structural analysis can possibly take. But, even in this imperfect form, thesis [I] can serve to show what is common to all the constants usually accepted as logical without dispute, which are logical according to this thesis, too. Moreover, together with the underlying assumptions about logic we have discussed, it shows that this common characteristic of logical constants proceeds from a certain conception of logic.

5   Thesis [II]

We stated in Section 2 that the double-line rule ($\rightarrow$) can serve to characterize implication in various logical systems: classical, intuitionistic, and relevant. In these characterizations ($\rightarrow$) is always the same: only assumptions concerning structural deductions are changed. We also mentioned that the situation is analogous for other logical constants we have considered. This situation naturally leads us to postulate the following thesis:

[II] Two logical systems are alternative if, and only if, they differ only in their assumptions on structural deductions.

This thesis can also be viewed as a consequence of assumptions [A], [B] and [C]. According to these assumptions, different systems of formal deductions can arise because they have either

(i) different structural deductions and logical constants ultimately analysed in the same way, or

(ii) the same structural deductions and logical constants ultimately analysed in different ways, or

(iii) both different structural deductions and logical constants ultimately analysed in different ways.

We suppose that the situation is best described by saying that in case (i) we are confronted with *alternative* logical systems, in case (ii) with logical systems that are *supplements*, and in case (iii) with logical systems that are both alternatives and supplements. For example, classical first-order logic and intuitionistic first-order logic are alternative logical systems, whereas the first-order modal logics S4 and S5 are supplements of classical first-order logic.

If the language M used for giving an analysis of α can be understood in two different ways (as happens when we assume different structural rules to be valid in M), so that in fact we have two languages, M_1 and M_2, then the analysis based on M_1 cannot be the same as the analysis based on M_2. However, it is clear that these two different analyses will have a common core. The expression α_1 with the analysis based on M_1 will not have the same meaning as the expression α_2 with the analysis based on M_2 (according to condition (3) for analysis, in Section 3), but we can say that α_1 and α_2 are *analytically identical*. This analytic identity is a kind of identity of function; in the case of logical constants this is identity of structural deductive function. This identity may be taken as the 'common denominator' of alternative logical systems. For example, we are justified in saying that both classical and intuitionistic implication are implications, because for both of them we assume the same structural deductive function, i.e. we assume a *deduction theorem* and *modus ponens*. Usually, this 'common denominator' of alternative logical systems is not clearly characterized, and a more or less vague resemblance between the alternatives is considered sufficient.

Two logical systems can 'differ only in their assumptions on structural deductions' not only when these assumptions are explicit, as in sequent-systems, but also when these assumptions are only implicit, as in Hilbert-style axiomatizations.

We shall summarize our discussion of thesis [II] by considering how it proceeds from thesis [I]. The import of thesis [I] is that a logical system is completely determined by its assumptions on structural deductions. Hence, to change logic, and not merely to supplement it by new 'punctuation marks', we must change structural deductions. An alternative logical system is obtained when the same 'punctuation marks' work in a different structural context.

6 Similar programs

Our attempt to analyse logical constants and thesis [I] should not be confused with the program of *defining* logical constants by syntactical means. First, the main goal of this program is to show that the *meaning* of logical constants can be given syntactically, whereas our analyses are neutral with respect to this claim, and are equally compatible with the view that the meaning of logical constants is to be given in a more conventional semantical framework. Second, the search for a criterion for being a logical constant does not always have a very important place in this program. If the problem of finding this criterion is considered at all, it is usually taken that logical constants will be just those expressions whose meaning can be given by syntactical means, which makes the search for a criterion dependent upon the main goal of the program. Thesis [I] is an attempt to formulate such a criterion without tying it to a thesis on the meaning of logical constants. On the other hand, it is clear that our analyses of logical constants and thesis [I] are congenial to this program. Presumably, the 'deductive structural function', which we think is demonstrated by our analyses, must be closely tied with the meaning of logical constants, even if we need not assume that it coincides exactly with this meaning.

The origins of this program can be traced to Gentzen, who made the following remark concerning the introduction and elimination rules of his natural deduction systems: 'Die Einführungen stellen sozusagen die „Definitionen"der betreffenden Zeichen dar, und die Beseitigungen sind letzen Endes nur Konsequenzen hiervon, ... ' ([18, section 5.13]).

In a series of papers (which he later called 'bad and ill fated') Popper attempted to use a certain sort of sequent-system to define logical constants, and to find a criterion for the demarcation of logic. (For references see [37], which reconstructs in great detail Popper's theory by divorcing it from the attempt to define logical constants syntactically, and tries only to derive from Popper's work a syntactical criterion for the demarcation of logic; it also contains an extensive bibliography on matters related to the program we are considering.) A program similar to Popper's was formulated by Kneale in [22] (see also [23]), who tried to formulate for that purpose a natural-deduction multiple-conclusion system. The program has been more recently pursued by Hacking in [20]. Hacking is concerned in principle with standard Gentzen-style sequent-systems with rules for introducing constants on the left and on the right of the turnstile, but he also tries to introduce a certain notion pertaining to the parametric parts of these rules that apparently makes it impossible for him to deal with modal constants. One of Hacking's aims is to show that quantum logic is logic.

That part of the proof-theoretical program of Prawitz (see [31] and [32]) that is relevant to our discussion is not so much concerned with the demarcation of logic, as with pursuing the idea expressed in Gentzen's remark on natural deduction introduction rules. This also holds for the relevant views of Dummett (see [16] and [17, pp. 389–403]).

Prior criticized this general program by giving in [33] natural-deduction rules for what we would call 'an inconsistent constant' (see Section 3). In the reply by Belnap [2], the requirements of conservativeness and uniqueness are stated for rules that pretend to define a constant (cf. [13]).

Our replacement of the term 'definition' by the term 'analysis' in the program above is not merely a verbal move. One substantial difference is that the requirement of conservativeness ceases to play for us the role it has to play in the former program. We don't want our double-line rules to give the meaning of the logical constants, but only a philosophically significant analysis. It is possible that something not very far from our notion of analysis was on Gentzen's mind when he made his brief remark on the *sozusagen Definitionen.*

The metaphor we have used to describe the function of logical constants is reminiscent of the following remarks of Wittgenstein from [44]:' Die logischen Operationszeichen sind Interpunktionen' (5.4611); '. . . in der Logik ist jeder Satz die Form eines Beweises' (6.1264). However, one would probably have to take these remarks out of their immediate context in order to connect them with the views expressed here.

References

[1] Aristotle, *Topica et Sophistici Elenchi,* edited by W. D. Ross, Oxford University Press, Oxford, 1958. English translation by W. D. Ross in *The Works of Aristotle,* vol. 1, Oxford University Press, Oxford, 1928.

[2] Belnap, N. D., Tonk, plonk and plink, *Analysis,* **22**, 130–134, 1962.

[3] Belnap, N. D., Display logic, *Journal of Philosophical Logic,* **11**, 375–417, 1982.

[4] Beth, E. W., *The Foundations of Mathematics,* North-Holland, Amsterdam, 1959.

[5] Bolzano, B., *Wissenschaftslehre,* Sulzbach, 1837. English translation *Theory of Science,* Blackwell, Oxford, 1972.

[6] Boolos, G. S., On second-order logic, *The Journal of Philosophy,* **72**, 509–527, 1975.

[7] Boričić, B., On sequence-conclusion natural deduction, *Journal of Philosophical Logic,* **14**, 359–377, 1985.

[8] Carroll, L., What the tortoise said to Achilles, *Mind*, **4**, 278–280, 1895.

[9] Došen, K., Logical Constants: An Essay in Proof Theory, D. Phil. thesis, University of Oxford, 1980.

[10] Došen, K., Sequent-systems for modal logic, *The Journal of Symbolic Logic*, **50**, 149–168, 1985.

[11] Došen, K., Higher-level sequent-systems for intuitionistic modal logic, *Publications de l'Institut Mathématique*, **39**(53), 3–12, 1986.

[12] Došen, K., Sequent-systems and groupoid models, *Studia Logica*, **47**, 353–385, 1988 (Addenda and corrigenda, *Studia Logica*, **49**, 614, 1990).

[13] Došen, K. and P. Schroeder-Heister, Conservativeness and uniqueness, *Theoria*, **51**, pp. 159–173, 1985 (Errata, *Theoria*, **52**, 127, 1986).

[14] Dummett, M., *Frege: Philosophy of Language,* Duckworth, London, 1973.

[15] Dummett, M., The significance of Quine's indeterminacy thesis, *Synthese*, **27**, 351–397, 1974.

[16] Dummett, M., The philosophical basis of intuitionistic logic. In *Logic Colloquium '73* (H. E. Rose and J. C. Shepherdson, eds), pp. 5–40, North-Holland, Amsterdam, 1975.

[17] Dummett, M., *Elements of Intuitionism*, Oxford University Press, Oxford, 1977.

[18] Gentzen, G., Untersuchungen über das logische Schliessen, *Mathematische Zeitschrift*, **39**, 176–210, 405–431, 1934. English translation in *The Collected Papers of Gerhard Gentzen*, North-Holland, Amsterdam, 1969.

[19] Grover, D. L., T. L. Camp, and N. D. Belnap, A prosentential theory of truth, *Philosophical Studies*, **17**, 73–125, 1975.

[20] Hacking, I., What is logic?, *The Journal of Philosophy*, **76**, 285–319, 1979.

[21] Kneale, W., Truths of logic, *Proceedings of the Aristotelian Society*, **46**, 207–234, 1946.

[22] Kneale, W., The province of logic. In *Contemporary British Philosophy* (H. D. Lewis, ed.), pp. 237–261, Allen and Unwin, London, 1956.

[23] Kneale, W. and M. Kneale, *The Development of Logic*, Oxford University Press, Oxford, 1962.

[24] Kojen, L., Categories and Analysis, D. Phil. thesis, University of Oxford, 1977.

[25] Lindenbaum, A. and A. Tarski, Über die Beschränkheit der Ausdrucksmittel deduktiver Theorien, *Ergebnisse eines mathematischen Kolloquiums*, **7**, 15–22, 1935. English translation in [41].

[26] Lindström, P., On extensions of elementary logic, *Theoria*, **35**, 1–11, 1969.

[27] Lindström, P., On characterizing elementary logic. In *Logical Theory and Semantic Analysis* (S. Stenlund, ed.), pp. 129–146, Reidel, Dordrecht, 1974.

[28] Mikeladze, Z. N., Ob odnom klasse logicheskikh poniatiĭ. In *Logicheskii vyvod* (V. A. Smirnov, ed.), pp. 287–299, Nauka, Moscow, 1979.

[29] Pascal, B., Fragments de l'esprit géométrique et extrait d'un fragment de l'introduction à la géométrie. In *Oeuvres de Blaise Pascal, vol. 9*, pp. 229–294, Hachette, Paris, 1914.

[30] Peano, G., Le definizioni in matematica, *Periodico di matematiche (4)*, **1**, 175–189, 1921. English translation in *Selected Works of Giuseppe Peano*, Allen and Unwin, London, 1973.

[31] Prawitz, D., Meaning and proofs: On the conflict between classical and intuitionistic logic, *Theoria*, **43**, 2–40, 1977.

[32] Prawitz, D., Proofs and the meaning and completeness of the logical constants. In *Essays on Mathematical and Philosophical Logic* (J. Hintikka *et al.*, eds), pp. 25–40, Reidel, Dordrecht, 1979.

[33] Prior, A. N., The runabout inference-ticket, *Analysis*, **21**, 38–39, 1969.

[34] Quine, W. V. O., Truth by convention. In *Philosophical Essays for A. N. Whitehead* (O. H. Lee, ed.), pp 90–124. Longman, New York, 1936.

[35] Quine, W. V. O., Two dogmas of empiricism, *Philosophical Review*, **60**, 20–43, 1951.

[36] Quine, W. V. O., *Philosophy of Logic*, Prentice- Hall, Englewood Cliffs, 1970.

[37] Schroeder-Heister, P., Popper's theory of deductive inference and the concept of a logical constant, *History and Philosophy of Logic*, **5**, 79–110, 1984.

[38] Scott, D. S., Completeness and axiomatizability in many-valued logic. In *Proceedings of the Tarski Symposium* (L. Henkin *et al.*, eds), pp. 411–435, American Mathematical Society, Providence, 1974.

[39] Shoesmith, D. J. and T. J. Smiley, *Multiple-Conclusion Logic*, Cambridge University Press, Cambridge, 1978.

[40] Tarski, A., O pojęciu wynikania logicznego, *Przegląd Filozoficzny*, **39**, 58–68, 1936. English translation in [41].

[41] Tarski, A., *Logic, Semantics, Metamathematics*, Oxford University Press, Oxford, 1956. Second Edition, Hackett, Indianapolis, 1983.

[42] Tarski, A., What are logical notions?, edited by J. Corcoran, *History and Philosophy of Logic*, **7**, 143–154, 1986.

[43] Wang, H., *From Mathematics to Philosophy*, Routledge, London, 1974.

[44] Wittgenstein, L., Logisch-philosophische Abhandlung, *Annalen der Naturphilosophie*, **14**, 185–262, 1921. English translation *Tractatus Logico-Philosophicus*, Routledge, London, 1961.

12

Finitary Inductively Presented Logics*

Solomon Feferman

1 Introduction

A notion of *finitary inductively presented (f.i.p.) logic* is proposed here,
which includes all syntactically described logics (formal systems) met in
practice. A f.i.p. theory FS_0 is set up which is universal for all f.i.p. logics;
though formulated as a theory of functions and classes of expressions, FS_0 is
a conservative extension of *PRA*. The aims of this work are (i) conceptual,
(ii) pedagogical and (iii) practical. The system FS_0 serves under (i) and (ii)
as a theoretical framework for the formalization of metamathematics. The
general approach may be used under (iii) for the computer implementation
of logics. In all cases, the work aims to make the details manageable in a
natural and direct way.

What is a logic? The question here is not 'What is logic?', which (ten-
dentiously) seeks to canonize some *one* distinguished system of reasoning
as being the only true one. But also, here, we are not after *any* logic—
only those that are *syntactically described,* or *formal,* as distinguished from
those that are *semantically described.* For the latter, a reasonable general
basic notion has evolved, that of *model-theoretic logic*; cf. e.g. Barwise-
Feferman [3]. Curiously (for a subject so devoted to foundational matters),
there is no corresponding generally accepted basic notion for the formal logics. Such should cover as special cases propositional and predicate calculi
of various kinds (classical, intuitionistic, many-valued, modal, temporal,
deontic, relevance, etc.) and styles (Hilbert, Gentzen natural deduction,
Gentzen sequential, linear, etc.), as well as equational calculi, lambda calculi, combinatory calculi (typed and untyped), and various applied logics

*Reprinted, with some minor corrections and additions, from *Logic Colloquium '88*
(R. Ferro, C. Bonotto, S. Valentini, and A. Zanardo, eds.), North-Holland Publishing
Co., Amsterdam (1989), pp. 191–220. Permission to reprint granted by Elsevier Science
Publishers, B.V.

(theories of arithmetic, algebraic systems, analysis, types, sets, etc.) and logics of programs.[1]

The first answer usually given is that by a syntactically described logic we mean a *formal system* i.e. a triple consisting of a *language, axioms* and *rules of inference,* all of these specified by their syntactic form. But what does this last mean? And what is a language anyhow? In practice, languages are themselves systems of interrelated syntactic categories including such notions as sorts, variables, terms, propositional operators, quantifiers, abstraction operators, atomic formulas, formulas, etc. So what do we mean by a *formal language system*?

Some answers to these questions have been proposed, but none so far has gained wide acceptance. Either they are too general, so that lots of things we would not ordinarily call logics are lumped in together and nothing interesting about them can be proved, or they are too specific, so that many logics met in practice are excluded, or they are too abstract, so that many significant particularities of logics in practice are simply ignored, or they are too coercive, so that everything is forced into one uncomfortable mould.

The aim here is to propose a comprehensive definition of a *finitary inductive system* which includes both languages and logics and which covers all examples met in practice, in a reasonably natural and direct way. As is to be expected for work of this nature, many of the ideas will have already been employed in the literature, in one way or another, for this and related purposes. The novelty here lies mainly in the particular combination of ideas, although there are some definitely new concepts which are introduced, the main one being that of a *presentation* of a finitary inductive system and thence of a *finitary inductively presented logic*.

The most closely related work by others is, on the one hand, that of Smullyan [23] (following Post [18]—cf. also [10]) and, on the other hand, that of Moschovakis [16], where the question dealt with—'What is an algorithm?'—is answered in terms of a more general class of inductive systems. The direct predecessor of this chapter is [8], 'Inductively presented systems and the formalization of meta-mathematics', which I refer to in the following as [IPS]. What is done below corrects, extends and improves [IPS] in certain respects, but is based on the same leading ideas; I shall refer to it frequently in the following.

There are three main reasons for pursuing our leading question:
(i) *Conceptual.* The topologists have their topological spaces, the algebraists have their algebraic structures (the *very* abstract algebraists have their categories), the analysts have their normed spaces, the probabilists

---

[1] Thus the approach here is neutral as to the reasons for choosing any particular logic for study, or for choosing one logic in preference to another.

have their measure spaces, the model-theorists have their model-theoretic logics, so the formal logicans ought to have their formal logics.

But the matter on the conceptual level goes deeper. Many subjects have been transformed by the search for the 'right way' to provide a manageable systematic development of their part of mathematics, even though some of the basic ideas and results are very intuitive. Examples are the exterior differential calculus as the framework for the ordinary and higher dimensional versions of Stokes' and Gauss' theorems, or the categorical theory of homology as the framework for combinatorial topology.

Where an exact notion of formal system is particularly needed in our subject is in the formalization of metamathematics, beginning with *Gödel's Second Incompleteness Theorem*. As we know, this is very sensitive to *how* the formal systems dealt with are *presented* (cf. [4] and [13, pp. 153–154]). While the two-line informal argument for Gödel's theorem is very convincing,[2] there is no really satisfactory presentation which is both detailed and sufficiently general. But, as anyone knows who has gone into proof theory at all, this is just the tip of the iceberg. For a number of other examples, see the concluding section of this chapter.

(ii) *Pedagogical.* This is simply an extension of (i). A good conceptual framework is necessary to explain the formalization of metamathematics in a reasonable and convincing way without excessive hand-waving. Students gain confidence when they see that various steps can be worked out systematically and in detail. This does not mean that the subject must be presented entirely at such a level, just that the mechanics of the details are at hand when confidence falters. As intuition and experience take over, the need for such recedes, but the existence of a manageable underlying framework is always reassuring.

(iii) *Practical.* There has been much talk in recent years of implementing various kinds of logics on computers, especially for the purposes of proof-checking. Examples for relatively specific logical systems are provided by projects of de Bruijn, Boyer and Moore, Constable, Ketonen, and others. The ELF (Edinburgh Logical Framework) project led by Plotkin (see [12] and [2]) aims to handle an enormous variety of formal logics, by a kind of reduction in each case to the typed lambda-calculus. However, in the ELF approach much preparatory work must be done by hand for each logic so that it can then be implemented on a computer. I believe the step from a logic, as it is presented in usual (humanly understandable) terms to its computer-ready presentation should be as natural and direct as possible. The use of some notion such as that of a (presented) finitary inductive system developed here, seems to me to be essential for this goal.

Because there is much ground to be covered, the work in the following

---

[2]See p.137 of Kleene's introductory note to *Gödel 1931* in [11].

concentrates on statements of notions and results; by necessity, proofs are omitted or only sketched.

2   The universe of tree expressions

The collection V of individuals dealt with is taken to be built up from a class U of *urelements* by closure under the operation P of pairing. We write P_1, P_2 for the left and right inverses of P, respectively, so that $P_i(P(x_1, x_2)) = x_i$, and x is a pair just in case $x = P(P_1x, P_2x)$. Thus U is the class of x such that $x \neq P(P_1x, P_2x)$. U has a distinguished element 0, and V_0 denotes the subclass of V generated from 0 by closure under pairing. Elements of V are called *(binary) tree expressions over U*, and elements of V_0 are called *pure tree expressions*.

The standard alternative approach to syntax takes the universe of expressions to be the class U^* of *finite strings*, or *words*, $u_0 \dots u_{n-1}$ with $u_i \in U$, thinking of U as a set of *basic symbols* or *alphabet* (cf. e.g. [23, 10]). These are represented here instead by finite sequences, defined below in terms of iterated pairing. The present approach builds in the tree structure of expressions met in practice, with x_1, x_2 being considered the immediate *subexpressions* of $P(x_1, x_2)$. The main advantage is that it provides for a more natural and direct introduction of syntactic functions, typically introduced by recursion (from subexpressions to expressions). The same approach is followed in the familiar list-processing programming language LISP.[3],[4]

For simplicity in the following we shall work entirely with pure tree expressions. There is no loss of generality for syntactic applications over any finite alphabet U, by representation of such U within V_0. The more general situation (V over any U) is useful if we want to develop recursion theory over an arbitrary structure $\langle U, \dots \rangle$, as is done e.g. in [15], as well as treat general model theory (as initiated in [IPS]). All of our work extends directly to the more general situation.

Abbreviations. $(x, y) := P(x, y)$

$$(x_1) := x_1 , \quad (x_1, \dots, x_n, x_{n+1}) := ((x_1, \dots, x_n), x_{n+1}) .$$

Note that this representation makes each n-tuple $(x_1, \dots, x_n)$ an m-tuple for each $m \leq n$, e.g. $(x_1, x_2, x_3, x_4, x_5) = ((x_1, x_2, x_3), x_4, x_5)$. Finite

---

[3]A third alternative (to the theory of trees as here, or to concatenation theory) is to work in some form of hereditarily finite set theory. However, sets must still be represented by trees or lists when it comes to effective implementation.

[4]Another reason for working with trees rather than sequences is that the former have a natural generalization to syntactically described infinitary logics; cf. also the concluding remarks to this chapter.

sequences will be represented below in a modified form in such a way that each finite sequence has a definite length.

As further abbreviations, we take

$$x' := (x, 0) , \quad 1 := 0' , \quad 2 := 1', \text{ etc.}$$

Note $x' \neq 0$ (by $(x, y) \neq 0$), and $x' = y' \Rightarrow x = y$.

3 Functions, classes, relations

Functions. We use f, g, h (with or without subscripts) to range over arbitrary unary functions from V_0 to V_0. Each unary f determines an n-ary $f^{(n)}$ by $f^{(n)}(x_1, \ldots, x_n) = fx$ for $x = (x_1, \ldots, x_n)$ i.e. $f^{(n)}$ is the restriction of f to the class of n-tuples. We do not distinguish $f^{(n)}$ from f; thus each f is simultaneously an n-ary function for all n. (This is an immediate advantage of the pairing structure of the universe.) Capital letters F, G, H are also used for specific functions.

Classes. We use A, B, C, X, Y, Z to range over arbitrary subclasses of V_0. The characteristic function $c_A : V_0 \to V_0$ of $A \subseteq V_0$ is given by
$c_A x = \begin{cases} 0 & x \in A \\ 1 & x \notin A \end{cases}$. Here, and in the following, '0' represents 'True' and '1', 'False'.

Relations. As with functions, each class A determines an n-ary relation $A^{(n)}$ given by:

$$(x_1, \ldots, x_n) \in A^{(n)} \text{ iff } x \in A , \quad \text{for } x = (x_1, \ldots, x_n) .$$

Again we shall not distinguish $A^{(n)}$ from A; thus each A acts simultaneously as an n-ary relation for each n. Following usual relational notation, we shall also write $A(x_1, \ldots, x_n)$ for $(x_1, \ldots, x_n) \in A$.

Functionals and collections. At the next level, script letters like $\mathcal{G}, \mathcal{H}$ will be used for certain specific functionals on and to functions or classes, as e.g. $\mathcal{G}(f, g) = h$, $\mathcal{H}(A, B) = C$, etc., and script letters like $\mathcal{F}(\mathcal{K})$ will be used for certain collections of functions (classes).

4 The explicit functions

The *basic functions* (on V_0) are I, K_0, D, P_1, P_2, where

$$Ix = x , \quad K_0 x = 0 \quad \text{all } x,$$

$$D(x_1, x_2, y_1, y_2) = \begin{cases} y_1 & \text{if } x_1 = x_2 \\ y_2 & \text{otherwise} \end{cases} \quad (Du = 0 \text{ if } u \text{ is not a 4-tuple}) ,$$

and P_1, P_2 are the inverses to pairing from Section 1.

The *explicit compounding functionals* are $\mathcal{P}$ (for pairing) and $\mathcal{C}$ (for composition), given by

$$\mathcal{P}(f,g)x = (fx, gx),$$
$$\mathcal{C}(f,g)x = f(gx).$$

We also write (f,g) for $\mathcal{P}(f,g)$ and $f \circ g$ for $\mathcal{C}(f,g)$.

A class $\mathcal{F}$ of functions is said to be closed under *explicit definition*, or $\mathcal{E}$-*closed*, if it contains I, K_0, D, P_1, P_2 and is closed under $\mathcal{P}$ and $\mathcal{C}$. We denote by $\mathcal{E}$ the least $\mathcal{E}$-closed class.

Throughout the following $\mathcal{F}$ is any $\mathcal{E}$-closed class.

(i) $P_{n,i} \in \mathcal{E}$ for each i, $1 \le i \le n$, with $P_{n,i}(x_1, \ldots, x_n) = x_i$.

(ii) $K_a \in \mathcal{E}$ for each $a \in V_0$, where $K_a x = a$.

(iii) $\mathcal{F}$ is closed under n-tupling of functions: $(g_1, \ldots, g_n)x = (g_1 x, \ldots, g_n x)$.

(iv) $\mathcal{F}$ is closed under general composition:

$$(f \circ (g_1, \ldots, g_n))x = f(g_1 x, \ldots, g_n x).$$

(Note then $(f \circ (g_1, \ldots, g_n))(x_1, \ldots, x_m) = f(g_1(x_1, \ldots, x_m), \ldots, g_n(x_1, \ldots x_m)).$)

(v) $E \in \mathcal{E}$, where $E(x_1, x_2) = \begin{cases} 0 & x_1 = x_2 \\ 1 & \text{otherwise} \end{cases}$ (and $E0 = 0$).

(vi) $E_a \in \mathcal{E}$ for each $a \in V_0$, where

$$E_a x = \begin{cases} 0 & x = a \\ 1 & \text{otherwise.} \end{cases}$$

(vii) $Q_a \in \mathcal{E}$ where $Q_a x = (x, a)$ for each $a \in V_0$.

(viii) The propositional functions *Neg, Cnj, Dsj* $\in \mathcal{E}$, where, for $x, y \in \{0, 1\}$ we have

$$Neg\ 0 = 1, \quad Neg\ 1 = 0,$$
$$Cnj\ (x, y) = 0 \Leftrightarrow x = 0 \wedge y = 0,$$
$$Dsj\ (x, y) = 0 \Leftrightarrow x = 0 \vee y = 0.$$

All these (i)–(viii) are easily established.

Remark. Speaking logically, every propositional combination of equations between terms built up from variables and 0 by the $\mathcal{E}$-closure conditions reduces to an equation of the form $t = 0$, by (v) and (viii).

5   Explicitly determined classes and relations

A class A is said to be *explicitly determined,* and we write $A \in \mathcal{E}$, if $c_A \in \mathcal{E}$; we do the same for a class B considered as a relation. The following are easily checked:

(i) $\{0\} \in \mathcal{E}$.

(ii) If $f \in \mathcal{E}$ and $A \in \mathcal{E}$ then $f^{-1}A(= \{x|fx \in A\})$ is in $\mathcal{E}$.

(iii) $\mathcal{E}$ is closed under $\cap, \cup$ and $-$ (complementation).

Exercises 5.1

1. For each $f \in \mathcal{E}$, $f^{-1}\{0\}(= \{x|fx = 0\})$ is in $\mathcal{E}$. Hence $V_0 = K_0^{-1}\{0\}$, $\emptyset = K_1^{-1}\{0\}$ and $\{a\} = E_a^{-1}\{0\}$ are in $\mathcal{E}$.

2. $A, B \in \mathcal{E} \Rightarrow A \times B \in \mathcal{E}$,

$$\text{by } A \times B = \{x|x = (P_1x, P_2x) \wedge P_1x \in A \wedge P_2x \in B\}$$
$$= \{x|E(x, (P_1x, P_2x)) = 0\} \cap P_1^{-1}A \cap P_2^{-1}B$$

Abbreviations. $A^1 := A$, $A^{n+1} := A^n \times A$.

A collection $\mathcal{K}$ of classes is said to be $\mathcal{F}$-*closed* if it contains $\{0\}$ and is closed under f^{-1} for each $f \in \mathcal{F}$, $\cup, \cap$ and $-$. $\mathcal{K}$ is said to be an $\mathcal{F}^+$-*closed collection* if it satisfies the same closure conditions except possibly for the complement operation. Note that $\mathcal{E}$ is the least $\mathcal{E}^+$-closed collection since if $A \in \mathcal{E}$ then $A = c_A^{-1}\{0\}$. Most closure conditions stated in the following apply to any $\mathcal{F}^+$-closed collection.

We shall represent $m+1$-tuples of classes $\langle A_0, \ldots, A_m \rangle$ by disjoint sums,

$$\langle A_0, \ldots, A_m \rangle := \bigcup_{i \le m} A_i \times \{i\} .$$

Thus $A_i = Q_i^{-1} \langle A_0, \ldots, A_m \rangle$. We also write $\langle A_i \rangle_{i \le m}$ (or simply $\langle A_i \rangle$) for $\langle A_0, \ldots, A_m \rangle$.

6   Primitive recursive functions and classes

The functional $\mathcal{R}$ for definition by primitive recursion is given by

$$\mathcal{R}(f, g) = h \text{ where } \begin{cases} h0 = 0 \\ h(x, 0) = fx \\ h(x, (y, z)) = g(x, y, z, h(x, y), h(x, z)) . \end{cases}$$

We consider this as primitive recursion with one parameter x. By the representation of n-tuples in Section 1, the very same functional yields primitive recursion with n-parameters for any $n \geq 1$:

$$h(x_1, \ldots, x_n, 0) = f(x_1, \ldots, x_n)$$
$$h(x_1, \ldots, x_n, (y, z)) = g(x_1, \ldots, x_n, y, z, h(x_1, \ldots, x_n, y), h(x_1, \ldots, x_n, z)) \,.$$

To obtain recursion with no parameters, i.e.

$$h0 = a,$$
$$h(y, z) = g(y, z, hy, hz) \,,$$

one applies $\mathcal{R}$ to suitable (f_0, g_0).

A collection $\mathcal{F}$ of functions is said to be $\mathcal{PR}$-(primitive recursively) closed if it is $\mathcal{E}$-closed and closed under $\mathcal{R}$. The least such collection is denoted $\mathcal{PR}$. A class A is said to be primitive recursive, and we write $A \in \mathcal{PR}$, if $c_A \in \mathcal{PR}$. The $\mathcal{PR}$ classes are also $\mathcal{E}$-closed. For any $\mathcal{F}$, $\mathcal{PR}(\mathcal{F})$ denotes the least $\mathcal{PR}$-closed collection of functions (and thence of classes) which contains $\mathcal{F}$; members of $\mathcal{PR}(\mathcal{F})$ are said to be primitive recursive in $\mathcal{F}$.

7 Presentation of primitive recursive functions

Informally, by a *presentation* of any specific $F \in \mathcal{PR}$ we mean a description of how F is defined in some particular way from the basic functions by successive application of the compounding functionals. Later, this will be specified by a *function term* in the formal system FS_0. However, there are other more *ad hoc* means of presentation, such as that provided by the following coding system C.

C is defined as the least class $X \subseteq V_0$ such that:

(1) $\begin{cases} (0, i) \in X \text{ for } i = 0, \ldots, 4, \text{ and} \\ c_1, c_2 \in X \Rightarrow (j, (c_1, c_2)) \in X \text{ for } j = 1, 2, 3 \,. \end{cases}$

With each $c \in C$ is associated a function $[c] \in \mathcal{PR}$ by:

(2) $\begin{cases} [(0,0)] := I, \quad [(0,1)] := K_0, \ [(0,2)] := D, \\ [(0,3)] := P_1, \ [(0,4)] := P_2, \\ [(1, (c_1, c_2))] := \mathcal{P}([c_1], [c_2]), \ [(2, (c_1, c_2))] := \mathcal{C}([c_1], [c_2]), \\ [(3, (c_1, c_2))] := \mathcal{R}([c_1], [c_2]) \,. \end{cases}$

Every $\mathcal{PR}$ function F is $[c]$ for some $c \in C$ (in fact for infinitely many $c \in C$). Presentations of explicit functions are obtained from the subclass

C_0 of C generated from the $(0, i)(i = 0, \ldots, 4)$ by closing under $(1, (c_1, c_2))$ and $(2, (c_1, c_2))$ only. Thus $F \in \mathcal{E}$ just in case $F = [c]$ for some $c \in C_0$.

It is interesting to note the following results concerning C, though they are not needed below.

(3) *Substitution ('s-1-1') theorem.* There is an operation $S \in \mathcal{PR}$ such that $c \in C$ implies $S(c, a) \in C$, and $[S(c, a)]x = [c](a, x)$ for all a, x.

(4) *Recursion theorem.* For each $\mathcal{PR}$ function $[f]$ we can find $e \in C$ with $[e]x = [f](e, x)$ for all x.

Proofs. The function S for (3) is simply given by $S(c, a) = (2, (c, (1, (K'a, (0, 0)))))$ where $K'0 = (0, 1)$, $K'(a, b) = (1, (K'a, K'b))$, so that $[K'a] = K_a$ for all a. Then (4) is proved by the usual diagonalization argument, taking $e = [S(c, c)]$ where $[c](z, x) = [f](S(z, z), x)$.

Note. Both (3) and (4) hold for the $\mathcal{E}$-closure of the single function K', in place of $\mathcal{PR}$.

8 Finitary inductive systems

We now come to a central concept of our work. By a *system of finitary inductive closure conditions* for classes $X_0, \ldots, X_m$ we mean a finite set of conditions of the form:

(1) (i) $A_i \subseteq X_i$ $(0 \leq i \leq m)$.

(ii) $$\frac{y_1 \in X_{k_1}, \ldots, y_{n_j} \in X_{k_{n_j}}}{x \in X_i} \quad B_j(x, y_1, \ldots, y_{n_j}) \quad (0 \leq j \leq p) .$$

Such a system is specified by two sequences of classes $\langle A_i \rangle_{i \leq m}$ (the *basis conditions*) and $\langle B_j \rangle_{j \leq p}$ (the *rules of inference*) and a *signature* σ, which is an assignment to each $j \leq p$ of an $(n_j + 1)$-tuple $(i, k_1, \ldots, k_{n_j})$ with $i \leq m$ and each $k_r \leq m$ $(1 \leq r \leq n_j)$. By the *finitary inductive system* Σ *of signature* σ for (1) we mean the pair $(\langle A_i \rangle_{i \leq m}, \langle B_j \rangle_{j \leq p})$ specifying these closure conditions.

In more logical form, the closure conditions (1) can be rewritten as:

(2) $\mathrm{Clos}^\sigma_\Sigma (X_0, \ldots, X_m) := \bigwedge_{i \leq m} \forall x (x \in A_i \Rightarrow x \in X_i)$
$\wedge \bigwedge_{j \leq p} \forall x, y_1, \ldots, y_{n_j}$
$\left[\bigwedge_{1 \leq r \leq n_j} (y_r \in X_{k_r}) \wedge B_j(x, y_1, \ldots, y_{n_j}) \Rightarrow x \in X_i \right] .$

Clearly there is a least $\langle X_0, \ldots, X_m \rangle$ satisfying these closure conditions; it is denoted

(3) $\mathcal{SI}^\sigma(\Sigma) := (\text{least}\langle X_0, \ldots, X_m \rangle)\ \text{Clos}^\sigma_\Sigma(X_0, \ldots, X_m).$

'$\mathcal{SI}$' is used for *simultaneous induction*. Note that for $\langle X_0, \ldots X_m \rangle = \mathcal{SI}^\sigma(\Sigma)$ we have each $X_i = Q_i^{-1}\mathcal{SI}^\sigma(\Sigma) = \{x | (x, i) \in \mathcal{SI}^\sigma(\Sigma)\}.$

Four measures of complexity of a simultaneous inductive definition $\mathcal{SI}^\sigma(\langle A_i \rangle_{i \leq m}, \langle B_j \rangle_{j \leq p})$ concern us in the following. The first is the number, $m+1$, of classes being determined simultaneously by the closure conditions (1). The second is the number, $p+1$, of rules of inference B_j being applied in (1). The third is the number $n = \max_{0 \leq j \leq p} n_j$, given by σ; we call n_j the *number of hypotheses* (or assumptions) of B_j, and n the *maximum number of hypotheses* of this inductive definition. The final measure is qualitative, namely as to how 'complicated' are the classes A_i, B_j; this will be described by different collections $\mathcal{K}$ from which these classes may be drawn.

When the signature σ is indicated by context, we shall omit it to simplify notation. We write $\mathcal{SI}_{\leq n}$ for $\mathcal{SI}^\sigma$ when the signature σ gives $n = \max_{0 \leq j \leq p} n_j$. The simplest case for m is that of $m = 0$, when we are dealing with a single inductively defined class, and in this case we write $\mathcal{I}_{\leq n}(A, \langle B_j \rangle_{j \leq p})$ for the result of the inductive definition. That is,

(4) $\mathcal{I}_{\leq n}(A, \langle B_j \rangle)$ is the least class X satisfying:

$\qquad$ (i) $A \subseteq X,$

$\qquad$ (ii) $\dfrac{y_1, \ldots, y_{n_j} \in X}{x \in X}\ B_j(x, y_1, \ldots y_{n_j})\ (0 \leq j \leq p),$

for $n = \max_{0 \leq j \leq p} n_j$. Finally, we write $\mathcal{I}_n(A, B)$ for the result of defining a single class using a single rule of inference with n hypotheses, that is,

(5) $\mathcal{I}_n(A, B)$ is the least class X satisfying:

$\qquad$ (i) $A \subseteq X,$

$\qquad$ (ii) $\dfrac{y_1, \ldots, y_n \in X}{x \in X}\ B(x, y_1, \ldots, y_n)\ .$

9   Reduction in the complexity of inductive definitions

In this section we shall show how to reduce the complexities of simultaneous inductive definitions according to the first three measures just described; then we shall accomplish a reduction in the complexity of basis conditions and rules of inference in the next section. The basic ideas, all quite simple, come from [IPS], pp. 101–102.

9.1 Reduction of $\mathcal{SI}_{\leq n}$ to $\mathcal{I}_{\leq n}$

To define $\mathcal{SI}_{\leq n}(\langle A_i \rangle_{i \leq m}, \langle B_j \rangle_{j \leq p})$ as $\mathcal{I}_{\leq n}(A', \langle B_j' \rangle_{j \leq p})$ we simply put conditions on $X = \langle X_0, \dots, X_m \rangle$ by treating $x \in X_i$ as $(x, i) \in X$. The desired closure conditions on X are then given in the form

(1)   (i) $\langle A_0, \dots, A_m \rangle \subseteq X$, and

(ii) $\dfrac{(y_1, k_1) \in X, \dots (y_{n_j}, k_{n_j}) \in X}{(x, i) \in X} \quad B_j(x, y_1, \dots, y_{n_j})\,.$

This is recast as

(2)   (i) $A' \subseteq X$, for $A' = \langle A_0, \dots, A_m \rangle$, and

(ii) $\dfrac{u_1, \dots, u_{n_j} \in X}{v \in X} \quad B_j'(v, u_1, \dots, u_{n_j})$

for $\begin{aligned} B_j'(v, u_1, \dots, u_{n_j}) &\Leftrightarrow B_j(P_1 v, P_1 u_1, \dots, P_1 u_{n_j}) \wedge v = (P_1 v, i) \wedge \\ u_1 &= (P_1 u_1, k_1) \wedge \dots \wedge u_{n_j} = (P_1 u_{n_j}, k_{n_j})\,. \end{aligned}$

Note that any $\mathcal{E}^+$-closed $\mathcal{K}$ which contains $\langle A_i \rangle, \langle B_j \rangle$, also contains $A', \langle B_j' \rangle$.

9.2 Reduction of $\mathcal{I}_{\leq n}$ to $\mathcal{I}_n$

Given $A, \langle B_j \rangle_{j \leq p}$ where the B_j are treated as n_j-ary relations, let $n = \max\limits_{0 \leq j \leq p} n_j$. Then replace B_j by B_j' where $B_j'(x, y_1, \dots, y_n) \Leftrightarrow B_j(x, y_1, \dots, y_{n_j}) \wedge y_{n_j+1} = \dots = y_n = y_1$. This makes $\mathcal{I}_{\leq n}(A, \langle B_j \rangle_{j \leq p}) = \mathcal{I}_{\leq n}(A, \langle B_j' \rangle_{j \leq p})$ with each B_j' n-ary. But then we simply have $\mathcal{I}_{\leq n}(A, \langle B_j' \rangle_{j \leq p}) = \mathcal{I}_n(A, B'')$ for $B'' = \bigcup\limits_{j \leq p} B_j'$. Again, any $\mathcal{E}^+$-closed $\mathcal{K}$ which contains $A, \langle B_j \rangle$ also contains A, B''.

9.3 Reduction of $\mathcal{I}_n$ to $\mathcal{I}_2$

The idea here is to replace the n-hypothesis rule of inference in $\mathcal{I}_n(A, B)$:

(1) $A \subseteq X; \quad \dfrac{y_1, \dots, y_n \in X}{x \in X} \quad B(x, y_1, \dots, y_n)\,,$

by the rule with single hypothesis:

(2) $A \subseteq X; \quad \dfrac{u \in X^n}{x \in X} \quad B(x, P_{n1} u, \dots, P_{nn} u)\,.$

However, X^n must be defined simultaneously with X, and for that we need to define X^k more generally simultaneously with X for each $k = 2, \ldots, n$. Thus consider the following conditions on classes $X_1, \ldots, X_n$:

$$(3) \quad \begin{cases} A \subseteq X_1 \; ; \quad \dfrac{y \in X_i, z \in X_1}{x \in X_{i+1}} \; x = (y,z), \quad \text{for } 1 \le i < n \; ; \\[2ex] \dfrac{y \in X_n}{x \in X_1} \; B(x, P_{n1}y, \ldots, P_{nn}y) \, . \end{cases}$$

The least $\langle X_1, \ldots, X_n \rangle$ satisfying this is of the form $\mathcal{SI}_{\le 2}(\langle A_i' \rangle_{1 \le i \le n}, \langle B_j' \rangle_{1 \le j \le n})$ where $A_1' = A$, $A_{i+1}' = \emptyset$, $B_j'(x, y_1, y_2) \Leftrightarrow x = (y_1, y_2)$ for $j < n$ and $B_n'(x, y_1, y_2) \Leftrightarrow B(x, P_{n1}y_1, \ldots, P_{nn}y_1) \wedge y_2 = y_1$. Moreover, $\mathcal{SI}_{\le 2}(\langle A_i' \rangle, \langle B_j' \rangle) = \langle X, X^2, \ldots, X^n \rangle$ where $X = \mathcal{I}_n(A, B)$ is the least solution of (1). Now by 9.1 and 9.2, we re-represent $\mathcal{SI}_{\le 2}(\langle A_i' \rangle, \langle B_j' \rangle)$ as $\mathcal{I}_2(A'', B'')$ for suitable A'', B'', so $X = Q_0^{-1}\mathcal{I}_2(A'', B'')$. Again, if $\mathcal{K}$ is $\mathcal{E}^+$-closed and contains A, B, we may obtain A'', B'' in $\mathcal{K}$.

10 Inductive closure and the normal form theorem

We define S-IND$(\mathcal{K})$ to be the least $\mathcal{PR}^+$-closed collection which contains $\mathcal{SI}^\sigma(\langle A_i \rangle, \langle B_j \rangle)$ for all $A_i, B_j \in \mathcal{K}$. Similarly, IND$_2(\mathcal{K})$ is defined to be the least $\mathcal{PR}^+$-closed collection which contains $\mathcal{I}_2(A, B)$ for all $A, B \in \mathcal{K}$. Finally, define $\mathcal{IND}$ to be the least $\mathcal{K}$ such that

$$\text{IND}_2(\mathcal{K}) \subseteq \mathcal{K} \, ,$$

i.e. the least $\mathcal{PR}^+$-closed $\mathcal{K}$ such that $\mathcal{K}$ is closed under $\mathcal{I}_2$. These notions can be relativized to any class $\mathcal{F}$ of functions in place of $\mathcal{PR}$, as S-IND$^{(\mathcal{F})}(\mathcal{K})$, IND$_2^{(\mathcal{F})}(\mathcal{K})$, and IND$^{(\mathcal{F})}$, and the following results hold for $\mathcal{E}$-closed $\mathcal{F}$ and $\mathcal{F}^+$-closed $(\mathcal{K})$.

First we can summarize the results of 9.1–9.3 by:

Theorem 10.1 *If $\mathcal{K}$ is $\mathcal{E}^+$-closed then* S-IND$(\mathcal{K})$ = IND$_2(\mathcal{K})$.

Corollary 10.2 S-IND$(\mathcal{IND})$ = $\mathcal{IND}$.

Our main result here is the following (which again holds for $\mathcal{IND}^{(\mathcal{F})}$, for any $\mathcal{E}$-closed $\mathcal{F}$ in place of $\mathcal{PR}$).

Theorem 10.3 (The normal form theorem for $\mathcal{IND}$[5]). *For each $X \in \mathcal{IND}$ we can find $A, B \in \mathcal{PR}$ with $X = Q_0^{-1}\mathcal{I}_2(A, B)$.*

---

[5]This result is analogous to (but formally simpler than) the reduction theorem of [15, p. 331] (also called a normal form theorem), for Moschovakis' inductive approach to the general notion of algorithm.

PROOF. It is simpler to first represent X in terms of $\mathcal{SI}_{\leq 2}$ and then apply the reductions of Section 9.

Lemma 10.4 *Each $X \in \mathcal{IND}$ is representable as $X = X_0$ for the least solution $\langle X_0, \ldots, X_m \rangle$ of closure conditions of the form*

$$A_i \subseteq X_i \; ; \quad \frac{y_1 \in X_j, \; y_2 \in X_k}{x \in X_i} \; B_{ijk}(x, y_1, y_2),$$

with $A_i, B_{ijk} \in \mathcal{PR}$. In other words $X = Q_0^{-1} \mathcal{SI}_{\leq 2}(\langle A_i \rangle, \langle B_{ijk} \rangle)$.

PROOF. This proceeds by induction on the generation of $\mathcal{IND}$ as the least $\mathcal{K}$ which is closed under $\mathcal{I}_2(A, B)$ for $A, B \in \mathcal{K}$.
(i) $X = \{0\}$; then $X = Q_0^{-1}$ (Least$\langle X_0 \rangle)(\{0\} \subseteq X_0)$. In the following, assume by induction hypothesis that $Y = Y_0$ for the least $\langle Y_0, \ldots, Y_m \rangle$ satisfying

$$(1) \qquad\qquad C_i \subseteq Y_i \; ; \quad \frac{y_1 \in Y_j, \; y_2 \in Y_k}{x \in Y_i} \; C'_{ijk}(x, y_1, y_2) \; ,$$

and that $Z = Z_0$ for the least $\langle Z_0, \ldots Z_q \rangle$ satisfying

$$(2) \qquad\qquad D_i \subseteq Z_i \; ; \quad \frac{u_1 \in Z_j, \; u_2 \in Z_k}{z \in Z_i} \; D'_{ijk}(z, u_1, u_2)$$

where all $C_i, D_i, C'_{ijk}, D'_{ijk} \in \mathcal{PR}$. We shall show that $X = f^{-1}Y$ (for $f \in \mathcal{PR}$), $X = Y \cup Z$, $X = Y \cap Z$ and $X = \mathcal{I}_2(Y, Z)$ satisfy the conclusion of the lemma in the following (ii)–(v).
(ii)   To show that $X = f^{-1}Y$ for $f \in \mathcal{PR}$ satisfies the lemma, we take $X = X_0$ for the least $\langle X_0, Y_0, \ldots, Y_m \rangle$ satisfying the closure conditions (1) and

$$\frac{y \in Y_0}{x \in X_0} \; y = fx \; .$$

(As in 9.2, this one-hypothesis rule is trivially transformed into a rule with two hypotheses; the same applies in the following.)
(iii)   To show $X = Y \cup Z$ satisfies the lemma, we take $X = X_0$ for the least $\langle X_0, Y_0, \ldots, Y_m, Z_0, \ldots, Z_q \rangle$ satisfying the closure conditions (1), (2) and, in addition,

$$\frac{y \in Y_0}{x \in X_0} \; y = x \; ; \quad \frac{y \in Z_0}{x \in X_0} \; y = x.$$

(iv)   To show $X = Y \cap Z$ satisfies the lemma, we represent $X = X_0$ for the least $\langle X_0, Y_0, \ldots, Y_m, Z_0, \ldots, Z_q \rangle$ satisfying the closure conditions (1), (2) and, in addition,

$$\frac{y_1 \in Y_0, \; y_2 \in Z_0}{x \in X_0} \; x = y_1 = y_2.$$

(v) To show $X = \mathcal{I}_2(Y, Z)$ satisfies this form, we consider first its given representation as the least X satisfying

$$Y \subseteq X \; ; \quad \frac{y_1, \, y_2 \in X}{x \in X} \; (x, y_1, y_2) \in Z \; .$$

Now in place of this, we take $X = X_0$ for the least $\langle X_0, Y_0, \ldots, Y_m, \, Z_0, \ldots, Z_q, W \rangle$ satisfying (1), (2) and the following conditions:

$$\frac{y \in Y_0}{x \in X_0} \; x = y \; ; \qquad\qquad \frac{y_1, y_2 \in X_0}{u \in W} \; u = (y_1, y_2) \; ;$$

$$\frac{u \in W, z \in Z_0}{x \in X_0} \; z = (x, P_1 u, P_2 u) \; .$$

The class W is introduced to make $W = X_0^2$ in the least solution and thus to keep to rules with two hypotheses.

This concludes the proof of the lemma.   ∎

Now the normal form theorem itself follows by the reduction methods of Section 9:

$$X = Q_0^{-1} \, \text{Least} \langle X_0, \ldots, X_m \rangle \, \text{Clos}_{\langle A_i \rangle \langle B_{ijk} \rangle}(X_0, \ldots, X_m)$$
$$= Q_0^{-1}(\text{Least } Y) \text{Clos}_{A', B'}(Y),$$

where $A' = \langle A_0, \ldots, A_m \rangle = \bigcup_i A_i \times \{i\}$ and

$$B'_{ijk}(v, u_1, u_2) \Leftrightarrow v = (P_1 v, i) \wedge u_1 = (P_1 u_1, j) \wedge u_2 = (P_1 u_2, k)$$
$$\wedge \, B_{ijk}(P_1 v, P_1 u_1, P_1 u_2) \; .$$

and $B' = \bigcup_{ijk} B'_{ijk}$.   ∎

In the following sections we turn to some interesting specific examples of classes defined by elementary closure conditions.

11   The natural numbers

We are using the abbreviation $x' = (x, 0)$ from Section 2; it follows that $x = P_1 x'$. Moreover, $x' \neq 0$, and $x' = y' \Rightarrow x = y$. Now N is defined as the least class X satisfying

$$0 \in X \; ; \quad \frac{y \in X}{x \in X} \; x = y' \; ,$$

that is, $N = \mathcal{I}_1(\{0\}, \{(x,y)|x = y'\})$. Hence we have:

Closure. $0 \in N \wedge \forall x(x \in N \Rightarrow x' \in N)$.

Induction. $0 \in A \wedge \forall x(x \in A \Rightarrow x' \in A) \Rightarrow N \subseteq A$.

Next note that N *is primitive recursive.* Its characteristic function c_N is defined by the primitive recursion (with no parameters):

$$c_N 0 = 0 \, , \qquad c_N(y,z) = \begin{cases} 0 & \text{if } z = 0 \wedge c_N y = 0 \\ 1 & \text{otherwise.} \end{cases}$$

This is because $(y,z) \in N \Leftrightarrow y \in N \wedge z = 0$.

Primitive recursion on N. We can define an operator $\mathcal{R}_N$ from $\mathcal{R}$ so that

$$h = \mathcal{R}_N(f,g) \Rightarrow h(x,0) = fx \text{ and } h(x,y') = f(x,y,\ h(x,y)) \, .$$

From this one obtains recursion on N with n parameters for any $n \geq 0$. *Note.* h is total on V_0; the equations only show how $h(x,y)$ acts for $x \in V_0$, $y \in N$.

It is immediate that all number-theoretic primitive recursive functions and relations are in $\mathcal{PR}$. But also many closure conditions on $\mathcal{PR}_N$ extend to arbitrary functions. For example, we have:

Bounded quantification. With each f is associated g such that for each $y \in N$ and $x \in V_0$:

$$g(x,y) = 0 \Leftrightarrow \forall z(z < y \Rightarrow f(x,z) = 0) \, .$$

g is defined by recursion on N, with

$$g(x,0) = 0 \, , \quad g(x,y') = \begin{cases} 0 & \text{if } g(x,y) = 0 \wedge f(x,y) = 0 \\ 1 & \text{otherwise} \end{cases} \, .$$

Similarly with each f is associated g such that for each $y \in N$ and $x \in V_0$,

$$g(x,y) = 0 \Leftrightarrow \exists z(z < y \wedge f(x,z) = 0) \, .$$

Finally, we can introduce the *bounded minimum*

$$g(x,y) = (\mu z < y)f(x,z) = 0$$

for $y \in N$, $x \in V_0$.

12 Sequences

Here we follow [IPS] Section 3.3: each $x \in V_0$ represents a sequence, with 0 representing the empty sequence and if y represents $\langle y_0, \ldots, y_{n-1} \rangle$ then (y,z) represents $\langle y_0, \ldots, y_{n-1}, z \rangle$.

Sequences from a class. For each class Z, the class $Seq(Z)$, or $Z^{<\omega}$, of finite sequences, all of whose terms belong to Z, is defined as the least class X satisfying:

$$0 \in X, \qquad \frac{y \in X}{x \in X} \; x = (y,z) \wedge z \in Z.$$

That is, $Seq(Z) = \mathcal{I}_1(\{0\}, \{(x,y) | x = (y, P_2 x) \wedge P_2 x \in Z\})$. Again we have the closure and induction principles for $Z^{<\omega}$. Moreover, $Z^{<\omega}$ is $\mathcal{PR}$ in Z.

Length. This is defined for arbitrary sequences (in other words, arbitrary members of V_0) by means of the primitive recursive definition:

$$Lh0 = 0, \qquad Lh(y,z) = Lh(y) + 1.$$

Then it is proved by induction on V_0 that $Lh : V_0 \to N$. The ith term of a sequence x, denoted $Val(x,i)$, is defined recursively by

$$Val(0,i) = 0, \qquad Val((y,z),i) = \begin{cases} Val(y,i) & \text{if } i < Lh(y) \\ z & \text{otherwise} \end{cases}$$

Thus if y represents $\langle y_0, \ldots, y_{n-1} \rangle$ we have $Lh(y) = n$ and $y_i = \mathrm{Val}(y,i)$. From now on, we write $y = \langle y_0, \ldots, y_{Lh(y)-1} \rangle$ or $y = \langle y_i \rangle_{i<Lh(y)}$ for arbitrary y, considered as a finite sequence. $y = \langle z \rangle$ is used for a sequence of length 1 with $y_0 = z$.

Concatenation. Again this applies to all sequences, with $x * y$ defined recursively by

$$x * 0 = x, \qquad x * (y,z) = (x * y, z).$$

Thus $x * y = \langle x_0, \ldots, x_{Lh(x)-1}, y_0, \ldots, y_{Lh(y)-1} \rangle$ and $x * \langle z \rangle = \langle x_0, \ldots, x_{Lh(x)-1}, z \rangle = (x, z)$.

Restriction of functions to sequences ('apply-to-all'). Define $f \upharpoonright x$ recursively by:

$$f \upharpoonright 0 = 0, \qquad f \upharpoonright (y,z) = (f \upharpoonright y) * \langle fz \rangle.$$

Thus $f \upharpoonright \langle x_0, \ldots, x_{Lh(x)-1} \rangle = \langle fx_0, \ldots, fx_{Lh(x)-1} \rangle$. (In [IPS] Section 5.4 we wrote $f \circ x$ for $f \upharpoonright x$.)

Sets from sequences. Given $x = \langle x_0, \ldots, x_{n-1} \rangle$, the set $\{x_0, \ldots, x_{n-1}\}$ can be identified with the class $\{x | x = x_0 \vee \ldots \vee x = x_{n-1}\}$. However, this is not an object in V_0. We can define equivalence of sequences if they determine the same set, by $x \equiv y := [x \subseteq y \wedge y \subseteq x]$, where $x \subseteq y := \forall i < Lh(x) \, \exists j < Lh(y) [x_i = y_j]$.

13   Inductive definitions with variably many hypotheses

In practice one also meets finitary inductive definitions with no pre-assigned bound to the number of hypotheses in the rules of inference e.g. when defining the class of terms in a language with function symbols of every arity. Using the representation of sequences in the preceding section, we show how such an inductive definition $\mathcal{I}_{<\omega}$ can be reduced to $\mathcal{I}_2$.

A rule of inference R between a conclusion x and a sequence $y = \langle y_0, \ldots, y_{Lh(y)-1} \rangle$ of hypotheses is simply of the form $R(x, y)$. Then we define $\mathcal{I}_{<\omega}(R)$ to be the least X such that

(1)
$$\frac{y \in X^{<\omega}}{x \in X} \; R(x, y).$$

Note that no separate base case is necessary, as $0 \in X^{<\omega}$ is always true; thus $A = \{x | R(x, 0)\}$ takes over the base case $A \subseteq X$.

The method of reduction is given in [IPS] Section 3.4(iv) (p.102). We can take $\mathcal{I}_{<\omega}(R) = X$ for the least $\langle X, Y \rangle$ satisfying the simultaneous inductive definition

(2)
$$0 \in Y; \quad \frac{y \in Y, z \in X}{u \in Y} \; u = (y, z) ; \quad \frac{y \in Y}{x \in X} \; R(x, y) ,$$

since the least Y here is then $X^{<\omega}$. This gives $\mathcal{I}_{<\omega}(R)$ in terms of an $\mathcal{SI}_{\leq 2}$, which is reduced to $\mathcal{I}_2$ by Section 9.

In the same way we can treat a simultaneous inductive definition of $\langle X_0, \ldots, X_m \rangle$ more generally with variably many hypotheses from each X_k.

14 Transitive closure

Informally, the transitive closure of x, $TC(x)$, is the set of ys below x in the build-up of x from 0. $TC(x) = \mathcal{I}_2(\{x\}, B)$ for suitable B. But $TC(x)$ is finite and we can define a function $tc \in \mathcal{PR}$ which gives for each x a sequence $tc(x)$ enumerating $TC(x)$ as follows:

(1)
$$tc(0) = 0 , \quad tc(y, z) = tc(y) * tc(z) * \langle y, z \rangle .$$

Thus we can also define $TC(x) := \{y | \exists i < Lh(tc(x))(y = (tc(x))_i)\}$. Another useful function is

(2)
$$p\ell(y, x) := \mu i < Lh(tc(x))[y = (tc(x))_i],$$

which gives the place of y in the sequence $tc(x)$ when $y \in TC(x)$. Finally, write $y \prec x$ for $y \in TC(x)$ and $y \preceq x$ for $y \prec x \lor y = x$; this relation is primitive recursive.

Induction with respect to $\prec$. This is the principle

(3)
$$\forall x [\forall y (y \prec x \Rightarrow y \in X) \Rightarrow x \in X] \Rightarrow \forall x (x \in X) ,$$

which follows from the above definition. In addition we have:

Recursion with respect to $\prec$. Given g we can obtain h primitive recursive (uniformly) in g, such that

(4) $$hx = g(x, h \upharpoonright tc(x)) \quad \text{for all } x .$$

The idea for this is to first define $\bar{h}x = h \upharpoonright tc(x)$ for each x, so that $hx = g(x, \bar{h}x)$ for each x. $\bar{h}$ is given by the primitive recursion:

$$\bar{h}0 = 0, \quad \bar{h}(y, z) = (\bar{h}y) * (\bar{h}z) * \langle g(y, \bar{h}y), g(z, \bar{h}z) \rangle .$$

Rank. Ordinary primitive recursion serves to define the function Rnk with

$$Rnk(0) = 0, \quad Rnk(y, z) = \max(Rnk(y), Rnk(z)) + 1 .$$

Thus $Rnk(x) = $ the height of x considered as a binary branching tree. We have $Rnk : V_0 \to N$ and $y \prec x \Rightarrow Rnk(y) < Rnk(x)$. There are only finitely many y with $Rnk(y) \leq Rnk(x)$. (Note that this is not true for the corresponding rank function on $V = U^*$ when we have an arbitrary class of urelements.) We can define a primitive recursive function on N which gives for each n a pair of sequences (r_n, r'_n) where r_n enumerates $\{x | Rnk(x) \leq n\}$ and r'_n enumerates $\{x | Rnk(x) = n\}$, since $\{x | Rnk(x) \leq n + 1\} = \{(y, z) | Rnk(y) \leq n \wedge Rnk(z) \leq n\}$ and $\{x | Rnk(x) = n + 1\} = \{(y, z) | (Rnk(y) \leq n \wedge Rnk(z) = n) \vee (Rnk(y) = n \wedge Rnk(z) \leq n)\}$.

15   Trees and derivations

In order to explain derivations for inductive definitions, we introduce *finitely branching labelled trees*. As all the inductive definitions dealt with here reduce to $\mathcal{I}_2$, it is sufficient to deal with *binary branching labelled trees*. The more general notion is treated in [IPS], pp.110–111, but the special case is simpler to deal with in certain respects.

The informal idea is that $(0, z)$ represents a tree with single node labelled z, and if y_1, y_2 represent (binary) trees then $x = ((y_1, y_2), z)$ represents the tree with label z at its tip and immediate subtrees y_1, y_2. Thus $Tree_2$ is the least X satisfying the closure conditions:

(1) $$(0, z) \in X \text{ for all } z ; \quad \frac{y_1, y_2 \in X}{x \in X} \, x = ((y_1, y_2), P_2 x).$$

The label of any $x \in Tree_2$ is just $P_2 x$, and its immediate subtrees are $y_i = P_i P_1 x$ when $P_1 x \neq 0$. Since each $y_i \prec x$ in the latter case, *recursion on trees* is just a special case of recursion with respect to $\prec$, in the following form.

(2)   For each f, g we can find h primitive recursive (uniformly) in f, g with $h(0, z) = fz$, and $h((y_1, y_2), z) = g(y_1, y_2, z, hy_1, hy_2)$.

In particular, we can define the *height* $|x|$ of tree by

(3) $|(0, z)| = 1, \quad |((y_1, y_2), z)| = \max(|y_1|, |y_2|) + 1$.

Given A, B we define the class $D(A, B) \subseteq Tree_2$ of $\mathcal{I}_2(A, B)$-derivations as the least X which satisfies the following closure conditions:

(4)   (i) $(0, x) \in X$ for each $x \in A$,

(ii) $\dfrac{d_1, d_2 \in X}{d \in X} \; B(P_2d, P_2d_1, P_2d_2) \wedge d = ((d_1, d_2), P_2d)$.

When $d \in D(A, B)$ and $P_2d = x$ we write $Der_{(A,B)}(d, x)$, or $d \vdash_{(A,B)} x$ or simply $d \vdash x$. (4(i)) expresses that when $x \in A$, the tree d with single node 0 and label x has $d \vdash x$, and (4(ii)) expresses that if $d_1 \vdash y_1$ and $d_2 \vdash y_2$ and $B(x, y_1, y_2)$ then the tree $d = ((d_1, d_2), x)$ has $d \vdash x$. It is thus seen that

(5) $x \in \mathcal{I}_2(A, B) \Leftrightarrow \exists d(d \in D(A, B) \wedge d \vdash x)$
              $\Leftrightarrow \exists d(d \in D(A, B) \wedge P_2d = x)$.

It will be shown in the next section that $D(A, B)$ is primitive recursive (uniformly) in A, B.

16   Deterministic and decidable inductive definitions

For implementation of logics on computers, we need to know that various syntactic classes dealt with are algorithmically decidable. We show how to do this for certain inductively defined classes of $\mathcal{I}_2$ form (see [IPS], pp.111–112 for the more general case $\mathcal{I}_{<\omega}$).

An inductive definition $\mathcal{I}_2(A, B)$ is said to be *deterministic* if for each $x \in \mathcal{I}_2(A, B)$ there is a unique $d \in D(A, B)$ with $d \vdash x$. A n.a.s.c. for this is that

(1) $\forall x \in \mathcal{I}_2(A, B)\{x \in A \vee \exists! y_1, y_2[y_1, y_2 \in \mathcal{I}_2(A, B) \wedge B(x, y_1, y_2)]\}$

Now for (1) it is *sufficient* that we have *predecessor functions* f_1, f_2 for B, in the sense that:

(2) $B(x, y_1, y_2) \Rightarrow y_1 = f_1x \wedge y_2 = f_2x$.

In this case, $\mathcal{I}_2(A, B)$ is called *functionally deterministic; f_1, f_2* are called *transitive predecessor functions* if (2) holds and

$$(3) \qquad\qquad B(x, y_1, y_2) \Rightarrow y_1 \prec x \wedge y_2 \prec x .$$

Theorem 16.1 *If B has transitive predecessor functions f_1, f_2 then $\mathcal{I}_2(A, B)$ is primitive recursive (uniformly) in A, B, f_1, f_2.*

PROOF. Let $J = \mathcal{I}_2(A, B)$. Its characteristic function c_J is defined by the $\prec$ recursion

$$c_J x = \begin{cases} 0 & \text{if } x \in A \text{ or } [B(x, f_1 x, f_2 x) \wedge c_J(f_1 x) = c_J(f_2 x) = 0] \\ 1 & \text{otherwise} . \end{cases}$$

∎

Corollary 16.2 *For each A, B, the class $D(A, B)$ of $\mathcal{I}_2(A, B)$-derivations is primitive recursive in A, B.*

PROOF. By the preceding section,

$$D(A, B) = \mathcal{I}_2(A', B'),$$

with $A' = \{(0, x) | x \in A\}$ and $B' = \{(d, d_1, d_2) | B(P_2 d, P_2 d_1, P_2 d_2) \wedge d = ((d_1, d_2), P_2 d)\}$. This has the $\mathcal{PR}$ transitive predecessor functions $f_1 d = P_1 P_1 d$, $f_2 d = P_2 P_1 d$. ∎

Note. The facts that $N \in \mathcal{PR}$ (Section 11), and that $A^{<\omega}$ is $\mathcal{PR}$ in A (Section 12), both follow from the theorem above.

We can carry out definition by recursion on classes $\mathcal{I}_2(A, B)$ satisfying the hypothesis of the theorem, so that for each g_1, g_2 we obtain h primitive recursive in g_1, g_2 with

$$h(x) = \begin{cases} g_1 x & \text{for } x \in A, \\ g_2(x, h(f_1 x), h(f_2 x)) & \text{for each } x \in \mathcal{I}_2(A, B) \text{ with } x \notin A. \end{cases}$$

This is again a special case of $\prec$-recursion.

17 The axiomatic theory FS_0 for functions and classes of expressions

We now set up a formal system FS_0 in which all the preceding work may be formalized directly. The language $L(FS_0)$ of this system is three-sorted, for *individuals, functions,* and *classes.* The symbols used for various entities in FS_0 will be similar to those used in the informal development Sections

2–16, except that we use Roman letters instead of italics; however, we shall still use script letters for the compounding functionals. Thus we use a, b, c, u, v, w, x, y, z for individual variables, f, g, h for function variables and A, B, C, X, Y, Z for class variables (in all cases with or without subscripts).[6] We denote by $InTm$ the class of *individual terms* (for which we use s, t,...), by $FnTm$ the class of *function terms* (F, G,...) and by $ClTm$ the class of *class terms* (R, S, T,...). $InTm$ and $FnTm$ are defined simultaneously as the smallest classes satisfying:

$InTm$

(i) Each individual variable is in $InTm$.

(ii) The constant $\bar{0}$ is in $InTm$.

(iii) If $t_1, t_2 \in InTm$ then $(t_1, t_2) \in InTm$.

(iv) If $F \in FnTm$ and $t \in InTm$ then $Ft \in InTm$.

$FnTm$

(i) Each function variable is in $FnTm$.

(ii) The constants I, D, P_1, P_2 are in $FnTm$.

(iii) If $t \in InTm$ then $K(t) \in FnTm$.

(iv) If $F, G \in FnTm$ then $\mathcal{P}(F, G), \mathcal{C}(F, G), \mathcal{R}(F, G) \in FnTm$.

Then $ClTm$ is defined as the smallest class satisfying:

$ClTm$

(i) Each class variable is in $ClTm$.

(ii) The constant $\{\bar{0}\} \in ClTm$.

(iii) If $F \in FnTm$ and $S \in ClTm$ then $F^{-1}S \in ClTm$.

(iv) If $S, T \in ClTm$ then $S \cap T, S \cup T$ and $\mathcal{I}_2(S, T) \in ClTm$.

The *atomic formulas* of $L(FS_0)$ are just those of the form $(t_1 = t_2)$ with $t_1, t_2 \in InTm$, and $t \in S$ with $t \in InTm$ and $S \in ClTm$.

The class of *formulas* $(\phi, \psi, \theta, \ldots)$ is the least class containing the atomic formulas and closed under $\neg, \wedge, \vee, \rightarrow, \forall, \exists$ (applied to variables of any sort). The underlying logic of FS_0 is that of three-sorted classical predicate calculus with $=$ in the first sort only.

---

[6]These are not the 'official' lists of variables.

Remark. We regard F = G as defined by $\forall x[Fx = Gx]$, and S = T as defined by $\forall x[x \in S \leftrightarrow x \in T]$. We could add = as a basic symbol in both these sorts and then take these (extensionality) statements as axioms.

The abbreviations introduced in Section 1 and Section 2 are also used in FS_0 and we write $S \subseteq T$ for $\forall x(x \in S \to x \in T)$.

AXIOMS OF FS_0

1. *Pairing, projections*

    1. (i)$(x_1, x_2) \neq \bar{0}$,

    2. (ii)$P_1(x_1, x_2) = x_1$, $P_2(x_1, x_2) = x_2$.

2. *Basic function axioms*

    (i) $Ix = x$.

    (ii) $K(a)x = a$.

    (iii) $[x_1 = x_2 \to D(x_1, x_2, y_1, y_2) = y_1] \wedge$
        $[x_1 \neq x_2 \to D(x_1, x_2, y_1, y_2) = y_2] \wedge$
        $(\neg \exists x_1, x_2, y_1, y_2[u = (x_1, x_2, y_1, y_2)] \to Du = \bar{0})$.

3. *Compound function axioms*

    (i) $h = \mathcal{P}(f, g) \to \forall x[hx = (fx, gx)]$,

    (ii) $h = \mathcal{C}(f, g) \to \forall x[hx = f(gx)]$.

4. *Recursion axiom*

    $h = \mathcal{R}(f, g) \to h\bar{0} = \bar{0} \wedge \forall x[h(x, \bar{0}) = fx]$
                     $\wedge \forall x, y, z[h(x, (y, z)) = g(x, y, z, h(x, y), h(x, z))]$

5. *Explicit class construction axioms*

    (i) $x \in \{\bar{0}\} \leftrightarrow x = \bar{0}$,

    (ii) $x \in f^{-1}A \leftrightarrow fx \in A$,

    (iii) $x \in A \cap B \leftrightarrow x \in A \wedge x \in B$,

    (iv) $x \in A \cup B \leftrightarrow x \in A \vee x \in B$.

6. *Inductive generation axiom*

  (i) $C = \mathcal{I}_2(A, B) \to A \subseteq C \wedge$
    $\wedge \forall x, y_1, y_2[y_1 \in C \wedge y_2 \in C \wedge (x, y_1, y_2) \in B \to x \in C]$,

(ii) $C = \mathcal{I}_2(A, B) \wedge A \subseteq X$
$\wedge \forall x, y_1, y_2[y_1 \in X \wedge y_2 \in X \wedge (x, y_1, y_2) \in B \rightarrow x \in X]$
$\rightarrow C \subseteq X$.

7. *Induction on the universe*

$$\bar{0} \in X \wedge \forall x, y[x \in X \wedge y \in X \rightarrow (x, y) \in X] \rightarrow \forall x(x \in X).$$

This completes the description of FS_0. We shall also consider the subsystem EFS_0 obtained by deleting the $\mathcal{R}$-operator and axiom 4.

18   Models and presentations

The standard model for Axioms 1 and 7 is the structure $\mathcal{V}_0 = \langle V_0, P, P_1, P_2, 0 \rangle$. We shall not be concerned here with non-standard models. The function axioms 2, 3 are satisfied by any $\mathcal{E}$-closed collection of functions $f : V_0 \rightarrow V_0$, in particular by $\mathcal{E}$ itself. Axioms 2–4 are satisfied by any $\mathcal{PR}$-closed collection of functions.[7] Axiom 5 is satisfied by any $\mathcal{E}^+$-closed collection of classes in EFS_0, and any $\mathcal{PR}^+$-closed collection of classes in FS_0 . Axiom 6 is satisfied in any collection of classes closed under $\mathcal{I}_2$. In particular, the class axioms are satisfied by $\mathcal{IND}$ (the least $\mathcal{PR}^+$-closed $\mathcal{K}$ which is closed under $\mathcal{I}_2$).

The minimal model of FS_0 is thus given by $\mathcal{V}_0, \mathcal{PR}$ and $\mathcal{IND}$. We shall use $[\![\cdot]\!]$ to associate with each formal term its corresponding informal interpretation in this model. A term of any sort is called *closed* if it contains no variables of any sort.

Each closed individual term t denotes an element $[\![t]\!]$ of V_0, and each $a \in V_0$ is denoted by a closed individual term $\bar{a}$, given by $\overline{(a, b)} = (\bar{a}, \bar{b})$; thus $[\![\bar{a}]\!] = a$.

Each closed function term F of FS_0 denotes a function $[\![F]\!]$ in $\mathcal{PR}$. We call F a *presentation of* $[\![F]\!]$. The term F shows exactly how $[\![F]\!]$ is built up from the basic functions by the compounding functionals.

Each closed class term S of FS_0 denotes a class $[\![S]\!]$ in $\mathcal{IND}$. We call S a *presentation of* $[\![S]\!]$. Again, the term S shows exactly how $[\![S]\!]$ is obtained by the explicit and inductive class construction axioms.

By a *presentation of a finitary inductive system* Σ (of signature σ), we mean a presentation of a pair $(\langle A_i \rangle_{i \leq m}, \langle R_j \rangle_{j \leq p})$ of classes specifying (with σ) the closure conditions for Σ.

---

[7]The operation $a \mapsto K(a)$, from individuals to functions, was not needed in $\mathcal{PR}$ since for each $a \in V_0$ we have $K(a) = K_a \in \mathcal{PR}$. However, if we just took K_0 in the axioms, we would not be able to define K(a) with 'a' variable. The latter is necessary if we are to prove that for each term t[x], $\exists f \forall x(fx = t[x])$, as well as recursion with no parameters.

19 Primitive recursive and inductive completeness of FS_0

C-$InTm(C$-$FnTm, C$-$ClTm)$ denotes the class of closed individual (function, class) terms. C-$InTm$ and C-$FnTm$ are obtained by a simultaneous inductive definition simply by omitting the basis condition for variables in Section 16; similarly for C-$ClTm$.

Lemma 19.1 *If $a, b \in V_0$ and $a \neq b$ then $EFS_0 \vdash \bar{a} \neq \bar{b}$.*

Theorem 19.2

(i) *If $t \in C$-$InTm$ and $[\![t]\!] = a$ then $FS_0 \vdash t = \bar{a}$.*

(ii) *If $F \in C$-$FnTm$ and $[\![F]\!]a = b$ then $FS_0 \vdash F\bar{a} = \bar{b}$.*

PROOF. This is carried out by induction on the simultaneous generation of C-$InTm$ and C-$FnTm$. In the cases where F has the form $\mathcal{R}(G, H)$, we carry out a subsidiary induction on its argument $a \in V_0$. ∎

Corollary 19.3

(i) *For each $t \in C$-$InTm$ there exists a with $FS_0 \vdash t = \bar{a}$*

(ii) *For each $F \in C$-$FnTm$ and each a there exists b with $FS_0 \vdash F\bar{a} = \bar{b}$.*

Note: the corollary may be proved directly without appeal to the semantic interpretations $[\![\cdot]\!]$.

Theorem 19.4 *If $S \in C$-$ClTm$ and $a \in [\![S]\!]$ then $FS_0 \vdash (\bar{a} \in S)$.*

PROOF. This is carried out by induction on the generation of C-$ClTm$. In the case where $S = \mathcal{I}_2(T, R)$ we have a subsidiary induction on the inductive generation of $[\![S]\!]$ from $[\![T]\!]$ by the rule $[\![R]\!]$. ∎

Similar results hold for EFS_0, when the terms are restricted to $L(EFS_0)$.

20 Functional and class abstraction

By the class of $\exists^+$-formulas of FS_0 we mean the smallest class which contains all equations $t_1 = t_2$, inequalities $t_1 \neq t_2$, as well as atomic formulas of the form $t \in T$ (t, t_1, t_2 individual terms, and T a class term), and closed under $\wedge, \vee,$ and $\exists x$ applied to any individual variable.

Theorem 20.1

(i) For each individual term t *with free variables included in* $\{x_1, \ldots, x_n\}$ *we can find a closed function term* F_t *such that*

$$FS_0 \vdash F_t(x_1, \ldots, x_n) = t \ .$$

(ii) For each function term G *with free variables included in* $\{x_1, \ldots, x_n\}$ *we can find a closed function term* F_G *such that*

$$FS_0 \vdash F_G(x_1, \ldots, x_n, y) = Gy \ .$$

(iii) For each $\exists^+$*-formula* ϕ *with free variables included in* $\{x_1, \ldots, x_n\}$ *we can find a closed class term* S_ϕ *such that*

$$FS_0 \vdash (x_1, \ldots, x_n) \in S_\phi \leftrightarrow \phi \ .$$

PROOF. Parts (i) and (ii) proceed by simultaneous induction. For part (iii), the essential new point is closure under $\exists$. This comes from the following observation. Given any B, we can define $\{x|\exists y B(x, y)\}$ as $Q_1^{-1}X$ where X is the least class satisfying:

$$(x, 0) \in X \text{ for all } x \ ; \quad \frac{(y, 0) \in X}{(x, 1) \in X} \ (x, y) \in B \ . \blacksquare$$

Remark 20.2 We may regard F_t as $\lambda(x_1, \ldots, x_n)t$, F_G as $\lambda(x_1, \ldots, x_n, y)$ Gy, and S_ϕ as $\{(x_1, \ldots, x_n)|\phi\}$.

21 Proof-theoretical strength of FS_0

By formalizing the inductive definition of the class N of natural numbers (Section 11) and the treatment of $\mathcal{PR}_N$ in terms of $\mathcal{PR}$, we can interpret the system *PRA* of primitive recursive arithmetic in FS_0. Moreover, the fragment Σ_1^0-*IA* of (first-order) Peano arithmetic based on *PRA* and the Σ_1^0-induction axiom are also contained in FS_0 under this interpretation. For, every Σ_1^0-formula is equivalent to an $\exists^+$-formula, and each such defines a class by Section 20. Since the induction axiom for N in the form

$$0 \in X \wedge \forall x(x \in X \rightarrow x' \in X) \rightarrow N \subseteq X$$

is a consequence of the induction axiom 7 for the universe, it follows that we have the induction scheme for all $\exists^+$-formulas.

Now it can also be shown that FS_0 is interpretable in Σ_1^0-*IA*. The idea for this is that we interpret individual, function, and class variables all as ranging over ω, with the pairing and projection functions taken to be primitive recursive with $(x, y) \neq 0$. We interpret fx as $[f](x)$ where the enumeration $[f]$ of primitive recursive functions is defined in terms of the more general enumeration $\{z\}$ of partial recursive functions. Finally $x \in z$ is interpreted as $\{z\}(x)\!\downarrow$, i.e. as $x \in W_z (= \{u | \exists y T_1(z, u, y)\})$.

These kinds of arguments lead to the following.

Theorem 21.1 FS_0 *is of the same proof-theoretical strength as* $(\Sigma_1^0\text{-}IA)$, *and hence of PRA.*[8]

Comparison with the system FM_0, and correction to [IPS]. The system FM_0 in [IPS] used only individual terms built up by pairing and projections, and class terms built up by class comprehension for $\exists^+$-formulas together with $\mathcal{I}_2$ inductive generation. FM_0 is easily seen to be a subsystem of FS_0, in fact already of EFS_0.[9] It was claimed in IPS that FM_0 contains the system $\Sigma_1^0\text{-}IA$. The idea was first to define a general recursion theory over the universe by means of an inductively defined three-placed relation $xy \simeq z$, and then to obtain primitive recursion as a special case. However, the unicity property for $\simeq$,

$$xy \simeq z_1 \wedge xy \simeq z_2 \rightarrow z_1 = z_2 \,,$$

in Section 3.5(vi) (p.102) of [IPS], does not seem to follow from FM_0 as asserted there. FM_0 can be expanded by a basic relation symbol $\simeq$ with the statements Section 3.5(i)–(vi) of [IPS] as axioms to give a system FM_0^* which *is* equivalent to $\Sigma_1^0\text{-}IA$. For, we can interpret $xy \simeq z$ via $\{x\}(y) \simeq z$ in o.r.t. Instead, we have chosen here to incorporate the primitive recursion part of the recursion theory into the formalism of FS_0. This is more intuitive and closer to the needs of logical practice.

It would be of interest to determine the exact proof-theoretical strength of the systems FM_0 and EFS_0 .

22   Finitary inductively presented logics

In the most general sense, a formal logic is just a finitary inductive system Σ, and a *finitary inductively presented (f.i.p.) logic* is just a presented finitary inductive system i.e. one represented by a class term S of FS_0 . By carrying out the arguments of Sections 9–10 in FS_0 , we can even take S in the normal form $Q_0^{-1} \mathcal{I}_2(T, R)$ where T, R are primitive recursive class terms.

---

[8]Parsons, [17] proved that $(\Sigma_1^0 - IA)$ and PRA are of the same proof-theoretical strength.

[9]The universe of FM_0 is U^* for an unspecified class U of urelements, with $0 \in U$.

Some among the variety of logics that are met in practice have been mentioned in the introduction. These can all be regarded as f.i.p. logics in the above sense and can be reasoned about in FS_0 . Notions and results about wide classes of logics might be considered to be part of the subject of meta-logic; these can also be formulated in FS_0 at various levels of generality. For example, one might study closure conditions on rules of inference (or consequence relations, as in [1]), the difference between derived rules and admissible rules, notions of schematic axioms and rules, interpretation of one logic into another, etc.

For illustrative purposes and to get quickly to Gödel's incompleteness theorems, we shall limit ourselves in the following to a very special case, namely logics based on many-sorted, first-order classical predicate calculus with equality (in some sorts). A number of details for the single-sorted case have been given in [IPS] Section 6 (pp.114–119) and will not be repeated here.[10] First one defines (in FS_0) the classes Var, Const, Fun and Rel of variables, constants, function symbols and relation symbols of arbitrary arities; these are all given explicitly. (In the many-sorted case these are supplemented by the class Sort of sorts, and arities are sequences from Sort.) By a *language* is meant an arbitrary subclass L of Const∪Fun∪Rel containing the relation symbol $r_{0,2}$ for equality. Note that L is treated as a variable class in FS_0. Then one defines Term(L), Atom(L) and Form(L) inductively, all of which have $\mathcal{PR}$ transitive predecessor functions and hence (by Section 13 and Section 16) are $\mathcal{PR}$ in L. Next one defines the general notions of being a free variable, and of being a term free for a variable in a formula, and the operation Sub of substitution of a term for a variable in a term or formula; Sub is defined by $\prec$-recursion and is primitive recursive. Finally one defines the ($\mathcal{PR}$) class LogAx of logical axioms, and takes LogAx(L)=LogAx∩Form(L), the class of *logical axioms in* L, which is $\mathcal{PR}$ in L. For the formulation of predicate calculus in [IPS], only two rules of inference were used: *modus ponens* (MP) and *universal generalization* (UG); these relations are in $\mathcal{E}$.

By an *axiomatic system* is meant a pair $S = \langle L, A \rangle$ where L is a language and $A \subseteq$ Form(L). A is considered to be the class of 'non-logical' *axioms of* S, denoted $A = Ax(S)$, and L is denoted L(S). Again L, A, S are treated as arbitrary (variable) classes in FS_0, subject to the given restrictions. The class Proof(S) is defined as the class of derivation trees for the class Prov(S) = $\mathcal{I}_2$(LogAx(L) ∪ Ax(S), MP ∪ UG); by Sections 15 and 16, Proof(S) is $\mathcal{PR}$ in S and

$$a \in \text{Prov}(S) \leftrightarrow \exists d[d \in \text{Proof}(S) \wedge a = P_2 d] \ .$$

---

[10]In IPS it was assumed that the class U of urelements contains eight basic symbols '0', 'v', 'c', 'f', 'r', '¬', '→', '∀'; these would be replaced here by '0',..., '7', resp.

We also write $\mathrm{Proof}_S(d, a)$ for $d \in \mathrm{Proof}(S) \wedge a = P_2 d$, and $\mathrm{Prov}_S(a)$ or $S \vdash a$ for $a \in \mathrm{Prov}(S)$.

Examples of elementary meta-logical theorems about $\mathrm{Prov}(S)$ which can be proved in FS_0 for arbitrary (variable) S are the deduction theorem and the finiteness theorem.

An axiomatic system is said to be *inductively presented* if it is given by a specific closed class term **S** of FS_0. In this case, all the notions leading up to $\mathrm{Prov}(\mathbf{S})$ are also f.i.p. **S** is said to be p.r.p. if it is given in the form $\mathbf{S} = \mathbf{F}^{-1}\{\bar{0}\} (= \{x|\mathbf{F}x = \bar{0}\})$ for a closed function term **F**; then all the notions leading up to $\mathrm{Proof}(\mathbf{S})$ are also p.r.p., while $\mathrm{Prov}(\mathbf{S})$ is f.i.p.

23 Gödel's incompleteness theorems for finitary inductively presented extensions of FS_0

With the notions of Section 22 suitably expanded to the many-sorted case, it is seen that FS_0 is itself a p.r.p. logic given by a $\mathcal{PR}$ class term $\mathbf{FS_0}$ of FS_0 .[11] Gödel's incompleteness theorems are formulated here for arbitrary, finitary, inductively presented extensions $S = \langle L, A \rangle$ of FS_0, given by a closed class term $\mathbf{S} = \langle \mathbf{L}, \mathbf{A} \rangle$. Each member ϕ of $Form(L)$ is identified with an element of V_0. Then $\bar{\phi}$ is the canonical closed term of $L(FS_0)$ which denotes ϕ. The function Sb which associates with each ϕ and a the result $Sb(\phi, a) = \phi(\bar{a})$ of substituting $\bar{a}$ for the variable x (or v_0) in ϕ, is in $\mathcal{PR}$, presented by a function term Sb. In particular, given $\phi(x)$ we can form $\psi(x) = \phi(Sb(x, x))$, so that for $\chi = \psi(\bar{\psi}) = Sb(\psi, \psi)$, we have

$$(1) \qquad\qquad FS_0 \vdash \chi \leftrightarrow \phi(\bar{\chi}) .$$

This gives the first ingredient of the incompleteness theorems, the construction of 'self-referential' statements. The second ingredient is the inductive completeness of FS_0 from Section 19, which is specialized here to $\mathrm{Prov}(\mathbf{S})$:

$$(2) \qquad\qquad S \vdash \phi \text{ implies } FS_0 \vdash \mathrm{Prov}_\mathbf{S}(\bar{\phi}) .$$

For Gödel's *First Incompleteness Theorem*, we apply (1) to form $\chi_\mathbf{S}$ with

$$(3) \qquad\qquad FS_0 \vdash \chi_\mathbf{S} \leftrightarrow \neg\mathrm{Prov}_\mathbf{S}(\bar{\chi}_\mathbf{S}) .$$

Then by the usual argument we have:

Theorem 23.1 *If* $S = [\![\mathbf{S}]\!]$ *is a consistent extension of* FS_0 *then* $S \not\vdash \chi_\mathbf{S}$.[12]

---

[11]In fact, $Ax(FS_0)$ is finite.

[12]This is the first half of Gödel's first incompleteness theorem; the second half is that if S is correct for statements of the form $\mathrm{Prov}_\mathbf{S}(\bar{\phi})$ then $S \not\vdash \neg\chi_\mathbf{S}$.

Let $\text{Con}_\mathbf{S} = \neg\text{Prov}_\mathbf{S}(\overline{\phi})$, for $\phi = \neg(\overline{0} = \overline{0})$, be the canonical consistency statement associated with the presentation $\mathbf{S}$ of S. Then what must be shown for Gödel's *Second Incompleteness Theorem* is:

Theorem 23.2 $FS_0 \vdash \text{Con}_\mathbf{S} \to \neg\text{Prov}_\mathbf{S}(\overline{\chi}_\mathbf{S})$, *for* $S = [\![\mathbf{S}]\!]$ *extending* FS_0 .

For the proof of Theorem 23.2 we need to formalize (2) in FS_0 and for this more generally we need to formalize Theorem 19.4. The details of that require a more extended presentation than is possible here. Only one point should be noted. In the proof of Theorem 19.4 we are carrying out a double induction, first on the closed class terms of FS_0 and then on $[\![\mathcal{I}_2(A, B)]\!]$ for each inductive class term. However, for fixed $\mathbf{S}$ there are only a finite number of subterms that must be considered, and so we are reduced to a finite number of individual inductions. Alternatively, using the normal form theorem of Section 10, we can reduce the inductive argument to a single one. Prior to that, one must establish a formal version of the primitive recursive completeness theorem of FS_0 (Theorem 19.2); again, only a finite number of inductions need to be made for each specific function.

24 Where do we go from here?

Returning to the three basic aims that we set for this work in the introduction—conceptual, pedagogical, and practical (computational)—what has been accomplished here lies mainly in providing a conceptual framework, with indications in the preceding paragraph, how this would be spelled out for a pedagogically reasonable exposition of Gödel's incompleteness theorems. That should be carried out in detail and extended to include other results in the 'arithmetization of metamathematics' and proof theory, for example concerning provable reflection principles (cf. [14, 22]), and proof-theoretical conservation results (cf. [9]). The use of infinitary methods in proof theory for which finitary formalizations can be given requires particular attention (cf. [7, pp. 93–95], and [19]). Another step into the transfinite, for which finitary treatments can be given (at least, in part) is provided by the iteration of (non-provable) reflection principles in recursive progressions of theories ([5, 6]). I believe that FS_0 provides a natural framework in which to re-develop these topics in a proper way. Finally, there should be an extension of FS_0 to a theory of *infinitely* branching trees (with primitive recursive functions and inductive classes of such) which would serve as a natural framework in which to formalize essentially infinitary logics, using inductive systems with infinitary closure conditions.

In another direction, one can form a non-finitist extension FS_1 of FS_0 (analogous to the extension FM_1 of FM_0 in [IPS]) by adding complementation as an operation on classes; the resulting system is a conservative extension of *PA*. As sketched in [IPS] Section 8, much countable model theory can be formalized in FS_1, in fact already in $FS_0 + WKL$ (Weak König's Lemma). The conservation result of Friedman for $\Sigma_1^0\text{-}IA + WKL$ over *PRA* gives conservation of $FS_0 + WKL$ over *PRA*, as can be established directly by finitist methods (e.g. those of Sieg [20]). But already in FS_0 and closely related systems one can develop non-trivial parts of countable model theory, thus generalizing portions of recursive model theory. Systematic work in this direction is being carried out by my doctoral student, Paolo Mancosu.

Finally, on the computational front, the work of Section 15 establishes implementability in principle, but clearly this is only the beginning. Whether implementation is feasible and what its value might be can only be judged by actually trying to carry it out. Good test cases for general topics are provided by the examples considered for the ELF project (cf. [2]). Elaboration of the preceding section could provide another test case, and here one has the work of Shankar [21] for an interesting comparison.

Added in proof

Following the original publication of this article in 1988, progress was made on several of the proposals in Section 24. The work of P. Mancosu mentioned there resulted in a PhD dissertation at Stanford University in 1989 and was later published as Mancosu [26]. The article Buchholz [24] provides one elegant way of carrying out the finitary formalization of infinitary proof theory. Finally, the paper [25] by Matthews, Smaill and Basin; and Chapter 13 in this volume by Matthews deal with questions of implementation of the system FS_0 as a logical framework and demonstrate its basic feasibility for that purpose.

References

[1] A. Avron, *Simple consequence relations*, LFCS Report Series 87–30, Laboratory for Foundations of Computer Science, University of Edinburgh, 1987.

[2] A. Avron, F.A. Honsell, and I.A. Mason, *Using typed lambda calculus to implement formal systems on a machine*, LFCS Report Series 87–31, Laboratory for Foundations of Computer Science, University of Edinburgh, 1987.

[3] J. Barwise and S. Feferman (eds.), *Model-theoretic logics*, (Springer-Verlag, Berlin), 1985.

[4] S. Feferman, Arithmetization of metamathematics in a general setting, *Fundamenta mathematica* **49**, 35–92, 1960.

[5] S. Feferman, Transfinite recursive progressions of axiomatic theories, *J. Symbolic Logic* **27**, 259–316, 1962.

[6] S. Feferman, Systems of predicative analysis, *J. Symbolic Logic* **29**, 1–30, 1964.

[7] S. Feferman, Lectures on proof theory, *Lecture Notes in Mathematics*, **70**, 1–107, 1967.

[8] S. Feferman, Inductively presented systems and the formalization of meta-mathematics, in *Logic Colloquium '80* (D. van Dalen *et al* eds., North-Holland, Amsterdam), pp. 95–128, 1982.

[9] S. Feferman, Hilbert's program relativized: proof-theoretical and foundational reductions, *J. Symbolic Logic*, **53**, 364–384, 1988.

[10] M. Fitting, *Computability theory, semantics and logic programming*, (Oxford University Press, New York), 1987.

[11] K. Gödel, *Collected Works, Volume I. Publications 1929–1936* (S. Feferman *et al*, eds., Oxford University Press, New York), 1986.

[12] R. Harper, F. Honsell and G. Plotkin, A framework for defining logics. In *Proc. Second Annual Conference on Logic and Computer Science*, Cornell 1987, pp. 193–204, IEEE, 1987.

[13] G. Kreisel, Mathematical logic, in *Lectures on Modern Mathematics III* (T. L. Saaty, ed., Wiley, New York), pp. 95–195, 1965.

[14] G. Kreisel and A. Levy, Reflection principles and their use for establishing the complexity of axiomatic systems, *Zeitschrift f. Mathematische Logik u. Grundlagen d. Mathematik* **14**, 97–142, 1968.

[15] Y. Moschovakis, Abstract first-order computability I, *Trans. Amer. Math. Soc.*, **138**, 427–464, 1969.

[16] Y. Moschovakis, Abstract recursion as a foundation for the theory of algorithms, *Lecture Notes in Mathematics*, vol. 1104, pp. 289–364, 1984.

[17] C. Parsons, On a number-theoretic choice schema and its relation to induction, in *Intuitionism and Proof Theory* (eds. J. Myhill *et al*, North-Holland, Amsterdam), pp. 459–474, 1970.

[18] E. Post, Formal reductions of the general combinatorial decision problem, *Amer. J. Math.*, **65**, 197–214, 1943.

[19] H. Schwichtenberg, Proof theory: some applications of cut-elimination, in *Handbook of Mathematical Logic* (J. Barwise ed., North-Holland, Amsterdam), pp. 867–895, 1977.

[20] W. Sieg, Fragments of arithmetic, *Annals of Pure and Applied Logic*, **28**, 33–72, 1985.

[21] N. Shankar, Towards mechanical metamathematics, *J. Automated Reasoning*, **1**, 407–434, 1985.

[22] C. Smorynski, The incompleteness theorems, in *Handbook of Mathematical Logic* (J. Barwise ed., North-Holland, Amsterdam), pp. 821–865, 1977.

[23] R. Smullyan, *Theory of formal systems* (Princeton University Press, Princeton), 1961.

[24] W. Buchholz, Notation systems for infinitary derivations, *Archive for Mathematical Logic*, **30**, 277–296, 1991.

[25] S. Matthews, A. Smaill, and D. Basin, Experience with FS_0 as framework theory, in *Logical Environments*, (eds. G. Huet and G. Plotkin) Cambridge University Press, Cambridge, pp. 61–82, 1993.

[26] P. Mancosu, Generalizing classical and effective model theory in theories of operations and classes, *Annals of Pure and Applied Logic*, **52**, 249–308, 1991.

13

A Theory and its Metatheory in FS_0

Seán Matthews

1 Introduction

Feferman, in the previous chapter, has proposed FS_0, a theory of finitary inductive systems, as a framework theory that allows a user to reason both in and about an encoded theory. I look here at how practical FS_0 really is. To this end I formalise a sequent calculus presentation of classical propositional logic, and show this can be used for work in both the theory and the metatheory. The latter is illustrated with a discussion of a proof of Gentzen's Hauptsatz.

1.1 Background

In order to be easier to use, proof development systems provide a range of facilities such as 'lemmas', tactic languages and uniform proof procedures, so that the work of building proofs can be automated as much as possible. For the most part, in fact, formal derivations of 'real' theorems can be built only because of such facilities, since they are so big that it is not practical for the user of a system to enter every atomic step by hand. In fact a lot of proofs are in essence not very big; most of the size of a formal derivation represents the work of fitting the original intuition into the given theory. A tactic language, or other similar facility, is a way for the user to automate some of this work, leaving him free to concentrate on the important parts of proofs, and also, incidentally, to speed things up, since a machine can usually build derivations much more quickly and reliably than a user manually entering rules.

Mathematics is not done with a proof development system in quite the same way as it is done in a textbook, even when the two look like one another. For instance in a book on algebra one might read

'If A is an abelian group, then, for all a, b in A, the equivalence

$$\overbrace{(a \circ b) \circ \cdots \circ (a \circ b)}^{n \text{ times}} = \overbrace{(a \circ \cdots \circ a)}^{n \text{ times}} \circ \overbrace{(b \circ \cdots \circ b)}^{n \text{ times}},$$

holds'

followed by a proof. This allows another, subsequent, proof to go, in one step,

$$
\begin{aligned}
a &= (b \circ c) \circ (b \circ c) \circ (b \circ c) \\
&= (b \circ b \circ b) \circ (c \circ c \circ c),
\end{aligned}
$$

with the step justified by an appeal to the theorem proved earlier. On the other hand, instead of a book, imagine a proof development system for algebra; there the theorem cannot be stated, since it is not a theorem of abelian group theory, it is, rather, a metatheorem, a theorem *about* abelian group theory.

Even if it is not possible to state the theorem though, it is still possible, in a sense, to state the proof. Since this is a description of how to effect the transformation inside the theory, it can be translated into the tactic language as a program that does that transformation. Then it is possible to build proofs in the system almost as before i.e.

$$
\begin{aligned}
a &= (b \circ c) \circ (b \circ c) \circ (b \circ c) \\
&\vdots \\
&= (b \circ b \circ b) \circ (c \circ c \circ c)
\end{aligned}
$$

where the gap is filled automatically by running the program. This looks the same as in the book, but there are important differences. First, there is no guarantee that the program will succeed in filling the gap, only the assurance of whoever wrote it. Secondly, even if the program succeeds, the safety of the step it allows is guaranteed by the fact that it actually builds the bridging proof, and this can take time—imagine if n is 65535.

Of course, even on a machine it is not always necessary to use a tactic; a lot of theorems can be stated in the language of group theory itself. For instance, one can say that

$$\forall a, b [\overbrace{(a \circ b) \circ \cdots \circ (a \circ b)}^{65535 \text{ times}} = \overbrace{(a \circ \cdots \circ a)}^{65535 \text{ times}} \circ \overbrace{(b \circ \cdots \circ b)}^{65535 \text{ times}}],$$

prove it, and store it as a lemma, then whenever an instance of this special fact is needed, the stored lemma can be recalled and instantiated with the appropriate a and b; there is no need to rebuild the proof. What is missing from most proof development systems is a facility like this, but at the 'metalevel', so that the general case can be stated, proved, and (re)used in the same way.

Proof development systems based on framework theories offer this possibility. Such systems are advertised as not specialised for proving theorems in some particular theory (such as group theory) but instead as easily adapted to different sorts of theories (first or higher order, classical, intuitionistic or linear, modal, etc.). Another way to look at them, however, is as being specialised for proving theorems in some *framework* theory designed for the express purpose of describing other theories. The idea being that, given a formal description of a theory written in the language of the framework, it is possible to build derivations in the theory via the framework. In fact the description of the theory in the framework is a metatheory, and theorems derived in a theory declared in the framework are really simple metatheorems in the metatheory. But if simple metatheorems can be proved, why not more complex ones e.g. the more general sorts proposed above?

1.2   Outline of the chapter

Not all the framework theories that have been proposed are very good for proving these 'real' metatheorems — they may have been designed with other ends in mind. However the theory FS_0, was designed, among other things, expressly as a tool not only for formalising and working in theories, but also for metatheoretic analysis of them; in other words, to do exactly the sort of things I have just described.

In this chapter I look at how well FS_0 behaves, in a worked example, in its designated rôles. The chapter is divided into three parts. The first part, Sections 2 to 5, is structured as follows: Section 2 is background detail about FS_0 and my notation, Section 3 describes the theory that I formalise, a sequent calculus for a complete fragment of classical propositional logic, Section 4 looks at a formalisation of this theory, and Section 5 looks briefly at how easy it is to build derivations in that formalisation. The second part, Sections 6 and 7 is a discussion of a proof in FS_0 of a fundamental metatheorem, Gentzen's Hauptsatz (also known as the cut elimination theorem), for the theory just formalised, and some possible applications. Finally the third part, Sections 8 and 9, looks at related and possible further work, and draws some conclusions.

2   The theory FS_0 and notational conventions

I refer to Feferman's paper [9] for details of FS_0. Here I give just a quick survey, together with a description of how my notation differs from what is described there.

2.1   What is FS_0

The theory FS_0 is a conservative extension of primitive recursive arithmetic, a weak second order theory of s-expressions and primitive recursive functions. It is like a version of *Pure Lisp* [15] where only certain functions can be defined, but that is supplemented with facilities for defining recursively enumerable classes, and with induction over such classes.

S-expressions are defined inductively as follows: O is an s-expression, and if a and b are s-expressions, then so is (a, b) — one can think of the comma as a function of arity two, the equivalent of cons in *Lisp*. For the sake of clarity, like Feferman, I take the comma as associating to the left, so that $(a, b, c) \equiv ((a, b), c)$. An important difference between FS_0 and *Lisp* is that in FS_0 the value O is used to stand for 'true', and anything else is 'false'; while in *Lisp* the situation is the other way about. Thus I can define abbreviations for particular s-expressions as

$$True \triangleq O$$
$$False \triangleq (O, O)$$

(I use $\triangleq$ to indicate a declaration of formal definitional equivalence and I write defined names with an initial capital letter and variables with an initial lower-case letter — the occasional exception to this is when I use single upper-case letters as class variables, but this use will always be clear in the context.)

A set of simple functions for operating on s-expressions is available including, for instance, projection functions π_1 and π_2, where $\pi_1(a, b) = a$ and $\pi_2(a, b) = b$, corresponding to car and cdr of *Lisp*. There are also second order combinators for functional composition, pairing and structural recursion. However I will not, for the most part, make explicit use of these — defining functions with them is a tedious exercise and my implementation of the system has a compiler available that can take sets of conditional equations and automatically build appropriate functions out of primitive components (assuming, of course, that it can see that the equations define a primitive recursive function). Instead I will use a notation similar to that of my implementation for the functions I define here. In that notation I can define an *And* function simply by saying that it is a solution to the equations

$$And(True, a) = a$$
$$And(False, a) = False$$

(for convenience sake, I assume that equations are read in the given order, and that the conditions on an equation implicitly include the negations of the conditions on all the previous equations — also notice that the definition is not typed, so there is no requirement, for instance, that a evaluate to something that looks like the boolean constants defined above).

In FS_0 comprehension is available for Σ_1^0-formulae, and in the same way that my implementation is able to build functions automatically from equational definitions, it is also able to build sets corresponding to the comprehension of such formulae. So I can write the definition of a class A, the extension of some predicate, as

$$A \triangleq \{ (a, b, c) \mid \exists d, e, \ldots P(a, b, c, d, e, \ldots) \}$$

(where $P(a, b, c, d, e, \ldots)$ is some quantifier free formula with no free variables other than $a, b, c, d, e, \ldots$), and the system will build the concrete definition itself.

Finally, I can define a class C, that is the closure of a class B under a rule

$$\frac{b \in C \quad c \in C}{a \in C} \exists d, e, \ldots P(a, b, c, d, e, \ldots)$$

(exactly as in Feferman's notation) as

$$C \triangleq \mathcal{I}_2(B, A).$$

And induction over such classes is provided by FS_0 with the axiom

$$B \subset X \to \forall x, y, z (y \in X \to z \in X$$
$$\to (x, y, z) \in A \to x \in X) \to \mathcal{I}_2(B, A) \subset X.$$

3   An informal description of Gentzen's calculus

The version of natural deduction invented by Gentzen, the sequent calculus, combines the virtues of being both practical to use for building derivations, and having good metatheoretic properties. This makes it perfect for the current purpose, since I want a theory in which I can prove theorems, and with which I can also hope to do useful metatheory. In this section I give an informal description of (one form of) the calculus such as one might find in a book.

3.1   The language

The language of wffs (well formed formulae) used here is just the $\vee, \neg$ fragment of the language of propositional logic i.e.

- The atomic propositions P_n are in the language.

- If A is in the language, then $\neg A$ is in the language,

- If A and B are in the language, then $A \vee B$ is in the language.

3.2   The calculus for classical propositional logic

In the following, A and B vary over wffs, Γ and Δ vary over lists of wffs, and a decorated Γ' or Δ'' indicates that it a permuted sublist of the undecorated form. A decorated wff, $A^\dagger$, is called principal.

A sequent is written

$$\Gamma \vdash \Delta,$$

which should be read as 'if all the wffs in Γ are true, then some wff in Δ is true'.

There is one class of axioms, which are called *basic*:

$$\frac{}{A^\dagger, \Gamma \vdash A^\dagger, \Delta} \ basic.$$

Then there are two rules (left, and right — depending on which side of the sequent they affect) for each connective. For negation these are

$$\frac{A^\dagger, \Gamma \vdash \Delta}{\Gamma \vdash \neg A^\dagger, \Delta} \ R\_neg \quad \text{and} \quad \frac{\Gamma \vdash A^\dagger, \Delta}{\neg A^\dagger, \Gamma \vdash \Delta} \ L\_neg,$$

and for disjunction,

$$\frac{\Gamma \vdash A^\dagger, B^\dagger, \Delta}{\Gamma \vdash A \vee B^\dagger, \Delta} \ R\_or \quad \text{and} \quad \frac{A^\dagger, \Gamma' \vdash \Delta' \quad B^\dagger, \Gamma'' \vdash \Delta''}{\Gamma, A \vee B^\dagger \vdash \Delta} \ L\_or.$$

To this set of rules a structural rule,

$$\frac{\Gamma' \vdash \Delta'}{\Gamma \vdash \Delta} \ struct,$$

and a cut rule,

$$\frac{\Gamma' \vdash A^\dagger, \Delta' \quad A^\dagger, \Gamma'' \vdash \Delta''}{\Gamma \vdash \Delta} \ cut,$$

are added.

It should be easy to see that these rules are enough so that for any valid formula A of the fragment of classical propositional logic I use, the sequent

$$\vdash A$$

is provable. The Hauptsatz says that if a formula can be proved using these rules, then it is can be proved without *cut*. The proof that Gentzen gives is essentially an algorithm for restructuring any derivation to remove all uses of *cut*.

4   Formalising the calculus

In Section 3 above, I have described a sequent calculus presentation of a fragment of classical propositional logic. That description is enough for an analysis in a book, but I have ignored details and taken things for granted. For instance I assume that you know what a list and what a permutation, or a sublist, of a list is; what rules are and what the closure of a set under a collection of rules is. But if I am to formalise the theory on a machine, I cannot assume any of this; I have exactly the resources that the framework theory, in this case FS_0, makes available, and all the 'missing' details in the last presentation have to be formalised along with everything else. So the first thing to do is describe the things that I took for granted: wffs, lists of wffs, permutations, etc. (some of this is directly — or almost directly — provided by FS_0 e.g. lists, or closure under a set of rules). In Section 4.1 I will describe these in FS_0, and then in Section 4.2 I will describe the theory itself.

4.1   Preliminaries

4.1.1   The class of wffs

The first class to define is that of wffs. The definition I gave in Section 3.1 can be easily translated, since it is already an inductively defined class where it is only ever necessary to appeal to at most two previous members and thus the basic facilities available in FS_0 can be used directly.

The translation from the syntax of Section 3.1 into FS_0 is as follows (I use a pair of square quotation marks $\ulcorner \cdot \urcorner$ to indicate the translation in a readable manner):

$$\ulcorner P_n \urcorner \ \equiv \ (Prop, \ulcorner n \urcorner)$$
$$\ulcorner \neg A \urcorner \ \equiv \ (Neg, \ulcorner A \urcorner)$$
$$\ulcorner A \vee B \urcorner \ \equiv \ (Disj, (\ulcorner A \urcorner, \ulcorner B \urcorner)),$$

where '*Prop*', '*Neg*' and '*Disj*' are the names of distinct s-expressions.

After assigning s-expressions to the three names the class of atomic propositions can be defined as

$$Atomic \triangleq \{ (Prop, a) \mid \top \}$$

(i.e. the class of all tuples where the left-hand part is the constant *Prop*, and the right-hand part is unconstrained — $\top$ is some tautology). This is a concise version of the equivalent definition

$$Atomic \triangleq \{ (b, a) \mid b = Prop \}.$$

And the rules for negated and disjoint formulae can be defined

$$Neg\text{-}gen \triangleq \{ ((Neg, a), a, a) \mid \top \}$$
$$Or\text{-}gen \triangleq \{ ((Disj, (a, b)), a, b) \mid \top \},$$

so that the definition of the class of wffs is simply

$$Wffs \triangleq \mathcal{I}_2(Atomic, Or\text{-}gen \cup Neg\text{-}gen).$$

4.1.2   The class of lists

Since s-expressions are already available, lists can be defined easily, taking O as the empty list. One rule,

$$Wff\text{-}list\text{-}gen \triangleq \{ ((a, g), g, g) \mid a \in Wffs \},$$

is needed, so that a definition of lists of wffs is

$$Wff\text{-}list \triangleq \mathcal{I}_2(\{O\}, Wff\text{-}list\text{-}gen).$$

Predicates for 'membership' and 'subset' (or 'permuted sublist') are also needed; these have the behaviour that the equivalent *Lisp* functions on lists would have, and can be defined simply as solutions to the equations

$$\begin{aligned} Member(a, O) &= False \\ Member(a, (a, g)) &= True \\ Member(a, (b, g)) &= Member(a, g) \end{aligned}$$

and

$$\begin{aligned} Subset(O, d) &= True \\ Subset(g, d) &= And(Member(\pi_1 g, d), \\ & \qquad Subset(\pi_2 g, d)). \end{aligned}$$

In order to make the presentation more readable, from now on I will abbreviate *Subset* as

$$g \sqsubset d \equiv Subset(g, d) = True.$$

4.1.3 Sequents

With facilities for treating primitive lists in hand, sequents can be defined as pairs of lists of wffs i.e.

$$\ulcorner \Gamma \vdash \Delta \urcorner \;\equiv\; (\ulcorner \Gamma \urcorner, \ulcorner \Delta \urcorner)$$

or, formally,

$$Seq \;\triangleq\; \{\, (g,d) \mid g \in \textit{Wff-list}, \, d \in \textit{Wff-list} \,\}.$$

4.2 Defining the theory

Now a sequent calculus for classical propositional logic can be formalised as a subclass of *Seq*.

4.2.1 The axioms

The class of basic sequents is then defined as

$$Basic \;\triangleq\; \{\, ((a,g),(a,d)) \mid ((a,g),(a,d)) \in Seq \,\}.$$

4.2.2 The rules

The rules can be defined in pretty much the same way. Since they are all fairly similar, I will give definitions of just three of them (those that I discuss later). The definitions here should be compared with the earlier informal ones.

First, take the most complex of the logical rules: *L_or*. This can be defined as

$$
\begin{aligned}
Lor\text{-}r \;\triangleq\; \{\, & ((((Disj,(a_L,a_R)),g),d),((a_L,g'),d'),((a_R,g''),d'')) \mid \\
& (((Disj,(a_L,a_R)),g),d) \in Seq, \\
& d' \sqsubset d, \, d'' \sqsubset d, \, g' \sqsubset g, \, g'' \sqsubset g \,\}
\end{aligned}
$$

(notice that the rule needs to check that the goal is a sequent, i.e. that nothing that is not a wff is accidentally included in g or d). Similarly, its dual, *R_or*, can be defined as

$$
\begin{aligned}
Ror\text{-}r \;\triangleq\; \{\, & ((g,((Disj,(a_L,a_R)),d)), \\
& (g,(a_L,(a_R,d))), \\
& (g,(a_L,(a_R,d)))) \mid \top \,\}.
\end{aligned}
$$

Notice that this definition takes two identical subderivations; this is because direct use is made of the facilities which *FS$_0$* provides for defining

338 S. Matthews

recursively enumerable classes (i.e. the $\mathcal{I}_2(\cdot,\cdot)$ constructor) when the theory itself is formalised. This does not affect the theory, though, as will be seen later, it does in a small way affect the way metatheory is done (this quirk has already appeared in the definitions of *Neg–gen* and *Wff–list–gen*).

A final example is the definition of the rule that is to be shown unnecessary: *cut*. This can be defined as

$$Cut\text{--}r \;\triangleq\; \{\; ((g,d),(g',(a,d')),((a,g''),d'')) \mid$$
$$(g,d) \in Seq,$$
$$g' \sqsubset g, d'' \sqsubset d, d' \sqsubset d, g'' \sqsubset g \;\}.$$

The definitions of the rules $(R\_neg, L\_neg, struct)$ are just variations on these patterns.

4.2.3 The theory

The theory of sequent calculus for classical propositional logic can now be defined simply as

$$Logic\text{--}r \;\triangleq\; Rneg\text{--}r \cup Lneg\text{--}r \cup Ror\text{--}r \cup Lor\text{--}r$$
$$SC \;\triangleq\; \mathcal{I}_2(Basic,\; Logic\text{--}r \cup Struct\text{--}r \cup Cut\text{--}r),$$

With this definition, a sequent $\Gamma \vdash \Delta$ is provable if and only if $\ulcorner\Gamma \vdash \Delta\urcorner \in SC$. It is easy to see that there is an isomorphism between derivations in the system described in Section 3 and derivations in SC.

5 Using SC

The class SC is a complete formal specification of the sequent calculus in FS_0, but being formal is not enough: a framework should allow *useable* formalisations of theories, so that proofs of theorems can actually be built, otherwise one could equally use *PRA*. I have not yet shown, and it is certainly not obvious, that the formalisation given here is usable.

One immediate criticism, for instance, is that it looks as if a lot of work has to be done every time a rule is applied e.g. four applications of the *Subset* predicate have to be evaluated at every application of *Lor–r*. Further, this is a function defined inside FS_0 rather than a part of the implementation, so it will be evaluated using a probably not very efficient interpreter, possibly written in a language that is itself interpreted or semi-interpreted. This means that the user is working two big steps away from the machine, and so will probably find that building proofs is tiresomely slow.

This sort of problem can be fixed by shifting as much of the work as possible from inside FS_0 to the supporting theorem prover, so that one (and probably, in terms of running time, by far the more costly) level of implementation can be 'stepped around'. This can be done by developing a clutch of lemmas corresponding to rule applications. For instance, a lemma that could be used for the *Lor–r* rule might look like

$$\forall a, b \in \text{\textit{Wffs}} \, \forall g, d \in \text{\textit{Wff–list}}$$
$$(((a, g), d) \in SC \rightarrow$$
$$((b, g), d) \in SC \rightarrow$$
$$(((\textit{Disj}, (a, b)), g), d) \in SC),$$

which, in terms of the abstract version of the theory described in Section 3, is, essentially, the derived rule

$$\frac{A, \Gamma \vdash \Delta \quad B, \Gamma \vdash \Delta}{A \vee B, \Gamma \vdash \Delta}.$$

Now it is no longer necessary to run any *Subset* tests; the work (once the lemma has been proven) is shifted from the implementation of SC to the lemma and substitution mechanisms of the implementation of FS_0, which might be in, for instance, *RPG*, *Fortran* or *COBOL*, and is (hopefully) much more efficient. Even if it is not efficient, it can probably be made efficient by being carefully rewritten, and such optimisation makes much more sense than optimising any particular piece of FS_0 itself, since it will work equally with any declared theory.

A further point about such collections of lemmas is that they can be extended in any direction; if some special style of proof search is needed, then a set of special lemmas tailored for it can be supplied, and these will be exactly as efficient as basic rules — in a sense the distinction between basic and derived rules has been blurred. In Section 6 I argue that it is practically possible in FS_0 to supply new rules of pretty much arbitrary complexity, derived or even just admissible, this way.

6 Doing metatheory

I now have a formalisation, SC, of classical propositional logic in FS_0 which I can use to build derivations of theorems. This is the first suggested use of FS_0. I still have to show that it can be used for the second: proving theorems *about* a formalised theory. To do this in this section I look at how one might go about formalising one of the basic metatheoretic results of logic in FS_0: Gentzen's Hauptsatz.

6.1   Expressing the theorem

The first thing I have to do is to express the theorem, and to do this a version of the theory that does not have the cut rule is needed. This can be defined simply in exactly the same way as SC, but with *cut* deleted, as

$$SCCF \ \triangleq \ \mathcal{I}_2(Basic, Logic\text{-}r \cup Struct\text{-}r)$$

and it is easy to see that

$$SCCF \ \subset \ SC.$$

The other direction,

$$SC \ \subset \ SCCF, \tag{1}$$

is the Hauptsatz, and the rest of this section discusses its proof.

6.2   An overview of the proof

Proofs of the Hauptsatz are easy to find in books on proof theory; for instance, Girard gives a detailed discussion in [10, Section 2.3], though the presentation in [20] is closer to that here. Those proofs however, cannot be directly translated into FS_0, since they make use of transfinite induction principles which it does not have. Alongside these proofs are, often, remarks to the effect that a proof in primitive recursive arithmetic *is* possible [10, Section 2.3.11], but not practical; Girard, for instance, describes the details as '... straightforward, but terribly long'. And since the proof is not practical, it is not given, only sketched. Part of the intended purpose of FS_0, which has only the same induction as primitive recursive arithmetic, is to make such proofs practical (even to the extent that they can be put on a machine).

Since I cannot use transfinite induction to prove the theorem directly, I have to find another, more indirect, way. I do this by mapping, inside FS_0, the usual transfinite ordering onto the natural numbers using a primitive recursive function, so that that part of the ordering that is needed for the proof is preserved (i.e. the mapping is not monotonic — that is not possible — but it suffices for the current purpose). I can then use the values that result from this as a 'complexity measure' to label derivations. I also ensure that the complexity of a derivation is 0 if and only if it does not use *cut*. Then I can show, using simple induction on the structure of derivations, that a derivation can be transformed into another with a lower complexity (unless the complexity is already 0) and, given this, that a derivation can be progressively transformed into another with a complexity of 0. The other parts of the proof i.e. the transformations performed on a derivation, are the same as one would need for a proof using ordinary transfinite induction.

6.2.1 Overview of the rest of this section

The rest of this section is structured as follows: in Section 6.3 I define the natural numbers, in Section 6.4 I define a measure of complexity on derivations, in Section 6.5 I show how to prove the central lemma of complexity reduction for proofs, and finally in Section 6.6 I quickly put everything together to get the main result.

6.3 The natural numbers

Since I will measure the complexity of derivations with natural numbers, the first thing I have to do is define them. A number n can be represented by a list of length $\underline{n}$; i.e.

$$\ulcorner 0 \urcorner \equiv O$$
$$\ulcorner s(n) \urcorner \equiv (O, \ulcorner n \urcorner),$$

so that a formal definition is just

$$Nat\text{-}gen \triangleq \{ ((O, n), n, n)T \}$$
$$Nat \triangleq \mathcal{I}_2(\{O\}, Nat\text{-}gen).$$

I also need an ordering relation and a function for addition; these can be defined as solutions to the sets of equations

$$Plus(m, O) = m$$
$$Plus(m, n) = (O, Plus(m, \pi_2 n))$$

and

$$Less(a, O) = False$$
$$Less(n, (O, n)) = True$$
$$Less(n, m) = Less(m, \pi_2 n).$$

Like *Subset* earlier, for the sake of readability I will abbreviate *Less* as

$$m < n \equiv Less(m, n) = True.$$

6.4 Attaching a measure to a derivation

A simple measure of the complexity of a derivation in an (inductively defined) class is just the number of steps in it. Given any class

$$C \triangleq \mathcal{I}_2(B, A),$$

a new class C_C can be defined as

$$B_C \triangleq \{ (x, \ulcorner 1 \urcorner) \mid x \in B \}$$
$$A_C \triangleq \{ ((x, l), (x', l'), (x'', l'')) \mid$$
$$(x, x', x'') \in A,$$
$$l = Plus(Plus(l', l''), \ulcorner 1 \urcorner) \}.$$
$$C_C \triangleq \mathcal{I}_2(B_C, A_C)$$

and it is easy to see that

$$x \in C \quad \leftrightarrow \quad \exists l((x, l) \in C_C),$$

where l is the number of steps taken in some derivation of x.

Such a simple measure cannot be used here; something more complicated is needed. As I said earlier, the usual way to prove the theorem is
with transfinite induction, and the well-ordering needed is a lexicographical ordering on the pair $\langle D, S \rangle$, where S is a measure of the size of the
derivation and D is a measure of the 'cut degree' (the complexity of the
cut formula). I can map this pair into the natural numbers as

$$\langle D, S \rangle \quad \mapsto \quad \left. 2^{2^{\cdot^{\cdot^{\cdot^{2^S}}}}} \right\} D+1$$

(i.e. a column D high of 2s). And this can easily be defined in FS_0 (using
primitive recursion on D) as the function

$$N\text{-}Ex(\ulcorner D \urcorner, \ulcorner S \urcorner).$$

Now a working measure of complexity can be associated with derivations,
as in the example above. In fact a pair of numbers $m = (c, l)$ is used, but
the complexity is measured just by c; the other number, l, is the size of
the derivation. First, I define the way the measure works with the 'logical'
rules. This can be done by defining classes as

$$M\text{-}Base \triangleq \{ (\ulcorner 0 \urcorner, \ulcorner 1 \urcorner) \}$$
$$M\text{-}Step \triangleq \{ ((c, l), (c', l'), (c'', l'')) \mid$$
$$l = Plus(Plus(l', l''), \ulcorner 1 \urcorner),$$
$$c = Cr1((c', l'), (c'', l'')) \},$$

where

$$Cr1((\ulcorner 0 \urcorner, l'), (\ulcorner 0 \urcorner, l'')) = \ulcorner 0 \urcorner$$
$$Cr1((c', l'), (\ulcorner 0 \urcorner, l'')) = (O, Plus(c', l''))$$
$$Cr1((\ulcorner 0 \urcorner, l'), (c'', l'')) = (O, Plus(l', c''))$$
$$Cr1((c', l'), (c'', l'')) = (O, Plus(c', c'')).$$

Then the 'logical' rules are extended as

$$Basic_C \triangleq \{ (s,m) \mid s \in Basic, m \in M\text{-}Base \}$$
$$Logic\text{-}r_C \triangleq \{ ((s,m),(s',m'),(s'',m'')) \mid$$
$$(s,s',s'') \in Logic\text{-}r \cup Struct\text{-}r,$$
$$(m,m',m'') \in M\text{-}Step \}.$$

Here $Struct\text{-}r$ has been added to the logical rules for the sake of convenience. With the definitions so far, c, the complexity measure, will not take any value other than $\ulcorner 0 \urcorner$. If it ever takes a value other than $\ulcorner 0 \urcorner$ then it will grow, but so long as only the 'logical' rules and $basic$ are used, this cannot happen. This is exactly the right behaviour, since a derivation that does not use cut will thus have a complexity measure of $\ulcorner 0 \urcorner$.

I want to use c to track information about cuts in the derivation, and the modified form of the cut rule has not been defined yet. Before doing so, a function that measures the number of connectives in a formula is needed, and this is defined as a solution to the equations

$$Comp(\ulcorner P_n \urcorner) = \ulcorner 0 \urcorner$$
$$Comp(\ulcorner \neg A \urcorner) = (O, Comp(\ulcorner A \urcorner))$$
$$Comp(\ulcorner A \vee B \urcorner) = (O, Plus(Comp(\ulcorner A \urcorner), Comp(\ulcorner B \urcorner))).$$

Then the new form of the cut rule can be defined as

$$Cut\text{-}r_C \triangleq \{ (((g,d),(c,l)),((g',(a,d')),(c',l')),(((a,g''),d''),(c'',l''))) \mid$$
$$(g,d) \in Seq,$$
$$g' \sqsubset g, \, d'' \sqsubset d, \, d' \sqsubset d, \, g'' \sqsubset g,$$
$$c = Cr2((c',l'),(c'',l''),Comp(a)),$$
$$l = Plus(Plus(l',l''),\ulcorner 1 \urcorner) \},$$

where

$$Cr2((\ulcorner 0 \urcorner,l'),(\ulcorner 0 \urcorner,l''),n) = N\text{-}Ex(n,Plus(l',l''))$$
$$Cr2((c',l'),(\ulcorner 0 \urcorner,l''),n) = N\text{-}Ex(n,Plus(c',l''))$$
$$Cr2((\ulcorner 0 \urcorner,l'),(c'',l''),n) = N\text{-}Ex(n,Plus(l',c''))$$
$$Cr2((c',l'),(c'',l''),n) = N\text{-}Ex(n,Plus(c',c''))$$

So the definition of SC_C is

$$SC_C \triangleq \mathcal{I}_2(Basic_C, Logic\text{-}r_C \cup Cut\text{-}r_C),$$

and I can show that

$$x \in SC \quad \leftrightarrow \quad \exists m((s,m) \in SC_C). \tag{2}$$

6.5   Reducing the complexity of a derivation

Now I prove the lemma,

$$(s, (c, l)) \in SC_C \to (s, (\ulcorner 0 \urcorner, l)) \in SC_C$$
$$\vee \exists c_1, l_1 [c_1 < c \wedge l_1 < c \wedge (s, (c_1, l_1)) \in SC_C], \qquad (3)$$

which is essentially the theorem itself; however, in order to do this I need to use induction, and induction is not available over such formulae in FS_0. The solution is to define a class,

$$SC_C^* \triangleq \{ (s, (c, l)) \mid (s, (\ulcorner 0 \urcorner, l)) \in SC_C$$
$$\vee \exists c_1, l_1 [c_1 < c \wedge l_1 < c \wedge (s, (c_1, l_1)) \in SC_C] \},$$

which is equivalent to the consequent of (3) and then then it is possible to prove the equivalent statement:

$$SC_C \subset SC_C^*.$$

6.5.1   The base case

The base case is trivial. I have to show that

$$s_C \in Basic_C \to s_C \in SC_C^*,$$

and can argue thus:

$$s_C \in Basic_C \to s_C = (s, m) \wedge s \in Basic \wedge m \in M\text{-}Base$$
$$\text{[for some } s \text{ and } m]$$
$$\to m = (\ulcorner 0 \urcorner, \ulcorner 1 \urcorner)$$
$$\to (s, (\ulcorner 0 \urcorner, \ulcorner 1 \urcorner)) \in SC_C$$
$$\to s_C \in SC_C^*.$$

6.5.2   The step case

This is more complicated. I have to show that, given

$$s_C' \in SC_C^*, \qquad (4)$$
$$s_C'' \in SC_C^*, \qquad (5)$$
$$(s_C, s_C', s_C'') \in Logic\text{-}r_C \cup Cut\text{-}r_C, \qquad (6)$$

it follows that

$$s_C \in SC_C^*.$$

I can do this by analysing a hierarchy of cases. The transformations are well known, and there seems little point in describing all of them, so I will give the general procedure, and then discuss one of the most complicated cases in detail; the others follow the same pattern.

By (4) and (5), given $s'_C = (s, (c, l))$ and $s''_C = (s'', (c'', l''))$, there are $(s', (c'_1, l'_1))$ and $(s'', (c''_1, l''_1))$ in SC_C and either one of c' and c'' is an encoded natural number other than $\ulcorner 0 \urcorner$ or both of them are $\ulcorner 0 \urcorner$.

Assuming the former, then either $c'_1 < c'$ and $l'_1 < c'$, and $c''_1 \leq c''$ and $l''_1 \leq c''$ (depending on whether or not $c'' = \ulcorner 0 \urcorner$), or vice versa. By (6) I can again separate into two subcases. If

$$(s_C, s'_C, s''_C) \in Logic\text{-}r_C,$$

then it is easy to show that

$$((s, (c_1, l_1)), (s', (c'_1, l'_1)), (s'', (c''_1, l''_1)) \in Logic\text{-}r_C,$$

where

$$
\begin{aligned}
c_1 &= Cr1((c'_1, l'_1), (c''_1, l''_1)) \\
l_1 &= (0, Plus(l'_1, l''_1))
\end{aligned}
$$

and to show that $s_C \in SC^*_C$ I have only to show that $c_1 < c$ and $l_1 < c$, which is a matter of simple manipulation.

Alternatively, if $(s_C, s'_C, s''_C) \in Cut\text{-}r_C$, then the argument follows the same pattern, except that the new values are

$$
\begin{aligned}
c_1 &= Cr2((c'_1, l'_1), (c''_1, l'')) \\
l_1 &= (0, Plus(l'_1, l''_1)).
\end{aligned}
$$

Now consider when both c' and c'' are $\ulcorner 0 \urcorner$. Again, by (6) there are two subcases: (s_C, s'_C, s''_C) is in either $Logic\text{-}r_C$ or $Cut\text{-}r_C$. In the first case it is easy to show that c is also $\ulcorner 0 \urcorner$. The cut rule is the interesting case — then the final derivation of $s_C = ((g, d), (c, l))$ has to be of the form

$$\frac{((g', (a, d')), (\ulcorner 0 \urcorner, l')) \quad (((a, g''), d''), (\ulcorner 0 \urcorner, l''))}{((g, d), (c, l))} \; Cut\text{-}r_C,$$

where

$$
\begin{aligned}
& g' \sqsubseteq g, \; d'' \sqsubseteq d, \; d' \sqsubseteq d, \; g'' \sqsubseteq g, \\
& c = Cr2((\ulcorner 0 \urcorner, l'), (\ulcorner 0 \urcorner, l''), Comp(a)), \\
& l = (0, Plus(l', l'')).
\end{aligned}
$$

The proof proceeds by analysing the ways that $((g', (a, d')), (\ulcorner 0 \urcorner, l'))$, or more briefly s'_C, might have been derived. Most of these cases are very similar, so only one (the most complicated, and the reason why transfinite induction is used) will be considered here. First note that, because $c' = \ulcorner 0 \urcorner$, s'_C cannot have been derived using $Cut\text{-}r_C$, and that there is a case for each of the other original rules of SC, i.e. *basic*, *Lor-r*, etc.

Consider the case where s'_C is derived by $Ror\text{-}r$, i.e. $a = (Disj, (a_L, a_R))$ and $s'_C = ((g', ((Disj, (a_L, a_R)), d')), then(\ulcorner 0 \urcorner, l'))$ is shown to be in SC_C by

$$\frac{((g', (a_L, (a_R, d'))), (\ulcorner 0 \urcorner, l'')) \quad ((g', (a_L, (a_R, d'))), (\ulcorner 0 \urcorner, l''))}{((g', ((Disj, (a_L, a_R)), d')), (\ulcorner 0 \urcorner, l'))} \; Ror\text{-}r.$$

Then there are two possible ways that $(((a, g''), d''), (\ulcorner 0 \urcorner, l''))$ could have been derived: either by a thinning or 'right' rule, or by $Lor\text{-}r$ — it is not possible for $Lneg\text{-}r$ to derive a sequent with a disjunction as principle formula. Consider the case when $Lor\text{-}r$ was the rule used; then the principle formula is $a' = a$ i.e. the derivation is:

$$\frac{(((a_L, g'''), d''), (\ulcorner 0 \urcorner, l''')) \quad (((a_R, g'''), d''), (\ulcorner 0 \urcorner, l'''))}{((((Disj, (a_L, a_R)), g''), d''), (\ulcorner 0 \urcorner, l''))} \; Lor\text{-}r,$$

where

$$g''' \sqsubseteq g'', \; d''' \sqsubseteq d'', \; g'''' \sqsubseteq g'', \; d'''' \sqsubseteq d''.$$

An alternative derivation for s_C is

$$\frac{((g, (a_R, d)), (c'_1, l'_1)) \quad (((a_R, g'''), d'''), (\ulcorner 0 \urcorner, l'''))}{((g, d), (c_1, l_1))} \; Cut\text{-}r_C,$$

where

$$\frac{((g', (a_L, (a_R, d'))), (\ulcorner 0 \urcorner, l'')) \quad (((a_L, g''), d''), (\ulcorner 0 \urcorner, l''))}{((g, (a_R, d)), (c'_1, l'_1))} \; Cut\text{-}r_C$$

Then all that is left to be done is to check that these are proper derivations and that $c_1 < c$ and $l_1 < c$, which is not hard.

6.6   Eliminating the cuts

Now, with lemma (3), it is an easy matter to prove that

$$(s, (a, l)) \in SC_C \quad \rightarrow \quad \exists l((s, (\ulcorner 0 \urcorner, l)) \in SC_C) \tag{7}$$

and, finally, that

$$(s, (\ulcorner 0 \urcorner, l)) \in SC_C \quad \rightarrow \quad s \in SCCF. \tag{8}$$

Then by composing (2), (7) and (8), the theorem, (1), follows.

7   Using metatheory

With a proof of the Hauptsatz available, the next question is: 'of what use is the result to practical people?'.[1]

The most immediate application is to show the consistency of SC; given (1) it is not hard to show that not every sequent is derivable in SC e.g.

$$ \ulcorner \vdash \neg(A \vee \neg A) \urcorner \notin SC, $$

since if a formula is in SC it is in $SCCF$, and an analysis of cases shows that this formula cannot be derived in $SCCF$.

This proof of the consistency is one example of a range of practical corollaries of the result. The most important after consistency is probably either Herbrand's theorem or the interpolation theorem [6]. The commonest justification for proof development systems is formal software verification, an activity which needs particularly powerful tools for structuring and combining collections of theories. The interpolation theorem is precisely the tool needed to track the relationships in such collections.

Showing the consistency of the implementation is something that can be done without considering the structure of the proof of the Hauptsatz itself, however an important point about the proof is that it is constructive. This is significant if, for instance, it is used to build a proof of the interpolation theorem, since one might then actually want to use the proof to extract interpolants. Unfortunately there are problems with this: if the proof here is considered as a program it is not a very good one — the problem is not the size of the complexity measure, which is a fairly accurate assessment[2] of the upper bound on the computation (and the bound is enormous — far outside the bounds of feasible computation — though it should be remembered that it is for a worst case), but that it is 'sloppily coded' i.e. from a programmer's point of view it does not do as much work on each iteration as it might, and it has bad normalisation properties. However these are programming rather than mathematical issues and (the second at least) can be addressed by the programmer's slogan, 'get it right, then make it fast' — a proof in hand can always be optimised if and as necessary.

---

[1]Strictly speaking, the answer to this question is: 'not much, since no one, in practice, is interested in propositional logic, and anyway the various corollaries discussed here all have, for the propositional case, easier proofs that do not need the Hauptsatz.' However scaling the proof up for predicate logic, where the same results much more usefully hold, is not hard; the problem of dealing with bound variables in predicate logic is an independent, though large, problem — bound variables do not introduce anything new into the proof presented here, though they do make case analysis quite a bit bigger. The issue of how to treat bound variables in FS_0 is explored in [13] and [14].

[2]At least for predicate logic — see the previous footnote.

8   Related work

Related work divides into several parts: there is complementary work that has been done in FS_0, and there is work on frameworks, and on doing, and using, metatheory in other proof development systems.

8.1   Using FS_0 as a framework

This chapter can be thought of as complementary to [14], where a full sequent calculus of first order logic is presented and the problems of working on a machine are discussed in more detail. In that chapter a much simpler metatheorem (the existence of equivalent prenex normal forms for formulae) is discussed — the intention of the paper is rather to look at how it is possible to work with a formalised binding mechanism. The issues are also examined in my thesis [13]. So far as I, or Feferman, knows, this is the only work which has been done on practical applications of FS_0 as a framework.

8.2   Other work similar to FS_0

The approach of FS_0 can be traced back to the work of Post in the 1930s. He was the first to formalise the idea of a proof system as a recursively enumerable set, and his work was built on by Smullyan in the 1960s. Their intention, however, was to capture the idea of a derived formula; they did not really look at the possibility of doing proof theory in their proposed systems, even in theory. Gödel, who had slightly different concerns at the time, must, for his incompleteness results, have been the first to do this. The first suggestion that such a theory might actually be used as the basis of a mechanical proof development system was by Davis and Schwartz [7], but their paper does not address the practical issues involved convincingly.

More recently Basin and Constable, in [2], have suggested an approach that is in many ways similar to what is described here: the chief difference is that they define a logic in terms of an abstract data type, rather than building it explicitly, and they do not concern themselves particularly with the logic used to treat this data type — they happen to use a type-theoretic approach (with abstract data types implemented as Σ-types) but this seems to be incidental; they insist only on a constructive metatheory sufficiently powerful to support such abstraction. They also point out that the FS_0 approach can be directly formulated in their system using inductive types. This is true, but ignores one intended purpose of FS_0, which is to give a simple, finite, description of what exactly a formal system is. Also, as is pointed out below in Section 9, while the enormous proof theoretic strength of their supporting system is useful, it does not seem to be necessary for most purposes. However, one definite advantage of using abstract data types is that there are no 'quirks' like those mentioned, for example, in the definition of $Ror-r$ above.

8.3   Research in type-theoretic frameworks

By far the largest body of work on theories suitable for use in framework proof development systems must be that based on type theories. This work goes back to the *Automath* project, which is surveyed in [8], and details of the theories that were used can be found in [24]. More recently, work at Edinburgh has built on this with the 'Edinburgh Logical Framework' (also called *LF*); details of the theory of this can be found in [11], and a collection of worked examples is described in [1].

The idea is to exploit the notion of an isomorphism between propositions and types, so that terms inhabiting a type are isomorphic to proofs of the corresponding proposition. The great advantage of this is that substitution for terms and formulae comes practically for free, since there is already a general substitution mechanism available in the lambda calculus facilities that come with the type theory. This is a very flexible approach, but it does have some problems: it is not always possible to take a presentation as given and encode it directly and intuitively in the *LF*; skill, and knowledge of proof theory may be needed, and the resulting encoding may not obviously correspond to the original presentation.

There is also the fact that the *LF* is not very good for doing metatheory: it cannot deal with the notion of an admissible rule (though simple derived rules are certainly possible). However it is not really fair to criticise the system for this, since it was developed with different concerns in mind. In particular the type theory it is based on was deliberately chosen to be as weak as possible so that it would be easier (or even just become possible) to develop various sorts of uniform proof procedures — it is intended to be used with tactics rather than metatheory; see, for instance, [19]. This does not mean that it is not possible to do general metatheory in any *LF* style system. *LF* is a fragment of the very powerful Calculus of Constructions, it is possible to move an encoding (carefully) into this and make use of the more powerful facilities there to develop metatheoretic results, such as admissible rules — in fact Taylor works through some small examples of this approach in [23], where he develops a pair of verified tactics for the theory of semigroups. Pollack, in unpublished work, has also considered a proof of the deduction theorem (this is also done with FS_0 in [13]). Similar ideas are implicit in the work of Basin and Howe [3], which looks at how to use a (very powerful) Martin-Löf style type of theory as a *LF* style framework.

Other work that uses lambda calculus style frameworks, but does not use the notion of propositions as types, can also be found in work on *Isabelle* [18], and *Lambda Prolog* [16], systems based on higher order intuitionistic logic.

Clearly then, it is a matter of choice and circumstance whether a type-theoretic, or Post style, framework is suitable for some particular piece of work.

8.4   Miscellaneous work

There is also other less classifiable work that should be mentioned. In [5], Boyer and Moore develop, and describe the implementation of, a metatheorem as an extension to their theorem prover, *Nqthm*. The work is very similar to the example explored in Section 1; their system relies on a uniform proof procedure supplemented with a powerful lemma facility, and they look at how it can be modified so that a whole class of lemmas characterised by a single metatheorem can be added so as to avoid having to add, piecemeal, each instance that is needed to prove some particular theorem. They do not do this by using a framework logic, but by taking advantage of the fact that their theorem prover is implemented in a system that is an extension of the system that it proves theorems about. Thus they use the system to prove the theorem and then 'reflect' (they do not use the word) it into the implementation. This is interesting, not only because it is a practical example of using metatheory to extend a theorem prover, but also because it works with a logic that is, in many ways, similar to FS_0 in that it resembles *Lisp* restricted to primitive recursive functions.[3]

Another example of metatheory in *Nqthm* is the proof, by Shankar [21], of the Church–Rosser theorem. The distinction here is that this is metatheory as mathematics for its own sake, rather than as a means for making work in the object theory easier. However it is one of the most substantial metatheoretic results that has been formalised and machine checked. Also, similar work done by Berardi in a *LF*-style framework is described in [4].

9   Conclusions

The point of this chapter is to try to show that FS_0 does what Feferman claims it should; it provides a simple and flexible characterisation of the idea of a formal theory, and it can be used as a framework in which it is practically possible to formalise a theory, prove theorems of that theory, and

---

[3]Since then, however, *Nqthm* has been extended with a more powerful induction principle using ordinal notations, though so far I know this has not as yet been needed.

also prove substantial metatheorems about it — especially metatheorems that might help a user in proving further theorems in the theory.

9.1   Doing metatheory

As I said earlier, Girard mentions in passing that a proof of the Hauptsatz in *PRA* is possible but impractically long. And this is after he has developed, in considerable detail, the machinery of a Gödel encoding of the sequent calculus, etc. The proof sketched here is developed from first principles in a theory which is a conservative extension of *PRA* and is a practical proposition for machine proof. (Admittedly, I only treat propositional logic here, not full predicate logic, but the proof can easily be extended, and as argued in [14], a binding mechanism can be dealt with in FS_0.) One can also argue that the Hauptsatz is almost a 'one off' piece of metatheory: the amount of effort needed to prove it is exceptional, since a lot of the other results that one might want are corollaries of it. In particular, many metatheorems corresponding to admissible rules become available with little more work.

One might wonder if the proof would have been easier if I had not been restricted to using only Σ_1^0-induction, and clearly this does make things slightly more complex than they would otherwise be e.g. there would be no need to worry about giving an explicit bound on the induction. But an explicit bound is a useful thing to have, since it provides a measure of the complexity of an algorithm (and in this case shows that in general it is far outside the limits of what is practically computable). If it was felt to be necessary, however, there are simple ways to extend FS_0 to allow much stronger induction principles — though at the cost of non-finitist proofs.

There are some problems with using FS_0 that perhaps cannot be properly fixed: any attempt to interpret the resulting proofs as programs is going to find that they do not have very good normalisation properties, simply because of the nature of a primitive recursive/inductive theory. There are some ways that the theory could be extended to improve the problem, but perhaps only at the cost of damaging it in other ways by making it much more complex, and such aesthetic considerations are practically important, for instance, for pedagogic reasons (another intention behind the theory) or if one were to try, as Feferman has suggested, to prove the second incompleteness theorem.

9.2   Further work

There are many possible directions of further work. My current intention is to implement a version of Talcott's theory of binding structures [22]. This is a sufficiently general framework so that it should be easily reusable for any particular theory that a user wants to implement and would provide an effective answer to the criticism that there is no facility for handling substitution in FS_0. Beyond that I have no specific plans. The obvious project is a full machine checked proof of cut elimination, and an exploration of some of its corollaries, such as the interpolation theorem. The other possibility is a machine checked proof of the second incompleteness theorem, the other basic result of syntactic metatheory. This would be interesting in itself, and the machinery developed along the way would, I believe, be independently useful.

Acknowledgements

I would like to thank Alan Smaill and Solomon Feferman for helpful criticism and comments. Paul Taylor's code for setting proofs was used.

References

[1] Arnon Avron, Furio Honsell, Ian Mason, and Robert Pollack. Using typed lambda calculus to implement formal systems on a machine. *Journal of Automated Reasoning*, 9:309–352, 1992.

[2] David Basin and Robert Constable. Metalogical frameworks. In [12].

[3] David Basin and Doug Howe. Some normalization properties of Martin-Löf's type theory, and applications. In Takayasu Ito and Albert R. Meyer, editors, *TACS '91, Theoretical Aspects of Computer Software*, volume 526 of *Lecture Notes in Computer Science*, pages 475–494. Springer, Tokyo, 1991.

[4] Stefano Berardi. Girard normalisation proof in LEGO. In [12].

[5] Robert Boyer and J. Strother Moore. Metafunctions: Proving them correct and using them efficiently as new proof procedures. In Robert Boyer and J. Strouther Moore, editors, *The Correctness Problem in Computer Science*, pages 103–184. Academic Press, New York, 1981.

[6] William Craig. Linear reasoning. A new form of the Herbrand–Genzen theorem. *Journal of Symbolic Logic*, 27:250–268, 1957.

[7] Martin Davis and Jacob T. Schwartz. Metamathematical extensibility for theorem verifiers and proof-checkers. *Computers and Mathematics with Applications*, 5:217–230, 1979.

[8] N. G. de Bruijn. A survey of the project Automath. In J. R. Hindley and J. P. Seldin, editors, *To H. B. Curry: Essays in Combinatory Logic, Lambda Calculus and Formalism*, pages 579–606. Academic Press, New York, 1980.

[9] Solomon Feferman. Finitary inductive systems. This volume.

[10] Jean-Yves Girard. *Proof Theory and Logical Complexity*, volume 1 of *Studies in Proof Theory*. Bibliopolis, Naples, 1987.

[11] Robert Harper, Furio Honsell, and Gordon Plotkin. A framework for defining logics. *Journal of the ACM*, 40(1):143–184, January 1993.

[12] Gérard Huet and Gordon Plotkin, editors. *Logical Environments*. Cambridge University Press, Cambridge, 1993.

[13] Seán Matthews. Metatheoretic and Reflexive Reasoning in Mechanical Theorem Proving. PhD thesis, University of Edinburgh, 1992.

[14] Seán Matthews, Alan Smaill, and David Basin. Experience with FS_0 as a framework theory. In [12].

[15] John McCarthy, Paul W. Abrahams, Daniel J. Edwards, Timothy P. Hart, and Michael I. Levin. *Lisp 1.5 Programmer's Manual*. M.I.T. Press, Cambridge, Massachusetts, 1965.

[16] Dale Miller. Abstractions in logic programs. In [17].

[17] Piergiorgio Odifreddi, editor. *Logic and Computer Science*, volume 31 of *APIC Studies in Data Processing*. Academic Press, London, 1990.

[18] Larry Paulson. Isabelle: the next 700 theorem provers. In [17].

[19] David J. Pym and Lincoln Wallen. Proof-search in the $\lambda\Pi$-calculus. In Gérard Huet and Gordon Plotkin, editors, *Logical Frameworks*, pages 309–340. Cambridge University Press, Cambridge, 1991.

[20] Helmut Schwichtenberg. Proof theory: Some applications of cut-elimination. In Jon Barwise, editor, *The Handbook of Mathematical Logic*, chapter D2. North-Holland, Amsterdam, 1977.

[21] Natarayan Shankar. A mechanical proof of the Church-Rosser theorem. *Journal of the ACM*, 35:475–522, 1988.

[22] Carolyn Talcott. A theory of binding structures and applications to rewriting. *Theoretical Computer Science*, 112:99–143, 1993.

[23] Paul Taylor. Using Constructions as a Metalanguage. Technical Report ECS–LFCS–88–70, Laboratory for Foundations of Computer Science, Department of Computer Science, University of Edinburgh, December 1988.

[24] D. T. van Daalen. The Language Theory of Automath. PhD thesis, Eindhoven University of Technology, 1980.

14

General Logics and Logical Frameworks

Narciso Martí-Oliet and José Meseguer

This chapter summarizes a theory of general logics first introduced in [39], in which different aspects, or components, of a logic such as its entailment relation, its proof theory, and its model theory are axiomatized. For the model-theoretic component, the theory of institutions of Goguen and Burstall [24] is adopted. Combinations of several such aspects of a logic are also supported by the theory. Special importance is given to the notion of mapping between logics that preserves the logical structure of some aspect, such as the entailment relation, or the satisfaction relation for the models. Such maps play for logics a role analogous to that played by group homomorphisms for groups. The notion of a logical framework, understood as a logic $\mathcal{F}$ in which many other logics can be represented, is then expressed in terms of appropriate representation maps $\mathcal{L} \longrightarrow \mathcal{F}$. The particular logical framework provided by rewriting logic [40] is introduced and discussed, and some of its good properties for representing logics and for reflecting aspects of its own metatheory are explained.

1 Introduction

An answer—hopefully in the form of a precise metamathematical axiomatization—to the question

What is a logic?

depends on the particular aspects of a logic that one has in mind. If one is, for example, interested in a logic's deductive aspects and assumes that they are presented in a finitary way, a possible answer may be an axiomatization such as Smullyan's theory of *formal systems* [56]. If one is instead interested in a logic's model-theoretic aspects, a suitable answer may consist of axioms for an *abstract model theory* such as those of Barwise [3], or the more general axioms of Goguen and Burstall for their theory of *institutions* [22, 24].

Section 2 of this chapter presents in summarized form a theory of *general logics* first proposed in [39] in which axiomatic notions formalizing the different aspects of a logic and of their combinations into fuller notions of logic are given. The theory is in a sense modular, in that it permits focusing on different aspects of a logic, as well as combining several aspects, depending on the particular applications. Three main aspects are considered. If only the entailment relation holding between a set of sentences used as axioms and a conclusion sentence is of interest, then the axiomatic notion of an *entailment system* is proposed. If the structure of the *proofs* of theorems, as specified by a given proof theory for a logic, is the focus of interest, then the notion of a *proof calculus* is put forward. If only the models and the satisfaction relation holding between sentences and models is considered, then the notion of *institution* provided by Goguen and Burstall [22] is used. Several of these aspects can be combined. For example, the combination of an entailment system and an institution yields a *logic*, but the same logic, or the same entailment system, can have different proof calculi. For example, first order logic has a variety of different proof calculi, such as Hilbert style and Gentzen style ones.

A mathematical insight by now obvious, although historically slow in emerging, is that, given any kind of structure, much can be learned about it, even to the point of fully characterizing it, by studying how it interacts with other similar structures by means of structure-preserving maps. For example, the study of the theory of groups can be best carried out by realizing that groups and group homomorphisms form a *category* [33]. This categorical point of view is also adopted in the theory of general logics, in which entailment systems, proof calculi, and institutions are viewed as mathematical structures, analogous to groups, that can be related to other such structures by means of structure-preserving maps. Thus, maps of entailment systems preserve the entailment relation, maps of proof calculi preserve both entailments and proofs, and maps of institutions (which in our sense are different from the institution morphisms of [22]) preserve the satisfaction relation. Section 2.6 summarizes these notions, and Section 2.7 explains how the concept of a *logical framework*, understood as a logic $\mathcal{F}$ in which many other logics can be represented, can be expressed in terms of appropriate representation maps $\mathcal{L} \longrightarrow \mathcal{F}$.

In recent work [34], we have discovered that *rewriting logic* [40] is a logical framework in precisely this sense, and that it allows particularly simple representations for a wide variety of logics. We give an introduction to the rules of deduction, proof theory, and semantics of rewriting logic in Section 3. By way of example—so as to give some flavor for its uses as a logical framework—we explain and illustrate a general method for representing sequent presentations of a logic in rewriting logic in Section 4, and illustrate some of the reflective capabilities of rewriting logic in Section 5. We should emphasize the limited character of our discussion of rewriting logic as a logical framework in this chapter, and refer the reader to [34] for a fuller account.

A discussion of related work on abstract model theory, institutions, and logical frameworks is postponed until Section 6. Finally, topics for future research are considered in Section 7.

2 General logics

A general axiomatic theory of logics should adequately cover all the key ingredients of a logic. These include: a *syntax*, a notion of *entailment* of a sentence from a set of axioms, a notion of *model*, and a notion of *satisfaction* of a sentence by a model. A flexible axiomatic notion of a *proof calculus*, in which proofs of entailments, not just the entailments themselves, are first class citizens should also be included. This section gives a brief review of the required notions and axioms; a more detailed account with many examples can be found in [39].

2.1 Syntax

Syntax can typically be given by a *signature* Σ providing a grammar on which to build *sentences*. For first order logic, a typical signature consists of a list of function symbols and a list of predicate symbols, each with a prescribed number of arguments, which are used to build up sentences by means of the usual logical connectives. For our purposes, it is enough to assume that for each logic there is a category **Sign** of possible signatures for it, and a functor *sen* assigning to each signature Σ the set $sen(\Sigma)$ of all its sentences.

2.2 Entailment systems

For a given signature Σ in **Sign**, *entailment* (also called *provability*) of a sentence $\varphi \in sen(\Sigma)$ from a set of axioms $\Gamma \subseteq sen(\Sigma)$ is a relation $\Gamma \vdash \varphi$ which holds if and only if we can prove φ from the axioms Γ using the rules of the logic. We make this relation relative to a signature.

In what follows, $|\mathcal{C}|$ denotes the collection of objects of a category $\mathcal{C}$.

Definition 2.1 [39] An *entailment system* is a triple $\mathcal{E} = (\mathbf{Sign}, sen, \vdash)$ such that

- **Sign** is a category whose objects are called *signatures*,

- *sen* : **Sign** $\longrightarrow$ **Set** is a functor associating to each signature Σ a corresponding set of Σ-*sentences*, and

- $\vdash$ is a function associating to each $\Sigma \in |\mathbf{Sign}|$ a binary relation $\vdash_\Sigma$ $\subseteq \mathcal{P}(sen(\Sigma)) \times sen(\Sigma)$ called Σ-*entailment* such that the following properties are satisfied:

  1. *reflexivity*: for any $\varphi \in sen(\Sigma)$, $\{\varphi\} \vdash_\Sigma \varphi$,

  2. *monotonicity*: if $\Gamma \vdash_\Sigma \varphi$ and $\Gamma' \supseteq \Gamma$ then $\Gamma' \vdash_\Sigma \varphi$,

  3. *transitivity*: if $\Gamma \vdash_\Sigma \varphi_i$, for all $i \in I$, and $\Gamma \cup \{\varphi_i \mid i \in I\} \vdash_\Sigma \psi$, then $\Gamma \vdash_\Sigma \psi$,

  4. $\vdash$-*translation*: if $\Gamma \vdash_\Sigma \varphi$, then for any $H : \Sigma \to \Sigma'$ in **Sign**, $sen(H)(\Gamma) \vdash_{\Sigma'} sen(H)(\varphi)$.

Except for the explicit treatment of syntax translations, the axioms are very similar to Scott's axioms for a consequence relation [55].

Definition 2.2 [39] Given an entailment system $\mathcal{E}$, its category **Th** of *theories* has as objects pairs $T = (\Sigma, \Gamma)$ with Σ a signature and $\Gamma \subseteq$ $sen(\Sigma)$. A *theory morphism* $H : (\Sigma, \Gamma) \to (\Sigma', \Gamma')$ is a signature morphism $H : \Sigma \to \Sigma'$ such that if $\varphi \in \Gamma$, then $\Gamma' \vdash_{\Sigma'} sen(H)(\varphi)$.

A theory morphism $H : (\Sigma, \Gamma) \longrightarrow (\Sigma', \Gamma')$ is called *axiom-preserving* if it satisfies the condition that $sen(H)(\Gamma) \subseteq \Gamma'$. This defines a subcategory **Th**$_0$ with the same objects as **Th** but with morphisms restricted to be axiom-preserving theory morphisms. Notice that the category **Th**$_0$ does not depend at all on the entailment relation $\vdash$.

2.3 Institutions

The axiomatization of a model theory is due to the seminal work of Goguen and Burstall on *institutions* [22, 24].

Definition 2.3 [22] An *institution* is a 4-tuple $\mathcal{I} = (\mathbf{Sign}, sen, \mathbf{Mod}, \models)$ such that

- **Sign** is a category whose objects are called *signatures*,

- *sen* : **Sign** $\longrightarrow$ **Set** is a functor associating to each signature Σ a set of Σ-*sentences*,

- **Mod** : **Sign** $\longrightarrow$ **Cat**^{op} is a functor that gives for each signature Σ a category whose objects are called Σ-*models*, and

- $\models$ is a function associating to each $\Sigma \in |\mathbf{Sign}|$ a binary relation $\models_\Sigma$ $\subseteq |\mathbf{Mod}(\Sigma)| \times sen(\Sigma)$ called Σ-*satisfaction* satisfying the following *satisfaction condition* for each $H : \Sigma \to \Sigma'$ in **Sign**: for all $M' \in |\mathbf{Mod}(\Sigma')|$ and all $\varphi \in sen(\Sigma)$,

$$M' \models_{\Sigma'} sen(H)(\varphi) \iff \mathbf{Mod}(H)(M') \models_{\Sigma} \varphi.$$

The satisfaction condition just requires that, for any syntax translation between two signatures, a model of the second signature satisfies a translated sentence if and only if the translation of this model satisfies the original sentence. Note that **Mod** is a contravariant functor, that is, translations of models go backwards.

Given a set of Σ-sentences Γ, we define the category $\mathbf{Mod}(\Sigma, \Gamma)$ as the full subcategory of $\mathbf{Mod}(\Sigma)$ determined by those models $M \in |\mathbf{Mod}(\Sigma)|$ that satisfy all the sentences in Γ i.e. $M \models_{\Sigma} \varphi$ for each $\varphi \in \Gamma$.

Since the definition above of the category of theories $\mathbf{Th}_0$ only depends on signatures and sentences, it also makes sense for an institution.

2.4   Logics

Defining a *logic* is now almost trivial.

Definition 2.4 [39] A *logic* is a 5-tuple $\mathcal{L} = (\mathbf{Sign}, sen, \mathbf{Mod}, \vdash, \models)$ such that:

- $(\mathbf{Sign}, sen, \vdash)$ is an entailment system,

- $(\mathbf{Sign}, sen, \mathbf{Mod}, \models)$ is an institution,

and the following *soundness condition* is satisfied: for any $\Sigma \in |\mathbf{Sign}|$, $\Gamma \subseteq sen(\Sigma)$, and $\varphi \in sen(\Sigma)$,

$$\Gamma \vdash_{\Sigma} \varphi \implies \Gamma \models_{\Sigma} \varphi,$$

where, by definition, the relation $\Gamma \models_{\Sigma} \varphi$ holds if and only if $M \models_{\Sigma} \varphi$ holds for any model M that satisfies all the sentences in Γ.

The logic is called *complete* if the above implication is in fact an equivalence.

2.5   Proof calculi

A given logic may admit many different proof calculi. For example, in first order logic we have Hilbert style, natural deduction, and sequent calculi among others, and the way in which proofs are represented and generated by rules of deduction is different for each of these calculi. It is useful to make proofs relative to a given theory T whose axioms we are allowed to use in order to prove theorems.

A proof calculus associates to each theory T a *structure* $P(T)$ of proofs that use axioms of T as hypotheses. The structure $P(T)$ typically has an *algebraic structure* of some kind so that we can obtain new proofs out of previously given proofs by operations that mirror the rules of deduction of the calculus in question. We need not make a choice about the particular types of algebraic structures that should be allowed for different proof calculi; we can abstract from such choices by simply saying that for a given proof calculus there is a category **Str** of such structures and a functor $P : \mathbf{Th}_0 \longrightarrow \mathbf{Str}$ assigning to each theory T its structure of proofs $P(T)$. Of course, it should be possible to extract from $P(T)$ the underlying set *proofs*(T) of all the proofs of theorems of the theory T, and this extraction should be functorial. Also, each proof, whatever it is, should contain information about what theorem it is a proof of; this can be formalized by postulating a 'projection function' π_T (parameterized by T in a natural way) that maps each proof $p \in proofs(T)$ to the sentence φ that it proves. Of course, each theorem of T must have at least one proof, and sentences that are not theorems should have no proof. To summarize, a *proof calculus* [39] consists of an entailment system together with:

- A functorial assignment P of a structure $P(T)$ to each theory T.

- An additional functorial assignment of a set *proofs*(T) to each structure $P(T)$.

- A natural function π_T assigning a sentence to each proof $p \in proofs(T)$ and such that, for Γ the axioms of T, a sentence φ is in the image of π_T if and only if $\Gamma \vdash \varphi$.

It is quite common to encounter proof systems of a specialized nature. In these calculi, only certain signatures are admissible as syntax, e.g. finite signatures, only certain sentences are allowed as axioms, and only certain sentences—possibly different from the axioms—are allowed as conclusions. The obvious reason for introducing such specialized (sub)calculi is that proofs are simpler under the given restrictions. In computer science the choice between an efficient and an inefficient calculus may have dramatic practical consequences. For logic programming languages, such calculi do (or should) coincide with what is called their *operational semantics*, and mark the difference between a hopelessly inefficient theorem-prover and an efficient programming language. In practice, of course, we are primarily interested in proof calculi and proof subcalculi that are computationally effective. This is axiomatized by the notion of an *(effective) proof subcalculus* which can be found in [39].

2.6 Mapping logics

The advantage of having an axiomatic theory of logics is that the 'space' of all logics (or that of all entailment systems, institutions, proof calculi, etc.) becomes well understood. This space is not just a collection of objects bearing no relationship to each other. In fact, the most interesting fruit of the theory of general logics outlined in this section is that it gives us a method for *relating* logics in a general and systematic way, and to exploit such relations in many applications. The simplest kind of relation is a *sublogic* (subentailment system, etc.) relation. Thus, first order equational logic and Horn logic are both sublogics of first order logic with equality. However, more subtle and general ways of relating logics are possible. For example, we may want to represent the universal fragment of first order logic in a purely functional way by taking all the predicates and formulas to be *functions* whose value is either *true* or *false* so that a universal formula then becomes an equation equating a given term to *true*. The general way of relating logics (entailment systems, etc.) is to consider *maps* that interpret one logic into another. A detailed treatment of such maps is given in [39]; here we summarize some of the key ideas.

Let us first discuss in some detail *maps of entailment systems*. Basically, a map of entailment systems $\mathcal{E} \longrightarrow \mathcal{E}'$ maps the language of $\mathcal{E}$ to that of $\mathcal{E}'$ in a way that respects the entailment relation. This means that signatures of $\mathcal{E}$ are functorially mapped to signatures of $\mathcal{E}'$, and that sentences of $\mathcal{E}$ are mapped to sentences of $\mathcal{E}'$ in a way that is coherent with the mapping of their corresponding signatures. In addition, such a mapping α must respect the entailment relations $\vdash$ of $\mathcal{E}$ and $\vdash'$ of $\mathcal{E}'$ i.e. we must have $\Gamma \vdash \varphi \Rightarrow \alpha(\Gamma) \vdash' \alpha(\varphi)$. It turns out that for many interesting applications, including the functional representation of first order logic sketched above, one wants to be more general and allow maps that send a signature of $\mathcal{E}$ to a *theory* of $\mathcal{E}'$. These maps extend to maps between theories, and in this context the coherence with the mapping at the level of signatures is expressed by the notion of *sensible functor* defined in [39].

Definition 2.5 [39] A *map of entailment systems* $(\Phi, \alpha) : (\mathbf{Sign}, sen, \vdash) \longrightarrow (\mathbf{Sign}', sen', \vdash')$ consists of a natural transformation $\alpha : sen \Rightarrow \Phi; sen'$ and an α-sensible functor[1] $\Phi : \mathbf{Th_0} \longrightarrow \mathbf{Th_0'}$ satisfying the following property:

$$\Gamma \vdash_\Sigma \varphi \implies \Gamma' \cup \alpha_\Sigma(\Gamma) \vdash'_{\Sigma'} \alpha_\Sigma(\varphi),$$

where, by convention, $(\Sigma', \Gamma') = \Phi(\Sigma, \Gamma)$.

We call (Φ, α) *conservative* when the above implication is an equivalence.

---

[1] We refer to [39] for the detailed definition of α-sensible functor. Basically, what is required is that the provable consequences of the theory $\Phi(\Sigma, \Gamma)$ are entirely determined by $\Phi(\Sigma, \emptyset)$ and by $\alpha(\Gamma)$.

The property of being conservative may be essential for many applications. For example, since proof calculi are in a sense computational engines on which the design and implementation of theorem-provers and logic programming languages can be based, we can view the establishment of a map of proof calculi having nice properties, such as conservativity, as a proof of correctness for a *compiler* that permits implementing a system based on the first calculus in terms of another system based on the second. Besides establishing correctness, the map itself specifies the compilation function.

A *map of institutions*[2] $\mathcal{I} \longrightarrow \mathcal{I}'$ is similar in its syntax part to a map of entailment systems. In addition, for models we have a natural functor $\beta : \mathbf{Mod}'(\Phi(\Sigma)) \longrightarrow \mathbf{Mod}(\Sigma)$ 'backwards' from the models in $\mathcal{I}'$ of a translated signature $\Phi(\Sigma)$ to the models in $\mathcal{I}$ of the original signature Σ, and such a mapping respects the satisfaction relations $\models$ of $\mathcal{I}$ and $\models'$ of $\mathcal{I}'$, in the sense that $M' \models' \alpha(\varphi) \iff \beta(M') \models \varphi$.

Definition 2.6 [39] A *map of institutions* $(\Phi, \alpha, \beta) : (\mathbf{Sign}, sen, \mathbf{Mod}, \models)$ $\longrightarrow (\mathbf{Sign}', sen', \mathbf{Mod}', \models')$ consists of a natural transformation $\alpha : sen \Rightarrow \Phi; sen'$, an α-sensible functor $\Phi : \mathbf{Th}_0 \longrightarrow \mathbf{Th}'_0$, and a natural transformation $\beta : \Phi^{op}; \mathbf{Mod}' \Rightarrow \mathbf{Mod}$ such that for each $\Sigma \in |\mathbf{Sign}|$, $\varphi \in sen(\Sigma)$, and $M' \in |\mathbf{Mod}'(\Phi(\Sigma, \emptyset))|$ the following property is satisfied:

$$M' \models'_{\Sigma'} \alpha_\Sigma(\varphi) \iff \beta_{(\Sigma, \emptyset)}(M') \models_\Sigma \varphi,$$

where Σ' is the signature of the theory $\Phi(\Sigma, \emptyset)$.

A *map of logics* now has a very simple definition. It consists of a pair of maps: one for the underlying entailment systems, and another for the underlying institutions, such that both maps agree on how they translate signatures and sentences.

Definition 2.7 [39] Given logics $\mathcal{L} = (\mathbf{Sign}, sen, \mathbf{Mod}, \vdash, \models)$ and $\mathcal{L}' = (\mathbf{Sign}', sen', \mathbf{Mod}', \vdash', \models')$, a *map of logics* $(\Phi, \alpha, \beta) : \mathcal{L} \longrightarrow \mathcal{L}'$ consists of a functor $\Phi : \mathbf{Th}_0 \longrightarrow \mathbf{Th}'_0$, and natural transformations $\alpha : sen \Rightarrow \Phi; sen'$ and $\beta : \Phi^{op}; \mathbf{Mod}' \Rightarrow \mathbf{Mod}$ such that:

- $(\Phi, \alpha) : (\mathbf{Sign}, sen, \vdash) \longrightarrow (\mathbf{Sign}', sen', \vdash')$ is a map of entailment systems, and

- $(\Phi, \alpha, \beta) : (\mathbf{Sign}, sen, \mathbf{Mod}, \models) \longrightarrow (\mathbf{Sign}', sen', \mathbf{Mod}', \models')$ is a map of institutions.

We call (Φ, α, β) *conservative* if and only if (Φ, α) is a conservative map of entailment systems.

There is also a notion of map of proof calculi, for which we refer the reader to [39].

---

[2]Such maps are different from the 'institution morphisms' considered by Goguen and Burstall in [22, 24].

2.7 The idea of a logical framework

Viewed from the perspective of a general space of logics that can be related to each other by means of mappings, the quest for a *logical framework*, understood as a logic in which many other logics can be represented, can in principle—although perhaps not in all approaches—be understood as the search within such a space for a logic $\mathcal{F}$ (the *framework* logic) such that many other logics (the *object* logics) such as, say, $\mathcal{L}$ can be represented in $\mathcal{F}$ by means of mappings $\mathcal{L} \longrightarrow \mathcal{F}$ that have good enough properties. The minimum requirement that seems reasonable to make on a representation map $\mathcal{L} \longrightarrow \mathcal{F}$ is that it should be a *conservative* map of entailment systems. Under such circumstances, we can reduce issues of provability in $\mathcal{L}$ to issues of provability in $\mathcal{F}$, by mapping the theories and sentences of $\mathcal{L}$ into $\mathcal{F}$ using the conservative representation map. Given a computer implementation of deduction in $\mathcal{F}$, we can use the conservative map to prove theorems in $\mathcal{L}$ by proving the corresponding translations in $\mathcal{F}$. In this way, the implementation for $\mathcal{F}$ can be used as a generic theorem-prover for many logics.

However, since maps between logics can, as we have seen, respect additional logical structure such as the model theory or the proofs, in some cases a representation map into a logical framework may be particularly informative because, in addition to being a conservative map of entailment systems, it is also a map of institutions, or a map of proof calculi. For example, when rewriting logic is chosen as a logical framework, appropriate representation maps for equational logic, Horn logic, and propositional linear logic can be shown to be maps of institutions also [34]. In general, however, since the model theories of different logics can be very different from each other, it is not reasonable to expect or require that the representation maps into a logical framework will always be maps of institutions.

The issue of whether, given a representation map $\mathcal{L} \longrightarrow \mathcal{F}$ that is a conservative map of entailment systems, proof calculi for $\mathcal{L}$ and $\mathcal{F}$ can be related in some way offers more hope. Assuming that the logical framework $\mathcal{F}$ comes equipped with a specified proof calculus, it is then possible, using a universal construction of Cerioli and Meseguer [9], to 'borrow' the proof calculus of $\mathcal{F}$ in order to endow $\mathcal{L}$ with a proof calculus in such a way that the representation map then becomes a map of proof calculi.

Having criteria for the adequacy of maps representing logics in a logical framework is not enough. An equally important issue is having criteria for the *generality* of a logical framework, so that it is in fact justified to call it by that name. That is, given a candidate logical framework $\mathcal{F}$, how many logics can be adequately represented in $\mathcal{F}$? We can make this question precise by defining the *scope* of a logical framework $\mathcal{F}$ as the class of entailment systems $\mathcal{E}$ having conservative maps of entailment systems $\mathcal{E} \longrightarrow \mathcal{F}$.

In this regard, the axioms of the theory of general logics that we have presented are probably too general; without adding further assumptions it is not reasonable to expect that we can find a logical framework $\mathcal{F}$ whose scope is the class of *all* entailment systems. A much more reasonable goal is finding an $\mathcal{F}$ whose scope includes all entailment systems of 'practical interest', having finitary presentations of their syntax and their rules of deduction. Axiomatizing such finitely presentable entailment systems and proof calculi so as to capture—in the spirit of the more general axioms that we have presented, but with stronger requirements—all logics of 'practical interest' (at least for computational purposes) is a very important research task.

In this chapter, we present rewriting logic as a logic that seems to have particularly good properties as a logical framework. The evidence we can give within the space constraints of this chapter is necessarily partial; further evidence can be found in [34]. We conjecture that the scope of rewriting logic contains all entailment systems of 'practical interest' for a reasonable axiomatization of such systems.

3   Rewriting logic

This section gives the rules of deduction, proof theory, and semantics of rewriting logic. Section 4 will explain how rewriting logic can be used as a logical framework in which to represent other logics.

3.1   Basic universal algebra

For the sake of simplifying the exposition, we treat the *unsorted* case; the many-sorted and order-sorted cases can be given a similar treatment. A set Σ of function symbols is a ranked alphabet $\Sigma = \{\Sigma_n \mid n \in \mathbb{N}\}$. A Σ-algebra is then a set A together with an assignment of a function $f_A : A^n \longrightarrow A$ for each $f \in \Sigma_n$ with $n \in \mathbb{N}$. We denote by T_Σ the Σ-algebra of ground Σ-terms, and by $T_\Sigma(X)$ the Σ-algebra of Σ-terms with variables in a set X. Similarly, given a set E of Σ-equations, $T_{\Sigma,E}$ denotes the Σ-algebra of equivalence classes of ground Σ-terms modulo the equations E; in the same way, $T_{\Sigma,E}(X)$ denotes the Σ-algebra of equivalence classes of Σ-terms with variables in X modulo the equations E. Let $[t]_E$ or just $[t]$ denote the E-equivalence class of t.

Given a term $t \in T_\Sigma(\{x_1, \ldots, x_n\})$, and terms $u_1, \ldots, u_n$, we denote by $t(u_1/x_1, \ldots, u_n/x_n)$ the term obtained from t by *simultaneously substituting* u_i for x_i, $i = 1, \ldots, n$. To simplify notation, we denote a sequence of objects $a_1, \ldots, a_n$ by $\bar{a}$; with this notation, $t(u_1/x_1, \ldots, u_n/x_n)$ can be abbreviated to $t(\bar{u}/\bar{x})$.

3.2   The rules of rewriting logic

A *signature* in rewriting logic is a pair (Σ, E) with Σ a ranked alphabet of function symbols and E a set of Σ-equations. Rewriting will operate on equivalence classes of terms modulo the set of equations E. In this way, we free rewriting from the syntactic constraints of a term representation and gain a much greater flexibility in deciding what counts as a *data structure*; for example, string rewriting is obtained by imposing an associativity axiom, and multiset rewriting by imposing associativity and commutativity. Of course, standard term rewriting is obtained as the particular case in which the set E of equations is empty.

Given a signature (Σ, E), *sentences* of the logic are 'sequents' of the form $[t]_E \longrightarrow [t']_E$, where t and t' are Σ-terms possibly involving some variables from the countably infinite set $X = \{x_1, \ldots, x_n, \ldots\}$. A *theory* in this logic, called a rewrite theory, is a slight generalization of the usual notion of theory as in Definition 2.2 in that, in addition, we allow the axioms—in this case the sequents $[t]_E \longrightarrow [t']_E$—to be labelled. This is very natural for many applications, and customary for automata—viewed as labelled transition systems—and for Petri nets, which are both particular instances of our definition.

Definition 3.1 A *rewrite theory* $\mathcal{R}$ is a 4-tuple $\mathcal{R} = (\Sigma, E, L, R)$ where Σ is a ranked alphabet of function symbols, E is a set of Σ-equations, L is a set of *labels*, and R is a set of pairs $R \subseteq L \times T_{\Sigma,E}(X)^2$ whose first component is a label and whose second component is a pair of E-equivalence classes of terms, with $X = \{x_1, \ldots, x_n, \ldots\}$ a countably infinite set of variables. Elements of R are called *rewrite rules*.[3] We understand a rule $(r, ([t], [t']))$ as a labelled sequent and use for it the notation $r : [t] \longrightarrow [t']$. To indicate that $\{x_1, \ldots, x_n\}$ is the set of variables occurring in either t or t', we write $r : [t(x_1, \ldots, x_n)] \longrightarrow [t'(x_1, \ldots, x_n)]$, or in abbreviated notation $r : [t(\overline{x})] \longrightarrow [t'(\overline{x})]$.

Given a rewrite theory $\mathcal{R}$, we say that $\mathcal{R}$ *entails* a sequent $[t] \longrightarrow [t']$, or that $[t] \longrightarrow [t']$ is a *(concurrent) $\mathcal{R}$-rewrite*, and write $\mathcal{R} \vdash [t] \longrightarrow [t']$ if and only if $[t] \longrightarrow [t']$ can be obtained by finite application of the following *rules of deduction*:

1. **Reflexivity.** For each $[t] \in T_{\Sigma,E}(X)$, $\dfrac{}{[t] \longrightarrow [t]}$.

---

[3]To simplify the exposition the rules of the logic are given for the case of *unconditional* rewrite rules. However, all the ideas presented here have been extended to conditional rules in [40] with very general rules of the form

$$r : [t] \longrightarrow [t'] \;\; \textit{if} \;\; [u_1] \longrightarrow [v_1] \wedge \ldots \wedge [u_k] \longrightarrow [v_k].$$

This increases considerably the expressive power of rewrite theories.

2. **Congruence.** For each $f \in \Sigma_n$, $n \in \mathbb{N}$,

$$\frac{[t_1] \longrightarrow [t'_1] \quad \ldots \quad [t_n] \longrightarrow [t'_n]}{[f(t_1,\ldots,t_n)] \longrightarrow [f(t'_1,\ldots,t'_n)]}.$$

3. **Replacement.** For each rule $r : [t(x_1,\ldots,x_n)] \longrightarrow [t'(x_1,\ldots,x_n)]$ in R,

$$\frac{[w_1] \longrightarrow [w'_1] \quad \ldots \quad [w_n] \longrightarrow [w'_n]}{[t(\overline{w}/\overline{x})] \longrightarrow [t'(\overline{w'}/\overline{x})]}.$$

4. **Transitivity**

$$\frac{[t_1] \longrightarrow [t_2] \quad [t_2] \longrightarrow [t_3]}{[t_1] \longrightarrow [t_3]}.$$

Rewriting logic is a logic for reasoning correctly about *concurrent systems* having *states*, and evolving by means of *transitions*. The signature of a rewrite theory describes a particular structure for the states of a system, e.g. multiset, binary tree, etc., so that its states can be distributed according to such a structure. The rewrite rules in the theory describe which *elementary local transitions* are possible in the distributed state by concurrent local transformations. The rules of rewriting logic allow us to reason correctly about which *general* concurrent transitions are possible in a system satisfying such a description. Clearly, concurrent systems should be the *models* giving a semantic interpretation to rewriting logic. Alternatively, however, we can adopt a logical viewpoint instead, and regard the rules of rewriting logic as *metarules* for correct deduction in a *logical system*. This second viewpoint will be particularly fruitful in our discussion of rewriting logic as a logical framework in Section 4. Both points of view are discussed in greater detail in our paper [34].

3.3 The models of rewriting logic

We first sketch the construction of initial and free models for a rewrite theory $\mathcal{R} = (\Sigma, E, L, R)$. Such models capture nicely the intuitive idea of a 'rewrite system' in the sense that they are systems whose states are E-equivalence classes of terms, and whose transitions are concurrent rewritings using the rules in R. By adopting a logical instead of a computational perspective, we can alternatively view such models as 'logical systems' in which formulas are validly rewritten to other formulas by concurrent rewritings which correspond to proofs for the logic in question. Such models have a natural *category* structure, with states (or formulas) as objects, transitions (or proofs) as morphisms, and sequential composition as morphism composition, and in them dynamic behavior exactly corresponds to deduction.

Given a rewrite theory $\mathcal{R} = (\Sigma, E, L, R)$, the model that we are seeking is a category $\mathcal{T}_{\mathcal{R}}(X)$ whose objects are equivalence classes of terms $[t] \in T_{\Sigma,E}(X)$ and whose morphisms are equivalence classes of 'proof terms' representing proofs in rewriting deduction i.e. concurrent $\mathcal{R}$-rewrites. The rules for generating such proof terms, with the specification of their respective domains and codomains, are given below; they just 'decorate' with proof terms the rules 1–4 of rewriting logic. Note that we always use 'diagrammatic' notation for morphism composition i.e. $\alpha; \beta$ always means the composition of α *followed by* β.

1. **Identities.** For each $[t] \in T_{\Sigma,E}(X)$, $\dfrac{}{[t] : [t] \longrightarrow [t]}$.

2. **Σ-structure.** For each $f \in \Sigma_n$, $n \in \mathbb{N}$,

$$\frac{\alpha_1 : [t_1] \longrightarrow [t'_1] \quad \cdots \quad \alpha_n : [t_n] \longrightarrow [t'_n]}{f(\alpha_1, \ldots, \alpha_n) : [f(t_1, \ldots, t_n)] \longrightarrow [f(t'_1, \ldots, t'_n)]}.$$

3. **Replacement.** For each rewrite rule $r : [t(\overline{x}^n)] \longrightarrow [t'(\overline{x}^n)]$ in R,

$$\frac{\alpha_1 : [w_1] \longrightarrow [w'_1] \quad \cdots \quad \alpha_n : [w_n] \longrightarrow [w'_n]}{r(\alpha_1, \ldots, \alpha_n) : [t(\overline{w}/\overline{x})] \longrightarrow [t'(\overline{w'}/\overline{x})]}.$$

4. **Composition** $\dfrac{\alpha : [t_1] \longrightarrow [t_2] \quad \beta : [t_2] \longrightarrow [t_3]}{\alpha; \beta : [t_1] \longrightarrow [t_3]}.$

Each of the above rules of generation defines a different operation taking certain proof terms as arguments and returning a resulting proof term. In other words, proof terms form an algebraic structure $\mathcal{P}_{\mathcal{R}}(X)$ consisting of a graph with nodes $T_{\Sigma,E}(X)$, with identity arrows, and with operations f (for each $f \in \Sigma$), r (for each rewrite rule), and $\_; \_$ (for composing arrows). Our desired model $\mathcal{T}_{\mathcal{R}}(X)$ is the quotient of $\mathcal{P}_{\mathcal{R}}(X)$ modulo the following equations:[4]

1. **Category**

    (a) *Associativity.* For all α, β, γ, $(\alpha; \beta); \gamma = \alpha; (\beta; \gamma)$.

    (b) *Identities.* For each $\alpha : [t] \longrightarrow [t']$, $\alpha; [t'] = \alpha$ and $[t]; \alpha = \alpha$.

2. **Functoriality of the Σ-algebraic structure.** For each $f \in \Sigma_n$,

    (a) *Preservation of composition.* For all $\alpha_1, \ldots, \alpha_n, \beta_1, \ldots, \beta_n$,

$$f(\alpha_1; \beta_1, \ldots, \alpha_n; \beta_n) = f(\alpha_1, \ldots, \alpha_n); f(\beta_1, \ldots, \beta_n).$$

---

[4] In the expressions appearing in the equations, when compositions of morphisms are involved, we always implicitly assume that the corresponding domains and codomains match.

(b) *Preservation of identities.* $f([t_1], \ldots, [t_n]) = [f(t_1, \ldots, t_n)]$.

3. **Axioms in** E. For $t(x_1, \ldots, x_n) = t'(x_1, \ldots, x_n)$ an axiom in E, for all $\alpha_1, \ldots, \alpha_n$, $t(\alpha_1, \ldots, \alpha_n) = t'(\alpha_1, \ldots, \alpha_n)$.

4. **Exchange.** For each $r : [t(x_1, \ldots, x_n)] \longrightarrow [t'(x_1, \ldots, x_n)]$ in R,

$$\frac{\alpha_1 : [w_1] \longrightarrow [w'_1] \quad \cdots \quad \alpha_n : [w_n] \longrightarrow [w'_n]}{r(\overline{\alpha}) = r(\overline{[w]}); t'(\overline{\alpha}) = t(\overline{\alpha}); r(\overline{[w']})}.$$

Note that the set X of variables is actually a parameter of these constructions, and we need not assume X to be fixed and countable. In particular, for $X = \emptyset$, we adopt the notation $\mathcal{T}_{\mathcal{R}}$. The equations in 1 make $\mathcal{T}_{\mathcal{R}}(X)$ a category, the equations in 2 make each $f \in \Sigma$ a functor, and 3 forces the axioms E. The exchange law states that any rewriting of the form $r(\overline{\alpha})$—which represents the *simultaneous* rewriting of the term at the top using rule r *and* 'below' i.e. in the subterms matched by the variables, using the rewrites $\overline{\alpha}$—is equivalent to the sequential composition $r(\overline{[w]}); t'(\overline{\alpha})$, corresponding to first rewriting on top with r and then below on the subterms matched by the variables with $\overline{\alpha}$, and is also equivalent to the sequential composition $t(\overline{\alpha}); r(\overline{[w']})$ corresponding to first rewriting below with $\overline{\alpha}$ and then on top with r. Therefore, the exchange law states that rewriting at the top by means of rule r and rewriting 'below' using $\overline{\alpha}$ are processes that are independent of each other and can be done either simultaneously or in any order. Since $[t(x_1, \ldots, x_n)]$ and $[t'(x_1, \ldots, x_n)]$ can be regarded as functors $\mathcal{T}_{\mathcal{R}}(X)^n \longrightarrow \mathcal{T}_{\mathcal{R}}(X)$, from the mathematical point of view the exchange law just asserts that r is a *natural transformation*.

Lemma 3.2 [40] For each rewrite rule $r : [t(x_1, \ldots, x_n)] \longrightarrow [t'(x_1, \ldots, x_n)]$ in R, the family of morphisms

$$\{r(\overline{[w]}) : [t(\overline{w}/\overline{x})] \longrightarrow [t'(\overline{w}/\overline{x})] \mid \overline{[w]} \in T_{\Sigma,E}(X)^n\}$$

is a natural transformation $r : [t(x_1, \ldots, x_n)] \Rightarrow [t'(x_1, \ldots, x_n)]$ between the functors $[t(x_1, \ldots, x_n)], [t'(x_1, \ldots, x_n)] : \mathcal{T}_{\mathcal{R}}(X)^n \longrightarrow \mathcal{T}_{\mathcal{R}}(X)$.

The category $\mathcal{T}_{\mathcal{R}}(X)$ is just one among many *models* that can be assigned to the rewrite theory $\mathcal{R}$. The general notion of model, called an $\mathcal{R}$-*system*, is defined as follows:

Definition 3.3 Given a rewrite theory $\mathcal{R} = (\Sigma, E, L, R)$, an $\mathcal{R}$-*system* $\mathcal{S}$ is a category $\mathcal{S}$ together with:

- a (Σ, E)-algebra structure given by a family of functors

$$\{f_{\mathcal{S}} : \mathcal{S}^n \longrightarrow \mathcal{S} \mid f \in \Sigma_n, n \in \mathbb{N}\}$$

satisfying the equations E i.e. for any $t(x_1, \ldots, x_n) = t'(x_1, \ldots, x_n)$ in E we have an identity of functors $t_S = t'_S$, where the functor t_S is defined inductively from the functors f_S in the obvious way.

- for each rewrite rule $r : [t(\overline{x})] \longrightarrow [t'(\overline{x})]$ in R a natural transformation $r_S : t_S \Rightarrow t'_S$.

An $\mathcal{R}$-*homomorphism* $F : S \longrightarrow S'$ between two $\mathcal{R}$-systems is then a functor $F : S \longrightarrow S'$ such that it is a Σ-algebra homomorphism i.e. $f_S * F = F^n * f_{S'}$, for each f in Σ_n, $n \in \mathbb{N}$, and such that 'F preserves R' i.e. for each rewrite rule $r : [t(\overline{x})] \longrightarrow [t'(\overline{x})]$ in R we have the identity of natural transformations[5] $r_S * F = F^n * r_{S'}$, where n is the number of variables appearing in the rule. This defines a category $\mathcal{R}$-**Sys** in the obvious way.

A detailed proof of the following theorem on the existence of initial and free $\mathcal{R}$-systems for the more general case of conditional rewrite theories is given in [40], where the soundness and completeness of rewriting logic for $\mathcal{R}$-system models is also proved.

Theorem 3.4 $\mathcal{T}_\mathcal{R}$ is an initial object in the category $\mathcal{R}$-**Sys**. More generally, $\mathcal{T}_\mathcal{R}(X)$ has the following universal property: Given an $\mathcal{R}$-system S, each function $F : X \longrightarrow |S|$ extends uniquely to an $\mathcal{R}$-homomorphism $F^\natural : \mathcal{T}_\mathcal{R}(X) \longrightarrow S$.

4 Rewriting logic as a logical framework

Our discussion of rewriting logic provides an example of the different aspects of a logic axiomatized in Section 2. Indeed, its entailment relation, its model theory, and even the structure of its proofs have all been discussed in detail. The question that we now wish to discuss is the privileged role of rewriting logic as a *logical framework*. That is, its good properties for the representation of other logics within it by means of conservative maps $\mathcal{L} \longrightarrow RWLogic$, where such maps are at least maps of entailment systems, but can in some cases preserve additional structure (maps of logics, maps of proof calculi).

In [34], we have shown the adequacy of rewriting logic as a logical framework in which other logics can be represented by means of conservative maps of logics or of entailment systems with relevant examples, including equational, Horn, and linear logic, a general approach to the treatment of quantifiers, and a very general method for representing sequent presenta-

---

[5]Note that we use diagrammatic order for the *horizontal*, $\alpha * \beta$, and *vertical*, $\gamma; \delta$, composition of natural transformations [33].

tions of a logic. Here, we present this last method in some detail, and in Section 5 we also show how rewriting logic can be represented in itself.

In what follows, we will use the syntax of Maude [40, 44, 42], a wide spectrum programming language directly based on rewriting logic, to present rewrite theories. In Maude, there are essentially two kinds of *modules*:[6]

- *Functional modules*, which are of the form fmod $\mathcal{E}$ endfm for an equational theory $\mathcal{E}$, and

- *System modules*, which are of the form mod $\mathcal{R}$ endm for a rewrite theory $\mathcal{R}$.

In functional modules, equations are declared with the keywords eq or ceq (for conditional equations), and in system modules with the keywords ax or cax. Certain equations, such as associativity, commutativity, or identity, for which rewriting modulo is provided, can be declared together with the corresponding function using the keywords assoc, comm, id. Rules can only appear in system modules, and are declared with the keywords rl or crl.

The version of rewriting logic used for Maude is *order-sorted*. This means that rewrite theories are typed (types are called *sorts*) and can have subtypes (subsorts), and that function symbols can be overloaded. In particular, functional modules are order-sorted equational theories [25] and they form a sublanguage similar to OBJ [27].

As in OBJ, Maude modules can be imported by other modules, and can also be parameterized by means of *theories* that specify semantic requirements for interfaces.

The map of entailment systems that we are about to describe can be applied to any sequent calculus, be it for intuitionistic, classical or any other logic. In general, we need an operation

```
op _|-_ : FormList FormList -> Sequent .
```

that turns two lists of formulas (multisets, or sets in some cases, depending on the structural rules of the entailment system in question) into a term representing a sequent. Then we have a sort Configuration representing multisets of sequents, with a union operator written using empty syntax. A sequent calculus rule

$$\frac{G_1 \vdash D_1, \ldots, G_n \vdash D_n}{G \vdash D}$$

becomes a rewrite rule

---

[6]There are also *object-oriented modules*, which can be reduced to a special case of system modules [42] and are not used here.

```
rl (G1 |- D1) ... (Gn |- Dn) => (G |- D) .
```

on the sort `Configuration`, that, using the fact that '---' introduces a comment,[7] can be written as

```
rl    (G1 |- D1) ... (Gn |- Dn)
   => --- ---------------------
             (G |- D) .
```

in order to make it even clearer that the rewrite rule and the sequent notations in fact capture the same idea. Sometimes the rewrite rule can be conditional to the satisfaction of some auxiliary side conditions.

As an example, we describe in full detail the representation within rewriting logic of a sequent calculus for classical propositional logic. The basic atoms are left as a parameter specified by a parameter theory ATOM.

```
fth ATOM is
   sort Atom .
endft
```

We can take advantage of several properties enjoyed by classical logic in order to have a more succint and elegant sequent calculus. First, using the double negation and De Morgan laws, we can push negation to the atomic level. Also, we can use one-sided sequents of the form $\vdash A_1, \ldots, A_n$, instead of the more usual double-sided sequents of the form $A_1, \ldots, A_n \vdash B_1, \ldots, B_m$, because such a sequent is equivalent to the one-sided sequent $\vdash \sim A_1, \ldots, \sim A_n, B_1, \ldots, B_m$, where the symbol $\sim$ denotes negation. One of the advantages of this presentation is that the number of rules is reduced to half. Furthermore, the contraction and permutation structural rules can be built into the sequent data structure by using sets of formulas instead of lists.

The first module defines the syntax of classical propositional logic, using the connectives of conjunction, disjunction, and negation. Other connectives can be defined in terms of these, or added to the module as desired. The equations in this functional module push negation to the atomic level.

```
fmod PROP[A :: ATOM] is
   sort Prop .
   subsort Atom < Prop .        --- atomic propositions
   ops tt ff : -> Prop .        --- truth values
   op ~_ : Prop -> Prop .       --- negation
   op _\/_ : Prop Prop -> Prop . --- disjunction
   op _/\_ : Prop Prop -> Prop . --- conjunction
```

---

[7]This displaying trick that makes it possible to write a sequent calculus rule in a similar way to the usual presentation in logical textbooks is due to K. Futatsugi.

```
    vars P Q : Prop .
    eq ~ tt = ff .
    eq ~ ff = tt .
    eq ~~ P = P .                    --- double negation
    eq ~(P \/ Q) = ~P /\ ~Q .        --- De Morgan laws
    eq ~(P /\ Q) = ~P \/ ~Q .
endfm
```

In order to define sequents, we assume a parameterized module SET[X] for finite sets, represented in the form A1,...,An i.e. the union operator has the syntax

```
    op _,_ : Set Set -> Set .
```

Then, a one-sided sequent is denoted by the syntax |- A1,...,An.

```
fmod SEQUENT[A :: ATOM] is
    protecting SET[PROP[A]] .
    sort Sequent .
    op |-_ : Set -> Sequent .
endfm
```

Finally, the following *system* module defines the sort Configuration of multisets of sequents as suggested above, and gives the corresponding rules for classical propositional logic.

```
mod SEQUENT-RULES[A :: ATOM] is
    protecting SEQUENT[A] .
    sort Configuration .
    subsort Sequent < Configuration .
    op empty : -> Configuration .
    op __ : Configuration Configuration -> Configuration
                                   [assoc comm id: empty] .
    vars R S : Set .
    vars P Q : Prop .

    --- Identity
    rl      empty
        => --- ------
           |- P,~P .
    --- Cut
    rl     (|- R,P)(|- S,~P)
        => --- --------------
              |- R,S .
```

```
--- Weakening
rl         |- R
   => --- ----
        |- R,P .
--- Disjunction
rl         |- R,P,Q
   => --- --------
        |- R,P \/ Q .
--- Conjunction
rl      (|- R,P)(|- S,Q)
   => --- ------------
        |- R,S,P /\ Q .
--- Truth values
rl      empty
   => --- --
        |- tt .
endm
```

Exactly the same technique has been used in [34] to represent a sequent calculus for Girard's linear logic [21].

As another example illustrating the generality of this approach, we sketch a presentation in rewriting logic of the *2-sequent calculus* defined by A. Masini and S. Martini in order to develop a proof theory for modal logics [36, 35]. In their approach, a *2-sequent* is an expression of the form $\Gamma \vdash \Delta$, where Γ and Δ are not lists of formulas as usual, but they are lists of lists of formulas, so that sequents are endowed with a vertical structure. For example,

$$\begin{matrix} A, B & & D \\ C & \vdash & E, F \\ & & G \end{matrix}$$

is a 2-sequent, which will be represented in rewriting logic as

$$A, B; C \vdash D; E, F; G.$$

We first define a parameterized module LIST[X] for lists, assuming a module NAT defining a sort Nat of natural numbers with zero 0, a successor function s_, an addition operation _+_, and an order relation _<=_.

```
fth ELEM is
  sort Elem .
endft
```

```
fmod LIST[X :: ELEM] is
  protecting NAT .
  sort List .
  subsort Elem < List .
  op nil : -> List .
  op _,_ : List List -> List [assoc id: nil] .
  op length : List -> Nat .
  var E : Elem .
  vars L L' : List .
  eq length(nil) = 0 .
  eq length(E) = s0 .
  eq length(L,L') = length(L) + length(L') .
endfm
```

In order to define 2-sequents, we instantiate twice the module LIST[X] above, using a sort of formulas Form whose definition is not presented here, and that should have an operation

```
op []_ : Form -> Form .
```

corresponding to the modality $\Box$.

```
make 2-LIST is
  LIST[LIST[Form]]*(sort List to 2-List,
                    op length to depth, op _,_ to _;_)
endmk
```

Note that in the 2-LIST module the concatenation operation _,_ is renamed to _;_ in the case of lists of lists of formulas, called 2-lists, whereas in the case of lists of formulas the notation _,_ is kept. Also, to emphasize the vertical structure of 2-sequents, the operation length for 2-lists is renamed to depth.

Now we can easily define 2-sequents as follows:

```
fmod 2-SEQUENT is
  protecting 2-LIST .
  sort 2-Sequent .
  op _|-_ : 2-List 2-List -> 2-Sequent .
endfm
```

The basic rules for the modality $\square$ are

$$
\frac{\begin{array}{c} \Gamma \\ \alpha \\ \beta, A \\ \Gamma' \end{array} \vdash \Delta}{\begin{array}{c} \Gamma \\ \alpha, \square A \\ \beta \\ \Gamma' \end{array} \vdash \Delta} \ (\square\text{-}L)
\qquad\qquad
\frac{\Gamma \vdash \begin{array}{c} \Delta \\ \alpha \\ A \end{array}}{\Gamma \vdash \begin{array}{c} \Delta \\ \alpha, \square A \end{array}} \ (\square\text{-}R)
$$

where Γ, Γ', Δ denote 2-lists, α, β denote lists of formulas, and the rule $\square$-R has the side condition that $depth(\Gamma) \leq depth(\Delta) + 1$ i.e. the formula A is the only formula in the last level of the 2-sequent.

These rules are represented in rewriting logic as follows:

```
mod 2-SEQUENT-RULES is
  protecting 2-SEQUENT .
  sort Configuration .
  subsort 2-Sequent < Configuration .
  op empty : -> Configuration .
  op __ : Configuration Configuration -> Configuration
                          [assoc comm id: empty] .

  vars R R' S : 2-List .
  vars L L' : List .
  var A : Form .

  rl     R ; L ; L',A ; R' |- S
     => --- --------------------
        R ; L,[]A ; L' ; R' |- S .

  rl     R |- S ; L ; A
     => --- ----------
        R |- S ; L,[]A
     if depth(R) <= s(depth(S)) .
endm
```

The dual rules for the modality $\lozenge$ are treated similarly.

This general method of viewing sequents as rewrite rules can even be applied to systems more general than traditional sequent calculi. Thus, besides the possibilities of being one-sided or two-sided, one-dimensional or two-dimensional, etc., a 'sequent' can, for example, be a sequent presentation of natural deduction, a term assignment system, or even any predicate defined by structural induction in some way such that the proof is a kind of tree, as, for example, the so-called structural operational semantics [49, 31], including type-checking systems. The general idea is to map a rule in the 'sequent' system to a rewrite rule over a 'configuration' of sequents or predicates, in such a way that the rewriting relation corresponds to provability of such a predicate. This idea is illustrated by means of several different examples in [34], where we apply it to Milner's *CCS* [45] and to Kahn's *natural semantics* for a small functional language [32].

5   Rewriting logic in rewriting logic

Rewriting logic can be used not only to represent what might be called the object level of a logic, but also to represent metalevel aspects such as proofs or theories. This capacity to *reflect* some metalevel aspects into the object level can be a very useful and powerful technique, as has been recently emphasized by Constable [10] in the context of the Nuprl system.

   This section presents a simple example of reflection in which the proofs of a rewrite theory are reflected into the object level. The process can be understood as a map $\mathcal{R} \mapsto \mathcal{R}^\sharp$ sending each rewrite theory $\mathcal{R}$ to a rewrite theory $\mathcal{R}^\sharp$ with the property that

$$\mathcal{R} \vdash [\alpha] : [t] \to [t'] \quad \Longleftrightarrow \quad \mathcal{R}^\sharp \vdash [\alpha^\sharp] : [empty] \to [\alpha : t \Rightarrow t'],$$

that is, a proof α of $[t] \to [t']$ can be derived in the original rewrite theory if and only if a proof $\alpha^\sharp$ of the rewrite from the $[empty]$ configuration to the term $[\alpha : t \Rightarrow t']$, which codifies both the rewrite and its proof, can be carried out in $\mathcal{R}^\sharp$.

   The map is illustrated for a very simple rewrite theory $\mathcal{R}$ having a single rewrite rule; however, the construction is entirely general.

   Consider a rewrite theory given by a signature consisting of a constant symbol c, a binary function symbol f, and an equation $t(x,y) = t'(x,y)$, and by a rewrite rule $n : [l(a,b)] \longrightarrow [r(a,b)]$, where t, t', l, r are terms in this signature involving the specified variables.

   Assuming a countable set of variables Var, defined in a module VAR including the declaration

```
ops x y a b : -> Var .
```

we can represent the signature using the following functional module:

```
fmod SIG is
   protecting VAR .
   sort Term .                --- terms
   subsort Var < Term .       --- variables are terms
   op c : -> Term .           --- constant symbol
```

```
op f : Term Term -> Term .   --- binary function symbol
eq t = t' .                  --- given axiom
endfm
```

First, we extend the signature by making explicit the substitution operation:

```
fmod SIG-SUBST is
   protecting SIG .
   op _[_/_] : Term Term Var -> Term . --- substitution
   vars X Y : Var .
   vars T U V : Term .
   eq X[T/X] = T .
   ceq Y[T/X] = Y if not(X == Y) .
   eq c[T/X] = c .                      --- for each constant
   eq f(U,V)[T/X] = f(U[T/X],V[T/X]) . --- for each function
endfm
```

Now, we can begin defining the algebraic structure $\mathcal{P}_{\mathcal{R}}(\text{Var})$ of proof terms presented in Section 3.3. We reserve the name 'proof term' for the label α together with the sequent $[t] \longrightarrow [t']$ and use 'proof label' for α alone. However, some of the equations involve both parts, and to handle this we introduce two auxiliary operations dom and cod (for domain and codomain) such that $\text{dom}(\alpha) = [t]$ and $\text{cod}(\alpha) = [t']$. Also, in the presentation in Section 3.3, the operation _;_ was partial while in the module below it is total; however, this does not affect the mapping at all, and in any case it could also be made partial if desired, using a *sort constraint* [43].

```
fmod PLABEL is
   protecting SIG-SUBST .
   sort Plabel .
   subsort Term < Plabel .
   op f : Plabel Plabel -> Plabel .   --- for each function
   op n : Plabel Plabel -> Plabel .   --- for each rewrite rule
   op _;_ : Plabel Plabel -> Plabel [assoc] .
   ops dom cod : Plabel -> Term .

   var T : Term .
   vars L M : Plabel .
   eq dom(T) = T .
   eq cod(T) = T .
   eq dom(L;M) = dom(L) .
   eq cod(L;M) = cod(M) .
```

```
   eq dom(f(L,M)) = f(dom(L),dom(M)) .
   eq cod(f(L,M)) = f(cod(L),cod(M)) .
   eq dom(n(L,M)) = l[dom(L)/a][dom(M)/b] .
   eq cod(n(L,M)) = r[cod(L)/a][cod(M)/b] .
endfm
```

Note that in the last two equations a and b are the variables in the rewrite rule $n : [l(a, b)] \longrightarrow [r(a, b)]$.

Again, the substitution operation needs to be made explicit now for the sort of proof labels:

```
fmod PLABEL-SUBST is
   protecting PLABEL .
   op _[_/_] : Term Plabel Var -> Plabel . --- substitution
   vars X Y : Var .
   vars U V : Term .
   var L : Plabel .
   eq X[L/X] = L .
   ceq Y[L/X] = Y  if  not(X == Y) .
   eq c[L/X] = c .                      --- for each constant
   eq f(U,V)[L/X] = f(U[L/X],V[L/X]) . --- for each function
endfm
```

Having available the substitution operation, we can impose on proof labels the corresponding set of equations listed in Section 3.3, as follows:

```
fmod PLABEL-ALG is
   using PLABEL-SUBST .
   vars L M L' M' : Plabel .
   eq dom(L);L = L .                              --- Identity 1
   eq L;cod(L) = L .                              --- Identity 2
   eq f(L;L',M;M') = f(L,M);f(L',M') .            --- Functoriality
   eq t[L/x][M/y] = t'[L/x][M/y] .                --- Given axiom
   eq n(dom(L),dom(M));r[L/a][M/b] = n(L,M) .--- Exchange 1
   eq l[L/a][M/b];n(cod(L),cod(M)) = n(L,M) .--- Exchange 2
endfm
```

Finally, we can define a system module in which rewriting logic proofs are made explicit at the object level. Rewriting logic rules are presented using the general technique for sequent systems described in Section 4.

```
mod RWL-PROOFS is
   protecting PLABEL-ALG .
   sort Pterm .
```

```
op _:_ ==> _ : Plabel Term Term -> Pterm .
sort Config .
subsort Pterm < Config .
op empty : -> Config .
op __ : Config Config -> Config [assoc comm id: empty] .

vars T T' U U' : Term .
vars L M : Plabel .

--- Identity/Reflexivity
rl        empty
   => --- ----------
      T : T ==> T .

--- SIG-structure/Congruence  (One rule for each function)
rl    (L : T ==> T')(M : U ==> U')
   => --- -------------------------
      f(L,M) : f(T,U) ==> f(T',U') .

--- Replacement  (One rule for each rewrite rule)
rl         (L : T ==> T')(M : U ==> U')
   => --- ------------------------------------
      n(L,M) : l[T/a][U/b] ==> r[T'/a][U'/b] .

--- Composition/Transitivity
rl    (L : T ==> T')(M : T' ==> U)
   => --- ----------------------
            L;M : T ==> U .
endm
```

Many variations are of course possible on this theme. One can instead reflect both proofs and theories simultaneously as terms, by defining a *universal rewrite theory* $\mathcal{U}$ in which each finitely presented rewrite theory $\mathcal{R}$ is represented as a term $\widehat{\mathcal{R}}$ in such a way that

$$\mathcal{R} \vdash [\alpha] : [t] \to [t'] \iff \mathcal{U} \vdash [\hat{\alpha}] : \langle \widehat{\mathcal{R}}, empty \rangle \longrightarrow \langle \widehat{\mathcal{R}}, \tilde{\alpha} : \tilde{t} \Rightarrow \tilde{t'} \rangle$$

for $\tilde{\alpha}, \tilde{t}, \tilde{t'}$ appropriate representations of α, t, t', respectively.

6 Related work

We briefly discuss related work on abstract model theory, institutions, and logical frameworks. Although we try to mention the most closely related work we are aware of, this is not a comprehensive survey; therefore, some relevant references may have been unintentionally overlooked.

6.1   Abstract model theory, institutions, and general logics

Barwise wrote a fundamental paper axiomatizing *abstract model theory* [3]. A key motivation was to make explicit what a wide variety of logics extending standard first order logic, such as second order logic, logics with generalized quantifiers, and infinitary logics, had in common, by developing an axiomatic framework in which all of them would fit. Barwise observed that certain properties of a logic were 'soft' in the sense that they could be proved with very minimal assumptions in his general axiomatic setting, rather than depending on properties unique to a particular logic. Much research has been done in this area since the appearance of Barwise's axioms. An excellent overview of the field can be gained from the collection of papers in [4], which also contains a very complete bibliography.

In a certain sense, abstract model theory is not abstract enough. The key limiting assumption built into the framework is that models are typical set-theoretic structures as those used in first order logic, that is, a set, or a many-sorted collection of sets, together with functions and relations defined on such a set or sets. Although much useful work can be done under those assumptions, there are other logics whose models are of a different nature. Therefore, a fully general and abstract model theory should make very minimal assumptions about the models of a logic. Goguen and Burstall's notion of *institution* [22, 23, 24] provides precisely an axiomatization of abstract model theory in which the class of models associated to a given syntax only satisfies the minimal assumption of forming a category (which in particular could be just a set or a class if the category is discrete). In addition, Goguen and Burstall showed that this notion can be very useful in computer science in a variety of ways, including the definition of specification languages with powerful modularity and parameterization mechanisms (see also [53, 54] for examples of related work on applying institutions to software specification).

Subsequent work by a number of authors has shown that Barwise's observation about the possibility of 'soft' proofs for properties of a logic remains true in the more general setting of institutions. For example, Tarlecki [57, 58, 59, 60] explores a number of such properties in an institutional framework, including the treatment of open formulae and universal quantification, free models, varieties and quasi-varieties, Craig's Interpolation Theorem, Robinson's Consistency Theorem, and Lindenbaum's Theorem. A careful study of Craig's Interpolation Theorem for institutions can be found in a more recent paper by Diaconescu, Goguen, and Stefaneas [11] (who also study modularity issues). Finally, an axiomatic study of the Löwenheim–Skolem Theorem has been presented by Salibra and Scollo [51] in their somewhat more general preinstitution framework.

An important notion in the theory of institutions is that of *institution morphism* by which one institution can be related to another. Besides the original notion proposed by Goguen and Burstall, other related notions have been proposed, such as *preinstitution transformation* [52], *simulation* [1], and *map of institutions* (see Section 2.6). Cerioli's thesis [8] contains a good discussion of these different notions and their relative advantages and disadvantages.

The notion of institution has been generalized in several ways. On the one hand, weaker notions such as those of *preinstitution* [52] relax the requirements that the satisfaction relation between models and sentences must meet, or do away with the satisfaction relation altogether, as in the case of *specification logics* [12]. On the other hand, the satisfaction relation can be enriched, so that instead of just assigning to a model and a sentence either *true* or *false*, a richer collection of truth values is used instead. Specifically, the poset formed by the two standard truth values can be replaced by a *category* of truth values. The first proposal for an enrichment of this kind was made by Mayoh with his notion of *gallery* [38]. This was later generalized by Goguen and Burstall [23] to the notion of $\mathcal{V}$-*institution*, where $\mathcal{V}$ is a category of values for the satisfaction relation. An even more ambitious generalization that uses indexed categories to take account of substitutions in formulas is provided by Poigné's notion of *foundation* [50].

The theory of institutions was primarily developed to axiomatize the model theory of logics in a general and flexible way. There are however other aspects of a logic quite different from its model theory, such as its entailment relation and its proof theory, that are also very important and are in addition very well suited for computational treatment. Although some aspects of deduction can be addressed using $\mathcal{V}$-institutions [23] and foundations [50], a promising alternative is to investigate such notions independently of the concept of institution, although in a similar spirit. In this way, a modular view of the different aspects of a logic such as its model theory, entailment relation, and proof theory can be developed, and appropriate notions of map preserving the logical structure of each aspect can be formulated. This is precisely the goal of the theory of general logics first presented in [39] and summarized in Section 2. For the case of entailment systems, which focus on the entailment relation between a set of sentences and a consequence sentence, two other related notions that have been proposed in the literature are π-*institution* [17] (recently generalized in [16]) and *logical system* [30].

A useful property enjoyed by the different categories of entailment systems, institutions, logics, and proof calculi, that cover the different aspects of a logic, is that they are related by adjoint functors that make it possible to add the missing logical structure by means of universal constructions [39]. This has been exploited by Cerioli and Meseguer [9] to define more general constructions in which a logic $\mathcal{L}$ lacking some of its logical structure (for example its proof theory) can be endowed with the missing structure by 'borrowing' it from another logic $\mathcal{L}'$ that has it, provided we are given a map $\mathcal{L} \longrightarrow \mathcal{L}'$.

The concepts of the theory of general logics have been applied to the axiomatization of a general notion of *logic programming language* in [39], and to the design of multiparadigm logic programming languages in [41]. They have also been applied by Bonacina and Hsiang [6] to the axiomatization of theorem-proving strategies. Fiadeiro and Costa [15] use the notion of *categorical logic* in [39] to give an elegant account of the relation between temporal logic theories and concurrent processes.

The recent work of Gabbay [18, 19] on *labelled deductive systems* has some interesting parallels with work on general logics. Roughly speaking, a labelled deductive system consists of a language, a consequence relation, which need not be monotonic, and an algebra of labels with deduction rules that show how labelled formulas can give rise to new labelled formulas. There is a parallel between Gabbay's consequence relation and the notion of entailment system, although to make the parallel closer entailment systems should be generalized so that monotonicity is not required. In a similar way, the labels on formulas and the rules to derive new labelled formulas from previous ones seem to provide the analogue of a proof calculus. It would be very worth while to explore further these, for the moment vague, analogies so as to obtain a precise understanding of the exact relationship between these two approaches.

6.2 Logical frameworks

Much work has already been done in this area, including the Edinburgh logical framework LF [28, 2, 20]. The basic idea of the LF framework is to represent a logic as a signature in an appropriate higher-order type theory, in such a way that provability of a formula in the original logic can be reduced to provability of a type inhabitation assertion in the framework type theory. A categorical formalization of representations of logics in LF as appropriate conservative maps of 'logical systems', which are similar to our conservative maps of entailment systems, has been given by Harper, Sannella, and Tarlecki in [30], and has been further extended to deal with open formulas and substitution in [29]. Other logical frameworks having some similarities with the LF framework include meta-theorem-provers such as Isabelle [47], λProlog [46, 14], and Elf [48], all of which adopt as framework logics different variants of higher-order logics or type theories.

There has also been important work on what Basin and Constable [5] call *metalogical* frameworks. These are frameworks supporting reasoning about the metalogical aspects of the logics being represented. Typically, this is accomplished by reifying as 'data' the proof theory of the logic being represented in a process that is described in [5] as *externalizing* the logic in question. This is in contrast to the more *internalized* form in which logics are represented in LF and in meta-theorem-provers, so that deduction in the object logic is mirrored by deduction—for example, type inference—in the framework logic. Work on metalogical frameworks includes the already mentioned paper by Basin and Constable [5], who advocate constructive type theory as the framework logic, work of Matthews, Smaill, and Basin [37], who use Feferman's FS_0 [13], a logic designed with the explicit purpose of being a metalogical framework, earlier work by Smullyan [56], and work by Goguen, Stevens, Hobley, and Hilberdink [26] on the 2OBJ meta-theorem-prover, which uses order-sorted equational logic [25, 27].

A difficulty with systems based on higher-order type theory such as LF is that it may be quite awkward and of little practical use to represent logics whose structural properties differ considerably from those of the type theory. For example, linear and relevance logics do not have adequate representations in LF, in a precise technical sense of 'adequate' [20, Corollary 5.1.8]. Since in metalogical frameworks a direct connection between deduction in the object and framework logics does not have to be maintained, they seem in principle much more flexible in their representational capabilities. However, this comes at a price, since the possibility of directly using an implementation of the framework logic to implement an object logic may be compromised.

In relation to this previous work, rewriting logic seems to have great flexibility to represent in a natural way many other logics, widely different in nature, including equational, Horn, and linear logics, and any sequent calculus presentation of a logic under extremely general assumptions about such a sequent presentation; moreover, quantifiers can also be treated without problems [34]. More experience in representing other logics is certainly needed, but we are encouraged by the naturalness and directness—often preserving the original syntax and rules—with which the logics that we have studied can be represented. This is due to the great simplicity and generality of rewriting logic, since in it all syntax and structural axioms are user-definable, so that the abstract syntax of an object logic can be represented as an algebraic data type, and is also due to the existence of only a few general 'metarules' of deduction relative to the rewrite rules given by a specification, where such a specification can be used to describe with rewrite rules the rules of deduction of the object logic in question. Given an implementation of rewriting logic, which can be accomplished using well-known rewrite rule implementation techniques, and given a conservative representation map from an object logic into rewriting logic, one can directly obtain a mechanized implementation of the object logic. Furthermore, given the directness with which logics can usually be represented, the task of proving conservativity is in many cases straightforward. Finally, externalization of logics using techniques such as reflection (see Section 5) and induction on the externalized data (which relies on the existence of initial models) can be used to support metalogical reasoning in rewriting logic, in addition to the internalized logical representation of standard mappings.

7   Future research directions

We point out some open problems whose solution would further advance the approach to general logics and logical frameworks proposed in this chapter.

As we pointed out in Section 2.7, the general logics axioms that we have presented are in a sense too general. The axiomatization in the same spirit, but with more specific requirements, of logics of 'practical interest', having finitary presentations of their syntax and their rules of deduction and being in principle amenable to implementation on a computer, seems a very worth while research problem. The notion of *effective proof calculus* in [39], as well as the ideas of Goguen and Burstall on *charters* and *parchments* [23] may be useful in the search for the appropriate axioms. Once an axiomatization of this kind is found and is justified as indeed capturing all logics of practical interest, we will have a good criterion for the generality of a logical framework, namely whether or not all such logics are within the scope of the framework, or what a subclass of such logics is. As we already pointed out, we conjecture that rewriting logic is a fully general framework in this sense.

Another important problem is that of combining logics. For example, a logic may be parameterized by another logic, or two logics may be combined together into a logic that extends both of them in a minimal way. Technically, these combinations are closely related to the existence of colimits, and in some cases limits, in the category of logics in question. Limits of institutions have been studied in [59, 61]; certain limits of logics and proof calculi are used in [9] to 'borrow' logical structure missing in one logic from another logic. The problem, however, is that—due to the generality of the axioms used to formalize logics—in some cases the logics obtained through these categorical constructions are in a sense too poor. For example, logical connectives coming from two different logics may only exist in a disjoint and independent way in a combination defined this way, instead of inter-acting with each other as they should. A more satisfactory solution can sometimes be found by combining not the logics, but their representations in a given framework logic. This is for example the approach taken in [30], where the framework logic is LF. Similar combinations of logics would also be possible in rewriting logic. However, solutions of this kind depend of course on the framework logic used and do not provide an intrinsic answer to the question of what the right combination should be for some given logics. We conjecture that a satisfactory solution to the problem of combining logics will be found as a byproduct of the quest for appropriate axioms for logics of 'practical use', because such a quest will lead to making explicit additional structure that is needed to define the right combination operations. As part of the general interest in a rapprochement between general logics and Gabbay's labelled deduction systems, the matter of how logics are combined in each approach and how these combinations relate to each other should be studied, taking into account Gabbay's ideas on the 'weaving' of logics in [19].

Modularity and compositionality mechanisms for theories in a logic should be further studied. Indeed, this was one of the initial motivations for defining institutions, so that the theory-combining operations of the Clear language [7] would be independent of the logic, and much work has followed since the original Clear proposal (see for example the discussion and references in [24] and [11] for some recent ideas on modularity issues). However, the search for more expressive specification and logic programming languages stimulates a corresponding search for a more powerful and expressive collection of theory-combining operations, which should of course remain independent of the logic as much as possible.

Finally, the very important topic of reflection should be further studied. Reflection is indeed a very powerful technique both theoretically and for implementation purposes. It can in particular be extremely useful for treating metalogical aspects because it permits bringing down to the object level metalevel notions such as proof or theory. For example, Section 5 has illustrated how reflection can be used to reify proofs in rewriting logic. A more systematic study of reflection in rewriting logic and also in the axiomatic setting of general logics seems a very worth while research direction.

Acknowledgements

The work reported in this chapter has been supported by Office of Naval Research Contracts N00014-90-C-0086 and N00014-92-C-0518, National Science Foundation Grant CCR-9224005, and by the Information Technology Promotion Agency, Japan, as a part of the Industrial Science and Technology Frontier Program 'New Models for Software Architecture' sponsored by NEDO (New Energy and Industrial Technology Development Organization).

References

[1] E. Astesiano and M. Cerioli. Relationships between logical frameworks. In M. Bidoit and C. Choppy, editors, *Recent Trends in Data Type Specification*, volume 655 of *Lecture Notes in Computer Science*, pages 126–143. Springer-Verlag, 1993.

[2] A. Avron, F. Honsell, I. A. Mason, and R. Pollack. Using typed lambda calculus to implement formal systems on a machine. *Journal of Automated Reasoning*, 9(3):309–354, December 1992.

[3] J. Barwise. Axioms for abstract model theory. *Annals of Mathematical Logic*, 7:221–265, 1974.

[4] J. Barwise and S. Feferman, editors. *Model-Theoretic Logics*. Springer-Verlag, 1985.

[5] D. A. Basin and R. L. Constable. Metalogical frameworks. In G. Huet and G. Plotkin, editors, *Logical Environments*, pages 1–29. Cambridge University Press, 1993.

[6] M. P. Bonacina and J. Hsiang. A category theory approach to completion-based theorem proving strategies. Unpublished manuscript presented at *Category Theory 1991*, Mc Gill University, Montréal, Canada, 1991.

[7] R. Burstall and J. Goguen. The semantics of Clear, a specification language. In D. Bjørner, editor, *Proc. 1979 Copenhagen Winter School on Abstract Software Specification*, volume 86 of *Lecture Notes in Computer Science*, pages 292–332. Springer-Verlag, 1980.

[8] M. Cerioli. Relationships between Logical Formalisms. PhD thesis, Technical Report TD-4/93, Dipartimento di Informatica, Università di Pisa, 1993.

[9] M. Cerioli and J. Meseguer. May I borrow your logic? In A. M. Borzyszkowski and S. Sokołowski, editors, *Proc. 18th. Int. Symp. on Mathematical Foundations of Computer Science, Gdánsk, Poland, Aug/Sept 1993*, volume 711 of *Lecture Notes in Computer Science*, pages 342–351. Springer-Verlag, 1993.

[10] R. L. Constable. Metalogical frameworks II: Using reflected decision procedures. Lecture at the Max Planck Institut für Informatik, Saarbrücken, Germany, July 1993.

[11] R. Diaconescu, J. A. Goguen, and P. Stefaneas. Logical support for modularisation. In G. Huet and G. Plotkin, editors, *Logical Environments*, pages 83–130, Cambridge University Press, 1993.

[12] H. Ehrig, M. Baldamus, and F. Orejas. New concepts of amalgamation and extension of a general theory of specifications. In M. Bidoit and C. Choppy, editors, *Recent Trends in Data Type Specification*, volume 655 of *Lecture Notes in Computer Science*, pages 199–221. Springer-Verlag, 1993.

[13] S. Feferman. Finitary inductively presented logics. In R. Ferro, S. Valentin, and A. Zanardo, editors, *Logic Colloquium'88*, pages 191–220. North-Holland, 1989.

[14] A. Felty and D. Miller. Encoding a dependent-type λ-calculus in a logic programming language. In M. E. Stickel, editor, *Proc. 10th. Int. Conf. on Automated Deduction, Kaiserslautern, Germany, July 1990*, volume 449 of *Lecture Notes in Computer Science*, pages 221–235. Springer-Verlag, 1990.

[15] J. Fiadeiro and J. Costa. Mirror, Mirror in my Hand: A Duality Between Specifications and Models of Process Behaviour. Research Report, DI-FCUL, Lisboa, Portugal, May 1994.

[16] J. Fiadeiro and T. Maibaum. Generalising interpretations between theories in the context of (π-)institutions. In G. Burn, S. Gay and M. Ryan, editors, *Theory and Formal Methods 93*, pp. 126–147. Springer-Verlag, 1993.

[17] J. Fiadeiro and A. Sernadas. Structuring theories on consequence. In D. Sannella and A. Tarlecki, editors, *Recent Trends in Data Type Specification*, volume 332 of *Lecture Notes in Computer Science*, pages 44–72. Springer-Verlag, 1988.

[18] D. Gabbay. Labelled deductive systems, Part I. Technical Report CIS-Bericht-90-22, Centrum für Informations- und Sprachverarbeitung, Universität München, December 1990. Draft of a book to be published by Oxford University Press.

[19] D. Gabbay. Fibred semantics and the weaving of logics 1. Unpublished manuscript, May 1993.

[20] P. Gardner. Representing Logics in Type Theory. PhD thesis, Technical Report CST-93-92, Department of Computer Science, University of Edinburgh, 1992.

388   *N. Martí-Oliet and J. Meseguer*

[21] J.-Y. Girard. Linear logic. *Theoretical Computer Science*, **50**:1–102, 1987.

[22] J. A. Goguen and R. M. Burstall. Introducing institutions. In E. Clarke and D. Kozen, editors, *Proc. Logics of Programming Workshop*, volume 164 of *Lecture Notes in Computer Science*, pages 221–256. Springer-Verlag, 1984.

[23] J. A. Goguen and R. M. Burstall. A study in the foundations of programming methodology: Specifications, institutions, charters and parchments. In D. Pitt, S. Abramsky, A. Poigné, and D. Rydeheard, editors, *Proc. Workshop on Category Theory and Computer Programming, Guildford, UK, September 1985*, volume 240 of *Lecture Notes in Computer Science*, pages 313–333. Springer-Verlag, 1986.

[24] J. A. Goguen and R. M. Burstall. Institutions: Abstract model theory for specification and programming. *Journal of the Association for Computing Machinery*, **39**(1):95–146, 1992.

[25] J. A. Goguen and J. Meseguer. Order-sorted algebra I: Equational deduction for multiple inheritance, overloading, exceptions and partial operations. *Theoretical Computer Science*, **105**:217–273, 1992.

[26] J. A. Goguen, A. Stevens, K. Hobley, and H. Hilberdink. 2OBJ: A meta-logical framework based on equational logic. *Philosophical Transactions of the Royal Society, Series A*, **339**:69–86, 1992.

[27] J. A. Goguen, T. Winkler, J. Meseguer, K. Futatsugi, and J.-P. Jouannaud. Introducing OBJ. Technical Report SRI-CSL-92-03, Computer Science Laboratory, SRI International, March 1992. To appear in J. A. Goguen, editor, *Applications of Algebraic Specification Using OBJ*, Cambridge University Press, 1994.

[28] R. Harper, F. Honsell, and G. Plotkin. A framework for defining logics. *Journal of the Association for Computing Machinery*, **40**(1):143–184, 1993.

[29] R. Harper, D. Sannella, and A. Tarlecki. Logic representation in LF. In D. H. Pitt, D. E. Rydeheard, P. Dybjer, A. M. Pitts, and A. Poigné, editors, *Category Theory and Computer Science, Manchester, UK, September 1989*, volume 389 of *Lecture Notes in Computer Science*, pages 250–272. Springer-Verlag, 1989.

[30] R. Harper, D. Sannella, and A. Tarlecki. Structure and representation in LF. In *Proc. Fourth Annual IEEE Symp. on Logic in Computer Science*, pages 226–237, Asilomar, California, June 1989. Expanded ver-

sion published as Technical Report CMU-CS-89-174, School of Computer Science, Carnegie Mellon University, July 1989.

[31] M. Hennessy. *The Semantics of Programming Languages: An Elementary Introduction Using Structural Operational Semantics.* John Wiley and Sons, 1990.

[32] G. Kahn. Natural Semantics. Technical Report 601, INRIA Sophia Antipolis, February 1987.

[33] S. Mac Lane. *Categories for the Working Mathematician.* Springer-Verlag, 1971.

[34] N. Martí-Oliet and J. Meseguer. Rewriting Logic as a Logical and Semantic Framework. Technical Report SRI-CSL-93-05, Computer Science Laboratory, SRI International, August 1993.

[35] S. Martini and A. Masini. A Computational Interpretation of Modal Proofs. Technical Report TR-27/93, Dipartimento di Informatica, Università di Pisa, November 1993.

[36] A. Masini. A Proof Theory of Modalities for Computer Science. PhD thesis, Technical Report TD-10/93, Dipartimento di Informatica, Università di Pisa, 1993.

[37] S. Matthews, A. Smaill, and D. Basin. Experience with FS_0 as a framework theory. In G. Huet and G. Plotkin, editors, *Logical Environments*, pages 61–82. Cambridge University Press, 1993.

[38] B. Mayoh. Galleries and Institutions. Technical Report DAIMI PB-191, Computer Science Department, Aarhus University, 1985.

[39] J. Meseguer. General logics. In H.-D. Ebbinghaus, J. Fernández-Prida, M. Garrido, D. Lascar, and M. Rodríguez Artalejo, editors, *Logic Colloquium'87*, pages 275–329. North-Holland, 1989.

[40] J. Meseguer. Conditional rewriting logic as a unified model of concurrency. *Theoretical Computer Science*, **96**:73–155, 1992.

[41] J. Meseguer. Multiparadigm logic programming. In H. Kirchner and G. Levi, editors, *Proc. Third Int. Conf. on Algebraic and Logic Programming, Volterra, Italy, September 1992*, volume 632 of *Lecture Notes in Computer Science*, pages 158–200. Springer-Verlag, 1992.

[42] J. Meseguer. A logical theory of concurrent objects and its realization in the Maude language. In G. Agha, P. Wegner, and A. Yonezawa, editors, *Research Directions in Object-Based Concurrency*, pages 314–390. The MIT Press, 1993.

[43] J. Meseguer and J. A. Goguen. Order-sorted algebra solves the constructor-selector, multiple representation and coercion problems. *Information and Computation*, **104**:114–158, 1993.

[44] J. Meseguer and T. Winkler. Parallel programming in Maude. In J. P. Banâtre and D. Le Métayer, editors, *Research Directions in High-Level Parallel Programming Languages*, volume 574 of *Lecture Notes in Computer Science*, pages 253–293. Springer-Verlag, 1992.

[45] R. Milner. *Communication and Concurrency*. Prentice Hall, 1989.

[46] G. Nadathur and D. Miller. An overview of λProlog. In K. Bowen and R. Kowalski, editors, *Fifth Int. Joint Conf. and Symp. on Logic Programming*, pages 810–827. The MIT Press, 1988.

[47] L. Paulson. The foundation of a generic theorem prover. *Journal of Automated Reasoning*, **5**:363–39, 1989.

[48] F. Pfenning. Elf: A language for logic definition and verified metaprogramming. In *Proc. Fourth Annual IEEE Symp. on Logic in Computer Science*, pages 313–322, Asilomar, California, June 1989.

[49] G. D. Plotkin. A Structural Approach to Operational Semantics. Technical Report DAIMI FN-19, Computer Science Department, Aarhus University, September 1981.

[50] A. Poigné. Foundations are rich institutions, but institutions are poor foundations. In H. Ehrig, H. Herrlich, H.-J. Kreowski, and g. Preuß, editors, *Categorical Methods in Computer Science with Aspects from Topology*, volume 393 of *Lecture Notes in Computer Science*, pages 82–101. Springer-Verlag, 1989.

[51] A. Salibra and G. Scollo. Compactness and Löwenheim-Skolem Properties in Pre-institution Categories. Technical Report LIENS-92-10, Laboratoire d'Informatique de l'Ecole Normale Supérieure, Paris, March 1992.

[52] A. Salibra and G. Scollo. A soft stairway to institutions. In M. Bidoit and C. Choppy, editors, *Recent Trends in Data Type Specification*, volume 655 of *Lecture Notes in Computer Science*, pages 310–329. Springer-Verlag, 1993.

[53] D. Sannella and A. Tarlecki. Specifications in an arbitrary institution. *Information and Computation*, **76**(2/3):165–210, 1988.

[54] D. Sannella and A. Tarlecki. Toward formal development of programs from algebraic specifications: Implementations revisited. *Acta Informatica*, **25**:233–281, 1988.

[55] D. Scott. Completeness and axiomatizability in many-valued logic. In L. Henkin, J. Addison, C. C. Chang, W. Craig, D. Scott, and R. Vaught, editors, *Proceedings of the Tarski Symposium*, pages 411–435. American Mathematical Society, 1974.

[56] R. M. Smullyan. *Theory of Formal Systems*, volume 47 of *Annals of Mathematics Studies*. Princeton University Press, 1961.

[57] A. Tarlecki. Free constructions in algebraic institutions. In M. P. Chytil and V. Koubek, editors, *Proc. Mathematical Foundations of Computer Science '84*, volume 176 of *Lecture Notes in Computer Science*, pages 526–534. Springer-Verlag, 1984.

[58] A. Tarlecki. On the existence of free models in abstract algebraic institutions. *Theoretical Computer Science*, **37**(3):269–304, 1985.

[59] A. Tarlecki. Bits and pieces of the theory of institutions. In D. Pitt, S. Abramsky, A. Poigné, and D. Rydeheard, editors, *Proc. Workshop on Category Theory and Computer Programming, Guildford, UK, September 1985*, volume 240 of *Lecture Notes in Computer Science*, pages 334–363. Springer-Verlag, 1986.

[60] A. Tarlecki. Quasi-varieties in abstract algebraic institutions. *Journal of Computer and System Sciences*, **33**(3):333–360, 1986.

[61] A. Tarlecki, R. M. Burstall, and J. A. Goguen. Some fundamental algebraic tools for the semantics of computation. Part 3: Indexed categories. *Theoretical Computer Science*, **91**:239–264, 1991.

15

General Algebraic Logic: A Perspective on 'What is Logic'

Istvan Németi and Hajnal Andréka

1 Introduction

What is logic? We find this an important question. We also doubt the availability of a simple one-sentence answer. The question invokes some responsibility, too: the answer given today might influence the shape in which logic will be tomorrow.

Johan van Benthem [46, p.271] writes 'Logic is the study of reasoning, both in the sense of description of reasoning practice and the sense of design of reasoning systems. (And as such, it is a discipline in its own right, without being a handmaiden to any special employer.)' We agree with this definition, though to reasoning we would like to add many aspects of cognition and of 'rational thinking'. So, there is a *subject matter of logic* which is 'out there in the world' and, roughly speaking, this subject matter is the phenomenon of reasoning, cognition and rational thinking (or at least many aspects of these). At this point we should mention that the subject matter of logic as we define it here is strictly broader than what the official definition had been some time ago. Indeed, defining logic as the science investigating inference practice(s) and consequence relation(s) against which one can measure these inference practices[1] is broad enough to cover what the subject matter of logic was 2000 years ago. However, in the meantime the subject grew, it became richer. (We think this is quite normal with healthy scientific disciplines.) We do not question the central importance of inference and of consequence for even modern logic. However, these are

---

[1] If someone wants to study the *valid* inferences (as the subject was often named), then he has to study two kinds of things, (i) inferences and (ii) validity (of inferences). Since inference is binary, i.e. we infer sentence φ from sentence ψ, in symbols $\psi \vdash \varphi$, to study validity of inference we need a binary relation, say $\psi \models \varphi$, called consequence relation.

only special parts or aspects of the phenomenon of cognition, reasoning, etc. and in our opinion, today, logic can (should) and does investigate a greater diversity of aspects, parts, mechanisms, questions, etc. of cognition than just inference and consequence.[2]

Having delineated what the subject matter of logic is, in our opinion, let us turn to the question of how logic studies its subject matter.

Barwise and Hammer [11] writes that the logician makes *mathematical models* of (parts or aspects of) the phenomenon which is the subject matter of logic. We agree with this. Some of these mathematical models are called *logical systems*. We also agree with Barwise and Hammer in that it is very important to keep in mind that 'there is a difference between a model and the thing being modelled'. Further we agree with them in that 'idealizations are necessary for mathematically modelling natural phenomena' and that this applies to logic, too. We find these considerations (difference between phenomenon and model, idealization and possible idealizations, their consequences, etc.) extremely important. They already played a central role in Sain [37] which investigated the question of what a logical system is, how it is related to the subject matter of logic (i.e. the phenomenon being modelled-studied) and what the rules of 'hygiene of' modelling are in the special area called logic. The above considerations (phenomenon, idealization, mathematical model, etc.) will be relied on throughout this paper (though often implicitly).

When we were first invited to contribute to this volume, we were told the title was 'What is logic'. Now the title is 'What is a logical system'. In our opinion, the two questions are not the same. The second one is easier. And is less general, less ambitious. If we tell what a logical system is we still have not told what logic is. Though, of course we contributed to obtaining a better understanding of the general question by answering the more specialized one. With saying all this, we do not deny the importance of logical systems. They are terribly important parts of logic. But logic is more than the collection of all logical systems, in our opinion. To give a simple-minded example: during our cognitive or thinking process, we not only use our logical systems, but we also improve them (i.e. change them, create new ones, etc.) This activity of 'improving' is part of our mental processes and belongs to the subject matter of logic. It is not clear to us how this 'improving process' could be studied naturally within the framework of

---

[2]Immanuel Kant writes in his Kritik Der reiner Vernunft e.g. in §I. Part II.I ('On logic in general') that logic is the formal science of thinking, of 'Verstand' and of 'Vernunft'. (He mentions that *certain* aspects or features of *human* thinking are studied by psychology instead of logic; and we agree, we never said that *all* aspects of thinking belong to logic.) Kant's conception of the subject of logic seems to be strictly broader than inference making and consequence relation. A similarly broader (than inference, etc.) view was held by logician and philosopher C.S. Peirce, and is also found e.g. in S. Haack: Philosophy of Logics, Cambridge University Press, 1992.

a logical system. This is so even if today logic has very little to say about this process of improving (though Dov Gabbay's research on combining logics, fibred semantics, investigation of the category whose objects are logical systems are existing research directions which are relevant to this, cf. e.g. [21], [18]).

All the same, we agree with the editors that it might be wiser to attack the easier question first, and 'go for the big one' only after having developed a firm grasp of the slightly easier topic. The present paper is organized accordingly. The main bulk of the paper is devoted to figuring out what logical systems are, then experimenting with the so obtained definitions, and then using the so obtained experience to refine the concept of a logical system, proving theorems about logical systems to see if they do what they should, etc. After all this (and some more) about logical systems, we return to the more ambitious question 'what is logic' in Section 5 of the chapter.

In Sections 2 and 3 below we will present our notions of logical systems in simplified forms for two reasons. These are: (i) lack of space and (ii) to make the paper easier to read, i.e. to abstract away from detail which is not absolutely necessary for the discussions at hand.

As a compensation, in Section 4 we briefly indicate how to recover the more general forms of a logical system from the ones discussed in Section 2. Finally, as we said, in Section 5 we turn to asking ourselves what logic is.

Convention: In the paper, for brevity we often write 'a logic' for 'a logical system'.

2   What is a logical system?

2.1   Defining the framework

Defining a logical system is an experience similar to defining a language. (This is no coincidence if you think about the applications of logic in e.g. theoretical linguistics.) So how do we define a language, say a programming language like Pascal. First one defines the *syntax* of Pascal. This amounts to defining the set of all Pascal programs. This definition tells us which strings of symbols count as Pascal programs and which do not. But this information in itself is not very useful, because having only this information enables the user to write programs but the user will have no idea what his programs will do. (This is more sensible if instead of Pascal we take a more esoteric language like ALGOL 68.) Indeed, the second, and more important step in defining Pascal amounts to describing what the various Pascal programs will do when executed. In other words, we have to define the meaning, or *semantics* of the language, e.g. of Pascal.

Defining semantics can be done in two steps, (i) we define the class M of
possible machines that understand Pascal, and then (ii) to each machine
$\mathcal{M}$ and each string φ of symbols that counts as a Pascal program we tell
what $\mathcal{M}$ will do if we 'ask' it to execute φ. In other words we define the
meaning $mng(\varphi, \mathcal{M})$ of program φ in machine $\mathcal{M}$.

The procedure remains basically the same if the language in question
is not a programming language but something like a natural language or
a simple declarative language like first-order logic. When teaching a for-
eign language, e.g. German, one has to explain which strings of symbols
are German sentences and which are not (e.g. 'Der Tisch ist rot' is a German sentence while 'Das Tisch ist rot' is not). This is called explaining
the syntax of German. Besides this, one has to explain what the German
sentences mean. This amounts to defining the semantics of German. If we
want to formalize the definition of semantics (for, say, a fragment of German) then one again defines a class M of possible situations or with other
words, 'possible worlds' in which our German sentences are interpreted,
and then to each situation $\mathcal{M}$ and each sentence φ we define the meaning
or denotation $mng(\varphi, \mathcal{M})$ of φ in situation (or possible world) $\mathcal{M}$.

At this point we could discuss the difference between a language and
a logical system, but we do not do that. For our present purposes it is
enough to say that the two things are very-very similar.[3]

Soon (in Definition 2.1 below) we will define what we mean by a logical
system.

Roughly speaking, a *logical system* L is a five-tuple

$$L = \langle F_L, \vdash_L, M_L, mng_L, \models_L \rangle,$$

where

- F_L is a set, called the set of all *formulas* of L;

- $\vdash_L$ is a binary relation between sets of formulas and individual for-
  mulas, that is, $\vdash_L \subseteq \mathcal{P}(F_L) \times F_L$ (for any set X, $\mathcal{P}(X)$ denotes the
  powerset of X); $\vdash_L$ is called the *provability relation* of L;

- M_L is a class, called the class of all *models* (or *possible worlds*) of L;

- mng_L is a function with domain $F_L \times M_L$, called the *meaning function*
  of L;

- $\models_L$ is a binary relation, $\models_L \subseteq M_L \times F_L$, called the *validity relation*
  of L.

---

[3]The philosophical minded reader might enjoy looking into the book [1], cf. e.g. B.
Partee's paper therein. More elementary ones are: Sain [38] and [36].

Intuitively, F_L is the collection of 'texts' or 'sentences' or 'formulas' that can be 'said' in the language L. For $\Gamma \subseteq F_L$ and $\varphi \in F_L$, the intuitive meaning of $\Gamma \vdash_L \varphi$ is that φ is provable (or derivable) from Γ with the syntactic inference system (or deductive mechanism) of L.

In all important cases, $\vdash_L$ is subject to certain conditions like $\Gamma \vdash_L \varphi$ and $\Gamma \cup \{\varphi\} \vdash_L \psi$ imply $\Gamma \vdash_L \psi$ for any $\Gamma \subseteq F_L$ and $\varphi, \psi \in F_L$. The meaning function tells us what the texts belonging to F_L mean in the possible worlds from M_L. The validity relation tells us which texts are 'true' in which possible worlds (or models) under what conditions. In all the interesting cases, from mng_L the relation $\models_L$ is definable. A typical possible definition of $\models_L$ from mng_L is the following.

$$\mathcal{M} \models_L \varphi \quad \text{iff} \quad (\forall \psi \in F_L)\big[mng_L(\psi, \mathcal{M}) \subseteq mng_L(\varphi, \mathcal{M})\big], \qquad (*)$$

for all $\varphi \in F_L$, $\mathcal{M} \in M_L$. However, in general there is *no* explicit connection required between mng_L and $\models_L$.

When no confusion is likely, we omit the subscripts L from F_L, $\vdash_L$, etc.

Usually F_L and $\vdash_L$ are defined by what is called grammars in mathematical linguistics. $\langle F_L, \vdash_L \rangle$ together with the grammar defining them is called the *syntactical part* of L, while $\langle M_L, mng_L, \models_L \rangle$ is the *semantical part* of L.

When defining a logical system, a typical definition of F has the following recursive form. Two sets, P and $Cn(L)$ are given; P is called the set of primitive or *atomic formulas* and $Cn(L)$ is called the set of *logical connectives* of L (these are operation symbols with finite or infinite ranks). Then we require F to be the smallest set H satisfying

(1). $P \subseteq H$, and

(2). for every $\varphi_1, \ldots, \varphi_n \in H$ and $f \in Cn(L)$ of rank n, $f(\varphi_1, \ldots, \varphi_n) \in H$.

For example, in propositional logic, if p_1 is a propositional variable (atomic formula according to our terminology), then $(\neg p_1)$ is defined to be a formula (where $\neg$ is a logical connective of rank 1).

For formulas $\varphi \in F$ and models $\mathcal{M} \in M$, $mng(\varphi, \mathcal{M})$ and $\mathcal{M} \models \varphi$ are defined in uniform ways (by some finite 'schemas').

Given a logical system L, for $\varphi \in F_L$ we say that φ is *valid* (in L), in symbols $\models_L \varphi$, iff $(\forall \mathcal{M} \in M_L)\mathcal{M} \models \varphi$. For φ as above and $\Gamma \subseteq F_L$ we say that φ is a *semantical consequence* of Γ, in symbols $\Gamma \models_L^c \varphi$, iff $(\forall \mathcal{M} \in M_L)[((\forall \psi \in \Gamma)\mathcal{M} \models \psi) \implies \mathcal{M} \models \varphi]$. One of the important topics of logic is the study of the connection between semantic consequence $\Gamma \models_L^c \varphi$ and the syntactic consequence $\Gamma \vdash_L \varphi$. If the two coincide, then $\vdash_L$ is said to be strongly complete and sound (for L). In subsection 2.2 we give several examples.

Now we turn to nailing down our definitions formally in the form we will use them.

Recall that for any set X, X^* denotes the set of all finite sequences ('words') over X. That is, $X^* \overset{def}{=} \bigcup_{n\in\omega} ({}^nX)$, where ω denotes the set of all natural numbers, and ${}^nX$ denotes the set of all X-termed sequences of length n.

Definition 2.1 (Logical system). By a *logical system* L we mean an ordered 5-tuple

$$L \overset{def}{=} \langle F_L, \vdash_L, M_L, mng_L, \models_L \rangle,$$

where (i)–(vi) below hold.

(i). F_L (called the set of *formulas*) is a subset of finite sequences (called *words*) over some set X (called the *alphabet* of L) that is, $F_L \subseteq X^*$;

(ii). $\vdash_L$ (called the *provability relation*) is a binary relation between sets of formulas and individual formulas, that is, $\vdash_L \subseteq \mathcal{P}(F_L) \times F_L$. (According to the tradition, instead of '$\langle \Gamma, \varphi \rangle \in \vdash_L$' we write '$\Gamma \vdash_L \varphi$'.);

(iii). M_L is a class (called the class of *models*);

(iv). mng_L is a function with domain $F_L \times M_L$ (called the *meaning function*);

(v). $\models_L$ (called the *validity relation*) is a relation between M_L and F_L that is, $\models_L \subseteq M_L \times F_L$. (According to the tradition, instead of '$\langle \mathcal{M}, \varphi \rangle \in \models_L$' we write '$\mathcal{M} \models_L \varphi$'.)

(vi). $\models_L$ depends on mng_L only, that is, for all $\varphi, \psi \in F_L$ and $\mathcal{M} \in M_L$ we have

$$[mng_L(\varphi, \mathcal{M}) = mng_L(\psi, \mathcal{M}) \text{ and } \mathcal{M} \models_L \varphi] \Longrightarrow \mathcal{M} \models_L \psi.$$

Remark 2.2 In the above definition, we nailed down the expression 'model of L' instead of the more suggestive one 'possible world of L' only for purely technical reasons, namely, to avoid a danger of potential ambiguity with the literature.

As we already indicated, in this chapter we will often write 'a logic' as a shorthand for 'a logical system'.

Definition 2.3 (Semantical consequence, valid formulas). Let $L = \langle F_L, \vdash_L, M_L, mng_L, \models_L \rangle$ be a logic. For every $\mathcal{M} \in M_L$ and $\Sigma \subseteq F_L$,

$$\mathcal{M} \models_L \Sigma \overset{def}{\Longleftrightarrow} (\forall \varphi \in \Sigma)\, \mathcal{M} \models_L \varphi,$$
$$Mod_L(\Sigma) \overset{def}{=} \{\mathcal{M} \in M_L : \mathcal{M} \models_L \Sigma\}.$$

$Mod_L(\Sigma)$ is called the class of models of Σ.

A formula φ is said to be *valid*, in symbols $\models_L \varphi$, iff $Mod_L(\{\varphi\}) = M_L$.
For any $\Sigma \cup \{\varphi\} \subseteq F_L$,

$$\Sigma \models_L^c \varphi \stackrel{def}{\Longleftrightarrow} Mod_L(\Sigma) \subseteq Mod_L(\{\varphi\}),$$

$$Csq_L(\Sigma) \stackrel{def}{=} \{\varphi \in F_L : \Sigma \models_L^c \varphi\}.$$

If $\varphi \in Csq_L(\Sigma)$ then we say that φ is a *semantical consequence* of Σ (in logic L). *Csq* abbreviates 'consequence'.

Definition 2.4 (Theory, set of validities). Let $L = \langle F_L, \vdash_L, M_L, mng_L, \models_L \rangle$ be any logic. For any $K \subseteq M_L$ let the *theory of* K be defined as

$$Th_L(K) \stackrel{def}{=} \{\varphi \in F_L : (\forall M \in K)\ M \models_L \varphi\}.$$

$Th_L(K)$ is called the theory of K in L. If $K = \{M\}$ for some $M \in M_L$ then instead of $Th_L(\{M\})$ we write $Th_L(M)$.

The set $Th_L(M_L)$ is called the *set of validities* of L.

For any set X^* of 'strings of symbols', the notion of a *decidable* subset $H \subseteq X^*$ is introduced in almost any introductory book on logic or on the theory of computation (see e.g. Monk [30]). The same applies to $H \subseteq X^*$ being *recursively enumerable (r.e.)*.

Definition 2.5 (Decidability of logics). We say that a logic $L = \langle F_L, \vdash_L, M_L, mng_L, \models_L \rangle$ is *decidable* iff the set $Th_L(M_L)$ of validities of L is a decidable subset of the set F_L of formulas.

Instead of the general conception of a logic outlined above, in many cases we will consider only four of its five components: F_L, M_L, mng_L and $\models_L$. Namely, we found that we can simplify the theory *without loss of generality* by not dragging $\vdash_L$ along with us for the following reason.

The validity relation $\models_L$ (or the function mng_L if you like) induces the *semantical consequence relation* $\models_L^c \subseteq \mathcal{P}(F_L) \times F_L$, given above in Definition 2.3. There is a natural temptation to try to replace $\vdash_L$ with $\models_L^c$ in the theory, though at several places (e.g. at completeness theorems) this would be a grave oversimplification. Surprisingly enough, we found that all the theorems we prove for $\models_L^c$ carry over to $\vdash_L$, whenever the theorems are not about connections between $\models_L^c$ and $\vdash_L$ (see explanation below). Therefore we decided to drop $\vdash_L$ for the time being and introduce it only where we must say something about $\vdash_L$ which cannot be said about $\models_L^c$ in itself.[4]

---

[4]These considerations, together with the ones which follow them, grew out from discussions with Willem Blok, Joseph M. Font, Ramon Jansana and Don Pigozzi. In particular, Remark 2.6 is due to Font and Jansana; for more information in this line see [20].

The reader interested in logics in the purely syntactical sense $\langle F_{\mathrm{L}}, \vdash_{\mathrm{L}} \rangle$ is invited to read our paper in the way described as follows.

Let $\mathrm{L}_s = \langle F, \vdash \rangle$ be a logic in the syntactical sense. To simplify the arguments below, we assume that L_s has a derived logical connective '$\leftrightarrow$' just as classical logics do. Of course, we assume the usual properties of '$\leftrightarrow$', e.g. $\{\varphi, (\varphi \leftrightarrow \psi)\} \vdash \psi$, etc. Intuitively, $(\varphi \leftrightarrow \psi)$ expresses that φ and ψ are equivalent. In Remark 2.6 below the present discussion, we will show how to eliminate the assumption of the expressibility of '$\leftrightarrow$'. (However, the reader may safely skip Remark 2.6, since we will not rely on it later.)

Assume we want to study the 'syntactical logic' $\mathrm{L}_s = \langle F, \vdash \rangle$. To be able to apply the theorems of the present paper, we will associate a class $M_\vdash$ of pseudo-models, a $mng_\vdash$, etc. to L_s. The class of *pseudo-models* is

$$M_\vdash \overset{def}{=} \{T \subseteq F \ : \ T \text{ is closed under } \vdash\}.$$

For any pseudo-model $T \in M_\vdash$ and formula $\varphi \in F$,

$$mng_\vdash(\varphi, T) \overset{def}{=} \{\psi \in F : T \vdash (\varphi \leftrightarrow \psi)\} \ .$$

Further, validity in pseudo-models $T \in M_\vdash$ is defined as

$$T \models_\vdash \varphi \quad \Longleftrightarrow \quad \varphi \in T.$$

Now, if we want to investigate the 'syntactic logic' $\langle F, \vdash \rangle$, we apply our theorems to the logic

$$\mathrm{L}_\vdash \overset{def}{=} \langle F, M_\vdash, mng_\vdash, \models_\vdash \rangle \ .$$

The semantical consequence relation $\models_\vdash^c$ induced by $\models_\vdash$ coincides with the original syntactical one $\vdash$. (This is easy to check.) Hence, applying the theorems to the logic $\mathrm{L}_\vdash$ yields results about $\langle F, \vdash \rangle$ as was desired. In other words, $\mathrm{L}_\vdash$ is an equivalent reformulation of the 'syntactic logic' $\langle F, \vdash \rangle$, hence studying $\mathrm{L}_\vdash$ is the same as studying $\langle F, \vdash \rangle$.

Remark 2.6 (Eliminating the assumption of the expressibility of '$\leftrightarrow$' in L). Here we show that in the above argument showing that our results can be applied to any syntactical logic $\mathrm{L}_s = \langle F, \vdash \rangle$, the assumption of expressibility of '$\leftrightarrow$' in L_s can be eliminated. It will turn out in Definition 3.1 in Section 3 that for any logic L, the set F_{L} of formulas has an algebraic structure, that is, F_{L} is the universe of an algebra $\mathcal{F}$. (The operations of $\mathcal{F}$ are the logical connectives of L collected in $Cn(\mathrm{L})$.) Let $T \in M_\vdash$ be given. Recall e.g. from [12] that the Leibniz congruence $\Omega(T) \subseteq F \times F$ associated to T is the biggest congruence relation of $\mathcal{F}$ with the property[5]

---

[5] $A \setminus B = \{x \in A : x \notin B\}$ denotes the set theoretical difference of the sets A and B, for any sets A and B.

$(\forall \varphi \in T)(\forall \psi \in F \setminus T)\langle \varphi, \psi \rangle \notin \Omega(T)$. Now we can define $mng_\vdash$ without using '$\leftrightarrow$':

$$mng_\vdash(\varphi, T) \overset{def}{=} \{\psi \in F : \varphi \,\Omega(T)\, \psi\}\,.$$

The rest of the definitions of $M_\vdash$, $\models_\vdash$ and the argumentation based on them remains the same. Since '$\leftrightarrow$' was not used anywhere except in the definition of $mng_\vdash$, this shows that no assumption (like the existence of '$\leftrightarrow$') is needed in our argument showing how to apply the present theory of 'semantical logics' $\langle F, M, mng, \models \rangle$ to the study of syntactical logics $\langle F, \vdash \rangle$.

Summing up, for a while we will concentrate our attention on the simplified form

$$\mathbf{L} = \langle F_\mathbf{L}, M_\mathbf{L}, mng_\mathbf{L}, \models_\mathbf{L} \rangle$$

of a logic. For the reasons outlined above, this temporary restriction of attention will not result in any loss of generality.

2.2 Examples

Now we define some basic logics. Some of them are well-known, but we recall their definitions for illustrating that they are special cases of the concept defined in Definition 2.1 above, and also for fixing our notation.

Definition 2.7 (Propositional or sentential logic $\mathbf{L}_S$). Let P be a set, called the set of *atomic formulas* of $\mathbf{L}_S$. Let $\{\wedge, \neg\}$ be a set disjoint from P, called the set of *logical connectives* of $\mathbf{L}_S$ (usually called *Boolean connectives*).

Propositional (or *sentential*) *logic* (corresponding to P) is defined to be a 5-tuple

$$\mathbf{L}_S \overset{def}{=} \langle F_S, \vdash_S, M_S, mng_S, \models_S \rangle,$$

for which conditions (i)–(iv) below hold.

(i). The set F_S of formulas is the smallest set H satisfying

- $P \subseteq H$
- $\varphi, \psi \in H \Longrightarrow (\varphi \wedge \psi), \neg\varphi \in H.$

(That is, the alphabet of this logic is $\{\wedge, \neg\} \cup P$.)

(ii). The class M_S of *models* of $\mathbf{L}_S$ is defined by

$$M_S \overset{def}{=} \{\langle W, v \rangle : W \text{ is a non-empty set and } v : P \to \mathcal{P}(W)\}.$$

If $\mathcal{M} = \langle W, v \rangle \in M_S$ then W is called the set of *possible states* (or *worlds*[6] or *situations*) of $\mathcal{M}$.

(iii). Let $\langle W, v \rangle \in M_S$, $w \in W$, and $\varphi \in F_S$. We define the binary relation $w \Vdash_v \varphi$ by recursion on the complexity of the formulas:

- if $p \in P$ then $\left(w \Vdash_v p \overset{def}{\Longleftrightarrow} w \in v(p) \right)$
- if $\psi_1, \psi_2 \in F_S$, then

$$w \Vdash_v \neg\psi_1 \quad \overset{def}{\Longleftrightarrow} \quad \text{not } w \Vdash_v \psi_1$$

$$w \Vdash_v (\psi_1 \wedge \psi_2) \quad \overset{def}{\Longleftrightarrow} \quad w \Vdash_v \psi_1 \text{ and } w \Vdash_v \psi_2.$$

If $w \Vdash_v \varphi$ then we say that φ is *true in* w, or w *forces* φ.

Now $mng_S(\varphi, \langle W, v \rangle) \overset{def}{=} \{ w \in W : w \Vdash_v \varphi \}$.

$\langle W, v \rangle \models_S \varphi$ (φ is *valid in* $\langle W, v \rangle$), iff for every $w \in W$, $w \Vdash_v \varphi$.

(iv). Let us turn to defining $\vdash_S$.

Throughout, we use $(\varphi \to \psi)$ as an abbreviation for $\neg(\varphi \wedge \neg\psi)$ and $(\varphi \leftrightarrow \psi)$ as that for $(\varphi \to \psi) \wedge (\psi \to \varphi)$. List a set Ax of valid formulas of L_S and call these *logical axioms*.[7] Possible elements of this list are $(\varphi \to \varphi)$ for all $\varphi \in F_S$, $(\varphi \wedge \psi) \to (\psi \wedge \varphi)$, $(\varphi \wedge \psi) \to \varphi$, $(\varphi \wedge \neg\varphi) \to (\psi \wedge \neg\psi)$, $\varphi \to (\psi \to \varphi)$, for all $\varphi, \psi \in F_S$. Having defined the set Ax of logical axioms, add the inference rule $\{\varphi, (\varphi \to \psi)\} \vdash \psi$ (for all $\varphi, \psi \in F_S$) which is called modus ponens. If one wishes, one may add similar rules like $\{\varphi, \psi\} \vdash (\varphi \wedge \psi)$ (but they are not really needed). For $\Gamma \subseteq F_S$, define $\Gamma \vdash_S \varphi$ to hold iff $\varphi \in H$ for the smallest set $H \subseteq F_S$ such that $\Gamma \cup Ax \subseteq H$ and H is closed under your inference rules, e.g. whenever $\psi, (\psi \to \rho) \in H$ then also $\rho \in H$. With this, $\vdash_S$ is defined.

It is important to note that the set P of atomic formulas is a parameter in the definition of L_S. Namely, in the definition above, P is a fixed but

---

[6]It is *important* to keep the two senses in which 'possible world' can be used separate. The elements $\langle W, v \rangle$ of M_S can be called possible worlds since we inherit this usage from the general concept of a logic. At the same time, the elements $w \in W$ can be called 'possible states or worlds' as a technical expression of modal logic. So there is a potential confusion here, which has to be kept in mind.

[7]If the instructions below would be too vague for the non-logician reader then s/he has three options: (i) Consult Definitions 3.6–3.9 together with the paragraph preceding Definition 3.6 in Section 3 herein. There we define and discuss inference systems $\vdash_L$ in detail, so that should suffice. (ii) Recall any of the known inference systems for propositional logic from the literature. (iii) Ignore this '$\vdash$-part' of this example, since we will not rely on it later.

arbitrary set. So in a sense L_S is a function of P, and we could write $L_S(P)$ to make this explicit. However, the choice of P has only limited influence on the behaviour of L_S, therefore, following the literature we write simply L_S instead of $L_S(P)$. From time to time, however, we will have to remember that P is a freely chosen parameter because in certain investigations the choice of P does influence the behaviour of $L_S = L_S(P)$.

In the rest of the examples we give the logics in the simplified form

$$L = \langle F_L, M_L, mng_L, \models_L \rangle \quad \text{or} \quad L = \langle F_L, M_L, \models_L \rangle$$

Definition 2.8 (Modal logic S5). The set of connectives of *modal logic* S5 is $\{\wedge, \neg, \Diamond\}$.

The set of formulas (denoted as F_{S5}) of S5 is defined as that of propositional logic L_S together with the following clause:

$$\varphi \in F_{S5} \implies \Diamond\varphi \in F_{S5}.$$

Let $M_{S5} \stackrel{def}{=} M_S$. The definition of $w \Vdash_v \varphi$ is the same as in the propositional case but we also have the case of $\Diamond$:

$$w \Vdash_v \Diamond\varphi \stackrel{def}{\iff} (\exists w' \in W) \; w' \Vdash_v \varphi.$$

Then $mng_{S5}(\varphi, \langle W, v \rangle) \stackrel{def}{=} \{w \in W : w \Vdash_v \varphi\}$, and the validity relation $\models_{S5}$ is defined as follows.

$$\langle W, v \rangle \models_{S5} \varphi \stackrel{def}{\iff} (\forall w \in W) \; w \Vdash_v \varphi.$$

Now, modal logic S5 is $S5 \stackrel{def}{=} \langle F_{S5}, M_{S5}, mng_{S5}, \models_{S5} \rangle$.

Remark 2.9 According to a rather respectable (and useful) tradition, an extra-boolean connective is called a *modality* iff it distributes over disjuction. This will not be true for all of our connectives that we will call modalities. Thus, regrettably, we sometimes ignore this useful tradition. For this tradition cf. e.g. Venema [48], Appendix A (pp. 143–152).

The following logic is discussed e.g. in Sain [39], [40], Venema [48], Roorda [34], but see also Segerberg [44] who traces this logic back to von Wright.

Definition 2.10 (Difference logic L_D). The set of connectives of *difference logic* L_D is $\{\wedge, \neg, D\}$.

The set of formulas (denoted as F_D) of L_D is defined as that of propositional logic L_S together with the following clause:

$$\varphi \in F_D \implies D\varphi \in F_D.$$

Let $M_D \overset{def}{=} M_{S5}(= M_S)$. The definition of $w \Vdash_v \varphi$ is the same as in the propositional case but we also have the case of D:

$$w \Vdash_v D\varphi \overset{def}{\Longleftrightarrow} (\exists w' \in W \setminus \{w\})\ w' \Vdash_v \varphi.$$

Then $mng_D(\varphi, \langle W, v \rangle) \overset{def}{=} \{w \in W : w \Vdash_v \varphi\}$, and the validity relation $\models_D$ is defined as follows.

$$\langle W, v \rangle \models_D \varphi \overset{def}{\Longleftrightarrow} (\forall w \in W)\ w \Vdash_v \varphi.$$

Now, difference logic L_D is $L_D \overset{def}{=} \langle F_D, M_D, mng_D, \models_D \rangle$. We note that L_D is also called *'Some-other-time logic'* (cf. Sain [40], Segerberg [44]).

The logics $L_{\kappa\text{-times}}$ to be introduced below play quite an essential rôle in Artificial Intelligence in the theory what is called there 'stratified logic', cf. e.g. works of H. J. Ohlbach, see e.g. [17].

Definition 2.11 (κ-times logic $L_{\kappa\text{-times}}$, twice logic Tw). Let κ be any cardinal. The set of connectives of *κ-times logic* $L_{\kappa\text{-times}}$ is $\{\wedge, \neg, \Diamond_\kappa\}$.

The set of formulas (denoted as $F_{\Diamond_\kappa}$) of $L_{\kappa\text{-times}}$ is defined as that of propositional logic L_S together with the following clause:

$$\varphi \in F_{\Diamond_\kappa} \implies \Diamond_\kappa \varphi \in F_{\Diamond_\kappa}.$$

Let $M_{\Diamond_\kappa} \overset{def}{=} M_{S5}(= M_S)$. The definition of $w \Vdash_v \varphi$ is the same as in the propositional case but we also have the case of $\Diamond_\kappa$:

$$w \Vdash_v \Diamond_\kappa \varphi \overset{def}{\Longleftrightarrow} (\exists H \subseteq W)(|H| = \kappa \text{ and } (\forall w' \in H)\ w' \Vdash_v \varphi).$$

Then $mng_{\Diamond_\kappa}(\varphi, \langle W, v \rangle) \overset{def}{=} \{w \in W : w \Vdash_v \varphi\}$, and the validity relation $\models_{\Diamond_\kappa}$ is defined as follows.

$$\langle W, v \rangle \models_{\Diamond_\kappa} \varphi \overset{def}{\Longleftrightarrow} (\forall w \in W)\ w \Vdash_v \varphi.$$

Now, κ-times logic $L_{\kappa\text{-times}}$ is $L_{\kappa\text{-times}} \overset{def}{=} \langle F_{\Diamond_\kappa}, M_{\Diamond_\kappa}, mng_{\Diamond_\kappa}, \models_{\Diamond_\kappa} \rangle$. We note that if $\kappa = 2$ then logic $L_{2\text{-times}}$ is also called *Twice logic* and is denoted as Tw.

Definition 2.12 below discusses various arrow logics. The field of arrow logics grew out of application areas in logic, language and computation, and plays an important rôle there, cf. e.g. van Benthem [46], [47], and the proceedings of the arrow logic day at the conference 'Logic at Work' (December 1992, Amsterdam (CCSOM of Univ. of Amsterdam)).

Definition 2.12 (Arrow logics L_{ARW0}, L_{ARROW}, L_{RA}). The set of connectives of *arrow logics* L_{ARW0}, L_{ARROW}, L_{RA} is $\{\wedge, \neg, \circ, \check{}, Id\}$, where $\circ$ is a binary, $\check{}$ is a unary, and Id is a zero-ary modality.

- The set of formulas (denoted as F_{ARW0}) of L_{ARW0} is defined as that of propositional logic L_S together with the following clauses:

$$\varphi, \psi \in F_{\text{ARW0}} \implies (\varphi \circ \psi), \ \varphi^{\smile} \in F_{\text{ARW0}}$$
$$Id \in F_{\text{ARW0}}$$

The models are those of propositional logic L_S enriched with three relations, called *accessibility relations*. That is,

$$M_{\text{ARW0}} \stackrel{def}{=} \{\langle \langle W, v \rangle, C_1, C_2, C_3 \rangle \ : \ \langle W, v \rangle \in M_S, \ C_1 \subseteq W \times W \times W,$$
$$C_2 \subseteq W \times W, \ C_3 \subseteq W\}.$$

For propositional connectives $\neg$ and $\wedge$ the definition of $w \Vdash_v \varphi$ is the same as in the propositional case. For the new connectives we have:

$$w \Vdash_v (\varphi \circ \psi) \quad \stackrel{def}{\Longleftrightarrow} \quad (\exists w_1, w_2 \in W)$$
$$\big(C_1(w, w_1, w_2) \text{ and } w_1 \Vdash_v \varphi \text{ and } w_2 \Vdash_v \psi\big)$$
$$w \Vdash_v \varphi^{\smile} \quad \stackrel{def}{\Longleftrightarrow} \quad (\exists w' \in W)\big(C_2(w, w') \text{ and } w' \Vdash_v \varphi\big)$$
$$w \Vdash_v Id \quad \stackrel{def}{\Longleftrightarrow} \quad w \in C_3.$$

As usual, $mng_{\text{ARW0}}(\varphi, \langle W, v \rangle) \stackrel{def}{=} \{w \in W \ : \ w \Vdash_v \varphi\}$, and the validity relation $\models_{\text{ARW0}}$ is defined as follows.

$$\langle W, v \rangle \models_{\text{ARW0}} \varphi \quad \stackrel{def}{\Longleftrightarrow} \quad (\forall w \in W) \ w \Vdash_v \varphi.$$

Then arrow logic is $L_{\text{ARW0}} \stackrel{def}{=} \langle F_{\text{ARW0}}, M_{\text{ARW0}}, mng_{\text{ARW0}}, \models_{\text{ARW0}} \rangle$.

- $F_{\text{ARROW}} \stackrel{def}{=} F_{\text{ARW0}}$.

- $M_{\text{ARROW}} \stackrel{def}{=} \{\langle W, v \rangle \in M_S : W \subseteq U \times U \text{ for some set } U\}$.

For propositional connectives $\neg$ and $\wedge$ the definition of $w \Vdash_v \varphi$ is the same as in the propositional case. For the new connectives we have:

$$\langle a, b \rangle \Vdash_v \varphi \circ \psi \quad \stackrel{def}{\Longleftrightarrow} \quad \exists c \big[\langle a, c \rangle, \langle c, b \rangle \in W$$
$$\text{and } \langle a, c \rangle \Vdash_v \varphi \text{ and } \langle c, b \rangle \Vdash_v \psi\big],$$
$$\langle a, b \rangle \Vdash_v \varphi^{\smile} \quad \stackrel{def}{\Longleftrightarrow} \quad \big[\langle b, a \rangle \in W \text{ and } \langle b, a \rangle \Vdash_v \varphi\big],$$
$$\langle a, b \rangle \Vdash_v Id \quad \stackrel{def}{\Longleftrightarrow} \quad a = b.$$

As usual, $mng_{\text{ARROW}}(\varphi, \langle W, v \rangle) \overset{def}{=} \{w \in W : w \Vdash_v \varphi\}$, and the validity relation $\models_{\text{ARROW}}$ is defined by

$$\langle W, v \rangle \models_{\text{ARROW}} \varphi \overset{def}{\Longleftrightarrow} (\forall w \in W) w \Vdash_v \varphi.$$

Arrow logic L_{ARROW} is defined by

$$L_{\text{ARROW}} \overset{def}{=} \langle F_{\text{ARROW}}, M_{\text{ARROW}}, mng_{\text{ARROW}}, \models_{\text{ARROW}} \rangle.$$

- $F_{\text{RA}} \overset{def}{=} F_{\text{ARROW}}$.

- $M_{\text{RA}} \overset{def}{=} \{\langle W, v \rangle \in M_S : W = U \times U \text{ for some set } U\}$.

  The definitions of $w \Vdash_v \varphi$, mng_{RA} and $\models_{\text{RA}}$ are the same as in the case of L_{ARROW}.

  Arrow logic L_{RA} is $L_{\text{RA}} \overset{def}{=} \langle F_{\text{RA}}, M_{\text{RA}}, mng_{\text{RA}}, \models_{\text{RA}} \rangle$. L_{RA} is also called as the *logic of relation set algebras*.

Definition 2.13 (First-order logic with n variables L_n). Let $V \overset{def}{=} \{v_0, \ldots, v_{n-1}\}$ be a set, called the set of *variables* of L_n. Let the set P of *atomic formulas* of L_n be defined as $P \overset{def}{=} \{r_i(v_0 \ldots v_{n-1}) : i \in I\}$ for some set I.

(1). The set F_n of formulas is the smallest set H satisfying

- $P \subseteq H$
- $(v_i = v_j) \in H$ for each $i, j < n$
- $\varphi, \psi \in H$, $v_i \in V \implies (\varphi \wedge \psi), \neg\varphi, \exists v_i \varphi \in H$.

(2). The class M_n of *models* of L_n is defined by

$$M_n \overset{def}{=} \{\langle M, R_i \rangle_{i \in I} : M \text{ is a non-empty set and } R_i \subseteq {}^nM \ (i \in I)\}.$$

If $\mathcal{M} = \langle M, R_i \rangle_{i \in I} \in M_n$ then M is called the *universe* (or *carrier*) of $\mathcal{M}$.

(3). Let $\mathcal{M} = \langle M, R_i \rangle_{i \in I} \in M_n, q \in {}^nM$ and $\varphi \in F_n$. We define the ternary relation $\mathcal{M} \models \varphi[q]$ by recursion on the complexity of φ as follows.

- $\mathcal{M} \models r_i(v_0 \ldots v_{n-1})[q] \overset{def}{\Longleftrightarrow} q \in R_i \ (i \in I)$
- $\mathcal{M} \models (v_i = v_j)[q] \overset{def}{\Longleftrightarrow} q_i = q_j \ (i, j < n)$

- if $\psi_1, \psi_2 \in F_n$, then

$$\mathcal{M} \models \neg\psi_1[q] \overset{def}{\Longleftrightarrow} \text{not } \mathcal{M} \models \psi_1[q]$$

$$\mathcal{M} \models (\psi_1 \wedge \psi_2)[q] \overset{def}{\Longleftrightarrow} \mathcal{M} \models \psi_1[q] \text{ and } \mathcal{M} \models \psi_2[q]$$

$$\mathcal{M} \models \exists v_i\psi_1[q] \overset{def}{\Longleftrightarrow} (\exists q' \in {}^nM)[(\forall i \neq j < n)$$
$$q'_j = q_j \text{ and } \mathcal{M} \models \psi_1[q']].$$

If $\mathcal{M} \models \varphi[q]$ then we say that the *evaluation q satisfies φ in the model* $\mathcal{M}$.

Now we define mng_n as follows.

$$mng_n(\varphi, \mathcal{M}) \overset{def}{=} \{q \in {}^nM : \mathcal{M} \models \varphi[q]\}.$$

(4). Validity is defined by

$$\mathcal{M} \models_n \varphi \overset{def}{\Longleftrightarrow} (\forall q \in {}^nM) \quad \mathcal{M} \models \varphi[q].$$

First-order logic with n variables

$$\mathrm{L}_n \overset{def}{=} \langle F_n, M_n, mng_n, \models_n \rangle$$

has been defined.

Intuitive explanation. Our L_n might look somewhat unusual because we do not allow substitution of variables in atomic formulas $r_i(v_0 \ldots)$. This does not restrict generality, because substitution is expressible by using quantifiers and equality. This is explained in more detail in Remark 2.15 (2) below.

Next we define first-order logic in a non-traditional form. Therefore, below the definition, we will give intuitive explanations for our present definition.

Definition 2.14 (First-order logic $\mathrm{L_{FOL}}$, rank-free formulation). Recall that ω denotes the set of natural numbers.

Let $V \overset{def}{=} \{v_i : i \in \omega\}$ be a set, called the set of *variables* of $\mathrm{L_{FOL}}$. As before, let P be an arbitrary set, called the set of *atomic formulas* of $\mathrm{L_{FOL}}$. (Now, we will think of atomic formulas as relation symbols, hence we write $R \in P$ instead of $p \in P$ as in the case of L_S.)

(1). The set F_{FOL} is the smallest set H satisfying

- $P \subseteq H$
- $(v_i = v_j) \in H$ for each $i, j \in \omega$
- $\varphi, \psi \in H$, $i \in \omega \implies (\varphi \wedge \psi), \neg\varphi, \exists v_i\varphi \in H$.

(2). The class M_{FOL} of *models* of L_{FOL} is

$$M_{FOL} \overset{def}{=} \{\mathcal{M} : \mathcal{M} = \langle M, R^{\mathcal{M}} \rangle_{R \in P}, \ M \text{ is a non-empty set and}$$
$$R^{\mathcal{M}} \subseteq {}^n M \text{ for some } n \in \omega \ (R \in P)\}.$$

If $\mathcal{M} \in M_{FOL}$ then M and $R^{\mathcal{M}}$ denote parts of $\mathcal{M}$ determined by the convention $\langle M, R^{\mathcal{M}} \rangle = \mathcal{M}$.[8]

(3). Validity relation $\models_{FOL}$.

In L_{S5} the 'basic semantical units' were the possible situations $w \in W$. In L_{FOL} the basic semantical units are the evaluations of individual variables into models $\mathcal{M}$, where $q \in {}^\omega M$ and q evaluates variables v_i as element $q_i \in M$ in the model $\mathcal{M}$. To follow model theoretic tradition, instead of $\mathcal{M}, q \Vdash \varphi$ we will write $\mathcal{M} \models \varphi[q]$ (though the former would be more in the line with our definitions of L_{S5}, etc.).

Let $\mathcal{M} = \langle M, R^{\mathcal{M}} \rangle_{R \in P} \in M_{FOL}$, $q \in {}^\omega M$ and $\varphi \in F_{FOL}$. We define the ternary relation '$\mathcal{M} \models \varphi[q]$' by recursion on the complexity of φ as follows:

- $\mathcal{M} \models R[q] \overset{def}{\Longleftrightarrow} \langle q_0, \ldots, q_{n-1} \rangle \in R^{\mathcal{M}}$ for some $n \in \omega$ $(R \in P)$

- $\mathcal{M} \models (v_i = v_j)[q] \overset{def}{\Longleftrightarrow} q_i = q_j$ $(i, j \in \omega)$

- if $\psi_1, \psi_2 \in F_{FOL}$, then

$$\mathcal{M} \models \neg\psi_1[q] \overset{def}{\Longleftrightarrow} \text{not } \mathcal{M} \models \psi_1[q]$$
$$\mathcal{M} \models (\psi_1 \wedge \psi_2)[q] \overset{def}{\Longleftrightarrow} \mathcal{M} \models \psi_1[q] \text{ and } \mathcal{M} \models \psi_2[q]$$
$$\mathcal{M} \models \exists v_i\psi_1[q] \overset{def}{\Longleftrightarrow} (\exists q' \in {}^\omega M)(\forall j \in \omega)$$
$$[j \neq i \Rightarrow (q'_j = q_j \text{ and } \mathcal{M} \models \psi_1[q'])].$$

If $\mathcal{M} \models \varphi[q]$ holds then we say that q *satisfies* φ in $\mathcal{M}$.

Now we define mng_{FOL} as follows.

$$mng_{FOL}(\varphi, \mathcal{M}) \overset{def}{=} \{q \in {}^\omega M : \mathcal{M} \models \varphi[q]\}.$$

---

[8]That is, if $\mathcal{M}$ given, then M denotes the universe of $\mathcal{M}$. Further, for $R \in P$, $R^{\mathcal{M}}$ denotes the meaning of R in $\mathcal{M}$.

(4). Validity is defined by

$$\mathcal{M} \models_{\text{FOL}} \varphi \quad \overset{def}{\Longleftrightarrow} \quad (\forall q \in {}^{\omega} M) \; \mathcal{M} \models \varphi[q].$$

(5). *First-order logic* (in rank-free form) is

$$\mathrm{L_{FOL}} \overset{def}{=} \langle F_{\text{FOL}}, M_{\text{FOL}}, mng_{\text{FOL}}, \models_{\text{FOL}} \rangle .$$

For more on $\mathrm{L_{FOL}}$ see e.g. Henkin–Tarski [24], Simon [45], Venema [48], Henkin–Monk–Tarski [23], §4.3.

Intuitive explanations for $\mathrm{L_{FOL}}$.
There are two kinds of explanations needed. Namely,

(1). Why does the definition go as it does?

(2). Why do we say that $\mathrm{L_{FOL}}$ is first-order logic? That is, what are the connections between $\mathrm{L_{FOL}}$ and the more traditional formulations of first-order logic?

We discuss (2) in Remark 2.15 below. Let us first turn to (1).

Let R be a relation symbol, i.e. $R \in P$. Then instead of the traditional formula $R(v_0, v_1, v_2, \ldots)$ we simply write R. That is, we treat R as a shorthand for $R(v_0, v_1, v_2, \ldots)$.

So this is why R is an atomic formula. The next part of the definition which may need intuitive explanation is the definition of the satisfaction relation's behaviour on R. That is, the definition of $\mathcal{M} \models R[k]$. So let $R^{\mathcal{M}} \subseteq {}^n M$ be given. Recall that R abbreviates $R(v_0, v_1, v_2, \ldots)$ here. Clearly we want $\mathcal{M} \models R[k]$ to hold if in the traditional sense $\mathcal{M} \models R(v_0, v_1, v_2, \ldots)[k]$ holds. But by the traditional definition this holds iff $\langle k_0, \ldots, k_{n-1} \rangle \in R^{\mathcal{M}}$. Which agrees with our definition. The rest of the definition of $\mathrm{L_{FOL}}$ coincides with the definition of the most traditional version of first-order logic.

Remark 2.15 (Connections between $\mathrm{L_{FOL}}$ and the more traditional form of first-order logic).
(1). The logic $\mathrm{L_{FOL}}$ is slightly more general than the more traditional forms of first-order logic in that here the *logic* does not tell us in advance which relation symbol has what rank (that is why it is called *rank-free*). This information is postponed slightly, because it is not considered to be purely logical. The information about the ranks of the relation symbols will be provided by the models, or equivalently, by the non-logical axioms of some theory. However, we can simulate the more traditional form of first-order logic in $\mathrm{L_{FOL}}$ as follows.

Any language (or similarity type) of traditional first-order logic is a *theory* of our L_{FOL}. Namely, such a language includes the rank $\varrho(R)$ of each relation symbol $R \in P$. So, a traditional language is given by a pair $\langle P, \varrho \rangle$. To such a language we associate the following theory T_ϱ:

$$T_\varrho \stackrel{def}{=} \{\forall v_i(\exists v_i R \to R) : R \in P \text{ and } i \geq \varrho(R)\}.$$

The theory T_ϱ spells out for each $R \in P$ that the rank of R is $\varrho(R)$. After T_ϱ has been postulated, whenever one sees R as a formula, one can read it as a shorthand for $R(v_0 \ldots v_{\varrho(R)-1})$. To *any* theory T it is usual to associate a 'sublogic' of L_{FOL} as follows:

$$L_T \stackrel{def}{=} \langle F_{FOL}, Mod(T), mng_{FOL}, \models_{FOL}\rangle.$$

For our T_ϱ, the sublogic L_{T_ϱ} is strongly equivalent with the most traditional first-order logic of language $\langle P, \varrho \rangle$.[9]

(2).   The other feature of traditional first-order logic which might seem to be missing from L_{FOL} is *substitution* of individual variables, that is, L_{FOL} includes atomic formulas with a fixed order of variables only. The reason for this is that Tarski discovered in the 1940s that substitution can be expressed with quantification and equality. Namely, if we want to substitute v_1 for v_0 in formula φ then the resulting formula is equivalent to $\exists v_0(v_0 = v_1 \wedge \varphi)$. E.g. $R(v_1, v_1, v_2)$ is equivalent to

$$\exists v_0 \big(v_0 = v_1 \wedge R(v_0, v_1, v_2)\big).$$

What happens if we want to *interchange* v_0 and v_1, i.e. we want to express $R(v_1, v_0, v_2)$. Then write

$$\exists v_3 \exists v_4 \big[v_3 = v_0 \wedge v_4 = v_1 \wedge \exists v_0 \exists v_1 \big(v_0 = v_4 \wedge v_1 = v_3 \wedge R(v_0, v_1, v_2)\big)\big].$$

Someone might object that *before* writing up the theory T_ϱ (cf. item (1) above) one cannot interchange variables. There are two answers: *(i)* This does not really matter if we want to simulate traditional first-order logic. *(ii)* This can be easily done by adding extra unary connectives p_{ij} ($i, j \in \omega$) to those of L_{FOL}. The semantics of p_{ij} is given by

$$\mathcal{M} \models p_{ij}\varphi[q] \stackrel{def}{\Longleftrightarrow} \mathcal{M} \models \varphi[\langle q_0, \ldots, q_{i-1}, q_j, q_{i+1}, \ldots, q_{j-1}, q_i, q_{j+1}, \ldots\rangle],$$

[9]This equivalence is the strongest possible one. The models are practically the same, and the formulas are alphabetical variants of each other in the following sense. To each absolutely classical formula ψ of $\langle P, \varrho \rangle$ there is $\varphi \in F_{FOL}$ such that their meanings coincide in every model. (Same holds in the other direction: for every $\varphi \in F_{FOL}$ there is a very classical ψ, etc.)

if $i \leq j$, and similarly otherwise. Adding such connectives does not change the basic properties of the logic.

For more on the properties of L_{FOL} see the Appendix of Blok–Pigozzi [12], Andréka–Gergely–Németi [2] and Henkin–Tarski [24], etc.

The following logics are of a different 'flavour' than the ones seen so far. They include Lambek calculus, some fragments of linear logic, Pratt's action logic, dynamic logic, different kinds of semantics than seen so far. The main purpose of giving them is to indicate that the methods of algebraic logic are applicable almost to any unusual logic coming from completely different paradigms of logical or linguistic or computer science research areas, and are not restricted to the kinds of logics discussed so far. If the reader is already convinced, then he may safely skip Definitions 2.16–2.19.

Definition 2.16 (Lambek calculus (slightly extended)). Recall the logics L_{ARROW} and L_{RA}. The connectives of Lambek Calculus L_{LC} are $\{\wedge, \circ, \backslash, /, \rightarrow\}$. This defines the formulas F_{LC} of Lambek Calculus. Now,

$$L_{LC} \stackrel{def}{=} \langle F_{LC}, M_{RA}, mng_{LC}, \models_{LC} \rangle,$$

where for all $\varphi, \psi \in F_{LC}$ and all $\mathcal{M} \in M_{RA}$

$$mng_{LC}(\varphi\backslash\psi, \mathcal{M}) = mng_{RA}(\neg(\varphi^{\smile} \circ \neg\psi), \mathcal{M}),$$
$$mng_{LC}(\varphi/\psi, \mathcal{M}) = mng_{RA}(\neg(\neg\varphi \circ \psi^{\smile}), \mathcal{M}),$$
$$mng_{LC}(\varphi \rightarrow \psi, \mathcal{M}) = mng_{RA}((\neg\varphi \vee \psi), \mathcal{M}),$$

$$mng_{LC}(\varphi \wedge \psi) = mng_{RA}(\varphi \wedge \psi), mng_{LC}(\varphi \circ \psi) = mng_{RA}(\varphi \circ \psi).$$

and $\models_{LC}$ is defined analogously to $\models_{RA}$.

Remark 2.17 Original Lambek Calculus is only a fragment of L_{LC} because in the original case the use of '$\rightarrow$' is restricted. (In any formula, '$\rightarrow$' can be used only once, and it is the outermost connective.)

The methods of the present work yielded quite a few results for Lambek Calculus and for some further fragments of Linear Logic, cf. Andréka–Mikulás [4].

Definition 2.18 (Language model for Lambek calculus and other logics (e.g. arrow logic)).

(1). *Notation:* A set $X \subseteq U^*$ is called a language (in the syntactic sense). Let $X, Y \subseteq U^*$. Then $X * Y = \{s \,^{\frown}q : s \in X \text{ and } q \in Y\}$, where $s \,^{\frown}q$ is the concatenation of s and q.

$$M_L \overset{def}{=} \{\langle U, f\rangle : U \text{ is a set and } f : P \longrightarrow U^*\}.$$

We write $mng(\varphi)$ instead of $mng_L(\varphi, \langle U, f\rangle)$.

$$
\begin{aligned}
mng(p_i) &= f(p_i) \text{ for } p_i \in P, \\
mng(\varphi \wedge \psi) &= mng(\varphi) \cap mng(\psi), \\
mng(\varphi \circ \psi) &= mng(\varphi) * mng(\psi), \\
mng(\varphi \to \psi) &= [U^* \setminus mng(\varphi)] \cup mng(\psi), \\
mng(\varphi \backslash \psi) &= \{q : (\forall s \in mng(\varphi))s \,^\frown q \in mng(\psi)\}, \\
mng(\varphi / \psi) &= \{s : (\forall q \in mng(\psi))s \,^\frown q \in mng(\varphi)\}.
\end{aligned}
$$

Now, $\models_L$ is defined as before.

(2). *Lambek Calculus with language models* is

$$\mathrm{L_{LCL}} = \langle F_{\mathrm{LC}}, M_L, mng_L, \models_L\rangle.$$

This is quite a well investigated logic, and in some respects behaves slightly differently from $\mathrm{L_{LC}}$.

Now we extend the definition of mng_L to the connectives $\neg, \breve{\ }$ and Id as follows:

$$
\begin{aligned}
mng(\neg\varphi) &= U^* \setminus mng(\varphi), \\
mng(\varphi^\breve{\ }) &= \{\langle s_n, \ldots, s_1\rangle : \langle s_1, \ldots, s_n\rangle \in mng(\varphi)\}, \\
mng(Id) &= \{\langle\rangle\}.
\end{aligned}
$$

(Here $\langle\rangle$ denotes the sequence of length 0.)

(3). *Extended Lambek calculus with language models*: $\mathrm{L_{LCL}^+}$ has all the Booleans as connectives in addition to F_{LC}, and the semantics described in (1) above.

$$\mathrm{L_{LCL}^+} = \langle F_{\mathrm{LC}}^+, M_L, mng_L, \models_L\rangle.$$

(4). *Arrow logic with language models* is

$$\mathrm{L_{ARROWL}} = \langle F_{\mathrm{ARROW}}^+, M_L, mng_L, \models_L\rangle.$$

Definition 2.19 (Dynamic arrow logic). Recall the definition of $\mathrm{L_{RA}}$. Add the unary connective $*$ sending φ to φ^*. The set of formulas (denoted as F_{DL}) of Dynamic Arrow Logic is defined as that of L_{RA} together with the following clause:

$$\varphi \in F_{DL} \implies \varphi^* \in F_{DL} .$$

The semantics of this connective is defined by

$$mng_{DL}(\varphi^*, \mathcal{M}) \stackrel{def}{=}$$
'reflexive and transitive closure of the relation $mng_{DL}(\varphi, \mathcal{M})$".

This defines $\models^*$ from $\models_{RA}$. Now, Dynamic Arrow Logic is

$$L_{DL} = \langle F_{DL}, M_{RA}, mng_{DL}, \models^* \rangle .$$

Pratt's original dynamic logic can easily and naturally be interpreted into L_{DL}. For more on dynamic arrow logic cf. e.g. van Benthem [47], M. Marx [27].

Below we give some *further logics*, which are even *less similar* to the ones discussed so far, e.g. infinite valued logics, relevant logics, partial logics, etc.

Definition 2.20 (Infinite valued logic L_∞). Let P be any set, the set of atomic formulas of L_∞. The logical connectives of L_∞ are $\wedge$, $\neg$, $\vee$ and $\rightarrow$. The set F_∞ of formulas is defined the usual way. Recall that $P \subseteq F_\infty$ is the set of atomic formulas.

$$M_\infty \stackrel{def}{=} \{f \ : \ (f : P \rightarrow [0,1])\} ,$$

where $[0,1]$ denotes the usual interval of real numbers.

Let $f \in M_\infty$. First we define $mn_f(\varphi)$:

$$mn_f(p) \stackrel{def}{=} f(p) \quad \text{for } p \in P$$

$$mn_f(\varphi \wedge \psi) \stackrel{def}{=} min\{mn_f(\varphi), mn_f(\psi)\}$$

$$mn_f(\neg\varphi) \stackrel{def}{=} 1 - mn_f(\varphi)$$

$$mn_f(\varphi \vee \psi) \stackrel{def}{=} max\{mn_f(\varphi), mn_f(\psi)\}$$

$$mn_f(\varphi \rightarrow \psi) \stackrel{def}{=} \begin{cases} 1 & \text{if } mn_f(\varphi) \leq mn_f(\psi) \\ 1 - (mn_f(\varphi) - mn_f(\psi)) & \text{else.} \end{cases}$$

For any $f \in M_\infty$, $\varphi \in F_\infty$,

$$mng_\infty(\varphi, f) \stackrel{def}{=} \{x \in [0,1] \ : \ x \leq mn_f(\varphi)\};$$

$$f \models_\infty \varphi \stackrel{def}{\iff} mng_\infty(\varphi, f) = [0,1].$$

With this the logic

$$L_\infty \overset{def}{=} \langle F_\infty, M_\infty, mng_\infty, \models_\infty \rangle$$

is defined.

Even in intuitionistic logic we have $\models \neg(\varphi \wedge \neg\varphi)$. However, in L_∞ this is not so, the truth value of $(\varphi \wedge \neg\varphi)$ can be as high as $1/2$. So in a sense, L_∞ tolerates contradictions (and by a cheap joke, we could call it 'dialectical' because of this, but we will not do so). Also $(\varphi \leftrightarrow \neg\varphi)$ can be valid in some of our models. This again cannot happen even in intuitionistic logic. Further, $mn_f(\varphi) \geq 1/2$ is expressible as $f \models_\infty (\neg\varphi \to \varphi)$, hence if we would want to have a new validity relation $\models_1$, where $f \models_1 \varphi$ iff $mn_f(\varphi) \geq 1/2$, then we can express this new $\models_1$ by $f \models_1 \varphi$ iff $mng_\infty(\neg\varphi \to \varphi) = mng_\infty(\varphi \to \varphi)$. That is, $\models_1$ is still expressible from mng as was required in our old definition of logic. We do not look into this new $\models_1$ any more, we only use it as an example of definability of $\models_1$ from mng without identifying truth with a greatest meaning or even with a single meaning.

Definition 2.21 (Relevance logic L_r). We obtain a new logic L_r from L_∞ by executing the following modifications in the definition. Replace $[0,1]$ with the set Q of rational numbers everywhere. Define $mn_f(\neg\varphi) \overset{def}{=} -mn_f(\varphi)$. Redefine the meaning of '$\to$' as follows:

$$mn_f(\varphi \to \psi) \overset{def}{=} \begin{cases} max\{-mn_f(\varphi), mn_f(\psi)\} & \text{if } mn_f(\varphi) \leq mn_f(\psi) \\ min\{mn_f(\varphi), -mn_f(\psi)\} & \text{else.} \end{cases}$$

For any $f \in M_\infty$, $\varphi \in F_\infty$,

$$mng_r(\varphi, f) \overset{def}{=} \{x \in Q \ : \ x \leq mn_f(\varphi)\};$$

$$f \models_r \varphi \overset{def}{\Longleftrightarrow} 0 \in mng_r(\varphi, f).$$

Now, relevance logic is

$$L_r = \langle F_r, M_r, mng_r, \models_r \rangle.$$

Next we define Partial Logic (L_P). Partial logics are designed to express the fact that in certain situations, certain statements may be meaningless. For example, the statement 'the integer 2 is of pink colour' may be meaningless in certain situations. If φ is meaningless then so is $\neg\varphi$. Also, according to the Copenhagen interpretation of quantum mechanics, in certain situations certain statements are meaningless, e.g. asking for the exact location of a particle in a situation where the particle has only a probability distribution of locations is meaningless.

Definition 2.22 (Partial logic, L_P). Connectives of L_P are: $\wedge$, $\vee$, $\neg$, N, where the new kind of formula $N(\varphi)$ intends to express that φ is either meaningless or false ('It is not the case that φ' or perhaps 'It is not the fact that φ'). (N is a very strong negation.)

- The set of formulas F_P is obtained from F_S by adding the new unary connective N.

- The class M_P of models is

$$M_P \overset{def}{=} \{f : f \text{ maps } P \text{ into } \{0,1,2\}\} \,.$$

Here $0, 1, 2$ are intended to denote the truthvalues 'false', 'true', and 'undefined' respectively. In the following we write $mng_f(\varphi)$ instead of $mng_P(\varphi, f)$.

- If $2 \notin \{mng_f(\varphi), mng_f(\psi)\}$, then mng_f of $(\varphi \wedge \psi)$, $(\varphi \vee \psi)$, $\neg\varphi$ are defined as in the case of L_S. Else (if 2 is one of the meanings) then mng_f of $(\varphi \wedge \psi)$, $(\varphi \vee \psi)$, $\neg\varphi$ is 2 (so all three are the same and they all are 2).

$$mng_f(N\varphi) \quad \overset{def}{=} \quad \begin{cases} 0 & \text{if } mng_f(\varphi) = 1 \\ 1 & \text{otherwise.} \end{cases}$$

$$f \models_P \varphi \quad \text{iff} \quad mng_f(\varphi) = 1 \,.$$

With this, $L_P = \langle F_P, M_P, mng_P, \models_P \rangle$ is defined.

L_P above is a quite important logic. It was introduced by Prior and was further investigated by I. Ruzsa (cf. e.g. [35]).

3 Fine-tuning the framework and algebraization

The idea of solving problems in logic by first translating them to algebra, then using the powerful methodology of algebra for solving them, and then translating the solution back to logic, goes back to Leibnitz and Pascal. Papers on the history of logic (e.g. Anellis–Houser [9], Maddux [26]) point out that this method was fruitfully applied in the nineteenth century not only to propositional logics but also to quantifier logics (De Morgan, Peirce, etc. applied it to quantifier logics, too). The number of applications has grown ever since (though some of these remained unnoticed e.g. the celebrated Kripke–Lemmon completeness theorem for modal logic w.r.t. Kripke models was first proved by Jónsson and Tarski in 1948 using algebraic logic).

For brevity, we will refer to the above method or procedure as 'applying Algebraic Logic (AL) to Logic'. This expression might be somewhat misleading since AL itself happens to be a part of logic, and we do not intend to deny this. We will use the expression all the same, and hope, the reader will not misunderstand our intention.

In items (i) and (ii) below we describe two of the main motivations for applying AL to logic.

(i) This is the more obvious one: When working with a relatively new kind of problem, it is often proved to be useful to 'transform' the problem into a well understood and streamlined area of mathematics, solve the problem there and translate the result back. Examples include the method of Laplace transform in solving differential equations (a central tool in electrical engineering).

At this point we would like to dispel a possible misunderstanding: In certain circles of logicians there seems to be a belief that AL applies only to syntactical problems of logic and that semantical and model-theoretic problems are not treated by AL or at least not in their original model-theoretic form. Nothing can be as far from the truth as this belief, as e.g. looking into the present work should reveal. A variant of this belief is that the main bulk of AL is about offering a cheap pseudo semantics to Logics as a substitute for intuitive, model-theoretic semantics. Again, this is very far from being true. (This is a particularly harmful piece of misinformation, because, this 'slander' is easy to believe if one looks only superficially into a few AL papers.) To illustrate how far this belief is from truth, the semantical-model-theoretic parts of the present work emphasize that they start out from a logical system L whose semantics is as intuitive and as non-algebraic as it wants to be, and then we transform L into algebra, paying special attention to not distorting its semantics in the process; and anyway, finally we translate the solutions back to the very original non-algebraic framework (including model theoretical semantics).

In the present part of the chapter we define the algebraic counterpart $\mathsf{Alg}_{\models}(L)$ of a logic L together with the algebraic counterpart $\mathsf{Alg}_m(L)$ of the semantical-model-theoretical ingredients of L. Then we prove equivalence theorems, which to essential logical properties of L associate natural and well investigated algebraic properties of $\mathsf{Alg}_{\models}(L)$ such that if we want to decide whether L has a certain property, we will know what to ask from our algebraist colleague about $\mathsf{Alg}_{\models}(L)$. The same devices are suitable for finding out what one has to change in L if one wants to have a variant of L having a desirable property (which L lacks). For example, if we want to decide whether L has the proof-theoretic property called Craig's interpolation property, then it is sufficient to decide whether $\text{Alg}_{\models}(\text{L})$ has the so-called amalgamation property (for which there are powerful methods in the literature of algebra). If the logical question concerns connections between several logics, say between L_1 and L_2, then the algebraic question will be about connections between $\text{Alg}_{\models}(\text{L}_1)$ and $\text{Alg}_{\models}(\text{L}_2)$.

(ii) With the rapidly growing variety of applications of logic (in diverse areas like computer science, linguistics, AI, law, etc.) there is a growing number of new logics to be investigated. In this situation AL offers us a tool for economy and a tool for unification in various ways. One of these is that $\text{Alg}_{\models}(\text{L})$ is always a class of algebras, therefore we can apply the same machinery, namely universal algebra, to study all the new logics. In other words, we bring all the various logics to a kind of 'normal form' where they can be studied by uniform methods. Moreover, for most choices of L, $\text{Alg}_{\models}(\text{L})$ tends to appear in the same 'area' of universal algebra, hence specialized powerful methods lend themselves to studying L. There is a fairly well understood 'map' available for the landscape of Universal Algebra. By using our algebraization process and equivalence theorems, we can project this 'map' back to the (far less understood) landscape of possible logics.

The definition of a logic in Section 2.1 is very wide. Actually, it is too wide for proving interesting theorems about logics. Now we will define a subclass of logics which we will call *nice logics*. Our notion of a nice logic is wide enough to cover the logics mentioned in the previous section, moreover, it is broad enough to cover almost all logics investigated in the literature. (Certain quantifier logics might need a little reformulation for this, but that reformulation does not affect the essential aspects of the logic in question as we will see.) On the other hand, the class of nice logics is narrow enough for proving interesting theorems about them, that is, we will be able to establish typical logical facts that hold for most logics studied in the literature.

Before reading Definition 3.1 below, it might be useful to contemplate the common features of the logics studied so far e.g. L_S, S5, L_n (cf. Section 2.2).

In almost all the logics studied so far the biconditional '↔' is available as a derived connective. In condition (3) of Definition 3.1 a new symbol '∇' will occur, denoting a derived connective of the logic in question. At first reading it is a good idea to identify '∇' with our old biconditional '↔'. Certainly, if we replaced condition (3) with the simpler assumption that '↔' is expressible in our logic L then all theorems would remain true. However, at a second reading of the definition it might be useful to observe that our condition (3) is a weaker assumption than expressibility of '↔' (and that this makes the class of nice logics broader).

We also note that the theorems below (based on the next definition) can be proved in a more general setting (cf. [7], [8] and Chapter 4 herein). Here we do restrictions in order to make the methodology more transparent. The reader who would find the definition below too restrictive is asked to consult Remark 3.5, where several conditions are either eliminated or it is explained how to eliminate them, and references are given where the elimination is done.

Definition 3.1 (Nice logic, strongly nice logic). Let $\langle F, M, mng, \models \rangle$ be a logic (i.e. F is a set, M is a class, mng is a function with domain $F \times M$, and $\models \subseteq M \times F$).

Convention: As we agreed below Remark 2.6, we will concentrate on the '$\vdash$'-free version $\langle F, M, mng, \models \rangle$ of our logic L. As indicated in the text between Definition 2.5 and subsection 2.2. Examples, this is *not an essential* decision; and '$\vdash$' can be systematically put back into L throughout the rest of the paper. If we do this (or if the reader carries this through), the theory remains essentially unchanged but it becomes somewhat richer. The most important change is that in Definition 3.4 below, instead of associating two classes $\mathsf{Alg}_\models(L)$ and $\mathsf{Alg}_m(L)$ to L (as is done now), we will have a third class $\mathsf{Alg}_\vdash(L)$ consisting of the so-called proof theoretical (or syntactical) Lindenbaum–Tarski algebras. If L is strongly sound then we will have $\mathsf{Alg}_\vdash(L) \supseteq \mathsf{Alg}_\models(L)$. The class $\mathsf{Alg}_\vdash(L)$ will turn out to be quite useful in developing the theory and in applying it to logic. Herein, however, we discuss only the restricted '$\vdash$'-free theory (except for remarks like the present one or Remark 3.3 below).
End of Convention.

We say that L is a *nice logic* if conditions (1–4) below hold for L.

(1). A set $Cn(L)$, called the set of *logical connectives* of L, is fixed. Every $c \in Cn(L)$ has some rank $rank(c) \in \omega$. The set of all logical connectives of rank k is denoted by $Cn_k(L)$.

There is a set P, called the set of *atomic formulas* (or *parameters* or *propositional variables*), such that F is the smallest set satisfying conditions (a)–(b) below:

(a) $P \subseteq F$,

(b) if $c \in Cn_k(L)$ and $\varphi_1, \ldots, \varphi_k \in F$ then $c(\varphi_1, \ldots, \varphi_k) \in F$.

The word-algebra generated by P using the logical connectives from $Cn(L)$ as algebraic operations is denoted by $\mathcal{F}$, that is, $\mathcal{F} = \langle F, c \rangle_{c \in Cn(L)}$ $\mathcal{F}$ is called the *formula algebra* of L.

(2). The function $mng_{\mathcal{M}} \overset{def}{=} \langle mng(\varphi, \mathcal{M}) : \varphi \in F \rangle$ is a homomorphism from $\mathcal{F}$, for every $\mathcal{M} \in M$.

(3). There are *'derived'* *connectives* 'ε' and 'δ' (unary) and '∇' (binary) of L with the following properties:

(i) $(\forall \mathcal{M} \in M)(\forall \varphi, \psi \in F)\left[\mathcal{M} \models (\varphi \nabla \psi) \iff mng_{\mathcal{M}}(\varphi) = mng_{\mathcal{M}}(\psi)\right]$.

(ii) $(\forall \mathcal{M} \in M)(\forall \varphi \in F)\left[\mathcal{M} \models \varepsilon(\varphi) \nabla \delta(\varphi) \iff \mathcal{M} \models \varphi\right]$.

(By 'derived' we mean that 'ε, δ' and '∇' are not necessarily members of $Cn(\mathrm{L})$. They are only 'built up' from elements of $Cn(\mathrm{L})$. But we do not know from which elements of $Cn(\mathrm{L})$ 'ε', 'δ', or '∇' are built up, or how. We do not care!)

(4). $(\forall \psi, \varphi_0, \ldots, \varphi_n \in F)(\forall p_0, \ldots, p_n \in P)\left[\models \psi(\overline{p}) \implies \models \psi(\overline{p}/\overline{\varphi})\right],$

where $\overline{p} = \langle p_0, \ldots, p_n \rangle$, $\overline{\varphi} = \langle \varphi_0, \ldots, \varphi_n \rangle$, and $\psi(\overline{p}/\overline{\varphi})$ denotes the formula that we get from ψ after simultaneously substituting φ_i for every occurrence of p_i $(0 \leq i \leq n)$ in ψ. We refer to this condition as '*L has the substitution property*'.

L is called *strongly nice* iff it is nice and satisfies condition (5) below.

(5). $(\forall s \in {}^P F)(\forall \mathcal{M} \in M)(\exists \mathcal{N} \in M)(\forall \varphi(p_{i_0}, \ldots, p_{i_n}) \in F)$

$$mng_{\mathcal{N}}(\varphi) = mng_{\mathcal{M}}\left(\varphi(p_{i_0}/s(p_{i_0}), \ldots, p_{i_n}/s(p_{i_n}))\right). \qquad (*)$$

Let $\hat{s} \in {}^F F$ be the natural extension of s to $\mathcal{F}$.

Then (*) says $mng_{\mathcal{N}}(\varphi) = mng_{\mathcal{M}}(\hat{s}(\varphi))$. If this property holds, then we say that the logic '*L has the semantical substitution property*' (the model $\mathcal{N}$ is the substituted version of $\mathcal{M}$ along substitution s).

Logics satisfying conditions (1), (2) and (5) above are called *structural* ones.

Structural logics nicely match the most general logics studied in the general theory of propositional logics, cf. Font–Jansana [20].

If $\mathcal{A}$ and $\mathcal{B}$ are two similar algebras, then $Hom(\mathcal{A}, \mathcal{B})$ denotes the set of all homomorphisms from $\mathcal{A}$ into $\mathcal{B}$. If $h \in Hom(\mathcal{A}, \mathcal{B})$, then $h(\mathcal{A})$ denotes the image of the algebra $\mathcal{A}$ along h i.e. $h(\mathcal{A})$ is the smallest subalgebra of $\mathcal{B}$ such that $h \in Hom(\mathcal{A}, h(\mathcal{A}))$.

Remark 3.2

(i) An equivalent form of (*) above is the very natural condition

$$(\forall h \in Hom(\mathcal{F}, \mathcal{F})) \, (\forall \mathcal{M} \in M)(\exists \mathcal{N} \in M) \, mng_{\mathcal{N}} = mng_{\mathcal{M}} \circ h \,.$$

Since h is just a substitution, this form makes it explicit that $\mathcal{N}$ is the h-substituted version of $\mathcal{M}$. Another equivalent version is the following.

$$(\forall \mathcal{M} \in M)\big(\forall h \in Hom(\mathcal{F}, mng_{\mathcal{M}}(\mathcal{F}))\big)(\exists \mathcal{N} \in M) \; mng_{\mathcal{N}} = h.$$

(ii) Item (2) of Definition 3.1 above is a purely logical criterion. Namely, it is Frege's principle of compositionality.

(iii) One can make the definition of a strongly nice logic more permissive by requiring in Definition 3.1 (3) the existence of $\nabla_1, \ldots, \nabla_k$ and $\varepsilon_0, \delta_0, \ldots, \varepsilon_n, \delta_n$ such that

(3)(i)$_0$ $\mathcal{M} \models \{(\varphi \, \nabla_i \, \psi) : i \leq k\} \Longleftrightarrow mng_{\mathcal{M}}(\varphi) = mng_{\mathcal{M}}(\psi),$

and

(3)(ii)$_0$ $\mathcal{M} \models \{(\varepsilon_j(\varphi) \, \nabla_i \, \delta_j(\varphi)) : i \leq k, j \leq n\} \Longleftrightarrow \mathcal{M} \models \varphi.$

(iv) In the presence of (3) of Definition 3.1 above, semantical substitution property (5) implies substitution property (4).

Remark 3.3 (Connections with the Blok–Pigozzi approach). Here we mention only a small part of these connections.

Let $L = \langle F_L, M_L, mng_L, \models_L \rangle$ be a logic. Recall that $\models_L^c$ denotes the semantical consequence relation $\models_L^c \subseteq \mathcal{P}(F) \times F$ induced by $\models_L$. Recall from the discussion of the connection between logics with $\vdash_L$ and without $\vdash_L$ preceding Definition 2.1 that the pair $\langle F_L, \models_L^c \rangle$ can be considered to be a logic in the purely syntactical sense. The $\langle F_L, \models_L^c \rangle$ part of a strongly nice logic L is always algebraizable in the sense of Blok and Pigozzi. Actually, their definition is more general. For example, they use the more general version outlined in Remark 3.2 (iii) above, which has $\nabla_0, \ldots, \nabla_n$ instead of a single ∇.

A small sample of references is Blok–Pigozzi [12], their papers in [5], Czelakowski [16], Font–Jansana [19].

For any class K of similar algebras,

$$\mathbf{I}K \overset{def}{=} \{\mathcal{A} : (\exists \mathcal{B} \in K) \; \mathcal{A} \text{ is isomorphic to } \mathcal{B}\}.$$

Definition 3.4 (Algebraic counterpart of a logic). Let $L = \langle F, M, mng, \models \rangle$ be a logic satisfying conditions (1),(2) of Definition 3.1.

(i) Let $K \subseteq M$.
Then for every $\varphi, \psi \in F$

$$\varphi \sim_K \psi \overset{def}{\Longleftrightarrow} (\forall \mathcal{M} \in K) \; mng_{\mathcal{M}}(\varphi) = mng_{\mathcal{M}}(\psi).$$

Then $\sim_K$ is an equivalence relation on F, which is moreover a congruence relation on $\mathcal{F}$ by condition (3). Now $\mathcal{F}/\sim_K$ denotes the factor-algebra of $\mathcal{F}$ when factorized by the congruence relation $\sim_K$.

$$\mathsf{Alg}_{\models}(L) \overset{def}{=} \mathbf{I}\{\mathcal{F}/\sim_K : K \subseteq M\}.$$

(ii)

$$\mathsf{Alg}_m(\mathrm{L}) \stackrel{def}{=} \{ mng_{\mathcal{M}}(\mathcal{F}) \ : \ \mathcal{M} \in M \},$$

where $mng_{\mathcal{M}}$ was defined in item (2) of Definition 3.1.

We note that
(i) $\mathsf{Alg}_m(\mathrm{L}_S) \subseteq$ 'class of all Boolean set algebras'
(ii) $\mathsf{Alg}_m(\mathrm{S}5) \subseteq$ 'class of all one-dimensional cylindric set algebras'

Remark 3.5 (Generalizations). First we will omit condition (3(ii)) from the definition of a nice logic. A logic L in the sense of Definition 2.1 is said to be *semi-nice* if it satisfies conditions (1), (2), (3(i)), (4) of Definition 3.1.

Semi-nice logics, even without condition (4) of Definition 3.1, were investigated in [7], but investigation of the relation $\models$ was restricted to formulas of the form $(\varphi \nabla \psi)$.

Below we indicate how to extend investigation to all formulas, i.e. how to extend the theory described in the present work to semi-nice logics.

To algebraize (in a reversible way) these more general logics, we add a new unary operation symbol 'c' to (the language of) our algebras. So the new version $\mathsf{Alg}_i^+(\mathrm{L})$ of $\mathsf{Alg}_i(\mathrm{L})$ ($i \in \{\models, m\}$) will consist of algebras which have an extra operation 'c' not available in $\mathsf{Alg}_i(\mathrm{L})$. However, in order to make our approach work, we have to permit 'c' to be a *partial operation*. This means that for certain elements of our algebras 'c' may not be defined. (A classical example of a partial operation is inversion $x \mapsto x^{-1}$ in the field of real numbers. Zero has no inverse, so $^{-1}$ is undefined at argument 0.) Universal algebra for partial algebras (i.e. algebras with partial operations) is well developed , cf. e.g. Burmeister [13], Andréka–Németi [6]. Therefore generalizing our previous theorems to the new algebras causes no real difficulty. Those readers who would prefer to avoid partial algebras are asked to consult the final part of this remark below. It is shown there how to eliminate the partial operation symbol 'c'.

For a semi-nice logic L we can define its 'algebraic counterpart' in the following way. Let $\mathrm{L} = \langle F, M, mng, \models \rangle$ be a logic. Assume L satisfies conditions (1), (2) in the definition of a nice logic (Definition 3.1). Recall that the algebras $\mathcal{F}$ and $mng_{\mathcal{M}}(\mathcal{F})$ were defined in Definition 3.1.

Let $K \subseteq M$. Then we define the partial function $c_K : F \to F$ in the following way. For any $\varphi \in F$,

if $K \models \varphi$ then $c_K(\varphi)$ is defined and $c_K(\varphi) = \varphi$; while
if $K \not\models \varphi$ then $c_K(\varphi)$ is undefined.

Clearly, $\langle \mathcal{F}, c_K \rangle$ is a partial algebra for every $K \subseteq M$. The equivalence relation $\sim_K$ (defined in Definition 3.4) is a congruence not only on $\mathcal{F}$ but also on $\langle \mathcal{F}, c_K \rangle$ (c_K was defined in a way to ensure this). Now,

$$\mathsf{Alg}_{\models}^{+}(\mathrm{L}) \stackrel{def}{=} \mathbf{I}\{\langle \mathcal{F}, c_K \rangle / {\sim_K} : K \subseteq M\}.$$

Let us turn to defining $\mathsf{Alg}_{m}^{+}(\mathrm{L})$. First we define a new partial function c on the algebra $\mathcal{A}(\mathcal{M}) \stackrel{def}{=} mng_{\mathcal{M}}(\mathcal{F})$ as follows. For every $\varphi \in F$,

$$c\big(mng_{\mathcal{M}}(\varphi)\big) \stackrel{def}{=} mng_{\mathcal{M}}(\varphi) \quad \text{if} \quad \mathcal{M} \models \varphi; \quad \text{else}$$
$$c\big(mng_{\mathcal{M}}(\varphi)\big) \quad \text{is undefined.}$$

The new partial algebra $\mathcal{A}^{+}(\mathcal{M})$ associated to $\mathcal{M}$ is

$$\mathcal{A}^{+}(\mathcal{M}) \stackrel{def}{=} \langle \mathcal{A}(\mathcal{M}), c \rangle.$$

Now

$$\mathsf{Alg}_{m}^{+}(\mathrm{L}) \stackrel{def}{=} \{\mathcal{A}^{+}(\mathcal{M}) : \mathcal{M} \in M\}.$$

If the reader would like to avoid using partial algebras, then the following equivalent, more natural approach works. Instead of 'c' we add a new unary predicate '$T(x)$' (T for truth). Imitating the definition of 'c_K', we let $T_K \stackrel{def}{=} \{\varphi \in F : K \models \varphi\}$ for any $K \subseteq M$. Similarly, the algebraic counterpart of a model $\mathcal{M}$ looks like $\langle \mathcal{A}, T \rangle$, where $\mathcal{A} \in \mathsf{Alg}_{m}(\mathrm{L})$ and $T \subseteq A$ such that

$$(\forall \varphi \in F)(\mathcal{M} \models \varphi \iff mng_{\mathcal{M}}(\varphi) \in T);$$

holds for T (cf. condition (vi) of Definition 2.1).

This approach is practically equivalent to the one using 'c' instead of 'T'. Further, this is very-very closely related to what is called 'matrix semantics' in Blok–Pigozzi [12] and in the works quoted therein. Blok and Pigozzi have several strong results about the presently outlined approach.

If we want to drop condition (3) of the definition of nice logic (Definition 3.1) altogether, then a possibility is to restrict the validity relation $\models$ to *sequents* ($\varphi \Rightarrow \psi$) of formulas (instead of having it for all formulas). Here '$\Rightarrow$' is not a logical connective, but rather a metalevel symbol. If $\varphi, \psi \in F$ then ($\varphi \Rightarrow \psi$) is a sequent (sequents are *not* formulas). Further,

$$\mathcal{M} \models (\varphi \Rightarrow \psi) \quad \text{iff} \quad mng_{\mathcal{M}}(\varphi) \subseteq mng_{\mathcal{M}}(\psi).$$

This approach is applicable to more logics, hence more kinds of algebras show up in $\mathsf{Alg}_{m}(\mathrm{L})$, $\mathsf{Alg}_{\models}(\mathrm{L})$. However, similarly to the way we had to introduce 'c' above to code validity in a model, now we have to introduce a pre-ordering '$\leq$' on our algebras to code '$\Rightarrow$'. However, this is not needed if we restrict the validity relation $\models$ a little bit more, namely to pairs

$\{(\varphi \Rightarrow \psi), (\psi \Rightarrow \varphi)\}$ of sequents. Then we do not need new symbols like '$\leq$' in our algebras. This approach is investigated e.g. in [7] to quite some extent.

We could also try to drop conditions (4), (5) of Definition 3.1, i.e. drop permutability of atomic formulas. This would enable us to treat traditional first-order logic more comfortably (with less preparation to do). This can be done, the only thing needed is the universal algebraic concept of a *free algebra over some defining relations*. The details are available in [7]. Cf. also Chapter 4 herein.

Next we turn to defining *Hilbert-style inference systems*. Inference systems in general are syntactical devices serving to recapture (or at least to approximate) the semantical consequence relation of the logic L. The idea is the following. Suppose $\Sigma \models^c_L \varphi$. This means that, in the logic L, the assumptions collected in Σ semantically imply the conclusion φ. (In any possible world $\mathcal{M}$ of L that is, in any $\mathcal{M} \in M_L$, whenever Σ is valid in $\mathcal{M}$, then also φ is valid in $\mathcal{M}$.) Then we would like to be able to reproduce this relationship between Σ and φ by purely syntactical, 'finitistic' means. That is, by applying some formal rules of inference (and some axioms of the logic L) we would like to be able to derive φ from Σ by using 'paper and pencil' only. In particular, such a derivation will always be a finite string of symbols.

Definition 3.6 (Formula scheme). Let L be a nice logic with the set $Cn(L)$ of logical connectives (cf. (1) of Definition 3.1). Fix a countable set $A = \{A_i : i < \omega\}$, called the set of *formula variables*. The set Fms_L of *formula schemes* of L is the smallest set satisfying conditions (a)–(b) below:

(a) $A \subseteq Fms_L$,
(b) if $c \in Cn_k(L)$ and $\Phi_1, \ldots, \Phi_k \in Fms_L$ then $c(\Phi_1, \ldots, \Phi_k) \in Fms_L$.

An *instance of a formula scheme* is given by substituting formulas for the formula variables in it.

Definition 3.7 (Hilbert-style inference system). Let L be a nice logic.

An *inference rule* of L is a pair $\langle \langle B_1, \ldots, B_n \rangle, B_0 \rangle$, where every B_i $(i \leq n)$ is a formula scheme. This inference rule will be denoted by

$$\frac{B_1, \ldots, B_n}{B_0}.$$

An *instance of an inference rule* is given by substituting formulas for the formula variables in the formula schemes occurring in the rule.

A *Hilbert-style inference system* (or *calculus*) for L is a finite set of formula schemes (called *axiom schemes* or *axioms*) together with a finite set of inference rules.

Definition 3.8 (Derivability). Let L be a nice logic and let $\vdash$ be a Hilbert-style inference system for L. Assume $\Sigma \cup \{\varphi\} \subseteq F_{\mathrm{L}}$. We say that φ is $\vdash$-*derivable* (or -*provable*) from Σ iff there is a finite sequence $\langle \varphi_1, \ldots, \varphi_n \rangle$ of formulas (an $\vdash$-*proof of φ from Σ*) such that φ_n is φ and for every $1 \le i \le n$

- $\varphi_i \in \Sigma$ or

- φ_i is an instance of an axiom scheme (an *axiom* for short) of $\vdash$ or

- there are $j_1, \ldots, j_k < i$, and there is an inference rule of $\vdash$ such that $\dfrac{\varphi_{j_1}, \ldots, \varphi_{j_k}}{\varphi_i}$ is an instance of this rule.

We write $\Sigma \vdash \varphi$ if φ is $\vdash$-provable from Σ. (We will often identify an inference system $\vdash$ with the corresponding derivability relation.)

Definition 3.9 (Complete and sound Hilbert-type inference system). Let L be a nice logic and let $\vdash$ be a Hilbert-type inference system for L. For any sets A and B, $A \subseteq_\omega B$ denotes that A is a finite subset of B. Then

- $\vdash$ is *weakly complete* for L iff

$$(\forall \varphi \in F_{\mathrm{L}})\, (\models_{\mathrm{L}} \varphi \implies \vdash \varphi);$$

- $\vdash$ is *finitely complete* for L iff

$$(\forall \Sigma \subseteq_\omega F_{\mathrm{L}})(\forall \varphi \in F_{\mathrm{L}})\, (\Sigma \models^c_{\mathrm{L}} \varphi \implies \Sigma \vdash \varphi);$$

that is, we consider only finite Σs;

- $\vdash$ is *strongly complete* for L iff

$$(\forall \Sigma \subseteq F_{\mathrm{L}})(\forall \varphi \in F_{\mathrm{L}})\, (\Sigma \models^c_{\mathrm{L}} \varphi \implies \Sigma \vdash \varphi);$$

- $\vdash$ is *weakly sound* for L iff

$$(\forall \varphi \in F_{\mathrm{L}})\, (\vdash \varphi \implies \models_{\mathrm{L}} \varphi);$$

- $\vdash$ is *strongly sound* for L iff

$$(\forall \Sigma \subseteq F_{\mathrm{L}})(\forall \varphi \in F_{\mathrm{L}})\, (\Sigma \vdash \varphi \implies \Sigma \models^c_{\mathrm{L}} \varphi).$$

3.1 Algebraic characterizations of completeness and other 'logical' properties of logics

First we give the general connection between the semantical consequence relation $\models_L^c$ of a logic L and validity of quasi-equations in the class $\mathsf{Alg}_m(L)$ of algebras.

Theorem 3.10 *Assume* $L = \langle F_L, M_L, mng_L, \models_L \rangle$ *is a strongly nice logic. Then for any formulas* $\varphi_0, \varphi_1, \ldots, \varphi_n \in F_L$, *(i) and (ii) below hold.*

(i)

$$\{\varphi_1 \ldots, \varphi_n\} \models_L^c \varphi_0$$
$$\Longleftrightarrow$$
$$\mathsf{Alg}_m(L) \models \big(\varphi_1 = (\varepsilon(\varphi_1)\nabla\delta(\varphi_1))\& \cdots \&\varphi_n = (\varepsilon(\varphi_n)\nabla\delta(\varphi_n))\big)$$
$$\rightarrow \varphi_0 = (\varepsilon(\varphi_0)\nabla\delta(\varphi_0)).$$

(ii) In particular,

$$\models_L \varphi_0 \Longleftrightarrow \mathsf{Alg}_m(L) \models \varphi_0 = (\varepsilon(\varphi_0)\nabla\delta(\varphi_0))$$

Intuitively, the theorem says that logical consequence $\Sigma \models_L^c \varphi$ (between formulas of L) translates to validity (in $\mathsf{Alg}_m(L)$) of algebraic quasi-equations after algebraization, if Σ is finite.

In Theorem 3.11 below, we will give a sufficent and necessary condition for a strongly nice logic to have a finitely complete Hilbert-style inference system.

Theorem 3.11
Assume L *is strongly nice and* $Cn(L)$ *is finite*[10]. *Then*

$$\mathsf{Alg}_m(L) \textit{ generates a finitely axiomatizable quasi-variety}$$
$$\Longleftrightarrow$$
$$(\exists \textit{ Hilbert-style } \vdash)(\vdash \textit{ is finitely complete and strongly sound for } L)$$

Having found the algebraic counterpart of 'finitely complete', let us try to characterize 'weakly complete'. Since weak completeness is slightly weaker than finite completeness, we have to weaken the algebraic counterpart of finite completeness for characterizing weak completeness. This way

---

[10]One can eliminate the assumption of $Cn(L)$ being finite. Then the finitary character of a Hilbert-style inference system has to be ensured in a more subtle way. Also, 'finitely axiomatizable quasi-variety' must be replaced by 'finite schema axiomatizable quasi-variety' in the second clause, cf. e.g. Monk [29], Németi [33].

we obtain condition (∗) below, where Eq_L and Qeq_L denote the set of all equations and the set of all quasi-equations, respectively, of the language of $\mathsf{Alg}_m(L)$:

$$(\exists Ax \subseteq_\omega Qeq_L)\left[(\forall e \in Eq_L)\,(\mathsf{Alg}_m(L) \models e \implies Ax \models e)\,\&\,\mathsf{Alg}_m(L) \models Ax\right].$$
(∗)

That is, the equational theory of $\mathsf{Alg}_m(L)$ is finitely axiomatizable by quasi-equations valid in $\mathsf{Alg}_m(L)$.

Theorem 3.12

> *Assume that* L *is nice and* $Cn(L)$ *is finite. Then*
>
> $$(\ast) \iff (\exists \text{ Hilbert-style} \vdash)$$
> $$(\vdash \text{ is weakly complete and strongly sound for } L).$$

In particular, if the equational theory of $\mathsf{Alg}_m(L)$ is finitely axiomatizable, then L admits a weakly complete Hilbert-style inference system.

Definition 3.13 (Compactness of a logic). Let $L = \langle F, M, mng, \models\rangle$ be a logic. We say that

(i) L is *satisfiability compact* (sat. compact for short), if

$$(\forall\Gamma \subseteq F)\left[(\forall\Sigma \subseteq_\omega \Gamma)\,(\Sigma \text{ has a model}) \implies (\Gamma \text{ has a model})\right], \text{ and}$$

(ii) L is *consequence compact* (cons. compact), if

$$\Gamma \models^c \varphi \implies (\exists\Sigma \subseteq_\omega \Gamma)\,\Sigma \models^c \varphi, \quad \text{for every } \Gamma \cup \{\varphi\} \subseteq F.$$

We note that even for nice logics we have

1. sat. compact $\not\Longrightarrow$ cons. compact;

2. sat. compact $\not\Longleftarrow$ cons. compact

(cf. [7] and [8]).

Recall that in Definition 3.1 (and also in the logics studied so far), there was a parameter P, which was the set of atomic formulas. The choice of P influenced what the set F of formulas would be. Thus in fact, our old definition of a logic yields a family

$$\langle\langle F^P, M^P, mng^P, \models^P\rangle : P \text{ is a set}\rangle$$

of logics.

Definition 3.14 (General logical system). A *general logical system* is a class

$$\underline{L} \stackrel{def}{=} \langle L^P \ : \ P \text{ is a set} \rangle,$$

where for each set P, $L^P = \langle F^P, M^P, mng^P, \models^P \rangle$ is a logical system in the sense of Definition 2.1, that is, F^P is a set, M^P is a class, mng^P is a function with domain $F^P \times M^P$, and $\models^P \subseteq M^P \times F^P$.

$\underline{L}$ is called a *(strongly) nice general logical system* iff conditions (1–4) below hold for $\underline{L}$.

1. L^P is a (strongly) nice logic (cf. Definition 3.1) for each set P, and P is the set of atomic formulas of logic L^P .

2. For any sets P and Q, $Cn(L^P) = Cn(L^Q) \stackrel{def}{=} Cn(\underline{L})$.

3. For any sets P, Q, if there is a bijection $f : P \to Q$ then logic L^Q is an 'isomorphic copy' of logic L^P that is, there are bijections f^F : $F^P \to F^Q$ and $f^M : M^P \to M^Q$ such that

   (a) f^F is an isomorphism from F^P onto F^Q extending f;

   (b) for all $\varphi \in F^P$, $\mathcal{M} \in M^P$

$$mng^P(\varphi, \mathcal{M}) \ = \ mng^Q\big(f^F(\varphi), f^M(\mathcal{M})\big)$$
$$\mathcal{M} \models^P \varphi \ \Longleftrightarrow \ f^M(\mathcal{M}) \models^Q f^F(\varphi).$$

4. For all sets $P \subseteq Q$

$$\big\{ mng^P_{\mathcal{M}} \ : \ \mathcal{M} \in M^P \big\} = \big\{ (mng^Q_{\mathcal{M}}) \lceil F^P \ : \ \mathcal{M} \in M^Q \big\}.$$

   Intuitively, this requirement says that L^P is the 'natural' restriction of L^Q.

Convention: For brevity we will write 'a general logic' instead of 'a general logical system'.

Remark 3.15

As a corollary of item (4) of Definiton 3.14 above we note that for all sets $P \subseteq Q$, if $\Gamma \cup \{\varphi\} \subseteq F^P$ then

$$\Gamma \models^P \varphi \ \Longleftrightarrow \ \Gamma \models^Q \varphi.$$

Definition 3.16 (Algebraic counterpart of a general logic). Let $\underline{L} = \langle L^P : P \text{ is a set} \rangle$ be a nice general logic. Then

$$\mathsf{Alg}_{\models}(\underline{\mathrm{L}}) \overset{def}{=} \bigcup \left\{ \mathsf{Alg}_{\models}(\mathrm{L}^P) \ : \ P \text{ is a set} \right\},$$

$$\mathsf{Alg}_m(\underline{\mathrm{L}}) \overset{def}{=} \bigcup \left\{ \mathsf{Alg}_m(\mathrm{L}^P) \ : \ P \text{ is a set} \right\}$$

(cf. Definition 3.4).

We note that
(i) $\mathsf{Alg}_m(\underline{\mathrm{L}}_S) = $ 'class of all Boolean set algebras'
(ii) $\mathsf{Alg}_m(\underline{\mathrm{L}}_{S5}) = $ 'class of all one-dimensional cylindric set algebras'
(cf. Definitions 2.7 and 2.8).

Theorem 3.17
For strongly nice general logics

$$\mathsf{Alg}_{\models}(\underline{\mathrm{L}}) = \mathbf{SP}\mathsf{Alg}_m(\underline{\mathrm{L}}),$$

where **S** *is the operator of taking subalgebras, and* **P** *is the operator of taking isomorphic copies of direct products.*

Definition 3.18 (Compactness of a general logic). A general logic $\underline{\mathrm{L}} = \langle \mathrm{L}^P : P \text{ is a set} \rangle$ is *satisfiability (consequence) compact* if for each set P the logic L^P is satisfiability (consequence) compact.

Our next theorem gives a sufficent condition for sat. compactness of a general logic.

Theorem 3.19 *Assume* $\underline{\mathrm{L}}$ *is a strongly nice general logic. Then*

$(\mathsf{Alg}_{\models}(\underline{\mathrm{L}})$ *is closed under taking ultraproducts*$) \Longrightarrow (\underline{\mathrm{L}}$ *is sat. compact*$)$.

Our next theorem states that the condition of Theorem 3.19 above is sufficient and also necessary for cons. compactness, and so for strong completeness (cf. Theorem 3.21 below).

Theorem 3.20 (cf. [7] Theorem 3.8).
Assume $\underline{\mathrm{L}}$ *is a strongly nice general logic. Then*

$(\mathsf{Alg}_{\models}(\underline{\mathrm{L}})$ *is closed under taking ultraproducts*$) \Longleftrightarrow (\underline{\mathrm{L}}$ *is cons. compact*$)$.

Theorem 3.21
Assume $\underline{\mathrm{L}} = \langle \mathrm{L}^P : P \text{ is a set} \rangle$ *is a strongly nice general logic and* $Cn(\underline{\mathrm{L}})$ *is finite.*[11] *Then*

$\mathsf{Alg}_{\models}(\underline{\mathrm{L}})$ *is a finitely axiomatizable quasi-variety*

---

[11]cf. the footnote of Theorem 3.11.

$$\Longleftrightarrow$$
$$(\exists \ Hilbert\text{-}style \ \vdash)(\forall \ set \ P)$$
$$(\vdash \ is \ strongly \ complete \ and \ strongly \ sound \ for \ \mathrm{L}^P).$$

Theorem 3.22

   Assume L *is strongly nice. Then*

   (i) L *is decidable* $\Longleftrightarrow$ *the equational theory* $Eq(\mathsf{Alg}_\models(\mathrm{L}))$ *is decidable. (Here by decidability of* L *we mean decidability of the validity problem of* L*.)*

   (ii) The validities of L *are recursively enumerable* $\Longleftrightarrow$ $Eq(\mathsf{Alg}_\models(\mathrm{L}))$ *is recursively enumerable.*

Beginning with pioneering works of Gabbay, weakly complete and weakly sound inference systems became popular recently, cf. e.g. Venema[48]. These inference systems are useful for logics to which there exists no strongly sound and weakly complete inference systems. The next theorem characterizes those logics for which weakly complete and weakly sound Hilbert style inference systems can be given.

Theorem 3.23 *Assume* $\underline{\mathrm{L}}$ *is a strongly nice general logic and* $Cn(\underline{\mathrm{L}})$ *is finite. Then (i) and (ii) below are equivalent.*

   (i) There is a weakly complete and weakly sound Hilbert-style inference system for $\underline{\mathrm{L}}$*.*

   (ii) There is a finitely axiomatizable quasivariety K *such that* $\mathbf{HSP}K = \mathbf{HSP}(\mathsf{Alg}_\models(\underline{\mathrm{L}}))$*.*

The above theorem motivates the following:

Open Problem 3.24 $K \subseteq RCA_n$ *such that* $\mathbf{H}K = RCA_n$?

In all the above we investigated only four logical properties: completeness, compactness, decidability and enumerability of validities. However, the literature contains similar theorems for a very large number of *further logical properties*. Such are e.g. Craig's interpolation property, the various definability properties (e.g. Beth's), the property of having a deduction theorem, the property of admitting Gabbay-style inference systems, to mention only a few; cf. e.g. [8], [7].

3.2 Other kinds of logical properties, their algebraic characterizations

We will look into logical properties, the algebraic characterization of which utilizes more strongly that we defined the algebraic counterpart $\mathsf{Alg}_m(\mathrm{L})$ of the model theory of L the way we did.

Definition 3.25 (K-morphism, K-epimorphism). Let K be a class of algebras. By a K-*morphism* (or briefly *morphism*) we understand a triple $\langle \mathcal{A}, h, \mathcal{B} \rangle$ where $\mathcal{A}, \mathcal{B} \in K$ and $h : \mathcal{A} \to \mathcal{B}$ is a homomorphism. Instead of '$\langle \mathcal{A}, h, \mathcal{B} \rangle$' we often write '$h : \mathcal{A} \to \mathcal{B}$' because this is more intuitive. Recall that $Hom(\mathcal{A}, \mathcal{B}) = \{h : (h : \mathcal{A} \to \mathcal{B} \text{ holds })\}$. A morphism $h : \mathcal{A} \to \mathcal{B}$ is a K-*epimorphism*, or an *epi* for short, iff for every $\mathcal{C} \in K$ and every pair $f, k \in Hom(\mathcal{B}, \mathcal{C})$ we have $(h \circ f = h \circ k \longrightarrow f = k)$.

Typical examples of epis are the surjections. But for certain choices of K there are K-epimorphisms which are not surjective. Such is the case e.g. when K is the class of distributive lattices.

For K we will always choose $\mathsf{Alg}_{\models}(\mathrm{L})$, for some L. If all epis are surjective in $\mathsf{Alg}_{\models}(\mathrm{L})$, then this implies that L has a certain logical property called the Beth definability property, cf. e.g. [23] Part 2.

Definition 3.26 (K-extensible). Let $K_0 \subseteq K$ be two classes of (similar) algebras. Let $h : \mathcal{A} \to \mathcal{B}$ be a K-morphism. h is said to be K_0-*extensible* iff for every $f : \mathcal{A} \to \mathcal{C} \in K_0$ there exist $g : \mathcal{B} \to \mathcal{N} \in K_0$ such that $\mathcal{C} \subseteq \mathcal{N}$ and $h \circ g = f$.

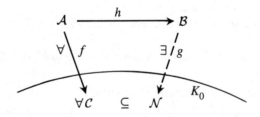

It is important here that $\mathcal{C}$ is a concrete subalgebra of $\mathcal{N}$ and *not* only is embeddable into $\mathcal{N}$.

The *weak Beth definability property* of a logic L was defined e.g. in Sain[41] and in Barwise-Feferman[10]. This property differs from the strong Beth property in that here if $\Sigma(R)$ is an implicit definition of R, then $\Sigma(R)$ implies not only uniqueness of R but also it implies existence of R (in every model of some pre-specified theory). We do not recall the definition in more detail.

Theorem 3.27 *Let $\underline{\mathrm{L}}$ be a strongly nice general logical system. Then, $\underline{\mathrm{L}}$ has the weak Beth definability property iff $\mathsf{Alg}_m(\mathrm{L})$ and $\mathsf{Alg}_{\models}(\mathrm{L})$ satisfy condition (1) below.*

1. For every $\mathsf{Alg}_m(\mathrm{L})$-extensible epimorphism $h : \mathcal{A} \to \mathcal{B}$ of $\mathsf{Alg}_{\models}(\mathrm{L})$, we *have that h is surjective, i.e. $Rg(h) = B$.*

In the formulation of Theorem 3.27 above, it is important that $\mathsf{Alg}_m(\mathrm{L})$ is not an abstract class in the sense that it is not closed under isomorphisms. When we defined the algebraic counterparts of a logic L, this was an essential difference between the way $\mathsf{Alg}_\vDash(\mathrm{L})$ and $\mathsf{Alg}_m(\mathrm{L})$ were defined, namely $\mathsf{Alg}_\vDash(\mathrm{L}) = \mathbf{I}\mathsf{Alg}_\vDash(\mathrm{L})$, while $\mathsf{Alg}_m(\mathrm{L}) \neq \mathbf{I}\mathsf{Alg}_m(\mathrm{L})$. The reason is that since $\mathsf{Alg}_m(\mathrm{L})$ is the class of the algebraic counterparts of the models (semantical domains) of L, we need these algebras as concrete algebras and replacing them with their isomorphic copies would lead to loss of information (about semantic-model theoretic matters).

The usefulness of theorems like Theorem 3.27 is perhaps illustrated by the fact that it was via this theorem that it was proved that the finite variable fragment L_n of first-order logic fails to have the weak Beth property if $n > 2$; cf. Sain-Simon[42]. A similar result applies to Propositional Dynamic Logic. It was via an analogous theorem that L_2 was proved to not have the strong Beth property. Because of the behaviour of the algebras involved, we conjecture that L_2 does enjoy the weak Beth property.

In a later version of this work we will discuss algebraic characterizations of further logical properties of L.

4   Refining the notion of a logical system

In Definition 3.14 we wrote that a general logic is an indexed system

$$\underline{\mathrm{L}} = \langle \mathrm{L}^P : P \text{ is a set} \rangle$$

where $\mathrm{L}^P = \langle F^P, \vdash^P, M^P, mng^P, \vDash^P \rangle$ is a logical system in the sense of Definition 2.1 and some conditions are satisfied on the connection between L^P and L^Q (P and Q are sets).

Intuitively, L^P is that 'instance' of $\underline{\mathrm{L}}$ which uses *vocabulary P*. (Sometimes P is called the set of *nonlogical constants* of L^P.) The idea is that when reasoning about something or some aspect of something, we use a set of certain primitive or 'atomic' words. When reasoning about some other aspect (or some other thing), we might use other atomic words. The set of atomic words we use in a certain stage of our reasoning is called a *vocabulary*. For example, sometimes we may reason about rabbits and foxes on an island, and may discuss the dynamics of their populations. So probably 'rabbit' and 'fox' and some other words will be in our vocabulary (but 'quark' and 'television' may not). At some other time we may discuss differential equations. Then we will probably use a different vocabulary (while speaking perhaps about the same phenomenon but in a different language). So during a certain period of our reasoning, we may use the instance L^P of the logical system $\underline{L}$. Some other time we may use another instance $L^{P'}$ of $\underline{L}$ (or another logical system $\underline{L}_1$ for that matter, but let us stay within $\underline{L}$ for a while). Roughly speaking, we may think of a theory T (of $\underline{L}$) as being built up in some L^P while another theory T' might be built up in $L^{P'}$. When investigating T, it might be convenient to be aware that T lives in L^P. This might be especially useful when investigating connections between theories, or investigating the way people use a network of relatively simple theories in trying to understand complex phenomena.

A further refinement of the concept of a logical system is when we allow vocabularies to have a structure of their own, so that they form a category (via structure preserving mappings). Then a logical system is

$$\underline{L} = \langle L^V : V \in Voc_{\underline{L}} \rangle$$

where $Voc_{\underline{L}}$ is the category of vocabularies (of $\underline{L}$) and conditions (3) and (4) of Definition 3.14 have to be refined in the obvious way. This was the approach taken in [7], in [3], [8], and it is very close to the one in [22], Salibra–Scollo [43], Meseguer [28], among others.

It is shown e.g. in [7], [8] that the results and constructions in Chapter 2 can be carried through after the generalization indicated above.

We do not discuss this direction (Sets $\mapsto$ $Voc_{\underline{L}}$) of generalization in more detail here, since it is well documented in the literature, as was indicated above. The point to discuss here is what the basic unit
$L^V = \langle F^V, \vdash^V, M^V, mng^V, \models^V \rangle$, (for $V \in Voc_{\underline{L}}$) should be and why. After that, the usual process of generalization can be applied to this unit. To mention a few points, it is worthwhile pointing out that mng^V is needed in L^V and $\models^V$ is not sufficient (as a replacement of mng^V).[12] Another issue is that it would not be satisfactory to restrict M^V to be a similarity class of first-order structures (as done e.g. in Barwise–Feferman [10]), because this would exclude many important logical systems.

Before closing this section, we note that already the generalization in Definition 3.14 enables us to define the category of all theories (and interpretations) of $\underline{L}$. Namely, we can define a theory of $\underline{L}$ to be a pair $\underline{T} = \langle L^P, T \rangle$ where $T \subseteq F^P$, and an interpretation of $\underline{T}_1$ in $\underline{T}_2$ is a function $f : P_1 \to F^{P_2}$ satisfying certain natural conditions (e.g. taking theorems to theorems). This category of theories has been investigated in [14], [3], [22], [28], etc. This kind of investigation can lead to an analysis of that part of our thinking process when we combine theories, decompose theories, create new theories. The latter can be done e.g. by computing the colimit of a diagram consisting of theories and interpretations, in the category of theories. This could be the beginning of accounting for the formation of

---

[12]This was discussed in Chapter 2 for some detail.

new concepts and new theories during cognition. There are two things to observe here: (i) This aspect of cognition *can* be considered as part of the subject matter of logic ever since the publication of [14]. (ii) This aspect of cognition does not seem to be a part of the process of making inferences. Putting (i) and (ii) together is one of the reasons why we claimed in the introduction that the subject matter of logic is broader than inference and consequence. But this is already the subject of Chapter 5.

5   Some thoughts on what logic is

Having discussed the special question of what logical systems are, we can turn to logic itself. Because of lack of space, we will have to be very brief and therefore incomplete and 'fragmentary'.

5.1

The social propagation of the belief that

$$\text{logic} = \text{the collection of logical systems}$$

sometimes produces unexpected side-effects. An example is the following.

Some time ago, people started to pay more and more attention to the so called non-monotonic parts/aspects of our thinking process. (A strong motivation came from A.I.) A simplified example[13] says that theoretical physicists had Newton's axioms in their theory. Then they learned a new axiom (saying that the speed of light is the same in all inertial systems), say from experimental physicists. The theoreticians applied their mental processes to the new set of axioms and eventually ended up with a theory in which Newton's axioms are no more provable. This is an instance of non-monotonicity, since adding axiom φ to a theory T resulted in a new theory T_1 which did not contain all theorems of T.

This kind of thing is of course an important ingredient of our thinking processes and therefore according to the views of the present chapter, logic should study this phenomenon. What is the phenomenon being discussed?

---

[13]DISCLAIMER: In the present discussion, non-monotonicity is only an illustrating example and not the target of our discussion. Therefore we are writing about only a particular kind of non-monotonicity here. There are many branches of the literature called nowadays 'non-monotonic reasoning' to which our considerations do not apply. Such is e.g. the logical analysis of *generics*. Another counterexample is probably the logic where we have a new unary logical connective '*Presumably*'. A typical inference here can be $\{\forall x[Bird(x) \rightarrow Presumably\ Fly(x)],\ Bird(\text{Tweety})\} \vdash Presumably\ Fly(\text{Tweety})$. Our remarks may *not* apply to this logic (we do not know; we did not think this over). A third and important counterexample is the Frame Problem first published in the famous Hayes–McCarthy paper of 1969 (in *Machine Intelligence* 4). Our remarks certainly do not apply to the Frame Problem.

Roughly, it is the following. We do not go on reasoning forever in a single, fixed theory. Instead, as a result of our reasoning/thinking we change our theories and *sometimes* the new theory is not a simple extension of the old one. Let us call this phenomenon non-monotonicity.

Believing something like 'logic = all logical systems' had the effect that people wanting to study the phenomenon of non-monotonicity in our thinking had no other choice than to invent a new logical system called 'non-monotonic logic'. Pushing this example a bit further, whenever we notice a new feature/phenomenon in our thinking process, say phenomenon X, then we invent the $n + 1$-th logical system, call it X-logic, and try to squeeze phenomenon X into the form of a logical system independently of the intrinsic nature of X.

Coming back to non-monotonicity, we fully agree that this is a subject of logic and should be studied in logic. However, we do not see why it would be self-evident that this should be done by squeezing non-monotonicity into the form of a new logical system $\mathcal{N} = \langle F_\mathcal{N}, \vdash_\mathcal{N}, \ldots \rangle$.

Indeed, the step in our thinking process responsible for the phenomenon of non-monotonicity is a step when we *change our theory*. (We change our axioms.) But manipulating, changing and handling theories is an important mental process in its own right. This process 'lives' on a different level of the hierarchy than the level on which the familiar inference process manipulating formulas (sentences, etc.) and deriving theorems lives. We argue that there are mental processes which manipulate bigger building blocks than formulas, namely they manipulate theories. Just as in physics where there are subatomic processes, there are macroscopic ones, there are solar systems each 'living' on its own scale of building blocks, etc.; we think that in the realm of logic, there are processes 'living' and working on the 'microscopic', 'macroscopic' or 'galactic' scale. Our traditional deductive processes represent only one of these 'scales'. We do not see why we assume that the process which manipulates theories (instead of formulas) would be best represented in the same form as our familiar deductive processes e.g. in the form of a logical system. Summing up, we believe that within logic, special calculi or some other effective mechanisms should be studied which manipulate theories in an analogous way as our deductive calculi manipulate formulas. These higher level 'calculi' (or whatever they will turn out to be) interact with the lower level deductive processes but they constitute mechanisms which have their special roles in the organization of our reasoning process and should be identified and studied on their own right (which does not exclude studying them as parts of the whole system). [14] It seems possible that a systematic study of this larger scale dynamics of

---

[14]There are some works available initiating the study of such higher level calculi. We already mentioned [14], [3], [31]. We should also mention the area known as 'Logic of

theory manipulation would provide insights into the phenomenon of non-monotonicity, and would provide answers more easily and smoothly than squeezing non-monotonicity into the form of an $n + 1$th logical system does.[15]

5.2

We wrote in the introduction that the subject matter of logic is a broader area of cognition (and thinking) than just inference making and consequence relation. We guess we should give at least a partial account of what makes us think so. We begin with examples (of aspects/parts of cognition and thinking belonging to logic but not necessarily to inference and cognition).

(i) One example was already given at the end of Chapter 3, namely, the mental activities of creating new theories from old ones in non-trivial ways, forming new concepts, etc. The mathematical model in which properties of these activities can be studied is not a formal system L^P but rather a structure whose building blocks are formal systems like L^P (more precisely, pairs $\langle L^P, T \rangle$ and interpretations between these).

(ii) Another example is the theory of definitions and definability. This part of model theory beginning with Beth's theorem, then Svenonius' Theorem of definability, Kueker's finite definability theorem, Chang and Makkai's theorem, [16] is quite illuminating in connection with certain parts of cognition. The concepts of implicit definition, the question of under what conditions such a definition is 'only an abbreviation', and the question of which definition-like texts really do define something seem to be relevant to our thinking process, in particular e.g. to concept formation. [17] Tarski's theorem about undefinability of truth is often (cf. e.g. Hofstadter [25]) considered almost as illuminating for our thinking process as Gödel's theorem

---

Theory Change' cf. e.g. Springer Verlag's *Lecture Notes in A.I.*, vol 465 (1991).

[15]The above sketched way of thinking in terms of various levels or 'scales' is explained and motivated in H.A. Simon's paper 'Architecture of complexity' available e.g. in his book *The Science of the Artificial*.

[16]Cf. Chang-Keisler [15] §5.3

[17]C.f. e.g. the recent volume *Definitions and Definability: Philos. Perspective*, Synthese Library Vol 216 (1991), especially the chapters by Rantala and Hintikka. For example, on p.155 of this book Rantala discusses a parallelism between the (branch of logic called) theory of definability and the theory of deduction. He also calls attention to the fact that this parallelism was much emphasized by Tarski.

Now, if definability theory is a branch of logic parallel with the theory of deduction, then the theory of deduction or inference can be only a *part* of logic (and hence cannot include the whole, because otherwise the whole [of logic] would turn out to be parallel with a branch of the whole turning logic into some kind of a nice fractal [which is not impossible but sounds unlikely in the context Rantala and Tarski used]).

is. At the same time, it seems to be a little bit artificial (if not impossible) to claim that all these are about inference making (or about the consequence relation between sentences). For example, in the case of the so-called weak Beth property (cf. [10]) we say that an implicit definition is correct iff it implies existence and uniqueness. Now, uniqueness can be reformulated in terms of consequence, but how about existence? Existence where? (Remember that the consequence relation is between objects of syntax.)

Instead of listing more examples, we would like to suggest some considerations.

Let us try to step back, and imagine that we are making a mathematical model of reasoning or of aspects of thinking. If somebody is reasoning, thinking, then probably he is thinking *about something*. So our picture of the thinking process will be more complete if we take into account that 'thing' that the thinker is thinking about (whatever this thing might be). Let us call this thing environment (independently of whether it is really his/its environment that our thinker is thinking about). This way we can develop an idealized picture consisting of an idealized thinker and an idealized environment which is the target or subject of the thinking process we are investigating. This idealized thinker need not be a single individual, it may be a set of individuals talking to each other, it may be a scientific society 'thinking about' say physics or something else in this line.

We may decide to consider only those thoughts which can be represented as syntactical entities e.g. which belong to some written language. From now on by the possible thoughts of our thinker we understand the expressions of this language.

Now, if we are analysing this thinking process, it might be relevant to know how the possible (or potential) thoughts of our thinker relate to its environment.

It seems to be a reasonable idea to build all these ingredients into our mathematical model. In the mathematical model, the thinker's language (its possible thoughts) will be represented by some kind of a formal language (or something like that), the thinker's inference mechanisms and other processes manipulating its 'thoughts' will be represented by calculi, rewrite rules, Turing machines and similar algorithmic or finitistic mathematical objects. But this is only a part of the model. There will be a mathematical model of the environment, and of course a mathematical representation of the connection between expressions of the thinker's language and the environment (to which they probably refer). But what should the mathematical model of the environment look like?

At this point we could decide that the thinker's language is represented by the syntax F_{L} of some logical system L, and the environment is represented by a model $\mathcal{M} \in M_{\mathrm{L}}$ of the same logical system, mng_{L} and $\models_{\mathrm{L}}$

representing the connection between the two. [18] But this would cause a problem:

Suppose we are interested in cognition. Then the question of how much the thinker knows about the environment, is a central one. That is, the model should represent the thinker's uncertainty, its lack of knowledge about the target of its thinking process, its environment. But the mathematical model representing the environment by the single structure [19] $\mathcal{M}$ does not tell us anything about uncertainty, lack of knowledge and things like that. At this point our mathematical model of the thinker-environment system is something like $\langle F_L, \mathcal{M}, mng_L, \models_L \rangle$ where $\mathcal{M} \in M_L$ is fixed. Our problem is that this particular mathematical model does not represent lack of knowledge.

To represent lack of knowledge mathematically, we could consider all the possible environments compatible with our thinker's actual knowledge and take their mathematical models, too. The class M_L can be taken as the class of mathematical models of possible environments (of our thinker). Now, we can mathematically represent the uncertainty, etc. of our thinker. Let $Ax \subseteq F_L$ be the thinker's knowledge at time t. Let $\mathcal{M}_0 \in M_L$ be the model of its environment. Then the class of possible environments compatible with the thinker's knowledge (at time t) is

$$Mod(Ax) = \{\mathcal{M} \in M_L : \mathcal{M} \models_L Ax\}.$$

If the thinker's knowledge is correct, then $\mathcal{M}_0 \in Mod(Ax)$. Now, our model of the situation (at time t) consists of

$$L = \langle F_L, \vdash_L, M_L, mng_L, \models_L \rangle, \quad Mod(Ax), \quad \mathcal{M}_0.$$

$Mod(Ax)$ represents the uncertainty of the thinker. At some later time instance $t_1 > t$, the thinker's knowledge may be Ax_1. If $\mathcal{M}_0 \in Mod(Ax_1)$ and $Mod(Ax_1) \subset Mod(Ax)$ is much smaller (in some sense) than $Mod(Ax)$, then the thinker has learned this much about its environment.

Metaphorically speaking, our thinker is in environment $\mathcal{M}_0$, but it does not know this. What it knows is that it is in one of the members of $Mod(Ax)$. [20]

---

[18]The concept of a logical system $L = \langle F_L, \ldots, mng_L, \models_L \rangle$ is in Definition 2.1 at the beginning of Chapter 2.

[19]To avoid ambiguity, we call the model theoretical models $\mathcal{M} \in M_L$ 'structures', so that they will not be confused with the mathematical model of the 'thinker-environment system' we are just building. (Same problem occurred in [11].)

[20]To avoid misunderstandings, we should mention that we do *not* associate physical existence to the possible environments represented by $\mathcal{M} \in M_L$ (if $\mathcal{M} \neq \mathcal{M}_0$). (Sometimes we write 'possible environment' instead of 'model of possible environment' for $\mathcal{M}$ when there is no danger of confusion.) Instead, the possible environments collected in M_L serve as technical-theoretical devices enabling us to represent conveniently some important aspect/parameter of the cognition process (lack of knowledge, universality of logical inference coded by $\vdash_L$, etc.) in our mathematical model.

One could call $\mathcal{M}_0$ the (model of the) [21] thinker's _real environment_. The other, possible environments $\mathcal{M} \in M_{\mathrm{L}}$ are possible in the sense (among others) that they are compatible with the thinker's reasoning/cognitive faculties. That is, figuratively speaking, [22] we could put the thinker into any one of these (imaginary) environments $\mathcal{M} \in M_{\mathrm{L}}$ and then the thinker's reasoning faculties/processes would be just as adequate for acquisition of knowledge about $\mathcal{M}$ as they are for the same about $\mathcal{M}_0$. (So, in this sense, 'largeness' of M_{L} represents universality of the logic L.)

Figure 1 below provides a schematic summary of what we have said so far about our idealized thinker, its language F_{L}, its inference mechanisms $\vdash_{\mathrm{L}}$, its 'real' environment $\mathcal{M}_0$, the class M_{L} of all possible environments, knowledge $Ax, Mod(Ax)$, etc. [23]

At this point we interrupt this description of our logical model of knowledge acquisition, because we think the reader can fill in the details. The main point is that model theory of L has a more explicit role in modelling aspects of cognition mathematically than just helping us to define the semantical consequence relation '$\Phi \models^c \varphi$'. Namely, model theory provides us with a mathematical model of the 'environment' our thinker is reasoning about and also with devices for representing the thinker's uncertainty, etc. (which are quite crucial for discussing such subjects as e.g. knowledge acquisition).

A related logical example is the model-theoretical notion $\equiv_{\mathrm{L}}$ of elementary equivalence of models. If $\mathcal{M}, \mathcal{M}_1 \in M$ are L-elementarily equivalent (in symbols $\mathcal{M} \equiv_{\mathrm{L}} \mathcal{M}_1$), then this is an important property of L as a framework for reasoning about our environment. Namely, somebody (or some society) using L for reasoning cannot distinguish between environments $\mathcal{M}$ and $\mathcal{M}_1$. (One could even say that the difference between $\mathcal{M}$ and $\mathcal{M}_1$ _does not exist_ for this person.) At the same time, another person (society, etc.) using a more expressive logic L_1 as the carrier of his/its thoughts might see the difference between $\mathcal{M}$ and $\mathcal{M}_1$ (and e.g. might take advantage of this). But they may pay a price, since the proof theory of L_1 might have undesirable properties. And the story of $\equiv_{\mathrm{L}}$ goes on, but we stop here. Our point is again that if we take model theory seriously as the mathematical model of the environment or 'world' or whatever our thinker is reasoning about, then we obtain a richer, more balanced picture of the reasoning or thinking process we are theorizing about, and this can be useful (especially in applied areas like A.I.).

---

[21] For brevity, we will drop this 'model of' part if there is no danger of confusion.

[22] In a sense, similarly to Einstein's 'gedanken Experimente'.

[23] The general model permits more reasoning mechanisms than the sole $\vdash_{\mathrm{L}}$ we included in the above 5-tuple. The model remains essentially the same if we include besides $\vdash_{\mathrm{L}}$ other Turing machines, calculi, and finitistic processes (as we often do; but not in this chapter).

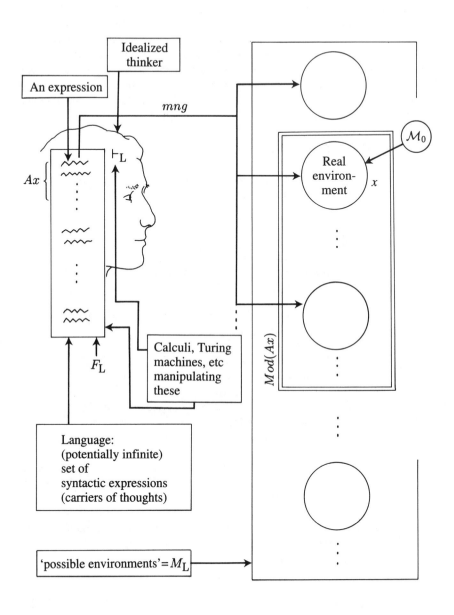

Figure 1:

Taking model theory to be more than just a device for defining the consequence relation '$\models$', means that instead of studying reasoning in isolation, we study reasoning together with the 'environment', which is, in a manner of speaking, the target of the reasoning process. Having a mathematical model which represents all essential 'factors' of the reasoning process seems to be more promising than representing only the 'heart' i.e. inference and consequence, because then this heart is sort of torn out of its environment.

Acknowledgements

Research supported by the Hungarian National Foundation for Scientific Research grant Numbers 1911 and T7255.

References

[1] *Possible Worlds in Humanities, Arts and Sciences.* W. de Gruyter, Berlin–New York, 1989.

[2] H. Andréka, T. Gergely, and I. Németi. On universal algebraic construction of logics. *Studia Logica*, 36:9–47, 1977.

[3] H. Andréka, T. Gergely, and I. Németi. Investigations in language hierarchies. Technical report, Math. Inst. Budapest, 1980.

[4] H. Andréka and Sz. Mikulás. Lambek calculus and its relational semantics: Completeness and incompleteness. *Journal of Logic, Language and Information (JoLLI)*, **3**, 1–37, 1994.

[5] H. Andréka, J.D. Monk, and I. Németi, editors. *Algebraic Logic.* (Proc. Conf. Budapest 1988) Colloq. Math. Soc. J. Bolyai Vol 54, North Holland, Amsterdam, 1991.

[6] H. Andréka and I. Németi. Generalization of variety and quasi–variety concepts to partial algebras through category theory. *Dissertationes Mathematicae (Rozprawy Math.)*, CCIV:1–56, 1982. PWN Polish Scientific Publisher, Warsaw, Poland.

[7] H. Andréka, I. Németi, I. Sain, and Á. Kurucz. Abstract model theoretic approach to algebraic logic. Technical report, Math. Inst. Budapest, 1984. updated in 1988, 1992; also in Proc. 1992 Summer Meeting of the Ass. Symb. Logic, D. Gabbay and L. Csirmaz, eds., Oxford Univ. Press, to appear.

[8] H. Andréka, I. Németi, I. Sain, and Á. Kurucz. *General Algebraic Logic (and General Theory of Logics)*. Lecture Notes Volume, Math. Inst. Budapest, 1993.

[9] I. H. Anellis and N. Houser. *The Nineteenth Century Roots of Universal Algebra and Algebraic Logic: A Critical–bibliographical Guide for the Contemporary Logician*, pages 1–36. In: [5], 1991.

[10] J. Barwise and S. Feferman, editors. *Model–theoretic Logics*. Springer–Verlag, Berlin, 1985.

[11] J. Barwise and E. Hammer. Diagrams and the concept of logical system. In *this volume*.

[12] W.J. Blok and D. Pigozzi. Algebraizable logics. *Memoirs Amer. Math. Soc.*, 77,396:vi+78 pp, 1989.

[13] P. Burmeister. *A Model Theoretic Oriented Approach to Partial Algebras*. Akademie–Verlag, Berlin, 1986.

[14] R. M. Burstall and J. A. Goguen. Putting theories together to make specifications. In *Procs. of 5th IJCAI, Boston, 1977*, pages 1045–1058.

[15] C. C. Chang and H. J. Keisler. *Model Theory*. North Holland, Amsterdam, 1973.

[16] J. Czelakowski. Logic, algebras and consequence operators. Technical report, 1993.

[17] L. F. del Cerro, D. Gabbay, A. Herzig, and H.J. Ohlbach. Overview on the current state of translation methods for non–classical logics. Technical report, Imperial College, 1993.

[18] Á. E. Eiben, A. Jánossy, and Á. Kurucz. Combining logics. In *Proceedings of the Applied Logic Conference Logic At Work, Amsterdam, Dec 1992*, page 24pp, 1992. Also available as a Preprint of Free Univ. Amsterdam, No. IR-319, 1992.

[19] J. M. Font and R. Jansana. A general algebraic semantics for deductive systems. Technical report, University of Barcelona, 1993. Also published in *Bulletin of the IGPL*, **2**, 55–76, 1994.

[20] J. M. Font and R. Jansana. On the identity of the notions of strongly nice general logic and regularly algebraizable deductive system. Technical report, University of Barcelona, 1993.

[21] D. M. Gabbay. Fibred semantics and the weaving of logics. Technical report, Imperial College, London, 1992.

[22] J.A. Goguen and R.M. Burstall. Introducing institutions. In E. Clarke and D. Kozen, editors, *Logics of Programs*, pages 221–256. Springer Lecture Notes in Computer Science Vol. 164, 1984.

[23] L. Henkin, J. D. Monk, and A. Tarski. *Cylindric Algebras Part I and Part II*. North Holland, Amsterdam, 1985.

[24] L. Henkin and A. Tarski. Cylindric algebras. In R. P. Dilworth, editor, *Lattice Theory, (Proc. of Symposia in pure mathematics, Vol 2)*, pages 83–113. American Mathematical Society, Providence, 1961.

[25] D. R. Hofstadter. *Gödel, Escher, Bach: An Eternal Golden Braid*. Basic Books, Inc., New York, 1979.

[26] R. Maddux. The origin of relation algebras in the development and axiomatization of the calculus of relations. *Studia Logica*, L(3/4):421–456, 1991.

[27] M. Marx. Dynamic arrow logic with pairs. In *Proceedings of the Applied Logic Conference Logic At Work, Amsterdam, Dec 1992*, page 13pp, 1992.

[28] J. Meseguer. General logics. In *this volume*.

[29] J. D. Monk. Nonfinitizability of classes of representable cylindric algebras. *J. of Symbolic Logic*, 34:331–343, 1969.

[30] J. D. Monk. *Mathematical Logic*. Springer–Verlag, 1976.

[31] I. Németi. Foundations for stepwise refinement of program specifications via cylindric algebra theory. *Diagrammes, Paris*, 8, 1982.

[32] I. Németi. Algebraization of quantifier logics, an introductory overview. *Studia Logica*, 50(3/4 (a special issue devoted to Algebraic Logic, eds.: W. J. Blok and D. L. Pigozzi)):485–570, 1991. Strongly updated and expanded [e.g. with proofs] version is [33].

[33] I. Németi. Algebraization of quantifier logics, an introductory overview, version 11.2. *CCSOM Reprint 91–67, Univerity of Amsterdam (Dept. of Statistics and Methodology)*, page 77 pp, 1993. also Preprint No. 50/1993 (November). An early, drastically shorter version appeared as [32].

[34] D. Roorda. *Resource Logics. Proof-Theoretical Investigations*. PhD thesis, Institute for Logic, Language and Computation, University of Amsterdam, 1991.

[35] I. Ruzsa. *Intensional Logic Revisited.* Published by the author, Budapest, 1991.

[36] I. Sain. Cognition, learning, (rats and) logic. (In Hungarian). 1978.

[37] I. Sain. There are general rules for specifying semantics: Observations on abstract model theory. *Computational Linguistics and Computer Languages (CL&CL)*, XIII:195–250, 1979.

[38] I. Sain. Dogmas on language. (in Hungarian), 1980.

[39] I. Sain. Successor axioms for time increase the program verifying power of full computational induction. Technical Report 23/1983, Math. Inst. Budapest, 1983.

[40] I. Sain. Is "some–other–time" sometimes better than "sometime" in proving partial correctness of programs? *Studia Logica*, XLVII(3):279–301, 1988.

[41] I. Sain. Beth's and Craig's properties via epimorphisms and amalgamation in algebraic logic In *Algebraic Logic and Universal Algebra in Computer Science, Springer Lecture Notes in Computer Science Vol 425*, C. H. Bergman, R. D. Maddux and D. L. Pigozzi, (Eds), (Proc. Conf. Ames USA, 1988), p. 209–226, Springer-Verlag, 1990.

[42] I. Sain and A.Simon. Weak Beth property fails in finite variable logics Mathematical Institute, Budapest, Preprint, 1990.

[43] A. Salibra and G. Scollo. A soft stairway to institutions. Technical report, Univ. of Pisa, Dip. Informatica, Corso Italia 40, I-56125 Pisa, Italy, 1992.

[44] K. Segerberg. "Somewhere else" and "Some other time", in Wright and Wrong, pp. 61–64, 1976.

[45] A. Simon. *Finite Schema Completeness for Typeless Logic and Representable Cylindric Algebras*, pages 665–670. In: [5], 1991.

[46] J. van Benthem. *Language in Action (Categories, Lambdas and Dynamic Logic)*. Studies in Logic and the Foundations of Mathematics Vol. 130. North Holland, 1991.

[47] J. van Benthem. Dynamic arrow logic. In *Logic and Information Flow*, Jan van Eijck and Albert Visser (eds.), pp. 15–29, MIT Press, 1994.

[48] Y. Venema. *Many–Dimensional Modal Logic*. University of Amsterdam, PhD thesis, 1992.

Index